Individual and Team Skill Decay

Skill and knowledge retention is a major issue and concern in learning and skill acquisition, especially when trained or acquired skills (or knowledge) are needed after long periods of nonuse. The goal of this book is to summarize and advance the thinking on critical issues related to skill retention and decay in the context of individual and team training on complex tasks. This volume will be of interest to researchers and practitioners in the fields of industrial and organizational psychology, human factors, organizational behavior, and human resources management.

Winfred Arthur, Jr. is Full Professor of Psychology and Management at Texas A&M University. He is a Fellow of the Society for Industrial and Organizational Psychology, the Association of Psychological Science, and the American Psychological Association. He is past Associate Editor of the *Journal of Applied Psychology* and currently serves on its editorial board along with *Personnel Psychology*, and *Industrial and Organizational Psychology*: *Perspectives on Science and Practice* as well. His research interests are in human performance; training development, design, implementation, and evaluation; team selection and training; acquisition and retention of complex skills; testing, selection, and validation; models of job performance; personnel psychology; and meta-analysis.

Eric Anthony Day is an Associate Professor of Psychology at the University of Oklahoma where he is part of the Doctoral program in Industrial and Organizational Psychology. His research interests primarily fall in the traditional areas of personnel psychology and human resources management, including personnel assessment, selection, and training and development. Much of his research involves the study of complex skill acquisition with emphases on individual differences, cognitive and social processes, expert–novice differences, decay and adaptability, and team-based training.

Winston "Wink" Bennett, Jr. is a Senior Research Psychologist and Technical Advisor for continuous learning and performance assessment research with the Air Force Research Laboratory Human Effectiveness Directorate in Dayton, Ohio. He is a Fellow of the Air Force Research Laboratory and is also a Fellow of the American Psychological Association. He has published over 90 research articles, textbooks, chapters, and technical reports in the Human Factors, Aviation, Industrial and Organizational Psychology literatures.

Antoinette M. Portrey is a Senior Scientist with L-3 Communications Link Simulation and Training. She leads her team in warfighter training research at the Air Force Research Laboratory Human Effectiveness Directorate, Warfighter Readiness Research Division in Dayton, Ohio. Her team facilitates the research, design, development, and integration of continuous learning training methodologies and technologies to be used with interactive, multi-fidelity, immersive training environments. Specialty areas include: human performance measurement; individual, team, and unit training effectiveness; training systems assessment; and integrated learning management technologies.

SERIES IN APPLIED PSYCHOLOGY

Series Editors
Jeanette N. Cleveland, Colorado State University
Kevin R. Murphy, Landy Litigation and Colorado State University

Edwin A. Fleishmann, Founding series editor (1987–2010)

Winfred Arthur, Jr., Eric Anthony Day, Winston Bennett, Jr., and Antoinette M. Portrey
Individual and Team Skill Decay: The Science and Implications for Practice

Gregory Bedny and David Meister
The Russian Theory of Activity: Current Applications to Design and Learning

Winston Bennett, David Woehr, and Charles Lance
Performance Measurement: Current Perspectives and Future Challenges

Michael T. Brannick, Eduardo Salas, and Carolyn Prince
Team Performance Assessment and Measurement: Theory, Research, and Applications

Jeanette N. Cleveland, Margaret Stockdale, and Kevin R. Murphy
Women and Men in Organizations: Sex and Gender Issues at Work

Aaron Cohen
Multiple Commitments in the Workplace: An Integrative Approach

Russell Cropanzano
Justice in the Workplace: Approaching Fairness in Human Resource Management, Volume 1

Russell Cropanzano
Justice in the Workplace: From Theory to Practice, Volume 2

David V. Day, Stephen Zaccaro, and Stanley M. Halpin
Leader Development for Transforming Organizations: Growing Leaders for Tomorrow's Teams and Organizations

Stewart I. Donaldson, Mihaly Csikszentmihalyi, and Jeanne Nakamura
Applied Positive Psychology: Improving Everyday Life, Health, Schools, Work, and Safety

James E. Driskell and Eduardo Salas
Stress and Human Performance

Manuel London
Leadership Development: Paths to Self-Insight and Professional Growth

Robert F. Morrison and Jerome Adams
Contemporary Career Development Issues

Michael D. Mumford, Garnett Stokes, and William A. Owens
Patterns of Life History: The Ecology of Human Individuality

Michael D. Mumford
Pathways to Outstanding Leadership: A Comparative Analysis of Charismatic, Ideological, and Pragmatic Leaders

Kevin R. Murphy
Validity Generalization: A Critical Review

Kevin R. Murphy and Frank E. Saal
Psychology in Organizations: Integrating Science and Practice

Kevin Murphy
A Critique of Emotional Intelligence: What Are the Problems and How Can They Be Fixed?

Susan E. Murphy and Ronald E. Riggio
The Future of Leadership Development

Susan E. Murphy and Rebecca J. Reichard
Early Development and Leadership: Building the Next Generation of Leaders

Margaret A. Neal and Leslie Brett Hammer
Working Couples Caring for Children and Aging Parents: Effects on Work and Well-Being

Robert E. Ployhart, Benjamin Schneider, and Neal Schmitt
Staffing Organizations: Contemporary Practice and Theory, Third Edition

Steven A. Y. Poelmans
Work and Family: An International Research Perspective

Erich P. Prien, Jeffery S. Schippmann, and Kristin O. Prien
Individual Assessment: As Practiced in Industry and Consulting

Robert D. Pritchard, Sallie J. Weaver, and Elissa L. Ashwood
Evidence-Based Productivity Improvement: A Practical Guide to the Productivity Measurement and Enhancement System

Ned Rosen
Teamwork and the Bottom Line: Groups Make a Difference

Eduardo Salas, Stephen M. Fiore, and Michael P. Letsky
Theories of Team Cognition: Cross-Disciplinary Perspectives

Heinz Schuler, James L. Farr, and Mike Smith
Personnel Selection and Assessment: Individual and Organizational Perspectives

John W. Senders and Neville P. Moray
Human Error: Cause, Prediction, and Reduction

Lynn Shore, Jacqueline Coyle-Shapiro, and Lois E. Tetrick
The Employee–Organization Relationship: Applications for the 21st Century

Kenneth S. Shultz and Gary A. Adams
Aging and Work in the 21st Century

Frank J. Smith
Organizational Surveys: The Diagnosis and Betterment of Organizations Through Their Members

Dianna Stone and Eugene F. Stone-Romero
The Influence of Culture on Human Resource Processes and Practices

Kecia M. Thomas
Diversity Resistance in Organizations

George C. Thornton III and Rose Mueller-Hanson
Developing Organizational Simulations: A Guide for Practitioners and Students

George C. Thornton III and Deborah Rupp
Assessment Centers in Human Resource Management: Strategies for Prediction, Diagnosis, and Development

Yoav Vardi and Ely Weitz
Misbehavior in Organizations: Theory, Research, and Management

Patricia Voydanoff
Work, Family, and Community

Mo Wang, Deborah A. Olson, and Kenneth S. Shultz
Mid and Late Career Issues: An Integrative Perspective

Mark A. Wilson, Winston Bennett, Shanan G. Gibson, and George M. Alliger
The Handbook of Work Analysis: Methods, Systems, Applications and Science of Work Measurement in Organizations

Individual and Team Skill Decay

The Science and Implications for Practice

Edited by

Winfred Arthur, Jr.
Texas A&M University

Eric Anthony Day
The University of Oklahoma

Winston Bennett, Jr.
Air Force Research Laboratory

Antoinette M. Portrey
Air Force Research Laboratory

Routledge
Taylor & Francis Group

NEW YORK AND LONDON

First published 2013
by Routledge
711 Third Avenue, New York, NY 10017

Simultaneously published in the UK
by Routledge
27 Church Road, Hove, East Sussex BN3 2FA

Routledge is an imprint of the Taylor & Francis Group, an informa business

© 2013 Taylor & Francis

Library of Congress Cataloging in Publication Data
    Individual and team skill decay: the science and implications for practice/
    edited by Winfred Arthur, Jr. . . . [et al.].
    p. cm.—(Applied psychology series) Includes bibliographical references and index.
    1. Performance. 2. Ability. 3. Employees—Training of. 4. Performance technology. I. Arthur, Winfred.
    BF481.I515 2013
    153.9—dc23
    2012038315

ISBN: 978-0-415-88578-2 (hbk)
ISBN: 978-0-415-82193-3 (pbk)
ISBN: 978-0-203-57607-6 (ebk)

Typeset in Minion and Optima by
Florence Production Ltd, Stoodleigh, Devon, UK

Printed and bound in the United States of America
by Edwards Brothers, Inc.

To Ian and Erika, and all the good friends I have who immensely enrich my life.

— Winfred Arthur, Jr.

My contribution to this book is dedicated to my wife, Amanda, for her never-decaying, but ever-growing patience, love, and support.

— Eric Anthony Day

I would like to thank my family for their endless support and for keeping things fun always. I would also like to thank the men and women of our research laboratory for their support and their dedication to the advance of science and practice in support of national defense.

— Winston "Wink" Bennett, Jr.

I would like to thank my team for their endless support and commitment to ensure the success of the Warfighter mission and, especially, to Mary Johnson for her tireless effort and dedication in support of this book.

— Antoinette M. Portrey

Contents

PART 1   Introduction and Foundational Issues

PART 2 Individual Skill Retention and Transfer on Complex Tasks with Extended Nonuse Intervals, the Factors that Influence Them, and How Skill Decay Can Be Mitigated

Series Foreword

Jeanette N. Cleveland and Kevin R. Murphy

The goal of the Applied Psychology series is to create books that exemplify the use of scientific research, theory, and findings to help solve real problems in organizations and society. Arthur et al.'s *Individual and Team Skill Decay: The Science and Implications for Practice* accomplishes this goal. This volume tackles the tough issues that are involved in understanding how, why, and over what time periods the skills of individuals and teams decay. It pulls together the basic science of skill development and decay with organizational efforts to build and sustain skills, and vividly demonstrates the interplay of science and practice in applying psychology to organizations.

The first section of this book introduces key concepts and findings from basic research on the development and assessment of skills, and the changes in these skills over time. A distinguished international team of authors lays out the critical questions being pursued in current research on skill development and decay. The next section examines the development and decay of individual skills in organizational settings, again drawing from broad international perspectives. The third section of this book looks at the definition, development, and decay of skills at the team level of analysis. The transition between individuals and teams changes the definition of what skills actually represent and how they can best be understood, and the comparison between individual and team-level skills discussed in this book represents one of its most distinctive contributions. The final chapter of this book discusses the past, present, and future of research and practice in the area of skill development and decay.

Individual and Team Skill Decay: The Science, and Implications for Practice integrates the perspectives of researchers and practitioners in an unusually broad array of settings. The authors include academics, consultants, military researchers, and practitioners in organizations around the world. We are very happy to add *Individual and Team Skill Decay: The Science and Implications for Practice* to the Applied Psychology series.

Preface

Winfred Arthur, Jr.

Skill and knowledge retention and decay is a major issue and concern in learning and skill acquisition, especially when trained or acquired skills (or knowledge) are needed after long periods of nonuse. Thus, this phenomenon is particularly salient and critical in situations where individuals and teams receive initial training on skills and knowledge that they may not be required to use or may not have the opportunity to perform for extended periods of time.

Hence, the identification of factors that enhance posttraining skill retention is potentially of vital importance and value. Unfortunately, a limitation that characterizes the learning, training, and educational literatures is the tendency to study learning (i.e., acquisition) and retention (and transfer) independently. However, contrary to this common practice, acquisition, retention, and transfer are recognized as related but separate phenomena which may yield different interpretations of the extent to which learning has taken place. Consequently, to fully understand the effects of a training intervention or manipulation, one must measure its effects in not only the acquisition phase, but also the retention and transfer phase. At odds with the criticality of this issue is the fact that what limited research there is on skill retention has predominantly involved relatively simple tasks with relatively short nonuse intervals focusing on individuals. Consequently, the objective of the present volume is to provide a compilation of chapters, the content of which updates and significantly advances the extant literature—both in terms of research and practice—by addressing and informing the reader on issues pertaining to the acquisition of skills and knowledge in complex performance domains, and their retention and sustainment over extended periods of time for both individuals and teams. Thus, our goal in this book is not only to summarize, but also to advance the thinking on critical issues related to skill retention and decay in the context of individual and team training on complex tasks.

This is the first volume in almost 25 years devoted exclusively to evidence-based ongoing research, solutions, and continuing challenges in the skill retention and decay area of human performance. As jobs and work become more complex, there is an increasing need to fully understand the implications of this complexity on human performance and on the sustainment of performance through periods of nonpractice and periods of competing task learning and performance. The contributors to this volume are internationally recognized researchers in their field who have been working in the training, skill acquisition, sustainment, and performance persistence area of research for some time. The unique focus of this text and the specific topics addressed by each of the contributors makes this text an important research and practice resource.

The book chapters are structured around empirical studies dealing with individuals and teams and with issues associated with how best to train, maintain, refresh, and monitor knowledge and skill retention and decay. Each chapter focuses on a specific task domain with specific examples of tasks, approaches to measuring performance and decay, and remediation. Although the examples are related to the specific domain of each chapter, applications and implications to other domains and tasks are highlighted and discussed. The focus on the specific domains and approaches also provides a rich source of past studies and research histories that we hope a variety of research and practice communities will find to be of substantial value.

About the Editors

Winfred Arthur, Jr. is a Full Professor of Psychology and Management at Texas A&M University. He received his Ph.D. in industrial/organizational psychology from the University of Akron in 1988. He is a Fellow of the Society for Industrial and Organizational Psychology, the Association of Psychological Science, and the American Psychological Association. He is past Associate Editor of *Journal of Applied Psychology* and currently serves on its editorial board along with *Personnel Psychology*, and *Industrial and Organizational Psychology: Perspectives on Science and Practice* as well. His research interests are in human performance; training development, design, implementation, and evaluation; team selection and training; acquisition and retention of complex skills; testing, selection, and validation; models of job performance; personnel psychology; and meta-analysis. He has extensive experience in conceptualizing, developing, and directing projects and research in these areas and has also published extensively in these areas. He also consults with a number of clients and consulting firms on the research, development, implementation, and evaluation of personnel and human resource management systems and programs for private, public, municipal, nonprofit, and volunteer organizations. He serves on several advisory boards and a full copy of his vita can be found at: http://people.tamu.edu/~w-arthur/vitae/ArthurVita.pdf.

Eric Anthony Day is an Associate Professor of Psychology at the University of Oklahoma where he is part of the Doctoral program in Industrial and Organizational (I–O) Psychology. He earned his Ph.D. in I–O Psychology from Texas A&M University, a M.S. in I–O Psychology from the University of Central Florida, and a B.S. in Psychology from James Madison University. He is a member of the American Psychological Association (APA), Association for Psychological Science, Academy of Management, the Society for I–O Psychology, and APA's Exercise and Sport Psychology Division 47. His research interests span both personnel psychology and organizational behavior, including topics in personnel assessment, selection, training and development, and group dynamics. Much of his research involves the study of human performance and complex skill acquisition with emphases on individual differences in ability and motivation, cognitive and social processes, expert–novice differences, decay and adaptability, and team-based training. He currently serves on the editorial board for *Journal of Applied Psychology*.

Winston "Wink" Bennett, Jr. is a Senior Research Psychologist and Technical Advisor for continuous learning and performance assessment research with the Air Force Research Laboratory Human Effectiveness Directorate in Dayton, Ohio. He is a Fellow of the Air Force Research Laboratory and is also a Fellow of the American Psychological Association. Wink and his team conduct and support core collaborative research programs and have garnered over $100M in outside funding investment. He and the team are actively involved in research related to performance evaluation, personnel assessment, training requirements identification, and quantifying the impact of organizational interventions—such as interactive, high fidelity immersive simulation environments and job redesign/restructuring and training systems' impacts on individual, team, and organizational learning and effectiveness. Wink maintains an active presence in the international research community through his work on various professional committees and his contributions in professional journals and forums. He has published over 90 research articles, textbooks, chapters, and technical reports in the Human Factors, Aviation, Industrial and Organizational Psychology literatures. He serves as a contributing editor and/or as a reviewer for several professional journals. His involvement with the larger psychological research community ensures that communication among international military, industry, and academic researchers remains consistent and of the highest quality.

Antoinette M. Portrey is a Senior Scientist with L-3 Communications Link Simulation and Training. She leads her team in warfighter training research at the Air Force Research Laboratory Human Effectiveness Directorate, Warfighter Readiness Research Division in Dayton, Ohio. Her team facilitates the research, design, development, and integration of continuous learning training methodologies and technologies to be used with interactive, multi-fidelity, immersive training environments. Specialty areas include: human performance measurement; individual, team, and unit training effectiveness; training systems assessment; and integrated learning management technologies. She completed her M.S. in Applied Psychology—Human Factors from Arizona State University in 2005 and an MBA in Project Management from Capella University in 2008.

About the Contributors

Dee Andrews
U.S. Army Research Institute for the Behavioral and Social Sciences

Maud Angelborg-Thanderz
Swedish Defence Agency, FOI

Winfred Arthur, Jr.
Department of Psychology
Texas A&M University

Winston Bennett, Jr.
Air Force Research Laboratory
Human Performance Wing
Human Effectiveness Directorate

Alok Bhupatkar
American Institutes for Research

Paul R. Boatman
Department of Psychology
University of Oklahoma

Jonathan Borgvall
Swedish Defence Research Agency, FOI

Lyle E. Bourne, Jr.
Department of Psychology and Neuroscience
University of Colorado

Elizabeth M. Boyd
Department of Psychology
India University-Purdue University Indianapolis

Martin Castor
Swedish Defence Research Agency, FOI

Nancy J. Cooke
Arizona State University
Applied Psychology

Eric Anthony Day
Department of Psychology
University of Oklahoma

Deborah DiazGranados
School of Medicine
Psychology Virginia Commonwealth University Theater Row

Jasmine Duran
Lumir Research Institute

Ryan M. Glaze
Department of Psychology
Texas A&M University

Kevin A. Gluck
Air Force Research Laboratory
Warfighter Readiness Research Division

Jamie C. Gorman
Department of Psychology
Texas Tech University

Scott D. Gronlund
Department of Psychology
University of Oklahoma

Alice F. Healy
Department of Psychology and Neuroscience
University of Colorado

Michael G. Hughes
Department of Psychology
University of Oklahoma

Tiffany S. Jastrzembski
Air Force Research Laboratory

Daniel R. Kimball
Department of Psychology
University of Oklahoma

James A. Kole
Department of Psychology and Neuroscience
University of Colorado

Attila J. Kovacs
Center for Complex Systems and Brain Sciences
Florida Atlantic University

Vanessa Kowollik
Department of Psychology
University of Oklahoma

Elizabeth H. Lazzara
Institute for Simulation and Training
University of Central Florida

Rebecca Lyons
Institute for Simulation and Training
University of Central Florida

Christopher W. Myers
Cognitive Models and Agents Branch
Air Force Research Laboratory

Frederick L. Oswald
Department of Psychology
Rice University

Antoinette M. Portrey
Air Force Research Laboratory
L-3 Communications
Human Effectiveness Directorate

Eduardo Salas
Institute for Simulation and Training
University of Central Florida

Vivian I. Schneider
Department of Psychology and Neuroscience
University of Colorado

Brian T. Schreiber
Lumir Research Institute

Matthew J. Schuelke
711th Human Performance Wing
Sensemaking and Organizational Effectiveness Branch

Ira Schurig
United States Special Operations Command

Charles H. Shea
Texas A&M University
Department of Health and Kinesiology

Kathleen M. Shea
Department of Psychology and Neuroscience
University of Colorado

Erland Svensson
Swedish Defence Agency, FOI

Anton J. Villado
Department of Psychology
Rice University

Xiaoqian Wang
Department of Psychology
University of Oklahoma

David J. Woehr
Department of Management
Belk College of Business
University of North Carolina Charlotte

Erica L. Wohldmann
Department of Psychology
California State University

Samuel R. Wooten, II
Department of Psychology
University of Central Florida

Part 1

Introduction and Foundational Issues

1

Introduction

Knowledge and Skill Decay in Applied Research

Winfred Arthur, Jr. and Eric Anthony Day

INTRODUCTION

Skill and knowledge retention and decay is a major issue and concern in learning and skill acquisition, especially when trained or acquired skills (or knowledge) are needed after long periods of nonuse. Thus, phenomena involving retention and decay are particularly salient and critical in situations where individuals and teams receive initial training on skills and knowledge that they may not be required to use or may not have the opportunity to perform for extended periods of time. Hence, the identification of factors that enhance posttraining skill retention and transfer is potentially of vital importance and value. Unfortunately, a limitation that characterizes the learning, training, and educational literatures is the tendency to study learning (i.e., acquisition), retention, and transfer independently. However, contrary to this common practice, acquisition, retention, and transfer are recognized as related but separate phenomena that may yield different interpretations of the extent to which learning has taken place. Consequently, to fully understand the effects of a training intervention or manipulation, one must measure its effects in terms of not only acquisition, but also of retention and transfer.

At odds with the criticality of this issue is the fact that what limited research there is on skill retention has predominantly involved relatively simple tasks with relatively short nonuse intervals focusing on individuals. Consequently, the objective of the present work is to provide a compilation of chapters, the content of which updates and significantly advances the extant literature—in terms of both research and practice—by addressing and informing the reader on issues pertaining to the acquisition of skills and knowledge in complex performance domains, and their retention and sustainment over extended periods of time for both individuals and teams. Thus, our goal in this book is to not only summarize, but also advance the thinking on critical issues related to skill retention and decay (and transfer) in the context of individual and team training on complex tasks.

IMPETUS FOR THIS VOLUME

The impetus for this volume arises from a large-scale individual and team complex skill acquisition, retention, and transfer research project undertaken in 2003 to 2008 funded at various stages by the Air Force Research Laboratory Human Effectiveness Directorate (AFRL/HE), the Defense Advanced Research Projects Agency (DARPA) (as part of the Universal-Persistent, On-Demand, Commodity-Computing-Devise-Based, Mostly Cognitive Individual/Team Training Wars (DARWARS) program), and the National Science Foundation (NSF). These awards were made primarily to the Texas A&M University team training and complex skill acquisition lab of the AFRL, Warfighter Training Research Division, University Consortium for Warfighter Research and were implemented in conjunction with the University of Oklahoma training and complex skill acquisition lab. The funding supported three objectives. The first was the design and implementation of specified large-scale empirical studies that investigated issues pertaining to individual and team complex skill acquisition, retention, and transfer after extended periods of nonuse. The second objective was to conduct a skill retention and decay mini-conference or workshop. The third objective was to develop and publish a comprehensive book that provided an opportunity to document and make available to the scientific, practitioner, and professional communities, the results of the multi-year work effort.

Consequently, the preceding historical context explains the preponderance of work in this volume from the Texas A&M University and University of Oklahoma training labs. In addition, because of the large-scale and multi-year nature of the empirical studies that were designed and implemented by these labs, attempts to address and speak to several research questions and issues were built into the data collection effort. Thus, the reader of the full volume will become cognizant of the fact there are some dependencies across the multiple chapters that are represented by these labs. So, although these chapters use the same dependent variables (i.e., individual and team performance) from the same data collection effort, each of them focuses on different independent variables and interventions that were the foci of the specific chapter.

Nevertheless, the reader will also realize that the works presented in the volume are broader and cover a wider range of issues than those represented by the Texas A&M University and University of Oklahoma training labs. Thus, for instance, participants at the workshop, which was held in September 2007 under the auspices of AFRL/HEA and Aptima, Inc. in Mesa, Arizona, included presentations by Cooke, Jastrzembski, Oswald, Shea, Svensson, and Woehr, all of whom have chapters in the present volume.

OBSERVATIONS ABOUT SOME CONCEPTS, TERMS, AND LABELS USED IN THIS VOLUME

Because of various usage in different literatures, we deemed it important to briefly provide and share some observations about some concepts, terms, and labels that are used in this volume. These pertain specifically to the concepts of decay and retention, the nonuse or retention interval, and transfer.

Decay, Loss, and Retention

We acknowledge that the term "decay" or "loss" is used most commonly in the present volume to refer to not a *process* but rather an *outcome* that is represented by the observed decrement in performance on trained or acquired knowledge and skills after a given period of nonuse (Arthur, Bennett, Stanush, and McNelly, 1998). The process and outcome distinction is an important one because, as noted by Gronlund and Kimball (Chapter 2, this volume), although the construct of decay is expedient as a colloquial description of what happens to memory over time, as a process variable, decay is inadequate as "an explanation of forgetting because the mechanism by which a memory [or skill] weakens is never specified" (p. 14). And, as further highlighted in their quotation of McGeoch (1932), "'Rust does not occur because of time itself, but rather from oxidation processes that occur with time.' To be viable, decay explanations of forgetting must specify the oxidation process" (pp. 32–33). That being said, and recognizing its limitations, as previously noted, the common usage of the term decay in this volume, refers to an outcome (not process) that is expressed as the effect size statistic d (i.e., the standardized difference between means), where for a within-subjects design:

$$d = \frac{M_{T2} - M_{T1}}{SD_{pooled}}$$

Thus, in this equation which represents the magnitude of decay, M_{T1} is the immediate posttest mean (i.e., at the end of a given training program), M_{T2} is the delayed posttest mean (i.e., at some time after training and the immediate posttest), and SD_{pooled} is the pooled standard deviation. A negative d reflects decay (or loss) after the nonuse interval (time between the immediate posttest and the delayed posttest), a positive d indicates gains after the nonuse interval, and a d of zero indicates that there was no decay or loss, but no gain either. Hence, decay and retention represent two sides of the same coin and are often used interchangeably. Specifically, higher or more decay is a reflection of lower or less retention and conversely, lower or less decay is a reflection of higher or more retention.

The Nonuse or Retention Interval

As reflected in and commented on by Arthur et al. (1998), the operational-ization and length of nonuse and retention intervals has been very varied in the extant literature, sometimes being as short as a few minutes. To ameliorate the lack of conceptual richness and ecological validity concerns associated with such short retention intervals, as highlighted in one of Wang, Day, Kowollik, Schuelke, and Hughes' (Chapter 4 this volume) inclusion criteria, for a criterion to be considered as assessing retention over time, the same measure had to be administered both immediately (i.e., within 1 hour) upon completion of training and some time later. In addition and more importantly, to formalize what we mean by a nonuse interval, the time interval between immediate and delayed posttest had to be *greater* than the time interval between the end of training and immediate posttest.

Transfer of Training

Transfer of training is the generalization of trained performance and as noted by Schmidt and Bjork (1992; see also Arthur, Bennett, Edens, and Bell, 2003; Arthur et al., 1998; Arthur, Day, Bennett, McNelly, and Jordan, 1997; Arthur et al., 2010) should be a key criterion for evaluating the effectiveness of training. However, a close reading of the extant literature indicates that industrial/ organizational (I/O) psychologists and cognitive psychologists—the two groups that are most immersed in and concerned with training and skill acquisition— have quite different conceptualizations and operationalizations of this concept. I/O psychologists' use of this term typically refers to the generalization of performance on a given task from the training environment to the work (or performance or operational) environment. Thus, the task is held constant or is the same, and the change is in the environment in which it is performed (e.g., how the demonstration of proficiency in a piece of software in training transfers to the use of that software in the workplace). Cognitive psychologists, on the other hand, typically use transfer to refer to how the acquisition or performance of a task facilitates or hinders the performance of different tasks (cf. Barnett and Ceci, 2002). Thus, the environment is held constant or is the same and the change is in the task that is to be performed (e.g., how proficiency in driving an automatic transmission vehicle transfers to driving one with a manual transmission). It is worth noting that the use of the term "transfer" in this volume is more consonant with the cognitive than the I/O psychologist's use of the term. Interestingly, in the context of the adaptive skills and adaptive performance literature, one can envisage situations in which transfer entails a change in *both* the task and the environment.

OVERVIEW OF CHAPTERS

The chapters in this volume are structured around primarily empirical studies dealing with individuals and teams and with issues associated with how best to train, maintain, refresh, and monitor knowledge and skill retention and decay. There are a handful of conceptual and review chapters as well. Each chapter focuses on a specific task domain with specific examples of tasks, approaches to measuring performance and decay, and remediation. While the examples are related to the specific domain of each chapter, applications and implications to other domains and tasks are highlighted and discussed. The focus on the specific domains and approaches also provides a rich source of past studies and research histories that a variety of research and practice communities will find of substantial value.

Within the context of its specific content issues, each chapter has been written to speak to the general issue of the state of the science and practice of individual and team skill retention and decay (and in some instances, transfer as well). The chapters are grouped into three categories according to the themes addressed and the issues they raise. The first part of the volume is composed of Chapters 1–5 with these chapters speaking primarily to foundational conceptual and methodological issues pertaining to skill decay and retention. Thus, with a focus on remembering and forgetting, Gronlund and Kimball (Chapter 2) review a wide range of basic research on human memory. They provide a discussion of three classificatory distinctions made in the memory literature (i.e., short-term versus long-term memory, implicit and explicit memory, and episodic versus semantic memory) along with an examination of several factors that influence retention and the mechanisms for forgetting. Gronlund and Kimball also present a discussion of the construct of decay as a colloquial description of what happens to memory over time and its inadequacies as an explanation for the process of forgetting.

Villado et al. (Chapter 3) describe and discuss performance on a complex command-and-control simulation task following periods of nonuse. Specifically, recognizing that the extant literature is characterized by research using simple tasks (e.g., memorizing word lists) over relatively short periods of nonuse (e.g., hours and minutes), it addresses these limitations by using paid participants who trained for approximately 10 hours on a command-and-control microworld simulation, and then examines the amount and trend of skill decay over periods of nonuse, ranging from 1 to 8 weeks. Based on their results, they conclude that skill decay on complex tasks may not parallel that of simple tasks and that skill on complex tasks may be more resistant to decay than previously thought.

Wang, Day, Kowollik, Schuelke, and Hughes (Chapter 4) present an update of Arthur et al.'s (1998) skill decay and retention meta-analysis and extend it to include an investigation of methodological and task factors that influence knowledge and skill decay in organizational training. Their results indicate that skill decay is not such a straightforward issue that is simply a matter of the length of the nonuse interval. Specifically, their results suggest that decay and retention are moderated by a number of factors such as task complexity, and the nature of the criterion (i.e., whether it is cognitive- vs. skill-based).

In Chapter 5, Schurig, Arthur, Day, and Woehr examine variance (in contrast to the mean) as an indicator of training effectiveness in the context of complex skill acquisition, retention, and transfer. Specifically, they investigate whether performance variance provides incremental diagnostic information over and above information provided by an investigation of group means by reanalyzing data from two previously published long-term skill retention studies involving different task platforms and performance tasks, criterion measures, and training protocols. They conclude that performance variance may provide some information about the nature of the task itself. However, as an indicator of training effectiveness, although it provides confirmatory evidence of training effectiveness it does *not* provide diagnostic information over and above that provided by an investigation of group means.

In the second part of the volume, which is composed of seven chapters, the emphasis is on individual skill retention and transfer on complex tasks with extended nonuse intervals, the factors that influence it, and how skill decay can be mitigated. Hence, in Chapter 6, Jastrzembski, Portrey, Schreiber, and Gluck report on recent efforts and progress by the U.S. Air Force Research Laboratory's Warfighter Readiness Research Division toward bringing together historically separate and conceptually distinct research investments into new technological capabilities for optimally scheduling training and rehearsal events to maintain skill and mitigate against decay.

The focus of Healy, Wohldmann, Kole, Schneider, Shea, and Bourne (Chapter 7) is on training for efficient, durable, and flexible performance in the military in the context of the acquisition, retention, and transfer of knowledge and skills. As they note, optimal learning should be efficient, durable, and flexible and the research they present identifies circumstances that lead to remarkable durability of what has been learned. However, these same conditions yield very poor flexibility, or the ability to generalize learning to new situations or contexts. Consequently, they propose a general theoretical framework that accounts for the high degree of specificity obtained in their studies but that also enables predictions of when learning will be generalizable rather than specific. In summary, it would seem that specificity (limited transfer) may occur for tasks based primarily on procedural information or skill, whereas generalizability (robust transfer) may occur for tasks based primarily on declarative information or facts. Thus, for skill learning, retention is strong but transfer is limited, whereas for fact learning, retention is poor but transfer is robust. It is noteworthy that these conclusions for retention are fairly consistent with the findings of Wang et al.'s meta-analysis (Chapter 4).

In Chapter 8, Shea and Kovacs critically review current theoretical perspectives on the representation, production, and modification of simple and complex movement sequences. This is followed by an empirical example illustrating the development of a sequence structure for a complex movement sequence and examples of practice conditions that facilitate or interfere with the development and maintenance of the sequence structure. It is Shea and Kovacs' position that the sequence structure provides the fundamental basis for efficient, effective, and durable performance and transfer under some task constraints, but also can impede transfer and relearning under others. They conclude by proposing future directions for the applied and theoretical study of movement sequences within the context of isolating the mechanism(s) by which performance on learned skills appears to decay over time.

Villado et al. (Chapter 9) describe and present data on the use of, reaction to, and efficacy of an observation rehearsal training program designed to enhance skill retention on a complex command-and-control simulation task. This study capitalizes on the fact that technological advances (e.g., internet-based training) may provide viable means by which nonuse interval training interventions are delivered. Thus, the efficacy of an observationally based refresher training program was investigated by examining the level of participation, individual differences that were related to participation, and the reaction to a voluntary observational rehearsal nonuse training intervention. They also examined the efficacy of the voluntary observationally based training intervention in enhancing skill retention in comparison to mandatory and no observational training. Interestingly, Villado et al. found that (a) only a small percentage (29 percent) of trainees utilized the voluntary training; (b) non-ability rather than ability-based individual differences were better able to differentiate those who availed themselves of the observationally based training intervention from those who did not; and (c) in general, reactions to the internet-based refresher training were positive. Finally, they also found that the efficacy of the training was dependent on the training outcome such that the observationally based training intervention improved training transfer, but not retention or reacquisition.

Similarly, Svensson, Angelborg-Thanderz, Borgvall, and Castor (Chapter 10) present the results of a number of skill decay and reacquisition training and transfer studies in the Swedish Air Force. Specifically, their program of research sought to answer the following questions: (1) What are the relationships between experience on an aircraft system, absence from a task/system, speed of skill decay, reacquisition training, and operational performance?; and (2) What are the transfer effects from simulated to real flight? Thus, this chapter presents a series of simulated and live studies comparing early retired fighter pilots with active pilots. The results of these studies demonstrate that pilots who had more experience with and less absence from the aircraft had better operational performance. In addition, consistent with Villado et al.'s (Chapter 3) observation that skill decay on complex tasks may be more resistant to decay than previously thought (see also Cooke, Gorman, Duran, Myers, and Andrews (Chapter 14); and Wang et al. (Chapter 4) as well), Svensson et al. also found that once skillful, pilots could be away from their systems for quite a while and make a successful comeback, provided that they got individualized and guided training, where the concrete results and performance measures were consistently used in briefings and as information feedback supervised by experienced instructors.

In Chapter 11, Day et al. investigate the relationships between individual differences in ability, personality, and motivation and the retention and transfer of skill on a complex command-and-control simulation task. Again, recognizing that the empirical skill retention literature is predominantly characterized by studies using simple tasks and short (e.g., 1 day) nonuse intervals, this study addresses a critical need by relating ability and non-ability individual differences to the performance of a cognitively complex task after a prolonged period of nonuse. Although none of the individual differences (i.e., assessments of ability, personality, and motivation) consistently predicted performance across each of the skill-based criteria, skill acquisition and self-efficacy scores taken immediately at the end of training as well as cognitive ability were generally the strongest predictors of performance after nonuse, especially in relation to skill retention. Declarative knowledge and openness were less consistent predictors. Conscientiousness and achievement motivation provided no predictive value. Day et al. discuss their results in terms of the need for more ecologically valid research examining how individual differences are related to skilled performance after extensive periods of nonuse.

In an attempt to broaden the consideration of individual differences within the skill decay literature, Boyd and Oswald (Chapter 12) present a laboratory study exploring the relationship between two cognitive and two non-cognitive individual difference characteristics and errors made during the training of a complex multitasking skill. Errors during training were proposed to be related to skill decay over time owing to the fact that they have repeatedly been shown in the literature on transfer of training to relate positively to learning and transfer outcomes. Their results indicated that working memory was related to errors of commission, perceptual speed was related to errors of omission, and anxiety was related to both types of error.

The third and final part of the volume consists of three chapters that focus on skill decay at the team and organizational level. Teams—two or more individuals who work independently, have specific role assignments, perform specific tasks, and interact and coordinate to achieve a common goal—have become an integral part of most organizations, especially the military. However, although there is a rich science and practice of team training and skill acquisition, minimal work has addressed the retention of team skill. For instance, an additional task and job characteristic not present with individuals is the nature and degree of interdependence that is required for successful task or job performance (Arthur, Glaze, Bhupatkar, Villado, Bennett, and Rowe, 2012). As a result of this, the presence of interdependence and the role of team-work processes suggests that there are aspects or characteristics of teams that may engender retention and transfer processes and outcomes that are quite different from those observed for individuals. Consequently, Arthur et al. (Chapter 13) describe and present a team skill acquisition and retention study in which they compare team- and individual-level acquisition, retention, and transfer data on a complex command-and-control simulation task with an 8-week nonuse interval. Their results indicated that teams and individuals displayed differing levels of skill acquisition and transfer, but similar levels of retention. Furthermore, the spacing of practice had a larger effect on individuals than teams. Finally, both teams and individuals displayed smaller levels of skill decay after an extended period of nonuse than researchers may be inclined to anticipate—a finding that they attributed to the complex nature of the task.

In contrast to Arthur et al. who focused on taskwork outcomes, Cooke, Gorman, Duran, Myers, and Andrews (Chapter 14) take a teamwork (in contrast to a taskwork) focus by investigating the retention of team coordination skill. Specifically, they present the results of a series of lab studies that indicate that team skill in a three-person unmanned aerial vehicle command-and-control task decays after a period of 10 weeks or sooner although the loss is short-lived. Cooke et al. further investigate the *source* of the observed team skill decay—specifically, is it owing to decay of individual team member skills or to a loss of team-level skills in the form of interaction or coordination among team members? Thus, these authors also examine the relative contributions of individual performance decay and loss of team interaction skills to the prediction of team performance decay. Their results indicate that team performance decay and/or retention is accounted for by differences in team member interaction, rather than individual competency. Hence, these results support the view that team performance is more than the sum of individual team member performance, and that differences in team retention can be attributed to team interaction processes.

Finally, starting with the observation that even the most capable teams do not always maintain optimal performance levels and demonstrate decay in said performance (i.e., a negative change in performance from a previously demonstrated positive performance level), DiazGranados, Lazzara, Lyons, Wooten, and Salas (Chapter 15) note that, whereas it is common to respond to decreases in performance after they have occurred, it would be more beneficial to combat team performance decay proactively, especially for teams that operate in critical, high-risk environments, where performance slips may be fatal. Consequently, they identify and discuss factors at the environmental, task, and team levels that are posited to influence the occurrence of team performance decay, and then propose strategies for reducing the occurrence or severity of team performance decay.

In the final chapter, Arthur and Day make a case that future research on skill retention is warranted and that the payoffs could be substantial from both applied and scholarly perspectives. Specifically, they note that the biggest payoffs can accrue from addressing two issues in particular: (1) how to build durable and efficient yet adaptable skills (a potential retention–transfer tradeoff?), and (2) filling notable gaps in the extant literature. They expound on these two issues by first reviewing the major conclusions that can be drawn from an integrative look across all the chapters in this volume in relation to the state of the science reflected in Farr's (1987) review. On the basis of this exposition, they then identify and discuss a set of specific issues that we believe would be most propitious to address in future applied research on skill retention.

In summary, this is the first book in almost 25 years (cf. Farr, 1987) devoted exclusively to evidence-based ongoing research, solutions, and continuing challenges in the skill retention and decay area of human performance. As jobs and work become more complex, there is an increasing need to fully understand the implications of this complexity on human performance and on the sustainment of performance through periods of nonpractice and periods of competing task learning and performance. Hence, the unique focus of this text and the specific topics addressed by each of the contributors makes this text an important research and practice resource.

REFERENCES

Arthur, W. Jr., Bennett, W. Jr., Edens, P. S., and Bell, S. T. (2003). Effectiveness of training in organizations: A meta-analysis of design and evaluation features. *Journal of Applied Psychology, 88*, 234–245.

Arthur, W. Jr., Bennett, W. Jr., Stanush, P. L., and McNelly, T. L. (1998). Factors that influence skill decay and retention: A quantitative review and analysis. *Human Performance, 11*, 57–101.

Arthur, W. Jr., Day, E. A., Bennett, W. Jr., McNelly, T. L., and Jordan, J. A. (1997). Dyadic versus individual training protocols: Loss and reacquisition of a complex skill. *Journal of Applied Psychology, 82*, 783–791.

Arthur, W. Jr., Day, E. A., Villado, A. J., Boatman, P. R., Kowollik, V., Bennett, W. Jr., and Bhupatkar, A. (2010). The effect of distributed practice on immediate posttraining, and long-term performance on a complex command-and-control simulation task. *Human Performance, 23*, 428–445.

Arthur, W. Jr., Glaze, R. M., Bhupatkar, A., Villado, A. J., Bennett, W. Jr., and Rowe, L. (2012). Team task analysis: Differentiating between tasks using team-relatedness and team workflow ratings as metrics of task interdependence. *Human Factors, 54*, 277–295.

Barnett, S. M., and Ceci, S. J. (2002). When and where do we apply what we learn? A taxonomy for far transfer. *Psychological Bulletin, 128*, 612–637.

Farr, M. J. (1987). *The long-term retention of knowledge and skill: A cognitive and instructional perspective.* New York: Springer-Verlag.

McGeoch, J. (1932). Forgetting and the law of disuse. *Psychological Review, 39*, 352–370.

Schmidt, R. A., and Bjork, R. A. (1992). New conceptualizations of practice: Common principles in three paradigms suggest new concepts in training. *Psychological Science, 3*, 207–217.

2

Remembering and Forgetting

From the Laboratory Looking Out

Scott D. Gronlund and Daniel R. Kimball

INTRODUCTION

This chapter provides an overview of basic research on memory and forgetting. Of course, that is a tall order given that there are entire books written on the subject (e.g., Baddeley, Eysenck, and Anderson, 2009; Tulving and Craik, 2000). Therefore, by necessity, we will be selective. Nevertheless, we will try to provide coverage of a wide range of memory phenomena, keeping in mind the interests of the readers of this book. Our goal is to provide an overview of empirical research and current theorizing that will benefit researchers interested in individual and team skill decay. We begin with three classificatory distinctions made in the memory literature—short-term versus long-term, implicit versus explicit, and episodic versus semantic memory. Next follows a discussion of standard memory tasks with a focus on recall and recognition and a related distinction between recollection and familiarity processes. The remainder of the chapter examines several factors that influence retention and the mechanisms of forgetting. The former includes encoding specificity and distinctiveness, prior knowledge, embodiment, and desirable difficulties. The latter begins with consideration of the construct of decay. Although expedient as a colloquial description of what happens to a memory over time, decay is inadequate as an explanation of forgetting because the mechanism by which a memory weakens is never specified. We also consider interference during storage (consolidation) and interference at retrieval. Interference at retrieval comprises several related constructs including retrieval failure, cue overload, and retrieval-induced forgetting. Finally, we discuss recent research on a possible suppression mechanism that may underlie certain forms of intentional forgetting. We conclude with practical recommendations for the skills researcher and the practitioner that include the use of formal models.

Koriat and Goldsmith (1996) proposed two metaphors that can be used to describe memory: a storehouse metaphor and a correspondence metaphor. The storehouse metaphor views memory as a repository of to-be-learned items and events and focuses on the quantity of what remains in the repository at test. The correspondence metaphor views memory as a description of the past and is concerned with evaluating the accuracy of that description. The focus of this book keeps our focus primarily on the storehouse metaphor and the question of *how much* is retained after a retention interval. However, we will touch on the reconstructive nature of memory when we think it is relevant to the readers of this volume. Overviews of the reconstructive aspects of memory are available (e.g., Koriat, Goldsmith, and Pansky, 2000; Schacter, 1999).

We begin with the primary classificatory distinctions made in the memory literature. These include short-term versus long-term, implicit versus explicit, and episodic versus semantic memory. Next follows a discussion of common tasks used to study memory with a focus on recall and recognition and the concomitant distinction between the processes of familiarity and recollection. Thereafter we take up various factors that influence retention including encoding specificity and distinctiveness, prior knowledge, and various desirable difficulties (Bjork, 1994). We follow this with an exploration of forgetting. We begin with decay and show why it is "intuitive but problematic" (Jonides et al., 2008, p. 207), owing to a failure to specify a mechanism by which a memory is weakened. We also consider more promising explanations of forgetting: disrupted consolidation (interference at storage), interference at retrieval, and suppression. Table 2.1 provides an overview of the key aspects of our discussion and some of the key citations. These papers would be an excellent place to start for a researcher wishing to capitalize on current knowledge in the basic memory domain. We conclude with practical recommendations for the skills researcher and practitioner with a focus on implications for research and practice. This includes discussion of the usefulness of formal quantitative modeling.

CLASSIFICATORY DISTINCTIONS

Short-term and Long-term Memory

One of the most influential ideas in the modern study of memory was the modal model (e.g., Atkinson and Shiffrin, 1968) that distinguished between long-term

TABLE 2.1

Overview of Key Findings and Cites

Distinctions	Key Citations
Explicit vs. Implicit	Schacter (1987); Shiffrin and Steyvers (1997)
Recollection vs. Familiarity	Wixted (2007); Yonelinas (2002)
Short-term vs. Long-term	Brown et al. (2007); Cowan (2000)
Episodic vs. Semantic	Anderson and Lebiere (1998); Schacter et al. (2007)
Influences on Retention	
Encoding Specificity and Distinctiveness	Hunt (2003); Nairne (2002)
Prior Knowledge	Chase and Simon (1973); Rawson and Overschelde (2008)
Embodiment	Glenberg (1997); Wilson (2002)
Desirable Difficulties	Bjork (1994); Roediger and Karpicke (2006a)
Mechanisms of Forgetting	
Disrupted Consolidation	Wixted (2005)
Interference at Retrieval	Anderson and Neely (1996); Crowder (1976)
Intentional Forgetting	MacLeod (1998); Sahakyan and Delaney (2003)
Suppression	Geiselman et al. (1983); Levy and Anderson (2002)

and short-term information stores. The former is thought to be relatively permanent but information in the latter is transient and will disappear quickly without refreshing. The original modal model included an undifferentiated short-term store, but Baddeley and Hitch's (1974) model of short-term working memory proposed information-specific storage buffers—the visuopatial sketchpad and the phonological buffer—and an executive system that operated on the information in the buffers. Baddeley (2000) added an episodic buffer, a workspace for the temporary integration of information from the stores and the executive system. There is general agreement about the idea of separate systems for storage and executive function in working memory, but there is debate about whether there are separate information stores for long-term and short-term memory systems (for a review see Jonides et al., 2008).

The primary data supporting a multistore approach comes from neuropsychology. Researchers have demonstrated a double dissociation between long-term (LTM) and short-term (STM) memory systems. That is, there exist patients with an impaired LTM but normal STM (e.g., Cave and Squire, 1992) as well as patients with an impaired STM but normal LTM (e.g., Shallice and Warrington, 1970). But these data have been challenged (Ranganath and Blumenfield, 2005) and alternative unitary models have been proposed.

In a unitary model, STM is considered as the activated part of LTM (e.g., Cowan, 2000; McElree, 2001), with a special status for information in the focus of attention. This was illustrated by a recent study by Öztekin, Davachi, and McElree (2010). They had participants view a rapid sequence of 12 words. After a masking stimulus, two test words were presented. One was from the prior list and one was a word not previously studied in the experiment. The participant's task was to indicate which word was from the prior list. The serial position of this studied word in the original studied sequence varied and functional magnetic resonance imaging (fMRI) assessed medial temporal lobe contributions for the test word at each serial position. Multistore accounts predict that medial temporal lobe activations support retrieval from LTM but not STM. Consequently, because the last 3–4 studied items should still be in STM, there should be no medial temporal lobe activations for these items. But Öztekin et al. showed that medial temporal lobe activations were present at all except the final serial position, consistent with a unitary store. The word in the final serial position is in the focus of attention (not STM) and need not be retrieved.

Brown, Neath, and Chater (2007) proposed a computational model that assumes a unitary store (SIMPLE, which stands for Scale Invariant Memory, Perception, and LEarning). Items are represented by their position in a multidimensional space (see also the Generalized Context Model for categorization by Nosofsky, 1986). The similarity between any two items is a function of the distance separating them in this multidimensional space. If we consider only a temporal dimension, the likelihood of recall is governed by the ratio of the times between the encodings of the items in question relative to the end of the retention interval. For example, as Brown and Lewandowsky (2010) describe, items encoded 1 and 2 seconds ago (ratio .5) are less confusable than items encoded 5 and 6 seconds ago (ratio .83).

In sum, although there is heuristic value to contemplating long-term and short-term memory as separate systems with unique properties, the data and theorizing indicate that the distinction may no longer be viable. From an accessibility perspective, there exists a very limited (one item) focus of attention that requires no retrieval, but the accessibility of all the remaining information in memory appears to be governed by the same underlying principles. What about an awareness perspective? Do memories of which we are unaware affect performance? We turn next to a consideration of implicit and explicit memory (Schacter, 1987; Squire, 1987).

Implicit and Explicit Memory

The explicit and implicit memory distinction (see a related distinction between declarative and procedural memory, Squire, 1992) refers to whether we are aware that a skill we are performing or an event we are reporting is being influenced by, or retrieved from, our past experiences. Implicit memory is memory without awareness and it has been demonstrated countless times. Patient H. M. had his hippocampus removed to stop debilitating epileptic seizures (Scoville and Milner, 1957). Post-surgery, H. M. was unable to report any new learning of which he was consciously aware yet he could learn new skills (Corkin, 2002). For example, H. M. performed normally on a second day of a mirror-tracing task despite having no memory for having previously performed the task. Jacoby (1983) provided a less dramatic example of the same phenomenon: After participants read a list of words, they were tested on their ability to identify additional words presented tachistoscopically. Some of these words had been spoken before, others had not. Participants were better able to name the words they had spoken in the first phase and this benefit occurred even for words that a participant failed to remember when asked directly.

There is no question that there exists information in memory that can influence our behavior and performance without our awareness. Moreover, this factor is important in skill learning. Robertson, Pascual-Leone, and Press (2004) had participants learn a finger-movement task explicitly or implicitly. Half the participants in each condition slept during a 12-hour retention interval and half did not. For those that learned the task explicitly, improvements during the retention interval occurred only for those individuals that slept. However, those that learned the task implicitly improved irrespective of whether they slept.

Most researchers believe that distinct processes underlie explicit and implicit memory based on the existence of functional, behavioral-level dissociations (e.g., Roediger and McDermott, 1993) or based on neuropsychological evidence that different neural structures support explicit and implicit memory (e.g., Bowers and Schacter, 1993). But recent evidence suggests that explicit and implicit memory interact more than was initially thought (e.g., Moscovitch, 2008). Westmacott and Moscovitch (2003) showed that recollection (an explicit process) contributed to an implicit task (speeded name reading). Participants completed a speeded reading task involving famous and non-famous names. The famous names were associated either with high or low recollective experience. For example, Princess Diana tended to evoke a high recollective experience because participants spontaneously recollected where they were when learning of her fatal crash. On the other hand, a name like George Bush Sr. evoked no such recollective experience. Despite both sets of names being equally famous and familiar, Westmacott and Moscovitch found that participants were faster to name the high recollective famous names, demonstrating that an explicit process (recollection) can influence an implicit one (speeded reading). Current theorizing fails to distinguish between explicit and implicit memory (REM—Retrieving Effectively from Memory: Shiffrin and Steyvers, 1997).

Episodic and Semantic Memory

The final classificatory distinction is between episodic and semantic memory (Tulving, 1972; Tulving and Schacter, 1990). Episodic memory contains events that happened in a particular temporal context: the list of words you just heard, the party you attended last week, the task you learned yesterday. Semantic memory contains atemporal knowledge, events or facts. Wheeler, Stuss, and Tulving (1997) examined neuroimaging studies and found that different brain regions generally appear to be involved when encoding or retrieving episodic versus semantic information (see also Tulving, 2002). But not all agree that episodic and semantic memory are distinct. McKoon and Ratcliff (1986; see also Westmacott and Moscovitch, 2003) demonstrated that episodic associations influenced semantic representations. Moreover, models of episodic memory have had success accounting for data thought to require the existence of semantic memory. For example, the MINERVA2 model can explain prototype effects in categorization (Hintzman, 1986). The Adaptive Control of Thought: Rational (ACT-R, Anderson and Lebiere, 1998) theory treats episodic and semantic memory as part of the same memory system.

A new development involving episodic memory involves research by Schacter, Addis, and Buckner (2007). Their constructive-episodic-simulation hypothesis proposes that episodic memory is not simply a repository for past experiences, but that these same internal representations (traces) play a role in simulating and imagining future episodes and scenarios. Addis et al. (2009) found significant neural overlap between remembering past events and imagining future events. Addis, Wong, and Schacter (2008) showed that recollection (or relational memory) played an important role in recombining past details into future scenarios. This new view of episodic memory likely has implications for skills researchers. For example, is there a benefit during training to imagining alternative methods of performing a task? It might enhance transfer of learning to new contexts or it might slow forgetting.

In sum, distinctions between short- and long-term, explicit and implicit, and episodic and semantic memory, all have heuristic value and need to be considered by skills researchers. Whether a researcher wishes to consider these distinctions as having more than heuristic value may turn on the goals of the researcher and the particular skill under study. On the one hand, there exist neural data supporting different underlying structures as well as behavioral and functional dissociations that support these distinctions. On the other hand, there also exist compelling data indicating that such distinctions are not needed or, at a minimum, that the two systems are highly interactive. Many computational models of memory (e.g., ACT-R: Anderson and Lebiere, 1998; SIMPLE: Brown et al., 2007; REM: Shiffrin and Steyvers, 1997) do not incorporate these distinctions. This could be the result of Occam's Razor (one distinction is simpler than two) or of theoreticians operating at different levels of analysis than empiricists (Marr, 1982). But irrespective of the reason, skills researchers should be aware of these distinctions in their empirical and theoretical work.

Now that we have reviewed the primary classificatory distinctions made in the memory literature, we turn next to several tasks used to explore how memory works. We begin with the most prominent ones: recall and recognition. However, in the course of discussing these two tasks, we introduce another distinction: recollection versus familiarity. We chose to separate the recollection/familiarity distinction from those we have discussed above because it is a process distinction. The three previously discussed distinctions have to do with the representation and storage of information; processes operate on the representations in storage (Atkinson and Shiffrin, 1968).

MEMORY TASKS

Recall and Recognition

Memory is cue-dependent, which means that what we retrieve is governed by the cues we use to access memory. In particular, the success of memory is governed in part by the degree to which the cues stored at encoding and retrieval overlap. Tulving and Thomson (1973) called this encoding specificity and we shall have more to say about it below.

Consider a simple list-learning experiment in which participants have read 20 words, completed a distractor task, and then are asked to recall all the words that they can. According to the Search of Associative Memory (SAM, Raaijmakers and Shiffrin, 1980) theory, a participant starts by generating a context cue that isolates the to-be-recalled list from everything else in memory. This context cue subsumes the situation, the rememberer's mood, the surroundings, etc., and defines a search set from which information can be sampled for possible retrieval. According to the SAM model, a trace representing specific information is always sampled from memory, but the recall or recovery of the label attached to the sampled trace may fail. In addition, a failure also results when a cue results in the resampling of a trace that already had been recalled or had been unsuccessfully sampled with that cue. Once a new trace is successfully recovered, the next iteration of the search process will include the context cue and this recovered item. These cues are combined multiplicatively to focus on information connected to both cues. The time course of the search process is governed by the accumulation of failures, which results in the switching of cues and the eventual stopping of the search (see Harbison, Davelaar, and Dougherty, 2008).

In contrast to the generative nature of recall, in recognition the target event is present during testing and the question is whether it is recognized as having been experienced previously. There are single- and dual-process approaches to how recognition decisions are made. The most successful single-process approaches are the global-matching models (see Clark and Gronlund, 1996, for a review). Hintzman's (1988) MINERVA2 model is one such instance. It assumes that recognition decisions rely on a scalar familiarity value that depends on the degree to which the target event matches everything in memory. The global-matching models use a signal detection metaphor (Banks, 1970) as a decision mechanism: If the familiarity value is above criterion, the event is judged familiar. Much current work is underway exploring how the recognition criterion is set and updated (e.g., Benjamin, Diaz, and Wee, 2009; Rhodes and Jacoby, 2007; Singer and Wixted, 2006).

Dual-process models such as Yonelinas (1994; for a review see Yonelinas, 2002) assume that recognition decisions rely on familiarity and recollection (which we equate with recall). Familiarity is a continuous index of memory strength but recollection is thought to be a threshold process that either results in successful retrieval verifying the prior occurrence of the event or in the failure to retrieve any information. But Wixted (2007) argued that recollection should be viewed as a continuous process, and proposed that familiarity and recollection signals could be added together and considered jointly using a signal detection decision mechanism. On the other hand, Moscovitch (2008; Shelden and Moscovitch, 2010) proposed that recollection is a two-stage process. The first stage is fast and operates outside of conscious awareness; the second stage is slower and conscious awareness of the output of this process results in the experience of recollection. The debate between single- and dual-process explanations of recognition continues (e.g., Diana, Reder, Arndt, and Park, 2006; Dunn, 2004; Malmberg, Zeelenberg, and Shiffrin, 2004), as do questions about the exact nature of recollection. But the consensus is that recollection does supplement familiarity in recognition (e.g., Migo et al., 2009; Wixted, 2007).

Other distinctions are related to the familiarity/recollection distinction, the most prominent being a distinction item (occurrence) and relational (or associative) information (e.g., Gronlund and Ratcliff, 1989; Hunt and Einstein, 1981). The retrieval of item information relies on familiarity and the retrieval of relational information relies on recollection. Recall that Addis et al. (2008) showed that relational information was necessary to simulate future events from past details. A type of relational information important for understanding the reconstructive aspects of memory involves source monitoring (Johnson, Hashtroudi, and Lindsay, 1993). That is, memory for source is required to determine that I learned about the effectiveness of a new drug treatment from a medical journal rather than an infomercial. However, a complicating factor is that separate events can be unitized rather than linked through association (breadbox vs. bread and box). Unitized information functions more like an item and appears to rely on familiarity rather than recollection (e.g., Quamme, Yonelinas, and Norman, 2007).

Direct and Indirect Tasks

A task distinction related to implicit and explicit memory is that between indirect and direct tasks. Direct tasks make direct reference to a prior experience while indirect tasks measure the influence of a prior experience without the person being asked (or likely being able) to explicitly recall that prior experience (Richardson-Klavehn and Bjork, 1988). For example, there are many examples whereby prior exposure to stimuli increases accuracy or decreases response latency upon re-presentation of these stimuli (without awareness of the prior exposure, e.g., Jacoby and Dallas, 1981). In indirect tasks involving generation (e.g., homophone spelling, word-fragment completion), prior exposure increases the likelihood that those same items will be generated at test (e.g., Eich, 1984; Tulving, Schacter, and Stark, 1982). Savings is one of many indirect tasks. Participants fail to remember having previously learned a skill (the Tower of Hanoi task) or a piece of information (a paired-associate) yet they demonstrate savings by performing it or relearning it more readily than a control group that had not learned the task or information initially (see Nelson, 1978).

Metamemory

There are several types of judgments that involve one's assessment of the state of one's own memory, and these are classified as metamemory judgments. Such judgments include confidence judgments, source judgments (e.g., where/when/from whom did I learn this?), remember–know judgments (recollecting specific contextual details or merely being familiar with information), feelings of knowing (likelihood that you will recognize an answer that is not now recall-able), and judgments of learning (how well will you be able to recall particular information on a later test?) (see Metcalfe, 2000; Dunlosky and Metcalfe, 2009). To the extent that such judgments guide further learning, their accuracy is widely thought to exert considerable influence on the efficacy of such further learning efforts. For example, delaying a judgment of learning rather than making the judgment immediately following initial learning has been shown to increase the accuracy with which one can discriminate between items that one will versus will not recall later (e.g., Nelson and Dunlosky, 1991). This is thought to imply that learners can benefit more from restudying items judged as poorly learned if the judgments are made at a delay than if they are made immediately following study (e.g., Dunlosky and Metcalfe, 2009). However, Kimball and Smith (2010) have demonstrated that any such advantage for delayed-judgment items is because the delay leads participants to select more items to restudy; the benefit for restudying any particular item is the same for items given immediate and delayed judgments.

Transfer Tasks

An important component of skill learning is the capability of taking what one has learned in one setting and transferring it to a different setting. There is an extensive history in the memory literature involving transfer in simple associative learning tasks (for a review see Crowder, 1976). But of greater interest here are more complex tasks for which participants often fail to transfer knowledge from one task to a related task. For example, Bassok and Holyoak (1989) taught students physics problems and found that they were unable to transfer what they learned in the physics problems to very similar arithmetic progression problems. Barnett and Ceci (2002) found that the likelihood of transfer was reduced if the original and transfer situations varied in any of six different ways (e.g., in knowledge domain, physical or temporal context, modality). Of particular importance is the similarity between surface features versus the causal structure of the tasks performed during learning and retrieval (for a review, see Kimball and Holyoak, 2000). Overall perceived similarity of features between the tasks will increase attempted transfer (e.g., Holyoak and Koh, 1987). However, overweighting the similarity of surface (goal-irrelevant) features relative to structural (goal-relevant) features can lead to negative transfer—that is, an attempt to transfer learning to an inappropriate task (e.g., Chi, Feltovich, and Glazer, 1981).

Before leaving the topic of transfer, it bears mentioning that some theoretical and empirical work has been done regarding the transfer of expertise (for a review, see Kimball and Holyoak, 2000). The general finding is that expertise is domain- and task-specific and cannot be transferred to novel domains and tasks (e.g., Chiesi, Spilich, and Voss, 1979). However, that finding pertains to what Hatano and Inagaki (1986) refer to as "routine expertise," in contrast to "adaptive expertise." Adaptive experts have a deeper understanding and more abstract causal representation of the domain, which means that they can reason from first principles rather than rely on more automated reasoning and actions. Training that promotes adaptive expertise is likely to involve task variability rather than stereotypicality, free rather than goal-specific exploration of the domain (Sweller, Mawer, and Ward, 1983), and the development of abstract skills including metacognition (Dorner and Scholkopf, 1991), mathematical skills (Novick, 1988), statistical and deductive reasoning (Nisbett, Fong, Lehman, and Cheng, 1987), and causal reasoning (Cheng, 1997).

As we shall discuss in the Influences on Retention section, making the initial learning more difficult can enhance the likelihood of transfer (Bjork, 1994). Schmidt and Bjork (1992) argued that good performance during initial learning might reflect superficial learning that is too tied to the learning context. However, slower and more effortful learning utilizing desirable difficulties could enhance the likelihood of transfer.

Knowledge Tasks

Various tasks are used when we want to assess the structure and influence of people's prior knowledge on memory. The most prominent among these is the Deese–Roediger–McDermott (Roediger and McDermott, 1995; Deese, 1959) paradigm (DRM). Participants are presented with a list of words all related to a theme word (e.g., *thread, thimble, sewing* but not *needle*). In a subsequent recall or recognition test, participants falsely recall or recognize *needle* at high rates. Two general explanations have been proposed. The activation-monitoring framework (Roediger, Balota, and Watson, 2001) assumes that the theme word (*needle*) is implicitly activated during encoding (Underwood, 1965) and then, owing to confusion in monitoring the source of that activation (Johnson et al., 1993), it is mistaken for a studied word. The second explanation is called fuzzy-trace theory (Brainerd and Reyna, 1998). Fuzzy-trace theory assumes that participants encode verbatim and gist traces during learning. Verbatim traces include surface details about an event (phonology, contextual information) and are tied more to the individual events or words. Gist traces include semantic information about the collection of events or words. Verbatim traces are relatively short-lived, leaving the gist traces to dominate retrieval during testing. Because all the items in a DRM list are related to the same theme (i.e., the gist), it makes the theme word likely to be retrieved at test. However, Kimball, Smith, and Kahana (2007) presented a computational model (fSAM) that relied on the use of a multiplicative combination of semantic and episodic associations at encoding and retrieval that explained a range of DRM effects. The fSAM model challenges both activation-monitoring and fuzzy trace, in terms of validity as well as comprehensiveness.

So far, we have described a number of classificatory distinctions that have been proposed in the memory literature. Although researchers are still trying to specify the exact nature of these distinctions, they possess heuristic value for understanding how memory works. We then discussed some tasks that are used to explore various aspects of memory. But the next section cuts across these distinctions, and these tasks, to deal more generally with variables that influence the retention of information and skills.

INFLUENCES ON RETENTION

Encoding Specificity and Distinctiveness

Reisberg (2010) describes a meta-experiment that crosses incidental and intentional learning with three different levels of processing. Research shows that the level of processing (Craik and Lockhart, 1972) influences the likelihood of retention but intention to learn does not. In other words, retention likelihood generally is better for information that we process for meaning (elaborative rehearsal) than information that is processed more superficially (e.g., do the words rhyme?). But the type of processing engaged in at encoding is only part of the story. More important is the degree of overlap between what is encoded and what the cues at retrieval make accessible. This is encoding specificity (Tulving and Thomson, 1973) or, more generally, transfer-appropriate processing (Morris, Bransford and Franks, 1977). According to transfer-appropriate processing, retention is best when the modes of encoding and retrieval match. For example, Morris et al. had participants make either a phonological or a semantic judgment for each word in a list. Words for which semantic judgments had been made resulted in better performance on a standard old–new recognition test but words for which phonological judgments had been made produced better performance on a phonological test measuring recognition of words that rhymed with studied words.

But the encoding–retrieval overlap is not the whole story either. As Nairne (2002) argued, although the relationship between deeper levels of encoding and successful retrieval, and between greater encoding–retrieval match and successful retrieval, is generally positive, the relationship is correlational, not causal. Instead, the causal factor governing successful retrieval is the extent to which a cue provides diagnostic information about a target event (Jacoby and Craik, 1979). In other words, retrieval likelihood for a target trace is determined by the extent to which the cue matches, or does not match, not just the target trace but also other traces stored in memory. We can appreciate the role of diagnosticity if we hold the cue–target overlap constant and compare two different cases. In one case the cue is associated to 10 other events (e.g., a list of unrelated words that share a common temporal context). In the other case the cue is associated only (or predominantly) to the target (e.g., each word on the list comes from a different category). Given the cue, the target is far more likely to be retrieved in the latter case.

A factor closely related to diagnosticity—distinctiveness—is another factor that influences retention (e.g., Valentine, 1991). The retrieval of distinctive information has been linked to recollection (Mäntylä, 1997): "Remember" judgments (indicative of recollection; see Gardiner, 1988) tend to be allied with distinctive faces and "know" judgments (indicative of familiarity) tend to be allied with nondistinctive faces (Brandt, Macrae, Schloerscheidt, and Milne, 2003).

A distinctive cue elicits a particular memory because such a cue is not overloaded (Watkins and Watkins, 1975). For example, assume we have 11 traces in memory, one target trace and 10 fillers. Let the degree of match between a cue and the target trace be strong (10 units); that same cue is a weak match to the remaining 10 traces (1 unit to each). According to a ratio sampling rule such as that used by SAM (Raaijmakers and Shiffrin, 1980), the likelihood of sampling the target given the cue is determined by how well the cue matches the target (10) divided by how well the cue matches everything in memory (10+10). However, if the cue is a strong match to the target plus two other traces, and a weak match to the remaining eight traces, the likelihood of sampling the target falls from 10/20 to 10/(10+10+10+8). Despite the degree of match between the cue and target not changing across these two examples, the likelihood of retrieving the target decreased because the cue was strongly connected to other traces. This is the same argument made by Nairne (2002).

Hunt (2003) demonstrated that distinctiveness was not a property of an item but a function of the relationship of the target to other items. He distinguished between two types of distinctiveness: item- and event-based. The picture superiority effect (Nelson, Reed, and Walling, 1976) is an example of item-based distinctiveness. Stimuli such as pictures are inherently distinctive and memorable, but nondistinctive stimuli can be made distinctive via encoding manipulations (i.e., through event-based distinctiveness). For example, Jacoby, Craik, and Begg (1979) had participants decide which of two words was most related to a third word. The choice between "lake" and "chair" vs. "water" was an example of an easy comparison; the choice between "lake" and "thirst" vs. "water" was a difficult comparison. Participants had better memory for the words that were part of the difficult choices because these words became more distinctive. For a similar reason, solving a word problem for the correct answer will lead to higher retention than memorization of the correct answer (the generation effect, Slamecka and Graf, 1978).

These views and findings generally comport with the more general view of retrieval as cue-dependent (Tulving, 1974). According to this view, information that is stored in memory remains available to a relatively permanent degree; however, the information is only accessible when the right cues are used to search memory. Notwithstanding how strongly information is associated to other information stored in memory, it may not be accessible if the retrieval cues are not sufficiently diagnostic to specify the desired information to the exclusion of other information.

Prior Knowledge

Prior knowledge in a domain also enhances memory. This is most clearly evident in the superior memory abilities of domain experts. For example, chess grandmasters can recall the positions of a large number of pieces after a brief exposure to a mid-game board (Chase and Simon, 1973), and Conrad the waiter could remember up to 20 meal orders without writing anything down (Ericsson and Polson, 1988). Some theories of skilled memory (e.g., Ericsson and Kintsch, 1995) propose that the greater knowledge possessed by experts allows for superior memory through the use of knowledge or retrieval structures that facilitate the encoding and subsequent retrieval of domain-relevant information. However, Rawson and van Overschelde (2008) proposed a distinctiveness theory of skilled memory that argued that it was the joint influence of distinctiveness and prior knowledge that produced the superior memory abilities of experts.

According to this distinctiveness theory, the role of prior knowledge is to support more distinctive processing of domain-relevant information through two mechanisms. The first mechanism capitalizes upon the similarities among a set of items using organizational processing of higher-order features (e.g., category membership, Conrad's entrées). The second mechanism engages item-specific processing of unique features of the items within a set (Einstein and Hunt, 1980). Consequently, a domain expert has superior memory because he or she can better delineate a memory set and because the discriminability of the items within that memory set are enhanced.

Rawson and van Overschelde (2008) tested individuals with high or low knowledge of NFL football and had them study lists of NFL-related items or cooking items. Participants processed these items in a manner that engaged organizational processing (category sorting), distinctive processing (i.e., item-specific pleasantness ratings), or both. Not surprisingly, performance by the NFL experts on a surprise free recall test was better on the NFL-related items; there were no memory differences on the cooking items. However, in support of distinctiveness theory, performance by the NFL experts was better when distinctive processing (i.e., both organizational and item-specific processing) was engaged than when only organizational processing was engaged. Moreover, secondary measures (e.g., items per category accessed) showed this benefit arose from greater distinctiveness among the NFL-related items by the NFL experts and not from better organizational processing of this information.

Prior knowledge generally will have positive impacts on memory and skill retention. However, the tendency for reconstructive memory to fill gaps, make inferences that become difficult to distinguish from reality, and a reliance on top-down expectations, may cause problems for an expert. For example, an air traffic controller can become confused regarding whether he or she told UAL123 to reduce speed or merely intended to do so. A nurse may administer an incorrect drug or an incorrect dosage by following a standard routine despite "knowing" that the standard routine is not appropriate for this particular drug (Green, 2004).

Embodiment

The embodied cognition approach holds that cognitive (and memory) processes are rooted in the body's interactions with the world (Glenberg, 1997; Wilson, 2002). That is, memories are not just abstract internal representations but often are grounded in the actions that created them. Moreover, embodiment positively influences retention. For example, memory is better for actions we perform (e.g., "pour the coffee") than for verbal descriptions of the same actions (e.g., Engelkamp and Zimmer, 1997). Noice and Noice (2001) had participants learn a script. Some were instructed to memorize it; others learned the script while simultaneously following a director's instructions. The latter group retained more of the script. Dijkstra, Kaschak, and Zwaan (2007) had participants retrieve autobiographical memories to several different probes (e.g., a time when you went to a dentist's office). These memories were retrieved after assuming a congruent body position (lie supine) or an incongruent body position (hands on hips). The former were retrieved more rapidly. More importantly, after a two-week delay, free recall by the younger participants was superior for those memories initially retrieved congruently. Encoding specificity is unlikely to be responsible because the benefit of the encoding–retrieval match is not viable two weeks later. It seems likely that an embodied trace is one that is encoded more strongly or more richly.

Desirable Difficulties

Many factors that affect retention involve introducing desirable difficulties into the learning process (Bjork, 1994). These factors typically harm immediate performance but enhance long-term retention. Such factors generally induce greater elaboration during encoding that in some cases involves effortful retrieval, and this elaboration and effort involves more transfer-appropriate processing—that is, processing similar to that used during subsequent retrieval efforts. One of these factors is spacing. Spaced learning generally results in better long-term retention (e.g., Greene, 1989; Hintzman, 1974). But the relationship is a joint function of the interstudy interval (ISI, the spacing between Study 1 and Study 2) and the retention interval (RI, the time between Study 2 and retrieval). Cepeda et al. (2006) used a 10-day RI and found that performance on a final recall test improved as the ISI increased from 15 minutes to 1 day, but then declined as the ISI increased further. For a 6-month RI, performance increased up to a 1-month ISI before declining. In other words, optimal performance is achieved when the ISI is 5–20 percent of the RI (see also Cepeda et al., 2008). A related factor involves overlearning material already mastered. If the overlearning is massed, it can result in performance gains if testing is done close in time to the overlearning. But after a delay, the benefit of massed overlearning disappears. For example, Rohrer et al. (2005) had participants learn novel paired-associates by cycling through them 5 or 10 times. There was a big performance gain for the overlearned pairs after one week, but this advantage was gone after a four-week RI. However, a positive effect of overlearning may be found if more sensitive dependent variables are used (e.g., such as response time, Logan and Klapp, 1991).

Another desirable difficulty involves varying the conditions of training as opposed to holding them constant. For example, Kerr and Booth (1978) trained 8-year-olds to toss a bean bag at a target from either a constant distance of 3 feet or from a mixture of 2- and 4-foot distances. Performance was worse during training in the variable condition than in the constant condition, but on a delayed transfer test from a 3-foot distance, participants with variable training outperformed those with constant training despite never having practiced from 3 feet during training.

There also is a difference in delayed performance as a function of whether the different versions of the task are practiced in separate blocks versus on a random, interleaved schedule: Interleaving of practice impairs performance during training but leads to better delayed performance than when such practice occurs in separate blocks for each version of the task. For example, Hall, Domingues, and Cavazos (1994) had college-level baseball players engage in blocked or interleaved (what they called random) practice. Blocked training consisted of hitting 15 fastballs, then 15 curve balls, and then 15 changeups; interleaved training involved the same number and type of pitches, administered in a random order. Although both types of training were superior to a control condition that received no extra batting practice, interleaved training resulted in more "solid hits" at an end-of-session transfer task. Because interleaved practice also tends to produce greater spacing among repetitions than does blocking, spacing might be the relevant factor. Taylor and Rohrer (2010) conducted a study that held spacing constant between blocking and interleaving and still found a positive impact of interleaving.

Another desirable difficulty that enhances retention occurs when to-be-learned information is tested rather than studied a second time (e.g., Roediger and Karpicke, 2006a). Roediger and Karpicke (2006b) had participants study a prose passage and followed that with a second study attempt or a test on the passage. Participants subsequently were tested immediately or 7 days later. As we saw above, the twice-studied (massed practice) group was superior on the immediate test but the tested group was superior after 7 days. Also, recall testing was more beneficial than recognition (i.e., multiple-choice) testing (Kang, McDermott, and Roediger, 2007). Kang et al. speculated that recall testing might be superior because it more deeply engages recollective processing.

In this section we have described a number of factors that positively enhance retention. These included the joint effects of encoding specificity and distinctiveness, prior knowledge, embodiment, and desirable difficulties. But inevitably, once we have learned something, we rapidly begin to forget it. We turn next to a discussion of forgetting and begin by reviewing research that sought to define the functional relationship between forgetting/retention and time. Then we turn to an exploration of what causes forgetting, considering the mechanisms of decay, consolidation, retrieval dynamics (which includes interference), and suppression.

FORGETTING

Functional Form

Since the time of Ebbinghaus (1885/1913), memory researchers have been fascinated by finding the function that would describe the loss of information or the loss of skills over time. A power function seems most adept at summarizing forgetting, in part because it makes conceptual sense: According to a power function, the rate of forgetting slows over time. In other words, one forgets a lot of information at first but that rate of forgetting slows over time. In contrast, an exponential function is characterized by a constant rate of loss. Also, a power function has an asymptote of 0 (e.g., Meeter, Murre, and Janssen, 2005; Wixted and Carpenter, 2007; but see Bahrick, 1992). A power law also is consistent with Jost's second law of forgetting (Jost, 1897; see Wixted, 2004), which states that the newer of two equally strong traces will lose strength more rapidly than will an older trace.

But the search goes on. Rubin and Wenzel (1996) tested among 105 different functions. Meeter et al. (2005) collected data from 14,000 participants. Cohen, Sanborn, and Shiffrin (2008) tried to improve the methodology. They subjected power and exponential functions to a series of simulations to examine their flexibility in fitting data. For aggregated data, the two functions were roughly equivalent in their ability to mimic one another; the exponential model was better able to fit individual forgetting functions. But we do not believe that more functions, more graphs of the functions, more data, or increasingly sophisticated quantitative scrutiny, will resolve the issue.

The goal is to explain why a memory or a skill is forgotten, and one cannot achieve that simply by describing the time course of retention. A depiction of forgetting is limited if it does not arise from a process-based explanation. For example, Brown and Lewandowsky (2010) indicated that making small changes to parameters of the SIMPLE model—changes that would not alter the model's underlying architecture—produced different forgetting curves. In other words, whether the forgetting function is a power function or an exponential function (or something else) does not specify the factor(s) responsible for the degree of forgetting observed. To gain that knowledge, we need to scrutinize our explanation and how the components of that explanation are affected. If we are correct that describing forgetting is insufficient and that we must explain it, what mechanisms of forgetting need to be considered?

Levy, Kuhl, and Wagner (2010) proposed five mechanisms of forgetting: (1) failure to encode, (2) disrupted consolidation, (3) retrieval competition, (4) resolving retrieval competition, and (5) ineffective retrieval cues. We reject the first because most researchers consider forgetting to be "the inability to recall something now that could be recalled on an earlier occasion" (Tulving, 1974, p. 74). In the next several sections, we will discuss the other four mechanisms, grouping the last three types of forgetting together because they all focus on the relationship between retrieval cues and target memories. However, before discussing those four mechanisms, we first discuss decay, which Levy et al. did not consider to be a viable mechanism, but which is a popular metaphor for forgetting. We explain why decay does not withstand scrutiny as a forgetting mechanism.

Decay

There is no doubt that our memories and the skills that we learn weaken with time. In a colloquial sense, we can say that they decay. But what is the evidence supporting the idea that the "wasting effects of time" (McGeoch, 1932) can stand as an explanation of forgetting. Jonides et al. (2008) referred to decay as "intuitive but problematic." The problem with decay as an explanation is that it does not specify a mechanism by which memories or skills are weakened. Moreover, when the passage of time is controlled, the density of events (e.g., number of intervening events) rather than the amount of time that has passed determines forgetting. A classic study by Jenkins and Dallenbach (1924) showed greater forgetting of verbal information after an equivalent period spent awake versus asleep. But to determine whether the passage of time alone is sufficient to produce forgetting, the ideal experiment requires that no processing and no rehearsal take place during a retention interval.

Berman, Jonides, and Lewis (2009) have approximated such an experiment. On each trial, participants studied four words. After a brief retention interval, they were tested with a single word (a test probe) and had to decide whether the test probe had been in the study set. The key manipulation occurred on trials when the test probe did not match any words from the current study set (trial N) but did match a word from the prior study set (trial N-1). Berman et al. also varied the intertrial interval from 1 to 13 seconds. The design of the task was such that there was no reason to rehearse words from any prior study sets because it would only serve to harm performance. Nevertheless, a test probe that matched a word from the trial N-1 study set did slow responding compared to a test probe that did not match the trial N-1 study set. More importantly, if decay was at work and no rehearsal was taking place, more decay should take place during the longer intertrial interval and performance should be worse. But Berman et al. found no evidence for time-based decay as a cause of short-term forgetting.

Functional arguments have been made for the usefulness of decay. For example, Anderson and Schooler (1991) showed that decaying activations track the likelihood that a target item will need to be retrieved in the future. Altmann and Gray (2002) argued that decay was necessary to reduce interference in a task-switching paradigm. Their participants had to complete hundreds of trials with no external cues to signal which task was current. Consequently, the burden fell on memory. Altmann and Gray (2008) proposed that to prevent the build-up of proactive interference across trials, the activation of the current task instructions must decay (i.e., lose activation). But as Jonides et al. (2008, p. 207) pointed out, McGeoch's (1932) criticism of decay theories still held: "Rust does not occur because of time itself, but rather from oxidation processes that occur with time." To be viable, decay explanations of forgetting must specify that oxidation process.

Disrupted Consolidation

Consolidation is a process by which a new trace is "gradually woven into the fabric of memory" (Baddeley et al., 2009, p. 196). If something interferes with the consolidation process, the result can be an event that is "forgotten." However, after examining 100 years of forgetting research, Wixted (2004) argued that memory researchers have come to support the wrong type of interference. The view of interference that came to the fore during this time was a cue overload interpretation (Watkins and Watkins, 1975). For example, a participant might be asked to learn a set of name–face associations. After learning this first set (denoted A–B), the same names are paired with new faces (A–D). In a control condition, learning A–B is followed by learning a new set of names and faces (C–D). Given the names as cues (A), recall of the faces (B) is worse in the A–B, A–D situation. The supposed reason was because the cues (the names) were overloaded (associated to two faces). According to this view, interference is a competitive phenomenon that occurs at retrieval. This is the view taken by most in the field and by us in this chapter, but is contrary to what Wixted (2005) proposed.

The alternative view of interference favored by Wixted (2005) was that interference operates at storage and hampers the formation—consolidation—of new memories. A primary implication of this view is that the encoding of new traces should interfere more with memories formed recently than those formed more remotely. That is, we should expect to see a temporal gradient of retroactive interference. The typical paradigm can be illustrated as follows: Imagine that a participant is taught three new skills and subsequently tested on this material 1 hour later. The key manipulation involves the time at which new interfering material is taught (e.g., learn to hum a short melody). The learning of this new material could immediately follow the teaching of the skills, occur halfway through the retention interval, or occur just prior to retrieval. The data show that performance was worst when learning the melody immediately followed the learning of the skills. From a consolidation perspective, the immediate condition interfered most because the learning of the new skills was at its most labile. But the SIMPLE model, relying on temporal distinctiveness and no consolidation mechanism, makes the same prediction: The more temporally crowded the learning of the melody with the three skills, the more confusable they all become.

In sum, we find consolidation to be an intriguing forgetting mechanism, one with much support in the psychopharmacology and neuroscience literatures, and an explanation warranting further consideration in the psychology literature. But at the present time we prefer the traditional cue overload interpretation and the notion that interference operates at retrieval to produce forgetting. We turn to an exploration of this mechanism next.

Interference at Retrieval

As noted previously, there is a long history in memory research for explanations of forgetting based on interference—the impairment in retrievability of items that is attributable to other items and/or associations stored in memory. Classic interference theories posited a number of mechanisms in an attempt to explain the wide range of interference effects reported in the literature (for a review, see Anderson and Neely, 1996).

Among the earliest proposed mechanisms was occlusion—the notion that, when using a particular cue to search memory, retrieval of a target is blocked by other items associated to the same cue that compete with the target for access. This retrieval competition is envisioned as being strength-dependent, such that the stronger a competitor is, the more the target suffers a competitive disadvantage at retrieval (e.g., Anderson, Bjork, and Bjork, 1994). For example, in the paired associate paradigm mentioned earlier, when two responses have been learned to the same cue (A–B, A–D), strengthening the second-learned response by repeated retrieval practice with A–D increases retroactive interference by rendering the D response hyper-accessible, which then blocks access from the cue A to the first-learned B response (McGeoch, 1932).

Whereas occlusion assumes that the strength of the original A–B association is unaffected by interference, an alternative mechanism—unlearning—assumes that this association becomes weaker in absolute terms. Melton and Irwin (1940) proposed that when learning the A–D association, the B response may come to mind and thus the A–B association may need to be suppressed. Consistent with this mechanism, the B response remains impaired even when participants are asked to provide both responses and are given a lengthy period to do so (Barnes and Underwood, 1959).

Some findings are consistent with both occlusion and unlearning. For example, retroactive interference is more pronounced than proactive interference on an immediate test (Melton and von Lackum, 1941), but proactive interference is more pronounced on a delayed test (Underwood, 1948). This pattern closely parallels extinction and spontaneous recovery of responses in classical conditioning, which have been explained in terms of unlearning. However, the pattern is also consistent with occlusion in that the learning of the A–D association can occlude the A–B association more initially, when the A–D association is strong, but then the *relative* strength of the A–B association recovers as the A–D association weakens over time owing to other intervening events.

Note also that this pattern is an instance of a more general shift from recency to primacy with a delay of testing, with recency items being favored in immediate testing and primacy items being favored in delayed testing—a pattern that holds across species, reflecting hard wiring (Bjork, 2001). This phenomenon should be of particular interest to skills researchers, in that earlier learned skills (response sets)—skills that have been replaced with new learning—may nevertheless re-emerge in situations encountered after a sufficiently long delay following the most recent use of the new learning, resulting in erroneous responses. For example, a pilot trained on new cockpit instrumentation who does not fly for some time (perhaps due to vacation, grounding, or furlough) may suffer upon returning to duty from a re-emergence of erroneous responses that are more appropriate to the old instrumentation.

Other explanations of interference involve suppression of the target items themselves, either individually or as a set. We will discuss item suppression later in connection with theories proposed to explain more recently studied forgetting paradigms. As an everyday example of response set suppression, commands learned for one version of a software program may need to be suppressed as a set to enable efficient access to the commands applicable to a replacement version of the program (see Anderson and Neely, 1996). This theory accounts for the finding of impaired recall of items that are unassociated to any cue or target in the first-learned set (learning C–D after learning A–B). The suppressed set remains in memory, as evidenced by good recognition performance (Postman and Stark, 1969). However, only pairs for which competitor responses were learned exhibited impairment; pairs for which there was no competing response exhibited no impairment.

Retrieval-induced forgetting: Whereas classical interference paradigms involved new learning interposed between initial learning and its testing, a related paradigm—the retrieval practice paradigm—involves retrieval of a subset of the initially learned material during a delay between the initial learning and testing (Anderson et al., 1994, Experiment 3). In this paradigm, participants study pairs of words—each pair comprising a category name followed by an example from that category, e.g., *fruit–ORANGE*—and then they practice retrieving half of the examples from half of the studied categories in response to category-stem cues (*fruit–OR_____*). On a final test, participants attempt to retrieve all the studied examples in response to category–letter cues (*fruit–O_____*). Anderson et al. (1994) reported that participants were less able to retrieve the unpracticed examples from practiced categories than they were the unpracticed examples from unpracticed categories.

The leading explanation for retrieval-induced forgetting is that unpracticed examples come to mind erroneously during retrieval practice; they must therefore be suppressed at that time, and the suppression carries over to be manifested in impairment during later testing when they have become the desired response. Thus, this is an instance of the item suppression hypothesis mentioned earlier in connection with classical interference research. Evidence in favor of this interpretation includes the following: (1) The greater impairment of stronger than of weaker examples of the category—the stronger being more likely to come to mind during retrieval practice and therefore more in need of suppression (Anderson et al., 1994); (2) The absence of impairment when examples are read rather than retrieved during pretest practice (e.g., Anderson, Bjork, and Bjork, 2000); (3) The impaired retrieval of examples that belong to an unpracticed category with which they are initially studied (*food–RADISH*) and a practiced category with which different examples are initially studied (*red–BLOOD*). This result is consistent with the unpracticed example (*RADISH*) incorrectly coming to mind during retrieval practice of the practiced category (*red–BL_____*) and therefore needing to be suppressed (Anderson and Spellman, 1995). However, recent results have challenged the generality of this suppression-based account. For example, Camp, Pecher, and Schmidt (2007) failed to find impairment of unpracticed items (e.g., *rat*) when they were tested using an unstudied cue word that is related to the target word but not categorically related (*poison–r_____*).

Part–set cuing: A paradigm that is similar procedurally to the retrieval practice paradigm just discussed is the part–set cuing paradigm. In this paradigm, a subset of the to-be-remembered set of items is presented during testing—rather than being retrieved prior to testing—and these part–set cues ostensibly serve as cues to facilitate retrieval of the remaining items in the set. However, the general finding is that such cues actually impair retrieval of the remaining items (Slamecka, 1968; for a review, see Nickerson, 1984). Besides being somewhat counterintuitive, this finding is not easily accommodated by general memory theories that assume cues facilitate retrieval during testing by increasing the accessibility of other items with which they have been associated (e.g., Collins and Loftus, 1975).

A number of theories have been proposed to explain impairment owing to part–set cuing. One theory assumes that the part–set cues disrupt the normal retrieval strategy formed during study (e.g., Basden and Basden, 1995). Evidence supporting this theory includes elimination of cue-induced impairment when the cues are consistent with the presumed retrieval strategy, such as when the cues comprised every other item from the study sequence (Sloman, Bower, and Rohrer, 1991). A second theory assumes that the cues become hyper-accessible, putting the remaining items at a disadvantage in the competition among items during retrieval. Evidence supporting this theory includes the finding that increasing the number of part–set cues that are drawn from a given set increases the impairment in retrieval of the remaining items (Roediger, 1974). The most recently offered theory assumes that processing the part–set cues suppresses access to the remaining items in the set, much as retrieval practice for a subset of items suppresses access to the remaining items in the set in retrieval-induced forgetting. Evidence supporting this theory includes the finding that impairment occurs even for non-cue target words (e.g., *robe*) that are cued with related but unstudied words (e.g., *clothing*), indicating that access to the target word itself has been impaired, purportedly via suppression (Aslan, Bäuml, and Grundgeiger, 2007).

Intentional forgetting: Although forgetting is usually thought of as something to be avoided, there are many circumstances in which it can be beneficial (Bjork, 1989). For example, after learning particular material, it is often important to forget that material. Such intentional or goal-directed forgetting can be motivated by a desire to update a category of information, such as forgetting your old telephone number when you get a new one or forgetting keystroke commands for functions in a word processing program after switching to a new one. Such forgetting also can be motivated by a desire to simply forget a past event, such as an incident of trauma. Experimental paradigms have been developed to investigate these types of goal-directed forgetting in the laboratory—the directed forgetting and think/no-think paradigms, respectively.

Directed forgetting: Two versions of the directed forgetting paradigm have been developed (for a review, see MacLeod, 1998). In one version—the item method—participants are given a cue to forget or remember a particular item following its presentation during learning, before presentation of the next item. The remember-cued items have an advantage over the forget-cued items in recall, recognition, and indirect tests (e.g., Basden and Basden, 1996), leading to the widespread consensus that differences in rehearsal during learning underlie this advantage (MacLeod, 1998).

In the other version of directed forgetting—the list method—the cue to remember or forget applies to an entire list of items and is delivered only after the entire list has been presented. Thus, this version is more analogous to an attempt to forget an entire episode or an entire integrated set of responses, such as the keystrokes for word-processing functions. Research has revealed a general advantage for remember-cued lists over forget-cued lists, but this advantage is subject to several important boundary conditions (Bjork, 1989). First, the remember-cue advantage is observed in recall but generally not in recognition (e.g., Geiselman, Bjork, and Fishman 1983), although recent studies have found effects in recognition under specific circumstances (see, e.g., Sahakyan, Waldum, Benjamin, and Bickett, 2009). This pattern suggests a role for retrieval processes in list-method directed forgetting, and not just learning-phase processes as with item-method directed forgetting. Second, the remember-cue advantage only occurs when the cue to forget previously learned material is followed by the learning of other, to-be-remembered material (Gelfand and Bjork, 1985). The general finding is that the subsequently learned material is recalled *better* following a forget cue than following a remember cue—in fact, it is recalled almost as well as if the first material had not been presented at all (e.g., Kimball and Bjork, 2002). This suggests that the original learning normally interferes proactively with subsequent learning but that this proactive interference is released upon delivery of the forget cue prior to the learning of to-be-remembered material. Third, the remember-cue advantage only occurs when the forget/remember cue is delivered prior to—not after—the learning of the new material (e.g., Bjork, 1970). Fourth, the remember-cue advantage is eliminated when recall is delayed by an intervening direct test of memory that requires participants to refer back to the originally learned material (Bjork and Bjork, 1996).

Leading theories of list-method directed forgetting posit cognitive mechanisms that include rehearsal differences favoring remember-cued material, suppression of forget-cued material, and combined changes in context and encoding strategies in response to the forget cue. The differential rehearsal hypothesis assumes that people intentionally forget material by devoting effort to processing new material in place of the old. This hypothesis gains support from the finding that new learning is a precondition to observing the remember-cue advantage (Gelfand and Bjork, 1985). The suppression hypothesis assumes that people forget intentionally by directing effort towards the entire originally learned list to inhibit retrieval access to it. A key piece of evidence supporting this hypothesis—and countering the differential rehearsal hypothesis—is the finding that typical directed forgetting effects are observed for material that is not to be rehearsed when such material is interleaved with material that is to be rehearsed (Geiselman et al., 1983). Finally, the context–strategy change hypothesis assumes that the forget cue has two effects. First, the cue changes the context to such a degree that there is then a mismatch between the testing and study contexts, rendering the testing context less effective as a cue for retrieving the original material—an example of the encoding specificity principle discussed earlier (Sahakyan and Kelley, 2002). Second, the hypothesis also assumes that the forget cue leads people to abandon ineffective encoding strategies in favor of more effective ones; this results in better memory for the newly learned material following a forget cue than a remember cue (Sahakyan and Delaney, 2003). Support for this dual process hypothesis comes from several studies that were able to dissociate the effects of the forget cue on the originally learned material versus the newly learned material (see Sahakyan and Goodmon, 2010).

Think/no-think: The think/no-think paradigm serves as an analog of an attempt to forget about an event simply by avoiding thinking about it. Anderson and Green (2001) noted that this mechanism probably comes closest to the Freudian notion of repression. In their study, participants initially studied unrelated word pairs (e.g., *ordeal–roach*), then were instructed to think or not think of the second word (*roach*) when the first word in the pair (*ordeal*) was presented. In the later think/no-think phase, the first words from think and no-think pairs were presented either 0, 1, 8, or 16 times. Participants then took a cued recall test in which they were to supply the second word in each studied pair when cued with the first word—for all pairs including think and no-think pairs. Results showed increasing recall of think items and decreasing recall of no-think items as a function of the number of the item's repetitions during the think/no-think phase. This pattern also occurred when the test used cues that—instead of being the first words from the studied pairs— instead were words related semantically to the second word (*insect–r_____*). This latter finding established that the impaired access to the item (*roach*) was owing to suppression of the item itself, rather than to impairment of the association between the two studied words or to competition at retrieval from other associations the participant may have formed to avoid thinking of the second word. The authors ruled out alternative explanations based on response withholding and demand characteristics. This study was important because it provided the first evidence that forgetting could be accomplished simply by avoiding thoughts of to-be-forgotten material.

IMPLICATIONS FOR PRACTICE, AND CONCLUSIONS

Why do skills decay? Despite its expediency as a description, decay is not responsible for skill decay. As our review indicated, skills "decay" (i.e., are forgotten) owing largely to interference and suppression. These mechanisms manifest themselves in many different forms of forgetting, including retrieval-induced forgetting, part–set cuing, and intentional forgetting. The question then becomes how these different forms of forgetting contribute to skill decay? To answer that question, we need to build and evaluate explanations of the mechanisms that underlie skill retention and decay. Consequently, to close our chapter, we briefly consider the contributions of cognitive modeling, with an eye to the role that modeling can play in explaining skill retention and decay when included in the repertoire of researchers in the field.

Cognitive Modeling

There are various types of formal models that can be used to enhance a researcher's ability to explore and understand data and the underlying mechanisms that give rise to it. These include computer simulation (e.g., Lewandowsky, 1993), computational models (e.g., Kimball et al., 2007), and mathematical models (e.g., Ratcliff, 1978; Riefer and Batchelder, 1988). When we apply these formal models to understand complex cognitive tasks, Busemeyer and Diederich (2010) refer to them as cognitive models. Cognitive models can be distinguished from conceptual and statistical models because a cognitive model seeks to understand the underlying cognitive processes that give rise to the phenomena of interest (e.g., the retention of skills). We made this same point above when we talked about the futility of trying to find the function that describes forgetting data.

Cognitive models, which are implemented in mathematical or computer languages, have several advantages over conceptual approaches or verbal explanations (see Hintzman, 1991), the foremost being that it is less equivocal to relate theoretical assumptions to empirical results. Cognitive models include parameters that measure latent variables and processes that are of interest to the researcher and informative about the impact of various variables on performance. At their most practical, cognitive models are tools to aid thinking, not only about the data that exist, but about new data that need to be collected to extend a model. For example, rather than imagining what the effects might be on skills retention of different training regimens, the degree of initial learning, or the method of testing, a cognitive model would give a researcher a powerful tool with which to implement these ideas, see their combined effects, and verify (and likely improve) his or her reasoning about the interaction of these factors.

We already have mentioned a number of cognitive models in our chapter (e.g., ACT-R, SAM, REM, MINERVA 2, SIMPLE). Most of these models focus on memory retrieval, which we think makes them excellent candidates for adaptation by the readers of this book. Adapting and extending existing models is an excellent way to begin, and is less intimidating than starting from scratch to build a new model. Both of the authors of this chapter have followed this advice. Kimball et al. (2007) expanded the SAM model (creating fSAM) to move it from explaining simple list learning experiments to explaining myriad false recall phenomena. It might at first glance seem unlikely that a model such as SAM that was wedded to the storehouse metaphor could be expanded to account for data evoking the correspondence metaphor. Gronlund and colleagues (Goodsell, Gronlund, and Carlson, 2010) applied a model to advance understanding of how best to conduct eyewitness identification lineups (see

Gronlund, Carlson, Dailey, and Goodsell, 2009). They used the WITNESS model (Clark, 2003), itself an extension of ideas from Hintzman's (1988) MINERVA 2 model. As an example for the readers of this book, we will describe the WITNESS model and illustrate how it can be used to explain data and deepen one's understanding of a domain.

WITNESS is ideal for applying to lineup decision-making tasks because its parameters connect to key components of the eyewitness task. In WITNESS, faces are represented as vectors of features. These are abstract features and not meant to represent specific features such as the shape of the nose or the color of the eyes. Most memory models make similar representational assumptions. More generally, models make a variety of simplifying assumptions. A model will deal explicitly only with some aspects of a task and make simplifying assumptions about other aspects. For example, WITNESS is concerned with retrieval and specifies how that is conducted. However, to be a functioning model, it needs something to retrieve. But rather than also specifying the mechanisms underlying encoding, Clark (2003) chose to focus on retrieval and assumed that the end result of an encoding process could be represented by a vector of features.

Our memory is not perfect, so how does WITNESS mimic the imperfect encoding of the perpetrator? The degree of overlap between the perpetrator and the memory of the perpetrator is governed by the parameter c, which specifies whether each feature of the vector representing the perpetrator is encoded correctly into memory (with probability c) or replaced with a random feature (with probability $1-c$). The better the encoding (the higher the value of c) the more the memory for the perpetrator resembles the perpetrator. The guilty suspect (the perpetrator) is placed into the perpetrator-present lineup and is assumed to be a perfect encoding of the perpetrator. An innocent suspect replaces the guilty suspect in the perpetrator-absent lineup and another parameter governs the similarity between the innocent suspect and the perpetrator. The remaining lineup members are called foils and the quality of the foils is governed by yet another parameter.

Now that we have described how the lineups are represented, we need to specify how retrieval takes place and we need the model to make a decision. The degree of match between each lineup member and the perpetrator's approximation stored in memory is based on the dot product of these two vectors (a sum of the products obtained by multiplying the values of corresponding features in the two vectors). A large match value signals strong overlap between a lineup member and memory for the perpetrator; a small match value signals that the lineup member bears little resemblance to memory for the perpetrator. Once a match value(s) is determined, it must be translated into a decision (i.e., make a choice or reject the lineup).

In a sequential lineup, lineup members are tested one at a time and the model chooses the first lineup member whose match value exceeds a criterion. If no match value exceeds the criterion, the model records a rejection. In a simultaneous lineup, the members are presented all at once. In this case, the witness's judgment might be influenced by the absolute degree of match between the remembered perpetrator and each lineup member, as well as by the relative degree of match obtained by comparing lineup members to each other. The model finds the lineup member that corresponds to the best match to the perpetrator (BEST), and the lineup member that corresponds to the next-best match (NEXT). The former represents the contribution of an absolute judgment process and its contribution to the decision is weighted by w_a. The relative judgment contribution is based on the difference between BEST and NEXT; its contribution to the decision is weighted by w_r (where $w_a + w_r = 1$). The BEST lineup member is chosen whenever $[w_a * \text{BEST} + w_r * (\text{BEST} - \text{NEXT})]$ exceeds the decision criterion. Otherwise, a rejection is recorded.

By adjusting the parameter values, we can mimic various situations and use a model to aid our thinking. For example, by varying the value of c, we can mimic situations in which a witness got a good or a poor look at the perpetrator. We can construct a lineup in which the innocent suspect is a dead-ringer or a poor match for the perpetrator. By adjusting the quality of the foils we can make the lineup fair or biased. By adjusting the value of the criterion we can mimic situations involving strict or lax responding. WITNESS (like any model) provides an explanation for the results of an experiment if the model's parameters can be adjusted to approximate the data. If a satisfactory approximation is achieved, the processes of the model plus the estimated parameter values provide insight into how participants might have solved this same problem.

Practical Implications

In closing, we highlight some practical implications to be taken from the research we reviewed. We divide these remarks into those that influence skill acquisition versus those that influence skill retention/forgetting.

Although most training practitioners are familiar with the classificatory distinctions we discussed, they likely are not familiar with new ideas (Schacter et al., 2007) that indicate that episodic memory is not simply a repository for past experiences, but that these same representations play a role in simulating and imagining future episodes. These ideas may provide new insights into skill transfer. Next, dual-process views of recognition memory are important to consider (Yonelinas, 2002). When trying to select the next action to take, what are the implications of being able to recollect that action versus selecting it because it "feels familiar"? Finally, new ideas about the role that distinctive processing plays in expertise (Rawson and van Overschelde, 2008) are worth examination. Prior knowledge results in superior memory not only owing to better organizational processing, but also owing to better item-specific, distinctive processing.

But, given the title of this volume, the most important practical implications for the training practitioner likely involve the review of forgetting research. First off, it is important to acknowledge that decay is merely a description of what happens to skills over time, it is not an explanation. Rather, the training practitioner must consider the mechanisms of forgetting. For example, an interference perspective allows one to understand the general shift from recency to primacy with a delay following learning, with recency items being favored immediately after learning and primacy items being favored after a delay (Bjork, 2001). This phenomenon makes clear that earlier learned skills may re-emerge in situations encountered after a delay, even when access to the original learning is not desired because it was superseded by later learning. Moreover, the consideration of suppression mechanisms (Anderson and Neely, 1996) and intentional forgetting (Bjork, 1989) provide ideas about how new skills can be learned by editing or even suppressing access to existing skills.

The goal of this chapter was to provide an up-to-date assessment of the basic memory literature—from the laboratory looking out. Throughout the chapter, we have highlighted findings that we believe can benefit the skills researcher, and conversely, topics about which the skills researcher can provide important new insights about the basic workings of memory. After all, the best chance for continued progress will result from the cooperation of basic and applied researchers, using the development and testing of cognitive models as their common language.

REFERENCES

Addis, D. R., Wong, A., and Schacter, D. L. (2008). Age-related changes in the episodic simulation of future events. *Psychological Science, 19*, 33–41.

Addis, D. R., Pan, L., Vu, M. A., Laiser, N., and Schacter, D. L. (2009). Constructive episodic simulation of the future and the past: Distinct subsystems of a core brain network mediate imagining and remembering. *Neuropsychologia, 47*, 2222–2238.

Altmann, E., and Gray, W. (2002). Forgetting to remember: The functional relationship of decay and interference. *Psychological Science, 13*, 27–33.

Altmann, E., and Gray, W. (2008). An integrated model of cognitive control in task switching. *Psychological Review, 115*, 602–639.

Anderson, J. R., and Lebiere, C. (1998). *The atomic components of thought.* Mahwah, NJ: Lawrence Erlbaum Associates.

Anderson, J. R., and Schooler, L. (1991). Reflections of the environment in memory. *Psychological Science, 2*, 396–408.

Anderson, M. C., and Green, C. (2001). Suppressing unwanted memories by executive control. *Nature, 410*, 131–134.

Anderson, M. C., and Neely, J. H. (1996). Interference and inhibition in memory retrieval. In E. L. Bjork and R. A. Bjork (Eds.), *Memory* (pp. 237–313). San Diego, CA: Academic Press.

Anderson, M. C., and Spellman, B. A. (1995). On the status of inhibitory mechanisms in cognition: Memory retrieval as a model case. *Psychological Review, 102*, 68–100.

Anderson, M. C., Bjork, E. L., and Bjork, R. A. (2000). Retrieval-induced forgetting: Evidence for a recall-specific mechanism. *Psychonomic Bulletin & Review, 7*, 522–530.

Anderson, M. C., Bjork, R. A., and Bjork, E. L. (1994). Remembering can cause forgetting: Retrieval dynamics in long-term memory. *Journal of Experimental Psychology: Learning, Memory, and Cognition, 20*, 1063–1087.

Aslan, A., Bäuml, K.-H., and Grundgeiger, T. (2007). The role of inhibitory processes in part–list cuing. *Journal of Experimental Psychology: Learning, Memory, and Cognition, 33*, 335–341.

Atkinson, R. C., and Shiffrin, R. M. (1968). Human memory: A proposed system and its control processes. In K. W. Spence and J. T. Spence (Eds.), *The psychology of learning and motivation*, Vol. 2 (pp. 89–195). New York: Academic Press.

Baddeley, A. D. (2000). The episodic buffer: A new component of working memory? *Trends in Cognitive Sciences, 4*, 417–423.

Baddeley, A. D., and Hitch, G. (1974). Working memory. In G. H. Bower (Ed.), *The psychology of learning and motivation: Advances in research and theory*, Vol. 8 (pp. 47–89). New York: Academic Press.

Baddeley, A. D., Eysenck, M., and Anderson, M. C. (2009). *Memory*. Hove, UK: Psychology Press.

Bahrick, H. P. (1992). Stabilized memory of unrehearsed knowledge. *Journal of Experimental Psychology: General, 121*, 112–113.

Banks, W. P. (1970). Signal detection theory and human memory. *Psychological Bulletin, 74*, 81–99.

Barnes, J. M., and Underwood, B. J. (1959). "Fate" of first-list associations in transfer theory. *Journal of Experimental* Psychology, *58*, 97–105.

Barnett, S. M., and Ceci, S. J. (2002). When and where do we apply what we learn?: A taxonomy for far transfer. *Psychological Bulletin, 128*, 612–637.

Basden, B. H., and Basden, D. R. (1996). Directed forgetting: Further comparisons of the item and list methods. *Memory, 4*, 633–653.

Basden, D. R., and Basden, B. H. (1995). Some tests of the strategy disruption interpretation of part–list cuing inhibition. *Journal of Experimental Psychology: Learning, Memory, and Cognition, 21*, 1656–1669.

Bassok, M., and Holyoak, K. J. (1989). Interdomain transfer between isomorphic topics in algebra and physics. *Journal of Experimental Psychology: Learning, Memory and Cognition, 15*, 153–166.

Benjamin, A. S., Diaz, M., and Wee, S. (2009). Signal detection with criterion noise: Applications to recognition memory. *Psychological Review, 116*, 84–115.

Berman, M., Jonides, J., and Lewis, R. (2009). In search of decay in verbal short-term memory. *Journal of Experimental Psychology: Learning, Memory, and Cognition, 35*, 317–333.

Bjork, R. A. (1970). Positive forgetting: The noninterference of items intentionally forgotten. *Journal of Verbal Learning and Verbal Behavior, 9,* 255–268.

Bjork, R. A. (1989). Retrieval inhibition as an adaptive mechanism in human memory. In H. L. Roediger III and F. I. M. Craik (Eds.), *Varieties of memory and consciousness: Essays in honour of Endel Tulving* (pp. 309–330). Hillsdale, NJ: Lawrence Erlbaum Associates.

Bjork, R. A. (1994). Memory and metamemory considerations in the training of human beings. In J. Metcalfe and A. Shimamura (Eds.), *Metacognition: Knowing about knowing* (pp. 185–205). Cambridge, MA: MIT Press.

Bjork, R. A. (2001). Recency and recovery in human memory. In H. L. Roediger, J. S. Nairne, I. Neath, and A. M. Surprenant (Eds.), *The nature of remembering: Essays in honor of Robert G. Crowder* (pp. 211–232). Washington, DC: American Psychological Association Press.

Bjork, E. L., and Bjork, R. A. (1996). Continuing influences of to-be-forgotten information. *Consciousness and Cognition, 5,* 176–196.

Bowers, J., and Schacter, D. L. (1993). Priming of novel information in amnesic patients: Issues and data. In P. Graf and M. Masson (Eds.), *Implicit memory: New directions in cognition, development, and neuropsychology* (pp. 303–326). Hillsdale, NJ: Lawrence Erlbaum Associates.

Brainerd, C. J., and Reyna, V. F. (1998). Fuzzy-trace theory and children's false memories. *Journal of Experimental Child Psychology, 71,* 81–129.

Brandt, K. R., Macrae, C. N., Schloerscheidt, A. M., and Milne, A. B. (2003). Remembering or knowing others? Person recognition and recollective experience. *Memory, 11,* 89–100.

Brown, G. D. A., and Lewandowsky, S. (2010). Forgetting in memory models: Arguments against trace decay and consolidation failure. In S. Della Sala (Ed.), *Forgetting* (pp. 49–75). Hove, UK: Psychology Press.

Brown, G. D. A., Neath, I., and Chater, N. (2007). A temporal ratio model of memory. *Psychological Review, 114,* 539–576.

Busemeyer, J. R., and Diederich, A. (2010). *Cognitive modeling.* Thousand Oaks, CA: Sage Publications.

Camp, G., Pecher, D., and Schmidt, H. G. (2007). No retrieval-induced forgetting using item-specific independent cues: Evidence against a general inhibitory account. *Journal of Experimental Psychology: Learning, Memory, and Cognition, 33,* 950–958.

Cave, C. B., and Squire, L. R. (1992). Intact verbal and nonverbal short-term memory following damage to the human hippocampus. *Hippocampus, 2,* 151–163.

Cepeda, N. J., Pashler, H., Vul, E., Wixted, J. T., and Rohrer, D. (2006). Distributed practice in verbal recall tasks: A review and quantitative synthesis. *Psychological Bulletin, 132,* 354–380.

Cepeda, N. J., Vul, E., Rohrer, D., Wixted, J. T., and Pashler, H. (2008). Spacing effects in learning: A temporal ridgeline of optimal retention. *Psychological Science, 19,* 1095–1102.

Chase, W. G., and Simon, H. A. (1973). Perception in chess. *Cognitive Psychology, 4,* 55–81.

Cheng, P. W. (1997). From covariation to causation: A causal power theory. *Psychological Review, 104,* 367–405.

Chi, M. T. H., Feltovich, P. J., and Glaser, R. (1981). Categorization and representation of physics problems by experts and novices. *Cognitive Science, 5,* 121–152.

Chiesi, H. L., Spilich, G. J., and Voss, J. F. (1979). Acquisition of domain-related information in relation to high and low domain knowledge. *Journal of Verbal Learning and Verbal Behavior, 18,* 257–274.

Clark, S. E. (2003). A memory and decision model for eyewitness identification. *Applied Cognitive Psychology, 17,* 629–654.

Clark, S. E., and Gronlund, S. D. (1996). Global matching models of recognition memory: How the models match the data. *Psychonomic Bulletin & Review, 3,* 37–60.

Cohen, A. L., Sanborn, A. N., and Shiffrin, R. M. (2008). Model evaluation using grouped or individual data. *Psychonomic Bulletin & Review, 15*(4), 692–712.

Collins, A. M., and Loftus, E. F. (1975). A spreading-activation theory of semantic processing. *Psychological Review, 82,* 407–428.

Corkin, S. (2002). What's new with the amnesic patient H.M.? *Nature Reviews Neuroscience, 3,* 153–160.

Cowan, N. (2000). The magical number 4 in short-term memory: A reconsideration of mental storage capacity. *Behavioral and Brain Science, 24,* 87–185.

Craik, F. I. M., and Lockhart, R. S. (1972). Levels of processing: A framework for memory research. *Journal of Verbal Learning and Verbal Behavior, 11,* 671–684.

Crowder, R. G. (1976). *Principles of learning and memory.* Hillsdale, NJ: Lawrence Erlbaum Associates.

Deese, J. (1959). On the prediction of occurrence of particular verbal intrusions in immediate recall. *Journal of Experimental Psychology, 58,* 17–22.

Diana, R., Reder, L. M., Arndt, J., and Park, H. (2006). Models of recognition: A review of arguments in favor of a dual-process account. *Psychonomic Bulletin & Review, 13,* 1–21.

Dijkstra, K., Kaschak, M., and Zwaan, R. (2007). Body posture facilitates retrieval of autobiographical memories. *Cognition, 102,* 139–149.

Dorner, D., and Scholkopf, J. (1991). Controlling complex systems; or, expertise as "grandmother's know-how." In K. A. Ericsson and J. Smith (Eds.), *Toward a general theory of expertise: Prospects and limits* (pp. 218–239). New York: Cambridge University Press.

Dunlosky, J., and Metcalfe, J. (2009). *Metacognition.* Thousand Oaks, CA: Sage Publications, Inc.

Dunn, J. C. (2004). Remember-know: A matter of confidence. *Psychological Review, 111,* 524–542.

Ebbinghaus, H. (1913). *Memory: A contribution to experimental psychology.* New York: Teachers College, Columbia University. (Original work published 1885)

Eich, E. (1984). Memory for unattended events: Remembering with and without awareness. *Memory & Cognition, 12,* 105–111.

Einstein, G. O., and Hunt, R. R. (1980). Levels of processing and organization: Additive effects of individual-item and relational processing. *Journal of Experimental Psychology: Human Learning and Memory, 6,* 588–598.

Engelkamp, J., and Zimmer, H. D. (1997). Sensory factors in memory for subject-performed tasks. *Acta Psychologica, 96,* 43–60.

Ericsson, K. A., and Kintsch, W. (1995). Long-term working memory. *Psychological Review, 102,* 211–245.

Ericsson, K. A., and Polson, P. G. (1988). A cognitive analysis of exceptional memory for restaurant orders. In M. T. H. Chi, R. Glaser, and M. J. Farr (Eds.), *The nature of expertise* (pp. 23–70). Hillsdale, NJ: Lawrence Erlbaum Associates.

Gardiner, J. M. (1988). Functional aspects of recollective experience. *Memory & Cognition*, *16*, 309–313.

Geiselman, R. E., Bjork, R. A., and Fishman, D. L. (1983). Disrupted retrieval in directed forgetting: A link with posthypnotic amnesia. *Journal of Experimental Psychology: General*, *112*, 58–72.

Gelfand, H., and Bjork, R. A. (1985, November). *On the locus of retrieval inhibition in directed forgetting*. Paper presented at the meeting of the Psychonomic Society, Boston, MA.

Glenberg, A. M. (1997). What memory is for: Creating meaning in the service of action. *Behavioral and Brain Sciences*, *20*, 41–50.

Goodsell, C. A., Gronlund, S. D., and Carlson, C. A. (2010). Exploring the sequential lineup advantage using WITNESS, *Law and Human Behavior*, *34*(6), 445–459.

Green, M. (2004). Nursing error and human nature. *Journal of Nursing Law*, *9*, 37–44.

Greene, R. L. (1989). Spacing effects in memory: Evidence for a two-process account. *Journal of Experimental Psychology: Learning, Memory, and Cognition*, *15*, 371–377.

Gronlund, S. D., and Ratcliff, R. (1989). The time course of item and associative information: Implications for global memory models. *Journal of Experimental Psychology: Learning, Memory, and Cognition*, *15*, 846–858.

Gronlund, S. D., Carlson, C. A., Dailey, S. B., and Goodsell, C. A. (2009). Robustness of the sequential lineup advantage. *Journal of Experimental Psychology: Applied*, *15*, 140–152.

Hall, K. G., Domingues, D. A., and Cavazos, R. (1994). Contextual interference effects with skilled baseball players. *Perceptual and Motor Skills*, *78*, 835–841.

Harbison, J. I., Davelaar, E. J., and Dougherty, M. R. (2008). Stopping rules and memory search termination decisions. In B. C. Love, K. McRae, and V. M. Sloutsky (Eds.), *Proceedings of the 30th Annual Meeting of the Cognitive Science Society* (pp. 565–570). Austin, TX.

Hatano, G., and Inagaki, K. (1986). Two courses of expertise. In H. Stevenson, H. Azuma, and K. Hakuta (Eds.), *Child development and education in Japan* (pp. 262–272). San Francisco: Freeman.

Hintzman, D. L. (1974). Theoretical implications of the spacing effect. In R. L. Solso (Ed.), *Theories in cognitive psychology: The Loyola Symposium* (pp. 77–99). Hillsdale, NJ: Lawrence Erlbaum Associates.

Hintzman, D. L. (1986). Schema abstraction in a multiple-trace memory model. *Psychological Review*, *93*, 429–445.

Hintzman, D. L. (1988). Judgments of frequency and recognition memory in a multiple-trace memory model. *Psychological Review*, *95*, 528–551.

Hintzman, D. L. (1991). Why are formal models useful in psychology? In W. E. Hockley and S. Lewandowsky (Eds.), *Relating theory and data: Essays on human memory in honor of Bennet B. Murdock* (pp. 39–56). Hillsdale, NJ, England: Lawrence Erlbaum Associates.

Holyoak, K. J., and Koh, K. (1987). Surface and structural similarity in analogical transfer. *Memory & Cognition*, *15*, 332–340.

Hunt, R. R. (2003). Two contributions of distinctive processing to accurate memory. *Journal of Memory and Language*, *48*, 811–825.

Hunt R. R., and Einstein G. O. (1981). Relational and item-specific information in memory. *Journal of Verbal Learning and Verbal Behavior*, *20*, 497–514.

Jacoby, L. L. (1983). Perceptual enhancement: Persistent effects of an experience. *Journal of Experimental Psychology: Learning, Memory, and Cognition*, *9*, 21–38.

Jacoby, L. L., and Craik, F. I. M. (1979). Effects of elaboration of processing at encoding and retrieval: Trace distinctiveness and recovery of initial context. In L. S. Cermak and F. I. M. Craik (Eds.), *Levels of processing and human memory*. Hillsdale, NJ: Lawrence Erlbaum Associates.

Jacoby, L. L., and Dallas, M. (1981). On the relationship between autobiographical memory and perceptual learning. *Journal of Experimental Psychology: General, 110*, 306–340.

Jacoby, L. L., Craik, F. I. M., and Begg, I. (1979). Effects of decision difficulty on recognition and recall. *Journal of Verbal Learning and Verbal Behavior, 18*, 586–600.

Jenkins, J. B., and Dallenbach, K. M. (1924). Oblivescence during sleep and waking. *American Journal of Psychology, 35*, 605–612.

Johnson, M. K., Hashtroudi, S., and Lindsay, D. S. (1993). Source monitoring. *Psychological Bulletin, 114*, 3–28.

Jonides, J., Lewis, R. L., Nee, D. E., Lustig, C. A., Berman, M. G., and Moore K. S. (2008). The mind and brain of short-term memory. *Annual Review of Psychology, 59*, 193–224.

Jost A. (1897). Die assoziationsfestigkeit in ihrer abhangigkeit von der verteilung der wiederholungen [The strength of associations in their dependence on the distribution of repetitions]. *Zeitschrift fur Psychologie und Physiologie Sinnesorgane, 16*, 436–472.

Kang, S. H. K., McDermott, K. B., and Roediger, H. L. (2007). Test format and corrective feedback modulate the effect of testing on memory retention. *European Journal of Cognitive Psychology, 19*, 528–558.

Kerr, R., and Booth, B. (1978). Specific and varied practice of a motor skill. *Perceptual and Motor Skills, 46*, 395–401.

Kimball, D. R., and Bjork, R. A. (2002). Influences of intentional and unintentional forgetting on false memories. *Journal of Experimental Psychology: General, 131*, 116–130.

Kimball, D. R., and Holyoak, K. J. (2000). Transfer and expertise. In E. Tulving and F. I. M. Craik (Eds.), *The Oxford handbook of memory* (pp. 109–122). New York: Oxford University Press.

Kimball, D. R., and Smith, T. A. (2010). *Delayed judgments of learning, improved self-regulation of study, and recall performance: A causal chain?* Manuscript in preparation.

Kimball, D. R., Smith, T. A., and Kahana, M. J. (2007). The fSAM model of false recall. *Psychological Review, 114*, 954–993.

Koriat, A., and Goldsmith, M. (1996). Monitoring and control processes in the strategic regulation of memory accuracy. *Psychological Review, 103*, 409–517.

Koriat, A., Goldsmith, M., and Pansky, A. (2000). Toward a psychology of memory accuracy. *Annual Review of Psychology, 51*, 481–537.

Levy, B. J., and Anderson, M. C. (2002). Inhibitory processes and the control of memory retrieval. *Trends in Cognitive Science, 6*, 299–305.

Levy, B. J., Kuhl, B. A., and Wagner, A. D. (2010). The functional neuroimaging of forgetting. In S. Della Sala (Ed.), *Forgetting* (pp. 135–163). Hove, UK: Psychology Press.

Lewandowsky, S. (1993). The rewards and hazards of computer simulations. *Psychological Science, 4*, 236–243.

Logan, G. D., and Klapp, S. T. (1991). Automatizing alphabet arithmetic: I. Is extended practice necessary to produce automaticity? *Journal of Experimental Psychology: Learning, Memory, and Cognition, 17*, 179–195.

McElree, B. (2001). Working memory and focal attention. *Journal of Experimental Psychology: Learning, Memory and Cognition, 27*, 817–835.

McGeoch, J. (1932). Forgetting and the law of disuse. *Psychological Review*, *39*, 352–370.

McKoon, G., and Ratcliff, R. (1986). The automatic activation of episodic information in a semantic memory task. *Journal of Experimental Psychology: Learning, Memory, and Cognition*, *12*, 108–115.

MacLeod, C. M. (1998). Directed forgetting. In J. M. Golding and C. M. MacLeod (Eds.), *Intentional forgetting: Interdisciplinary approaches* (pp. 1–57). Mahwah, NJ: Lawrence Erlbaum Associates.

Malmberg, K. J., Zeelenberg, R., and Shiffrin, R. M. (2004). Turning up the noise or turning down the volume? On the nature of the impairment of episodic recognition memory by Midazolam. *Journal of Experimental Psychology: Learning, Memory, and Cognition*, *30*, 540–549.

Mäntylä, T. (1997). Recollections of faces: Remembering differences and knowing similarities. *Journal of Experimental Psychology: Learning, Memory, and Cognition*, *23*, 1203–1216.

Marr, D. (1982). *Vision: A computational investigation into the human representation and processing of visual information.* New York: Freeman.

Meeter, M., Murre, J., and Janssen, S. (2005). Remembering the news: Modeling retention data from a study with 14,000 participants. *Memory & Cognition*, *33*, 793–810.

Melton, A. W., and Irwin, J. M. (1940). The influence of degree of interpolated learning on retroactive inhibition and the transfer of specific responses. *American Journal of Psychology*, *53*, 173–203.

Melton, A. W., and von Lackum, W. J. (1941). Retroactive and proactive inhibition in retention: Evidence for a two-factor theory of retroactive inhibition. *American Journal of Psychology*, *54*, 157–173.

Metcalfe, J. (2000). Metamemory: Theory and data. In E. Tulving and F. I. M. Craik (Eds.), *The Oxford handbook of memory* (pp. 197–211). London: Oxford University Press.

Migo, E., Montaldi, D., Norman, K. A., Quamme, J., and Mayes, A. R. (2009). The contribution of familiarity to recognition memory is a function of test format when using similar foils. *Quarterly Journal of Experimental Psychology*, *62*, 1198–1215.

Morris, C. D., Bransford, J. D., and Franks, J. J. (1977). Levels of processing versus transfer-appropriate processing. *Journal of Verbal Learning and Verbal Behavior*, *16*, 519–533.

Moscovitch, M. (2008). The hippocampus as a "stupid" domain-specific module: Implications for theories of recent and remote memory, and of imagination. *Canadian Journal of Experimental Psychology*, *62*, 62–79.

Nairne, J. S. (2002). Remembering over the short-term: The case against the standard model. *Annual Review of Psychology*, *53*, 53–81.

Nelson, D. L., Reed, U. S., and Walling, J. R. (1976). Pictorial superiority effect. *Journal of Experimental Psychology: Human Learning and Memory*, *2*, 523–528.

Nelson, T. O. (1978). Detecting small amounts of information in memory: Savings for nonrecognized items. *Journal of Experimental Psychology: Human Learning and Memory*, *4*, 453–468.

Nelson, T. O., and Dunlosky, J. (1991). When people's judgments of learning (JOLs) are extremely accurate at predicting subsequent recall: The "delayed-JOL effect." *Psychological Science*, *2*, 267–270.

Nickerson, R. S. (1984). Retrieval inhibition from part-set cuing: A persisting enigma in memory research. *Memory & Cognition*, *12*, 531–552.

Nisbett, R. E., Fong, G. T., Lehman, D. R., and Cheng, P. W. (1987). Teaching reasoning. *Science*, *238*, 625–631.

Noice, H., and Noice, T. (2001). Learning dialogue with and without movement. *Memory & Cognition, 29*, 820–827.

Nosofsky, R. M. (1986). Attention, similarity, and the identification–categorization relationship. *Journal of Experimental Psychology: General, 115*, 39–57.

Novick, L. R. (1988). Analogical transfer, problem similarity, and expertise. *Journal of Experimental Psychology: Learning, Memory and Cognition, 14*, 510–520.

Öztekin, I., Davachi, L., and McElree, B. (2010). Are representations in working memory distinct from those in long-term memory? Neural evidence in support of a single store. *Psychological Science, 21*, 1123–1133.

Postman, L., and Stark, K. (1969). The role of response availability in transfer and interference. *Journal of Experimental Psychology, 79*, 168–177.

Quamme, J., Yonelinas, A., and Norman, K. (2007). Effect of unitization on associative recognition in amnesia. *Hippocampus, 17*, 192–200.

Raaijmakers, J. G. W., and Shiffrin, R. M. (1980). SAM: A theory of probabilistic search in associative memory. In G. H. Bower (Ed.), *The psychology of learning and motivation: Advances in research and theory*, Vol. 14 (pp. 207–262). New York: Academic Press.

Ranganath, C., and Blumenfield, R. S. (2005). Doubts about double dissociations between short- and long-term memory. *Trends in Cognitive Science, 9*, 374–380.

Ratcliff, R. (1978). A theory of memory retrieval. *Psychological Review, 85*, 59–108.

Rawson, K. A., and Van Overschelde, J. P. (2008). How does knowledge promote memory? The distinctiveness theory of skilled memory. *Journal of Memory and Language, 58*, 646–668.

Reisberg, D. (2010). *Cognition: Exploring the science of the mind.* New York: W. W. Norton & Company.

Richardson-Klavehn, A., and Bjork, R. A. (1988). Measures of memory. *Annual Review of Psychology, 39*, 475–543.

Riefer, D. M., and Batchelder, W. H. (1988). Multinomial modeling and the measurement of cognitive processes. *Psychological Review, 95*, 318–339.

Robertson, E. M., Pascual-Leone, A., and Press, D. Z. (2004). Awareness modifies the skill-learning benefits of sleep. *Current Biology, 14*, 208–212.

Roediger, H. L. (1974). Inhibiting effects of recall. *Memory & Cognition, 2*, 261–269.

Roediger, H. L., and Karpicke, J. D. (2006a). The power of testing memory: Basic research and implications for educational practice. *Perspectives on Psychological Science, 1*, 181–210.

Roediger, H. L., and Karpicke, J. D. (2006b). Test-enhanced learning: Taking memory tests improves long-term retention. *Psychological Science, 17*, 249–255.

Roediger, H. L., and McDermott, K. B. (1993). Implicit memory in normal human subjects. In F. Boller and J. Grafman (Eds.), *Handbook of neuropsychology*, Vol. 8 (pp. 63–131). Amsterdam: Elsevier.

Roediger, H. L., and McDermott, K. B. (1995). Creating false memories: Remembering words not presented in lists. *Journal of Experimental Psychology: Learning, Memory and Cognition, 21*, 803–814.

Roediger, H. L., Balota, D. A., and Watson, J. M. (2001). Spreading activation and the arousal of false memories. In H. L. Roediger, J. S. Nairne, I. Neath, and A. M. Surprenant (Eds.), *The nature of remembering: Essays in honor of Robert G. Crowder* (pp. 95–115). Washington, D.C.: American Psychological Association Press.

Rhodes, M. G., and Jacoby, L. L. (2007). On the dynamic nature of response criterion in recognition memory: Effects of base rate, awareness, and feedback. *Journal of Experimental Psychology: Learning, Memory, and Cognition, 33*, 305–320.

Rohrer, D., Taylor, K., Pashler, H., Wixted, J. T, and Cepeda, N. J. (2005). The effect of overlearning on long-term retention. *Applied Cognitive Psychology, 19*, 361–374.

Rubin, D. C., and Wenzel, A. E. (1996). One hundred years of forgetting: A quantitative description of retention. *Psychological Review, 103*, 734–760.

Sahakyan, L., and Delaney, P. F. (2003). Can encoding differences explain the benefits of directed forgetting in the list-method paradigm? *Journal of Memory and Language, 48*, 195–201.

Sahakyan, L., and Goodmon, L. H. (2010). Theoretical implications of extralist probes for directed forgetting. *Journal of Experimental Psychology: Learning, Memory, and Cognition, 36*, 920–937.

Sahakyan, L., and Kelley, C. M. (2002). A contextual change account of the directed forgetting effect. *Journal of Experimental Psychology: Learning, Memory, and Cognition, 28*, 1064–1072.

Sahakyan, L., Waldrum, E. R., Benjamin, A. S., and Bickett, S. P. (2009). Where is the forgetting with list-method directed forgetting in recognition? *Memory & Cognition, 37*, 464–476.

Schacter, D. L. (1987). Implicit memory: History and current status. *Journal of Experimental Psychology: Learning, Memory, and Cognition, 13*, 501–518.

Schacter, D. L. (1999). The seven sins of memory: Insights from psychology and cognitive neuroscience. *American Psychologist, 54*, 182–203.

Schacter, D. L., Addis, D. R., and Buckner, R. L. (2007). Remembering the past to imagine the future: The prospective brain. *Nature Reviews Neuroscience, 8*, 657–661.

Schmidt, R. A., and Bjork, R. A. (1992). New conceptualizations of practice: Common principles in three paradigms suggest new concepts for training. *Psychological Science, 3*, 207–217.

Scoville, W. B., and Milner, B. (1957). Loss of recent memory after bilateral hippocampal lesions. *Journal of Neurology, Neurosurgery and Psychiatry, 20*, 11–21.

Shallice, T., and Warrington, E. K. (1970). Independent functioning of verbal memory stores: A neuropsychological study. *Quarterly Journal of Experimental Psychology, 22*, 249–253.

Shelden, S. A., and Moscovitch, M. (2010). Recollective performance advantages for implicit memory tasks. *Memory, 18*, 681–697.

Shiffrin, R. M., and Steyvers, M. (1997). A model for recognition memory: REM—Retrieving effectively from memory. *Psychonomic Bulletin & Review, 4*, 145–166.

Singer, M., and Wixted, J. T. (2006). Effect of delay on recognition decisions: Evidence for a criterion shift. *Memory & Cognition, 34*, 125–137.

Slamecka, N. J. (1968). An examination of trace storage in free recall. *Journal of Experimental Psychology, 76*, 504–513.

Slamecka, N. J., and Graf, P. (1978). The generation effect: Delineation of a phenomenon. *Journal of Experimental Psychology: Human Learning and Memory, 4*, 592–604.

Sloman, S., Bower, G., and Rohrer, D. (1991). Congruency effects in part-list cuing inhibition. *Journal of Experimental Psychology: Learning, Memory, and Cognition, 17*, 974–982.

Squire, L. R. (1987). *Memory and brain*. New York: Oxford University Press.

Squire, L. R. (1992). Declarative and nondeclarative memory: Multiple brain systems supporting learning and memory. *Journal of Cognitive Neuroscience, 4*, 232–243.

Sweller, J., Mawer, R. F., and Ward, M. R. (1983). Development of expertise in mathematical problem solving. *Journal of Experimental Psychology: General, 112*, 639–661.

Taylor, K., and Rohrer, D. (2010). The effects of interleaved practice. *Applied Cognitive Psychology, 24*, 837–848.

Tulving, E. (1972). Episodic and semantic memory. In E. Tulving and W. Donaldson (Eds.), *Organization of memory*. New York: Academic Press.

Tulving, E. (1974). Cue-dependent forgetting. *American Scientist, 62*, 74–82.

Tulving, E. (2002). Episodic memory: From mind to brain. *Annual Review of Psychology, 53, 1–25.*

Tulving, E., and Craik, F. I. M. (Eds.) (2000). *The Oxford handbook of memory*. London: Oxford University Press.

Tulving, E., and Schacter, D. L. (1990). Priming and human memory systems. *Science, 247*, 301–306.

Tulving, E., and Thomson, D. M. (1973). Encoding specificity and retrieval processes in episodic memory. *Psychological Review, 80*, 352–373.

Tulving, E., Schacter, D. L., and Stark, H. A. (1982). Priming effects in word-fragment completion are independent of recognition memory. *Journal of Experimental Psychology: Learning, Memory, and Cognition, 8*, 336–342.

Underwood, B. J. (1948). "Spontaneous recovery" of verbal associations. *Journal of Experimental Psychology, 38*, 429–438.

Underwood, B. J. (1965). False recognition produced by implicit verbal responses. *Journal of Experimental Psychology, 70*, 122–129.

Valentine, T. (1991). A unified account of the effects of distinctiveness, inversion and race in face recognition. *Quarterly Journal of Experimental Psychology, 43A*, 161–204.

Watkins O. C., and Watkins M. J. (1975). Buildup of proactive inhibition as a cue-overload effect. *Journal of Experimental Psychology: Human Learning and Memory, 1*, 442–452.

Westmacott, R., and Moscovitch, M. (2003). The contribution of autobiographical significance to semantic memory. *Memory & Cognition, 31*, 761–774.

Wheeler, M., Stuss, D. T., and Tulving, E. (1997). Toward a theory of episodic memory: The frontal lobes and autonoetic consciousness. *Psychological Bulletin, 121*, 331–354.

Wilson, M. (2002). Six views of embodied cognition. *Psychonomic Bulletin & Review, 9*, 625–636.

Wixted, J. T. (2004). The psychology and neuroscience of forgetting. *Annual Review of Psychology, 55*, 235–269.

Wixted, J. (2005). A theory about why we forget what we once knew. *Current Directions in Psychological Science, 14*, 6–9.

Wixted, J. T. (2007). Dual-process theory and signal-detection theory of recognition memory. *Psychological Review, 114*, 152–176.

Wixted, J. T., and Carpenter, S. K. (2007). The Wickelgren power law and the Ebbinghaus savings function. *Psychological Science, 18*, 133–134.

Yonelinas, A. P. (1994). Receiver operating characteristics in recognition memory: Evidence for a dual process model. *Journal of Experimental Psychology: Learning, Memory, and Cognition, 20*, 1341–1354.

Yonelinas, A. P. (2002). The nature of recollection and familiarity: A review of 30 years of research. *Journal of Memory and Language, 46*, 441–517.

3

Complex Command-and-Control Simulation Task Performance Following Periods of Nonuse

Anton J. Villado, Eric Anthony Day, Winfred Arthur, Jr., Paul R. Boatman, Vanessa Kowollik, Alok Bhupatkar, and Winston Bennett, Jr.

INTRODUCTION

Skill retention is an important consideration, especially when trained skills are needed after an extended period of time (Arthur, Bennett, Stanush, and McNelly, 1998; Arthur, Day, Bennett, McNelly, and Jordan, 1997). The retention or decay of skill is a particularly relevant and problematic concern in domains where training is followed by an extended period of nonuse. For example, reserve personnel in the military may receive formal training only once or twice a year with the expectation that they will only need a limited amount of refresher training to reacquire any skill that has been lost when they are called up for active duty (Wisher, Sabol, Hillel, and Kern, 1991). Likewise, disaster teams and first responders may work for years without evacuating residents from affected areas, managing evacuation routes, and rescuing and treating survivors of major disasters. Military reserves, first responders, and emergency management personnel are all vulnerable to skill decay given the extended intervals spanning the training and execution of specified skills (Arthur et al., 1998). Although these personnel may experience extended periods of nonuse, they are still expected to perform at high proficiency levels—with no retraining—should an emergency or disaster arise.

Despite the critical role of military reserves, first responders, and emergency management personnel during emergency disasters, the training literature provides limited information regarding the retention or decay of these types of skills (i.e., cognitively complex decision-making skills). Researchers and training professionals are left to assume that the retention or decay of cognitively complex decision-making skills is similar to that of the cognitively simple skills upon which most of the skill retention and decay literature is based. We believe that this assumptions that cognitively *complex* skills are similar to cognitively *simple* skills needs, to be empirically investigated. Therefore, the purpose of the present study is to examine the retention or decay of complex, decision-making skills during periods of nonuse. Using 192 paid participants who trained for approximately 10 hours on a command-and-control microworld simulation, we examined the amount and trend of skill decay over periods of nonuse, ranging from 1 to 8 weeks. Our results suggest that skill decay on complex tasks may not parallel that of simple tasks. Moreover, skill on complex tasks may be more resistant to decay than previously thought. The present study begins to address gaps in the extant literature by using a complex task and an extended nonuse interval.

Skill Retention/Decay Literature

Skill decay occurs when individuals receive initial training on skills that they may not be required to use or may not have the opportunity to perform for extended periods of time (Arthur et al., 1998; Arthur et al., 1997). Arthur et al. (1998) identified a core set of factors that influence the retention of trained skills over extended periods of nonuse and categorized them as either methodological or task-related factors. Methodological factors are those factors that can be modified in the training or learning context to enhance retention. Examples of methodological factors include the instructional strategies, degree of overlearning, retention interval, conditions of retrieval, and methods for testing original learning and retention. Task-related factors are inherent characteristics of the task and are typically not amenable to modification by the trainer or researcher. Examples of these factors include characteristics such as the distinction between closed- versus open-looped tasks, physical versus cognitive tasks, and natural versus artificial tasks. Meta-analytic estimates generally indicate that all of these factors influence skill decay (Arthur et al., 1998). However, research has also demonstrated that characteristics of the task may exert varying influences on skill retention or decay. For example, Arthur et al. (1998) reported that the 95 percent confidence intervals around their meta-analytic estimate of the task characteristics included zero.

Most relevant to the issue of complex skill retention and decay is the decay associated with cognitive tasks. Arthur et al. (1998) found that cognitive tasks (versus physical tasks) suffer a large degree of skill decay, $d = -1.18$. However, although the magnitude of skill decay for cognitive tasks was large, the

95 percent confidence interval included zero (lower CI d = –2.98, upper CI d = 0.48). Furthermore, the range of effects varied largely (d = –5.24–0.99). Based on these findings, in some instances cognitive skills were susceptible to decay, whereas in other instances, cognitive skills were immune to decay and in others, cognitive skills improved during some period of nonuse. These findings suggest that additional moderators within the cognitive task classification may be present in these studies. Perhaps not all cognitive tasks are equally susceptible to skill decay. Unfortunately, limited research exists on the decay of skills on cognitively complex tasks. In other words, the majority of the skill decay literature has focused on simple tasks (Cepeda, Pashler, Vul, Wixted, and Rohrer, 2006). Furthermore, the literature on the retention of complex skills over extended periods of nonuse is virtually nonexistent.

In addition to the task-related factors, the length of time between training and opportunity-to-perform also influences the degree of skill decay (Arthur et al., 1998). Progressive skill decay is a seemingly robust phenomenon when skills are not used or exercised (Arthur et al., 1998; Arthur et al., 1997). In general, the longer the period of nonuse, the greater the amount or extent of decay (Annett, 1979; Arthur et al., 1998; Arthur et al., 1997; Farr, 1987; Gardlin and Sitterley, 1972; Hurlock and Montague, 1982; Naylor and Briggs, 1961; Prophet, 1976). Arthur et al. (1998) reported a large positive correlation between skill decay (corrected mean d) and the length of the retention interval (r = .51).

Despite the robust nature of the positive relationship between skill decay and the length of nonuse interval, it is important to note that this relationship has typically only been investigated within the context of relatively short nonuse intervals. For example, across all task types, Arthur et al. (1998) found that 70 percent of the studies in their quantitative review utilized nonuse intervals of 28 days or less. In fact, nonuse intervals of 1 day or less are common. In addition, research investigating *complex* skill decay is even more limited.

Since Arthur et al.'s (1998) quantitative review of the factors that influence skill decay, only a few studies have investigated the decay of complex skills (e.g., Day, Arthur, and Gettman, 2001; May, and Kahnweiler, 2000; Shebilske, Goettl, Corrington, and Day, 1999), and fewer have investigated the decay of cognitively complex skills over an extended period of nonuse (e.g., Saucer, Hockey, and Wastell, 2005). Despite the limited number of studies investigating complex skill decay, the results reported in the literature would tend to suggest that the decay of simple skills may not generalize to complex skills. For example, Saucer et al. (2005) found that skill on their complex task did not decay over a 32-week nonuse period. And although Saucer et al. did not vary the degree of nonuse, their study does provide some initial evidence that complex skills may not be susceptible to the rate of decay typically associated with simple skills. Consonant with this is Gabriele and Shea's (2002) review of the motor task literature in which the authors noted that learning principles concerning simple motor tasks may not generalize to the learning of complex motor tasks.

Present Study

Given the lack of empirically based guidance regarding complex skill retention over extended periods of nonuse and the rate of skill decay for complex tasks, researchers and training professionals are left to assume that the retention characteristics of complex skills are similar to those of the skills required to perform simple tasks. The present study sought to empirically test this premise by assessing the retention of skills on a cognitively complex task over varying periods of nonuse, and comparing the decay of those skills to the decay of skills reported for simple tasks. Additionally, we sought to document the rate of complex skill decay during varying periods of nonuse.

METHOD

Participants

The initial sample consisted of 236 volunteers (23 percent female) from the university and campus communities at Texas A&M University and the University of Oklahoma. The mean age of participants was 20.90 ($SD = 3.58$). Participants were paid $16.00 per hour. They also competed for three bonuses of $100, $60, and $40, which were awarded to the three trainees with the highest average task performance scores.

Participants were assigned to one of two acquisition training conditions (long or short interstudy [practice] interval), one of three rehearsal conditions during the 8-week nonuse interval (mandatory, voluntary, or no-rehearsal), and one of two reacquisition training conditions (long or short interstudy interval) for a total of 12 training conditions.

A total of 29 participants withdrew from the study after training began (13 percent attrition). Attrition rates were roughly equal across conditions. Specifically, 15 participants in the longer interstudy acquisition condition withdrew from the study and 14 participants in the shorter interstudy acquisition condition withdrew from the study. In addition, data from 15 participants were excluded from the analyses because the participants consistently did not follow the training instructions. Consequently, the final sample size was 192 (22 percent female) with a mean age of 20.94 years

(SD = 3.67). All of the participants completed 10 hours of acquisition training, separated into 10 training sessions.

Performance Task

Jane's Fleet Command. The performance task was Jane's Fleet Command (Sonalysts, Inc., 2004, Air Force Research Laboratory ver. 1.55). Fleet Command is a PC-based real-time micro-simulation of modern naval warfare featuring ships, aircraft, submarines, and airbases on land. Fleet Command provides the user with the ability to wargame carrier battle group strategy, tactics, and resource allocations and enables flexible, immersed, and interactive training.

The objective of Fleet Command is to complete a mission by completing mission objectives and achieving mission goals. To complete a mission, users must formulate a strategy, issue orders to various platforms to carry out the strategy, monitor mission progress, revise the strategy in response to the environment (enemy and neutral forces), and ensure that the objectives and goals are met by the end of the mission. Trainees operate the simulator using a monitor, keyboard, and mouse. Trainees are provided with a top-down, map-like view of the mission space. The map depicts the geographical features and various platforms (e.g., ships, aircraft, land bases, and weapons). Navy Tactical Data System (NTDS) symbols are used to represent the various contacts on the map. The map is also used to operate the simulator by assigning orders or tasks to each of the platforms under a trainee's command. Orders are issued to platforms using a series of menus. For example, to order an aircraft to engage another aircraft, a trainee would right-click on one of the aircraft under their command, select ENGAGE from the menu, and then left-click on the enemy aircraft. The psychomotor requirement of Fleet Command is equal to that of most PC-based word processing programs.

Fleet Command meets the requisite criteria for cognitive complexity and information processing demands (Ericsson and Charness, 1994; Ericsson, Krampe, and Tesch-Roemer, 1993; Schneider, 1985) including short- and long-term memory load, high workload, dynamic attention allocation, decision making, prioritization, and resource management. Consequently, it is an ecologically valid laboratory analogue of the types of cognitive, information-processing, and decision-making tasks and activities present in operational command-and-control environments in military, civilian first-responder, and other similar settings. This is highlighted by the use of Fleet Command for training purposes by several groups such as the U.S. Naval Academy, the Surface Warfare Development Group, the Surface Warfare Officers School Command, and the U.S. Naval Academy Division of Professional Development. Figure 3.1 presents a Fleet Command screen capture.

FIGURE 3.1

Fleet Command screen capture.

Task performance was operationalized as the mission effectiveness of test missions. Specifically, the mission effectiveness represents a ratio of the points earned relative to the total points possible within a mission. Participants gained points for destroying enemy platforms (aircraft, surface ships, submarines, and land bases) and completing assigned goals, and lost points for destroying friendly or neutral platforms. The number of points earned (i.e., points gained minus points lost) was divided by the total number of points available in the mission. The ratio of points earned to points possible was multiplied by 100 to rescale the value to approximate a percentage of points earned during the mission. However, because trainees could lose more points than they could gain during a mission (e.g., an unharmed enemy destroying all friendly and neutral platforms), trainees could earn a score less than –100 but not greater than 100.

Jane's Fleet Command missions. Six different missions were created for the overall data collection effort (referred to as Missions A–F in the tables). Each of the six missions was slightly modified to produce three to four variations, depending on the number of times the mission was used across the different training sessions. Trainees practiced using one variation of a mission and then tested using another variation of the same mission. The variations of a particular mission differed only in the location of own-side and enemy platforms. For example, a trainee might have been attacked by an enemy fleet from the North during the practice mission, but attacked from the West during the test mission; otherwise, the missions were identical.

Using a progressive-part training approach, the missions were presented to trainees in an order of increasing difficulty. As the study progressed, the missions required trainees to implement new strategies and systems as well as those presented and learned in the preceding training sessions (e.g., SONAR, RADAR, specialized platforms, and/or specialized weapons). In addition, as the study progressed, mission goals required an increasingly greater degree of planning, the mission tasks required greater accuracy in navigation, and trainees were required to coordinate and monitor more platforms (both own-side and enemy). Thus, the mission played during the baseline session, Session 1, and Session 2 was the least difficult (Mission A), while the mission played during Session 11 was the most complex and difficult (Mission F; also considered to be the transfer mission) and required trainees to implement all of the strategies and techniques presented in all of the preceding training sessions.

Procedure

Table 3.1 provides an overview and summary of the training procedures. Upon being recruited, trainees were informed during a screening and scheduling session that they would be training to perform a complex decision-making computer-based performance task. The screening session also entailed the completion of a demographic and contact information form, and a video/computer game experience measure. The intention of the video/computer game experience measure was to exclude trainees who reported extensive experience and familiarity with Fleet Command. However, no one was eliminated on this basis. Trainees were selected into the study based on their availability and then randomly assigned to their specified condition. Although we attempted to assign all the trainees randomly to their respective training conditions, random assignment was not always possible owing to difficulties encountered with accommodating participants' weekly schedules and 4-month calendars.

Prior to training on the first day of the study, trainees completed the baseline mission (Session 0) of Fleet Command. For this baseline mission (A), trainees were simply given time to read the standard mission briefing, which specified the goals and objectives of the mission. No other instructions were provided. After completing the baseline mission, trainees then received instruction and tutorials on how to "play" Fleet Command. Training was delivered by an instructor who guided trainees through the training sessions

TABLE 3.1

Overview of Study Procedures

10 Sessions of Skill Acquisition

Session	Activity	Mission
0	JFC baseline	A
1	JFC tutorial, practice and test mission	A
2	JFC tutorial, practice and test mission	A
3	JFC tutorial, practice and test mission	B
4	JFC tutorial, practice and test mission	B
5	JFC tutorial review, practice, and test mission	C
6	JFC practice and test mission	C
7	JFC practice and test mission	D
8	JFC practice and test mission	D
9	JFC practice and test mission	E

8-Week Nonuse Interval

Retention	JFC retention tests at varying periods of nonuse	E

7 Sessions of Skill Retention, Transfer, and Reacquisition

Session	Activity	Mission
10	JFC retention test mission	E
11	JFC transfer test mission	F
12	JFC tutorial review, practice, and test mission	B
13	JFC practice and test mission	C
14	JFC practice and test mission	D
15	JFC practice and test mission	E
16	JFC transfer test mission	F

JFC = Jane's Fleet Command.

as trainees followed along on their individual workstations using a fully functional Fleet Command mission. Following the training portion of a session, trainees then completed a practice mission followed by a test mission. Subsequent sessions (1–9) and missions (A–E) followed the training sequence presented in Table 3.1. Sessions were scheduled to be an hour long, consisting of 20 minutes of practice and 25 minutes of testing—unless there was a tutorial or training which used up approximately 15 minutes and the practice and testing were then 15 minutes and 25 minutes long, respectively. Training for approximately half of the participants took place over a 1-week period (shorter interstudy practice interval), while the training for the second half of the sample took place over a 2-week period (longer interstudy practice interval). The effects of these manipulations are not the focus of the present chapter; however, they are discussed in Chapter 13 of this volume.

After completing training, trainees began their specific nonuse period. Nonuse periods varied from 1 to 8 weeks in length. Following the nonuse period, trainees returned to the lab and immediately completed a single test mission (Session 10). The test mission (E) was the same mission used at the end of acquisition and during the nonuse period. The purpose of repeating this mission was to further assess skill retention. After the test of retention, trainees completed a test of transfer, 6 hours of reacquisition training, followed by a second test of transfer. The protocol for the assessment of retention, transfer, and reacquisition is presented in the bottom half of Table 3.1.

RESULTS

Figure 3.2 presents the mean mission effectiveness scores during the acquisition session and nonuse intervals. Table 3.2 presents the descriptive statistics and standardized mean differences for task performance during the last acquisition (Session 9) and retention session.

Overall Skill Decay

To test for skill decay following the nonuse period, we first examined the difference between the last acquisition session (Session 9) and retention session performance (see Table 3.2). Using a t-test for dependent scores, the mean difference between the last acquisition session and the retention session performance scores was statistically different, $t(180) = -2.58, p < .05, d = -0.23$. These results suggest a moderate amount of skill decay during the nonuse period. Also presented in Table 3.2 are the standardized mean differences between acquisition and retention session performance for each of the nonuse intervals. These results indicate that for the majority of nonuse intervals, there was not a consistent, clear, interpretable pattern of skill decay. In contrast, there were appreciable levels of skill decay present at the 7- and 8-week nonuse intervals.

Skill Decay Trend

The trend of skill decay was assessed using the trainees' retention session performance scores. As depicted in Figure 3.1, retention session performance across the 8-week nonuse period displayed a slight negative trend (see

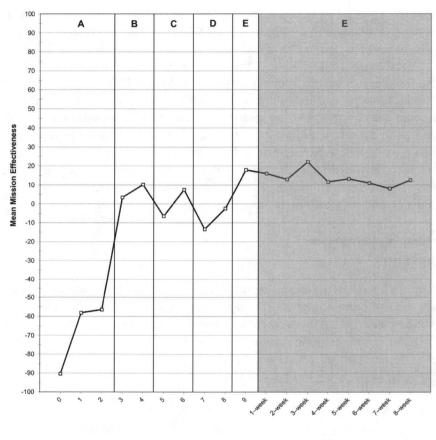

Acquisition Session   **Nonuse Interval**

FIGURE 3.2

Mean mission effectiveness scores by session and nonuse interval. $N = 192$. A–E =
Missions A–Mission E. Missions A–Mission E were progressively more difficult and
complex. Means for the nonuse intervals are based upon subsets of the entire study
sample. 1-week: $n = 28$; 2-week: $n = 20$; 3-week: $n = 19$; 4-week: $n = 25$; 5-week: $n = 23$;
6-week: $n = 25$; 7-week: $n = 19$; 8-week: $n = 21$.

Figure 3.1). Although the nature of these data (between-subjects) precluded
trend analyses, we were able to test for mean differences between the eight
nonuse intervals using a one-way analysis of variance (ANOVA), with eight
groups (length of nonuse interval). We failed to detect a significant effect for
length of nonuse interval, indicating that performance scores across the varying
nonuse intervals did not differ, $F(7, 173) = 0.87, p > .05, \eta^2 = .03$.

To further explore the effect of nonuse interval length on skill decay, we
tested for mean differences between the last acquisition session and the

TABLE 3.2

Descriptive Statistics and Standardized Mean Differences for Task Performance by Nonuse Interval

| Nonuse Interval | n^a | Acquisition[b] | | Retention[c] | | d |
		Mean	SD	Mean	SD	
1	29	17.96	20.20	16.00	18.49	−0.10
2	20	12.53	14.96	12.95	18.60	0.02
3	19	19.47	27.92	22.21	14.73	0.12
4	25	19.23	18.58	11.64	22.58	−0.37
5	23	15.22	15.09	13.22	18.96	−0.12
6	25	12.57	21.48	11.00	24.87	−0.07
7	19	20.89	15.22	8.11	22.52	−0.66*
8	21	26.39	16.11	12.57	16.56	−0.85*
Overall	181	17.89	19.24	13.44	20.01	−0.23*

[a]Total sample size does not sum to $N = 192$ owing to technical difficulties that resulted in data loss during the retention session. [b]Last acquisition session (Session 9). [c]Retention session. d = standardized mean difference for correlated scores. * $p < .05$, two-tailed.

retention session performance scores for each of the nonuse intervals. Using a 2 (session) × 8 (nonuse interval) mixed ANOVA we obtained a significant within-subjects main effect indicating that performance differed across the two sessions $F (1, 173) = 7.01$, $p < .05$, $\eta^2 = .04$. Consistent with the overall test for differences between the nonuse intervals, the between-subjects effect for session was not statistically significant, $F (7, 173) = 0.84$, $p > .05$, $\eta^2 = .03$, indicating that the eight groups (1-week through 8-week nonuse interval) did not differ in performance. Consistent with the nonsignificant within-subjects effect for interval lengths, performance did not decay differentially between groups; that is, the session × nonuse interval length interaction was not significant, $F (7, 173) = 1.46$, $p > .05$, $\eta^2 = .05$.

Long-Term Skill Retention

As an additional and exploratory assessment, trainees were contacted and invited to return to evaluate their long-term retention. Trainees' long-term retention was assessed after either a 9-, 19-, or 27-week interval. Upon returning, trainees completed a single test mission. The test mission (Mission E) was the same mission used during the second to last mission of reacquisition. The means, standard deviations, and standardized mean differences are presented in Table 3.3. Using *t*-tests for dependent scores, the mean difference

TABLE 3.3

Descriptive Statistics and Standardized Mean Differences for Task Performance by Long-Term Retention Interval

Long-Term Interval	n	Session 15		Long-Term Retention		
		Mean	SD	Mean	SD	d
9 weeks	10	14.70	13.66	8.60	18.68	−0.37
19 weeks	8	22.75	16.26	19.38	9.44	−0.25
27 weeks	21	16.20	16.57	9.29	17.12	−0.41

d = Standardized mean difference for correlated scores. None of the ds were statistically significant.

between second to last mission of reacquisition and the long-term retention session performance was not statistically different, at either the 9-week, $t(9) = -1.31$, $p > .05$, $d = -0.37$, 19-week, $t(7) = -0.49$, $p > .05$, $d = -0.25$, or 27-week interval, $t(20) = -1.54$, $p > .05$, $d = -0.41$. Although exploratory and of low statistical power, these results suggest that skill demonstrated moderate, but nonsignificant decay following a 9-, 19-, or 27-week nonuse interval.

DISCUSSION

The assumption that all skills decay over various periods of nonuse has reached the status of received doctrine. However, this seems to be based almost exclusively on simple skills over relatively short periods of nonuse. Given that most organizational training programs involve the application of skills learned at some later time (Arthur, Bennett, Edens, and Bell, 2003) potentially in a different environment (i.e., transfer), complex skill retention over extended periods of nonuse merits investigation. The purpose of our study was to examine the retention of a complex skill over an extended period of nonuse. Contrary to the large degree of skill decay that has been reported for simple tasks, we observed a moderate degree of skill decay on the complex task we used. Furthermore, the moderate degree of complex skill decay was more intriguing in that the nonuse interval spanned a period of 8 weeks. The moderate degree of complex skill decay was still present at the 9-, 19-, or 27-week nonuse intervals. These results are in contrast to what the skill decay literature would have suggested if the degree and trend of decay witnessed for simple tasks generalizes to complex tasks. For example, Arthur et al.'s (1998) meta-analysis of the skill decay literature reports a d of −0.65 for a nonuse interval similar to our 8-week nonuse interval; our comparative effect as −0.23.

Consequently, our results suggest that compared to skills on simple tasks, skills on complex tasks may be more resistant to decay over extended periods of nonuse.

There are several possible explanations for why more cognitively complex tasks would be associated with less skill loss compared to simple tasks. For instance, it is possible that the dynamic stimulus-response patterns associated with complex tasks inherently induces deeper, more elaborative processing, which in turn leads to greater skill retention compared to superficial, rote processing (Craik and Lockhart, 1972; Schmidt and Bjork, 1992). Likewise, cognitively complex tasks may be inherently more meaningful (i.e., natural), and meaningfulness may lead to higher levels of motivation as well as deeper, more elaborative processing (Wexley and Latham, 2002). Furthermore, individuals may be more naturally inclined to mentally rehearse tasks that are more meaningful during periods of nonuse (cf. Driskell, Copper, and Moran, 1994; Ryan and Simons, 1981). Finally, complex tasks may mask skill loss. That is, complex tasks by their very nature require more time to perform than their simpler counterparts. Therefore, to fully capture performance on complex tasks, longer tests of performance are required. Longer tests of retention naturally provide individuals with the opportunity to reacquaint themselves with the task. Thus, the time necessary to perform a complex task may confound tests of retention. Although one could argue that no such confounding occurs as long as the tests of performance before and after the nonuse period are equal, we contend that there would be a sharp contrast in performance during the early periods of both tests, with less of a contrast occurring during later periods. Consequently, longer tests of retention will not be sensitive to the amount of skill loss *immediately* following nonuse. In the present study, performance tests lasted 25 minutes, which is in sharp contrast to the typical skill decay study that entails a simple task with a performance test lasting no more than a few minutes. Therefore, it is difficult to say whether the overall low level of skill loss in the present study is owing to the nature of the task or the length of the performance test.

Implications for Practice, and Conclusions

Our findings have implications for researchers and training professionals alike. The moderate degree of skill decay on a complex skill, such as that used in our study, calls into question the assumption that the decay of skill on complex tasks is similar to the decay of skill on simple tasks. Skill decay research based upon simple tasks will probably not accurately capture the decay and retention of complex skills. Therefore, research aimed at assessing and documenting the acquisition, decay, and retention of complex skills is needed.

In terms of practical implications, our findings suggest that complex skill training may not be as susceptible to decay as we had once thought. If skills on complex tasks are more resistant to decay, refresher training may still be necessary; however, the interval between initial training and a refresher may be lengthened, thus reducing costs and increasing the utility of skills training on complex tasks.

In summary, although researchers generally agree that skills decay over periods of nonuse, the characteristics and patterns of decay for complex skills are less clear. Consequently, the present study investigated the decay of complex skills necessary to perform a command-and-control task over an extended period of nonuse. Our results suggest that complex skills may not decay at the same rate as simple skills over extended periods of nonuse. Hence, this pattern of results suggests that complex skills may be less susceptible to skill decay and that estimates of skill decay based upon simple tasks may not generalize to complex tasks.

REFERENCES

Annett, J. (1979). Memory for skill. In M. M. Grunberg and P. E. Morris (Eds.), *Applied problems in memory* (pp. 215–247). London: Academic.

Arthur, W. Jr., Bennett, W. Jr., Edens, P. S., and Bell, S. T. (2003). Effectiveness of training in organizations: A meta-analysis of design and evaluation features. *Journal of Applied Psychology, 88,* 234–245.

Arthur, W. Jr., Bennett, W. Jr., Stanush, P. L., and McNelly, T. L. (1998). Factors that influence skill decay and retention: A quantitative review and analysis. *Human Performance, 11,* 57–101.

Arthur, W. Jr., Day, E. A., Bennett, W. Jr., McNelly, T. L., and Jordan, J. A. (1997). Dyadic versus individual training protocols: Loss and reacquisition of a complex skill. *Journal of Applied Psychology, 82,* 783–791.

Cepeda, N. J., Pashler, H., Vul, E., Wixted, J. T., and Rohrer, D. (2006). Distributed practice in verbal recall tasks: A review and quantitative synthesis. *Psychological Bulletin, 132,* 354–380.

Craik, F. I., and Lockhart, R. S. (1972). Levels of processing: A framework for memory research. *Journal of Verbal Learning and Verbal Behavior, 11,* 671–684.

Day, E. A., Arthur, W. Jr., and Gettman, D. (2001). Knowledge structures and the acquisition of a complex skill. *Journal of Applied Psychology, 86,* 1022–1033.

Driskell, J. E., Copper, C., and Moran, A. (1994). Does mental practice enhance performance? *Journal of Applied Psychology, 79,* 481–492.

Ericsson, K. A., and Charness, N. (1994). Expert performance: It's structure and acquisition. *American Psychologist, 49,* 725–747.

Ericsson, K. A., Krampe, R. T., and Tesch-Roemer, C. (1993). The role of deliberate practice in the acquisition of expert performance. *Psychological Review, 100,* 363–406.

Farr, M. J. (1987). *The long-term retention of knowledge and skills: A cognitive and instructional perspective.* New York: Springer-Verlag.

Gabriele, W., and Shea, C. H. (2002). Principles derived from the study of simple skills do not generalize to complex skills training. *Psychonomic Bulletin & Review, 9*, 185–211.

Gardlin, G. R., and Sitterley, T. E. (1972). *Degradation of learned skills: A review and annotated bibliography* (D180-15081-1, NASA-CR-128611). Seattle, WA: Boeing.

Hurlock, R. E., and Montague, W. E. (1982). *The contribution of part-task training to the relearning of a flight maneuver* (Report No. NAVTRADEVCEN TR-297-2). Port Washington, NY: U.S. Naval Training Device Center.

May, G., and Kahnweiler, W. M. (2000). The effect of a mastery practice design on learning and transfer in behavioral modeling training. *Personnel Psychology, 53*, 353–373.

Naylor, J. C., and Briggs, G. E. (1961). *Long-term retention of learned skills: A review of the literature* (ASD TR 61–390). Columbus: Ohio State University, Laboratory of Aviation Psychology.

Prophet, W. W. (1976). *Long-term retention of flying skills: A review of the literature* (HumPRO Final Rep. No. 76–35). Alexandria, VA: Human Resources Research Organization (ADA036077).

Ryan, E. D., and Simons, J. (1981). Cognitive demand, imagery, and frequency of mental rehearsal as factors influencing acquisition of motor skills. *Journal of Sport Psychology, 3*, 35–45.

Saucer, J., Hockey, G. R. J., and Wastell, D. G. (2000). Effects of training on short- and long-term skill retention in a complex multiple-task environment. *Ergonomics, 43*, 2043–2064.

Schmidt, R. A., and Bjork, R. A. (1992). New conceptualizations of practice: Common principles in three paradigms suggest new concepts in training. *Psychological Science, 3*, 207–217.

Schneider, W. (1985). Training high-performance skills: Fallacies and guidelines. *Human Factors, 27*, 285–300.

Shebilske, W. L., Goettl, B. P., Corrington, K., and Day, E. A. (1999). Interlesson spacing and task-related processing during complex skill acquisition. *Journal of Experimental Psychology: Applied, 5*, 413–437.

Sonalysts, Inc. (2004). *Jane's Fleet Command Air Force Research Laboratory ver. 1.55* [Computer software]. Redwood City, CA: Electronic Arts.

Wexley, K. N., and Latham, G. P. (2002). *Developing and training human resources in organizations* (3rd ed.). Upper Saddle, NJ: Prentice Hall.

Wisher, R. A., Sabol, M. A., Hillel, H., and Kern, R. P. (1991). *Individual ready reserve (IRR) call-up: Skill decay* (ARI Research Rep. No. 1595). Alexandria, VA: U.S. Army Research Institute.

AUTHORS' NOTES

This research was sponsored by contracts and grants from the U.S. Air Force Research Laboratory, Human Effectiveness Directorate, Warfighter Training Research Division, Mesa, AZ, the Defense Advance Research Project Agency, and the National Science Foundation awarded to Winfred Arthur, Jr. The views expressed herein are those of the authors and do not necessarily reflect the official position or opinion of the sponsors or their respective organizations.

4

Factors Influencing Knowledge and Skill Decay after Training

A Meta-Analysis

Xiaoqian Wang, Eric Anthony Day,
Vanessa Kowollik, Matthew J. Schuelke,
and Michael G. Hughes

INTRODUCTION

Training is an essential endeavor in many organizations. Based on a 2009 report by the American Society for Training and Development, an estimated $134.1 billion was spent on formal training among U.S. organizations (Paradise and Patel, 2009). However, it is commonly thought that only 10 percent of these dollars invested in training results in "enduring behavioral change" (Wexley and Latham, 2002, p. 261). These low returns on investment are costly to organizations. From an organization's perspective, maximizing the amount of posttraining knowledge and skills retained is directly linked to achieving a high return on investment. Consequently, the present chapter presents a meta-analysis of existing organizationally relevant training research on knowledge and skill decay. Results based on 111 independent effects retrieved from 35 reports suggested an overall moderate decay effect ($d = -0.38$). The amount of decay was minimal for periods of nonuse less than 1 day ($d = -0.08$). For longer periods of nonuse, decay was moderate to large (ds ranged from $= -0.24$ to -0.84), but there was no straightforward monotonic relationship between the amount of decay and length of nonuse. That is, beyond 1 day, a greater length of nonuse did not always translate into greater decay. Decay was related to several methodological factors. Specifically, decay was greater when the operationalization of acquisition was criterion- versus duration-based, for cognitive versus skill-based criteria, and when the instructional environment was less structured. Furthermore, posttraining decay-prevention interventions showed strong decay-mitigating effects with large gains in performance after formal training. Decay was also related to the combination of cognitive and physical (i.e., psychomotor) task demands as well as task complexity. Tasks with moderate cognitive demands and minimal physical demands were associated with the greatest decay, whereas tasks with minimal cognitive demands but strong physical demands were associated with the least decay. Complex tasks were associated with modest levels of decay that were unlikely to be moderated by additional factors, but for simpler tasks decay effects were less robust and dependent upon other factors. Regression analysis indicated that decay was primarily related to the length of nonuse, amount of cognitive task demands, and the closed-/open-looped distinction such that longer periods of nonuse, greater cognitive demands, and closed-looped tasks were associated with greater decay. These results are discussed with respect to Arthur, Bennett, Stanush, and McNelly's (1998) previous meta-analysis of decay effects. Practical and theoretical implications are also discussed.

Skill and Knowledge Decay

Consonant with its usage throughout this volume, decay is used to refer to not the process but rather the observed decrement in performance on trained or acquired knowledge and skills after a given period of nonuse (Arthur, Bennett, Stanush, and McNelly, 1998; see Gronlund and Kimball, Chapter 2 this volume, for a discussion of decay as a process). As shown in Equation 1, decay and retention represent two sides of the same coin.

$$d = \frac{M_{T2} - M_{T1}}{SD_{pooled}}$$

Magnitude of decay is expressed as the effect size statistic, d, where M_{T1} is the immediate posttest mean (i.e., at the end of a given training program), M_{T2} is the delayed posttest mean (i.e., at some time after training and the immediate posttest), and SD_{pooled} is the pooled standard deviation. A negative d reflects decay after the retention interval (i.e., period of nonuse as indicated by the time between posttests), with larger effects indicating more decay (or less retention). A positive d indicates gains after the nonuse interval, while a d of zero indicates no loss, but no gain either. Hence, both terms—decay and retention—are often used interchangeably.

With one exception (i.e., Arthur et al., 1998), existing reviews of decay and retention have been qualitative in nature (e.g., Farr, 1987; Naylor and Briggs, 1961). Both qualitative and quantitative reviews suggest that decay increases as the retention interval extends (cf. Gronlund and Kimball, Chapter 2 this volume). Specifically, Arthur et al.'s (1998) meta-analysis showed that the correlation between the retention interval and corrected mean d was -0.51, indicating that decay increases as the retention interval increases. In addition, several other factors, such as degrees of overlearning and certain task characteristics, have also been shown to influence decay after periods of nonuse in both qualitative and quantitative reviews. Arthur et al. (1998) differentiated methodological factors from task-related factors that influence decay. Results for the methodological factors showed less decay for behavioral criteria ($d = -0.77$) than for learning criteria ($d = -1.04$); less decay when conditions of retrieval were similar to those during original learning ($d = -0.94$) than when those were different ($d = -2.07$); and a small difference in the amount of decay for studies that used recognition tests ($d = -0.85$) versus recall tests ($d = -0.96$). Owing to limited data at the time, no conclusive statements were made by Arthur et al. regarding the influence of degrees of overlearning on decay. The findings of task-related factors indicated more decay for open-looped tasks ($d = -1.04$) than for closed-looped tasks ($d = -0.71$); more decay for cognitive ($d = -1.15$) than for physical tasks ($d = -0.75$); and more decay for accuracy ($d = -1.00$) than for speeded tasks ($d = -0.32$). Additionally, Arthur et al. suggested exploring in future research the effect of additional moderators, such as task complexity, structure of training and practice, and decay-prevention interventions during retention intervals.

Arthur et al.'s (1998) initial efforts were not without limitations, partially owing to the limited number of empirical studies available at the time. Also, the dichotomization of each of the task-related characteristics studied in their meta-analysis could be considered coarse, failing to capture the multi-dimensional nature of task-related characteristics. Furthermore, Arthur et al. (1998) showed that several of the examined variables covaried, and thus their moderator analyses were confounded. For example, physical tasks were more likely to be speeded than accuracy-based with an even distribution of open-versus closed-looped tasks, whereas cognitive tasks were more likely to be accuracy-based than speeded and open- rather than closed-looped. In addition, Arthur et al. (1998) focused only on studies with a strict nonuse retention interval, while not addressing posttraining factors, such as decay-prevention interventions, which have been demonstrated to mitigate decay both in theoretical models and empirical studies (e.g., Baldwin and Ford, 1988; Gaudine and Saks, 2004).

The purpose of the present study was to conduct a meta-analysis of organizationally relevant training research to determine the methodological and task factors most likely to influence the decay of trained knowledge and skills. Given that the Arthur et al. (1998) meta-analysis is now over 10 years old, an updated meta-analysis seems appropriate. Additionally, to address the limitations of Arthur et al.'s (1998) study, we (1) examined methodological and task factors previously not examined, (2) used a more nuanced, multidimensional approach to coding task characteristics that involved coding dimensions along a 3-point scale (0–2), and (3) performed analyses that took into account the covariation among task-related characteristics as well as methodological factors. With respect to methodological factors, like Arthur et al. (1998), we examined the length of the retention interval, the degree of overlearning, condition of retrieval, and type of evaluation criteria. To expand on Arthur et al. (1998), we also examined the influence of how acquisition was operationalized, degree of training structure, and decay-prevention interventions. With respect to task-related characteristics, we examined differences in decay as a function of task-content demands and task complexity. To further expand on Arthur et al. (1998), content demands were expanded beyond cognitive and physical demands to include interpersonal demands as well. Our examination of complexity expanded on Arthur et al.'s (1998) closed- versus open-looped distinction by also including performance discretion, dynamic complexity, and component complexity.

METHODOLOGICAL FACTORS AFFECTING DECAY

Retention Interval

Retention interval refers to the duration between criterion assessments after the most recent training session and some specified period of nonuse (Driskell, Willis, and Copper, 1992; Ebbinghaus, 1885, 1913). Generally speaking, performance is negatively related to the retention interval length, with longer retention intervals resulting in worse performance than shorter retention intervals owing to the increased possibilities of interference and forgetting during the extended delay between acquisition and retrieval (Driskell et al., 1992; Farr, 1987). Consistent with the findings in Arthur et al. (1998), we examined the following hypothesis.

H1: There will be a negative relationship between the length of the retention interval and retention, such that longer retention intervals will be associated with more decay.

Operationalization of Acquisition

Knowledge and skill acquisition is a vital prerequisite of knowledge and skill retention (Arthur et al., 1998; Farr, 1987; cf. Schmidt and Bjork, 1992), yet it is not equivalent to permanent or long-lasting changes (Kraiger, 2003). Theoretically, there are three stages of skill acquisition. According to the Anderson's ACT* model (adaptive control of thought, Anderson, 1987, 1996), these skill acquisition stages progress from acquiring *declarative knowledge* (memory-based), to *knowledge compilation* (sequencing steps required to perform a task), and eventually to acquiring *procedural knowledge* (auto-mated performance). Despite the argument for automaticity as indications for competent performance (Howell and Cooke, 1989), the distinction between these stages in empirical studies is rather arbitrary.

Depending on the purpose of a given training intervention, trainees are expected to achieve a specified level of performance (i.e., criterion-based training) or to spend a specific amount of time (i.e., duration-based training) in training (Adams and Hufford, 1962; Arthur, Day, Bennett, McNelly, and Jordan, 1997; Rohrer, Taylor, Pashler, Wixted, and Cepeda, 2005). Many applied researchers use a measure of performance immediately after training as an operationalization of skill acquisition. Arthur et al. (1998) did not directly examine how skill acquisition was operationalized as a methodological moderator in their meta-analysis, but they did suggest that future research should pay more attention to acquisition as a prerequisite for retention. Without having acquisition clearly defined or operationalized, discussions of decay are less meaningful. Therefore, the current meta-analysis examined whether decay differed depending on how acquisition was operationalized. Specifically, the following research question was examined.

Q1: Will the amount of decay differ depending on whether the operational-ization of acquisition is criterion-based or duration-based?

Overlearning

Overlearning refers to deliberate learning and practice beyond the point of initial mastery, which can be either completing the first error-free trial or reaching a set criterion performance (Ebbinghaus, 1885, 1913). In other words, overlearning is relevant only in criterion-based training. Driskell et al.'s (1992) meta-analysis of overlearning showed that greater overlearning led to less decay of newly learned cognitive (e.g., remembering verbal information) and physical skills (e.g., balancing on a stabilometer), and overlearning was more effective for retaining cognitive skills compared to physical skills. Consistent with the findings of Driskell et al. (1992), Arthur et al. (1998) hypothesized a positive relationship between overlearning and skill retention, but they did not find support for this hypothesis. Given a relatively weak effect that was based on 30 studies (17 percent of the entire data points) with a limited range of degree of overlearning, Arthur et al. (1998) cautioned readers against making firm conclusions regarding the small differences in decay they found as the degree of overlearning increased. It should also be noted that a large portion of studies included in both meta-analyses involved tasks, such as remembering verbal information or balancing on a stabilometer, that were simple and straightforward. For those tasks, it was easy to identify when the first error-free trial (i.e., initial mastery) occurred. However, the determination of initial mastery would be challenging for complex and dynamic tasks in the context of organizational training, which is the focus of the current meta-analysis. Nevertheless, based on the existing literature on the facilitating effect of overlearning on retention, the following hypothesis was examined.

H2: The amount of decay will decrease as the degree of overlearning increases in criterion-based training.

Conditions of Retrieval

Conditions of retrieval refers to the similarity between the performance context on a test of retrieval (i.e., decay) and the context where learning and acquisition take place. According to the encoding specificity principle (Tulving, 1983; Tulving and Thompson, 1973) and identical-elements theory (Thorndike and Woodworth, 1901), the likelihood of information retrieval increases as the similarity increases between the retention testing and original learning contexts. Similarities between these two contexts provide cues and stimuli that facilitate information retrieval. Machin (2002) suggested that one should ensure that training incorporates procedures that are similar to those in the workplace, in order to maximize skill retrieval after training. Indeed, Arthur et al. (1998) found that decay was greater when the retrieval conditions were different from those of initial acquisition. Therefore, we examined the following hypothesis.

H3: The amount of decay will be greater when the conditions at the assessments of acquisition and retrieval are different compared to when they are similar.

Evaluation Criteria

There are two major models of training evaluation criteria commonly used by training practitioners and applied researchers. First, Kirkpatrick's typology

(Kirkpatrick, 1959, 1976, 1996) differentiates reaction (i.e., trainees' enjoyment and perceived utility of training), learning (i.e., measures of knowledge and skill specified as training objectives), behavioral (i.e., on-the-job performance), and results criteria (i.e., utility of training in terms of meeting organizations' objectives). Second, Kraiger, Ford, and Salas's (1993) model extends Kirkpatrick's typology by incorporating a more construct-centered model of training evaluation criteria. Although the two models exhibit some conceptual overlap, there are important distinctions. The Kraiger et al. (1993) model, which is more consistent with learning theory, provides a more theoretically viable framework in evaluating training by distinguishing between different types of affective, cognitive, and skill-based outcomes. For example, Kraiger et al.'s (1993) affective outcomes reflect an expansion of Kirkpatrick's reaction criteria by also including attitudinal (e.g., respect for diversity) and motivational (e.g., self-efficacy) outcomes rather than equating all attitudinal outcomes with mere reactions (cf. Alliger and Janak, 1989; Alliger, Tannenbaum, Bennett, Traver, and Shotland, 1997; Kirkpatrick, 1959, 1976, 1996). In terms of cognitive outcomes, the Kraiger et al. (1993) model extends Kirkpatrick's learning criteria by distinguishing knowledge organization and cognitive strategies from verbal knowledge (e.g., declarative and procedural). Similarly, based on theories of skill development (e.g., Anderson, 1996), the Kraiger et al. (1993) model makes distinctions between (a) skill proceduralization (i.e., reproduction of trained skills), (b) skill composition, adaptability, and generalization (i.e., application of trained skills in a new context or with new contingencies), and (c) skill automaticity (i.e., performing a task without conscious monitoring or performing a task while simultaneously performing a secondary interference task).

Only learning and behavior criteria under Kirkpatrick's typology were used by Arthur et al. (1998) in their meta-analysis of skill decay. They found that the amount of decay was less for behavioral ($d = -0.77$) than for learning criteria ($d = -1.04$). The current meta-analysis used the more construct-centered Kraiger et al. (1993) model, and focused on cognitive and skill-based outcomes. Although cognitive and skill-based criteria under the Kraiger et al. (1993) model are loosely similar to learning and behavioral criteria under the Kirkpatrick's typology, we proposed the following research questions rather than framing them as hypotheses owing to the lack of past research in this regard.

Q2: Will the amount of decay differ for cognitive criteria compared to skill-based criteria?
Q3: Will the amount of decay differ for different types of cognitive criteria?
Q4: Will the amount of decay differ for different types of skill criteria?

Degree of Structure in the Instructional Environment

Structure of the training refers to the extent to which instructors (or instructional environments, in general) provide guidance, clarification, and feedback and objectives for trainees, and the extent to which instructors exert control over how the materials are delivered as well as trainees' learning process (Campbell and Kuncel, 2001). In general, with highly structured training, trainees have little control over the learning process, whereas trainees have more control over their learning in less structured training, particularly with respect to exploratory or discovery-based learning. It is commonly thought that some degree of structure is needed to ensure that trainees fully engage all the material to be learned and focus their attention in a manner that facilitates basic learning and skill acquisition (Bell and Kozlowski, 2002; Mayer, 2004; Salas, Cannon-Bowers, Rhodenizer, and Bowers, 1999). However, recent research on adaptive guidance and active learning suggests that too much structure can be detrimental to learning, particularly in terms of the generalization of knowledge and skills (e.g., Bell and Kozlowski, 2008; Dormann and Frese, 1994; McDaniel and Schlager, 1990). Therefore, to examine how structure of training is related to decay, we trichotomized degree of structure into low, moderate, and high categories and examined the following research question.

Q5: What is the relationship between training structure and the amount of decay?

Decay-prevention Interventions

The purpose of posttraining *decay-prevention interventions* is to promote effective transfer of training to the job environment by helping trainees set transfer goals, creating a supportive transfer climate, monitoring posttraining performance, and providing relapse prevention training (Foxon, 1993, 1994; Goldstein and Ford, 2002; Machin, 2002; Salas et al., 1999). For example, goal setting and self-management are the most commonly used posttraining decay-prevention interventions. Goal setting posits that difficulty and specificity are the two components of goals that positively influence performance (Locke and Latham, 1990). Self-management training is related to relapse-prevention interventions that were originally advocated in the treatment of addictions (Marx, 1982). Self-management training is a cognitive-behavioral strategy that encourages trainees to identify obstacles and strategies to overcome said obstacles. As supported by findings from relevant primary studies and qualitative reviews, both goal setting and self-management interventions have been found to be effective in promoting retention in training on negotiation, customer service, and supervisory skills (Gist, Stevens, and Bavetta, 1991; Hutchins and Burke, 2006; Noe, Sears, and Fullenkamp, 1990; Richman-Hirsch, 2001; Tews and Tracey, 2008). Therefore, the following hypothesis was examined:

H4: The use of posttraining decay-prevention interventions will be associated with less decay.

TASK-RELATED FACTORS AFFECTING DECAY

Task-content Demands

Task-content demands concern the nature of tasks that trainees are expected to learn in training. Depending on the specific learning objectives and task requirements, task-content demands can fall into the following three categories: cognitive, physical, and interpersonal (Farina and Wheaton, 1973; Fleishman and Quaintance, 1984; Goldstein and Ford, 2002). Cognitive demands involve information processing, problem solving, sense making, idea generation, and decision making. Physical demands require the use of the musculoskeletal system to perform a range of physical and psychomotor movements. Interpersonal demands relate to interacting with others including co-workers, clients, and customers. However, the content demands of many tasks involve some mix or combination of cognitive, physical, or interpersonal components.

Although previous research has shown that effectiveness of different kinds of training depends upon the content of the training (Aguinis and Kraiger, 2009; Arthur, Bennett, Edens, and Bell, 2003; Wexley and Latham, 2002), such investigations have not specifically addressed training effectiveness with respect to decay. Moreover, Arthur et al.'s (1998) meta-analysis only compared decay by treating task content as a categorical variable, specifically either cognitive or physical in nature. Their results showed an overall greater amount of decay for cognitive tasks ($d = -1.15$) than for physical tasks ($d = -0.75$). In the present study, instead of making a categorical distinction, task content was treated as a multidimensional construct. As such, cognitive, physical, and interpersonal demands were each scored on a three-point scale (0 = low [minimally applicable/involved]; 1 = moderate [somewhat applicable/involved]; 2 = high [very applicable/involved]).

Arthur et al.'s (1998) dichotomization of cognitive versus physical tasks can be represented as tasks with high cognitive and low physical demands versus tasks with low cognitive and high physical demands under the current coding scheme. Accordingly, we examined the following hypothesis.

H5: There will be more decay for high cognitive/low physical tasks than for low cognitive/high physical tasks.

Furthermore, the multidimensional coding scheme of task content allowed us to examine the following research questions:

Q6: Will the amount of decay be related to the strength of each of the content demands?
Q7: Will the amount of decay differ as a function of the combination of cognitive, physical, and interpersonal demands?

Task Complexity

Task complexity is a function of objective characteristics of tasks and has been found to be an important determinant of learning and performance (e.g., Haerem and Rau, 2007; Wood, 1986). The most commonly used framework of task complexity, with a focus on individual task performance, was articulated by Wood (1986). Under this model, three components comprise task complexity: *component complexity* (the number of distinct acts and distinct information cues or information elements that are needed to perform a task), *coordinative complexity* (the form and strength of the relationships between the components of a task and the sequencing of the inputs), and *dynamic complexity* (the need to adapt to potential changes in the means–ends hierarchy during the performance of a task).

Task complexity, as defined using Wood's model, is often studied as a moderator in meta-analyses. For example, Wood, Mento, and Locke (1987) showed that the magnitude of goal setting on performance was moderated by task complexity, such that the magnitude of goal effects was greater on simple tasks (e.g., recall task) than on complex tasks (e.g., business game simulation). Chen, Casper, and Cortina (2001) found that self-efficacy partially mediated the relationships of cognitive ability and conscientiousness with performance on simple tasks, but not on complex tasks. In addition, the relationships of cognitive ability and conscientiousness with performance were stronger for more complex tasks, while self-efficacy was not related to complex task performance after controlling for cognitive ability and conscientiousness (Chen et al., 2001).

A similar model was used in a meta-analysis of the distributed practice effect by Donovan and Radosevich (1999). Based on the results from a cluster analysis of task characteristics, Donovan and Radosevich categorized tasks into different types along the following three dimensions. First, *overall task complexity* was operationalized as the number of distinctive behaviors required, number of choices needed, and degree of uncertainty involved to complete a task. This dimension was adapted from Wood's (1986) aggregated task complexity. The other two dimensions, *mental requirements of the task* and *physical requirements of the task*, were unique dimensions that resulted from their cluster analysis. These two dimensions were not included in the operationalization of task complexity in the current meta-analysis because they are captured under the aforementioned factor of task-content demands (i.e., cognitive, physical and interpersonal tasks). Results from Donovan and Radosevich's (1999) meta-analysis on spacing practice indicated that the superiority of spaced practice over massed practice diminished as complexity of tasks on all three dimensions increased from low to high ($d = 0.97$ to $d = 0.07$).

The current meta-analysis adapted the conceptualization of task complexity proposed by Wood (1986) and Donovan and Radosevich's (1999) operationalization of overall task complexity as well as the distinction between closed- and open-looped tasks, yielding four dimensions of complexity: (1) closed-/open-looped, (2) discretion, (3) dynamic complexity, and (4) component complexity. Except for the closed-/open-looped distinction, which was dichotomously coded, task complexity was scored on a 3-point scale (0 = low [minimally applicable/involved]; 1 = moderate [somewhat applicable/involved]; 2 = high [very applicable/involved]) for each of the three other complexity dimensions. This coding scheme allowed us to examine decay as a function of each dimension of task complexity as well as in combination.

With respect to our first dimension of complexity, an *open-looped* task refers to a task without a clear and distinct end, which is contingent on time, and requires constant monitoring of the discrepancies between a current and desired state. On the other hand, a *closed-looped* task is one with an un-ambiguous ending that is not contingent on time (Naylor and Briggs, 1961). For example, monitoring a nuclear reactor is an open-looped task that requires ongoing comparison between the current and desired state of the reactor. The end of such tasks is usually marked by specific time limits. However, delivering a package is closed-looped because the task is complete when the package reaches the addressee's hands. Closed-looped tasks often involve discrete responses that have a definite beginning and end, whereas open-looped tasks typically involve continuous responses that are repeated, or constant monitoring without a definite beginning or end.

Results from primary studies and narrative reviews (e.g., Farr, 1987) generally suggest that open-looped tasks are more resistant to decay than closed-looped tasks. Compared to closed-looped tasks, open-looped tasks are more coherent and continuous in nature, so they are more natural and meaningful to people (Naylor and Briggs, 1961). Based on previous reviews, Arthur et al. (1998) hypothesized that closed-looped tasks would decay more than open-looped tasks, but their meta-analytic findings indicated an opposite trend such that open-looped tasks generally decayed more ($d = -1.06$) than closed-looped tasks ($d = -0.71$). However, this inconsistent finding may be largely owing to the covariation and confounding among three types of task characteristic moderators examined (closed-/open-looped, physical/cognitive, and natural/artificial). Specifically, Arthur et al. (1998) found that physical tasks were more likely to be speeded than accuracy-based with an even distribution of open- and closed-looped tasks, whereas cognitive tasks were more likely to be accuracy-based than speeded and open- rather than closed-looped.

Discretion, the second dimension of complexity, refers to the number of choices or approaches that can be adopted to perform a task and reach an end goal. We adapted this dimension from the coordinative complexity dimension under Wood's (1986) model and aspects of overall complexity in the Donovan and Radosevich (1999) framework. Our third dimension, *dynamic complexity*, as specified under Wood's (1986) model, refers to the dynamic nature of the task environment. Task elements are dynamic in cases where inconsistent information exists or there is inconsistency in information processing and decision execution. In other words, a task with dynamic elements is characterized by the extent of not knowing what will happen or what to expect, and the requirement of constantly paying attention to different components in the task environment. Last, our fourth dimension, *component complexity*, as specified by Wood (1986), refers to the total number of distinct processes and behaviors required to execute a task, and the total number of distinct information cues that must be processed in performing actions.

As task complexity increases, the knowledge and skill requirements for performing tasks also increase. The characteristics of complex tasks are inherently more meaningful to individuals. Rather than performing rote tasks, individuals are motivated to engage in deeper and more elaborative processing during training, and consequently should achieve better retention given the nature of complex tasks (Arthur et al., 1998; Craik and Lockhart, 1972; Schmidt and Bjork, 1992; Wexley and Latham, 2002). Therefore, the following hypothesis was examined:

H6: Decay will be smaller for more complex tasks than for less complex tasks across all four dimensions of complexity and combinations of complexity dimensions.

Covariation among Moderators

Although Arthur et al. (1998) showed that several task-related factors covaried in their sample of studies, they did not undertake any analyses to examine the independent effects of the different moderating factors. Instead, Arthur et al.

reported how data points for a given analysis (e.g., closed- versus open-looped tasks) were disproportionately represented by levels of another moderating factor (e.g., cognitive versus physical tasks), and then they commented on the possible confounding influences. Furthermore, Arthur et al. (1998) only examined the possibility of confounding influences for the subset of their analyses involving task-related factors. They did not examine the possibility of confounding with respect to methodological factors. Therefore, to extend the methodological approach taken by Arthur et al. (1998), we (1) calculated the correlations among all the moderating variables examined in this meta-analysis, as well as the correlations between the moderators and the study effect sizes (i.e., amount of decay), and (2) examined the independent effects of all the moderators by regressing the study effect sizes on all the moderators.

METHOD

Literature Search

An extensive literature search was conducted, both electronically and manually through the year 2007, to identify empirical studies that investigated knowledge and/or skill decay. The electronic search covered nine computer databases (Academic Search Elite, Business Source Elite, Defense Technical Information Center, Dissertation Abstract, Econlit, Educational Research Information Center, Government Printing Office, PsycINFO, and SocINDEX). The electronic search was supplemented by a manual search of reference lists of recent training literature reviews (Aguinis and Kraiger, 2009; Alliger and Janak, 1989; Alliger et al., 1997; Arthur et al., 1998; Arthur et al., 2003; Colquitt, LePine, and Noe, 2000), as well as conference presentations of the Society for Industrial and Organizational Psychology. The following key words were used: *knowledge/skill retention, knowledge/skill maintenance, knowledge/skill perishability, knowledge/skill deterioration, knowledge/skill decay, knowledge/skill degradation, knowledge/skill acquisition, training evaluation, training efficiency, training effectiveness,* and *training.* The initial search resulted in approximately 10,459 English language citations, out of which 38 reports were retained based on the inclusion criteria. The final dataset was comprised of the following sources: 29 journal articles, four dissertations, four technical reports, and one unpublished manuscript submitted for review.

Inclusion Criteria

A set of decision rules was used to determine whether to retain studies, given the purpose of the current meta-analysis. First, to be included in the meta-analysis, a study must have investigated the effectiveness of an organizational-relevant training program over time. The study could have occurred either in a field or laboratory setting. Laboratory studies were included if it was judged that the author intended to generalize the findings to organizationally relevant settings. Studies published in educational journals were excluded unless the researchers specifically sought to generalize their findings to organizational settings. In addition, studies using simple tasks, such as memorizing nonsense syllables (e.g., Mandler and Heineman, 1956) or drawing lines blindfolded (e.g., Trowbridge and Cason, 1932), were not included because findings from such studies are less likely to have implications for organizational contexts. Second, participants had to be 18 years or older. Third, studies must have clearly indicated that the training was completed either because trainees reached training goals or underwent a specific amount of time as required by the training program. Fourth, the study had to report enough information to allow reasonable judgments about the structure of the training to be made. Fifth, for a criterion to be considered as assessing retention over time, the same measure had to be administered both immediately (i.e., within 1 hour) upon completion of training and some time later. The time interval between immediate and delayed posttest had to be greater than the time interval between the end of training and immediate posttest. Sixth, studies had to report statistics that allow for the computation of d. In other words, studies had to report sample sizes along with means and standard deviations for the immediate and delayed criterion test, or present sufficient statistical information to permit the computation of d (e.g., effect sizes can also be calculated if dependent t-statistics are reported along with the correlation between the immediate and delayed posttests; Dunlap, Cortina, Vaslow, and Burke, 1996). Last, the current meta-analysis only focused on individual-level effects.

Dataset

Nonindependence. The inclusion criteria led to an initial dataset consisting of 209 data points (ds) from 38 reports. However, not all of these data points were independent, because many of them involved the same group of participants. In the context of meta-analysis, nonindependence can be problematic because it can reduce the observed variability of effect sizes, artificially inflate sample sizes and effect sizes, and overweight the contributions of studies with multiple nonindependent data points (Arthur, Bennett, and Huffcutt, 2001). For analysis examining overall effects (e.g., retention interval and decay), data points were averaged across all types of criteria if they were from the same group of participants under the same manipulation in the same study. However, in examining differences as a function of criterion type (e.g., whether decay differed for cognitive versus skill-based criteria), effects from the same group of participants on different criterion measures were considered independent if the different criterion measures reflected different criterion types that could contribute to a specific meta-analytic comparison (e.g., cognitive versus skill-based and proceduralized skill versus adaptive skill). Consequently, nonindependent data points were averaged, and this resulted in 114 independent data points from 38 reports. Out of the 114 independent data points, three reports involved posttraining interventions, thus they were excluded from the final dataset except for addressing Hypothesis 4 (the use of posttraining decay-prevention interventions will be associated with lower levels of decay). Therefore, the final dataset used to address the majority of the hypotheses and research questions consisted of 111 independent data points from 35 reports. The sources of these data points were as follows: 66.7 percent from journal articles, 20.7 percent from technical reports, 11.7 percent from dissertations, and 0.9 percent from unpublished manuscripts.

Outliers. As in primary studies, the presence of outliers poses a concern for meta-analyses. Accordingly, we used the sample-adjusted meta-analytic deviancy (*SAMD*; Huffcutt and Arthur, 1995) statistic to detect outliers. *SAMD* statistics were computed for each of the 111 independent data points, resulting in a mean *SAMD* of −0.08 ($SD = 1.82$). The resulting *SAMD* scree plot suggested a total of five outliers. However, these five data points, which constituted 4.5 percent of the 111 effect sizes in the dataset, were retained because (1) a detailed review failed to identify any peculiar characteristics to the studies to justify their exclusion, and (2) they were originally included in Arthur et al.'s (1998) meta-analysis. One of these studies was from a journal article by Reynolds and Bilodeau (1952), two were from a technical report by Thompson, Morey, Smith, and Osborne (1981), and two were from a technical report by Grimsley (1969).

Because one of the objectives of the current meta-analysis was to provide an update of Arthur et al.'s (1998) meta-analysis, efforts were made to extract all 53 reports coded by Arthur et al. However, ultimately, only eight were retained in the current meta-analysis (including the three reports yielding data points that were identified as potential outliers in the *SAMD* scree plot). Out of Arthur et al.'s 53 reports, hard copies of 10 could not be found, 17 did not report relevant statistics to calculate effect sizes per our inclusion criteria, and another 18 failed to meet one or more of the other inclusion criteria. It is important to note a difference between our inclusion criteria and those of Arthur et al. (1998) pertaining to reports providing enough statistical information needed to compute effect sizes. Arthur et al. (1998) adopted the approach recommended by Glass, McGaw, and Smith (1981) to convert *p*-values to effect sizes for reports that did not report other relevant statistics (e.g., means, standard deviations, and correlations; W. Arthur, Jr., personal communication, April 8, 2010). We did not adopt this approach for several reasons. One, *p*-values are sensitive to study design and sample sizes. Two, different study designs or sample sizes can result in changes in *p*-values but have no effect on the population effect size. Three, exact *p*-values are rarely accurately reported (Kraemer, 2005).

Methodological Factors

Retention interval. The retention intervals between immediate posttests and delayed posttests were coded in terms of hours. To compare the results related to the retention intervals from the current meta-analysis with those from Arthur et al. (1998), the same categorization scheme was used to break number of hours into different retention interval categories: (1) less than 1 day; (2) greater than or equal to 1 day, but less than or equal to 7 days; (3) greater than 7 days, but less than or equal to 14 days; (4) greater than 14 days, but less than or equal to 28 days; (5) greater than 28 days, but less than or equal to 90 days; (6) greater than 90 days, but less than or equal to 180 days; (7) greater than 180 days, but less than or equal to 365 days; and (8) greater than 365 days (see Table 4.1). None of the studies included in the current meta-analysis involved retention intervals in the last two categories.

Operationalization of acquisition. If participants in a study were required to reach some stated performance level to complete training, then such studies were coded as criterion-based. If participants simply completed a specified training program without having to pass a criterion assessment, then such studies were coded as duration-based.

TABLE 4.1

Retention Interval Categories

Retention Interval	Number of Days
1	Less than 1 day
2	Greater than or equal to 1 day; less than or equal to 7 days
3	Greater than 7 days; less than or equal to 14 days
4	Greater than 14 days; less than or equal to 28 days
5	Greater than 28 days; less than or equal to 90 days
6	Greater than 90 days; less than or equal to 180 days
7*	Greater than 180 days; less than or equal to 365 days
8*	Greater than 365 days

* No studies meeting the inclusion criteria were obtained for Intervals 7 and 8.

Overlearning. The degree of overlearning was calculated only for studies that were coded as criterion-based, using the formula previously used by Driskell et al. (1992) and Arthur et al. (1998). As an example, if reaching a criterion level requires five trials and the overlearning condition involves five additional trials, then the degree of overlearning is 100 percent. A zero score for overlearning indicates no overlearning occurred.

Conditions of retrieval. The contexts of the immediate and delayed posttests were dichotomously coded as being the same or different based on the descriptions provided in primary studies.

Type of evaluation criteria. Dependent variables in primary studies were classified as cognitive or skill-based outcomes according to Kraiger et al.'s (1993) model of evaluation criteria. In addition, the cognitive criteria were further broken down to declarative knowledge, procedural knowledge, strategic knowledge, knowledge organization, and cognitive strategies criteria. Skill criteria were coded as either proceduralized skill or adaptive skill. No studies included explicit tests of skill automaticity (or resistance to secondary task interference).

Training structure. The degree of structure was a composite of six dimensions scored on a 0–2 scale (0 = little if any [e.g., the dimension of structure involved less than 10 percent of training time], 1 = moderate degree [e.g., more than 10 percent of training time but less than 50 percent], 2 = large degree [e.g., more than 50 percent of training time]). These six were (1) instructor control of activities (the instructor [this could also be the computer in computer-based training] determines the sequence of activities, announcing to the trainees when to move on to a new activity), (2) instructional messages (explicit information about the training content and how to approach the learning of it), (3) clarification of material (the instructor provides clarifying and elaborative information that extends basic instruction), (4) personal assistance from the instructor (the instructor provides personalized hands-on assistance to individual trainees in the form of advice or demonstrations), (5) breakdown of training into modules (training content is divided into components or modules that help trainees direct and focus their attention), and (6) detailed training objectives (information is provided to trainees in terms of what they should know or be able to do as a result of training activities). Although scores could range from 0 to 12, the distribution of overall structure scores ranged from 0 to 9. Thus, none of the data points in this meta-analysis involved a sample that underwent highly structured (i.e., guided) training. Based on the frequency distribution, the overall structure scores were trichotomized: low structure = 0 to 2 (k = 38), medium structure = 3 to 4 (k = 58), and high structure = 5 to 9 (k = 15). A trichotomous rather than a dichotomous scheme was used to examine the possibility of a curvilinear association between structure and decay.

Decay-prevention intervention. Information about whether there was any decay-prevention intervention (e.g., refresher training) implemented during the retention interval was dichotomously coded.

Task-related Factors

Task-content demands. Three types of task-content demands (i.e., cognitive, physical, and interpersonal) were each coded using a 3-point scale (0 = low [minimally applicable/involved]; 1 = moderate [somewhat applicable/involved]; 2 = high [very applicable/involved]) to reflect the nature of the demands. For example, training on negotiation would be coded as 1 for cognitive, 0 for physical, and 2 for interpersonal. Word processing would be coded as 1 for cognitive, 2 for physical, and 0 for interpersonal. It should be noted that the physical demands in the vast majority of studies included in the present meta-analysis were psychomotor in nature more so than gross-motor or stamina-based.

Task complexity. Based on the previously reviewed definitions, the open-/closed-looped distinction was dichotomously coded, whereas discretion, dynamic complexity, and component complexity were coded using a 3-point scale (0 = low [minimally applicable/involved]; 1 = moderate [somewhat applicable/involved]; 2 = high [very applicable/involved]), with a higher number indicating higher levels of complexity. For example, training on giving presentations would be coded as closed-looped, 2 for discretion, 1 for dynamic complexity, and 1 for component complexity. Air traffic control would be coded as open-looped, 2 for discretion, 2 for dynamic complexity, and 2 for component complexity.

Coding Interrater Agreement

Having received 20 hours of training using a training manual developed for the current meta-analysis, three graduate students coded the data. All coders were assigned a common set of nine reports, which were used to assess interrater agreement by comparing the values and categorizations assigned by each coder for all variables of concern. As shown in Table 4.2. The levels of agreement were generally high, with a mean overall agreement of 97.17 percent ($SD = 5.29$). As a means a further training, discrepancies and disagreements related to this set of nine reports were resolved through consensus meetings involving all three graduate student coders.

TABLE 4.2

Interrater Agreement for Major Study Variables

Variable	Percent agreement
d	100.00
N	100.00
Initial acquisition	100.00
Overlearning	100.00
Conditions of retrieval	100.00
Type of evaluation criteria	
Cognitive	
Declarative knowledge	98.40
Declarative and procedural knowledge	95.27
Skill	
Proceduralized	98.40
Adaptive	98.40
Structure*	92.76
Practice opportunities	100.00
Decay-prevention intervention	100.00
Task content	
Cognitive	92.60
Physical	92.60
Interpersonal	100.00
Task complexity	
Open-looped	77.80
Amount of discretion	100.00
Dynamic complexity	100.00
Component complexity	100.00

* Percent agreement reported for structure was an average of percent agreement of all six dimensions. ICC for structure composite score among three coders was .94.

Computation of Effect Sizes

We conducted meta-analytic calculations following the recommendations of Hunter and Schmidt (1990) as outlined by Arthur et al. (2001). Specifically, we used the effect size statistic, d, as the common metric to aggregate decay effects across all studies. Effect sizes were sample-weighted and corrected for the attenuating effect of unbalanced sample sizes. The standard deviation of effects, percentage of variance explained by sampling error, and 95 percent confidence intervals were also calculated.

Moderator Analyses. To assess the impact of each proposed factor on decay, studies were separated into different subsets based on specific levels of a proposed moderating factor. For the current meta-analysis, a factor was considered a meaningful moderator if the difference between level effects (respective sample-weighted mean *d*s) was equal to or greater than 0.20 and the confidence intervals for each effect did not substantially overlap.

RESULTS

As shown in Table 4.3, across 111 independent effects, there was an overall moderate degree of decay ($d = -0.38$). However, the 95 percent confidence interval was rather large, covering a range from strong levels of decay ($d = -1.50$) to moderately strong levels of retention ($d = 0.75$). Furthermore, there was a small amount of variance accounted for by sampling error (30.85 percent), suggesting that the investigation of moderators was warranted.

TABLE 4.3

Meta-analysis Results for Retention Interval

Retention interval	k	N	d	SD d	% var.	Min. d	Max. d	95% CI L	95% CI U
Overall	111	3152	−0.38	0.57	30.85	−3.71	1.74	−1.50	0.75
1. RI < 1 day	10	252	−0.08	0.31	62.97	−0.72	1.74	−0.68	0.53
2. 1 day ≤ RI ≤ 7 days	48	1283	−0.42	0.27	8.14	−1.62	1.29	−0.94	0.11
3. 7 days < RI ≤ 14 days	8	259	−0.31	0.00	100.00	−0.40	0.07	−0.31	−0.31
4. 14 days < RI ≤ 28 days	14	278	−0.84	0.84	24.14	−3.71	0.24	−2.49	0.81
5. 28 days < RI ≤ 90 days	28	966	−0.24	0.81	15.32	−2.66	0.72	−1.83	1.35
6. 90 days < RI ≤ 180 days	3	114	−0.71	0.00	100.00	−0.85	−0.60	−0.71	−0.71

k = number of independent data points. N = number of participants. d = sample-weighted mean effect size. SD d = standard deviation of the estimated true effect size. % var. = percentage of variance explained by sampling error. Min. d = minimum effect size. Max. d = maximum effect size. 95% CI = 95% confidence interval (L = lower, U = upper).

Methodological Factors

Retention interval. The first hypothesis involved examining the effect of the length of nonuse retention interval on the amount of decay. Specifically, it was hypothesized that the length of the retention intervals would be negatively related to the amount of retention. In support of Hypothesis 1, the correlation between the retention interval and the sample-weighted mean effect size (d) was −0.58 ($p > .05$), indicating longer intervals were associated with more decay. Being based on only six data points (i.e., six retention interval categories), it is not surprising that this correlation was not statistically significant. Nevertheless, the direction of the relationship was consistent with Hypothesis 1. The results presented in Table 4.3 indicated that there was almost no decay ($d = -0.08$) when the retention interval was less than 1 day. Beyond 1 day, higher levels of decay were found for Retention Intervals 2 through 6 compared to Retention Interval 1. However, there was not a monotonic trend for the amount of decay with longer retention intervals. For instance, Retention Interval 5 (i.e., greater than 28 days, but less than or equal to 90 days) yielded less decay than Retention Intervals 2, 3, and 4. Overall, the results in Table 4.3 reflect mixed support for Hypothesis 1. The shortest retention interval was associated with less decay than any other retention interval, but there was no clear pattern of greater decay as retention interval increased beyond 1 day. However, the relatively small amount of variance accounted for by sampling error for Retention Intervals 2, 4, and 5 suggests the presence of additional moderators.

Operationalization of acquisition. Research Question 1 asked whether decay would differ depending on the operationalization of initial acquisition as criterion- or duration-based. Based on an analysis of seven studies that operationalized initial acquisition as criterion-based, the results showed there was more decay for criterion-based training ($d = -1.43$) than for duration-based training ($d = -0.35$). The absolute difference between these two effects was greater than 0.20, and the confidence intervals for each effect did not substantially overlap (Table 4.4). Therefore, there was a meaningful difference in decay depending on whether the operationalization of initial acquisition is criterion-based or duration-based. However, the percentage of variance accounted for by sampling error was relatively small for both effects, suggesting the presence of additional moderators.

Overlearning. Hypothesis 2 posited that higher degrees of overlearning in criterion-based training would be associated with less decay. However, there were only seven studies ($N = 52$) that were criterion-based training, out of which no information regarding degree of overlearning was reported. Therefore, Hypothesis 2 could not be tested in the current meta-analysis.

TABLE 4.4

Meta-Analysis Results for Methodological Factors

Methodological factor	k	N	d	SD d	% var.	Min. d	Max. d	95% CI L	U
Overall	111	3152	−0.38	0.57	30.85	−3.71	1.74	−1.50	0.75
Initial acquisition									
Criterion-based	7	52	−1.43	1.25	33.15	−3.71	0.22	−3.87	1.02
Duration-based	104	3100	−0.35	0.52	34.19	−2.66	1.74	−1.37	0.66
Condition of retrieval									
Similar	108	3004	−0.37	0.58	30.58	−3.71	1.74	−1.52	0.77
Different	3	148	−0.38	0.30	48.22	−0.85	1.11	−0.97	0.21
Type of evaluation criteria									
Cognitive	38	1135	−0.60	0.24	71.05	−1.99	0.47	−1.07	−0.12
Declarative	21	716	−0.46	0.13	87.42	−1.99	0.17	−0.72	−0.20
Declarative and procedural	14	359	−0.93	0.00	100.00	−1.62	−0.39	−0.93	−0.93
Skill	73	2017	−0.25	0.66	25.46	−3.71	1.74	−1.54	1.04
Proceduralized	68	1768	−0.23	0.68	25.31	−3.71	1.74	−1.56	1.11
Adaptive	5	249	−0.43	0.42	32.53	−1.01	0.47	−1.24	0.39
Structure									
Low	38	948	−0.68	0.63	30.26	−2.66	0.47	−1.92	0.56
Moderate	58	1443	−0.27	0.23	76.26	−1.99	1.74	−0.72	0.17
High	15	761	−0.18	0.76	12.10	−3.71	0.72	−1.67	1.31
Decay-prevention intervention									
No	111	3152	−0.38	0.57	30.85	−3.71	1.74	−1.50	0.75
Yes	3	376	0.82	0.00	100.00	0.64	0.86	0.82	0.82

k = number of independent data points. N = number of participants. d = sample-weighted mean effect size. $SD\ d$ = standard deviation of the estimated true effect size. % var. = percentage of variance explained by sampling error. Min. d = minimum effect size. Max. d = maximum effect size. 95% CI = 95% confidence interval (L = lower, U = upper). Low = 0 to 2 on a 0-to-12 scale. Moderate = 3 or 4 on a 0-to-12 scale. High = 5 to 9 on a 0-to-12 scale. No studies found for the factors of overlearning and practice opportunities.

Conditions of retrieval. Hypothesis 3 posited that decay would be greater when the conditions at the assessments of acquisition and retrieval are different compared to when they are similar. As shown in Table 4.4, the results did not support Hypothesis 3. The amount of decay when the conditions between the original and retrieval assessment were different (d = −0.38) was not different from when they were similar ($d = -0.37$). However, it should be noted that the estimated effect for different conditions was based on only three data points.

Criterion type. Three research questions were proposed regarding the degree of decay and different types of criteria as specified in the Kraiger et al. (1993) taxonomy. Research Question 2 asked whether amounts of decay would differ for cognitive criteria compared to skill-based criteria. To address Research Question 2, all specific types of cognitive and skill criteria were collapsed, respectively. As shown in Table 4.4, the results indicated greater decay for cognitive criteria ($d = -0.60$) compared to skill criteria ($d = -0.25$). It should also be noted that the range of the confidence interval associated with skill criteria (-1.54 to 1.04) was larger than that with cognitive criteria (-1.07 to -0.12). Furthermore, the confidence interval associated with skill criteria suggested the possibility of no decay or even improvement after a period of nonuse. The same conclusion could not be drawn regarding cognitive criteria. Therefore, there was more decay for cognitive criteria compared to skill-based criteria.

Research Question 3 asked whether amounts of decay would differ for different types of cognitive criteria. A comparison was only made between two specific types of cognitive criteria, namely declarative knowledge versus a combination of declarative and procedural knowledge. No studies were found that involved a pure procedural knowledge criterion. Also, there were not enough studies involving other types of cognitive criteria (e.g., knowledge organization, cognitive strategy) to warrant meaningful analyses. Results showed less decay for declarative knowledge ($d = -0.46$) than for a criterion assessing both declarative and procedural knowledge ($d = -0.93$), and their confidence intervals did not overlap. The percentage of variance accounted for by sampling error not only increased after separating cognitive criteria into these two specific cognitive criterion types, but also the high percentage of variance accounted for by sampling error suggested the low likelihood of additional moderators that would make a meaningful difference.

Research Question 4 asked whether rates of decay would differ for different types of skill criteria. Results indicated there was less decay for proceduralized skill criteria ($d = -0.23$) compared to adaptive skill criteria ($d = -0.43$), but their confidence intervals overlapped substantially. In addition, the percentage of variance accounted for by sampling error barely increased after breaking skill criteria into proceduralized and adaptive skill criteria. The small percentages of variance explained coupled with the large overlapping confidence intervals suggest that additional unknown moderators are likely influencing the relationship between decay and different types of skill criteria.

The results regarding Research Questions 2, 3, and 4 together show that criterion type does appear to be an important moderator of decay. Decay for cognitive criteria was stronger than that for skill criteria; declarative and procedural knowledge criteria decayed more than declarative knowledge; and adaptive skill criteria decayed more than proceduralized skill criteria. In addition, findings related to specific types of cognitive criteria were more robust than those for specific types of skill criteria.

Training structure. Research Question 5 asked whether training structure would influence decay. Results showed that the amount of decay increased as the level of structure decreased from high to low ($d = -0.18$, -0.27, and -0.68 for high, moderate, and low structure categories, respectively). The greatest difference was found between high and low structure, followed by the difference between moderate and low structure. But the difference between moderate and high structure was less than 0.20. The small percentage of variance accounted for by sampling error for low and high structure suggests the presence of additional moderators. Therefore, structure appears to have a moderating influence, but its influence also depends on other variables.

Decay-prevention interventions. Hypothesis 4 posited that posttraining decay-prevention interventions would be associated with lower levels of decay. Results presented in Table 4.4 supported Hypothesis 4. There was no decay when decay-prevention interventions were implemented. In fact, decay-prevention interventions were associated with a boost in performance from the immediate posttest to the delayed posttest ($d = 0.82$). However, the findings for decay-prevention interventions were based on only three data points ($N = 376$). Nevertheless, it appears that decay-prevention interventions are effective in mitigating decay.

Task-related Factors

Task-content demands. Hypothesis 5 posited that decay would be greater for high cognitive/low physical tasks than for low cognitive/high physical tasks. As presented in Table 4.5, the results supported Hypothesis 5 indicating more decay for high cognitive/low physical tasks ($d = -0.35$) than for low cognitive/high physical tasks ($d = 0.23$). One hundred percent of the variance was explained by sampling error for high cognitive/low physical tasks, suggesting that the small to moderate amount of decay for such tasks is robust and unlikely to depend on other factors. In contrast, the small positive amount of retention for low cognitive/high physical tasks is not robust. Only 47 percent of the variance was explained by sampling error, and the 95 percent confidence interval ranged from -0.67 to 1.13.

Owing to the limited number of data points ($k = 2$), interpersonal task demands were excluded from the exploratory moderator analyses concerning task-content demands. Research Question 6 asked whether decay would be

TABLE 4.5

Meta-Analysis Results for Task-content Demands

Task-content demands	k	N	d	SD d	% var.		Min. d	Max. d	95% CI L	U
Overall	111	3152	−0.38	0.57	30.85		−3.71	1.74	−1.50	0.75
Cognitive demands										
Low	8	176	0.23	0.46	46.97		−0.72	1.74	−0.67	1.13
Moderate	66	1886	−0.49	0.71	22.74		−3.71	0.72	−1.87	0.90
High	35	1025	−0.29	0.00	100.00		−1.68	0.42	−0.29	−0.29
Physical demands										
Low	43	1231	−0.62	0.21	77.03		−1.99	0.47	−1.04	−0.21
Moderate	40	723	−0.30	0.46	52.47		−3.71	0.47	−1.19	0.60
High	26	1133	−0.17	0.78	13.17		−2.66	1.74	−1.71	1.37
Demand combinations										
Cognitive = low, Physical = low[a]	–	–	–	–	–		–	–	–	–
Cognitive = low, Physical = mod.[a]	–	–	–	–	–		–	–	–	–
Cognitive = low, Physical = high	8	176	0.23	0.46	46.97		−0.72	1.74	−0.67	1.13
Cognitive = mod., Physical = low	34	880	−0.73	0.17	85.22		−1.99	0.47	−1.07	−0.40
Cognitive = mod., Physical = mod	21	422	−0.30	0.66	32.46		−3.71	0.47	−1.59	0.98
Cognitive = mod., Physical = high	11	584	−0.25	1.05	6.53		−2.66	0.72	−2.31	1.80
Cognitive = high, Physical = low	9	351	−0.35	0.00	100.00		−1.05	0.11	−0.35	−0.35
Cognitive = high, Physical = mod.	19	301	−0.30	0.00	100.00		−1.68	0.42	−0.30	−0.30
Cognitive = high, Physical = high	7	373	−0.23	0.00	100.00		−0.57	−0.04	−0.23	−0.23

k = number of independent data points. N = number of participants. d = sample-weighted mean effect size. $SD\ d$ = standard deviation of the estimated true effect size. % var. = percentage of variance explained by sampling error. Min. d = minimum effect size. Max. d = maximum effect size. 95% CI = 95% confidence interval (L = lower, U = upper). Low = 0 (minimally applicable/involved); mod. = moderate = 1 (somewhat applicable/involved); high = 2 (very applicable/involved). [a] No studies found.

related to the strength of each of the content demands. Based on the available data, the results (see Table 4.5) regarding Research Question 6 indicated that amount of decay decreased as the physical demands increased across levels of cognitive demands. But no obvious linear trend was found as the cognitive demands increased across levels of physical demands. Tasks with moderate cognitive demands yielded the most decay ($d = -0.49$), followed by tasks with high cognitive demands ($d = -0.29$), but no decay was found for tasks with low cognitive demands ($d = 0.23$). Together, these results show that the degree of both cognitive and physical task demands have an influence on decay. However, the relatively small percentage of variance explained by sampling error associated with certain levels of physical (i.e., moderate and high) as well as cognitive demands (i.e., low and moderate) also suggest that additional moderators may be operating.

Combinations of task-content demands. The intent of Research Question 7 was to explore whether decay would differ for tasks that have greater combined demands than for tasks with lower combined demands. To examine this research question, all three levels of cognitive demands were crossed with all three levels of physical demands to create categories with different combinations of both demands. As shown in Table 4.5, there was no simple trend showing that greater combined demands were associated with either less or more decay compared to fewer combined demands. For instance, for tasks with moderate cognitive demands, there was less decay when there were also physical demands; but for tasks with high cognitive demands, the degree of decay did not differ much depending on the degree of physical demands. The most decay occurred for moderate cognitive/low physical tasks ($d = -0.73$); and retention (actually, improved performance) was found for low cognitive/ high physical tasks ($d = 0.23$). Additionally, the effect for moderate cognitive/low physical tasks is fairly robust as 85.22 percent of the variance was explained by sampling error. It should be noted that the findings regarding decay for tasks with high cognitive demands combined with each level of physical demands are also relatively robust because the percentage of variance explained by sampling error was 100 percent for all the effects. Moreover, none of the confidence intervals for the effects for tasks with high cognitive demands overlapped with the confidence interval for the effect for moderate cognitive/low physical tasks. Therefore, even though no straightforward pattern was found for the relationship between overall combined task demands and decay, certain combinations of cognitive and physical demands appear to be make meaningful differences in decay.

Task complexity. Hypothesis 6 posited that decay would be less for more complex tasks than for less complex tasks. As previously described, task complexity in the current meta-analysis was conceptualized along four dimensions: (1) closed- versus open-looped, (2) discretion, (3) dynamic complexity, and (4) component complexity. In testing Hypothesis 6, the pattern of effects for each dimension was examined separately, and then the pattern of effects for combinations of dimensions was examined.

As shown in Table 4.6, across the four dimensions separately, the pattern of effect sizes showed mixed support for Hypothesis 6. First, consistent with Hypothesis 6, open-looped tasks were associated with less decay ($d = -0.30$) compared to closed-looped tasks ($d = -0.44$); however, the difference between the effects was small (0.14). Second, in contradiction to Hypothesis 6, more decay was found for tasks with high discretion ($d = -0.45$) compared to tasks with moderate discretion ($d = -0.37$), which had more decay compared to tasks with low discretion ($d = -0.29$); however, all of the differences between these effects were small (< 0.16). Third, in mixed support of Hypothesis 6, less decay was found for tasks with high dynamic complexity ($d = -0.26$) compared to tasks with low dynamic complexity ($d = -0.50$) but not compared to tasks with moderate dynamic complexity ($d = -0.18$). Fourth, in support of Hypothesis 6, less decay was found for tasks with high component complexity ($d = -0.20$) compared to tasks with moderate component complexity ($d = -0.37$), which in turn had less decay compared to tasks with low component complexity ($d = -0.61$). It is important to note that the effects for all four indicators of high complexity—open-looped, high discretion, high dynamic complexity, and high component complexity—are fairly robust given that 100 percent of the variance was explained by sampling error for each of these indicators. Across the four dimensions, sampling error did not account for much of the variance in the effects for the low and moderate complexity levels (all < 37 percent). These results suggest that decay for complex tasks is less influenced by other moderating factors compared to decay for simpler tasks.

Combinations of task complexity dimensions. A complete examination of how different combinations of task complexity dimensions are related to decay would involve calculating meta-analytic statistics for all possible combinations of the four dimensions of complexity. However, this was not possible given that no studies (effects) were obtained for many of the combinations. Therefore, discretion, dynamic complexity and component complexity were dichotomized by combining 1 and 2 on the original 0–2 rating scale in order to create a 2 × 2 × 2 × 2 matrix. This matrix is shown in Table 4.7. Despite collapsing complexity scores in this matter, almost half of the combinations (i.e., combinations involving low discretion) did not have any data, and the combination of open-looped, high discretion, high dynamic complexity, and low to moderate component complexity only had one data point.

TABLE 4.6

Meta-Analysis Results for Task Complexity Factors

Task complexity factor	k	N	d	SD d	% var.	Min. d	Max. d	95% CI	
								L	U
Overall	111	3152	−0.38	0.57	30.85	−3.71	1.74	−1.50	0.75
Closed vs. open-looped									
Closed-looped	63	1769	−0.44	0.76	20.47	−3.71	1.74	−1.93	1.05
Open-looped	48	1383	−0.30	0.00	100.00	−1.68	1.29	−0.30	−0.30
Discretion									
Low	23	420	−0.29	0.63	36.25	−3.71	0.47	−1.53	0.95
Moderate	66	2256	−0.37	0.62	23.65	−2.66	1.74	−1.60	0.85
High	22	476	−0.45	0.00	100.00	−1.68	0.42	−0.45	−0.45
Dynamic complexity									
Low	4	1745	−0.50	0.64	27.27	−3.71	1.74	−1.76	0.75
Moderate	23	833	−0.18	0.58	25.32	−1.55	0.72	−1.31	0.94
High	24	574	−0.26	0.00	100.00	−1.68	0.42	−0.26	−0.26
Component complexity									
Low	30	728	−0.61	0.82	20.64	−2.66	1.74	−2.22	1.01
Moderate	41	1450	−0.37	0.62	23.53	−3.71	0.72	−1.58	0.83
High	40	974	−0.20	0.00	100.00	−1.68	0.42	−0.20	−0.20

k = number of independent data points. N = number of participants. d = sample-weighted mean effect size. $SD\ d$ = standard deviation of the estimated true effect size. % var. = percentage of variance explained by sampling error. Min. d = minimum effect size. Max. d = maximum effect size. 95% CI = 95 confidence interval (L = lower, U = upper). Low = 0 (minimally applicable/involved); moderate = 1 (somewhat applicable/involved); high = 2 (very applicable/involved).

Given the lack of data points for many combinations of the complexity dimensions, it was not possible to draw clear conclusions regarding the relationship between decay and the combinations of complexity and overall task complexity. However, in the majority of comparisons, combinations yielding overall higher amounts of complexity were associated with less decay compared to combinations yielding lower complexity. Also, given high discretion, decay varied more based on combinations of dynamic and component complexity for closed-looped tasks than for open-looped tasks. In sum, no clear support was found for Hypothesis 6, although the general pattern of effects suggests that decay more times than not will be smaller for tasks with higher complexity compared to tasks with lower complexity.

TABLE 4.7

Meta-Analysis Results for Task Complexity Factors in Combination

			Closed-looped		Open-looped	
			Low discretion	Mod./high discretion	Low discretion	Mod./high discretion
Low component complexity	Low dynamic complexity	d (k)	–[a]	-0.91 (14)	–[a]	-0.25 (9)
		% Var.		13.33		60.49
		CI		(-2.91, 1.09)		(-0.84, 0.35)
	Mod./high dynamic complexity	d (k)	–[a]	-0.39 (6)	–[a]	0.43 (1)
		% Var.		100.00		100.00
		CI		(-0.39, -0.39)		(0.43, 0.43)
Mod./high component complexity	Low dynamic complexity	d (k)	-0.29 (23)	-0.91 (14)	–[a]	-0.42 (12)
		% Var.	63.28	65.57		100.00
		CI	(-1.53, 0.95)	(-1.14, -0.17)		(-0.42, -0.42)
	Mod./high dynamic complexity	d (k)	–[a]	-0.18 (14)	–[a]	-0.24 (26)
		% Var.		16.48		100.00
		CI		(-1.46, 1.10)		(-0.24, -0.24)

d = sample-weighted mean effect size. k = number of independent data points. % Var. = percentage of variance explained by sampling error. CI = 95% confidence interval. Low = 0 (minimally applicable/involved); mod. to high = 1 (somewhat applicable/involved) or 2 (very applicable/involved). [a] No studies found.

Correlation and Regression Analyses

As an alternative to the traditional meta-analytic approach, correlations between amount of decay (i.e., study effect sizes) and each of the moderator variables were examined, and a multiple regression analysis was also conducted to examine the unique influence of each moderator variable on decay. As shown in Table 4.8, amount of decay was significantly correlated with criterion type and physical task demands. Skill criteria were associated with less decay than cognitive criteria, and stronger physical demands were associated with less decay. None of the other moderator variables were significantly correlated with the amount of decay.

There were also statistically significant correlations among many of the moderator variables. First, retention interval covaried with the closed-/open-looped distinction, with open-looped tasks tending to have longer retention intervals than closed-looped tasks. Second, criterion type was significantly

TABLE 4.8

Descriptive Statistics and Correlations of Effect Sizes and Moderators

Variable	M	SD	Skewness	Kurtosis	1	2	3	4	5	6	7	8	9
1. d	-0.43	0.74	-1.51	5.87	—								
2. Retention Interval (weeks)	3.39	4.45	3.08	12.08	-.12	—							
3. Criterion Type[a]	0.66	0.48	-0.67	-1.58	.23*	-.11	—						
4. Structure	3.26	1.69	-0.57	0.75	-.01	.19	.19*	—					
5. Cognitive Task Demands[b]	1.23	0.60	-0.12	-0.44	-.08	.12	-.01	.16	—				
6. Physical Task Demands[b]	0.79	0.79	0.31	-1.31	.29**	-.04	.69**	.03	-.07	—			
7. Closed/Open-looped[c]	0.43	0.50	0.28	-1.96	.13	.29**	-.21*	.10	.56**	-.07	—		
8. Amount of Discretion[b]	0.99	0.64	0.01	-0.50	.01	.11	-.10	.20*	.46**	-.20*	.56**	—	
9. Dynamic Complexity[b]	0.64	0.82	0.76	-1.08	.04	.06	.31**	.20*	.61**	.13	.45**	.62**	—
10. Component Complexity[b]	1.09	0.79	-0.16	-1.39	.06	.08	.32**	.12	.59**	.20*	.25**	.02	.50**

[a] cognitive criterion = 0, skill criterion = 1. [b] 0 = low (not applicable/involved); 1 = moderate (somewhat applicable/involved); 2 = high (very applicable/involved). [c] closed-looped = 0, open-looped = 1. *$p < .05$, **$p < .01$, two-tailed.

correlated with structure, physical task demands, and all task complexity dimensions except for discretion. The covariation between criterion type and physical task demands was particularly noticeable ($r = 0.69, p < .01$), indicating the learning of tasks with higher physical demands was more likely to be assessed with skill-based criteria. Third, structure was positively correlated with discretion and dynamic complexity, suggesting training for tasks with higher discretion and dynamic complexity were likely to be more structured. Fourth, cognitive task demands shared significant positive correlations with all four dimensions of task complexity, indicating tasks with higher cognitive demands also tended to be more complex. Fifth, physical task demands were negatively correlated with discretion, but positively correlated with component complexity. In other words, as the physical demands of a task increased, the number of approaches that can be adopted to accomplish tasks with higher physical demands was limited, but the requirement for number of distinct acts and information cues needed to perform such tasks increased. Last, the closed-/open-looped distinction was significantly correlated with the other three dimensions of task complexity, with open-looped tasks being higher in other dimensions than closed-looped tasks. Discretion also covaried with component complexity but not dynamic complexity.

Because many of the moderator variables were correlated with each other, it could be argued that the meta-analytic results previously presented do not provide a clear picture of which variables are predominantly related to decay. Therefore, multiple regression was warranted to examine the unique influence of each moderator variable. As shown in Table 4.9, the results indicated that the closed-/open-looped distinction ($sr^2 = .06$), retention interval ($sr^2 = .02$), and cognitive demands ($sr^2 = .02$) were the variables that made the strongest contributions to explaining decay. Although not presented in Table 4.9, we examined the possibility that the relationship between retention interval and decay might exhibit a power function (cf. Gronlund and Kimball, Chapter 2 this volume), but the results did not show a statistically significant quadratic effect. In support of Hypothesis 1, longer retention intervals were associated with more decay ($\beta = -0.17, p < .05$, one-tailed). Stronger cognitive demands were associated with more decay ($\beta = -0.25, p < .05$, one-tailed). This result is consistent with Hypothesis 5, which posited more decay for high cognitive/low physical tasks than for low cognitive/high physical tasks. In support of Arthur et al.'s (1998) hypothesis and Hypothesis 6, open-looped tasks were associated with lower levels of decay ($\beta = 0.37, p < .01$, one-tailed). However, it is important to recognize that interpretations based on these regression results should be made with caution, given the unbalanced distribution of data points across levels of the variables examined.

TABLE 4.9

Summary of Multiple Regression Results

Model	B	SE	β	sr^2
Retention Interval (weeks)	−.03	.02	−.17*	.02
Criterion Type[a]	.30	.24	.19	.01
Structure	−.01	.04	−.03	.00
Cognitive Task Demands[b]	−.31	.18	−.25*	.02
Physical Task Demands[b]	.17	.13	.18	.01
Closed-/Open-looped[c]	.55	.20	.37**	.06
Amount of Discretion[b]	.11	.18	.10	.00
Dynamic Complexity[b]	−.15	.15	−.16	.01
Component Complexity[b]	.10	.13	.11	.00
R^2	.19**			

B = Unstandardized regression weights. A negative weight indicates the predictor variable was inversely related to retention (i.e., yielding more decay). SE = Standard error. β = Standardized regression weights. sr^2 = Squared semi-partial correlation. *$p < .05$, **$p < .01$, one-tailed. [a] cognitive criterion = 0, skill criterion = 1. [b] 0 = low (not applicable/involved); 1 = moderate (somewhat applicable/involved); 2 = high (very applicable/involved). [c] closed-looped = 0, open-looped = 1.

DISCUSSION

Training is known to be an essential yet expensive endeavor, so organizations investing in training expect durable results or long-term retention of trained knowledge and skill after the completion of training. The impact of poor retention can be particularly salient in the context of training emergency responders or military reserves given that the probability of immediate and frequent application of trained knowledge and skills tends to be fairly low. The meta-analytic review conducted by Arthur et al. (1998) was the first systematic attempt to quantify the differential influence of various methodological and task-related factors on decay. Since this initial effort is more than 10 years old and is not without limitations, the current meta-analysis intended to provide an update and extend the investigation of decay to additional methodological and task-related factors that were not previously examined. In addition, a more nuanced, multidimensional coding scheme was used in the current meta-analysis to reflect the multidimensional nature of task-related characteristics, leading to the examination of the covariation among methodological and task-related factors as well as their independent effects.

The following discussion will relate findings from the current meta-analysis to those reported in Arthur et al.'s (1998) meta-analysis by comparing the overall effect, as well as moderating effects related to methodological and task-related factors on decay. Integrative conclusions as well as theoretical and practical implications will then be discussed. Lastly, discussion of the limitations of the current meta-analysis will be followed by recommendations for future research.

Overall Decay Effect

Both the current meta-analysis and that conducted by Arthur et al. (1998) showed performance decay after a period of nonuse. However, the overall decay found in the current meta-analysis across all retention interval categories ($d = -0.38$; 95 percent CI = [-1.50 to 0.75]) was smaller than that found by Arthur et al. ($d = -0.97$; 95 percent CI = [-2.35 to 0.44]). Such differences may partially be owing to the lack of overlap in studies included in both meta-analyses.

The larger overall effect found by Arthur et al. (1998) might be a result of using p-values and sample sizes to calculate effect sizes for some reports that were not included in the current meta-analysis. Alternatively, perhaps Arthur et al.'s (1998) sample of data points included a higher proportion of moderate cognitive/low physical tasks, which were shown to have the most decay in the present meta-analysis. Nevertheless, it should be noted that the overall effect size from the current meta-analysis was within the confidence interval around Arthur et al.'s overall effect, and vice versa. Therefore, decay indeed occurs, and how to promote knowledge and skill retention is a worthwhile topic for research as well as a legitimate concern for practitioners of organizational training.

Methodological Factors

Retention interval. Consistent with the proposed hypothesis and findings from Arthur et al. (1998), the results from the current meta-analysis indicated a negative relationship between retention and the length of the retention interval (i.e., a positive relationship between decay and length of nonuse). Although the effect sizes found for each of the retention intervals were larger in Arthur et al.'s meta-analysis than those in the current investigation, both meta-analyses found minimal or no decay when the retention interval was less than 24 hours. In addition, there was no clear trend suggesting a linear relationship between decay and the length of the retention interval, nor was there a trend suggesting either a power or exponential function (cf. Gronlund and Kimball,

2013). Therefore, one can reasonably expect the amount of decay to be negligible when the length of nonuse is less than 24 hours. Although one might expect larger amounts of decay with longer nonuse intervals, the lack of a clear and strong relationship between length of nonuse and decay suggests that factors other than the length of nonuse (e.g., task characteristics) are also important to consider given periods of nonuse greater than 24 hours.

Conditions of retrieval. In line with encoding specificity principle (Tulving, 1983; Tulving and Thompson, 1973) and the identical-elements theory (Thorndike and Woodworth, 1901), the similarity of retrieval conditions was identified as the most important moderator by Arthur et al. (1998). However, the results from the current meta-analysis did not replicate this finding. Thus, the hypothesis positing that the amount of decay would meaningfully differ depending on whether the conditions between the original and retrieval assessments are similar or different was not supported. The discrepancies in findings between the two meta-analyses may be owing to the lack of overlap in studies included in the analyses coupled with differences in other methodological factors or task characteristics (e.g., task complexity) covarying with the effects. Hence, no conclusive statements can be made regarding the influence of the similarity of retrieval conditions on decay.

Criterion type. In contrast to the Kirkpatrick typology used by Arthur et al. (1998), a more construct-centered model by Kraiger et al. (1993) was adopted in the current meta-analysis to categorize training evaluation criteria into cognitive and skill-based outcomes. Using this framework, the results of the current meta-analysis showed (a) more decay for cognitive criteria than for skill-based criteria, (b) criteria involving a combination of declarative and procedural knowledge decayed more than declarative knowledge, and (c) adaptive skill criteria decayed more than proceduralized skill criteria.

The greater decay in criteria reflecting a combination of declarative and procedural knowledge compared to criteria reflecting only declarative knowledge may be owing to the covariation between criterion type and other task-related factors, such as cognitive demands, physical demands, and the closed-/open-looped distinction. Specifically, an inspection of the data points involved in this comparison revealed that when a combination of declarative and procedural knowledge was used to assess learning, 92.9 percent ($k = 13$) of these studies also involved moderate cognitive/low physical tasks that displayed the most decay compared to tasks reflecting other combinations of cognitive and physical demands. In addition, 78.6 percent ($k = 11$) of these studies were closed-looped tasks that were found to decay more than open-looped tasks. On the other hand, for data points involving only declarative knowledge criteria, 42.9 percent ($k = 9$) studies involved moderate cognitive/low physical tasks, and 23.8 percent ($k = 5$) involved closed-looped tasks.

Therefore, it seems likely that the greater decay for criteria reflecting a combination of declarative and procedural knowledge was an artifact of task characteristics.

Nevertheless, although Arthur et al. (1998) used Kirkpatrick's less construct-focused scheme, their results were similar to those of the present meta-analysis in that they found more decay for learning criteria ($d = -1.07$), which are typically more knowledge-based, than for behavioral criteria ($d = -0.78$), which are more reflective of skill. Thus, although the results from the two meta-analyses were not directly comparable because of the use of different training criterion models, both meta-analyses show that criterion type is an important moderator to consider.

Operationalization of acquisition. In response to Arthur et al.'s (1998) call for additional research, an additional set of methodological moderators was examined in the present meta-analysis. Specifically, Arthur et al. (1998) suggested that future research should focus on the operationalization of acquisition because it is an important prerequisite of retention. In fact, the operationalization of acquisition—either criterion- or duration-based—produced one of the largest differences in effect sizes for all the moderators examined, suggesting more decay for criterion-based than for duration-based training. Like the confounding of the results for criterion type by task-related factors, one possible explanation for this finding could be the differences in task-related factors for studies in which initial acquisition was criterion- versus duration-based. Specifically, given the limited number of studies, all tasks ($k = 7$) used in criterion-based training were closed-looped tasks with minimal dynamic and moderate component complexity, which were associated with more decay than open-looped tasks or tasks with higher dynamic and component complexity. On the other hand, studies that involved duration-based training had a more even distribution of data points across levels of these task-related factors (e.g., 53.8 percent were closed-looped). Therefore, it seems likely that the lower amount of decay that was observed for duration-based training may have been an artifact of task complexity.

Training structure. Training structure is another methodological factor that was not considered by Arthur et al. (1998). Results from the current meta-analysis showed that training with higher structure was found to be associated with less decay. However, at first glance, such a finding may be viewed as inconsistent with the beneficial effects found in some research regarding learner-centered or active learning approaches, which give learners more responsibility for managing their learning with some guidance from the instructional environment. It is important to note that active learning is not the same as discovery learning or open-learning, which provide minimal structure and guidance to trainees (Salas et al., 1999; Mayer, 2004). With active learning, some guidance from the instructional environment is provided to ensure that trainees properly focus their attention and fully engage all the training content (Bell and Kozlowski, 2008; Frese et al., 1988). In training using active learning approaches, trainees are offered flexibility and control over their knowledge construction through exploration and experimentation. Although exploration and experimentation do not necessarily translate into effective performance during training, they are likely to facilitate retention and adaptive transfer (Kozlowski, Chao, and Jensen, 2009; Smith, Ford, and Kozlowski, 1997). Nonetheless, results from the present meta-analysis suggest that unstructured training programs (i.e., the low structure category) are not effective in promoting retention. This provides additional support for the possible detrimental effects found for discovery training with no or minimal structure on learning as suggested by Mayer (2004).

Decay-prevention interventions. One last methodological factor we examined that was not included in Arthur et al.'s (1998) meta-analysis was the effectiveness of posttraining decay-prevention interventions. Our findings support the use of posttraining decay-prevention interventions, showing actual gains rather than decay, or even mere retention, after formal training. Of course, these results are not surprising given the inherent nature of decay-prevention interventions. However, it should be noted that this beneficial effect should be considered fairly robust given that all the studies in the current meta-analysis that implemented decay-prevention interventions involved moderate cognitive/low physical tasks, which the other meta-analytic results showed were the kinds of tasks that displayed the most decay. Therefore, findings from the current meta-analysis provide further support for the value of such interventions in addition to what has been demonstrated in primary studies (e.g., Hutchins and Burke, 2006; Richman-Hirsch, 2001; Tews and Tracey, 2008).

Task-related Factors

Task-content demands. Arthur et al. (1998) showed that decay was greater for cognitive tasks than for physical tasks. The results of the current meta-analysis showed a more complex relationship between decay and cognitive and physical task demands. Rather than dichotomizing tasks into physical versus cognitive tasks, a more nuanced, multidimensional approach was used to code different levels of cognitive and physical demands, which allowed examinations of different combinations of cognitive and physical demands to be conducted. Also, our original intent was to expand on Arthur et al. (1998) by adding interpersonal demands to our examination, but we were unable to conduct meaningful analyses of interpersonal demands owing to a limited number of data points. Results showed that low cognitive/high physical tasks were retained better than high cognitive/low physical tasks. This finding not only supported the proposed hypothesis, but it was also consistent with the conclusion reached by Arthur et al. (1998) regarding decay using the dichotomized distinction between cognitive and physical tasks.

Combinations of task-content demands. As an extension to Arthur et al.'s (1998) meta-analysis, the multidimensional coding scheme used in the present investigation allowed for an examination of whether the amount of specific task demands or the extent of combined demands had differential effects on decay. Our results did not show a simple linear relationship between the sheer amount of combined cognitive and physical task demands and decay. No decay was found for low cognitive/high physical tasks. Moderate cognitive/low physical tasks decayed the most. However, minimal differences were found in decay for moderate cognitive/moderate physical tasks compared to moderate cognitive/high physical tasks. Furthermore, less decay was found for tasks with high cognitive demands across all levels of physical demands than for moderate cognitive/low physical tasks. These differences are robust given the percentage of variance explained by sampling error for all effect sizes was high and the confidence intervals did not overlap. Therefore, decay does not appear to be simply a function of the sheer amount of combined cognitive and physical demands. Rather, decay appears to be more a function of the particular combination of cognitive and physical demands.

Task complexity. Arthur et al. (1998) only focused on the closed- versus open-looped distinction, and did not examine other aspects of task complexity. The current meta-analysis took a multidimensional approach to operationalize task complexity with four dimensions including the closed- versus open-looped distinction. As a result, examinations of decay as a function of each dimension of task complexity as well as in combination were conducted. Overall, mixed support was found for the hypothesis that there would be less decay for more complex tasks than for less complex tasks. Specifically, less decay was found for open-looped tasks than for closed-looped tasks. This finding was inconsistent with Arthur et al.'s (1998) results, but supportive of their original hypothesis and previous reviews of the literature (e.g., Farr, 1987).

Combinations of task complexity dimensions. Regarding combinations of task complexity dimensions, although almost half of the combinations could not be examined owing to a lack of data points, the general pattern of effects suggests a negative relationship between decay and levels of combined task complexity, with less decay for more complex tasks. Furthermore, given high discretion, decay varied more based on combinations of dynamic and component complexity for closed-looped tasks than for open-looped tasks. One possible explanation may be owing to the nature of closed- versus open-looped tasks. Closed-looped tasks are ones with an unambiguous ending that is not contingent on time, and they often involve discrete responses that have a definite beginning and end. On the other hand, open-looped tasks do not have a clear and distinct end, and they require constant monitoring of the discrepancies between the current and desired state. Therefore, open-looped tasks are more dynamic and are likely to be higher in component complexity than closed-looped tasks. Put another way, the open-looped distinction in and of itself reflects a large degree of task complexity. Overall, the obtained results are consistent with the notion that training involving tasks with greater complexity requires trainees to engage in deeper and more elaborative processing during acquisition, which consequently leads to better retention (Craik and Lockhart, 1972; Schmidt and Bjork, 1992; Wexley and Latham, 2002).

LIMITATIONS AND FUTURE RESEARCH

There are a few limitations with the current meta-analysis that should be noted. First, the number of empirical studies that met the current set of inclusion criteria was limited compared to that of Arthur et al. (1998). Consequently, the hypothesis regarding the impact of overlearning could not be tested. Also, owing to the lack of data, many hierarchical moderator analyses could not be undertaken. For example, tasks that were low in discretion were only reflected in one combination with the other three task complexity dimensions. Hence, not all possible combinations of task complexity dimensions could be examined in the current meta-analysis. Furthermore, the limited data available did not allow for the meaningful interpretation of the effects of some moderators (e.g., different retrieval conditions) on decay. Therefore, additional training research that examines both immediate and delayed assessments of learning in relation to potential moderators of decay is greatly needed. In spite of the limited number of primary studies examining decay, another main cause of the small number of studies included in the current meta-analysis was the lack of necessary statistics to calculate effect sizes. Therefore, researchers should be more mindful and consistent in reporting necessary statistics in primary studies so that future meta-analyses can provide more stable estimates.

Second, additional moderators are likely given the relatively sizable standard deviations of the sample-weighted mean effect size, along with the small percentages of variance accounted for by sampling error, in some of the moderator analyses. For example, no support was found for the hypothesis positing more decay when the original and retrieval assessment conditions are different than when they are similar, but the small percentage of variance explained by sampling error suggests that the effect of retrieval conditions is likely moderated by one or more other variables.

Third, the range of structure of training included in the current meta-analysis was rather restricted. Therefore, present findings regarding the high structure category should not be generalized to highly structured (i.e., guided) training. Although results from the current meta-analysis suggest less decay for training with higher structure, additional research is needed to explore decay in training programs that fall on the high end of the spectrum of the training structure composite in order to examine whether there is a point of diminishing returns for the beneficial effect of structure.

Finally, examinations of decay should be extended to the team level in response to the recent call for studying training and transfer using a multilevel framework (Aguinis and Kraiger, 2009). Although a team comprises a group of individuals, team performance is not a simple composite of individual performance. Overall team performance is a combination of individual team member task performance and teamwork performance, such as coordination, team monitoring, and backup behaviors among team members (Marks, Mathieu, Zaccaro, 2001; Salas, Burke, and Cannon-Bowers, 2002). Hence, future examinations of decay at the team level should explore whether decay is more a function of individual task performance deterioration or degradation of teamwork capabilities.

Implications for Practice, and Conclusions

In summary, results from the current meta-analysis suggest that decay is a real phenomenon and how to promote the retention of trained knowledge and skill should be on the agenda of both training researchers and practitioners. There is minimal decay when the length of periods of nonuse is less than 24 hours. However, as periods of nonuse extend beyond 24 hours, other factors, especially task-related factors, appear to play more important roles. Although the regression results indicated a slight negative relationship between length of nonuse and retention, conclusions regarding this relationship should be made with caution. Rather than simply considering the length of nonuse as the critical factor of decay, it is also important, perhaps even more important, to consider how task demands are associated with decay. With respect to future research, the independent effects of and interactions between task demands and the length of nonuse might be better examined via primary investigations rather than meta-analysis.

In particular, upon closer inspection of the data, it appeared that the effects of the retention interval covaried with the effects of the combined cognitive and physical demands (this was not the case with respect to dimensions of task complexity). Accordingly, it was necessary to examine the effect of the retention interval on decay separately for each combination of cognitive and physical demands. As shown in Table 4.10 and Figure 4.1, there were no clear linear trends of increasing decay as the period of nonuse increased for any of the types of tasks. High cognitive/moderate physical tasks showed somewhat of a trend of increasing decay across retention intervals, but none of the other combinations showed such trends, and in some cases longer periods of nonuse were associated with less decay or even improved performance. Together, the results shown in Table 4.10 and Figure 4.1 indicate that combinations of cognitive and physical demands may well exert more influence than length of nonuse on decay after the completion of training. However, it is difficult to make strong conclusions regarding the relative importance of length of nonuse versus task demands given the lack of data points for many of the different retention intervals within each of the various combinations of cognitive and physical demands.

Nonetheless, the overall pattern of findings suggests that decay is most likely to occur for relatively simple cognitive tasks. In contrast, decay does not appear to be as much of a problem or issue for more cognitively complex tasks or tasks that are predominantly physical in nature. This conclusion is based on the following findings. In the meta-analysis, (a) cognitive criteria were associated with greater decay than skill-based criteria, (b) decay was by far the strongest for moderate cognitive/low physical tasks than for any other combination of cognitive and physical demands, and (c) higher levels of task complexity were generally associated with less decay. In the regression analysis, decay was (d) stronger with higher levels of cognitive demands, yet (e) weaker for open-looped versus closed-looped tasks.

It would appear then that decay is more of a problem for the performance of tasks that mostly require the recall of basic facts or mundane cognitive processes than it is for the performance of tasks that demand information integration or engagement in multiple cognitive processes. In addition, although such a conclusion cannot be generalized to all types of task complexity combinations given the limited data points available, it is important to note that the effects for all four indicators of high complexity—open-looped, high discretion, high dynamic complexity, and high component complexity—are fairly robust as reflected in the percentages of variance explained by sampling error and the confidence intervals, suggesting less decay for more complex tasks. Unlike methodological factors, task-related factors cannot be easily manipulated. Thus, results from the current meta-analysis imply the importance of conducting appropriate task analyses in order to understand different task characteristics, and to consequently incorporate relevant methodological factors that promote retention for tasks of concern. From a researcher's

TABLE 4.10

Meta-Analysis Results for Task-content Demands by Retention Interval

Task-content demands/ retention interval	*k*	*N*	*d*	*SD d*	% var.	Min. *d*	Max. *d*	95% CI L	U
Cognitive = low, Physical = high[a]									
1. RI < 1 day	6	136	0.09	0.41	52.35	−0.72	1.74	−0.70	0.88
2. 1 day ≤ RI ≤ 7 days	2	40	0.69	0.29	72.39	0.15	1.29	0.12	1.25
Cognitive = mod., Physical = low									
2. 1 day ≤ RI ≤ 7 days	27	696	−0.71	0.00	100.00	−1.62	0.29	−0.71	−0.71
4. 14 days < RI ≤ 28 days	3	60	−1.22	0.43	57.52	−1.99	−0.35	−2.05	−0.38
6. 90 days < RI ≤ 180 days	3	114	−0.71	0.00	100.00	−0.85	−0.60	−0.71	−0.71
Cognitive = mod., Physical = mod.									
2. 1 day ≤ RI ≤ 7 days	15	340	−0.16	0.00	100.00	−0.44	0.16	−0.16	−0.16
4. 14 days < RI ≤ 28 days	3	34	−2.49	0.92	45.71	−3.71	−0.62	−4.29	−0.69
5. 28 days < RI ≤ 90 days	2	38	0.39	0.00	100.00	0.23	0.47	0.39	0.39
Cognitive = mod., Physical = high									
5. 28 days < RI ≤ 90 days	11	584	−0.25	1.05	6.53	−2.66	0.72	−2.31	1.80
Cognitive = high, Physical = low									
3. 7 days < RI ≤ 14 days	5	229	−0.35	0.00	100.00	−0.40	−0.35	−0.35	−0.35
5. 28 days < RI ≤ 90 days	3	102	−0.21	0.16	81.68	−0.74	0.11	−0.53	0.11
Cognitive = high, Physical = mod.									
2. 1 day ≤ RI ≤ 7 days	2	29	−0.10	0.00	100.00	−0.18	−0.03	−0.10	−0.10
3. 7 days < RI ≤ 14 days	2	20	0.01	0.00	100.00	−0.09	0.07	0.01	0.01
4. 14 days < RI ≤ 28 days	7	164	−0.32	0.00	100.00	−0.99	0.24	−0.32	−0.32
5. 28 days < RI ≤ 90 days	8	88	−0.39	0.00	100.00	−1.68	0.42	−0.39	−0.39
Cognitive = high, Physical = high									
1. RI < 1 day	3	106	−0.35	0.00	100.00	−0.57	−0.13	−0.35	−0.35
2. 1 day ≤ RI ≤ 7 days	2	178	−0.05	0.00	100.00	−0.07	−0.04	−0.05	−0.05
5. 28 days < RI ≤ 90 days	2	89	−0.43	0.00	100.00	−0.46	−0.41	−0.43	−0.43

k = number of independent data points. *N* = number of participants. *d* = sample-weighted mean effect size. *SD d* = standard deviation of the estimated true effect size. % var. = percentage of variance explained by sampling error. Min. *d* = minimum effect size. Max. *d* = maximum effect size. 95% CI = 95% confidence interval (L = lower, U = upper). [a] Low = 0 (minimally applicable/involved); mod. = moderate = 1 (somewhat applicable/involved); high = 2 (very applicable/involved).

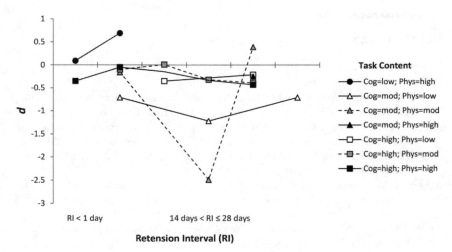

FIGURE 4.1

Meta-analytic results for task content by retention interval. *d* = sample-weighted mean effect size.

perspective, additional research that examines task-related factors in greater detail as well as possible boundary effects of various training methodologies in relation to different task-related factors is needed. From a practitioner's perspective, results from an appropriately conducted task analysis can inform when decay is more likely to be problematic, and consequently whether or when specific interventions are needed and likely to be cost-effective in preventing decay.

In sum, there are two primary conclusions that can be drawn from this meta-analysis. One, decay is not simply a matter of how long individuals go without performing a task (cf. Gronlund and Kimball, Chapter 2 this volume). It is also important, perhaps even more important, to consider how task characteristics, such as complexity and the combination of cognitive and physical demands, are associated with decay. Two, the small number of studies found shows that substantially more research is needed before a clear theory of skill decay can be articulated. Nevertheless, the results of the present study suggest that task analysis should be an important part of determining the extent to which decay might indeed be a potential problem and subsequently whether decay prevention strategies (both in training and after training) should be incorporated in the design of training programs.

REFERENCES

* Reports included in the meta-analysis.

Adams, J. A., and Hufford, L. E. (1962). Contribution of a part-task trainer to the learning and relearning of a time-shared flight maneuver. *Human Factors, 4*, 159–170.

Aguinis, H., and Kraiger, K. (2009). Benefits of training and development for individuals and teams, organizations, and society. *Annual Review of Psychology, 60*, 451–474.

Alliger, G. M., and Janak, E. A. (1989). Kirkpatrick's level of training criteria: Thirty years later. *Personnel Psychology, 42*, 331–342.

Alliger, G. M., Tannenbaum, S. I., Bennett, W. Jr., Traver, H., and Shotland, A. (1997). A meta-analysis of the relations among training criteria. *Personnel Psychology, 50*, 341–358.

Anderson, J. R. (1987). Skill acquisition: Compilation of weak-method problem solutions. *Psychological Review, 94*, 192–210.

Anderson, J. R. (1996). ACT: A simple theory of complex cognition. *American Psychologist, 51*, 355–365.

*Anger, W. K., Patterson, L., Fuchs, M., Will, L. L., and Rohlman, D. S. (2009). *Learning and recall of worker protection standard (WPS) training in vineyard workers*. Unpublished manuscript.

*Anger, W. K., Stupfel, J., Ammerman, T., Tamulinas, A., Bodner, T., and Rohlman, D. S. (2006). The suitability of computer-based training for workers with limited formal education: a case study from the US agricultural sector. *International Journal of Training and Development, 10*, 269–284.

*Anshel, M. H. (1978). Effect of aging on acquisition and short-term retention of a motor skill. *Perceptual and Motor Skills, 47*, 993–994.

Arthur, W. Jr., Bennett, W. Jr., Edens, P. S., and Bell, S. T. (2003). Effectiveness of training in organizations: A meta-analysis of design and evaluation features. *Journal of Applied Psychology, 88*, 234–245.

Arthur, W. Jr., Bennett, W. Jr., and Huffcutt, A. I. (2001). *Conducting meta-analysis using SAS*. Mahwah, NJ: Lawrence Erlbaum Associates.

Arthur, W. Jr., Bennett, W. Jr., Stanush, P. L., and McNelly, T. L. (1998). Factors that influence skill decay and retention: A quantitative review and analysis. *Human Performance, 11*, 234–245.

*Arthur, W. Jr., Day, E. A., Bennett, W., Jr., McNelly, T. L., and Jordan, J. A. (1997). Dyadic versus individual training protocols: Loss and reacquisition of a complex skill. *Journal of Applied Psychology, 82*, 783–791.

* Arthur, W., Jr., Day, E. A., Villado, A. J., Boatman, P. R., Kowollik, V., Bennett, W., Jr., and Bhupatkar, A. (2007). *Decay, transfer, and the reacquisition of a complex skill: An investigating of practice schedules, observational rehearsal, and individual differences* (Rep No. AFRL-RH-AZ-2008–0001). Mesa, AZ: Air Force Research Laboratory.

Baldwin, T. T., and Ford, J. K. (1988). Transfer of training: A review and directions for future research. *Personnel Psychology, 41*, 63–105.

Bell, B. S., and Kozlowski, S. W. J. (2002). Adaptive guidance: Enhancing self-regulation, knowledge, and performance in technology-based training. *Personnel Psychology, 55*, 267–306.

Bell, B. S., and Kozlowski, S. W. J. (2008). Active learning: Effects of core training design elements on self-regulatory processes, learning, and adaptability. *Journal of Applied Psychology, 93*, 296–316.

*Boker, R. J. (1974). Immediate and delayed retention effects of interspersing questions in written instructional passages. *Journal of Educational Psychology, 66*, 96–98.

Campbell, J. P., and Kuncel, N. R. (2001). Individual and team training. In N. Anderson, D. S. Ones, H. K. Sinangil, and C. Viswesvaran (Eds.), *Handbook of Industrial, Work and Organizational Psychology* (pp. 278–313). London: Sage.

*Campbell, M. (2007). Error management training from a resource allocation perspective: An investigation of individual differences and the training components that contribute to transfer. Unpublished doctoral dissertation. Rice University, Texas.

Chen, G., Casper, W. J., and Cortina, J. M. (2001). The roles of self-efficacy and task complexity in the relationships among cognitive ability, conscientiousness, and work-related performance: a meta-analytic examination.

Colquitt, J. A., LePine, J. A., and Noe, R. A. (2000). Toward an integrative theory of training motivation: A meta-analytic path analysis of 20 years of research. *Journal of Applied Psychology, 85*, 678–707.

Craik, F. I., and Lockhart, R. S. (1972). Levels of processing: A framework for memory research. *Journal of Verbal Learning and Verbal Behavior, 11*, 671–684.

*Davis, F. D., and Yi, M. Y. (2004). Improving computer skill training: Behavior modeling, symbolic mental rehearsal, and the role of knowledge structure. *Journal of Applied Psychology, 89*, 509–523.

*Day, E. A., Arthur, W., Jr., and Gettman, D. (2001). Knowledge structures and the acquisition of a complex skill. *Journal of Applied Psychology, 86*, 1022–1033.

*Decker, P. J. (1980). Effects of symbolic coding and rehearsal in behavioral-modeling training. *Journal of Applied Psychology, 65*, 627–634.

Donovan, J. J., and Radosevich, D. J. (1999). A meta-analytic review of the distribution of practice effect: Now you see it, now you don't. *Journal of Applied Psychology, 84*, 795–805.

Dormann, T., and Frese, M. (1994). Error training: Replication and the function of exploratory behavior. *International Journal of Human–Computer Interaction, 6*, 365–372.

Driskell, J. E., Willis, R. P., and Copper, C. (1992). Effect of overlearning on retention. *Journal of Applied Psychology, 77*, 615–622.

Dunlap, W. P., Cortina, J. M., Vaslow, J. B., and Burke, M. J. (1996). Meta-analysis of experiments with matched groups or repeated measures designs. *Psychological Methods, 1*, 170–177.

*Dunn, S. (2000). Effects of a simulation game on trainees' knowledge and attitudes about age-related changes in learning and work behaviors of older workers. Unpublished doctoral dissertation. University of North Texas, Texas.

*Dupuis, R. J., and Struthers, C. W. (2007). The effects of social motivational training following perceived and actual interpersonal offenses at work. *Journal of Applied Social Psychology, 37*, 426–456.

Ebbinghaus, H. (1885). *Memory: A contribution to experimental psychology.* New York: Columbia University.

Ebbinghaus, H. (1913). *Memory: A contribution to experimental psychology.* New York: Columbia University.

*Eckerman, D. A., Lundeen, C. A., Steele, A., Fercho, H. L., Ammerman, T. A., and Anger, W. K. (2002). Interactive training versus reading to teach respiratory protection. *Journal of Occupational Health Psychology, 7*, 313–323.

*Espejo, J., Day, E. A., and Scott, G. (2005). Performance evaluations, need for cognition, and the acquisition of a complex skill: an attribute–treatment interaction. *Personality and individual differences, 38*, 1867–1877.

*Fante, R. M. (2008). A comparison of three training methods on the acquisition and retention of automotive product knowledge. Unpublished Doctoral Dissertation, Western Michigan University, Kalamazoo, MI.

Farina, A. J. Jr., and Wheaton, G. R. (1973). Development of a taxonomy of human performance: The task-characteristics approach to performance prediction. *JSAS Catalog of Selected Documents in Psychology, 3*, 26–27.

Farr, M. J. (1987). *The long-term retention of knowledge and skills: A cognitive and instructional perspective.* New York: Springer-Verlag.

*Fein, E. C., and Day, E. A. (2004). The PASS theory of intelligence and the acquisition of a complex skill: A criterion-related validation study of Cognitive Assessment System scores. *Personality and Individual Differences, 37*, 1123–1136.

Fleishman, E. A., and Quaintance, M. K. (1984). *Taxonomies of human performance: The description of human tasks.* Orlando, FL: Academic Press.

Foxon, M. J. (1993). A process approach to the transfer of training: Part I: The impact of motivation and supervisor support on transfer maintenance. *Australian Journal of Educational Technology, 9*, 130–143.

Foxon, M. J. (1994). A process approach to the transfer of training: Part II: Using action planning to facilitate the transfer of training. *Australian Journal of Educational Technology, 10*, 1–18.

Frese, M., Albrecht, K., Altmann, A., Lang, J., Papstein, P. V., Peyerl, R. et al. (1988). The effects of an active development of the mental model in the training process: Experimental results in a work processing system. *Behavior and Information Technology, 7*, 295–304.

Gaudine, A. P., and Saks, A. M. (2004). A longitudinal quasi-experiment on the effects of posttraining transfer interventions. *Human Resource Development Quarterly, 15*, 57–76.

*Gist, M. E., Stevens, C. K., and Bavetta, A. G. (1991). Effects of self-efficacy and posttraining intervention on the acquisition and maintenance of complex interpersonal skills. *Personnel Psychology, 44*, 837–861.

Glass, G. V., McGaw, B., and Smith, M. L. (1981). *Meta-analysis in social science research.* Beverly Hills, CA: Sage.

Goldstein, I. L., and Ford, J. K. (2002). *Training in organizations: Needs assessment, development and evaluation* (4th ed.). Canada: Wadsworth Group.

*Goodwin, J. E., Grimes, C. R., Eckerson, J. M., and Gordon, P. M. (1998). Effect of different quantities of variables practice on acquisition, retention, and transfer of an applied motor skill. *Perceptual and Motor Skills, 87*, 147–151.

*Grimsley, D. L. (1969). *Acquisition, retention, and retraining: group studies on using low fidelity training devices* (HumPRO Tech. Re. 69–12). Alexandria, VA. Human Resources Resource Organization.

Gronlund, S. D., and Kimball, D. R. (2013). Remembering and forgetting: From the laboratory looking out. In W. Arthur, Jr., E. A. Day, W. Bennett, Jr., and A. Portrey (Eds.), *Individual and team skill decay: The science and implications for practice* (pp. 14–52). New York: Taylor & Francis.

Haerem, T., and Rau, D. (2007). The influence of degree of expertise and objective task complexity on perceived task complexity and performance. *Journal of Applied Psychology, 92,* 1320–1331.

Howell, W. C., and Cooke, N. J. (1989). Training the human information processor: A review of cognitive models. In I. L. Goldstein (Ed.), *Training in Development and Organizations.* San Francisco, CA: Jossey-Bass.

Huffcutt, A. I., and Arthur, W. Jr. (1995). Development of a new outlier statistic for meta-analytic data. *Journal of Applied Psychology, 80,* 327–334.

Hunter, J. E., and Schmidt, F. L. (1990). *Methods of meta-analysis: Correcting error and bias in research findings.* Newbury Park, CA: Sage Publications, Inc.

Hutchins, H. M., and Burke, L. A. (2006). Has relapse prevention received a fair shake? A review and implications for future transfer research. *Human Resource Development Review, 5,* 8–24.

Kirkpatrick, D. L. (1959). Techniques for evaluation training programs. *Journal of the American Society for Training Directors, 13,* 3–9.

Kirkpatrick, D. L. (1976). Evaluation of training. In R. L. Craig (Ed.), *Training and Development Handbook: A Guide to Human Resource Development* (2nd ed.) (pp. 301–319). New York: McGraw-Hill.

Kirkpatrick, D. L. (1996). Invited reaction: Reaction to Holton article. *Human Resource Development Quarterly, 7,* 23–25.

*Konoske, P. J. (1985). Cognitive factors in learning and retention of procedural tasks. Unpublished doctoral dissertation. Wayne State University, Detroit, MI.

Kozlowski, S. W. J., Chao, G. T., and Jensen, J. M. (2009). Building an inference structure in organizational training: A multilevel approach. In S. W. J. Kozlowski and E. Salas (Eds.) *Learning, training, and development in organizations.* New York: Routledge Academic.

Kraemer, H. C. (2005). A simple effect size indicator for two-group comparisons? A comment on $r_{equivalent}$. *Psychological Methods, 10,* 413–419.

Kraiger, K. (2003). Perspectives on training and development. In W. C. Borman, D. R. Ilgen, R. J. Klimoski, and I. B. Weiner (Eds.), *Handbook of Psychology* (pp. 171–192). Hoboken, NJ: John Wiley & Sons, Inc.

Kraiger, K., Ford, J. K., and Salas, E. (1993). Application of cognitive, skill-based, and affective theories of learning outcomes to new methods of training evaluation. *Journal of Applied Psychology, 78,* 311–328.

*Lim, D. H., and Morris, M. L. (2006). Influence of trainee characteristics, instructional satisfaction, and organizational climate on perceived learning and training transfer. *Human Resource Development Quarterly, 17,* 85–115.

Locke, E. A., and Latham, G. P. (1990). *A theory of goal setting and task performance.* Englewood Cliffs, NJ: Prentice-Hall.

McDaniel, M. A., and Schlager, M. S. (1990). Discovery learning and transfer of problem-solving skills. *Cognition and Instruction, 7,* 129–159.

Machin, M. A. (2002). Planning, managing, and optimizing transfer of training. In K. Kraiger (Ed.), *Creating, implementing, and managing effective training and development: State-of-art lessons for practice* (pp. 263–301). San Francisco, CA: Jossey-Bass.

*McLeod, D. B., and Briggs, J. T. (1980). Interactions of field independence and generatl reasoning with inductive instruction in mathematics. *Journal for Research in Mathematics Education, 11,* 94–103.

Mandler, G., and Heineman, S. H. (1956). Effect of overlearning of a verbal response on transfer of training. *Journal of Experimental Psychology, 52,* 39–46.

Marks, M. A., Mathieu, J. E., and Zaccaro, S. J. (2001). A temporally based framework and taxonomy of team processes. *Academy of Management Review, 26*, 356–376.

Marx, R. D. (1982). Relapse prevention for managerial training: A model for maintenance of behavior change. *Academy of Management Review, 7*, 433–441.

Mayer, R. E. (2004). Should there be a three-strikes rule against pure discovery learning? The case for guided methods of instruction. *American Psychologist, 59*, 14–19.

*Morin, L., and Latham, G. P. (2000). The effect of mental practice and goal setting as a transfer of training intervention on supervisors' self-efficacy and communication skills: An exploratory study. *Applied Psychology: An International Review, 49*, 566–578.

Naylor, J. C., and Briggs, G. E. (1961). *Long-term retention of learned skills: A review of the literature* (ASD TR 61–390). Columbus: Ohio State University, Laboratory of Aviation Psychology.

Noe, R., Sears, J., and Fullenkamp, A. (1990). Relapse training: Does it influence trainees' posttraining behavior and cognitive strategies? *Journal of Business and Psychology, 4*, 319–328.

*Overdorf, V., Schweighardt, R., Page, S. J., and McGrath, R. E. (2004). Mental and physical practice schedules in acquisition and retention of novel timing skills. *Perceptual and Motor Skills, 99*, 51–62.

Paradise, A., and Patel, L. (2009). *State of the industry: ASTD's annual review of trends in workplace learning and performance.* Alexandria, VA: ASTD.

*Payne, D. A., Krathwohl, D. R., and Gordon, J. (1967). The effect of sequence on programmed instruction. *American Educational Research Journal, 4*, 125–132.

*Rabbitt, P., Cumming, G., and Vyas, S. (1979). Improvement, learning, and retention of skill at a visual search. *Quarterly Journal of Experimental Psychology, 31*, 441–459.

*Rawls, J. R., Perry, O., and Timmons, E. O. (1966). A comparative study of conventional instruction and individual programmed instruction in the college classroom. *Journal of Applied Psychology, 50*, 388–391.

*Reynolds, B., and Bilodeau, I. M. (1952). Acquisition and retention of three psychomotor tests as a function of distribution of practice during acquisition. *Journal of Experimental Psychology, 44*, 19–26.

Richman-Hirsch, W. L. (2001). Posttraining interventions to enhance transfer: the moderating effects of work environments. *Human Resource Development Quarterly, 12*, 105–120.

*Rohlman, D. S., Eckerman, D. A., Ammerman, T. A., Fercho, H. L., Lundeen, C. A., Blomquist, C., and Amger, W. K. (2005). Quizzing and feedback in computer-based and book-based training for workplace safety and health. *Journal of Organizational Behavior Management, 24*, 1–26.

Rohrer, D., Taylor, K., Pashler, H., Wixted, J. T., and Cepeda, N. J. (2005). The effect of overlearning on long-term retention. *Applied Cognitive Psychology, 19*, 361–374.

*Ryan, E. D. (1962). Retention of stabilometer and pursuit rotor skills. *The Research Quarterly, 33*, 593–598.

Salas, E., Burke, C. S., and Cannon-Bowers, J. A. (2002). What we know about designing and delivering team training: Tips and guidelines. In K. Kraiger (Ed.), *Creating, implementing, and managing effective training and development* (pp. 234–259). San Francisco, CA: Jossey-Bass.

Salas, E., Cannon-Bowers, J. A., Rhodenizer, L., and Bowers, C. A. (1999). Training in organizations: Myths, misconceptions, and mistaken assumptions. *Research in Personnel and Human Resources Management, 17*, 123–161.

Schmidt, R. A., and Bjork, R. A. (1992). New conceptualizations of practice: Common principles in three paradigms suggest new concepts in training. *Psychological Science, 3*, 207–217.

*Simon, S. J., and Werner, J. M. (1996). Computer training through behavior modeling, self-paced, and instructional approaches: A field experiment. *Journal of Applied Psychology, 81*, 648–659.

Smith, E. M., Ford, J. K., and Kozlowski, S. W. J. (1997). Building adaptive expertise: Implications for training design. In M. A. Quiñones and A. Dudda (Eds.), *Training for a Rapidly Changing Workplace: Applications of Psychological Research* (pp. 89–118). Washington, D. C.: APA Books.

*Smith-Jentsch, K. A., Campbell, G. E., Milanovich, D. M., and Reynolds, A. M. (2001). Measuring teamwork mental models to support training needs assessment, development, and evaluation: Two empirical studies. *Journal of Organizational Behavior, 22*, 179–194.

Swanson, R. A. (2001). *Assessing the financial benefits of human resource development.* Cambridge, MA: Perseus.

*Swezey, R. W., Perez, R. S., and Allen, J. A. (1988). Effects of instructional delivery system and training parameter manipulations on electromechanical maintenance performance. *Human Factors, 30*, 751–762.

*Swezey, R. W., Perez, R. S., and Allen, J. A. (1991). Effects of instructional strategy and motion presentation conditions on the acquisition and transfer of electromechanical troubleshooting skill: Training theory, methods, technology. *Human Factors, 33*, 309–323.

Tews, M. J., and Tracey, J. B. (2008). An empirical examination of posttraining on-the-job supplements for enhancing the effectiveness of interpersonal skills training. *Personnel Psychology, 61*, 375–401.

*Thompson, T. J., Morey, J. C., Smith, S., and Osborne, A. D. (1981). *Basic rifle marksmanship skill retention: Implications for retention research* (Report no. AD-A134017). U.S. Army Research Institute for the Behavioral and Social Sciences, GA: ARI Field Unit at Fort Benning.

Thorndike, E. L., and Woodworth, R. S. (1901). The influence of improvement in one mental function upon the efficiency of other functions. *Psychological Review, 8*, 247–261.

Trowbridge, M. H., and Cason, H. (1932). An experimental study of Thorndike's theory of learning. *Journal of General Psychology, 7*, 245–260.

Tulving, E. (1983). *Elements of episodic memory.* New York: Oxford University Press.

Tulving, E., and Thomson, D. M. (1973). Encoding specificity and retrieval processes in episodic memory. *Psychological Review, 80*, 352–373.

*Wetzel, S. K., Konoske, P. J., and Montague, W. E. (1983). *Estimating skill loss throughout a Navy technical training pipeline* (Final Rep. No. ADA1366368XSP). San Diego, CA: Navy Personnel Research and Development Center.

*Wexley, K. N., and Baldwin, T. T. (1986). Posttraining strategies for facilitating positive transfer: An empirical exploration. *The Academy of Management Journal, 29*, 503–520.

Wexley, K. N., and Latham, G. P. (2002). *Developing and training human resources in organizations.* New York: HarperCollins.

*Wood, E., Willoughby, T., Specht, J., Stern-Cavalcante, W., and Child, C. (2002). Developing a computer workshop to facilitate computer skills and minimize anxiety for early childhood educators. *Journal of Educational Psychology, 94*, 164–170.

Wood, R. E. (1986). Task complexity: Definition of the construct. *Organizational Behavior and Human Decision Processes, 37*, 60–82.

Wood, R. E., Mento, A. J., and Locke, E. A. (1987). Task complexity as a moderator of goal effects: A meta-analysis. *Journal of Applied Psychology, 72*, 416–425.

AUTHORS' NOTE

This research was conducted as part of Xiaoqian Wang's doctoral dissertation at the University of Oklahoma under the supervision of Eric Day.

5

Variance as an Indicator of Training Effectiveness in the Context of Complex Skill Acquisition, Retention, and Transfer

*Ira Schurig, Winfred Arthur, Jr.,
Eric Anthony Day, and David J. Woehr*

INTRODUCTION

Although comparison of group means is by far the most commonly used method of assessing training effectiveness, it has been suggested that investigating differences between group means may not be the only way of assessing training effectiveness. Specifically, an investigation of differences in performance variance may reveal important conclusions not revealed by an analysis of group means. The present chapter presents the results of an investigation of whether performance variance provides incremental diagnostic information over and above information provided by an investigation of group means in the context of complex skill acquisition, retention, and transfer by reanalyzing data from two previously published long-term skill-retention studies involving different performance tasks, criterion measures (i.e., skill-based performance and declarative knowledge), and training protocols. In general, the results indicate that performance variance may provide inform-ation regarding the nature of the task itself. However, as an indicator of training effectiveness, variance provides confirmatory evidence of training effectiveness but does not provide diagnostic information over and above information provided by an investigation of group means in the context of complex skill acquisition, retention, and transfer.

Training effectiveness is most commonly operationalized as a change in mean performance as a function of training and most training effectiveness studies use group means (either gain scores or between-groups measures) as measures of training effectiveness. Indeed, of the training effectiveness studies described in this book, all report group means as the primary measures of training effectiveness, skill decay, and skill retention. So, the effectiveness of training may involve the comparison of a single group's mean performance before and after training. Or, it may involve the comparison of two groups' mean performance after each receives some sort of training intervention or lack thereof (i.e., control condition).

It has been suggested, however, that investigating differences between group means may not be the only way of assessing training effectiveness. Alliger and Katzman (1997) observed that there are alternative means of assessing training effectiveness, and an assessment of training effectiveness via these alternative means may uncover important conclusions not revealed by an analysis of group means. For example, in some research designs, an assessment of some characteristic of a group of trainees as a whole is not of interest. Instead, researchers may be interested in analyzing an individual's change over a period of time via an individual growth model. In addition, although the goal of many training programs is an improvement in performance and evidence of such an improvement is an increase in mean task performance, the distribution of individuals' task performance (i.e., performance variance) may also be worth exploring because it may be an indicator of the effectiveness of the training protocol (Alliger and Katzman, 1997). However, to our knowledge, there have been no comparative investigations of the mean and variance as training evaluation criteria, especially in the context of complex skill acquisition, retention, and transfer. Therefore, the purpose of the present study is to investigate whether variance is a viable indicator of training effectiveness. In doing this, we (a) briefly discuss the potential role of variance as an indicator of training effectiveness, (b) provide some background on the factors that affect variance, (c) reanalyze datasets from two previously published empirical studies on long-term retention and transfer, and (d) discuss any implications that using variance as a training effectiveness metric has for training program evaluation, especially in the context of complex skill acquisition, retention, and transfer.

THE CASE FOR VARIANCE AS AN INDICATOR OF TRAINING EFFECTIVENESS

Conceptually, the use of variance as an indicator of training effectiveness seems sound. In fact, some training protocols may be explicitly designed to bring about variation in performance outcomes and, as such, variance is an appropriate dependent variable. In some cases, training may be implemented to reduce variance. For example, in a training protocol designed to instill group consensus, a reduction in opinion variation might be a desired outcome (Watson, DeSanctis, and Poole, 1988). Rater training is designed to reduce variance in raters' responses without affecting mean ratings (Woehr and Huffcutt, 1994). Mastery training likewise results in decreased performance variance across trainees because of the ceiling on performance such a training paradigm imposes (Goldberg, Drillings, and Dressel, 1981). Conversely, training may be designed to increase variance. For example, creativity training helps increase idea generation (Scott, Leritz, and Mumford, 2004). Similarly, organizations implement diversity training to increase cultural awareness (Roberson, Kulik, and Pepper, 2001). As these examples demonstrate, the use of variance as a dependent variable is not unprecedented; in fact, in some studies, it may be the only appropriate measure of training effectiveness.

Although the literature is limited, some researchers have theorized about the use of performance variability as a metric. Thorndike (1908) first suggested that an investigation of the effect of training on performance variability was worthwhile. Based on an examination of the effect of training on individual differences, he concluded that general intelligence would predict rate of change in performance owing to training more strongly for complex tasks than for simple tasks (Thorndike, 1910). Reed (1931) later summarized the purpose of her own and Thorndike's (1910) investigations by posing the question, "Does equal training make a group of individuals more alike or more different in their achievement? More exactly, does it increase or decrease the variability of a group of individuals?" (p. 1). This stream of inquiry became, and remained, inactive until Ackerman (1987) integrated his own work on performance variance with these previous findings and concluded that if individuals' scores converged (i.e., variance decreased), then it was assumed that with sufficient practice, all individuals could perform at similar levels. In contrast, if individuals' scores diverged (i.e., variance increased), then the more able would show greater improvement than those less able. This phenomenon, in which "the amplification of any initial advantage . . . leads to cumulative differences that widen preexisting gaps" (Ceci and Papierno, 2005, p. 149), has been dubbed the *Matthew effect* and is a prime example of a case in which the analysis of performance variance complements more traditional analysis of group means.

These examples illustrate that it may be important for researchers to avoid the temptation to assess training effectiveness solely in terms of changes in group means. It is important to note that although an assessment of variance may complement an assessment of group means, analysis of group means still provides perhaps the most important evidence of training effectiveness. In most training effectiveness studies, a change in group means owing to training provides evidence that the group as a whole has changed its position on some relevant dependent variable (Alliger and Katzman, 1997) and this conclusion cannot be reached solely by investigating performance variance.

Finally, although there is a substantial training literature dealing with the nature and appropriateness of evaluation criteria (e.g., Alliger and Janak, 1989; Alliger and Katzman, 1997; Arthur, Bennett, Edens, and Bell, 2003), this literature has focused primarily on the type or level of a criterion (e.g., Alliger and Janak, 1989; Alliger, Tannenbaum, Bennett, Traver, and Shotland, 1997; Kirkpatrick 1959a, 1959b, 1960a, 1960b). Regardless of the specific criterion used (e.g., motor performance, reaction time, declarative knowledge), the vast majority of studies report changes in group means as evidence of training effectiveness (Arthur et al., 2003). Alliger and Katzman (1997) highlighted this lack of attention to other metrics and noted that it has occurred "despite the implications that a change in variability may have for assessing mean differences, and the importance of variability effects per se for understanding the effects of organizational training" (p. 226). Specifically, they argued that whereas a change in group means owing to training indicates that the group as a whole has changed, a change in the variability of trainees' performance may provide some insight over and beyond conclusions drawn from an investigation of group means.

FACTORS INFLUENCING POSTTRAINING VARIANCE

A detailed reading of the literature reveals a number of potential challenges associated with using the variance to provide diagnostic information over and beyond mean performance levels because many factors influence how training might affect posttraining performance variance. For instance, depending on the factors specific to a training protocol, one might expect either no change in performance variance, an increase in performance variance, or a decrease in performance variability. It is also important to note that these changes in variability can be observed at different levels of analysis—either by evaluating the performance variance of individual persons (e.g., through the use of growth curves) or by evaluating the performance variance of a group of persons (e.g., program evaluation). In this study, our goal is to explore the feasibility of using variance reduction as a viable indicator of training effectiveness for groups of individuals undergoing training. As such, our focus is on program evaluation and not on modeling the performance of individual trainees.

Drawing on the automatic-controlled information processing perspective (Shiffrin and Schneider, 1977), skill acquisition theory (Anderson, 1982), and Norman and Bobrow's (1975) performance-resource function, Ackerman (1987) proposed a model for predicting variance in skill learning. Skill learning was operationalized as increased task proficiency over trials for tasks that were "simple" in terms of information-processing requirements, such as cancelling "A"s, mental multiplication, and memory scanning. He defined tasks in terms of whether they placed consistent or inconsistent demands on an individual's cognitive resources and posited that the demands that consistent, simple tasks placed on individuals' cognitive resources changed with practice; as an individual practiced a task that places consistent demands on cognitive abilities, less and less conscious effort was required to perform the task and such a task therefore became less resource dependent. He submitted that as individuals practice a task and the task becomes less resource dependent, individuals would show a decreased variance in performance on the task (i.e., they will become more alike in terms of task performance). He based his explanation on the following reasoning: differences in cognitive ability caused initial differences in task performance, but as a task that places consistent demands on an individual's cognitive ability becomes less resource dependent, the decreasing demand on cognitive ability permitted similar performance for most individuals. Thus, individuals performed more similarly to each other and performance variance after training was smaller than performance variance before training. Conversely, a task that places inconsistent demands on an individual's cognitive ability remained resource dependent—the demands placed on cognitive ability did not decrease, and individual differences in cognitive ability led to increased variability in performance on the task. This initial line of reasoning would later be integrated into Alliger and Katzman's (1997) taxonomy of factors influencing the variance of training outcomes. In addition, Ackerman's emphasis on the consistency of task demands would serve as the foundation of his later work (Ackerman, 2007), emphasizing the influence of both task and individual characteristics on performance variability.

Ackerman's (1987) theory emphasized task characteristics as important to an understanding of variability effects. But, seeking to further an understanding of the conditions under which a change in variability would be a useful indicator of training effectiveness, Alliger and Katzman (1997) subsequently built on Ackerman's work in an attempt to identify the boundary conditions critical to a more complete understanding of variability effects. They proposed that five factors were likely to influence posttraining outcomes with respect to variance across trainees. Specifically, these factors are: (a) the degree to which differences in ability relevant to performance are present, (b) the degree of initial true differences among individuals on the dependent variable,

(c) characteristics of measures, (d) type of training, and (e) characteristics of the task to be trained.

Differences in Ability Relevant to Performance

With respect to differences in ability, differences among trainees on any set of knowledge, skills, abilities, or other individual characteristics relevant to skill acquisition are likely to lead to an increase in posttraining variability as early advantages accumulate over time and the "rich get richer" while the poor do not (Ackerman, 2007). For example, with all other things being equal, if training success requires cognitive ability (g), individuals higher in g would experience more gains from training than individuals lower in g. This is the model underlying the aptitude–treatment interaction (ATI) paradigm (Thorndike, 1908). The classic ATI seen in this situation (a "fan–shaped" interaction) is observed in an analysis of *subgroup means*, but ATIs also have implications for performance variance. Specifically, the presence of an ATI indicates that a training protocol has different effects on different trainees; this implies the presence of posttraining variance in the group of trainees *as a whole*. Without an a priori rationale for dividing a group of trainees into separate subgroups based on some underlying attribute, a group consisting of trainees who vary on some ability related to training would show an increase in posttraining variance because underlying abilities would become more manifest as training progressed. By way of analogy, consider a meta-analysis. A sample-weighted effect size associated with a substantial amount of variance unaccounted for by statistical or measurement artifacts may indicate the presence of substantive moderators. A moderator analysis performed on subgroups of studies may indicate different effect sizes for the subgroups. Similarly, a large increase in posttraining variance may indicate the presence of an ATI; in other words, the training is more effective for some trainees than others.

Initial True Differences on a Dependent Variable

The degree of initial true differences among individuals on the dependent variable also influences the degree of difference between pre and posttraining variability. In general, if trainees exhibit substantial initial differences on the dependent variable, then convergence from pretest to posttest will be more likely than if initial differences are small. In an extreme example, if every trainee in a group undergoing training had identical scores on a baseline performance measure, then it would be impossible to detect a decrease in variance owing to training.

Characteristics of Measures

Although individual differences (on both training-relevant attributes and baseline performance measures) may influence the degree of variability observed after training, a related concept—how performance is measured— may also influence conclusions drawn from observations of posttraining variability. Researchers have noted that degree of posttraining variance depends on the type of performance measure used (Ackerman, 1987; Alliger and Katzman, 1997). Ackerman (1987) notes that almost all performance measures are ultimately based on either reaction time or attainment measures, but "variability changes found in an experiment with one type of measure seem to be at odds with changes in variability found in experiments with the other type of measure" (p. 8); thus, the two measures may answer the question of whether variability changed in different ways. In addition, Arthur, Bennett, Stanush, and McNelly (1998) noted that speed and accuracy are both used as dependent measures of performance, but the two measures may differentially impact posttraining variance. Specifically, accuracy measures approach asymptote more rapidly than speed measures and will therefore show reduced performance variance more quickly.

Type of Training

In addition to type of measurement, type of training may also influence observed posttraining variance. For example, mastery training would initially result in an increase in variance because initial individual differences would be expected to impact performance, but as all individuals eventually approached mastery, the variance observed between individuals would decrease. In contrast, when trainees undergo training for a specified period of time or number of trials, the performance of some trainees may not approach asymptote because the impact of initial individual differences may preclude substantial early training gains. Therefore, in such a limited number of training trials, an increase in posttraining variance would be observed.

Task Characteristics

Finally, the nature of the task itself may affect variability. In an attempt to answer the question of whether practice on a task makes individuals "more similar to one another or more different," Ackerman (2007, p. 235) speculated that the answer depended on a small number of task characteristics. First, performance variance is affected by the degree to which a task depends on speed and accuracy of motor movement. Most tasks that involve speed and accuracy of motor movements tend to be relatively consistent in terms of the demands on cognitive resources and show decreased performance variance among individuals after training. Performance differences between individuals may be large for novices, but tend to be much smaller after practice because with practice on such tasks individuals improve speed and accuracy on the task, become more alike in performance, and hence, variability between individuals decreases. However, as these tasks become more complex, the demands they place on cognitive resources become more inconsistent. Consequently, training may lead to improvements for some individuals (especially those with higher levels of attributes related to training) but not for others (those with lower levels of attributes related to training). In this situation, posttraining variance would increase as individuals who grasped optimal solution strategies would improve, and those who did not would be left farther and farther behind.

In contrast to tasks that depend on speed or accuracy, variance on a task in which domain (or declarative) knowledge is necessary for successful performance is largely influenced by the degree to which the task is "closed" or "open" (Ackerman, 2007). Closed tasks tend to be those associated with a reasonably finite domain of knowledge (e.g., learning to identify friend or foe in a combat simulation). As individuals mastered all aspects of such a closed task, they would become more alike (in terms of performance scores) and variance would therefore decrease. Open tasks, on the other hand, are characterized by an unbounded domain of knowledge. For example, after mastering an identification task, another new task (e.g., deciding which weapon to employ) is added to the training protocol, followed by additional tasks, until all tasks to be trained have been introduced. In this manner, the knowledge demands of each closed task would have a cumulative effect; individuals would build on the domain knowledge gained in mastering prior tasks. As some individuals mastered these closed tasks more quickly or more fully, these differences in prior knowledge would have a large effect on the acquisition of new knowledge. In contrast, individuals who did not master early tasks quickly or fully would not develop a strong foundation upon which new knowledge could be placed and these individuals would fall behind. Therefore, open tasks would show more posttraining variance than closed tasks.

VARIANCE IN THE CONTEXT OF SKILL RETENTION

As obvious from previous research (e.g., Arthur et al., 1997, 2010; Schmidt and Bjork, 1992) and earlier chapters in this volume, discussions of training effectiveness have to date not been limited to the context of skill acquisition.

Assessing skill acquisition is fundamental in determining the effectiveness of training; however, in many domains skill acquisition may be followed by a nonuse interval before trainees are expected to perform the skills they have acquired (Arthur et al., 1998; Wisher, Sabol, Hillel, and Kern, 1991). Arthur et al. (2003) argued that evaluating the effectiveness of training in the context of skill retention is a logical extension of any research effort in which researchers seek to assess the effectiveness of training protocols. In addition, Schmidt and Bjork (1992) noted that training protocols that maximize skill acquisition may not necessarily be associated with higher retention and transfer, and therefore skill acquisition and skill retention are inseparable and must both be considered in investigations of skill acquisition.

Arthur et al. (1998) note that a pervasive problem in the skill loss literature is the lack of consensus concerning the criteria used to determine the point at which skill acquisition should cease and the retention interval should begin. In addition, they note that several dimensions of performance have been used throughout the literature to identify the end of skill acquisition. For example, some primary studies have trained individuals to one error-free trial (e.g., Goldberg et al., 1981) while other studies have defined mastery as a predetermined percentage of trainees correctly performing the task (e.g., Shields, Goldberg, and Dressel, 1979). Other studies have not specified a particular criterion that must be reached before terminating skill acquisition; instead, trainees were required to practice a task for a certain amount of time (Arthur et al., 1997). As an alternative to these criteria, variance might also be a potential indicator of mastery. When performance approaches asymptote, variance decreases and this may indicate a point of diminishing returns for training. Therefore, as an indicator of training effectiveness, variance could be useful in skill acquisition, retention, and transfer studies. For example, variance might provide information regarding how long to train or—in conjunction with group means—provide convergent evidence of mastery.

PRESENT STUDY

Based on arguments that performance variance may be diagnostic as an indicator of training effectiveness, we reanalyzed data to explore whether performance variance provides diagnostic information over and above information provided by an investigation of group means in the context of complex skill acquisition, retention, and transfer. In addition, the nature of these data also permitted an investigation of this issue in terms of acquisition and long-term retention on different performance tasks and training protocols. Both datasets also included both skill-based and declarative knowledge criterion measures. As Villado et al. noted in Chapter 3, the training literature provides limited information regarding the retention and decay of cognitively complex, decision-making skills. Both sets of data that we reanalyzed were obtained from previously published studies (Arthur et al., 1997; Arthur et al., 2010) involving these types of tasks. As such, the current investigations provide a measure of ecological validity relative to the cognitive, information-processing, and decision-making tasks and activities present in (a) a complex perceptual-motor skill task representative of a dynamic aviation environment and (b) a PC-based, real-time micro-simulation of modern naval warfare featuring ships, aircraft, submarines, and airbases on land that are both analogues of operational environments in military, civilian first-responder, and other similar settings.

STUDY 1—ARTHUR ET AL. (1997)

Arthur et al. (1997) originally completed a replication and extension of Shebilske, Regian, Arthur, and Jordan's (1992) active interlocked modeling (AIM) dyadic training protocol—defined as "observational learning in the context of actively performing a task in harmony with a partner" (Arthur et al., 1997, p. 784)—to assess whether the amount and rate of skill acquisition (at the end-of-acquisition) and the amount and rate of skill loss (after an 8-week nonuse interval) would be the same for participants trained in dyads with an AIM protocol when compared to participants trained individually. They expected that, at worst, the AIM–dyad protocol would result in the same rates and amounts of skill acquisition and loss; hence, they sought to demonstrate the increased efficiency of the AIM protocol—as compared to the individual protocol—by demonstrating an increase in the effective use of time and resources in relation to trainee-to-simulator ratio and amount of trainee hands-on practice.

Participants

The Arthur et al. (1997) sample consisted of 89 participants. This sample (100 percent young adult males), from the campus and surrounding community of Texas A&M University, completed approximately 9 hours of training on a complex perceptual-motor skill task representative of a dynamic aviation environment task and assessments of ability, personality, and motivation. After an 8-week nonuse interval, they returned for tests of skill retention, transfer, and reacquisition.

Measures and Procedure

Performance Task—Space Fortress. The performance task was Space Fortress (Mane and Donchin, 1989), a PC-based, complex psychomotor task involving 3-button mouse and joystick controls in which participants controlled a spaceship to battle a fortress. Skilled performance on Space Fortress was operationalized as a composite score obtained on test sessions prior to training (i.e., baseline), at the end of approximately 9 hours of training (i.e., skill acquisition), after an 8-week nonuse period (i.e., long-term skill retention), and under novel performance demands (i.e., skill transfer) immediately after the test of long-term retention. Similar missions were used for the tests of baseline performance, acquisition, retention, and transfer. In the baseline, acquisition, and retention missions, participants used a joystick to control their ship in Space Fortress; however, in the transfer session, participants used a keyboard to control their ship. The keyboard version was identical in all respects to the joystick version except that joystick control was replaced by keyboard control. Arthur et al. (1997) provide a more complete description of Space Fortress, the scoring method used, and the composition of training and test sessions.

Declarative Knowledge. Arthur et al. (1997) and Arthur, Bennett, Day and McNelly (2002) developed a 30-item, two to four alternative multiple-choice test to assess knowledge of Space Fortress instructions, procedural rules, and information presented during training. The test was scored by summing the number of items answered correctly. Trainees completed this test prior to training (after initial instruction but prior to practice), at the end of approximately 10 hours of training, and after an 8-week nonuse period.

Procedure. Trainees were assigned to either an individual ($n = 49$) or a dyadic ($n = 40$) training protocol. Individuals in the individual-based protocol underwent training individually; individuals assigned to the AIM–dyad protocol were paired with a training partner and each trainee was required to perform each half of a task (i.e., mouse and joystick controls) alternately with his partner, who performed the other half. Regardless of training conditions, performance was assessed individually—at baseline, after approximately 9 hours of acquisition training, after an 8-week nonuse interval, and on a transfer task following the nonuse interval.

Results

Arthur et al. (1997) found that both the amount and rate of skill acquisition appeared to be the same for the AIM–dyad and individual-based protocols ($d = -0.18$). Furthermore, after an 8-week nonpractice interval, AIM–dyad participants' level of skill loss and rate of skill reacquisition were not different from participants in the individual-based protocol ($d = -0.12$). Although they found the training effectiveness of both training protocols to be roughly equivalent, Arthur et al. (1997) demonstrated the robustness of the efficiency gains associated with the AIM–dyad protocol by showing that a 100 percent increase in the effective use of time and resources (Shebilske et al., 1992) was still present after an extended period of nonpractice.

STUDY 2—ARTHUR ET AL. (2010)

Our second dataset was obtained from Arthur et al.'s (2010) study comparing the effectiveness of two different distributed practice schedules. They sought to compare the effectiveness of two distributed training protocols in terms of performance immediately following training, and after an 8-week nonuse interval. However, they also sought to investigate the effect of these distributed training protocols on a complex task—in contrast to a simple one—because of a lack of consensus regarding the ability to generalize from simple laboratory tasks to real-world training environments. Specifically, they hypothesized that the deeper information processing associated with longer interstudy intervals would lead to acquisition of skills more resilient to skill loss. The training task used was Jane's Fleet Command, a cognitively complex command-and-control microworld simulation of modern naval warfare (Sonalysts, Inc., 2004, Air Force Research Laboratory ver. 1.55).

Participants

The sample consisted of the 192 participants described in Villado et al. (Chapter 3 of this volume). This sample (77 percent young adult males) from the campuses and surrounding communities of Texas A&M University and the University of Oklahoma completed approximately 10 hours of training on a cognitively complex command-and-control simulation task and assessments of ability, personality, and motivation. After an 8-week nonuse interval, they returned for tests of skill retention, transfer, and reacquisition.

Measures and Procedure

Performance Task—Jane's Fleet Command. As described in Chapter 3, the performance task was Jane's Fleet Command (Sonalysts, Inc., 2004, Air Force Research Laboratory ver. 1.55), a PC-based real-time micro-simulation of modern naval warfare featuring ships, aircraft, submarines, and airbases on land. Skilled performance on Jane's Fleet Command was operationalized as the mission effectiveness of test missions prior to training (i.e., baseline), at the end of approximately 10 hours of training (i.e., skill acquisition), after an 8-week nonuse period (i.e., long-term skill retention), and on a novel mission (i.e., skill transfer) immediately after the test of long-term retention. Similar missions were used for the tests of baseline performance, acquisition, and long-term retention. The test of transfer involved a very different mission consisting of both novel and overwhelming performance demands. The transfer mission was the most complex and difficult mission faced by trainees. It required trainees to implement all of the strategies and techniques presented in all of the preceding training sessions and test missions. Whereas in other missions trainees may have used proficiency in one area (e.g., sensor and weapons use, strike coordination, and resource management) to compensate for a deficiency in another area, effective performance on the test of transfer required proficiency in all tasks simultaneously. Furthermore, this transfer mission also presented trainees with an environment that was novel, both in terms of the platforms under their command and the strategy necessary to achieve the mission objectives and goals. This mission required trainees to employ new platforms with unique capabilities, search for and engage an enemy fleet that was defended unlike any other previous fleet they had engaged, while for the first time defending their fleet from two separate attacks simultaneously. Villado et al. (Chapter 3 of this volume) provide a more complete description of Jane's Fleet Command, the scoring method used, and the composition of training and test missions.

Declarative Knowledge. Arthur et al. (2007, 2010) developed a 21-item, 3-alternative multiple-choice test to assess knowledge of Jane's Fleet Command instructions, procedural rules, and information presented during training. The test was scored by summing the number of items answered correctly. Trainees completed this test prior to training (after initial instruction but prior to practice), at the end of approximately 10 hours of training, and after an 8-week nonuse period.

Procedure. Trainees were assigned to one of two distributed training conditions—one with longer interstudy intervals between practice sessions ($n = 100$), and one with shorter interstudy intervals between practice sessions ($n = 92$). Performance was assessed at baseline, after 9 hours of acquisition training, after an 8-week nonuse interval, and at transfer.

Results

Arthur et al. (2010) found that both types of interstudy intervals achieved higher immediate posttraining than pretraining mission effectiveness scores (longer interstudy interval $d = 3.25$, shorter interstudy interval $d = 3.27$). In addition, the longer interstudy interval achieved higher levels of skill at the end of training than the shorter interstudy interval ($d = 0.24$). With respect to long-term retention, performance after an 8-week nonuse interval decreased in the shorter interstudy interval condition ($d = -0.28$), but not in the longer interstudy interval condition ($d = -.06$). Finally, they found that the longer interstudy interval resulted in higher skill levels than the shorter interstudy interval condition after the 8-week nonuse interval ($d = 0.46$).

In summary, an investigation of the extant literature indicates that training features have differential impacts on posttraining variance and this variance may be of diagnostic value. In addition, we are unaware of any research that provides empirical evidence for or against the usefulness of variance as a training evaluation criterion or that compares means and variances to determine whether variance (as an indicator of training effectiveness) is of diagnostic value, especially in the context of skill acquisition, retention, and transfer. Therefore, the purpose of the present study was to undertake a comparative assessment of the mean and variance as training effectiveness metrics and further investigate how they may supplement or complement each other. This was accomplished by analyzing two datasets from previously published studies (Arthur et al., 1997, 2010) involving different training designs and criterion tasks.

DATA ANALYTIC APPROACH

We calculated means, standard deviations, and correlations using raw data from Arthur et al. (1997) and Arthur et al. (2010). The objective of the current investigation was to explore whether performance variance provided incremental diagnostic information over and above information provided by an investigation of group means in the context of complex skill acquisition, retention, and transfer. As such, we assessed differences between mean performance scores across training protocols (i.e., in Study 1, the difference between AIM–dyad and individual training scores, and in Study 2, the difference between longer and shorter interstudy interval training scores) at pretraining, end-of-acquisition, long-term retention, and transfer using independent samples t-tests and Cohen's (1988) between-groups effect sizes; we assessed differences between variances across training protocols using Levene's (1960) test for homogeneity of variances. All variance comparisons involved two groups, so to indicate which variance was larger in each comparison, we converted each F statistic (which does not indicate the larger variance in each comparison) obtained from Levene's test into a t statistic (which can indicate the larger variance in each comparison). Because of the exploratory nature of this study, we performed 2-tailed tests of significance when comparing variances, and for consistency, we also performed 2-tailed tests of significance when comparing group means.

We assessed skill acquisition and loss within each training protocol (e.g., the difference between mean pretraining and end-of-acquisition scores within a single training protocol) using paired samples *t*-tests and Cohen's (1988) within-subjects effect sizes; we assessed differences between variances within each training protocol (e.g., the difference between performance variances at pretraining and end-of-acquisition within a single training protocol) using Pitman's (1939) test for equality of variances in correlated samples.

RESULTS

Study 1—Arthur et al. (1997)

Table 5.1 shows the means, standard deviations, and correlations obtained by reanalyzing performance scores from Arthur et al. (1997). Recall that in this study, individuals were assigned to either an AIM–dyad or an individual training protocol and performance was assessed pretraining, after 9 hours of training (end-of-acquisition), after an 8-week nonuse interval (long-term retention), and at transfer (immediately after the test of long-term retention).

Along the diagonal in Table 5.1, there are two stacked values. The upper value in each cell indicates the standardized mean difference between training protocols, with positive values indicating that the AIM–dyad training protocol was more effective than the individual training protocol. The lower value in each cell is an index of difference in variances (assessed via Levene's test of homogeneity of variances) between training protocols, with positive values indicating that the AIM–dyad training protocol had a larger variance than the individual training protocol. Although the AIM–dyad training protocol resulted in higher mean performance scores than the individual training protocol at transfer, this difference was not statistically significant. In fact, results indicated that there were no statistically significant mean differences between training conditions (*d*s ranged from –0.18 to 0.29). Similarly, the results of Levene's test indicated that variances were not significantly different in the two training protocols, although variances were consistently lower in the AIM–dyad training protocol once training began. Hence, an examination of differences between variances provided evidence confirming the results obtained through an analysis of mean differences. This is especially evident in Figure 5.1: the effectiveness of the training protocols was about the same,

TABLE 5.1

Space Fortress Pretraining, End-of-Acquisition, Long-Term Retention, and Transfer Performance—Descriptive Statistics, Standardized Mean Differences Between Interstudy Interval Conditions, and Standardized Mean Differences Within Interstudy Interval Conditions

Session		Session 1 (Pretraining)	9 (End-of-Acquisition)	10 (Long-Term Retention)	12 (Transfer)
		M = −1402.64** SD = 947.62**	M = 3936.74** SD = 1665.71**	M = 3206.73** SD = 1555.12**	M = 515.64** SD = 1454.08**
1 (Pretraining)	M = −1468.12 SD = 1028.34	d = −0.07** t = 0.28**	d = 3.95** t = 5.02** r = .59**	d = 3.72** t = 4.44** r = .61**	d = 1.38** t = 3.29** r = .39**
9 (End-of-Acquisition)	M = 3648.27 SD = 1521.68	d = 4.25** t = 3.15** r = .62**	d = −0.18 t = −0.84**	d = −0.86** t = −0.94** r = .86**	d = −2.46** t = −1.18** r = .61**
10 (Long-Term Retention)	M = 3028.24 SD = 1507.14	d = 3.65** t = 2.98** r = .59**	d = −0.71** t = −0.11** r = .83**	d = −0.12** t = −0.21**	d = −2.03** t = −0.58** r = .62**
12 (Transfer)	M = 929.25 SD = 1385.67	d = 1.85** t = 2.10** r = .46**	d = −2.39** t = −0.81** r = .70**	d = −1.88** t = −0.73** r = .71**	d = 0.29** t = −0.96**

In the *leftmost column* of stacked values, the upper value in each cell is the mean and the lower value in each cell is the standard deviation for *AIM–dyad training* protocol (n = 40) session performance scores. In the *topmost row* of stacked values, the upper value in each cell is the mean and the lower value in each cell is the standard deviation for *Individual training* protocol (n = 49) session performance scores. Along the diagonal, upper values indicate the AIM–dyad training protocol is more effective. Along the diagonal, lower values are results of Levene's test of homogeneity of variances (converted to t-values) for comparisons of variances between AIM–dyad and Individual training protocols for a specific trial. Positive values indicate the AIM–dyad training protocol has a larger variance. In the solid box below the diagonal, upper values are repeated measures effect sizes for comparisons across AIM–dyad training protocol trials. Positive values indicate greater performance scores for the higher numbered trial. Middle values are results of Pitman's test of homogeneity of variances for comparisons of variances across AIM–dyad training protocol trials. Positive values indicate greater performance variance for the higher numbered trial. Lower values are correlations between performance scores between trials. In the dashed box above the diagonal, upper values are repeated measures effect sizes for mean comparisons across Individual training protocol trials. Positive values indicate greater performance scores for the higher numbered trial. Middle values are results of Pitman's test of homogeneity of variances for comparisons of variances across Individual training protocol trials. Positive values indicate greater performance variance for the higher numbered trial. Lower values are correlations between performance scores between trials. *p < .05, **p < .01, two-tailed.

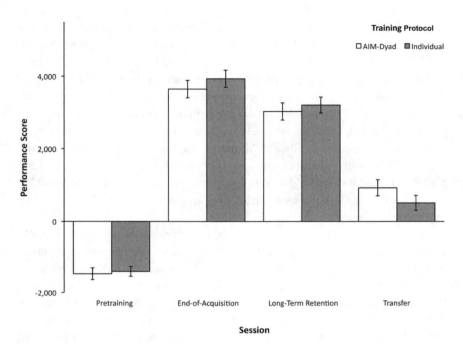

FIGURE 5.1

Space Fortress pretraining, end-of-acquisition, long-term retention, and transfer session performance scores based on data from Arthur et al. (1997). Error bars represent one standard error.

and this lack of difference is evident in both mean performance scores and performance variances.

Results from the individual training protocol are located in the dashed box above the diagonal in Table 5.1. Within the individual training protocol, mean performance scores (t [48] = 27.66, $p < .01$, $d = 3.95$ [two-tailed]) and performance variance (t [47] = 5.02, $p < .01$ [two-tailed]) both increased significantly from pretraining to end-of-acquisition.[1] Mean performance scores (t [48] = –6.03, $p < .01$, $d = –0.86$ [two-tailed]) and performance variance (t [47] = –0.94, $p > .05$ [two-tailed]) both decreased after the 8-week nonuse interval, but only the decrease in mean performance scores was statistically significant. Finally, mean performance scores (t [48] = 14.24, $p < .01$, $d = –2.03$ [two-tailed]) and performance variance (t [47] = –0.58, $p > .05$ [two-tailed]) both decreased at transfer, but only the decrease in mean performance scores was statistically significant.

Results from the AIM–dyad training protocol are located in the solid box below the diagonal in Table 5.1. Within the AIM–dyad training protocol, we observed largely the same pattern of differences as were observed in the individual training protocol. Mean performance scores (t [39] = 26.91, $p < .01$, $d = 4.25$ [two-tailed]) and performance variance (t [38] = 3.15, $p < .01$ [two-tailed]) both increased significantly from pretraining to end-of-acquisition. After the 8-week nonuse interval, mean performance scores (t [39] = −4.47, $p < .01$, $d = −0.71$ [two-tailed]) and performance variance (t [38] = −0.11, $p > .05$ [two-tailed]) both decreased, but only the decrease in mean performance scores was statistically significant. Similar to the results seen at transfer in the individual training protocol, mean performance scores (t [39] = −11.91, $p < .01$, $d = −1.88$ [two-tailed]) and performance variance (t [38] = −0.73, $p > .05$ [two-tailed]), both decreased at transfer, although only the decrease in mean performance was statistically significant.

Overall, mean performance scores and performance variance consistently covaried—as mean performance scores increased, performance variance increased, and as mean performance scores decreased, performance variance decreased. In addition, an examination of performance variances did not seem to provide information differing from that provided by an examination of differences between means—neither group means nor performance variances differed between training protocols. It is interesting, however, that mean performance in both training protocols increased at acquisition and this increase was accompanied by a corresponding increase in performance variance. Finally, although neither difference reached significance, comparisons of means and variances at transfer indicated that—in terms of mean performance increase—the AIM–dyad training protocol was more effective than the individual training protocol and this increase in training effectiveness was accompanied by less performance variance in the AIM–dyad protocol than in the individual protocol.

Although Arthur et al. (1997) originally examined skill-based training effectiveness outcomes (Kraiger, Ford, and Salas, 1993) by looking at differences in mean performance, they also assessed cognitive training effectiveness outcomes via a declarative knowledge test at pretraining, after 9 hours of training (end-of-acquisition), and after an 8-week nonuse interval (long-term retention). Table 5.2 shows the means, standard deviations, and correlations obtained by analyzing declarative knowledge test scores from Arthur et al. (1997).

Along the diagonal in Table 5.2, there are two stacked values. The upper value in each cell indicates the standardized mean difference between training protocols, with positive values indicating more learning in the AIM–dyad training protocol than the individual training protocol. The lower value in each cell is an index of difference in learning variances between training protocols, with positive values indicating more variance in learning in the AIM–dyad

TABLE 5.2

Space Fortress Pretraining, End-of-Acquisition, and Long-Term Retention Declarative Knowledge—Descriptive Statistics, Standardized Mean Differences Between Interstudy Interval Conditions, and Standardized Mean Differences Within Interstudy Interval Conditions

Session		Session 1 (Pretraining)	9 (End-of-Acquisition)	10 (Long-Term Retention)
		M = 27.84**	M = 28.16**	M = 27.27**
		SD = 2.07**	SD = 1.28**	SD = 1.77**
1 (Pretraining)	M = 27.02 SD = 2.28	d = −0.38** t = 1.38**	d = 0.18** t = −4.04** r = .54**	d = −0.27** t = −1.18** r = .41**
9 (End-of-Acquisition)	M = 28.02 SD = 1.25	d = 0.60** t = −5.45** r = .69**	d = −0.11** t = −0.41**	d = −0.92** t = 4.21** r = .85**
10 (Long-Term Retention)	M = 27.40 SD = 1.37	d = 0.20** t = −3.94** r = .56**	d = −0.54** t = 0.74** r = .62**	d = 0.08** t = −1.51**

In the *leftmost column* of stacked values, the upper value in each cell is the mean and the lower value in each cell is the standard deviation for *AIM–dyad training* protocol (n = 40) declarative knowledge scores. AIM = active interlocked modeling.

In the *topmost row* of stacked values, the upper value in each cell is the mean and the lower value in each cell is the standard deviation for *Individual training* protocol (n = 49) declarative knowledge scores.

Along the diagonal, upper values are effect sizes for comparisons declarative knowledge scores between AIM–dyad and Individual training protocols for a specific trial. Positive values indicate the AIM–dyad training protocol is more effective. Along the diagonal, lower values are results of Levene's test of homogeneity of variances (converted to t-values) for comparisons of variances between AIM–dyad and Individual training protocols for a specific trial. Positive values indicate the AIM–dyad training protocol has a larger variance.

In the solid box area below the diagonal, upper values are repeated measures effect sizes for mean comparisons across AIM–dyad training protocol trials. Positive values indicate greater declarative knowledge scores for the higher numbered trial. Middle values are results of Pitman's test of homogeneity of variances for comparisons of variances across AIM–dyad training protocol trials. Positive values indicate greater declarative knowledge variance for the higher numbered trial. Lower values are correlations between declarative knowledge scores between trials.

In the dashed box area above the diagonal, upper values are repeated measures effect sizes for mean comparisons across Individual training protocol trials. Positive values indicate greater declarative knowledge scores for the higher numbered trial. Middle values are results of Pitman's test of homogeneity of variances for comparisons of variances across Individual training protocol trials. Positive values indicate greater declarative knowledge variance for the higher numbered trial. Lower values are correlations between declarative knowledge scores between trials.

*p < .05, **p < .01, two–tailed.

training protocol than the individual training protocol. The effect sizes shown along the diagonal indicate that there were no mean differences in learning between training protocols (*d*s ranged from –0.38 to 0.08), nor were there any differences in performance variance between training protocols. Hence, an examination of differences between variances again provided evidence confirming the results obtained through an analysis of mean differences, and this confirmatory nature of the information provided by a comparison of performance variance is seen in Figure 5.2.

Results from the individual training protocol are located in the dashed box above the diagonal in Table 5.2. Mean declarative knowledge scores increased (*t* [48] = 1.31, *p* > .05, *d* = 0.18 [two-tailed]) at the end-of-acquisition while variance in these scores decreased (*t* [47] = –4.04, *p* < .01 [two-tailed]), although only the change in performance variance was statistically significant. After an 8-week nonuse interval, mean declarative knowledge scores

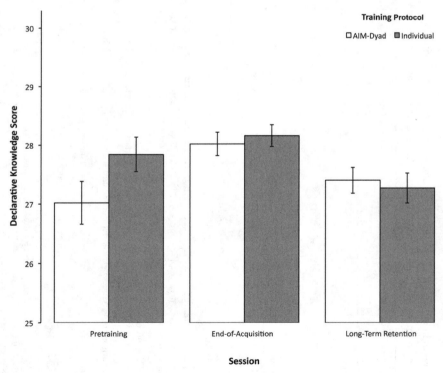

FIGURE 5.2

Space Fortress pretraining, end-of-acquisition, and long-term retention session declarative knowledge test scores based on data from Arthur et al. (1997). Error bars represent one standard error.

significantly decreased (t [48] = −6.53, p < .01, d = −0.92 [two-tailed]) while declarative knowledge variance increased significantly (t [47] = 4.21, p < .01 [two-tailed]).

Results from the AIM–dyad training protocol are located in the solid box below the diagonal in Table 5.2. Within this training protocol, mean declarative knowledge scores significantly increased (t [39] = 3.76, p < .01, d = 0.60 [two-tailed]), while variance in these scores significantly decreased (t [38] = −5.45, p < .01, [two-tailed]) at the end-of-acquisition. After the 8-week nonuse interval, mean declarative knowledge scores decreased significantly (t [39] = −3.45, p < .01, d = −0.54 [two-tailed]) while declarative knowledge variance increased (t [38] = 0.74 p > .05, [two-tailed]), although this increase in variance was not significant.

Overall, mean declarative knowledge scores and variance consistently covaried, but in a manner opposite of that seen for mean performance scores and performance variance. Specifically, as mean declarative knowledge scores increased, variance in these scores decreased, and as mean declarative knowledge scores decreased, variance in these scores increased. In addition, an examination of variances in declarative knowledge scores did not seem to provide information differing from that provided by an examination of differences between means—neither group means nor variances differed between training protocols. Finally, although neither difference reached significance, comparisons of means and variances at transfer indicated that – in terms of mean change in declarative knowledge—the AIM–dyad training protocol was more effective than the individual training protocol and this increase in mean declarative knowledge scores was accompanied by less variance in the AIM–dyad protocol than in the individual protocol.

Study 2—Arthur et al. (2010)

Table 5.3 shows the means, standard deviations, and correlations obtained by reanalyzing performance scores from Arthur et al. (2010). Recall that in this study, individuals were assigned to either a longer or shorter interstudy interval (ISI) training protocol and performance was assessed pretraining, after 10 hours of training (end-of-acquisition), after an 8-week nonuse interval (long-term retention), and at transfer (immediately after the test of long-term retention).

Along the diagonal in Table 5.3, there are two stacked values. The upper value in each cell indicates the standardized mean difference between training protocols, with positive values indicating that the longer ISI training protocol was more effective than the shorter ISI training protocol. The lower value in each cell is an index of the difference in variances between training protocols,

TABLE 5.3

Fleet Command Pretraining, End-of-Acquisition, Long-Term Retention, and Transfer Performance—Descriptive Statistics, Standardized Mean Differences Between Interstudy Interval Conditions, and Standardized Mean Differences Within Interstudy Interval Conditions

Session		Session 1 (Pretraining)	9 (End-of-Acquisition)	10 (Long-Term Retention)	11 (Transfer)
		M = -90.97** SD = 41.60**	M = 15.58** SD = 18.07**	M = 11.01** SD = 17.98**	M = -14.56** SD = 16.49**
1 (Pretraining)	M = -89.74 SD = 42.83	d = 0.03** t = 0.49**	d = 2.44** t = -8.91** r = .11**	d = 2.21** t = -8.94** r = -.05**	d = 1.71** t = -10.08** r = .01**
9 (End-of-Acquisition)	M = 20.26 SD = 19.45	d = 2.45** t = -8.71** r = .12**	d = 0.24** t = 1.14**	d = -0.19** t = -0.05** r = .14**	d = -1.29** t = -0.87** r = .09**
10 (Long-Term Retention)	M = 19.02 SD = 16.81	d = 2.47** t = -10.76** r = .13**	d = -0.06** t = -1.55** r = .34**	d = 0.46** t = -0.04**	d = -1.02** t = -0.82** r = -.05**
11 (Transfer)	M = -13.63 SD = 16.08	d = 1.78** t = -11.53** r = .19**	d = -1.48** t = -1.93** r = .19**	d = -1.46** t = -0.44** r = .07**	d = 0.06** t = -0.58**

In the *leftmost column* of stacked values, the upper value in each cell is the mean and the lower value in each cell is the standard deviation for *longer ISI training* protocol ($n = 100$) session performance scores. ISI = interstudy interval. In the *topmost row* of stacked values, the upper value in each cell is the mean and the lower value in each cell is the standard deviation for *shorter ISI training* protocol ($n = 92$) session performance scores. Along the diagonal, upper values are effect sizes for comparisons of performance scores between longer and shorter ISI training protocols for a specific trial. Positive values indicate longer ISI is more effective. Along the diagonal, lower values are results of Levene's test of homogeneity of variances (converted to *t*-values) for comparisons of variances between longer and shorter ISI training protocols for a specific trial. Positive values indicate longer ISI has a larger variance. In the solid box below the diagonal, upper values are repeated measures effect sizes for mean comparisons across longer ISI training protocol trials. Positive values indicate greater performance scores for the higher numbered trial. Middle values are results of Pitman's test of homogeneity of variances for comparisons of variances across longer ISI training protocol trials. Positive values indicate greater performance variance for the higher numbered trial. Lower values are correlations between performance scores between trials. In the dashed box above the diagonal, upper values are repeated measures effect sizes for mean comparisons across shorter ISI training protocol trials. Positive values indicate greater performance scores for the higher numbered trial. Middle values are results of Pitman's test of homogeneity of variances for comparisons of variances across shorter ISI training protocol trials. Positive values indicate greater performance variance for the higher numbered trial. Lower values are correlations between performance scores between trials. *p < .05, **p < .01, two-tailed.

with positive values indicating that the longer ISI training protocol had a larger variance than the shorter ISI training protocol. Results indicate that there were no significant differences in means or variances at pretraining or end-of-acquisition.[2] In terms of mean differences, the longer ISI protocol was more effective than the shorter ISI protocol at long-term retention (t [190] = 3.19, $p < .01$, $d = 0.46$ [two-tailed]), but performance variances did not differ significantly (t [190] = -0.04, $p > .05$ [two-tailed]). Finally, neither mean performance scores nor performance variances were significantly different at transfer. A graphical depiction of these results is shown in Figure 5.3. Neither training protocol resulted in a significantly different performance variance than the other protocol, even though the longer ISI showed higher mean performance scores than the shorter ISI protocol after the 8-week nonuse interval. With the exception of performance after the 8-week nonuse interval, though, it does not appear (at least in terms of group differences) that an examination of variances provides any diagnostic information over and beyond that provided by an examination of differences between means.

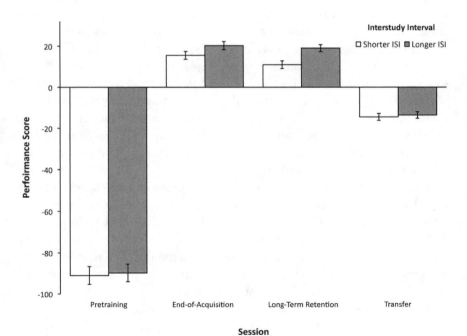

FIGURE 5.3

Fleet Command pretraining, end-of-acquisition, long-term retention, and transfer session performance scores based on data from Arthur et al. (2010). Error bars represent one standard error.

Results from the shorter ISI training protocol are located in the dashed box above the diagonal in Table 5.3. Within the shorter ISI training protocol, mean performance scores increased significantly from pretraining to end-of-acquisition (t [91] = 23.45, $p < .01$, $d = 2.44$ [two-tailed]), while performance variance decreased significantly, (t [90] = −8.91, $p < .01$ [two-tailed]). Between end-of-acquisition and long-term retention, both mean performance (t [91] = −1.86, $p > .05$, $d = −0.19$ [two-tailed]) and performance variance decreased (t [90] = −0.05, $p > .05$ [two-tailed]), although neither decrease was statistically significant. Finally, between long-term retention and transfer, both mean performance (t [91] = −9.80, $p < .01$, $d = −1.02$ [two-tailed]) and performance variance (t [90] = −0.82, $p > .05$ [two-tailed]) decreased, although only the decrease in mean performance was statistically significant.

Results from the longer ISI training protocol are located in the solid box below the diagonal in Table 5.3. Within the longer ISI training protocol, we observed that mean performance scores significantly increased (t [99] = 24.44, $p < .01$, $d = 2.45$ [two-tailed]) between pretraining and end-of-acquisition, while performance variance decreased significantly (t [98] = −8.71, $p < .01$ [two-tailed]) during this period. Between end-of-acquisition and long-term retention, both mean performance (t [99] = −0.50, $p > .05$, $d = −0.05$ [two-tailed]) and performance variance (t [98] = −1.55, $p > .05$ [two-tailed]) decreased, although neither decrease was statistically significant. Finally, between long-term retention and transfer, both mean performance (t [99] = −14.58, $p < .01$, $d = −1.46$ [two-tailed]) and performance variance (t [98] = −0.44, $p > .05$ [two-tailed]), decreased, although only the decrease in mean performance was statistically significant. Overall, the same pattern of results can be seen in both training protocols—mean performance peaked at acquisition, then declined at both long-term retention and transfer, while performance variance consistently declined after pretraining.

Although Arthur et al. (2010) originally examined skill-based training effectiveness outcomes (Kraiger, Ford, and Salas, 1993) by looking at differences in mean performance, they also assessed cognitive outcomes via a declarative knowledge test at pretraining, after 10 hours of training (end-of-acquisition), and after an 8-week nonuse interval (long-term retention). Table 5.4 shows the means, standard deviations, and correlations obtained by analyzing declarative knowledge test scores from Arthur et al. (2010).

Along the diagonal in Table 5.4, there are two stacked values. The upper value in each cell indicates the standardized mean difference between training protocols, with positive values indicating more learning in the longer ISI training protocol than the shorter ISI training protocol. The lower value in each cell is an index of difference in learning variances between training protocols, with positive values indicating more variance in learning in the

TABLE 5.4

Fleet Command Pretraining, End-of-Acquisition, and Long-Term Retention Declarative Knowledge—Descriptive Statistics, Standardized Mean Differences Between Interstudy Interval Conditions, and Standardized Mean Differences Within Interstudy Interval Conditions

Session		Session 1 (Pretraining)	9 (End-of-Acquisition)	10 (Long-Term Retention)
		$M = 11.22^{**}$	$M = 17.17^{**}$	$M = 16.45^{**}$
		$SD = 2.67^{**}$	$SD = 2.58^{**}$	$SD = 2.39^{**}$
1 (Pretraining)	$M = 11.68$ $SD = 2.44$	$d = 0.18^{**}$ $t = -0.93^{**}$	$d = 2.15^{**}$ $t = -0.32^{**}$ $r = .44^{**}$	$d = 1.92^{**}$ $t = -1.09^{**}$ $r = .42^{**}$
9 (End-of-Acquisition)	$M = 17.57$ $SD = 1.64$	$d = 2.42^{**}$ $t = -4.32^{**}$ $r = .34^{**}$	$d = 0.19^{**}$ $t = -2.47^{**}$	$d = -0.34^{**}$ $t = -0.91^{**}$ $r = .63^{**}$
10 (Long-Term Retention)	$M = 16.52$ $SD = 2.27$	$d = 1.79^{**}$ $t = -0.76^{**}$ $r = .34^{**}$	$d = -0.53^{**}$ $t = 3.87^{**}$ $r = .53^{**}$	$d = 0.03^{**}$ $t = -0.30^{**}$

In the *leftmost column* of stacked values, the upper value in each cell is the mean and the lower value in each cell is the standard deviation for *longer ISI training* protocol ($n = 100$) declarative knowledge scores. ISI = interstudy interval.

In the *topmost row* of stacked values, the upper value in each cell is the mean and the lower value in each cell is the standard deviation for *shorter ISI training* protocol ($n = 92$) declarative knowledge scores.

Along the diagonal, upper values are effect sizes for comparisons of declarative knowledge scores between longer and shorter ISI training protocols for a specific trial. Positive values indicate longer ISI is more effective. Along the diagonal, lower values are results of Levene's test of homogeneity of variances (converted to *t*-values) for comparisons of variances between longer and shorter ISI training protocols for a specific trial. Positive values indicate longer ISI has a larger variance.

In the solid box area below the diagonal, upper values are repeated measures effect sizes for mean comparisons across longer ISI training protocol trials. Positive values indicate greater declarative knowledge scores for the higher numbered trial. Middle values are results of Pitman's test of homogeneity of variances for comparisons of variances across longer ISI training protocol trials. Positive values indicate greater declarative knowledge variance for the higher numbered trial. Lower values are correlations between declarative knowledge scores between trials.

In the dashed box area above the diagonal, upper values are repeated measures effect sizes for mean comparisons across shorter ISI training protocol trials. Positive values indicate greater declarative knowledge scores for the higher numbered trial. Middle values are results of Pitman's test of homogeneity of variances for comparisons of variances across shorter ISI training protocol trials. Positive values indicate greater declarative knowledge variance for the higher numbered trial. Lower values are correlations between declarative knowledge scores between trials.

$^{*}p < .05$, $^{**}p < .01$, two-tailed.

longer ISI training protocol than the shorter ISI training protocol. The effect sizes shown along the diagonal indicate that there were no mean differences in learning between training protocols (*d*s ranged from 0.03 to 0.19), but at the end-of-acquisition, participants in the shorter ISI training protocol showed more variation in declarative knowledge scores than their counterparts in the longer ISI training protocol (*t* [190] = –2.47, *p* < .01 [two-tailed]). However, this difference in performance variances was not evident at pretraining or long-term retention. A graphical depiction of these results is shown in Figure 5.4.

Results from the shorter ISI training protocol are located in the dashed box above the diagonal in Table 5.4. Mean declarative knowledge scores significantly increased (*t* [91] = 20.61, *p* < .01, *d* = 2.15 [two-tailed]) at the end-of-acquisition while variance in these scores decreased (*t* [90] = –0.32, *p* > .05 [two-tailed]), although not significantly so. After an 8-week nonuse interval, a significant decrease in mean declarative knowledge scores (*t* [91] = –3.24, *p* < .01, *d* = –0.34 [two-tailed]) was accompanied by a decrease in variance (*t* [90] = –0.91, *p* > .05 [two-tailed]), but this variance decrease was not statistically significant.

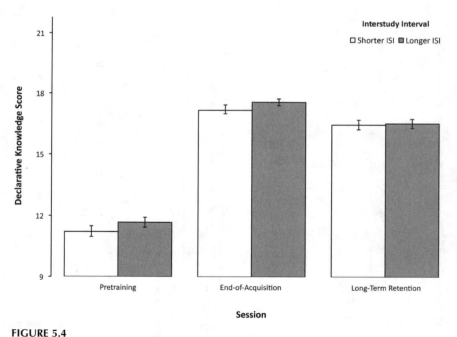

FIGURE 5.4

Fleet Command pretraining, end-of-acquisition, and long-term retention session declarative knowledge test scores based on data from Arthur et al. (2010). Error bars represent one standard error.

Results from the longer ISI training protocol are located in the solid box below the diagonal in Table 5.4. Within this training protocol, mean declarative knowledge scores significantly increased (t [99] = 24.22, $p < .01$, $d = 2.42$ [two-tailed]), while variance in these scores significantly decreased (t [98] = -4.32 $p < .01$, [two-tailed]) at the end-of-acquisition. After the 8-week nonuse interval, a significant decrease in mean declarative knowledge scores (t [99] = -5.29, $p < .01$, $d = -0.53$ [two-tailed]) was accompanied by a significant increase in variance (t [98] = 3.87 $p < .01$, [two-tailed]).

Overall, mean performance and performance variance seem to behave similarly regardless of training protocol. Mean declarative knowledge increased at end-of-acquisition, then decreased after a period of nonuse. However, variance in declarative knowledge scores was decreased at end-of-acquisition, then slightly increased after a period of nonuse. In addition, participants' performance on the test of declarative knowledge mirrored the results seen previously with skill-based performance—although neither difference reached significance, a comparison of means and variances at end-of-acquisition and at retention indicated that the longer ISI training protocol was more effective than the shorter ISI training protocol and this increase in training effectiveness—based on differences between group means—was accompanied by less performance variance in the longer ISI protocol than in the shorter ISI protocol.

DISCUSSION

Although comparison of group means is by far the most commonly used and widely accepted method of assessing training effectiveness, it has been suggested (Alliger and Katzman, 1997) that there are alternative means of assessing training effectiveness, and an assessment of training effectiveness via these alternative means may uncover important conclusions not revealed by an analysis of group means. However, the extant literature contains no investigations of the utility of these alternative measures. The purpose of many types of training is to eliminate behaviors that do not contribute to successful task performance, and these extraneous behaviors increase variance in performance. Thus, this study contributes to the extant literature by investigating the potential role of variance as an indicator of training effectiveness in the context of complex skill acquisition, retention, and transfer. In addition, the nature of these data also permitted investigations of this issue in terms of different performance tasks, criterion measures (i.e., skill-based performance and declarative knowledge), and training protocols, all of which contribute to the generalizability of our conclusions.

In general, our conclusion is that an investigation of performance variance as a training effectiveness metric provides confirmatory evidence of training effectiveness, and may provide information that supplements that provided by an investigation of group means. We base this conclusion primarily on the consistency with which differences in mean performance between training protocols were accompanied by differences in performance variance between training protocols. In addition, we observed that, in comparisons of training protocols, the protocol resulting in higher mean level of training effectiveness also tended to result in lower variance. We compared the effectiveness of different training protocols on skill-based performance at four different times (pretraining, end-of-acquisition, long-term retention, and transfer) on two different task platforms utilizing different performance tasks—eight comparisons in all. In only one comparison was a significant difference in group means accompanied by a nonsignificant difference between performance variances. In all other comparisons, nonsignificant differences between group means were accompanied by nonsignificant differences between performance variances. In addition, we also examined differences in declarative knowledge between two different training protocols at three separate times on two different task platforms. In only one of these six comparisons did we observe a significant difference in declarative knowledge variance that was accompanied by a nonsignificant difference between mean declarative knowledge scores. In summary, only twice in 14 separate comparisons of training outcomes was there an incongruence between mean differences and variance differences.

In addition to these between group comparisons, we also investigated changes in performance across time within training protocols. On all four training protocols (conducted using two different performance tasks), we observed that mean performance peaked at the end-of-acquisition, then decreased after a period of nonuse and further decreased on a transfer task. However, the type of performance task seemed to moderate the pattern of performance variance. In both training protocols on Fleet Command, a task that places high demands on decision-making skills and domain knowledge, performance variance was highest at baseline, decreased at the end-of-acquisition, decreased even more after a period of nonuse, and decreased further still on a transfer task; in addition, performance variance was significantly lower at all three of these times than it was prior to training. In contrast, in both training protocols on Space Fortress, a task that places a heavier demand on psychomotor than on decision-making skills, performance variance increased at the end of acquisition, then decreased after a period of nonuse and decreased further on a transfer task. Performance variance on Space Fortress, however, was significantly higher at these three times than it was prior to training.

Mean declarative knowledge scores exhibited patterns similar to those seen in skill-based outcomes—regardless of task type or training protocol, mean declarative knowledge scores peaked at the end of acquisition then decreased after a period of nonuse. However, variances in these declarative scores did not mirror the patterns seen in performance variances. In fact, it is difficult to discern any stable pattern in these variances, except for the fact that variance in declarative knowledge scores was greatest prior to training and smaller after training began, regardless of task type or training protocol. It is possible, however, that the inconsistent patterns seen in performance variance could stem from the ceiling on Space Fortress declarative knowledge scores and the corresponding reduction in these scores' variance.

In summary, performance variance may not tell us as much about performance on a task as it does about the task itself. The two task platforms we investigated were qualitatively different—although Space Fortress (Arthur et al., 1997) places some demands on decision-making skills, it places considerably more demands on psychomotor skills. In contrast, Fleet Command (Arthur et al., 2010) places more of a demand on decision-making skills and has very low psychomotor skill demands. Ackerman (2007) posited that the degree to which a task demands cognitive resources and the degree to which a task is open or closed would influence how much performance on the task varied. In both Space Fortress training protocols, performance variance tended to increase as mean performance increased. In both Fleet Command training protocols, performance variance decreased throughout all training phases (acquisition, retention, and transfer). Ackerman's ideas regarding the influence of task characteristics may provide an explanation for these results. If individuals were able to quickly master the psychomotor demands (i.e., how to manipulate entities within the task platform) of Fleet Command, then this source of performance variance would have been minimized and variance owing to the required decision-making skills would have remained. In contrast, if individuals were not able to fully master the psychomotor demands of Space Fortress, then this source of variance, in addition to any variance owing to decision-making skills, would have remained. Therefore, an investigation of performance variance may inform the type and/or degree of resources demanded by a task.

IMPLICATIONS FOR PRACTICE, AND CONCLUSIONS

Organizations do not train for training's sake; training prepares individuals to perform at high proficiency levels at some time after training. Arthur et al.

(2003) stressed the importance of training effectiveness in the context of skill retention and other researchers (e.g., Schmidt and Bjork, 1992) have noted that factors that maximize skill acquisition may not necessarily be associated with higher retention and transfer; therefore, acquisition, retention, and transfer must all be considered in investigations of training effectiveness. Given Ackerman's (2007) work and reasoning regarding the influence of task characteristics on performance variance, it may also be possible that different task characteristics may affect performance variance differently at the end of skill acquisition, retention, and transfer.

We examined differences in performance variance after an extended period of nonuse and found that regardless of the type of outcome (skill-based or cognitive), in a comparison of two training protocols, the training protocol that resulted in higher mean performance also resulted in lower perform- ance variance (although it should be noted that these differences in variance between training protocols were not statistically significant). Thus, per- formance variance could serve to supplement mean performance as a training effectiveness metric because the goal of training protocols similar to those examined in these studies is to simultaneously increase performance *and* reduce variability. For example, given two different training protocols with similar levels of training effectiveness (based on trainees' mean level of performance), the protocol that results in less variance within a group of trainees may be the more desirable one to implement. Therefore, information about performance variance could provide practitioners additional informa- tion on which to rely when making decisions regarding adoption and imple- mentation of training.

In addition, a pervasive problem in the skill loss literature is the lack of consensus concerning the criteria used to determine the point at which skill acquisition should cease and the retention interval should begin (Arthur et al., 1998). In both of the studies discussed here, individuals trained for a specific, predetermined amount of time. However, other studies have defined mastery to be one error-free trial (e.g., Schendel and Hagman, 1982) or a predetermined percentage of trainees correctly performing a task (e.g., Holmgrem, Hilligoss, Swezey, and Eakins, 1979). These situations are analogous to real-world training in which individuals attend a course (i.e., train for a predetermined amount of time) or are required to exhibit error-free performance (i.e., train to an error-free trial). In the case of training for a predetermined amount of time, it is conceivable that variance could be used as evidence that a group of trainees are (or are not) approaching mastery. For example, based on Ackerman's (2007) reasoning, the variance in performance for a group of individuals on a closed task should decrease as training progresses. After training for a predetermined amount of time on such a closed task without any other mastery criterion, significant variance in trainees' performance could potentially provide evidence that the trainees as a group were not approaching mastery.

In summary, our findings have implications for both researchers and training professionals. The current study raises questions about the nature of performance variance as a function of task complexity. Ackerman's (2007) model provides a basis for understanding how specific task dimensions (e.g., open vs. closed, simple vs. complex) influence performance variance, but does not address how variance will increase or decrease when training involves numerous tasks that vary on multiple dimensions simultaneously. Further research would be necessary to explore the interactive effect of multiple tasks on performance variance. In addition, the extant literature contains very little research concerning the value of using performance variance as an indicator of training effectiveness at the end of acquisition, retention, and transfer, especially in the context of training complex tasks. By reanalyzing data from previously published studies involving skill acquisition and long-term retention on different task platforms, performance tasks, and training protocols, we undertook a comparative assessment of the mean and variance as training effectiveness metrics to investigate how they may supplement or complement each other. Our results suggest that performance variance provides confirmatory evidence of training effectiveness, but does not provide diagnostic information over and above information provided by an investigation of group means in the context of complex skill acquisition, retention, and transfer.

NOTES

1   The results of Pitman's test for equality of variances in correlated samples are distributed as a t-distribution with $n-2$ degrees of freedom (Pitman, 1939).

2   At first, this conclusion seems to contradict the conclusion Arthur et al. (2010) reached regarding differences in mean performance at the end of acquisition. They found (based on a directional hypothesis) that the longer ISI protocol was more effective than the shorter ISI protocol. In the current investigation, we made no directional predictions regarding performance variance. As such, tests of significant differences between performance variances were two-tailed and, for the sake of consistency, tests of significant differences between means were also two-tailed.

REFERENCES

Ackerman, P. L. (1987). Individual differences in skill learning: An integration of psychometric and information processing perspectives. *Psychological Bulletin, 102*, 3–27.

Ackerman, P. L. (2007). New developments in understanding skilled performance. *Current Directions in Psychological Science, 16*, 235–239.

Alliger, G. M., and Janak, E. A. (1989). Kirkpatrick's levels of training criteria: Thirty years later. *Personnel Psychology, 42*, 331–342.

Alliger, G. M., and Katzman, S. (1997). When training affects variability: Beyond the assessment of mean differences in training evaluation. In J. K. Ford and S. W. J. Kozlowski (Eds.), *Improving training effectiveness in work organizations* (pp. 223–246). Mahwah, NJ: Lawrence Erlbaum Associates.

Alliger, G. M., Tannenbaum, S. I., Bennett, W. Jr., Traver, H., and Shotland, A. (1997). A meta–analysis of the relations among training criteria. *Personnel Psychology, 50*, 341–358.

Anderson, J. E. (1982). Limitations of infant and preschool tests on the measurement of intelligence. *Journal of Psychology, 10*, 203–212.

Arthur, W. Jr., Bennett, W. Jr., Day, E. A., and McNelly, T. L. (2002). *Skill decay: A comparative assessment of training protocols and individual differences in the loss and reacquisition of complex skills* (Tech. Rep. No. AFRL–HE–AZ–TR–2002–0004). Mesa, AZ: Air Force Research Laboratory.

Arthur, W. Jr., Bennett, W. Jr., Edens, P. S., and Bell, S. T. (2003). Effectiveness of training in organizations: A meta-analysis of design and evaluation features. *Journal of Applied Psychology, 88*, 234–245.

Arthur, W. Jr., Bennett, W. Jr., Stanush, P. L., and McNelly, T. L. (1998). Factors that influence skill decay and retention: A quantitative review and analysis. *Human Performance, 11*, 57–101.

Arthur, W. Jr., Day, E. A., Bennett, W. Jr., McNelly, T. L., and Jordan, J. A. (1997). Dyadic versus individual training protocols: Loss and reacquisition of a complex skill. *Journal of Applied Psychology, 82*, 783–791.

Arthur, W. Jr., Day, E. A., Villado, A. J., Boatman, P. R., Kowollik, V., Bennett, W. Jr., and Bhupatkar, A. (2007). *Decay, transfer, and the reacquisition of a complex skill: An investigation of practice schedules, observational rehearsal, and individual differences* (Tech. Rep. No. AFRL–HE–AZ–TR–2008–0001). Mesa, AZ: Air Force Research Laboratory.

Arthur, W. Jr., Day, E. A., Villado, A. J., Boatman, P. R., Kowollik, V., Bennett, W. Jr., and Bhupatkar, Alok. (2010). The effect of distributed practice on immediate posttraining, and long-term performance on a complex command-and-control simulation task. *Human Performance, 23*, 428–445.

Ceci, S. J., and Papierno, P. B. (2005). The rhetoric and reality of gap closing: When the "Have-nots" gain but the "Haves" gain more. *American Psychologist, 60*, 149–160.

Cohen, J. (1988). *Statistical power analysis for the behavioral sciences* (2nd ed.). Hillsdale, NJ: Lawrence Erlbaum Associates.

Goldberg, S. L., Drillings, M., and Dressel, J. D. (1981). *Mastery training: Effect on skill retention* (Tech. Rep. No. 513). Alexandria, VA: U.S. Army Research Institute for the Behavioral and Social Sciences.

Holmgrem, J. R., Hilligoss, R. E., Swezey, R. W., and Eakins, R. (1979). *Training effectiveness and retention of training extension course instruction in the combat arms* (Research Rep. No. 1208). Alexandria, VA: U.S. Army Research Institute.

Kirkpatrick, D. L. (1959a). Techniques for evaluating training programs. *Journal of ASTD, 13*(11), 3–9.

Kirkpatrick, D. L. (1959b). Techniques for evaluating training programs: Part 2–Learning. *Journal of ASTD, 13*(12), 21–26.

Kirkpatrick, D. L. (1960a). Techniques for evaluating training programs: Part 3–Behavior. *Journal of ASTD, 14*(1), 13–18.

Kirkpatrick, D. L. (1960b). Techniques for evaluating training programs: Part 4–Results. *Journal of ASTD, 14*(2), 28–32.

Kraiger, K., Ford, J. K., and Salas, E. (1993). Application of cognitive, skill-based, and affective theories of learning outcomes to new methods of training evaluation. *Journal of Applied Psychology, 78*, 311–328.

Levene, H. (1960). Robust tests for equality of variances. In I. Olkin (Ed.), *Contributions to probability and statistics* (pp. 278–292). Palo Alto, CA: Stanford University Press.

Mane, A. M., and Donchin, E. (1989). The Space Fortress game. *Acta Psychologica, 71*, 17–22.

Norman, D. A., and Bobrow, D. B. (1975). On data–limited and resource–limited processes. *Cognitive Psychology, 7*, 44–64.

Pitman, E. J. G. (1939). A note on normal correlation. *Biometrika, 31*, 9–12.

Reed, H. B. (1931). The influence of training on changes in variability in achievement. *Psychological Monographs, 41* (Whole No. 185).

Roberson, L., Kulik, C. T., and Pepper, M. B. (2001). Designing effective diversity training: Influence of group composition and trainee experience. *Journal of Organizational Behavior, 22*, 871–885.

Schendel, J. D., and Hagman, J. D. (1982). On sustaining skills over a prolonged retention interval. *Journal of Applied Psychology, 67*, 605–610.

Schmidt, R. A., and Bjork, R. A. (1992). New conceptualizations of practice: Common principles in three paradigms suggest new concepts in training. *Psychological Science, 3*, 207–217.

Scott, G., Leritz, L. E., and Mumford, M. D. (2004). The effectiveness of creativity training: A quantitative review. *Creativity Research Journal, 16*, 361–388.

Shebilske, W. L., Regian, J. W., Arthur, W. Jr., and Jordan, J. A. (1992). A dyadic protocol for training complex skills. *Human Factors, 34*, 369–374.

Shields, J. L., Goldberg, S. L., and Dressel, J. D. (1979). *Retention of basic soldiering skills* (Research Rep. No. 1225). Alexandria, VA: U.S. Army Research Institute.

Shiffrin, R. M., and Schneider, W. (1977). Controlled and automatic human information processing: Perceptual learning, automatic attending, and a general theory. *Psychological Review, 84*, 127–190.

Sonalysts, Inc. (2004). *Jane's Fleet Command Air Force Research Laboratory ver. 1.55* [Computer software]. Redwood City, CA: Electronic Arts.

Thorndike, E. L. (1908). The effect of practice in the case of a purely intellectual function. *American Journal of Psychology, 19*, 374–384.

Thorndike, E. L. (1910). Practice in the case of addition. *American Journal of Psychology, 21*, 483–486.

Villado, A. J., Day, E. A., Arthur, W. Jr., Boatman, P. R., Kowollik, V., Bhupatkar, A., and Bennett, W. Jr. (2013). Complex command-and-control simulation task performance following periods of nonuse. In W. Arthur, Jr., E. A. Day, W. Bennett, Jr., and A. Portrey (Eds.), *Individual and team skill decay: The science and implications for practice* (pp. 53–67). New York: Taylor & Francis.

Watson, R. T., DeSanctis, G., and Poole, M. S. (1988). Using a GDSS to facilitate group consensus: Some intended and unintended consequences. *MIS Quarterly, 12*, 463–478.

Wisher, R. A., Sabol, M. A., Hillel, H., and Kern, R. P. (1991). *Individual ready reserve (IRR) call-up: Skill decay* (ARI Research Rep. No. 1595). Alexandria, VA: U.S. Army Research Institute.

Woehr, D. J., and Huffcutt, A. I. (1994). Rater training for performance appraisal: A quantitative review. *Journal of Occupational and Organizational Psychology, 67,* 189–205.

AUTHORS' NOTE

This research was sponsored by contracts and grants from the U.S. Air Force Research Laboratory, Human Effectiveness Directorate, Warfighter Training Research Division, Mesa, AZ, the Defense Advance Research Project Agency, and the National Science Foundation awarded to Winfred Arthur, Jr. The views expressed herein are those of the authors and do not necessarily reflect the official position or opinion of the sponsors or their respective organizations.

Part 2

Individual Skill Retention and Transfer on Complex Tasks with Extended Nonuse Intervals, the Factors that Influence Them, and How Skill Decay Can Be Mitigated

6

Improving Military Readiness

Evaluation and Prediction of Performance to Optimize Training Effectiveness

Tiffany S. Jastrzembski, Antoinette M. Portrey, Brian T. Schreiber, and Kevin A. Gluck

Integrating historically separate and conceptually distinct research invest-ments at the Air Force Research Laboratory's Warfighter Readiness Research Division, we present a new technological capability for predicting how much knowledge and skill decay will occur for an individual, team, or squadron after an extended period of nonuse or practice, utilizing that information to more optimally schedule future training and rehearsal events. We align Mission Essential Competencies (MECs) research, which provide expert-driven identification of key enablers for operational success, with the Performance Evaluation Tracking System (PETS) line of research—a fine-resolution performance measurement tool used in high-complexity, time-pressured, mission-relevant domains—to provide a performance measurement founda-tion to adequately equip our third line of research—the predictive performance equation (PPE). The co-dependence among the MECs, PETS, and PPE research lines provide us with the methods, metrics, and models required to achieve our vision for optimally adaptive, individualized training and rehearsal experiences. This chapter seeks to showcase how the integration of these research foci will be used in the application of psychological science to improve the readiness of our forces.

INTRODUCTION

It is often stated that its people are an organization's most important asset. To the extent that this is true, investments in improving the effectiveness and efficiency of the people in an organization are among the most justifiable, understandable, and worthwhile investments an organization can make. The Air Force Research Laboratory (AFRL) has understood this for quite some time, with research investments in human-centered sciences stretching as far back as World War II. Today AFRL's Human Effectiveness Directorate has a diverse portfolio of investments that are improving the design of systems that people will use, improving training and rehearsal for the people who will use those systems, and improving our ability to protect the people who are carrying out the Air Force's operational missions.

This chapter reports on recent efforts and progress towards bringing together historically separate and conceptually distinct research investments into a new technological capability for optimally scheduled training and rehearsal events. To achieve this ambitious goal, AFRL's Warfighter Readiness Research Division has been conducting research into a carefully selected set of methods, metrics, and models. The first of these lines of research is an expert-driven method for identifying MECs that are key enablers for operational success. The second line of research is in the creation of a PETS, as a fine-resolution performance measurement tool in high-complexity, time-pressured, mission-relevant domains. The third line of research is in the development of a PPE that calibrates cognitive parameters on the basis of historical performance data and uses those parameters to predict future performance as a function of the predicted loss of knowledge or skills following periods of nonuse or practice, and prescribe training and rehearsal schedules designed to meet training goals (i.e., minimize decay and maximize retention, ensure desired mission-effectiveness is achieved by a specified date, schedule just-in-time training refreshers when knowledge/skills are expected to decay below a specified threshold, etc.). There is a co-dependence among the MECs, PETS, and PPE research lines that we both acknowledge and celebrate in this chapter. It has only recently become clear that our vision for optimally adaptive, individualized training and rehearsal experiences is unachievable without the success of all three of these methods, metrics, and models. In this chapter we will describe them briefly and show how a MEC-motivated, PETS-driven, PPE integrative approach will be used in the application of psychological science to improve the readiness of our forces, having the potential to enhance skill retention and mitigate skill decay.

DISTRIBUTED MISSION OPERATIONS (DMO), MECS, AND PETS

Distributed, simulation-based training environments are designed and built with the intention of increasing trainees' knowledge, skills, and relevant experiences, in order to better prepare them to perform their mission. However, it is not enough merely to insert advanced modeling and simulation and high-bandwidth networks into the training environment and hope for the best. This chapter describes some of the applied cognitive science research that will enable the next generation of immersive, distributed training and rehearsal systems to adapt in response to individual and team performance profiles to an extent previously inconceivable on any large scale. In this section of the chapter we provide background information on the measurement portion of the capability, in the form of MECs and PETS.

Mesa Distributed Mission Operations Training Facility

The DMO Training Research facility at the AFRL's Mesa Research Site provides warfighters the opportunity to participate in simulated air combat missions with teammates across the nation and with coalition partners around the world. This immersive training research testbed allows for realistic recreations of real-world mission environments. This realism and relevance has been achieved in a laboratory setting that enables experimental control sufficient for the careful study of distinct proficiencies and teamwork skills, such as situational awareness and communication (Bennett and McCall, 2006; Schreiber, Watz, Portrey, and Bennett, 2003). During a training research week at AFRL/Mesa, pilots arrive early Monday morning for five days of DMO participation. Upon arrival, the pilots are given an in-brief on the objectives and procedures of DMO and the simulators, a tour of the facilities, and then given a research administrative session where they complete a series of research procedures, including a battery of subjective measurement tools, and are assigned an anonymous research identification number. Pilots participate in one of two similar syllabi; each syllabus consists of nine 3.5 hour sessions, beginning with session one on Monday morning and ending with session nine on Friday morning. There are two sessions each day of a standard 5-day training research week, except on Friday which is a single morning session. Each session entails a 1-hour briefing period, an hour of flying multiple engagements of the same mission genre, and an hour and a half debriefing period. The syllabi scenarios are either defensive or offensive and the flight of four F-16s can face up to 24 threat entities in a single engagement by the end of the week. The scenarios are designed with trigger events and situations to specifically train MECs (Colegrove and Alliger, 2003; Symons, France, Bell, and Bennett, 2005). The syllabi were developed using full mission rehearsal scenarios across a spectrum of air-to-air and air-to-ground mission types and threats while increasing the complexity of the missions as the training research week progressed (Schreiber, Stock, and Bennett, 2006).

The first session on Monday morning, for both syllabi, begins with a familiarization flight to help orient pilots to the DMO simulator environment specifics, such as visual ID characteristics and cockpit differences that may be associated with F-16 block number type or mission software. Session two on Monday begins with benchmarks, scenarios of equal complexity designed as pretest scenarios to measure pretraining performance. The training research week ends on Friday, session nine, with posttest benchmark scenarios to measure posttraining performance. Friday's benchmark scenarios are exact mirror-images of Monday's benchmark scenarios. Strict data collection rules govern all benchmarks in order to maintain a realistic combat environment (see Schreiber, Stock, and Bennett (2006), for a complete description). Benchmark scenarios are terminated when: 1) all F-16s are dead, 2) all threats are dead, 3) enemy strikers reach their target, or 4) 13 minutes have elapsed.

The pilots' overriding goal for the benchmark scenarios is to prevent the enemy strikers/bombers from reaching the base, with the second and third most important goals being to minimize friendly mortalities and maximize adversary kills. The benchmark scenarios were selected because: 1) they have very clear goals and measures of success, 2) they all have equivalent levels of complexity, 3) the same pilots have the same cockpit assignments for the pre and posttesting, and 4) the scenarios are flown under real-time kill removal and strict data collection rules (Schreiber et al., 2006).

Each MEC-based training research syllabus provides a building block approach to training, which begins right after the benchmark scenarios on Monday and continues throughout the course of the week. The sessions increase in complexity via increases in number of threats, different types of threats, different levels of threat autonomy, and increases in vulnerability time. Teams are exposed to between four and eight scenarios within each hour session, depending on the complexity of the scenarios. Teams experience 30–35 scenarios over the training research week between the Monday and Friday benchmarks. Finally, before departure, teams are given a performance out-brief after their last session. This out-brief consists of graphs from a number of objective measures collected by the PETS, a system that will be described next, demonstrating the team's observed performance changes between Monday and Friday benchmarks (Schreiber et al., 2006).

Objective Performance Measurement. Over the past three decades within the air combat distributed environments, there have been many research endeavors focusing on subjective and objective measurement of air combat performance (Brecke and Miller, 1991; Kelly, 1988; Schreiber, Watz, Portrey, and Bennett, 2003). Researchers have consistently reported success at reliably observing and measuring air combat outcomes, which have included shot/kill ratios, bombs on target, fratricides, and mortalities; however, when research has focused on process measures of performance, less success has been documented (Schreiber, Stock, and Bennett, 2006). Traditionally, air combat performance has been assessed by having subject matter experts (SMEs) provide observations and subjective ratings on numerous process indicators of engagement performance, the sum of which are often combined into a single composite measure for data analysis (Seaman, 1999). The resulting composite measures have provided little understanding into what specific processes are leading to successful or unsuccessful outcomes over multiple training scenarios (Brecke and Miller, 1991). There are concerns about the validity and reliability of measuring distinct processes required in air combat owing to their subjectivity; concerns including inter-rater reliability, sensitivity, and grader bias (Krusmark, Schreiber, and Bennett, 2004).

Many of these research endeavors also explored the objective collection of data within standalone simulators or small distributed environments (Brecke and Miller, 1991; Brictson, Ciavarelli, Pettigrew, and Young, 1978; Gehr, Schreiber and Bennett, 2004; Kelly, 1998; Schreiber, Watz, Portrey, and Bennett, 2003; Waag, Raspotnik, and Leeds, 1992; Wooldridge et al., 1982). Process measures of air combat performance were collected from simulators by computers in real time, which presumably allowed for a more reliable assessment of the process. This objective data research mostly included summary measures of both positional advantage and aircraft state (basically who has the positional advantage during a confrontation). These measures were found to be related to engagement outcomes such as shot/kill ratios and fatalities (Brecke and Miller, 1991; Kelly, 1988; McGuinness, Forbes, and Rhoads, 1984; Waag et al., 1992), and were shown to improve between pre and posttraining assessments (McGuinness, Bouwman, and Puig, 1982). However, as in the case of air-to-air combat, a number of measurements were considered too complex to be measured subjectively or objectively. An example of this type of complex measure would be "controls intercept geometry." To calculate this complex measure, the measurement system would need to know the positional information of both the friendly aircraft and the threat aircraft. The system would then calculate the aspect angle of the threat to the friendly aircraft, using rules such as (Schreiber et al., 2006):

- Is threat an enemy fighter aircraft?
- Is the aspect angle greater than 120 degrees?
- If so, then what is the threat's altitude, weapon type, latitude, and longitude coordinates (for determining relative position)?
- Based on this information, is the range less than that of the configuration table value?
- If yes, then the friendly aircraft is in danger of being hit by a threat missile.

Complex measures such as this are very important in providing more detailed feedback to the learner and a better diagnostic metric for instructors and researchers.

Another issue to contend with is that systems that gather objective data are mostly focused on providing immediate feedback to the learner. This however, does not permit quantifying learning as a part of a formal training effectiveness evaluation. These systems are also single simulator-based performance measurement systems, not able to follow the learner to different platforms or tasks. Given these shortcomings, a measurement system capable of automatically aggregating performance over scores of trials and learners for feedback and analysis is required (Schreiber, Watz, Portrey, and Bennett, 2003).

Performance Evaluation Tracking System

To meet this complex requirement for objective measurement in a distributed environment, researchers and engineers at AFRL/Mesa developed an objective measurement system called the Performance Evaluation and Tracking System (PETS). PETS was developed to collect data from a distributed network via the information passed on that network (e.g., Distributive Interactive Simulation (DIS), High Level Architecture (HLA), Test and Training Enabling Architecture (TENA), etc.), and then utilize the data inputs in calculating different algorithms from simple outcome measures to more complex process measures. These measures can be used to achieve a variety of desirable ends, such as training feedback, simulator/model validation, and quantitative analyses (Watz, Keck, and Schreiber, 2004; Watz, Schreiber, Keck, McCall, and Bennett, 2003).

There are three overarching goals for the PETS application (Watz et al., 2003). First, it must be capable of objective measurement over multiple platforms (e.g. F-16, F-15, A-10), including live, virtual, and constructive exercises. Second, PETS must be flexible and configurable to serve multiple purposes, such as human performance assessment, database storage for empirical research studies, simulation technology validation, threat model validation, etc. Third, it must operate on multiple levels in training, including measurements designed for individuals, teams, teams of teams, whole forces, and security, unclassified and classified (Portrey, Keck, and Schreiber, 2005).

Structure. PETS is designed as a modular, multithreaded application capable of robustly handling high volumes of network entities, has the ability to customize default entity properties, and handles custom-developed entity types and measurements. PETS listens to the distributed network, collecting data that is stored in a MYSQL database, within tables called Data Objects. These Data Objects are then used to create various output files called

Summaries, allowing single or aggregated use of the files for statistical analyses, real-time feedback to the learner as an individual or as a team, and tracking performance over time (Figure 6.1). A more detailed description of the structure of PETS can be found in Watz et al. (2004) and Watz, Schreiber, Keck, McCall, and Bennett (2003).

Types of Measurements. Currently PETS collects both performance outcome measures and process measures for air-to-air combat and air-to-ground combat for the F-16 platform. In development are metrics for the F-15E, F-15C, F-22, A-10, two Airborne Warning and Control System (AWACS) positions, and the Joint Terminal Attack Controller (JTAC). Examples of the types of objective data collected are shown in Table 6.1 (Schreiber, Watz, Portrey, and Bennett, 2003). A more complete list can be found in Schreiber et al. (2006). Measures in PETS are established through a structured SME interview process and go through a rigorous validation process (Portrey et al., 2005; Schreiber et al., 2003; Watz et al., 2004).

Measurement Validation Process. Initial conceptual validity of a measure is established by experienced operational warfighters during a workshop. During the workshop, the operational warfighters define what measures should be used to assess proficiency. Then, engineers code the identified rule sets and

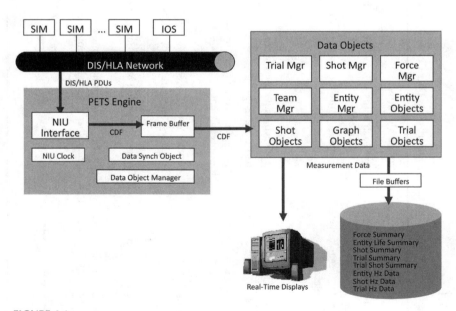

FIGURE 6.1

Architectural overview of PETS. Pathway of data from simulation network to Summary files or real-time displays.

TABLE 6.1

Examples of DMO Objective Training Effectiveness Data Currently Available in PETS

Outcome Measures	Process Measures	Munition Employment
Bombers reaching 2nm of target	Time each entity spent within Minimum Out Range (MOR)	Who shot what type of weapon at whom
Minimum distance to target bombers achieved	Time each entity spent within Minimum Abort Range (MAR)	Result (hit, miss, and some types of misses). Also records distance of misses for missiles. For bombs, records left/right and long/short error distances
Fratricides	Time each entity spent within N-pole (notch range)	2D and 3D range of shot
Mortalities	Chaff/Flare usage	Altitude at release
Enemy fighters killed	AIM-9 Clear Avenue of Fire (possible fratricides), measured by angles	F-pole (distance from firing entity to the target entity at either: a) munitions impact, or b) munitions miss) for hits and misses
Enemy strikers killed	AMRAAM Clear Avenue of Fire (possible fratricides), measured by distances	A-pole (The distance between a missile-firing platform and its target at the instant the missile becomes autonomous.)
Missiles fired that resulted in a kill	Wingman position in relation to lead	Loft angle (the angle between the horizon (horizontal axis) and the aircraft body) at release
Scenario demographics (e.g., number of threats presented, etc.)	How often and for how long flight "steps-on" one another when talking on mic	Mach (speed) at release
Pilot demographics (e.g., flight hours, flight qualification)		G-load (the additional gravitational force exerted on the aircraft and its operator by in-flight moves such as high-speed maneuvers and/or rapid changes in vertical and/or horizontal acceleration) at release

algorithms for each measure. Testing then consists of pilots often flying scenarios that target the specific measurements. Engineers record network traffic from the simulators and reuse the recordings for regression testing. After the initial variable validation, engineers continuously review feedback from pilots and look for anomalies. Researchers also plot larger distributions of data to look for outliers, given the nature of the measure and the contexts in which they were measured. A formal blind study of the reliability of outcome measures has been conducted. The results revealed that the outcome measures from PETS were actually more valid than human observation of outcomes (Schreiber et al., 2006). We refer the reader to that study for a more detailed discussion of the validation process and for additional data that shows the relationship between outcome and process measures.

Skill Retention Research. The Air Force Research Laboratory is currently preparing a final report on a skill retention study. Four-ship teams of pilots fly in week-long training, as discussed earlier, with Monday/Friday mirror-image benchmarks. The primary independent variable is decay interval, with each team returning for additional testing either 3 or 6 months after the initial training. The 2.5 day return visit consists of other, nearly identical mirror-image benchmarks. A number of PETS variables, for use as dependent measures and for use as demographics/descriptors have been collected during the course of the study, including Minimum Abort Range (MAR) and N-pole (notch range) counts/times (total count and duration in which an entity is within the weapon engagement zone of a threat), bomb drop errors, communication errors, kills, mortalities, fratricides, missile hit ratios, etc. Primary questions of interest in the study include: How much of what pilots learn is retained after 3 and 6 months?

- Training gains: Does pilot performance significantly improve as a result of 5 days of DMO training (replication of Schreiber, Stock, and Bennett, 2006)?
- Skill decay: How much of what pilots learn during DMO training is retained after retention intervals of 3 and 6 months?
- Skill reacquisition: How much of the skill loss can be recovered in 2 days of refresher DMO training?
- Factors moderating skill decay: What factors moderate or lessen the degree of skill decay?

Analyses are currently underway, and data will directly feed into the predictive modeling and validation work that is described in the next section of this chapter.

MATHEMATICAL COGNITIVE MODELING FOR PERFORMANCE TRACKING AND PREDICTION

Training people to stable levels of high performance in specialized skills requires a great deal of investment in both time and capital. This is particularly true in highly complex domains such as military operations, where a warfighter may receive years of training before achieving mission ready status. Given the length, complexity, and cost of warfighter training, it is ironic and disappointing that warfighter readiness status is often defined by simple numbers of training hours completed or by subjective ratings of performance using checklists, rather than through objective means (see Gebicke, 1995; Rosales, 2006; Tactical Air Command Regulation 50–31, 1983; Waag, Pierce, and Fessler, 1987). Thus, it may be the case that two individual warfighters appear identical on paper in terms of training history, but operationally, quantitatively, and qualitatively function at very different levels of effectiveness.

To address the challenge of assessing individual performance objectively PETS was developed as a proof-of-concept tool to demonstrate that warfighter skill sets are amenable to precise, quantitative measurement and tracking even in highly immersive, ecologically valid, multi-platform warfighting domains, such as the DMO testbed. PETS provides the necessary measurement foundation for achieving even more ambitious, long-term training optimization goals that the Department of Defense would like to achieve; such as precisely assessing individual warfighter skill and knowledge sets, predicting when threshold levels of performance effectiveness will be attained, optimizing training opportunities and regimens to minimize performance decrements over periods of nonuse, and reducing the total number of costly training opportunities required for warfighters to achieve and maintain threshold levels of performance effectiveness.

The Predictive Performance Equation

Progress towards these goals may be achieved by combining the objective measurement functionality of PETS with new breakthroughs in the field of cognitive science. Specifically, a newly developed mathematical model, termed the Predictive Performance Equation (PPE), synthesizes findings from over a century's worth of research in experimental, cognitive, and mathematical psychology to help understand the dynamics of skill learning and decay, and has extended the capabilities of previous modeling efforts that handled only retrospective fits to human performance into the predictive realm (Jastrzembski, Gluck, and Gunzelmann, 2006a, 2006b; Jastrzembski, Rodgers, and Gluck, 2009). As such, the PPE first provides the ability to track past and current levels of trainee performance proficiency and then utilizes known training history to calibrate trainee model parameters and extrapolate knowledge state transformation under specified future training regimens. This method allows the model to predict performance at specific future points in time based on the unique learning history and performance parameters with which the model was initially calibrated.

The PPE has demonstrated its ability to validly track and precisely predict performance in a variety of published experimental tasks and research domains associated with knowledge and skill acquisition and retention (Jastrzembski et al., 2006a, 2006b; Jastrzembski et al., 2009), and the time is therefore ripe to validate the efficacy of this tool in the context of a more complex, militarily-relevant domain, with clear real-world applications and utilities. We will turn our discussion, in a moment, to validation in the DMO testbed, utilizing PETS as fodder for the PPE modeling approach.

To provide some insight concerning each component parameter and the functional form that makes up the PPE, we now turn to a brief explanation of the mathematical model itself. Built upon Anderson and Schunn's (2000) General Performance Equation, our equation captures effects of recency and frequency on the human memory system. Additionally, unlike the General Performance Equation, our equation also captures the spacing effect, which is the robust finding that retention of knowledge is better when learning repetitions are spaced farther apart temporally, rather than massed together in short succession (e.g., Arthur, et al., 2007; Bahrick and Phelps, 1987).

Until quite recently, computational models have been unable to reproduce the effects of spacing (e.g., massed versus distributed practice), and have quantitatively revealed learning trajectories that are inconsistent with human empirical findings found robustly across the spacing literature. This suggests that underlying cognitive process model mechanisms implemented within these models must possess a fundamental flaw in representing how human memory actually functions under differential training lag conditions. To remedy these failures, Pavlik and Anderson (2005) developed and integrated an activation-based decay mechanism that nicely accounted for effects of spacing and resulted in great improvements over prior computational cognitive process model instantiations. As such, their model continually changed forgetting rates over the course of training as a function of how highly activated a given memory trace was estimated to be at each training opportunity. Thus, as periods of time *increased* between consecutive training opportunities, activation values possessed by individual memory traces *diminished*. This then translated to lower forgetting rates (higher retention) between increasingly spaced training opportunities. This ultimately results in more stable retention and of course simulates human empirical data very effectively.

However, Pavlik and Anderson's (2005) activation-based model requires knowledge of each training point to calculate the activation of individual memory traces and corresponding decay rates for each point in time. Thus, the model fits data in a retrospective and post hoc manner. Our mathematical model extends the aforementioned research efforts in a novel way, such that the model's implementation allows the flexibility and utility to make precise, quantitative *predictions* of performance at later points in time. Equation 1 shows the formal structure of the model:

$$S \cdot St \cdot N^c \cdot T^{-d}$$

where S is a free scalar parameter to allow fits and predictions to any type of dependent variable (e.g., percentages, response times, proportions), St represents a calculated rate of knowledge and skill stability to capture expected differences in retention as a function of how closely initial practice occurred (see formalization of Equation 2), N is the amount of practice up to the current training point, c is the rate of learning, T is the amount of time passed since learning, and d represents the rate of decay.

$$St_i = \frac{Max\left(lag_{Cal}\right)/Min\left(lag_{Cal}\right)}{\#CalEvents} \cdot \frac{\left(T_i - T_{i-1}\right)^2}{T_i^2} + 1$$

As shown above, Equation 2 calculates how stable knowledge and skill sets are expected to be on the basis of the historical training baseline, and uses that value to modify how likely knowledge and skills will be expected to decay across extended periods of nonuse or practice. In detail, the stability term captures effects of spacing by calculating the experience amassed as a function of the temporal training distribution and true time passed. This term provides the model with knowledge of how stable learning is or will be during training, and determines how quickly memory traces will fade as a result of how much practice has been amassed. This calculation is then used to precisely and quantitatively predict performance after a training lag.

It must be noted that the PPE has been modified since our earlier publications (Jastrzembski et al., 2006a, 2006b; Jastrzembski et al., 2009). This change occurred after extensive tests of the equations' generalizability across both real datasets (e.g., data obtained from the human performance literature) and hypothetical datasets (e.g., data that spanned large positive and negative numbers simultaneously, data that were saw-toothed in nature). The modification to this parameter was made in order to more effectively capture the principled underlying mathematical regularities of learning in a robust way, and to make valid predictions of data that would not be specific to any one kind of dataset.

In summary, this mathematical model possesses a function form that weighs the overall amount of practice amassed during training with how tightly practices are spaced in time. This allows the model to measure the stability of that learning, such that the rate of forgetting rises and falls as practice opportunities are less spaced versus more spaced in time, respectively.

Validation in the DMO Testbed

It is of critical importance to the military and individual warfighters themselves, to know *when* they have received enough training to perform reliably at a high level, and also to know the probability is very high (near certain) that they will achieve success in specific missions at future points in time. Additionally, it is of high importance to know how much reacquisition training will be necessary when extended periods of nonuse are expected. The PPE may be a means for providing warfighters and instructors with precise, accurate future performance predictions, because the mechanics and implementation of the model balance the performance benefits of training and rehearsal experiences with the performance costs of periods of nonuse in a psychologically principled, theoretically motivated manner. However, surmising that a model is valid is not the same thing as formally evaluating its validity. In this section of the chapter we describe recent research on evaluating the validity of the PPE.

At the Air Force Research Laboratory in Mesa, two studies have been run to collect PETS data for teams in the Distributed Mission Operations (DMO) testbed, using F-16 pilots and AWACS controllers in air-to-air combat scenarios. Given the breadth of objective data (PETS collects hundreds of variables at up to 60 Hz) collected, this testbed provides and equips the PPE with a unique opportunity to assess the real-world applicability of the mathematical modeling tool to the warfighter domain.

In more detail, the first study examines objective performance changes over the course of one week of simulator training (Schreiber, Stock, and Bennett, 2006), and the second study examines retention of skills after a training lag of either 3 or 6 months, upon completion of a full week of simulator training. These two studies provide data that may be utilized to assess and validate individual model components of the PPE; namely, the first study will be utilized to assess knowledge and skill tracking capability, and the second study will be utilized to assess the model's capability to make accurate and precise predictions after a pre-specified training lag.

Previous statistical analyses from the first DMO testbed study examined differences between the first and last day of training only (see Schreiber et al., 2006). Simple pre and posttest analyses would be inadequate to equip the PPE properly, so this is why great care must go into examining learning changes over the course of each individual training session and over the course of the entire training week. This allows the model to garner fine-tuned mathematical regularities of knowledge and skill changes over time, as a function of the recency and frequency of training opportunities, and delays in the training regimen.

Furthermore, individual and composite variables from the weeklong training study must be investigated to identify exactly *which* skills are being honed at the team or warfighter level, as improvements across unique skill sets may be expected to vary according to level of individual or team experience/ expertise, or to individual differences within learners themselves. Thus, identification of proper learning variables for each team or individual is essential, as is determining which variables or skill sets may best measure learning changes and be meaningful for predictive purposes.

In summary, in order to apply the PPE to the DMO testbed, care must be taken to ensure that learning variables are correctly identified from the start and that the model is indeed able to track performance over the training week. Doing so will help provide the foundation for equipping the mathematical modeling tool with detailed training histories, so that warfighter or team parameters may be properly calibrated and fine-tuned, based upon unique individual or team learning curves.

Predictive Capabilities. A preliminary investigation using a small sample of variables in an unclassified PETS dataset from a highly experienced team has revealed promising results, such that at the team level, effectiveness steadily improved with regard to the number of times the MAR was violated as a function of the number of threats (see Figure 6.2, Calibration Panel). Accounting for the number of threats across missions was necessary to examine learning, because scenario difficulty increased over the course of the training week and the number of threats was therefore never constant. Thus, data were normalized by dividing by number of threats (a measure for complexity of the mission) to better gauge how much learning was occurring over the course of training.

Assuming adequate learning variables are identified from the full PETS database and that the model is able to adequately track performance changes throughout the weeklong training regimen (initial results are promising that they will be), it will then be possible to utilize the skill retention data from the second DMO training study (which as mentioned above, requires a team to

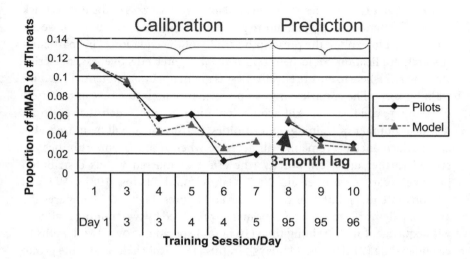

FIGURE 6.2

Validation of the PPE in the DMO testbed.

return either 3 or 6 months after the baseline training week, and reassesses performance over the course of 2 additional training days) and assess the validity of mathematical model performance predictions. Using the minimized unclassified dataset described above, and the identification of the variable composite proportion of times in MAR to the number of threats, predictive capability of the mathematical modeling tool also reveals initial promising results (see Figure 6.2, Prediction Panel). It must be noted, however, that additional validation must occur across more dependent variables, more teams, and at the individual grain of analysis, to assess the model's overall utility and applicability.

A major scientific and technical challenge associated with validating model predictive capabilities within this study is that it may be unknown precisely what training opportunities warfighter participants engage in during the delay between acquisition and retention, and the timings of those training opportunities are also not likely to be provided—pieces of information the PPE must have in order to be properly equipped. This limits the model's ability to make accurate predictions, because any training that hones the skill set being modeled must be explicitly entered into the model, along with specific timing information of that training opportunity. We argue that calling for more detailed records of individual training experiences will help bypass this potential limiting factor, and will also aid in making retention study conclusions easier to interpret.

Prescriptive Capabilities. Given the preliminary successes of the PPE to track past performance and predict future performance in the DMO testbed, we are encouraged to explore the prescriptive utility of the equation. This particular research application could help optimize warfighter effectiveness, prescribe training refreshers to ensure effectiveness is maintained, and potentially reduce training costs. The empirical human performance literature reveals the effect of training schedules on skill acquisition and retention, such that given an identical number of training opportunities, performance will be more stable and performance decrements will decrease when training opportunities are spaced further apart temporally (the effect of massed versus distributed practice) (e.g., Arthur et al., 2007; Bahrick and Phelps, 1987). We will demonstrate this point over the next several figures. Figure 6.3 compares the anticipated improvements in performance predicted by two training regimens with equivalent total training time (16 hours) spread out over two lengths of calendar time (71 days vs. 141 days). In this analytical trade study one group receives 2 hours of training per training opportunity, compared to the other group receiving 1 hour of training per training opportunity. Not surprisingly, the "massed" practice condition (training 2 hours per day) is predicted to show a faster improvement rate, reaching a notional performance effectiveness level above 0.95, twice as fast as the "distributed" condition (training 1 hour per day).

At a relative, qualitative level, this is fairly intuitive. People who train more intensively (2 hours per training opportunity) improve more quickly than those who train less intensively, according to the model. It is hard to imagine not predicting that qualitative relationship. However, the advantage of the mathematical model is that it allows us to be precise in predicting exactly how quickly people will improve, given different training programs, and at what specific point they will achieve a particular level of proficiency.

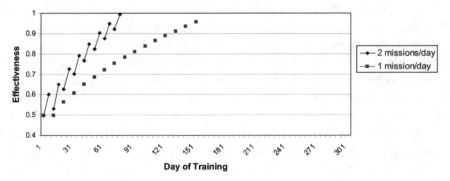

FIGURE 6.3

Depiction of knowledge/skill acquisition as a function of training regimen.

An important characteristic of the PPE is that it predicts both learning *and* forgetting. It is here that the implications of the spacing effect are most important and the predictions of the model become less obvious. The key cognitive effect is that greater temporal spacing produces lower decay rates, and therefore more stable knowledge and skill. An implication of this is that refresher training is not necessary as often when the skills to be refreshed were learned over a longer initial period of time, even holding formal training time constant. This point is shown in Figures 6.4 and 6.5.

These notional training scenarios reveal the impact of massed (2 simulator hours per training opportunity) (see Figure 6.4) versus distributed (1 simulator hour per training opportunity) (see Figure 6.5) practice on performance retention, and additionally provide predictions for when training "refreshers" must be scheduled to ensure performance effectiveness is maintained over a specified effectiveness threshold (in this scenario, 90 percent effectiveness). These depictions also reveal the fact that when levels of knowledge and skill reach higher states of stability (therefore resulting in a lower rate of forgetting), refreshers are needed on a less frequent basis and may additionally be spaced further apart in time. These effects may translate to significantly reduced costs for the military as a result. In this particular notional example, where initial amounts of training are equivalent (16 hours are trained in each condition— the only variable is the timing between events), 43 percent fewer training refreshers are required to keep trainees in the distributed condition at the same level of performance as those in the massed condition, for the same amount of calendar time.

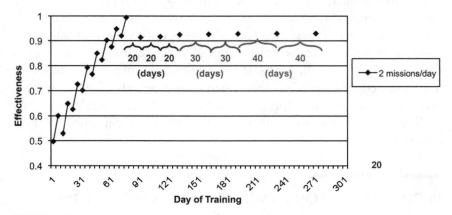

FIGURE 6.4

When training opportunities are massed (2 simulator hours of training per opportunity), training refreshers to maintain 90 percent effectiveness must be provided at 20-day intervals for the first 3 months, 30-day intervals for the next 2 months, and 40-day intervals for subsequent 2 months.

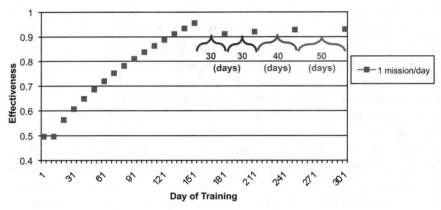

FIGURE 6.5

When training opportunities are distributed (1 simulator hour of training per opportunity), training refreshers to maintain 90 percent effectiveness must be provided at 30-day intervals for the first 2 months, a 40-day interval for the next month, and a 50-day interval for the subsequent month.

As demonstrated by the notional scenarios depicted above, the PPE provides a very nice functionality for illustrating the interplay of skill acquisition and skill retention, such that specified training regimens may be precisely compared, in both qualitative and quantitative manners. Thus, an instructor may examine fine training distinctions to decide which regimen would produce the desired training goals most efficiently. For instance, the tool may be used to help determine the best way to space training opportunities when only a limited amount of resources or training opportunities are available (e.g., simulator training). It may help prescribe the optimal spacing of training to ensure a warfighter is trained to a threshold level of effectiveness by a given date or within a specified timeframe. Additionally, it may be utilized to minimize performance decrements when known periods of down time are anticipated, and prescribe optimally spaced training "refreshers" to maintain performance effectiveness with minimal levels of reacquisition training required.

IMPLICATIONS FOR PRACTICE, AND CONCLUSIONS

In this chapter we described the MEC, PETS, and PPE research efforts and the fact that the convergence of them creates entirely new capabilities in adaptive, individualized training and rehearsal, designed to improve the readiness of our warfighters.

It is worth emphasizing the point that, although some of the data presented here come from the air-to-air domain that has been the showcase application area for DMO research for many years, the MEC, PETS, and PPE approaches are all fully generalizable to other domains. Indeed, MEC analyses and PETS development have already been completed and validated in a variety of other domains and the scalar parameter in the PPE makes it agnostic to context. Progress to date reveals increased levels of predictive validity across contexts and domains, and continued evaluations and explorations of the validity of these research products, both separately and in conjunction with one another, suggest that we are on a productive and useful path. There remain some challenges, however, that must be addressed before the full power and flexibility of the integrated system will be realized. We describe four of these challenges here in the concluding section of the chapter, and provide some thoughts on what this research implies for the practice of warfighter training and rehearsal.

CHALLENGES

The first challenge is in creating the ability for transfer among related skills to influence the performance predictions of the system. Currently, PPEs assume that exactly the same fixed set of knowledge and skills is required at each training and rehearsal event, both in the historical data and in the predicted future events. To the extent that this is true, the validity of the model increases, as do the accuracy of its predictions. Unfortunately, in environments as complex and dynamic as military operations, it is highly unlikely that only a specific subset of identical knowledge and skills will be required for each of many consecutive training, rehearsal, and operational experiences. There are bound to be differences in the detailed requirements of specific missions and engagements. To the extent that happens, this important underlying assumption in the model becomes incorrect and its predictions will likely become less accurate. Addressing this challenge will require establishing some form of similarity, or transfer metrics for all of the skills and knowledge elements that comprise all of the possible competencies required in a particular mission. We will need automated approaches for defining similarities among skill and knowledge elements, because large number of relationships among elements in a military mission space make it impractical to define them manually.

A second challenge in this research program is in mapping individual and team-level performance metrics to the probability of mission success. This is important because, at the end of the day, having a direct, positive impact on the probability of mission success is what we are trying to achieve for the Air

Force. It is a challenge because the probability of mission success is actually the joint probability of hundreds, perhaps thousands, of contributing factors and events. Clearly the ability of people to perform at reliably high levels of competence is an important contributing factor in predicting mission success, but it is still just one of many. We have only just begun to consider how one might identify a central set of factors that serve to define mission success in a domain of interest, or how one might elaborate the full space of important factors and their relationships to one another as predictors of mission success.

A third challenge is that the inherent, ubiquitous variability in human performance imposes limits on predictive accuracy. Stochastic processes run rampant through the human system. There is always variability from one trial to the next when human performance is measured. People are not deterministic systems. This clearly creates a theoretical and practical upper bound on our ability to predict what people will do and precisely how accurately and/or quickly they will do it. We do not yet have a comprehensive analytical assessment of what the theoretical limits are on our ability to predict future human performance, but there is no question that the reality of the human condition bounds the predictive validity of any system of this sort.

A fourth major scientific and technical challenge, which also limits our predictive powers, is that it may be unknown precisely what training opportunities warfighter participants engage in during the delay between acquisition and retention tests/assessments, and the timings of those training opportunities are also not likely to be provided—pieces of information the PPE and predictive performance optimizer (PPO) must have in order to maximize predictive validity. The lack of documented training may translate to effectively limiting the model's scope to make accurate predictions, because any training being engaged in that hones the skill set being modeled must be explicitly entered into the model, along with specific timing information of that training opportunity. We argue that calling for more detailed records of individual training experiences will help bypass this potential limiting factor, and will also aid in making retention study conclusions easier to interpret.

IMPLICATIONS FOR PRACTICE

Military training has historically adopted a one-size-fits-all, checkbox approach. The fact that PETS, MECS, and PPE provide tools to *objectively* quantify, evaluate, and track performance provides operational decision makers and training practitioners the opportunity to examine, validate, and institutionalize tailored training to fit specific trainee needs and mission requirements. With further validation, the tailoring that is now possible may one day streamline the training pipeline according to the needs of individual learners, and could additionally provide principled guidance concerning how training should optimally be spaced to achieve desired training goals.

The convergence of the PETS, MECS, and PPE lines of research holds real *promise* for training future generations of warfighters more efficiently and effectively. Given the lack of data available to accurately assess the real-world utility of our approach, we argue it should be a priority for the military to collect objective performance measures in applied, military contexts, so that a more thorough validation effort may be undertaken. This is necessary in order to allow extensive examination of the benefits that we believe could be gained by shifting away from the military training status quo.

REFERENCES

Anderson, J. R., and Schunn, C. D. (2000). Implications of the ACT-R learning theory: No magic bullets. In R. Glaser (Ed.), *Advances in instructional psychology: Educational design and cognitive science, Vol. 5*. Mahwah, NJ: Erlbaum.

Arthur, W. J., Day, E. A., Villado, A. J., Boatman, P. R., Kowollik, V., Bennett, W., and Bhupatkar, A. (2007). Decay, transfer, and the reacquisition of a complex skill: An investigation of practice schedules, observational rehearsal, and individual differences. *AFRL-RH-AZ-2008–0001*. Available online at: www.dtic.mil.

Bahrick, H., and Phelps, E. (1987). Retention of Spanish vocabulary over 8 years. *Journal of Experimental Psychology: Learning, Memory, and Cognition, 13*, 344–349.

Bennett, W. Jr., and McCall, J. M. (2006). Learning management for competency-based training: Issues and challenges for consideration (06F-SIW-073). In *Proceedings for the Fall Simulation Interoperability Workshop*. Orlando, FL: SIW.

Brecke, F. H., and Miller, D. C. (1991). *Aircrew performance measurement in the air combat maneuvering domain: A critical review of the literature* (AL-TR-1991–0042) Williams Air Force Base, AZ: Aircrew Training Research Division, Armstrong Laboratory.

Brictson, C. A., Ciavarelli, A. P., Pettigrew, K. W., and Young, P. A. (1978). *Performance assessment methods and criteria for the Air Combat Maneuvering Range (ACMR): Missile envelope recognition*. Special Report No. 78–4 (Confidential). Pensacola, FL: Naval Aerospace Medical Research Laboratory.

Colegrove, C. M., and Alliger, G. M. (2003, March). *Mission essential competencies: Defining combat mission readiness in a novel way*. Paper presented at the Thirteenth International Occupational Analyst Workshop, San Antonio, TX.

Gebicke, M. (1995). Military readiness: Improved assessment measures are evolving. *Testimony before the Subcommittee on Readiness, Committee on National Security, House of Representatives*, GAO/T-NSIAD-95–117.

Gehr, S. E., Schreiber, B. T., and Bennett, W. Jr. (2004) Within-simulator training effectiveness evaluation. In *Proceedings of the Interservice/Industry Training, Simulation and Education Conference (I/ITSEC)* (pp. 1652–1661). Orlando, FL: National Security Industrial Association.

Jastrzembski, T. S., Gluck, K. A., and Gunzelmann, G. (2006a). Knowledge tracing and prediction of future trainee performance. I/ITSEC annual meetings, Orlando, December 4–7.

Jastrzembski, T. S., Gluck, K. A., and Gunzelmann, G. (2006b). Mathematical models of spacing effects in memory: Applications in education and training. Society for Mathematical Psychology annual meeting: Vancouver.

Jastrzembski, T. S., Rodgers, S., and Gluck, K. A. (2009). Improving military readiness: A state-of-the-art cognitive tool to predict performance and optimize training effectiveness. *Proceedings of the I/ITSEC* annual meetings, Orlando, Florida.

Kelly, M. J. (1988). Performance measurement during simulated air-to-air combat. *Human Factors, 30(4)*, 495–506.

Krusmark, M., Schreiber, B. T., and Bennett, W. Jr. (2004). The effectiveness of a traditional gradesheet for measuring air combat performance in simulated distributed mission operations. *AFRL-HE-AZ-TR-2004–0090*. Available online at: www.dtic.mil.

McGuinness, J., Bouwman, J. H., and Puig, J. A. (1982). Effectiveness evaluation for air combat training. In *Proceedings of the 4th Interservice/Industry Training Equipment Conference* (pp. 391–396). Washington D.C.: National Security Industrial Association, 16–18 November, 1982.

McGuinness, J., Forbes, J. M., and Rhoads, J. E. (1984). *Air combat maneuvering performance measurement system design.* (AFHRL-TP-83–56) Williams Air Force Base, AZ: Operations Training Division, Armstrong Laboratory.

Pavlik, P. I, and Anderson, J. R. (2005). Practice and forgetting effects on vocabulary memory: An activation based model of the spacing effect. *Cognitive Science, 29*, 559–586.

Portrey, A. M., Keck, L. M., and Schreiber, B. T. (2005). Challenges in developing a performance measurement system for the global virtual environment. In *Proceedings of the 2005 Spring Simulation Interoperability Workshop.* San Diego, CA: SISO, Inc.

Rosales, R. (2006). A legacy of excellence: The USAF Weapons School's challenge to maintain standards. Unpublished thesis. Available online at: www.dtic.mil.

Schreiber, B. T., Stock, W. A., and Bennett, W. (2006). Distributed mission operations within-simulator training effectiveness baseline study: Metric development and objectively quantifying the degree of learning. *AFRL-HE-AZ-TR-2006–0015-Vol II.* Available online at: www.dtic.mil.

Schreiber, B. T., Watz, E., Portrey, A. M., and Bennett, W. Jr. (2003). Development of a distributed mission training automated performance tracking system. In *Proceedings of the Behavioral Representations in Modeling and Simulation (BRIMS) Conference.* Scottsdale, AZ.

Seaman, K. A. (1999). *Improving F-15C air combat training with distributed mission training (DMT) advanced simulation.* (AU/ACSC/183/1999–04). Air Command and Staff College Air University. Maxwell Air Force Base, AL.

Symons, S., France, M., Bell, J., and Bennett, W. Jr. (2005). *Linking knowledge and skills to mission essential competency-based syllabus development for distributed mission operations (AFRL-HE-AZ-TR-2006–0041; ADA453737).* Mesa AZ: Air Force Research Laboratory, Warfighter Readiness Research Division.

Tactical Air Command Regulation 50–31 (1983). *Training records and performance evaluations in formal flying training programs.* Langley Air Force Base, VA: HZ TAC.

Waag, W. L., Pierce, B. J., and Fessler, S. (1987). Performance measurement requirements for tactical aircrew training. *AFHRL-TR-86–62.* Available online at: www.dtic.mil.

Waag, W. L., Raspotnick, W. B., and Leeds, J. L. (1992). *Development of a Composite Measure for Predicting Engagement Outcome During Air Combat Maneuvering* (AL-TR-1992–0002) Williams Air Force Base, AZ: Aircrew Training Research Division, Armstrong Laboratory.

Watz, E., Keck, L., and Schreiber, B. T. (2004). Using PETS software to capture complex objective measurement data from distributed mission operations (DMO) environments. In *Proceedings of the 2004 Spring Simulation Interoperability Workshop.* Arlington, VA. Paper available as 04S-SIW-143.

Watz, E., Schreiber, B. T., Keck, L., McCall, J. M., and Bennett, W. Jr. (2003). *Performance Measurement Challenges in Distributed Mission Operations Environments.* [Electronic Version] Simulation Technology Newsletter. 03F-SIW-022. March 16, 2004.

Wooldridge, L., Obermayer, R. W., Nelson, W. H., Kelly, M. J., Vreuls, D., and Norman, D. A. (1982). *Air combat maneuvering performance measurement state space analysis* (AFHRL-TR-82–15).

7

Training for Efficient, Durable, and Flexible Performance in the Military

Alice F. Healy, Erica L. Wohldmann,
James A. Kole, Vivian I. Schneider,
Kathleen M. Shea, and Lyle E. Bourne, Jr.

INTRODUCTION

There are three aspects of learning that we should consider when we are trying to optimize performance. First is the efficiency of training. Because of the high costs of training, we certainly want to be sure that training is accomplished as quickly as possible. However, optimizing training speed should not be the only, or even the most important, goal. If individuals have successfully learned how to perform a task during training but then forget how to perform it some time later, the training has clearly been ineffective. Passing a test at the end of training does not guarantee later success in the field. Long-term retention of the trained knowledge and skills is essential. Learning needs to be durable as well as efficient. But even durable training will not be sufficient if the learned knowledge and skills cannot be applied to situations different from those encountered during training. Training can rarely capture the full set of circumstances under which tasks are subsequently encountered. Another important goal for learning then is transfer or flexibility. Thus, optimal learning should be efficient, durable, and flexible. This chapter discusses research on the training, retention, and transfer of knowledge and skills, and also reviews research that we have been conducting on training for efficient, durable, and flexible performance in the military.

In the research discussed here, circumstances have been found leading to remarkable durability of what has been learned. Those same conditions, however, yield very poor flexibility, or the ability to generalize learning to new situations or contexts. A general theoretical framework is proposed that can account for the high degree of specificity obtained in these studies but that also enables predictions of when learning will be generalizable rather than specific. The chapter is centered on five separate lines of research. The first three lines demonstrate a high degree of specificity of learning.

We have identified certain circumstances leading to remarkable durability of what has been learned. But those same conditions yield very poor flexibility, or the ability to generalize learning to new situations or contexts. We present empirical findings illustrating specificity and briefly summarize our theoretical explanations of them for the particular tasks we investigated. The chapter ends with a summary of the results from the last two lines of research, which demonstrate, in support of the theoretical framework, situations showing robust transfer of learning. In summary, it is proposed that specificity (limited transfer) may occur for tasks based primarily on procedural information, or skill, whereas generalizability (robust transfer) may occur for tasks based primarily on declarative information, or facts. Thus, for skill learning, retention is strong but transfer is limited, whereas for fact learning, retention is poor but transfer is robust.

We conclude with a short discussion of the relevance of this work to military training.

THEORETICAL FRAMEWORK

We propose a general theoretical framework, called *procedural reinstatement*, that can account for both the high degree of specificity obtained in the initial set of three studies and the high degree of generalizability found in the final set of two studies. The procedural reinstatement framework also accounts for differences in the durability, or long-term retention, of the information learned in the two sets of studies. This framework derives in part from two related principles proposed in the literature on list learning and memory tasks both of which are consistent with the specificity of training we observed in our first three studies. By the *encoding specificity principle* (Tulving and Thomson, 1973), retrieval is successful to the extent that the encoding cues and operations during learning of the list items correspond with those available at retrieval of the list items during subsequent retention testing. Similarly, by the *transfer appropriate processing principle* (McDaniel, Friedman, and Bourne, 1978; Morris, Bransford, and Franks, 1977; Roediger, Weldon, and Challis, 1989), retention test performance depends more on the match in the processing occurring during list acquisition and the processing occurring during retention testing of the list than on the level of processing (the extent to which processing is deep rather than shallow) during list acquisition (cf. Craik and Lockhart, 1972). Likewise, this framework derives in part from models of transfer, including the classic theory of identical elements proposed by Thorndike (1906), according to which transfer takes place only to the extent that there is a match in elements between training and retention testing. The elements for Thorndike were stimulus–response associations. Subsequently, similar identical elements models were proposed for cognitive skills in general by Singley and Anderson (1989), who viewed production rules as elements, and for arithmetic skills in particular by Rickard and Bourne (1995), who viewed operands and operators as elements.

As a consequence of our earlier research on the long-term retention and transfer of knowledge and skills, we proposed the *procedural reinstatement principle* (Healy and Bourne, 1995; Healy, Wohldmann, and Bourne, 2005). According to this principle, procedural information (knowing how to do something) is more durable than declarative information (knowing that something is the case). However, durable performance lacks generality because performance at a retention test is optimal only when the procedures acquired during training are duplicated during retention testing.

The high degree of specificity of training implied by these principles and models needs to be tempered with an acknowledgment of the generality of training found in many other studies. Indeed the specificity of training we have shown in the first three studies we summarize is actually quite surprising given the findings from many other investigations reported in the literature (e.g., Harlow, 1949) as well as the strong transfer of learning found in the last two studies we summarize. Thus, a distinction should be made between specificity and generality of training. An expansion of the procedural reinstatement principle provides a working hypothesis (Healy, 2007) about when there will be specificity or generality of training. Specificity, or limited transfer, occurs for tasks based primarily on procedural information, or skill, whereas generality, or robust transfer, occurs for tasks based primarily on declarative information, or facts. Thus, for skill learning, retention is strong but transfer is limited, whereas for fact learning, retention is poor but transfer is robust.

SPECIFICITY

We now review three studies showing strong specificity of training, thus documenting the first part of our working hypothesis—that for skill learning retention is strong but transfer is limited.

Speeded Aiming

The first line of investigation (Healy, Wohldmann, Sutton, and Bourne, 2006) illustrates clearly the striking specificity of learning. This study involved a speeded aiming task, in which participants saw on a computer screen a clock face display with a central start position surrounded by a circle of digits, shown in Figure 7.1. A target digit was displayed above the start position, and participants used a computer mouse to move a cursor from the start position to the location of the digit around the circumference of the clock face. The task was made more difficult by reprogramming the computer mouse to introduce stimulus–response incompatibilities. Three reprogrammed mouse conditions were used: Either only horizontal movements were reversed (so when the mouse went left the cursor went right and vice versa), only vertical movements were reversed (so when the mouse went up the cursor went down and vice versa), or horizontal and vertical reversals were combined (so when

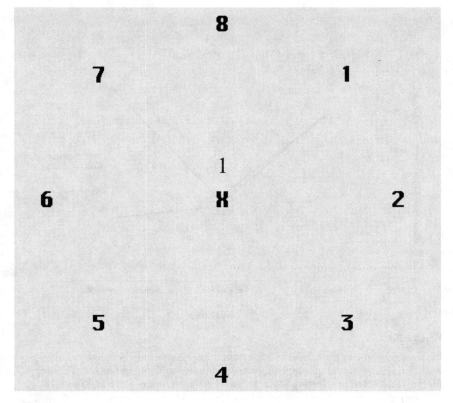

FIGURE 7.1

Clock face stimulus display used in study of speeded aiming.

the mouse went in any direction the cursor went in the opposite direction). (Although this is a simple laboratory task, there are many situations in everyday life, including military situations, that require movement reversals, such as those required by U.S. drivers who must drive in England, where the manual controls are on the opposite side of the car and driving is done on the opposite side of the street.) Participants were trained in one condition for five blocks of 80 trials and then returned 1 week later for retention testing for another five blocks of 80 trials in either the same or a different reprogrammed mouse condition.

The results are summarized in Figure 7.2 for the measure of movement time, which is the time to move from the start position to the target location. Comparisons of performance at the start and end of training showed a large decrease in movement time, demonstrating learning of this skill. Comparisons of performance at the end of training and the beginning of retention testing 1 week later for those participants who were in the same reprogrammed mouse condition in both weeks also showed a small but significant decrease

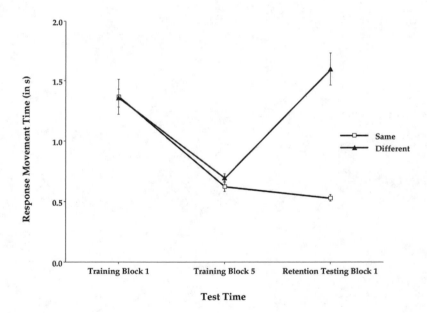

FIGURE 7.2

Response movement time (in s) as a function of the relationship between training and retention testing in reprogrammed mouse conditions for Training Block 1, Training Block 5, and Retention Testing Block 1. Error bars represent positive and negative standard errors of the mean. From study of speeded aiming by Healy et al. (2006, Experiment 1).

Note: Lower scores reflect better performance.

in movement time, reflecting perfect retention and dissipation of fatigue across the 1-week delay. However, for those participants who were in different reprogrammed mouse conditions in training and retention testing, there was actually a trend for movement time at the start of retention testing to increase relative to that at the start of training. Although participants learned much during training, they could not transfer the skill they learned to training on a new condition a week later.

To understand the processes responsible for the severe specificity of training, we examined performance on the first block of training and on the first block of retention testing as a function of the specific reprogrammed mouse conditions employed for those participants who were in different conditions in the 2 weeks. Figure 7.3 shows these results, where H represents the horizontal condition, V the vertical condition, and C the combined condition. Because the combined condition includes both types of reversals whereas the horizontal and vertical conditions include only a single reversal each, the first two sets

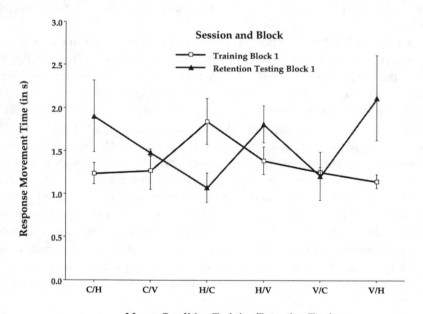

FIGURE 7.3

Response movement time (in s) for the first block of training and the first block of retention testing as a function of transfer condition for only those participants who had a reprogrammed mouse in each session and switched reversal conditions across sessions. Error bars represent positive and negative standard errors of the mean. C = combined, H = horizontal, V = vertical. From study of speeded aiming by Healy et al. (2006, Experiment 1).

Note: Lower scores reflect better performance.

of bars (labeled C/H and C/V) represent a change in the direction from combined reversals to a single reversal (which can be thought of as analogous to whole–part transfer, in which training is done with the whole set of reversals and retention testing is done with only part of the set of reversals). Clearly there was interference in this case, with movement times at the start of retention testing slower than those at the start of training. Likewise, the bars labeled H/V and V/H represent a change in the direction from one single reversal to another single reversal (which can be thought of as analogous to part–part transfer, in which training is done with one part of the set of reversals and retention testing is done with a different part of the set of reversals) and show interference. The only bars showing some positive transfer, where movement time at the start of retention testing is somewhat faster than that at the start of training, are labeled H/C and V/C and represent a change in the direction from a single reversal to combined reversals (which can be thought of as analogous to part–whole transfer, in which training is done with one part of the set of reversals and retention testing is done with the whole set of reversals).

Further insight into the underlying processes is derived from an examination of the type of movement made as a function of condition. Three different movement types are compared in Figure 7.4 as a function of reversal condition for performance at the start of training. Movement is either made to a target along the horizontal dimension (2 or 6), to a target along the vertical dimension (4 or 8), or to a target along one of the diagonals (1, 3, 5, or 7). It is interesting to note that participants in the horizontal condition are actually faster for pure horizontal movements, which are reversed, than for pure vertical movements, which require no reversal. Similarly, participants in the vertical condition are faster for pure vertical movements, which are reversed, than for pure horizontal movements, which require no reversal. Note also that for participants in these two conditions, the movements are slowest along the diagonal. In contrast, diagonal movement is no slower than vertical or horizontal movement for participants in the combined condition, and participants in the combined condition are faster for movement along the diagonal than are participants in the horizontal or vertical conditions.

We proposed a global inhibition hypothesis to explain these results (Healy et al., 2006). According to this hypothesis, whenever the mouse is reprogrammed, participants apply a global inhibition strategy, inhibiting normal movements in *both* dimensions. When only one dimension is reversed, a further step is then required to disinhibit responses on the non-reversed dimension. This strategy can explain why we saw positive part–whole transfer and negative or no transfer in the part-to-part or whole-to-part directions. For part–whole transfer, the global inhibition strategy applies directly to the

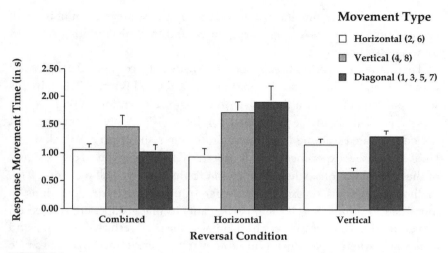

FIGURE 7.4

Response movement time (in s) for Training Block 1 as a function of reversal condition and movement type. Error bars represent positive standard errors of the mean. From study of speeded aiming by Healy et al. (2006, Experiment 1).

Note: Lower scores reflect better performance.

transfer task, and there is no need for disinhibition during retention testing. In contrast, for part–part transfer, the inhibited and disinhibited dimensions must be exchanged between training and retention testing, and for whole–part transfer, one of the previously inhibited dimensions must be disinhibited during retention testing.

The global inhibition hypothesis can also explain why movement times are faster along a purely reversed dimension than along a dimension requiring no reversal in the horizontal and vertical conditions. According to the global inhibition hypothesis, inhibition is applied globally whenever some reversal is required, so that a further step is needed when only one dimension is reversed. Responses on the intact dimension must be disinhibited in these cases, causing slower responding on the non-reversed than on the reversed dimension and faster responding on diagonal movements in the combined condition (when no disinhibition is required) relative to the single reversal conditions (when disinhibition is required along one dimension).

Although the global inhibition hypothesis was developed to account for performance in the simple laboratory speeded aiming task, a similar global inhibition strategy might be adopted by anyone in everyday life who encounters a device with stimulus–response incompatibilities. That is, realizing that the device does not work normally, so that there are reversals in responses required to stimuli, people might start by using the simple strategy of inhibiting all normal movements, reversing all responses, and then disinhibiting reversed movements as required.

To test the global inhibition hypothesis, we recently conducted a new study with the speeded aiming task (Wohldmann, Healy, and Bourne, 2008). In this study participants were always given training and retention testing for 192 experimental trials in the horizontal condition. Also, only a 5-minute rest period separated training from retention testing rather than a 1-week delay. Unlike the earlier experiment, in this new study, training involved only a subset of the target locations, whereas retention testing involved all locations. This method allowed us to examine transfer from trained target locations to untrained locations. Specifically, participants in one group were trained on two dimensions (either the pure horizontal or the pure vertical dimension and a diagonal), whereas participants in another group were trained on only a single dimension (either pure horizontal, pure vertical, or a diagonal). Both groups of participants were given a retention test on all dimensions. According to the global inhibition hypothesis, positive transfer to the untrained targets along the diagonal axis should be evident whenever training involves moving along a diagonal axis because both the trained and untrained targets along that axis demand that horizontal movements be inhibited and vertical movements be disinhibited in the same way. The global inhibition hypothesis would thus not predict any differences in transfer for trained and untrained movements. However, the strong degree of specificity found in the earlier study suggests that the learned skill may depend on the particular target locations practiced as well as on such strategies as global inhibition. If specificity does apply in this case, then we should find faster movement times at the retention test to the trained than to the untrained targets on the diagonal axes.

One possible way to overcome specificity of training and to promote transfer is to introduce variability into the practice routine (e.g., Schmidt and Bjork, 1992). The new study also enabled us to evaluate this variability of practice hypothesis. For this evaluation, we examined retention test performance on diagonal targets and we compared training on only one dimension with more variable training on two dimensions. In both cases retention testing was conducted on all four dimensions. We broke down performance into subblocks of 16 experimental trials (two trials with each target). This analysis was limited to participants who trained with one diagonal and were given a retention test with both diagonals. As shown in Figure 7.5, we found general task improvements across blocks of retention testing. Importantly, we also found that movement to old targets was significantly faster than movement to new targets, documenting specificity of training. Naturally, there was much more

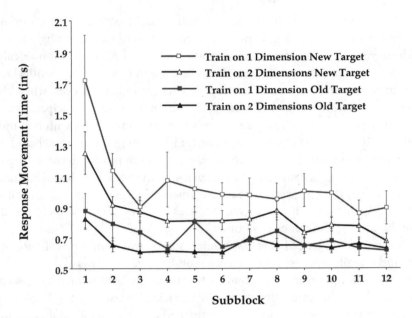

FIGURE 7.5

Response movement time (in s) during retention testing for diagonal movements as a function of participant group, target type (old, new), and subblock (1–12). Error bars represent positive and negative standard errors of the mean. From study of speeded aiming by Wohldmann et al. (2008, Experiments 1 and 2).

Note: Lower scores reflect better performance.

improvement across subblocks for new targets than for old ones. Also of interest with respect to the variability of practice hypothesis was the significant interaction between target type and participant group, reflecting a larger advantage of training with two dimensions than training with only one dimension for new targets than for old targets. Thus, variability of practice does seem to enhance transfer of training to new targets. In any event, finding specificity of training in this situation cannot be explained solely on the basis of the global inhibition hypothesis. Presumably participants learned a strategy of inhibiting all normal movements but disinhibiting those along the vertical axis. In addition, however, they must have learned special, unique movement tactics to reach the targets along the trained diagonal, and those movement tactics could not be fully transferred to targets along the untrained diagonal.

Time Production

The high degree of specificity found for the task involving speeded aiming movements was surprising. However, perhaps even more surprising was the high degree of specificity we found in a second line of investigation (Healy, Wohldmann, Parker, and Bourne, 2005) because in this case we found a lack of transfer across different secondary, or background, tasks even when the primary, or foreground, task was held constant. In this study, participants were trained to produce time intervals expressed in arbitrary units, with one unit equal to 783 ms. Participants were not told how long a unit was, but they learned how to produce intervals by feedback on each response. For example, on a given trial, participants may be told that after the beep they should estimate 32 units. They then pressed the space bar when they thought that 32 units had elapsed. At that point they received feedback, such as "Your estimate was 29 units" and "The difference is –3 units."

Participants practiced this task under one of two conditions. In the *no alphabet* condition, they performed no secondary task, whereas in the *alphabet* condition, they performed a secondary task in which they counted backwards through the alphabet by threes. When participants reached the beginning of the alphabet, they were to revert to the end of the alphabet and continue from that point. For example, if they were given the letter cue *s*, they were to say *s, p, m, j, g, d, a, x*. This is clearly a difficult secondary task. Participants were trained in one condition for six blocks of six trials, and then they returned 1 week later for six blocks of six trials of retention testing in a condition that was either the same as the training condition (training and retention testing either both involved the alphabet task or both involved no secondary task) or different from the training condition (training involved the alphabet task and retention testing involved no secondary task or training involved no secondary task and retention testing involved the alphabet task). We used as our measure of performance for this task the *proportional absolute error*, which is the absolute (or unsigned) difference between the produced interval and the specified interval divided by the specified interval. This index provides a normalized assessment of error magnitude. Figure 7.6 allows us to compare performance in terms of proportional absolute error at the start and end of training and shows that participants improved their skill of time production during training. Also, comparing performance at the end of training and the start of retention testing when participants were in the same condition in training and retention testing reveals no decrement in performance, thereby showing perfect skill retention. However, when participants were in different conditions in training and retention testing, performance did suffer across the 1-week delay, so that, in fact, performance at the start of retention testing was

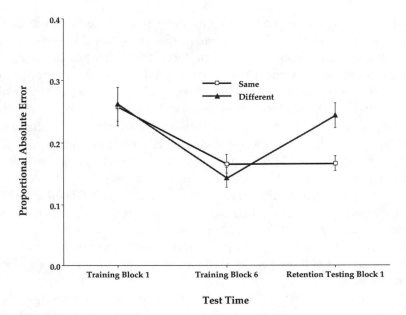

FIGURE 7.6

Proportional absolute error as a function of the relationship between training and retention testing in time production conditions for Training Block 1, Training Block 6, and Retention Testing Block 1. Error bars represent positive and negative standard errors of the mean. From time production study of Healy et al. (2005, Experiment 2).

Note: Lower scores reflect better performance.

comparable to that at the start of training. Thus, again, as with the clock face task involving speeded aiming movements, there was perfect retention but no transfer of this time production skill from one condition to another, even though the required skill did not change; instead the only change was in the secondary, background task.

We explained the high degree of specificity in this case by assuming that what participants learned about time production incorporated the secondary alphabet task so if the secondary task was changed (even if it was simply removed) the participants could not benefit at all from training. More generally, we proposed a functional task hypothesis, according to which secondary task requirements are often integrated with primary task requirements during learning, resulting in the acquisition of a single functional task rather than two separate tasks. For example, participants might learn not that a given unit is about 3/4 s but rather how many letters in the alphabet task they should count before a given number of units has elapsed.

We recently completed another experiment aimed to provide a test of this functional task hypothesis (Wohldmann, Healy, and Bourne, 2010). One basic prediction from the functional task hypothesis is that if performance on the secondary task is affected by a change in that task, then there should be a corresponding, congruent change in performance on the primary task, and there should be no trade-off in performing the two tasks. Specifically, participants were trained to produce three different intervals of time while performing one of two versions of the alphabet counting task. In the *fixed* alphabet condition, the starting letter was always the same (*M*), whereas in the *random* alphabet condition, the starting letter varied randomly across trials. In this experiment, unlike the last one (Healy et al., 2005), participants typed the letters for the secondary task—they did not just say them aloud—so we could easily measure performance on the secondary task as well as on the primary task. After six blocks of training, each including six trials, participants engaged in an irrelevant letter detection task during a retention interval, which lasted about 15 min. Then participants were given a retention test under the same conditions as those encountered during training for another six blocks of six trials.

We expected accuracy on the time production task to improve across blocks of trials and, based on the findings from our earlier experiment, we also expected perfect retention for the time production task between training and retention testing. Of greater interest was the relationship between the changes in performance on the two tasks. According to the functional task hypothesis, we expected performance on both the time production and alphabet-counting task to be better when the starting letter was fixed rather than randomly changing from trial to trial. This expectation was based on the assumption that participants develop a strategy for time production that is based on the number of letters counted for a given interval. That strategy should be easier to employ with a fixed starting letter because participants could simply learn on what letter to stop for each of the three time intervals used when the starting letter is fixed but they would have to learn many more rules of that type when the starting letter is random. However, fixing the starting letter might also have an adverse effect on time production if that condition promotes a continuous increase across trials in the number of letters typed for a given time interval. Under those circumstances, there might be a negative bias in time production so that the intervals produced would be shorter than those prescribed. Finding these specific patterns for the comparison of the fixed versus random conditions would be evidence for the functional task hypothesis and inconsistent with the alternative notion that primary and secondary tasks trade off with each other because of limited cognitive resources (e.g., Gopher, Brickner, and Navon, 1982).

The results are summarized in Figure 7.7, which has three panels. The top panel shows primary task performance in terms of proportional absolute error, the normalized index of error magnitude. The middle panel shows primary task performance in terms of proportional relative error, an index of response bias. This measure is the signed difference between the produced interval and the specified interval divided by the specified interval. The proportional relative error is just like the proportional absolute error but uses signed differences instead of absolute differences. When the produced interval is longer than the specified interval, there is positive bias by this index, whereas when the produced interval is shorter than the specified interval, there is negative bias. The bottom panel shows performance on the secondary task as a function of the number of letters typed per s. We found that on the secondary task participants typed many more letters per s when the starting letter was fixed than when it was random. Also, the number of letters typed per s showed a large, steady increase across blocks in training when the starting letter was fixed but a minimal increase when the starting letter was random. Despite the changes in performance on the secondary task with the fixed starting letter, performance on the primary time production task showed significantly less proportional absolute error with the fixed than with the random starting letter, especially during retention testing. This result can be explained by assuming that participants counted the number of letters said in the secondary task as a means to gauge how much time had elapsed. However, if participants used a strategy that required them to stop after a certain number of letters were counted, then they would stop earlier whenever they were able to go through the alphabet more quickly. This strategy would lead the participants to produce shorter time intervals than those prescribed when the number of letters typed per s increased, resulting in a negative bias in the participants' time judgments. Thus, participants should show a negative bias on the primary task in terms of proportional relative error whenever the number of letters said per s on the secondary task increased. Consistent with this reasoning is the finding for the fixed condition that as the number of letters said per s increased during training there was a negative bias. During retention testing following the 15-minute retention interval filled with the irrelevant distractor task, the number of letters said per s did not change markedly, and there was little bias.

The results of this experiment, thus, provide clear-cut evidence that improvements in the secondary task do have an influence on the level of improvement in the primary task, in accordance with the functional task hypothesis. Changes in secondary task performance (an increase in the number of letters said per s across blocks in the fixed alphabet condition) were generally consistent with changes in primary task performance (negative bias across blocks during training and lower error across blocks during retention testing in the fixed alphabet condition). Thus, it did not appear that participants traded

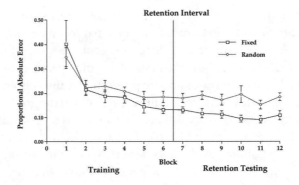

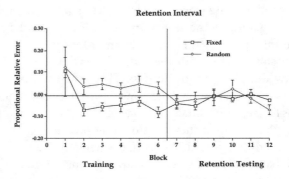

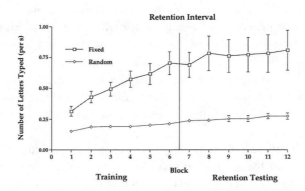

FIGURE 7.7

Proportional absolute error for the primary task (top panel), proportional relative error for the primary task (middle panel), and number of letters typed per s on the secondary task (bottom panel) as a function of session half, block, and alphabet condition in Experiment 1. Error bars represent positive and negative standard errors of the mean. From time production study of Wohldmann et al. (2010, Experiment 1).

Note: Lower scores reflect better performance in top and middle panels; higher scores reflect better performance in bottom panel.

off one task for the other, but rather, they seemed to develop a strategy that combined the requirements of the two tasks. The functional task hypothesis then helps explain why there is so much specificity, or lack of transfer, in time production. In essence, changing the background requirements during time production changes the functional task that participants must perform, and training participants with one functional task does not necessarily help them perform a different functional task.

Navigation

Although the functional task hypothesis can help us understand the high degree of specificity we found for the time production task, this hypothesis does little to help us understand the specificity that we recently found in an experiment in another line of investigation. We have been studying a situation meant to mimic communication between air traffic controllers and flight crews, which involves giving and receiving navigation instructions (Barshi and Healy, 2002; Schneider, Healy, and Barshi, 2004). Flight crews often make errors resulting from this communication, and these errors can lead to serious accidents. Thus, our research has the eventual goal to determine ways to reduce such critical errors.

In our task, participants receive messages instructing them to make movements in a space shown on the computer screen. Figure 7.8 shows on the left the three-dimensional space that is depicted on the computer screen by the grid of matrices shown on the right. In our experimental task, the messages vary in length from one to six commands. Figure 7.9 provides a sample display showing movements for a message with three commands (Length 3): Left 2 squares, down 2 levels, forward 1 step. Participants in our experiments typically hear the commands; they do not see them. Their task is to repeat back immediately the commands heard and then to follow them by clicking, with a computer mouse, on the appropriate squares of the grid, as illustrated on the figure with numbers for each required click. (Note that commands to move left or right require horizontal movements, whereas both commands to move up or down and commands to move forward or back require vertical movements, with the up/down commands requiring vertical movements from one matrix to another and the forward/back commands requiring vertical movements within a single matrix.) In the experiment just completed, we were interested in how best to train participants to perform this task (Schneider, Healy, Barshi, and Bourne, 2007). We wondered whether it would be better to provide *easy* training (restricted to short message lengths 1–3), *hard* training (restricted to long message lengths 4–6), or *mixed* training (with all six message lengths 1–6). Retention testing occurred following a

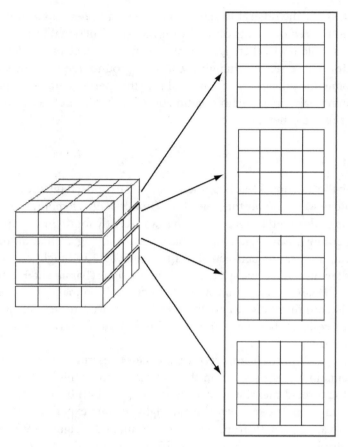

FIGURE 7.8

On the left is the three-dimensional space that is depicted on the computer screen by the grid of matrices shown on the right. From navigation study of Schneider et al. (2007).

10-minute retention interval filled with an irrelevant distractor task and in all conditions was in the mixed format involving all six message lengths. We used an all-or-none scoring system to measure performance in terms of the proportion of correct responses. All required clicks had to be made in order for a given trial to be scored as correct.

This experiment allowed us to test again for the advantage of variability of practice and also to see whether specificity of training applies in this paradigm. On the basis of the predicted advantage for variability of practice, participants should do better at the retention test with the more variable mixed training than with either easy or hard training. Because retention testing involves all

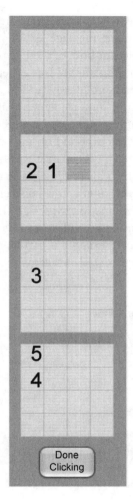

Left 2 squares
Down 2 levels
Forward 1 step

FIGURE 7.9

A sample display showing movements for a message with three commands (Length 3). The written commands are not shown to the participants. The numbers, which are also not shown to participants, illustrate the required clicks. From navigation study of Schneider et al. (2007).

Note: Up/down commands lead to vertical movements from one matrix to another, whereas forward/back commands lead to vertical movements within a single matrix. In the messages to participants, right/left movement is always described in terms of squares, up/down movement in terms of levels, and forward/back movement in terms of steps.

six lengths, finding an advantage at the retention test for mixed training would also be consistent with specificity of training. Further, on the basis of specificity of training, at the retention test with short message lengths participants should do better with easy than with hard training, but with long message lengths they should do better with hard than with easy training. Thus, there should be an interaction between training condition and message length.

As shown in Figure 7.10, there was evidence for both of these hypothesized patterns of results at the retention test. First, note that in this experiment, as in others we have conducted with this paradigm (Barshi and Healy, 2002; Schneider et al., 2004), there is a huge effect of message length, with performance dropping off markedly when the number of commands per message increases from three to four. Also note that, as expected on the basis of the predicted advantage for variability of practice, performance was best in the mixed condition at almost all message lengths. This finding is also consistent with specificity of training, as is the observed interaction between training condition and message length, and this interaction was significant even when considering only the easy and hard training conditions. It is clear that participants given easy training performed better than did participants given hard training on the short message lengths 1–3, whereas participants

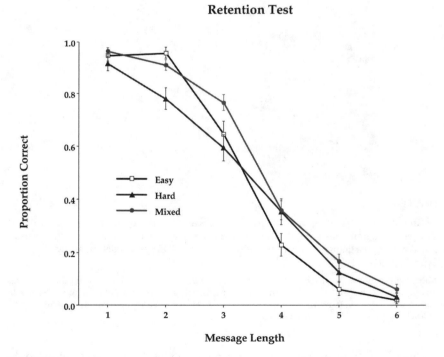

FIGURE 7.10

Proportion correct on the retention test as a function of training condition and message length. Error bars represent positive and negative standard errors of the mean. From navigation study of Schneider et al. (2007).

given hard training performed better than did participants given easy training on the long message lengths 4–6. Therefore, retention test performance on a given set of message lengths was better for participants trained with those lengths than for participants trained with the other set of lengths. Thus, we have shown that training is specific even to the length of messages that need to be understood and executed.

GENERALIZABILITY

We have reviewed studies documenting the first part of our working hypothesis by showing excellent retention but limited transfer for learning skills. Now we turn to studies documenting the second part of our working hypothesis—that for fact learning retention is poor but transfer is robust—by showing strong generalizability of knowledge. These studies demonstrate that learning is facilitated whenever pre-existing knowledge can be employed as a mediator in the process of acquisition.

Fact Learning

The first study of this type that we review shows just how powerful transfer can be for such a task. In this study (Kole and Healy, 2007, Experiment 1), participants started with a listing procedure in which they gave us the names of 12 individuals, half male and half female, whom they know very well, such as their friends or relatives. Later, all participants in each of three groups learned a total of 144 fictitious facts, consisting of 12 facts about each of 12 individuals. Participants in the *high knowledge* group learned facts about the 12 well-known individuals whom they had listed earlier. Participants in the *low knowledge* group learned facts about 12 relatively unfamiliar individuals; the names used in this group were drawn from the fields of professional beach volleyball and off-Broadway plays. Participants in the *mediated knowledge* group also learned facts about 12 unfamiliar individuals, the same set as in the low knowledge group, but these participants associated each unfamiliar individual with a well-known individual. Specifically, after the listing procedure, participants in the mediated knowledge group completed association training, during which they were trained to associate the 12 people whom they had just listed with the 12 unfamiliar individuals whom they would learn about later, in a paired-associate task, to a criterion of three consecutive study-test cycles with perfect accuracy.

Each of the facts that participants learned was unique. There were 12 fact categories used. The fact category exemplars were all one word in length, and were common instances of the category. So, for example, if Alice Healy was a participant in the high knowledge group, she might learn that her daughter Charlotte Healy likes to play lacrosse (which is certainly not true). If she was in the low knowledge group, she might learn that Nancy Reno likes to play lacrosse, and if she was in the mediated knowledge group, she might also learn that Nancy Reno likes to play lacrosse, but she would be encouraged to think of Charlotte Healy while learning this fact. These 144 facts were presented in a learning phase, which consisted of a study-test procedure. Each sentence was presented individually, in blocks of 12 sentences. After each block there was a cued recall test over the 12 facts in the block. The presentation and testing of the entire set of 144 sentences constituted one learning round, and participants completed three learning rounds altogether. After the three learning rounds, participants were given a final cued recall task as a retention test, during which they were examined on all 144 facts without further study.

The results for the final retention test are summarized in Figure 7.11. First, note that overall performance was quite poor in this task, documenting the poor retention of facts that are learned. Second, note that there was a significant main effect of knowledge group, reflecting highest accuracy for the high knowledge group and lowest accuracy for the low knowledge group, with the mediated knowledge group in between. The difference between the mediated and low knowledge groups was significant. We conclude that prior knowledge can aid in the learning of new information. Furthermore, the facilitative effect of using prior knowledge to learn new information was found even when the prior knowledge played only a mediating function, rather than a direct function.

In this experiment, prior knowledge was used to learn new information conceptually related to the prior knowledge. That is, participants used their prior knowledge of people to learn about people. Thus, the question arises whether the facilitative effect of mediated learning depends on whether the information to be learned is conceptually related to the prior knowledge. For example, conceptually unrelated mediated learning might be using one's knowledge of people to learn about countries. The next experiment (Kole and Healy, 2007, Experiment 3) addressed this question. In this experiment, the domain, or the type of facts, that participants learned was manipulated. As in the previous experiment, participants learned a total of 144 facts. In the person domain, participants learned fictitious facts about 12 unfamiliar individuals, and in the country domain, participants learned true facts about 12 relatively unfamiliar countries. Knowledge group was also varied, with participants in the low knowledge group learning facts about these unfamiliar individuals or countries, and those in the mediated knowledge group learning the same facts while associating the unfamiliar countries or individuals with well-known

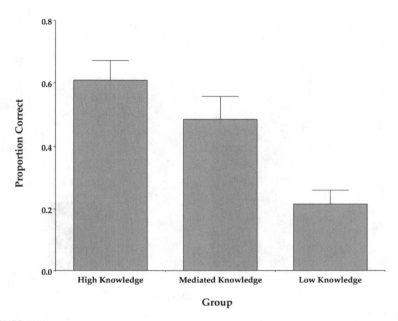

FIGURE 7.11

Proportion correct during the final retention test phase as a function of knowledge group. Error bars represent positive standard errors of the mean. From fact learning study by Kole and Healy (2007, Experiment 1).

individuals. The stimuli employed were constructed such that the fact category exemplars learned were the same across conditions. So, for example, in the person domain, participants learned that Linda Hanley's monthly income is $2200, and in country domain, they learned that Singapore's gross domestic product per capita is $2200. The method was largely the same as in the previous experiment: Again, there was a listing procedure, during which all participants listed the names of 12 individuals whom they know well. Only participants in the mediated knowledge groups completed association training, whereby they were trained to associate the 12 unfamiliar individuals or countries with the names of the 12 familiar individuals. The number of association training rounds was fixed at eight. Then the learning phase and retention test phase proceeded as before except that participants were tested with a cued recognition task. Specifically, participants were provided with a sheet giving all the possible answers for each of the 12 fact categories.

As shown in Figure 7.12, the proportion of correct responses on the retention test for mediated knowledge participants, who had been trained to associate the unfamiliar items with familiar individuals, was overall more than twice as high as that for low knowledge participants, who had not received

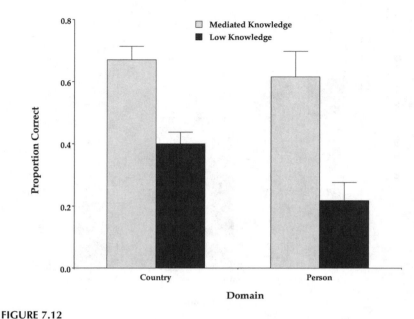

FIGURE 7.12

Proportion correct during the final retention test phase as a function of knowledge group and domain. Error bars represent positive standard errors of the mean. From fact learning study by Kole and Healy (2007, Experiment 3).

such association training, and this advantage for mediated learning was just about as large for learning facts about countries (which are conceptually unrelated to the familiar individuals) as for learning facts about other people. Also, prior knowledge about familiar individuals aided learning facts about unfamiliar individuals even though the facts were unlikely to be true about the familiar individuals with whom they were associated. We explained these results in terms of a mental model approach, following Johnson-Laird (1983) and Radvansky and Zacks (1991). Specifically, prior knowledge about well-known individuals can be viewed as mental models or integrated representations, and the new facts learned can be incorporated easily within these well-established, integrated representations, thereby minimizing interference both from other facts learned about the same individuals and from similar facts learned about other individuals.

Memory for Order Information

More recently, we conducted an experiment in another series in which we also found a surprising ability to transfer information from prior knowledge to learn a new set of declarative facts (Healy, Shea, Kole, and Cunningham, 2008).

In this line of investigation we are attempting to understand the processes underlying the bow-shaped serial position function evident in studies of memory for order information. Earlier experiments in this series examined memory for information either learned outside the laboratory or learned in a single list presentation in the laboratory. In our new experiment, we used a novel training procedure in which list items were presented two to four times each. With this procedure we compared the relative contributions of two variables postulated to affect the serial position functions: familiarity of the items and distinctiveness of the positions. Another novel aspect of the present study was that it tested memory for spatial order, rather than memory for temporal sequence. Specifically, each item occurred individually on a different numbered line in a vertical array. Thus, unlike earlier studies, position distinctiveness was not confounded with temporal distinctiveness.

Participants learned the spatial positions of a list of 20 names. Half of these names were familiar names of friends and relatives, which we obtained using the same listing procedure that we had employed in our last study (Kole and Healy, 2007). The remaining half of the names were unfamiliar ones, taken from the set of professional beach volleyball players and actors from off-Broadway plays that we had also used in our study of fact learning (Kole and Healy, 2007). We compared two different familiarity conditions. In both of these conditions, the familiar and unfamiliar names alternated in pairs. In the *familiar first* condition, familiar names were assigned to the first two list positions, unfamiliar names were assigned to the next two list positions, and so on throughout the list of 20 names. The opposite assignment of names to list positions was used for the *unfamiliar first* condition. Following other procedures we developed earlier, at a retention test following a delay filled with a distractor task, participants were asked to reconstruct the order of only a 12-name subset of the full list of 20 names. There were three serial position conditions that differed in terms of the 12-name subset of positions used for the reconstruction of order task: 1–12, 5–16, and 9–20. Participants were given the 12 names in the subset, listed alphabetically, and had to type one of the 12 possible position numbers beside each name.

As shown in Figure 7.13, there was a striking effect of serial position condition on the shape of the serial position function at the retention test, with a strong primacy effect only for the 1–12 condition (where the primacy items are the first items in the list of 20) and a strong recency effect only for the 9–20 condition (where the recency items are the last items in the list of 20). This pattern of results suggests that distinctiveness of the entire set of 20 list positions, rather than that of the subset of 12 tested list positions, contributes to the bow-shaped serial position functions. These results also document the poor retention of fact learning because overall accuracy was quite low. Most

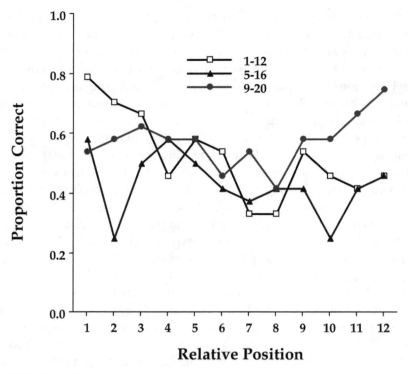

FIGURE 7.13

Proportion of correct responses in the reconstruction of order retention test as a function of relative serial position and serial position condition. From study of memory for order information by Healy et al. (2008, Experiment 3).

interesting are the effects on the retention test of familiarity condition shown in Figure 7.14. There were huge effects of familiarity. For the familiar first condition, the first two positions are much higher than the next two positions, and so on throughout the list, whereas the opposite pattern is found for the unfamiliar first condition. This scalloped pattern reveals that reconstruction of order performance at the retention test is almost twice as high on average for the familiar names as for the unfamiliar names. These effects of item familiarity vividly illustrate that participants can use their prior knowledge about items to learn the spatial locations of the items. Again a mental model account of memory can be used to explain the results, according to which prior knowledge of individuals can be viewed as integrated representations, and new facts about the individuals (in this case those pertaining to spatial location information) can be incorporated within these integrated representations. Thus, for example, Alice Healy could use her extensive knowledge of Charlotte Healy to elaborately encode her position.

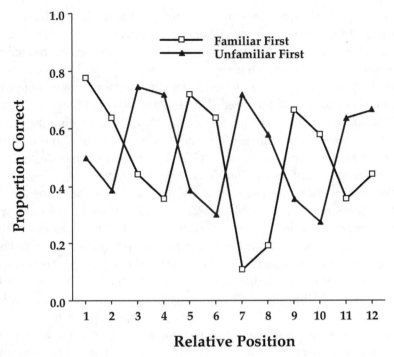

FIGURE 7.14

Proportion of correct responses in the reconstruction of order retention test as a function of relative serial position and familiarity condition. From study of memory for order information by Healy et al. (2008, Experiment 3).

IMPLICATIONS FOR PRACTICE, AND CONCLUSIONS

In any event, these last two lines of investigation show that, despite poor overall retention of declarative information, we can indeed use prior learning to aid in new learning of declarative information. These dramatic benefits of prior learning for declarative information stand in contrast to the surprising lack of benefits for procedural information found in the first three lines of investigation, which also documented the strong retention of procedural information. Together these studies support our working hypothesis based on the procedural reinstatement framework. In summary, it seems that specificity (limited transfer) occurs for tasks based primarily on procedural information, or skill, whereas generality (robust transfer) occurs for tasks based primarily on declarative information, or facts. Thus, for skill learning, retention is strong but transfer is limited, whereas for fact learning, retention is poor but transfer is robust. In our present research we are conducting further tests of this working hypothesis, and we are trying to develop interventions to facilitate long-term retention and transfer of training to novel circumstances. Specifically, we are searching for new ways, such as the variability of practice that we explored in both the speeded aiming study (Wohldmann et al., 2008) and the navigation study (Schneider et al., 2007), to overcome the limited transfer of procedural information, and new ways, such as the mediated knowledge that we explored in the fact learning study (Kole and Healy, 2007), to leverage the robust transfer for declarative information.

The research summarized in this chapter has implications for practice that might be used to drive applied research. To illustrate this potential symbiosis between basic and applied research, we give two brief examples. First, our research has demonstrated a high degree of specificity from training to subsequent application. In fact, we have shown that training is specific even to the length of messages that need to be understood and executed in the navigation task (Schneider et al., 2007). Retention test performance was best following training with all possible message lengths. These findings have crucial implications for military training because instructors may assume that teaching a particular task through a limited number of examples will generalize fully to an entire domain even when the examples differ in a fundamental respect (e.g., length) from the test situations. However, our findings imply that, to be effective, training should incorporate a full range of examples on critical task dimensions. Although the tasks used in our research are often components of military tasks, they are not the real military tasks currently being trained in the Army. We hope that applied research units are interested in testing whether the principles we have developed would apply to such real tasks and whether the methods we hope to develop for overcoming the problem of training specificity could be adapted to improve military training.

Second, we have shown that prior knowledge of friends and relatives can be used to enhance the learning and retention of facts about unknown individuals or countries (Kole and Healy, 2007) as well as the learning and retention of spatial position information (Healy et al., 2008). We are presently conducting research to explore the boundaries of effective prior knowledge utilization. Would learning and retention be improved for other tasks as well by relating task components to well-known friends and relatives? The use of prior knowledge also needs to be examined in the context of real military tasks, and we hope that applied research units will be willing and able to take on this examination.

REFERENCES

Barshi, I., and Healy, A. F. (2002). The effects of mental representation on performance in a navigation task. *Memory & Cognition, 30,* 1189–1203.

Craik, F. I. M., and Lockhart, R. S. (1972). Levels of processing: A framework for memory research. *Journal of Verbal Learning and Verbal Behavior, 11,* 671–684.

Gopher, D., Brickner, M., and Navon, D. (1982). Different difficulty manipulations interact differently with task emphasis: Evidence for multiple resources. *Journal of Experimental Psychology, Human Perception and Performance, 8,* 146–157.

Harlow, H. F. (1949). The formation of learning sets. *Psychological Review, 56,* 51–65.

Healy, A. F. (2007). Transfer: Specificity and generality. In H. L. Roediger, III, Y. Dudai, and S. M. Fitzpatrick (Eds.), *Science of memory: Concepts* (pp. 271–275). New York: Oxford University Press.

Healy, A. F., and Bourne, L. E., Jr. (Eds.). (1995). *Learning and memory of knowledge and skills: Durability and specificity.* Thousand Oaks, CA: Sage.

Healy, A. F., Shea, K. M., Kole, J. A., and Cunningham, T. F. (2008). Position distinctiveness, item familiarity, and presentation frequency affect reconstruction of order in immediate episodic memory. *Journal of Memory and Language, 58,* 746–764.

Healy, A. F., Wohldmann, E. L., and Bourne, L. E., Jr. (2005). The procedural reinstatement principle: Studies on training, retention, and transfer. In A. F. Healy (Ed.), *Experimental cognitive psychology and its applications* (pp. 59–71). Washington, DC: American Psychological Association.

Healy, A. F., Wohldmann, E. L., Parker, J. T., and Bourne, L. E., Jr. (2005). Skill training, retention, and transfer: The effects of a concurrent secondary task. *Memory & Cognition, 33,* 1457–1471.

Healy, A. F., Wohldmann, E. L., Sutton, E. M., and Bourne, L. E., Jr. (2006). Specificity effects in training and transfer of speeded responses. *Journal of Experimental Psychology: Learning, Memory, and Cognition, 32,* 534–546.

Johnson-Laird, P. N. (1983). *Mental models: Towards a cognitive science of language, inference, and consciousness.* Cambridge, MA: Harvard University Press.

Kole, J. A., and Healy, A. F. (2007). Using prior knowledge to minimize interference when learning large amounts of information. *Memory & Cognition, 35,* 124–137.

McDaniel, M. A., Friedman, A., and Bourne, L. E. Jr. (1978). Remembering the levels of information in words. *Memory & Cognition, 6,* 156–164.

Morris, C. D., Bransford, J. D., and Franks, J. J. (1977). Levels of processing versus transfer appropriate processing. *Journal of Verbal Learning and Verbal Behavior, 16,* 519–533.

Radvansky, G. A., and Zacks, R. T. (1991). Mental models and the fan effect. *Journal of Experimental Psychology: Learning, Memory, and Cognition, 17,* 940–953.

Rickard, T. C., and Bourne, L. E., Jr. (1995). An identical-elements model of basic arithmetic skills. In A. F. Healy and L. E. Bourne, Jr. (Eds.), *Learning and memory of knowledge and skills: Durability and specificity* (pp. 255–281). Thousand Oaks, CA: Sage.

Roediger, H. L., III, Weldon, M. S., and Challis, B. H. (1989). Explaining dissociations between implicit and explicit measures of retention: A processing account. In H. L. Roediger, III, and F. I. M. Craik (Eds.), *Varieties of memory and consciousness: Essays in honour of Endel Tulving* (pp. 3–41). Hillsdale, NJ: Lawrence Erlbaum Associates.

Schmidt, R. A., and Bjork, R. A. (1992). New conceptualizations of practice: Common principles in three paradigms suggest new concepts for training. *Psychological Science, 3*, 207–217.

Schneider, V. I., Healy, A. F., and Barshi, I. (2004). Effects of instruction modality and readback on accuracy in following navigation commands. *Journal of Experimental Psychology: Applied, 10*, 245–257.

Schneider, V. I., Healy, A. F., Barshi, I., and Bourne, L. E., Jr. (2007, November). *Effects of difficulty, specificity, and variability on training to follow navigation instructions.* Poster presented at the 48th Annual Meeting of the Psychonomic Society, Long Beach, CA.

Singley, M. K., and Anderson, J. R. (1989). *The transfer of cognitive skill.* Cambridge, MA: Harvard University Press.

Thorndike, E. L. (1906). *The principles of teaching: Based on psychology.* New York: A. G. Seiler.

Tulving, E., and Thomson, D. M. (1973). Encoding specificity and retrieval processes in episodic memory. *Psychological Review, 80*, 352–373.

Wohldmann, E. L., Healy, A. F., and Bourne, L. E., Jr. (2008). Global inhibition and midcourse corrections in speeded aiming. *Memory & Cognition, 36*, 1228–1235.

Wohldmann, E. L., Healy, A. F., and Bourne, L. E., Jr. (2010). Task integration in time production. *Attention, Perception, & Psychophysics, 72*, 1130–1143.

AUTHORS' NOTE

This work was supported by Army Research Institute Contract DASW01–03–K-0002 and Army Research Office Grant W911NF-05-1-0153 to the University of Colorado.

8

Complex Movement Sequences

How the Sequence Structure Affects Learning and Transfer

Charles H. Shea and Attila J. Kovacs

INTRODUCTION

The purpose of this chapter is to critically review current theoretical perspectives on the representation, production, and modification of simple and complex movement sequences. This is followed by an empirical example illustrating the development of a sequence structure for a complex movement sequence and examples of practice conditions that facilitate or interfere with the development and maintenance of the sequence structure. It is our position that the sequence structure provides the fundamental basis for efficient, effective, and durable performance and transfer under some task constraints, but also can impede transfer and relearning under others.

Much scientific inquiry has been devoted to understanding the processes involved in the fluent production of sequential movements such as those involved in speech, handwriting, typing, drumming, playing the piano, driving an automobile, or operating complex equipment for a number of theoretical and applied reasons. From a theoretical perspective this is important because sequential movements are thought to be initially composed of a number of relatively independent elements that through practice are concatenated, consolidated, or otherwise organized into what appear to be a smaller number of subsequences (termed motor chunks by Verwey, 1994). Lashley (1951) proposed that sequential actions were structured such that the order and organization of the movement elements were determined independent of the nature of the movement elements (also see Keele, Jennings, Jones, Caulton, and Cohen, 1995; Klapp, 1995; Schmidt, 1975). This notion of hierarchical control of movement sequences was further developed as a result of a series of experiments and theoretical models by Rosenbaum and colleagues (e.g., Rosenbaum, Kenny, and Derr, 1983; Rosenbaum, Saltzman, and Kingman, 1984; Rosenbaum and Saltzman, 1984; Rosenbaum, Hindorff, and Munro, 1986; Rosenbaum, 1990) in the 1980s and 1990s. Hierarchical control of movement sequences was conceptualized using an inverted tree/branch metaphor such that higher levels (nodes), which were thought to transmit sequence information, branched into lower levels, where specific element/ effector information was stored (also see Nissen and Bullemer, 1987; Povel and Collard, 1982). The memorial representation of this information was thought to be retrieved, unpacked, parameterized, and/or edited (depending on the theoretical perspective) prior to execution so as to meet the specific demands in the movement environment. These models seemed to account fairly well for, at least some of, the time delays between the executions of the discrete individual and/or grouped elements in the sequence.

From a practical standpoint the study of sequential movements is also important because sequential movements make up a large percentage of our learned movement repertoire and often represent some of the most complicated and difficult to learn movements we face. Improved understanding of the processes involved in the performance, learning, and transfer of movement sequences should lead to the design of more effective and efficient training procedures that exploit the way performers structure, execute, and ultimately store in memory movement sequences. In our opinion, the sequence learning literature has now developed to the degree that it can provide strong guidance to research aimed at maximizing the effectiveness, flexibility, and efficiency of sequence learning.

In this chapter we first review theoretical perspectives on sequence representation that shed some light on how movement sequences are represented in memory and processed by the central nervous system. These perspectives provide important clues as to the ways in which movement sequences can be adapted to new (unpracticed) movement demands and the degree to which movement sequences are specific to conditions imposed during practice. This will be followed by an example illustrating the development of a sequence structure for a complex movement sequence and examples of practice conditions that facilitate or impede this development. Finally, we will describe experiments that illustrate the ways in which the sequence structure impacts movement production and transfer.

SEQUENCE REPRESENTATION

Numerous theoretical perspectives have proposed that independent codes, representations, coordinate systems, and/or processing modules contribute to sequence production. Further, these perspectives often argue that the development of and reliance on these codes changes over practice. These movement codes have been variously labeled relative and absolute (e.g., Schmidt, 1975), invariant and variant (Schmidt, 1985, 1988), structural and metrical (Kelso, 1981), higher and lower order (e.g., Fowler and Turvey, 1978), and essential and non-essential (Gelfand and Tsetlin, 1971; Kelso, Putnam, and Goodman, 1983; Langley and Zelaznik, 1984), extrinsic and intrinsic (e.g., Criscimagna-Hemminger, Donchin, Gazzaniga, and Shadmehr, 2003; Lange, Godde, and Braun, 2004), visual–spatial and motor (Hikosaka et al., 1999; Bapi, Doya, and Harner, 2000), and cognitive and motor (Keele et al., 1995; Shea and Wulf, 2005; Verwey, 1995). These distinctions not only imply that these codes are relatively independent, but also that one set of codes (or coordinate system, processing module, or representation) is more abstract, develops more quickly, and is more available to consciousness (e.g., extrinsic, visual–spatial, cognitive) than the other (e.g., intrinsic, motor).

For example, Keele et al. (1995; also see Keele et al., 2003) proposed a modular theory of sequence processing. They proposed that sequential tasks are processed in two independent processing modules which were termed the cognitive (ventral) and motor (dorsal) modules. The cognitive processing module was responsible for computing successive spatial locations and organization of the elements in the sequence. The motor processing module was responsible for selecting effectors and computing activation patterns to achieve these locations. Similarly, Verwey (1995, 2003) proposed that movement sequences were represented in memory in two coding schemes which he also labeled cognitive and motor. The cognitive representation contained information on how the individual elements in the sequence were ordered and organized into chunks. The motor representation maintains information related to the selection and muscle activation of the various effectors.

Hikosaka et al. (1999; also see Bapi et al., 2000) have also provided evidence that movement sequence learning involves both a fast developing and effector-independent component coded in visual–spatial coordinates (e.g., spatial locations of end effectors and/or sequential target positions), and a slower developing effector-dependent motor component that is coded in motor coordinates (e.g., activation patterns of the agonist/antagonist muscles—joint angles). The Hikosaka et al. model, which is based on both experimental and brain imaging data, proposes that the processing of a movement sequence is distributed in the brain in independent spatial and motor coordinate systems with different neural substrates subserving each class of processing. In terms of the neural substrate, the Hikosaka et al. model proposed that intracortical serial connections between the association cortex, motor cortex, basal ganglia, and cerebellum develop over practice with visual–spatial processing supported by distinct loop circuits. During this early stage of learning, explicit knowledge related to the visual–spatial characteristics of the sequence seem to be available to consciousness and attention requirements are relatively high. On the other hand, the circuits within the motor system appear to develop more slowly and at a more implicit level. Hikosaka et al. propose that eventually practice results in a shift from loops specific to visual–spatial coordinate processing to loops associated with motor coordinate processing. At this stage explicit information about movement production and attention demands appears to be substantially reduced relative to earlier in practice.

The Hikosaka model appears to have many similarities to previous and contemporary theoretical perspectives that propose intrinsic and extrinsic coordinate or coding systems (e.g., Criscimagna-Hemminger et al., 2003; Krakauer, Ghilardi, and Ghez, 1999). The intrinsic coordinates are thought to be represented in terms of an internal model of joint representations (Criscimagna-Hemminger et al., 2003), musculoskeletal forces and dynamics (Krakauer et al., 1999), and/or orientation of body segments relative to each other (Lange et al., 2004). This type of coordinate system is thought to be effector dependent to the extent that biomechanical, neurological, and dynamic properties of the effectors used on the transfer test are dissimilar to those used during practice. The extrinsic coordinates are thought to reflect Cartesian coordinates of the task space with respect to the body and visual display. Thus, this type of coordinate system is thought to be effector independent when the extrinsic coordinates are reinstated during effector transfer tests, even though intrinsic characteristics of the required transfer movement may have been altered.

Each of these perspectives argue that two types of processing modules, representations, or coordinate systems are developed independently, at different rates during practice, and limit transfer to different degrees, although some evidence exists that suggests that sequence knowledge is represented in only one coordinate system (e.g., Bischoff-Grethe, Goedert, Willingham, and Grafton, 2004; Russeler and Rosler, 2000). There is also evidence that suggests that hemispheric specialization limits the development and/or the utilization of one or more codes depending on which limb is used during practice and subsequently used on an effector transfer test. The left hemisphere appears to play a dominant role in movement organization, selection (Rushworth, Krams, and Passingham, 2001; Schluter, Rushworth, Passingham, and Mills, 1998) and learning (Grafton, Hazeltine, and Ivry, 2002). The right hemisphere has been implicated in the development of spatial memory, learning, response selection (Schumacher, Elston, and D'Esposito, 2003) and specification of final position of movement (Sainburg, 2002). Additionally, left hemisphere processing appears to be guided by internal representations, whereas right hemisphere processing is driven by the external environment (Goldberg, Podell, and Lovell, 1994). Thus, the transfer of the various representations may be asymmetric across limbs. In right-dominant participants for example, transfer from right to left has been argued to occur predominantly for intrinsic coordinates during movement preparation (Lange et al., 2004; see Criscimagna-Hemminger et al., 2003 for an alternate outcome) whereas transfer from left to right occurs mainly for extrinsic coordinates during movement execution (Lange, Braun, and Godde, 2006).

EXPIRICAL EXAMPLE OF CHUNKING AND CONCATENATION

A popular way to study sequential movements over the last 20 years has been to have participants sequentially depress keys corresponding to visual signals presented on a computer monitor (e.g., Nissen and Bullemer, 1987; Povel and Collard, 1982). This type of task has been called a serial reaction time task (SRT) because participants initially must react to the visual signals much as they would do in a choice reaction time paradigm. However, when the stimuli are presented in a repeating sequence the participant begins to anticipate the upcoming stimuli—thus reducing the time required to respond. As more and more of the sequence is learned the time required to complete the sequence is further reduced. With additional practice it is assumed that the participants become less reliant on the visual stimulus because it is fully anticipated resulting in even more rapid and fluid response production. An explanation for the decreased reaction times was that participants "chunk" or "package" two or more elements together in such a way that the elements could be executed as an independent subsequence.

In these experiments it was common to include either a control group (e.g., Nissen and Bullemer, 1987) or control blocks (e.g., Keele et al., 1995) composed of randomly presented elements at various stages throughout practice. The reduction over practice in response time for the random sequences indicates general improvements in performance that can be attributed to familiarity with the device, the learning of lower order probabilities, and other task-specific information not related to sequence order. The reduction in performance of the repeated sequence relative to the random sequence is used as an index of the amount of sequence knowledge acquired. This allows general improvements in performance to be separated from the gains accrued as a result of learning the specific sequence.

Similar findings occur for movement sequences. To demonstrate how these sequences are learned a sample task and data from Park and Shea (2005) will be presented. The task was to move a lever in an attempt to "hit" targets projected onto the table top (Figure 8.1, right). In this experiment a 16-element movement sequence (Figure 8.1, left) was presented although participants were not informed that there was a sequence. Participants were simply instructed to move the lever from target to target as quickly and smoothly as possible. Figure 8.2 provides an example of the displacement, velocity, and acceleration profiles produced at various stages of practice. From these figures it is easy to see that the movement sequence is produced more quickly and smoothly over practice. Indeed, the movement pattern could be describe as multiple discrete steps early in practice but much more continuous (harmonic) later in practice.

What is particularly interesting is the patterns of element durations, which we refer to as the sequence structure. The development of the sequence structure is clearly seen early in acquisition (Figure 8.3). The differences between the time required to complete the individual elements comprising the sequences were relatively small on the first block of practice with the repeated sequence. However, on the subsequent blocks (Block 2–3) the participants began to decrease the duration of some elements, but not others. This pattern of selective improvement suggests that participants were beginning to impose a structure on the elements comprising the sequence. That is, participants began grouping elements into functional subsequences (termed motor chunks). Subsequences are typically characterized by a relatively slow response to one element followed by a faster response to one or more

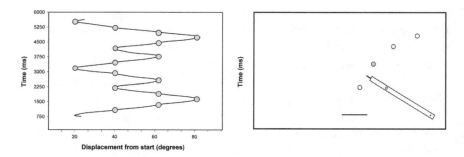

FIGURE 8.1

Illustration of the lever and position of the targets (left) and example of the displacement pattern (right).

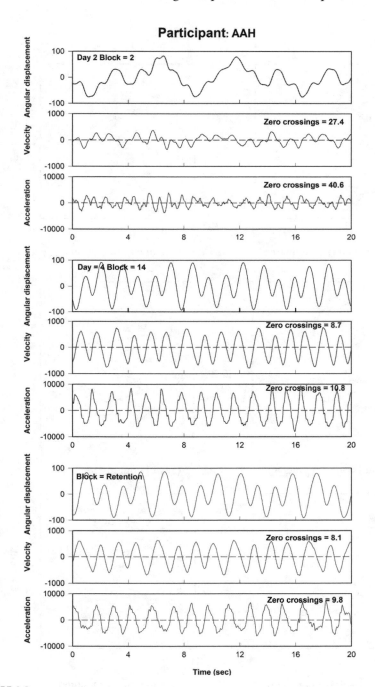

FIGURE 8.2

Example of displacement, velocity, and acceleration profiles for one participant on Day 1 Block 2 (top), Day 4, Block 14 (middle), and on the retention test (bottom).

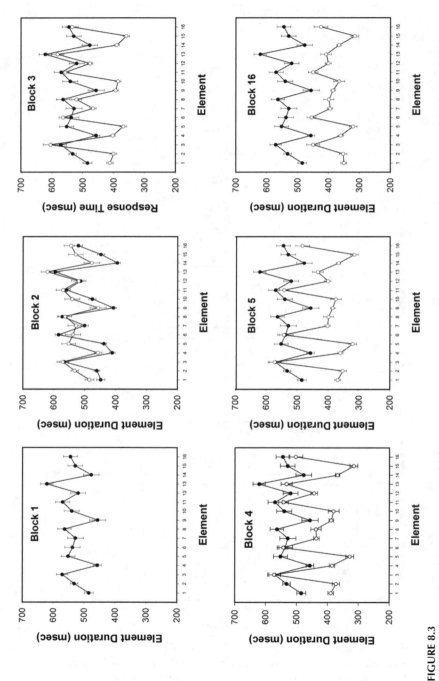

FIGURE 8.3

Mean element durations for Blocks early and late in practice. The element durations for Block 1 are repeated in subsequent figures (from Park and Shea, 2005).

subsequent elements. The first element is slowed because of the additional processing required to retrieve, organize, and initiate the subsequence, but the subsequent elements were produced more rapidly because the processing and articulatory activities required for their execution were completed in advance. Note on Block 3 (Figure 8.3) that Elements 3, 6, 8, 12, and 14 were produced somewhat more slowly than one or more of the following elements. Indeed, the major decreases in movement time across blocks for Block 2 to Block 3 accrue from the elements within a subsequence and not from the elements that marked the beginning of the subsequences. On Block 4 decreases in movement time were again accomplished by further decreasing the time required to traverse the elements within the subsequences. Interestingly, there appears to be further consolidation of subsequences in Block 4. This consolidation process is best seen in Element 8, which initially appeared in Blocks 2 and 3 as if it were the beginning of an independent subsequence, but by the end of Block 4 appeared to be consolidated into the preceding subsequence. Remember, also, that the repeated sequence continued for 160 elements (10 repetitions of the 16 element sequence) within each block. This allows participants to group elements from the end of a sequence with elements at the beginning of the sequence. Indeed, this appears to be the case with Elements 16, 1, and 2 being grouped together in a single subsequence.

After the sequence structure is developed, a second important process occurs which has been referred to as concatenation (Verwey, 1994) and coactivation (Jordan, 1995). The result of this additional processing was to speed up and smooth the transition from one subsequence to the next. This is thought to occur because participants after structuring the sequence can reallocate processing resources during the production of one subsequence to the processing of the subsequent subsequence. The result is a relatively smooth and seamless response production. The result of the concatenation process could be viewed as further consolidation of the subsequences into one larger chunk but various perturbations indicated that this does not seem to be the case. For example, when resource demands are increased through the inclusion of a secondary task the first element in the subsequence is again slowed and glitches occur in the movement trace, but the elements within the subsequence are unaffected.

FACTORS INFLUENCING THE LEARNING OF A SEQUENCE STRUCTURE

In the following section we describe a few experiments that illustrate how the structure becomes the basis for effective and efficient sequence production and transfer. These experiments illustrate how retroactive and proactive interference and facilitation, contextual interference, and part–whole practice influence the development of the movement structure.

Interference and facilitation. Movement sequences are often learned and later modified as circumstances dictate throughout one's lifetime. After initially learning to perform a movement sequence we may be required to perform a slightly different but related sequence. For example, after learning to shift gears in a standard transmission car, we may be required to operate a farm tractor where the gears are aligned in slightly different positions or drive an auto in a different country where the driver sits on the right rather than the left. Likewise, after learning to play a musical score on a standard piano, we may be required to play the same score on an electronic keyboard where the spacing between keys is slightly different than on the standard piano or type on a foreign computer keyboard where one or two keys are in different positions.

In a recent paper (Panzer, Wilde, and Shea, 2006) we determined the effect of making a subtle change in a previously learned movement sequence. Two hypotheses were proposed. First, because the sequences were so similar, proactive and retroactive interference could degrade the performance of both sequences. Previous research in the verbal (e.g. Melton and van Lackum, 1941; Underwood, 1957) and motor learning (e.g., Bock, Schneider, and Bloomberg, 2001; Holding, 1976; Schmidt and Young, 1987; Walter and Swinnen, 1994) literatures has demonstrated that similarity plays a role in increasing interference effects. Alternatively, because the two sequences were so similar, it seemed logical that a previously learned movement sequence could be modified to produce a slightly different movement sequence (e.g. Schmidt and Young, 1987, see also Malfait, Shiller and Ostry, 2002). If the latter were true, proactive facilitation would be evident in the performance of the new sequence. Indeed, this notion is consistent with belief that "lead-up" games and practice activities, which are slightly different from the movement pattern used by the skilled athlete, form the building blocks for the later skilled performance even though the specific movement sequences used in the training activities may be subtly different from those used by the skilled performer.

Panzer et al. (2006) had participants practice a 16-element movement sequence on one day (S1) and then practice a similar sequence on a second day (S2). The second sequence was constructed by only switching the positions of two of 16 elements in the sequence (Figure 8.4). This subtle change in the sequence was designed so as to increase the potential for transfer on the one hand and interference on the other. Note also that practice on the two sequences was separated by 24 hours. This was done to allow consolidation of the stored information for the first sequence prior to introducing the second sequence (e.g., Brashers-Krug, Shadmehr, and Bizzi, 1996). According

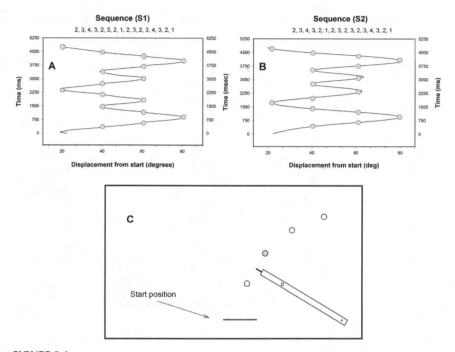

FIGURE 8.4

Illustration of the lever and position of the targets (bottom) and examples of the two displacement patterns (top).

to the consolidation hypothesis, 24 hours would provide sufficient time to allow consolidation, and thus afford the sequences protection from mutual interference. The results indicated that participants modified the first sequence to accommodate the changes in the second sequence (Figure 8.5). This resulted in the participant essentially "overwriting" the memory states responsible for the productions of the first sequence. This conclusion seemed warranted as the performance on the first sequence for the group that had practiced both sequences was no better than that for a control group that only practiced the second sequence. Thus, retroactive inference was so complete that an "overwriting" explanation seemed justified.

In a second experiment Muehlbauer, Panzer, and Shea (2007) used an interference paradigm with the same two complex arm movement sequences used in the previous experiment. As in the first experiment, the sequences were identical except that two of the 16 elements were reversed in the second sequence. However, the experimental group in this experiment practiced S1 for 2 days prior to practice with S2 on Day 3. In Panzer et al. (2006) only 1 day of practice was permitted on the first sequence. We hypothesized that

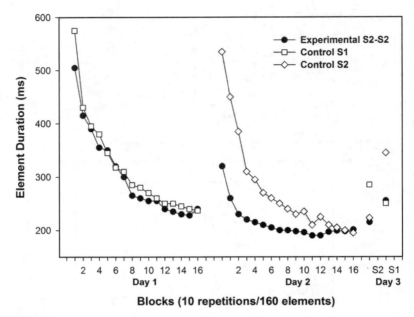

FIGURE 8.5

Mean element duration for Day 1 (Sequence S1), Day 2 (Sequence S2) and on the retention tests (from Panzer et al., 2006).

with an additional day of practice the memory states underpinning the first sequence would be developed to the point that these memory states would be more resistant to interference. However, there is evidence in the literature that additional practice actually increases the potential for interference between sequences. Adams (1987, p. 50), for example, in a review of transfer of training, concludes that

> interference increases with the amount of original learning and the amount of interpolated learning. It might seem that the greater the original learning the greater the resistance should be to the interfering action of the interpolated task, but this is not so. As motor response becomes increasingly refined, it appears to acquire a sensitivity to interference.

If Adams' conclusions are true then we would expect even stronger retroactive interference when additional practice is provided on the first sequence (also see Lewis, McAllister, and Adams, 1951).

The results found no indications that S2 practice positively or negatively influenced S1 performance on the retention test. In terms of element duration, zero crossings, and the movement structure, S1 for the experimental group performed similarly to S1 for the S1 control group on the retention test. Indeed, the pattern of element durations for the experimental group was remarkably similar to the pattern observed at the end of S1 practice on Day 2 and on the S1 retention test on Day 4.

Contextual interference. The initial works on contextual interference found that while blocked practice resulted in enhanced acquisition performance, retention and transfer performances were superior following random practice (e.g., Lee and Magill, 1983; Shea and Morgan, 1979; Shea and Zimny, 1983). However, later research, which considered the timing or regulation of force for the individual movement segments comprising the movement sequence, demonstrated that the retention and transfer benefits of random practice over constant practice were limited to an increased ability to rescale the response and how quickly a given task variation could be produced. This research demonstrated that blocked practice enhanced the participants ability to develop a movement plan that incorporated both the timing and forces required to effectively produce the sequence (e.g., Lai and Shea, 1998; Whitacre and Shea, 2000). The finding that blocked and constant practice compared to serial and random practice results in enhanced relative timing learning led to the proposal of the "stability hypothesis" by Shea, Wulf, Park, and Gaunt (2001). This hypothesis proposed that factors that increase trial-to-trial consistency (e.g., constant or blocked practice) will benefit relative time learning compared to those practice conditions that introduce trial-to-trial change (e.g., random practice).

In an attempt to reap relative timing benefits from constant practice and absolute timing benefits from random practice, Lai, Shea, Wulf, and Wright (2000, Experiment 2; also see Han and Shea, 2008) not only had participants practice under constant and random practice schedules, but also combined these practice schedules such that one group practiced constant practice for the first half of practice and random practice for the second half. A random–constant practice condition was also included in these experiments to serve as a control. Combined practice schedules were formulated because Lai et al. (2000) reasoned that the relative timing structures of a timing sequence were best developed prior to learning to scale the absolute timing of the entire sequence. If this logic was true, they reasoned that the constant-random practice would result in superior relative and absolute timing compared to the random-constant practice condition. Consistent with their hypothesis the results indicated that the constant-random practice schedule resulted in relative and absolute timing learning that was significantly better than the random-constant practice. Indeed relative timing learning for the constant-random group was similar to that of the constant practice group and absolute timing was similar to that of the random practice group. This result was recently replicated by Han and Shea (2008) using blocked and random practice schedules. In sum (considering both relative and absolute timing), the performance of the constant-random group was superior to the other groups tested on the retention test and the advantages of constant-random practice were even larger on the transfer tests. These experiments were not only informative about the independent development of relative and absolute timing, but also proposed a practice scheme that could optimize the development of both relative and absolute timing.

Wilde, Magnuson, and Shea (2005) investigated the contextual interference phenomenon using three movement sequences (six elements each) that have been shown to be structured by participants differently when blocked practice was used (Povel and Collard, 1982). Povel and Collard originally designed the sequences so that they created generally the same movement demands (as the sequences were identical except for the placement of one element). However, under blocked practice the sequence structures adopted by participants allowed one of the sequences (C1) to be performed more rapidly than the other two. Wilde et al. proposed that this advantage and unique structure, which had been shown to occur in blocked practice, may not emerge during random practice. During random practice of the three sequences (C1, C2, and C3) participants may attempt to structure the three practiced sequences similarly, given the obvious superficial similarities in the movement sequences. A uniform response structure could be an effective strategy to reduce the reconstructive processes that are proposed to occur from trial to trial during random practice (e.g., Lee and Magill, 1983; 1985) and should be beneficial from a processing load standpoint because a different sequence structure would not have to be retrieved and processed for each sequence. In traditional contextual interference terms, the decision to structure the sequences could be facilitated by intertask comparisons (elaborative processing) that focus on the obvious similarities in the sequences (Shea and Zimny, 1983).

Consistent with earlier contextual interference research the blocked practice group performed the sequences more rapidly than the random practice group early in acquisition, but this difference was lost by the end of practice (Figure 8.6). Interestingly, however, the random practice group's performance on the non-repeated sequence blocks (Blocks 1, 22, and 43) improved across acquisition while the performance of the blocked group did not. Non-repeated sequence blocks have been used in the sequence learning literature (e.g., Nissen and Bullemer, 1987; Povel and Collard, 1972; Keele et al., 1995) to separate general improvements related to task performance and lower order probabilities from improvements related to learning the specific repeated sequences. This finding indicates that random practice enhances general

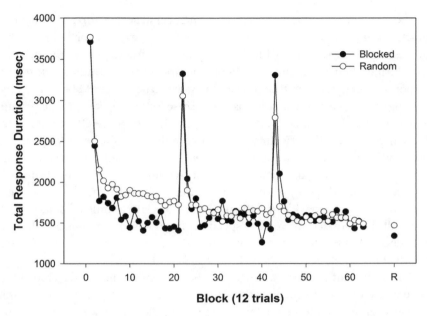

FIGURE 8.6

Total response duration during acquisition and retention under blocked and random practice schedules. Random sequences were tested on Blocks 1, 22, and 42 (from Wilde et al., 2005).

performance capabilities to a greater extent than blocked practice while blocked practice leads to enhanced sequence specific capabilities.

On the retention test, which was the critical test of learning, the blocked practice group performed the repeated sequences on average more rapidly than the random practice group. The difference between groups, however, was not uniform across sequences. The blocked practice group performed Sequence C1 nearly 350 ms faster than the random practice group. Total response duration for Sequences C2 and C3 were similar for the blocked and random groups. Interestingly, mean total response durations for each of the sequences were similar for the random practice groups, but not the blocked practice group.

The difference between groups can be accounted for by the manner in which the blocked and random practice groups structured the sequences. As hypothesized, the pattern of element durations (termed sequence structure) across sequences suggests that random practice resulted in participants structuring each of the sequences in a remarkably similar manner while blocked practice permitted the participants the opportunity to differentially structure the sequences, presumably in an attempt to optimize specific aspects of the sequence. Adopting the same sequence structure for all sequences practiced in a random format could be an effective strategy for reducing the processing load associated with changing the response sequence from trial to trial during acquisition. That is, rather than retrieving and processing different response structures from trial to trial, the same structure could be utilized by loading different elements. This was not the case for the blocked practice group which appeared to utilize a different structure for Sequence C1 compared to Sequences C2 and C3. It is important to note that the blocked group would not require a new sequence to be retrieved and processed from trial to trial, at least not during acquisition, and therefore would not accrue benefits during practice from adopting a single structure. In any event, the decreased processing associated with structuring the responses in a similar fashion failed to result in increased movement speed on the retention test—especially for Sequence C1, although it may have reduced the processing demands during acquisition.

The important question was why did the sequence structure developed for Sequence C1 under blocked practice lead to more rapid response production? The answer appears to be related to the way Sequence C1 was structured in blocked and random practice. Under blocked practice Sequence C1 was structured as two subsequences while under blocked practice C1 was structured as one subsequence. Remember subsequences have been defined as a relatively long duration element followed by one or more short duration elements. According to this viewpoint additional time is required to retrieve, unpack, parameterize, or otherwise prepare the upcoming subsequence for execution. This substantially slows the production of the first element in the subsequence. Subsequent elements in the subsequence are performed more rapidly because they are not encumbered with the additional retrieval and processing delays. However, the time required to prepare a longer subsequence for production and the speed with which the individual elements within a subsequence are produced increases as the length of the subsequence increases (sequence length effect; Sternberg, Monsell, Knoll, and Wright, 1978; Verwey, 1994; 1996). By adopting a unique movement structure for Sequence C1 under blocked practice the total movement time was decreased.

In summary, the present data suggest that random practice results in participants adopting a uniform response structure while blocked practice allows participants to exploit unique sequential aspects of the individual tasks. This may allow the random practice participants to reduce trial to trial processing associated with loading the subsequences during random practice, but this does not allow the participant to exploit other unique sequential characteristics of the individual sequences being learned. Accordingly, random practice may result in enhanced performance when the tasks being practiced together effectively conform to like structures but not when they can benefit from unique sequential solutions.

Part–whole practice. Several part–whole practice schemes (e.g., fractionation, segmentation, simplification; Wightman and Lintern, 1985) are commonly used. However, a large proportion of the part–whole practice research does not appear to support the benefits of part–whole practice in terms of learning (see Templet and Hebert, 2002 for a recent meta-analysis). The compelling logic is that complex movement sequences can best be taught by partitioning the whole sequence into smaller more manageable units which can later be combined to produce a consolidated sequence.

In order to study part–whole practice, a 16-element movement sequence was arbitrarily decomposed into two 8-element parts. The first eight elements were termed Sequence A and the second eight elements were termed Sequence B. Thus, the whole sequence was labeled Sequence AB. On the first day of practice one group practiced only Sequence A (part sequence practice) while the other practiced Sequence AB (whole sequence practice). On the second day of practice both groups practiced Sequence AB. On the third day, all participants completed a retention test on Sequence AB and two transfer tests. The transfer tests involved producing Sequence A and B independently (tests counter-balanced). Based on past literature on part–whole practice we hypothesized a small (e.g., Ash and Holding, 1990; Watters, 1992), if any (e.g., Knapp and Dixon, 1952; Lersten, 1968), advantage for the part practice group on the retention test. However, we hypothesized that part–whole practice would accrue additional subtle advantages that are not typically assessed with traditional part–whole practice research but are predicted by the sequence learning literature. Specifically, we anticipated that the part–whole practice group, because of the way practice was structured, would be more effective in producing the parts of the sequence than the whole practice group. While this may not be as apparent when producing Sequence A, because the whole sequence could be prepared with the final elements simply aborted or edited out (Rosenbaum and Saltzman, 1984), the performance on Sequence B should be especially informative. Evidence that the part–whole practice participants can execute Sequence B more rapidly than whole practice participants, even though they received only 1 day of practice on Sequence B compared to 2 days, would suggest that the 8-element sequences have retained their identity even though they appeared to have been effectively concatenated during the second day of practice.

In addition, it will be informative to determine how quickly Sequence A and B can be produced relative to the respective elements in Sequence AB. Verwey (2001) argued that the processing of later parts of a sequence can occur during the execution of the earlier parts when the cognitive processor is allocated to higher order sequence processing. This must occur in order for subsequences to be effectively concatenated, but results in a general slowing down of the subsequences because the cognitive and motor processors are allocated to different aspects of the task. However, if Sequence A and B are completed more rapidly when produced separately than when combined, without specific increases/decreases in subsequence production, then the residual effects of the other subsequences would have been eliminated. In this case Verwey would argue that the cognitive processor was reallocated to assist in response execution processing. Alternatively, if only the first element in a subsequence is produced more rapidly in the shorter sequences notions related to resource load and/or retrieval are implicated as the reason for producing the longer sequences more slowly.

On the retention test, which was conducted approximately 24 hrs after the completion of practice, the participants in Practice groups A and AB performed similarly (Figure 8.7). This similarity was observed not only in terms of mean element duration but also in terms of the sequence structure. In fact, the

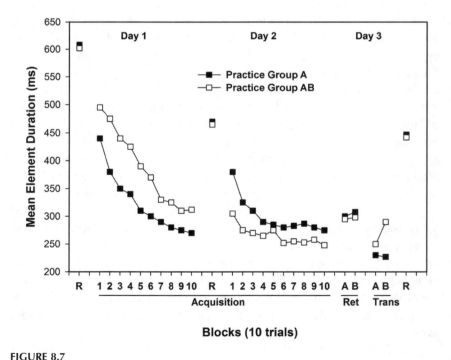

FIGURE 8.7

Mean element duration during acquisition and retention/transfer. Note that random (R) were tested before each day of practice and following the retention/transfer tests (from Park, Wilde, and Shea, 2004).

patterns of element duration were nearly identical for the two groups. After completing the retention test, two transfer tests were conducted to examine participants' ability to independently produce Sequences A and B. We initially hypothesized that the participants in Practice group A might demonstrate an advantage in producing the two 8-element sequences because they had some experience in producing Sequence A independently prior to practicing the combined Sequence AB. This could occur if participants structured the longer sequence differently depending on whether they initially received part or whole sequence practice. However, given the similarity in the way participants structured the 16-element sequence (AB) on the retention test, it seemed unlikely that the practice groups would differentially respond to the 8-element sequences. In addition, we were interested in determining the costs, if any, associated with producing the 16-element sequence relative to the 8-element sequences.

Participants in both Practice groups A (68 ms per element) and AB (44 ms per element) produced Sequence A on the transfer test significantly faster than when the same elements were included in Sequence AB (retention test). While this represents what has been referred to as the "sequence length effect" (e.g., Sternberg et al., 1978), the increased speed seems to suggest that both groups were able to produce the first eight elements without costs associated with the additional elements in the longer sequence. However, the results from the transfer test on Sequence B suggest that this interpretation may not be quite so straightforward. Participants in Practice group AB were able to produce Sequence A substantially faster than when combined in Sequence AB, but were not able to produce Sequence B alone any faster than when combined in Sequence AB (–5 ms). This was not the case for participants in Practice group A, who were able to produce both Sequence A and B alone more rapidly than when combined in Sequence AB (75 ms per element).

The finding that participants in Practice group AB were able to produce Sequence A, but not Sequence B, faster than when the same elements were combined in Sequence AB, is particularly noteworthy. This finding is consistent with the notion that in order to produce Sequence B participants in Practice group AB had to load the entire 16-element sequence and thus incurred costs associated with the initial eight elements. However, this position does not seem compatible with the finding that Sequence A was produced more rapidly than the same elements in Sequence AB. This conflict could be resolved if one assumes that participants can effectively truncate elements at the end of a sequence but not at the beginning. Elements/subsequences at the beginning of a series may provide important cues and context necessary for the readying of later subsequences and, thus may be difficult to edit out prior to execution. In some ways this may be like the waiter who has memorized the nightly menu.

It is no problem to fluently present the first part of the menu and stop at any point but it is difficult to start in the middle without going back through beginning of the list. Similarly you can easily name the first number of your phone number without much hesitation but in order to recall a number later in the sequence you must silently work through the preceding elements before specifying the number requested. Rosenbaum and colleagues (Rosenbaum, Inhoff, and Gordon, 1984; Rosenbaum and Saltzman, 1984) proposed a hierarchical editor model whereby learned movement sequences can be edited with some limitations prior to execution. The present data suggest that the cost associated with this editing process is less when the latter part of the sequence was truncated than when the beginning was edited out. The fact that participants in Practice group A did not seem to accrue these costs suggests that they were able to independently produce either Sequence A or B without cost associated with loading the entire sequence.

It is also interesting to note that from a part–whole training perspective, Practice condition A (part–whole practice) could be considered more efficient than Practice condition AB (whole practice). More efficient training results when the "costs" in terms of money, time, effort, potential injury, etc. are reduced. When practice effectiveness is equal across practice conditions, as was the case on the retention test in the present experiment, practice efficiency becomes a key consideration in deciding on a practice scheme. In the present experiment participants in Practice group A were required to respond to 25 percent fewer targets during acquisition than participants in Practice group AB without a loss in terms of learning effectiveness. Indeed, when viewed in terms of the capability of participants in Practice group A to produce not only the whole sequence (AB) but also the individual components (A or B), this adds to the efficiency benefits of the part–whole practice condition.

In summary, part–whole practice failed to result in advantages or disadvantages relative to whole practice in terms of learning the whole (16-element) movement sequence. However, part–whole practice resulted in more effective transfer to Sequence B (last eight elements) but not Sequence A (first eight elements) than whole practice. This is important theoretically because it demonstrates that the whole practice group was able to truncate elements at the end, but not the beginning, of the learned sequence without incurring processing costs associated with the whole sequence. Part–whole practice allowed participants to effectively eliminate either the first or last half of the response without incurring processing costs associated with longer sequence.

Scaling and effector transfer. The extent to which a learned movement sequence can be adapted is also of considerable theoretical interest because observing how performers change learned movement sequences when faced with new constraints should provide a window through which to observe the fundamental ways in which movement sequences are structured, stored, and executed. By imposing new requirements on learned movement sequences we feel important new theoretical insights into the control and learning of movement sequences can be gained. Furthermore, determining the boundary conditions for effective transfer and the conditions under which movement sequences can be effectively modified will allow for further *theoretical* development and may ultimately lead to more effective training and retraining protocols.

Proportional and non-proportional transfer: Scaling effects. The focus of this section provides some insight into the extent to which movement sequences can be transferred when the spatial requirements of the sequence are changed—sequence order unchanged. We predicted that participants can effectively transfer to new spatial requirements when the changes were proportional across the movement sequence, but not when the changes were non-proportional. Proportional in this context means that the relationships between elements in the sequence maintain the same proportional amplitudes to each other but that the overall scale of the movement sequence could be increased or decreased. Non-proportional changes involve changing the relationship between amplitudes of the elements. We make this prediction because we believe the movement structure that is developed over practice can be maintained in proportional transfer conditions by simply rescaling the sequence, but the movement structure must be altered to effectively produce a non-proportional change.

In these experiments as in a number of other experiments involving sequence learning (e.g., Keele et al., 1995; Park and Shea, 2002, 2003, 2005), we also have participants periodically in acquisition perform a block involving randomly presented elements. This is done in order to determine whether differences arise between groups in terms of general performance capabilities unrelated to acquiring repeated sequence. That is, improvements over practice or differences observed in the retention or transfer tests on the random sequence indicate general task improvements while the difference between the performance on the random blocks and the repeated blocks/tests indicated improvements resulting from sequence knowledge. Most importantly, from a design standpoint, the random blocks in retention/transfer using the various amplitude combinations, provide a reference upon which to determine the extent to which sequence knowledge (and the associated response structure) contributes to the increased sequence production speed.

The Experiment 1 data from Wilde and Shea (2006), which involved 1 day of practice prior to retention and transfer testing, demonstrated participants could successfully transfer to both proportional and non-proportional transfer conditions. Indeed, contrary to our initial predictions, performance on the non-proportional transfer test was as effective as the group that practiced with that spatial configuration on Day 1. This suggests that participants at this stage of practice were relying primarily on sequence order information and had not yet optimized the motor commands to the specific movement requirements. However, after 4 days of practice, participants were only effective in transferring to the proportional transfer conditions. Performance on the non-proportional transfer test after 4 days of practice was no better than transfer after 1 day of practice (Figure 8.8). That is, additional practice incremented performance on the proportional transfer tests, but not the non-proportional transfer tests. These results demonstrated that the specificity of the sequence production increases over practice, but that participants remain capable of rescaling the spatial characteristics of the movement sequence even after extended practice.

Clearly a perceptual motor system that initially permits a great deal of movement flexibility early in the learning processing, but is capable of optimizing movement specifics with additional practice has a great deal of intuitive appeal. The results of these experiments suggest that the independence of the movement structure and movement scaling may be lost over practice with the movement structure and the force/time characteristics becoming more closely integrated. It seems reasonable after initial practice with this type of task that participants attempt to exploit the unique characteristics of the specific effectors and dynamic characteristics of the specific task, and this exploitation benefits response production when the same spatial characteristics are reinstated but increasingly limits the extent to which the response sequence is adaptable to new non-proportional spatial demands (also see Proteau, Marteniuk, Girouard, and Dugas, 1987; Proteau, Marteniuk, and Levesque, 1992).

Effector transfer of movement sequences. Schema theory, originally proposed by Schmidt in 1975, posited that the effectors (i.e., muscle or muscle groups) that were used to produce the movement were selectable in much the same way as other absolute characteristics (e.g., absolute time, absolute force) of the response were selected prior to movement execution. This was quite different from many of the earlier notions of motor programs (e.g., Henry and Rogers, 1960) where it was implied that the muscle activation patterns were directly controlled by the motor program. In reference to Merton's (1972; also see Raibert, 1977) demonstration that individuals can produce the same signature on a check or 10 times larger on a blackboard, Schmidt stated that schema theory explains this phenomenon by proposing that a generalized motor program requires certain specifications in order to produce a given movement sequence that meets a unique set of environmental constraints. These later became known as the variant (selectable) characteristics of the motor program (e.g., absolute time, absolute force, and specific effectors), which were

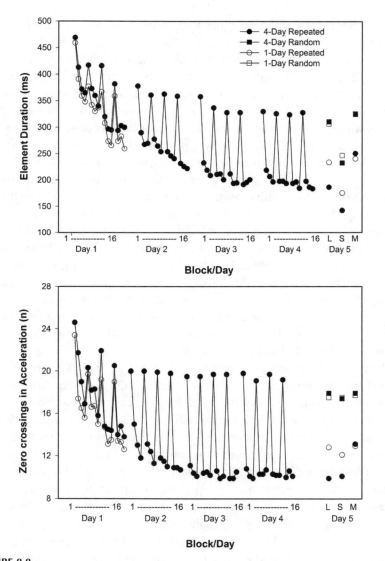

FIGURE 8.8

Mean element durations (top) and zero crossings on the acceleration trace (bottom) during each day of practice and on the retention/transfer tests (from Wilde and Shea, 2006).

contrasted with the invariant characteristics (e.g., order of the elements, relative time, relative force) that defined the GMP. The ability to effectively select new effectors is the focus of this section.

Although Merton (1972) and Raibert (1977) provided interesting demonstrations that individuals can produce their signature using different muscle groups, there was no attempt, other than visual inspection, to determine the degree to which the signatures matched. Some years later, Wright (1990) and Castiello and Stelmach (1993) provided careful kinematic analyses of handwriting using different effectors and generally concluded that there were striking similarities in the shape of the letters, but also some important differences across muscle groups. Thus, this important prediction of schema theory, which has come to be known as "effector independence," had not been systematically studied until recently. The more recent attempts to study this prediction were prompted not only by schema theory but also by recent theoretical perspectives that have proposed that the memory state or processing mechanism—depending on the theoretical perspective—responsible for organizing elements in a sequence is more abstract than the memory state or processing mechanism responsible for the direct articulatory activities that produce the movement outcome (Keele et al., 1995; Verwey, 1999; also see Klapp, 1996; MacKay, 1982). In addition, researchers using the dynamical system perspective have studied this question (e.g., Kelso and Zanone, 2002) noting, similarly to researchers from more cognitively oriented perspectives, that high-level dynamic representation of skilled behavior proves to be largely effector independent. In the next subsections we will briefly outline some of the recent effector transfer experiments.

Park and Shea (2002) allowed participants to practice producing a force–time waveform using one set of effectors and then compared delayed retention performance using the same set of effectors with performance on a transfer test where a different set of effectors was required. In Experiments 1 and 2 contralateral or ipsilateral effector transfer tests were conducted. The contralateral test involved transfer to the opposite limb while the ipsilateral effector transfer test involved transfer where the agonist and antagonist muscle switched roles. In Experiment 3, participants practiced the static, force production task used in Experiments 1. After completing the delayed retention test, participants were asked to produce a dynamic version of the task. This transfer condition involved considerably different muscle activation patterns, but the relative timing and relative force requirements were the same.

The results were remarkably similar across the three experiments regardless of whether transfer was to a new limb, a different muscle group on the same limb, or whether transfer was from static to dynamic versions of the task. Under all conditions, the sequence structure was maintained across the effector transfer test. These effects were virtually the same regardless of which condition (left or right hand; triceps-push or biceps-pull) the participant practiced under. The data suggest that the sequence structure was stored in an abstract, effector-independent manner while the scaling of the force was specific to the muscle group used during practice. Interestingly, this result has been replicated by

Park and Shea (2003) using a 16-element arm movement sequence. After 1 day of practice with the right limb, participants were able to effectively produce the movement pattern with their left limb. Likewise, using a timing sequence, Lai, Shea, Bruechert, and Little (2002) found that participants produced nearly identical sequence structures when the role of the fingers was reversed, different fingers were used, or when a single finger was moved from key to key. These results provided strong empirical support for the notion of effector independence at least with respect to the sequence structure.

While a number of recent studies (Park and Shea, 2002, 2005) have demonstrated that the relative characteristics of simple movement sequences could be effectively transferred to new muscle groups, Park and Shea (2003) conducted another experiment to determine the effect of practice on the extent to which simple response sequences practiced using one set of effectors could be effectively produced using a new set of effectors. Further, they were interested in whether or not the sequence structure and scaling characteristics of the task were differentially affected on the effector transfer test after extended practice. Given additional practice, it is possible that in an attempt to optimize movement production, effector information becomes more directly linked to the response structure than was observed early in practice (e.g., Park and Shea, 2002). This general phenomenon has been termed coarticulation (Jordan, 1995) and has been shown to influence the production of well-learned movement sequences in speech (e.g., Benguere and Cowan, 1974), key pressing (Verwey and Wright, 2004), and in skilled typing (e.g., Gentner, Larochelle, and Grudin, 1988). The effect of additional practice then would be a more effective response when the same muscle groups were used but of little additional benefit when a new set of effectors was required. In the extended practice experiment delayed contralateral and ipsilateral effector transfer tests were compared to a delayed retention test (effector transfer tests counterbalanced). The use of contralateral and ipsilateral effector transfer tests in the same experiment also permitted hemispheric/handedness specificity questions to be addressed (e.g., Henningsen, Henningsen, and Gordon, 1995), because the ipsilateral effector transfer task is primarily controlled by the hemisphere/hand used to control the practice and delayed retention tests, and the contralateral effector transfer task is governed primarily by the other hemisphere/hand.

The retention and transfer results of the 1-day group replicated the results of Park and Shea (2002). However, these results were restricted to the 1-Day acquisition group. Following 4 days of practice, the sequence structure on the effector transfer test was different than that on the retention test. This suggests that, as the movement sequence was refined during the additional practice, the movement structure became less effector independent than it was earlier in practice.

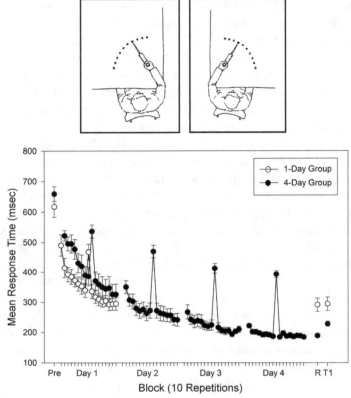

FIGURE 8.9

Illustration of the lever and position of the targets (left) and participant during acquisition and effector transfer (top). Mean element durations (top) and zero crossings on the acceleration trace (bottom) during each day of practice and on the retention/transfer tests (from Park and Shea, 2003).

Park and Shea (2003) also provide evidence using a 16-element repeated sequence that after extended practice participants structured their response (consolidated or concatenated elements) on an effector transfer test differently than on the retention test. This was not the case after one practice session. In fact, the sequence organization that was used on the effector transfer test after extended practice was similar to that observed much earlier in practice. In the Park and Shea (2003) experiment, this position is supported by the finding that not only the movement structure, but also the specification of force, was equally effective on the effector transfer tests for the 1- and 4-day groups. Additional practice resulted in a more refined and better scaled movement sequence, which was also less adaptable to effector transfer conditions. When faced with producing the response using a different set of effectors the additional practice resulted in no additional benefit in terms of the response structure and the specification of force. The results of these experiments suggest that the independence of the movement structure and movement scaling may be lost over practice with the movement structure and the force characteristics becoming more closely integrated. It seems reasonable that after initial practice with this type of task that participants attempt to exploit the unique characteristics of the specific effectors and this exploitation benefits response production when the same effectors are used but increasingly limits the extent to which the response sequence is effector independent (also see Proteau et al., 1987, 1992).

Asymmetries in effector transfer and multiple coding effects. In a series of three experiments using a 14-element movement sequence Kovacs, Muehlbauer and Shea (2009) attempted to determine how the representation of movement sequences change over practice. They predicted, based upon the Hikosaka et al. (1999) model and recent sequence learning experiments (e.g., Bapi et al., 2000; Grafton et al., 2002; van Mier and Petersen, 2006; Willingham, Wells, Farrell, and Stemwedel, 2000), that relatively early in practice movement sequences would be coded in visual–spatial coordinates (also termed extrinsic codes/ coordinates), but with more extensive practice codes based in motor coordinates (also termed intrinsic codes/coordinates) would be developed, resulting in less reliance on visual–spatial codes. The task consisted of practicing the sequential task with one limb (dominant or non-dominant) and transfer to the contralateral limb in a visual–spatial condition with visual–spatial cues reinstated or a motor (mirror) condition with motor coordinates reinstated.

In three experiments utilizing 1, 4, and 12 days of practice, the results were consistent with the predictions of the Hikosaka model relative to development and reliance on visual–spatial coordinates at early and mid stages of practice. That is, after 1 and 4 days of practice transfer to the same visual-spatial condition was much more effective than for the transfer that necessitated the same muscle activation pattern. In fact, improvement on the motor transfer from 1 to 4 days of practice was noticed only for the group that had practiced with their non-dominant arm/hand and consequently transferred to their dominant arm/hand. This asymmetric transfer pattern was thought to be due to two factors: first, that practice even after 4 days was insufficient (at least with a more complicated dynamic task) for motor codes to sufficiently develop, and/or, second that the transfer of visual–spatial and/or motor codes is inherently limited by asymmetries between hemispheres. In right dominant participants for example, transfer from right to left has been argued to occur predominantly for intrinsic coordinates during movement preparation (Lange et al., 2004; see Criscimagna-Hemminger et al., 2003 for an alternate outcome) whereas transfer from left to right occurs mainly for extrinsic coordinates during movement execution (Lange et al, 2006).

Considering the possibility that motor codes haven't sufficiently developed in Experiment 2, Kovacs et al. had participants practice the task for 12 days, which is rather unusual in this type of experimental settings. Additionally, a "blind" transfer test was also performed in which the visual array (target display) was removed, emphasizing the reliance on motor codes. Contrary to the findings after 4 days of practice, after 12 days of practice performance on the mirror transfer test was symmetric. However, performance on the blind mirror transfer test (visual cues removed) had no effect for the right limb acquisition group but resulted in a relatively large decrement in performance for the left limb acquisition group. In other words the group that had practiced with their right (dominant) hand and consequently transferred to their left (non-dominant) hand had no performance decrements when visual cues were removed compared to when visual cues were available, indicating a strong reliance on motor codes. Performance of the left-hand acquisition group however was poorer when visual cues were removed. Considering that with visual cues available no differences were detected between the left- and right-hand acquisition groups, the results of the "blind" tests seem to indicate that motor codes cannot be effectively transferred from the non-dominant to the dominant hand. Thus, it seems that performance on a mirror transfer (with regard to the body midline) relies predominantly on motor codes for dominant to non-dominant limb transfer, whereas both motor and transformed visual–spatial codes are utilized in a transfer from non-dominant to dominant limb (Lange et al., 2004, 2006).

Additionally, imaging data suggest that in right-hand dominant performers motor representations transfer better from dominant to non-dominant limb because practice with the right arm produces representations in the left hemisphere with neural elements tuned both to the right and the left arm. In contrast, motor representations acquired during non-dominant (left) limb practice are represented in the non-dominant (right) hemisphere with neural elements that are not accessible for the control of the right arm (Criscimagna-Hemminger et al., 2003; Gazzaniga, 2000; Hlustik et al., 2002). Thus, the dominant hemisphere can effectively control the non-dominant limb but not vice versa.

The results of Kovacs et al. indicated that visual–spatial cues developed relatively early in practice and continued to be refined across 12 days of practice. Alternatively, the motor code did not appear to develop until much later in practice and appeared to be less effectively transferred from the dominant to non-dominant limb than vice versa. Importantly, the present data are consistent with a multiple code explanation for sequence production. A multiple coding explanation would argue that each code potentially adds to retention and transfer performance. After 1 and 4 days of practice the visual–spatial transfer test was performed more efficiently than the motor transfer test. However, the motor transfer test had only one valid code (motor) on which to base transfer performance. Alternatively, the visual–spatial transfer condition provided both the same visual display of the targets and the same spatial positions as were used in practice. These two codes (visual and spatial) resulted in better performance than one code (motor). Indeed, when the visual information was not provided on the blind spatial transfer test after 12 days of practice, performance was reduced to the level observed for the motor code alone. Consistent with this logic, performance on the motor transfer test, where the visual display was altered, was unaffected by the withdrawal of the visual display. In fact, on the retention test, where all codes were valid, removal of the visual display resulted in reduced performance. These data are consistent with the notion that retention and transfer performance are determined by multiple codes that act together to enhance performance rather than the pure dominance of a single, most salient code.

IMPLICATIONS FOR PRACTICE, AND CONCLUSIONS

Movement sequences comprise a large percentage of our learned movement skills and these sequences often require a substantial amount of practice to be effectively acquired. From a practical standpoint the current research provides a substantial amount of guidance in how the training of these skills can be facilitated and how important certain characteristics of training are, not only to the development of a specific skill but also to the ability of the performer to transfer or modify that skill to accommodate some new conditions or requirements. For example, the literature on contextual interference provides strong evidence that, when a group of related skills are practiced in a random order (termed random practice) during each practice session rather than practicing one skill during one training session then practicing another in a subsequent session (termed blocked practice), the time required to effectively learn the skill decreases and the memories that underpin each of the movements' segments become interrelated in a way that resists forgetting. In addition, random practice results in a substantially more flexible movement pattern so that movement sequences trained this way are more flexibly modified when transferred to new unpracticed conditions or altered to accommodate unforeseen conditions that may arise. Using blocked practice results in a very strong but specific movement production but is relatively inflexible when modifications are required.

Similarly, the literature presented on part–whole practice provides some guidelines as to when it is effective to teach a complex movement sequence in parts (a common practice in training) and when this technique is counter-productive to learning. For example, a movement sequence taught as a whole results in a movement plan that can be quite effective but is also less adaptable and is less likely to be used to facilitate the learning of other movement sequences that may share movement segments. Part–whole practice, on the other hand, formulates the movement commands in segments which can provide the building blocks for new skills. Note also that learned movement sequences can be rescaled in force, time, and amplitude to accommodate new conditions but the process of rescaling requires that the whole movement be rescaled. When only one segment of a movement sequence is rescaled, relearning of the skill would be required rather than being able to spontaneously rescale response production.

In sum, the factors discussed in this chapter shed light on how practice should be designed to facilitate the learning of simple and complex movement sequences and to engender the development of flexible patterns of movement that can be altered when situations demand modification of the learned movement sequence.

Clearly the learning of complex movement sequences is enhanced when participants impose a structure on the elements in the sequence. This structure allows the entire sequence can be produced quickly and fluidly with little or no hesitation between elements. However, while this structure allows successful transfer when changes are proportional across limb and/or homologous muscle groups are used, it severely restricts transfer when transfer conditions are nonproportional or different activation patterns are required. The sequence scaling and effector transfer findings also suggest that the way in which movement sequences are represented in memory changes across practice. Early in practice the response structure appears to be represented in a relatively abstract way resulting in scaleable, effector independent performance capabilities. Later in practice, as muscle-specific characteristics are exploited in an attempt to refine the movement pattern, the movement sequence becomes more literally represented, resulting in enhanced performance when the practice conditions are reinstated and the same muscle groups are used but less effective when circumstances require the response to be rescaled or executed using a new muscle group. In addition, the present findings suggest that the sequence structure should be considered when studying the effectiveness of various practice schemes such as contextual interference and part–whole practice.

REFERENCES

Adams, J. A. (1987). Historical review and appraisal of research on the learning, retention, and transfer of human motor skills. *Psychological Bulletin, 101*, 41–74.

Ash, D. W. and Holding, D. H. (1990). Backward versus forward chaining in the acquisition of a keyboard skill. *Human Factors, 32*, 139–146.

Bapi, R. S., Doya, K., and Harner, A. M. (2000). Evidence for effector independent and dependent representations and their differential time course of acquisition during motor sequence learning. *Experimental Brain Research, 132*(2), 149–162.

Benguere, A. P., and Cowan, H. A. (1974). Coarticulation of upper lip protrusion in French. *Phonetica, 30*(1), 41–55.

Bischoff-Grethe, A., Goedert, K. M., Willingham, D. T., and Grafton, S. T. (2004). Neural substrates of response-based sequence learning using fMRI. *Journal of Cognitive Neuroscience, 16*(1), 127–138.

Bock, O., Schneider, S., and Bloomberg, J. (2001). Conditions for interference versus facilitation during sequential sensorimotor adaptation. *Experimental Brain Research, 138*(3), 359–365.

Braden, H., Panzer, S. and Shea, C. H. (2008). The effects of sequence difficulty and practice on proportional and non-proportional transfer. *Quarterly Journal of Experimental Psychology, 61*, 1321–1339.

Brashers-Krug, T., Shadmehr, R., and Bizzi, E. (1996). Consolidation in human motor memory. *Nature, 382*, 252–255.

Castiello, U., and Stelmach, G. E. (1993). Generalized representation of handwriting: Evidence of effector independence. *Acta Psychologica, 82*(1–3), 53–68.

Criscimagna-Hemminger, S. E., Donchin, O., Gazzaniga, M. S., and Shadmehr, R. (2003). Learned dynamics of reaching movements generalize from dominant to non-dominant arm. *Journal of Neurophysiology, 89*(1), 168–176.

Fowler, C. A., and Turvey, M. T. (1978). Concept of command neurons in explanations of behavior. *Behavioral and Brain Sciences, 1*, 20–22.

Gazzaniga, M. S. (2000). Cerebral specialization and interhemispheric specialization. *Brain, 123*, 1293–1326.

Gelfand, I. M., and Tsetlin, M. (1971). Mathematical modeling of mechanisms of the central nervous system. In I. M. Gelfand, V. Gurfinkel, S. Fomin, and M. Tsetlin (Eds.), *Models of the structural-functional organization of certain biological systems* (pp. 1–22). Cambridge, MA: MIT Press.

Gentner, D. R., Larochelle, S., and Grudin, J. (1988). Lexical, sublexical, and peripheral effects in skilled typewriting. *Cognitive Psychology, 20*(4), 524–548.

Goldberg, E., Podell, K., and Lovell, M. (1994). Lateralization of frontal-lobe functions and cognitive novelty. *Journal of Neuropsychiatry and Clinical Neurosciences, 6*(4), 371–378.

Grafton, S. T., Hazeltine, E., and Ivry, R. B. (1998). Abstract and effector-specific representations of motor sequences identified with PET. *Journal of Neuroscience, 18*(22), 9420–9428.

Grafton, S. T., Hazeltine, E., and Ivry, R. B. (2002). Motor sequence learning with the nondominant left hand: A PET functional imaging study. *Experimental Brain Research, 146*(3), 369–378.

Han, D.-W., and Shea, C. H. (2008). Auditory model: Effects on learning under random and blocked practice schedules. *Research Quarterly for Exercise and Sports, 79*, 476–486.

Henningsen, H., Henningsen, B., and Gordon, A. M. (1995). Asymmetric control of bilateral isometric finger forces. *Experimental Brain Research, 105*(2), 304–311.

Henry, F. M., and Rogers, D. E. (1960). Increased response latency for complicated movements and a "memory drum" theory of neuromotor reaction. *Research Quarterly, 31*, 448–458.

Hikosaka, O., Nakahara, H., Rand, M. K., Sakai, K., Lu, X. F., Nakamura, K., et al. (1999). Parallel neural networks for learning sequential procedures. *Trends in Neurosciences*, *22*(10), 464–471.

Hlustik, P., Solodkin, A., Gullapalli, R. P., Noll, D. C., and Small, S. L. (2002). Functional lateralization of the human premotor cortex during sequential movements. *Brain and Cognition*, *49*(1), 54–62.

Holding, D. H. (1970). Approximate transfer surface. *Journal of Motor Behavior*, *8*, 1–9.

Jordan, M. I. (1995). The organization of action sequences: Evidence from a relearning task. *Journal of Motor Behavior*, *27*(2), 179–192.

Keele, S. W., Ivry, R., Mayr, U., Hazeltine, E., and Heuer, H. (2003). The cognitive and neural architecture of sequence representation. *Psychological Review*, *110*(2), 316–339.

Keele, S. W., Jennings, P., Jones, S., Caulton, D., and Cohen, A. (1995). On the Modularity of Sequence Representation. *Journal of Motor Behavior*, *27*(1), 17–30.

Kelso, J.A.S. (1981). Contrasting perspectives on order and regulation in movement. In J. Long and A. Baddeley (Eds.), *Attention and performance IX* (pp. 437–457). Hillsdale, NJ: Lawrence Erlbaum Associates.

Kelso, J. A. S., and Zanone, P. G. (2002). Coordination dynamics of learning and transfer across different effector systems. *Journal of Experimental Psychology: Human Perception and Performance*, *28*(4), 776–797.

Kelso, J. A. S., Putnam, C. A., and Goodman, D. (1983). On the nature of human interlimb coordination. *Quarterly Journal of Experimental Psychology*, *35A*, 347–375.

Klapp, S. T. (1995). Motor response programming during simple and choice reaction time: The role of practice. *Journal of Experimental Psychology: Human Perception and Performance*, *21*, 1015–1027.

Klapp, (1996). Reaction time analysis of central motor control. In H. N. Zelaznik (Ed.), *Advances in Motor Learning and Control* (pp. 13–35). Champaign, IL: Human Kinetics.

Knapp, C. G. and Dixon, W. R. (1952). Learning to juggle II: A study of whole and part methods. *Research Quarterly*, *23*, 398–401.

Kovacs, A. J., Muehlbauer, T., and Shea C. H. (2009). The coding and effector transfer of movement sequences. *Journal of Experimental Psychology: Human Perception and Performance*, *35*, 390–407.

Krakauer, J. W., Ghilardi, M. F., and Ghez, C. (1999). Independent learning of internal models for kinematic and dynamic control of reaching. *Nature Neuroscience*, *2*(11), 1026–1031, *Journal of Experimental Psychology: Human Perception and Performance*, *35(2)*, 390–407.

Lai, Q. and Shea, C. H. (1998). Generalized motor program (GMP) learning: Effects of reduced frequency of knowledge of results and practice variability. *Journal of Motor Behavior*, *30*, 51–59.

Lai, Q., Shea, C. H., Bruechert, L., and Little, M. (2002). Modeled auditory information enhances relative timing learning. *Journal of Motor Behavior*, *34*, 299–308.

Lai, Q., Shea, C. H., Wulf, G., and Wright, D. L. (2000). Optimizing generalized motor program and parameter learning. *Research Quarterly for Exercise and Sport*, *71*, 10–24.

Lange, K., Braun, C., and Godde, B. (2006). Coordinate processing during the left-to-right hand transfer investigated by EEG. *Experimental Brain Research*, *168*(4), 547–556.

Lange, R. K., Godde, B., and Braun, C. (2004). EEG correlates of coordinate processing during intermanual transfer. *Experimental Brain Research*, *159*(2), 161–171.

Langley, D. J., and Zelaznik, H. N. (1984). The acquisition of time properties associated with a sequential motor skill. *Journal of Motor Behavior*, *16*, 275–301.

Lashley, K. S. (1951). The problem of serial order in behavior. In L. A. Jeffress (Ed.), *Cerebral Mechanisms in Behavior* (pp. 112–136). New York: John Wiley & Sons.

Lee, T. D., and Magill, R. A. (1983). The locus of the contextual interference effect in motor skill acquisition. *Journal of Experimental Psychology: Learning, memory, and cognition, 9,* 730–746.

Lee, T. D., and Magill, R. A. (1985). On the nature of movement representation in memory. *British Journal of Psychology, 76,* 175–182.

Lersten, K. C. (1968). Transfer of movement components in a motor learning task. *Research Quarterly, 39,* 575–581.

Lewis, D., McAllister, D. E., and Adams, J. A. (1951). Facilitation and interference in performance on the modified mashburn apparatus: 1. The effects of varying the amount of original learning. *Journal of Experimental Psychology, 41*(4), 247–260.

MacKay, D. G. (1982). The problem of flexibility and fluency in skilled behavior. *Psychological Review, 89,* 483–506.

Malfait, N., Shiller, D. M., and Ostry, D. J. (2002). Transfer of motor learning across arm configurations. *Journal of Neuroscience, 22*(22), 9656–9660.

Melton, A. W., and von Lackum, W. J. (1941). Retroactive and proactive inhibition in retention: Evidence for a two-factor theory of retroactive inhibition. *American Journal of Psychology, 54,* 157–173.

Merton, P. A. (1972). How we control the contraction of our muscles. *Scientific American, 226,* 30–37.

Muehlbauer, T., Panzer, S., and Shea, C. H. (2007). The transfer of movement sequences: Effects of decreased and increased load. *Quarterly Journal of Experimental Psychology, 60,* 770–778.

Nissen, M. J., and Bullemer, P. (1987). Attentional requirements of learning: Evidence from performance-measures. *Cognitive Psychology, 19*(1), 1–32.

Panzer, S., Wilde, H., and Shea, C. H. (2006). Learning of similar complex movement sequences: Proactive and retroactive effects on learning. *Journal of Motor Behavior, 38*(1), 60–70.

Park, J. H., and Shea, C. H. (2002). Effector independence. *Journal of Motor Behavior, 34*(3), 253–270.

Park, J. H., and Shea, C. H. (2003). Effect of practice on effector independence. *Journal of Motor Behavior, 35*(1), 33–40.

Park, J. H., and Shea, C. H. (2005). Sequence learning: Response structure and effector transfer. *Quarterly Journal of Experimental Psychology Section a: Human Experimental Psychology, 58*(3), 387–419.

Park, J. H., Wilde, H., and Shea, C. H. (2004). Part–whole practice of movement sequences. *Journal of Motor Behavior, 36*(1), 51–61.

Povel, D. and Collard, R. (1982). Structural factors in patterned finger tapping. *Acta Psychologica, 52,* 107–123.

Proteau, L., Marteniuk, R. G., Girouard, Y., and Dugas, C. (1987). On the type of information used to control and learn an aiming movement after moderate and extensive practice. *Human Movement Science, 6,* 181–199.

Proteau, L., Marteniuk, R. G., and Levesque, L. (1992). A sensorimotor basis for motor learning: Evidence indicating specificity of practice. *Quarterly Journal of Experimental Psychology, 44,* 557–575.

Raibert, M. H. (1977). *Motor control and learning in a state space model.* Technical Report AI-M-351, Massachusetts Institute of Technology. NTIS AD-A026–960.

Rosenbaum, D. A. (1990). On choosing between movement sequences: Comments on Rose (1988). *Journal of Experimental Psychology: Human Perception and Performance, 16,* 439–444.

Rosenbaum, D. A. and Saltzman, E. (1984). A motor-program editor. In W. Prinz and A. Sanders (Eds.), *Cognition and motor processes VIII* (pp. 93–106). Berlin: Springer.

Rosenbaum, D. A., Hindorff, V., and Munro, E. M. (1986). Programming of rapid finger sequences. In H. Heuer and C. Fromm (Eds.), *Generation and Modulation of Action Patterns* (pp. 64–71). Berlin: Springer-Verlag.

Rosenbaum, D. A., Inhoff, A.W., and Gordon, A. M. (1984). Choosing between movement sequences: A hierarchical editor. *Journal of Experimental Psychology: General, 113,* 372–393.

Rosenbaum, D. A., Kenny, S., and Derr, M. A. (1983). Hierarchical control of rapid movement sequences. *Journal of Experimental Psychology: Human Perception and Performance, 9,* 86–102.

Rosenbaum, D. A., Saltzman, E., and Kingman, A. (1984). Choosing between movement sequences. In S. Kornblum and J. Requin (Eds.), *Preparatory states and processes* (pp. 119–134). Hillsdale, NJ: Lawrence Erlbaum Associates.

Rushworth, M. F. S., Krams, M., and Passingham, R. E. (2001). The attentional role of the left parietal cortex: The distinct lateralization and localization of motor attention in the human brain. *Journal of Cognitive Neuroscience, 13*(5), 698–710.

Russeler, J., and Rosler, F. (2000). Implicit and explicit learning of event sequences: evidence for distinct coding of perceptual and motor representations. *Acta Psychologica, 104*(1), 45–67.

Sainburg, R. L. (2002). Evidence for a dynamic-dominance hypothesis of handedness. *Experimental Brain Research, 142*(2), 241–258.

Schluter, N. D., Rushworth, M. F. S., Passingham, R. E., and Mills, K. R. (1998). Temporary interference in human lateral premotor cortex suggests dominance for the selection of movements: A study using transcranial magnetic stimulation. *Brain, 121,* 785–799.

Schmidt, R. A. (1975). Schema theory of discrete motor skill learning. *Psychological Review, 82*(4), 225–260.

Schmidt, R. A. (1985). The search for invariance in skilled movement behavior. *Research Quarterly for Exercise and Sport, 56*(2), 188–200.

Schmidt, R. A. (1988). *Motor control and learning.* Champaign, IL: Human Kinetics.

Schmidt, R. A. and Young, D. E. (1987). Transfer of movement control in motor learning. In S. M. Cormier and J. D. Hagman (Eds.), *Transfer of learning* (pp 47–79), Orlando, FL: Academic Press.

Schumacher, E. H., Elston, P. A., and D'Esposito, M. (2003). Neural evidence for representation-specific response selection. *Journal of Cognitive Neuroscience, 15*(8), 1111–1121.

Shea, C. H., and Wulf, G. (2005). Schema theory: A critical appraisal and reevaluation. *Journal of Motor Behavior, 37*(2), 85–101.

Shea, C. H., Wulf, G., Park, J.-H., and Gaunt, B. (2001). Effects of an auditory model on the learning of relative and absolute timing. *Journal of Motor Behavior, 33,* 127–138.

Shea, J. B. and Morgan, R. B. (1979). Contextual interference effects on the acquisition, retention, and transfer of a motor skill. *Journal of Experimental Psychology: Human Learning and Memory, 5,* 179–187.

Shea, J. B. and Zimny, S. T. (1983). Context effects in memory and learning movement information. In R. A. Magill (Ed.), *Memory and control of action* (pp. 145–166). Amsterdam: North Holland.

Sternberg, S., Monsell, S., Knoll, R. L., and Wright, C. E. (1978). The latency and duration of rapid movement sequences: Comparisons of speech and typewriting. In G. E. Stelmach (Ed.), *Information processing in motor control and learning* (pp. 117–152). New York: Academic Press.

Templet, E., and Hebert, E. (2002, March). *A meta-analysis of part–whole research on motor skill acquisition and learning.* Paper presented at the annual meeting of the American Association of Health, Physical Education, Recreation, and Dance in San Diego.

Underwood, B. J. (1957). Interference and forgetting. *Psychological Review, 64,* 49–60.

van Mier, H. I., and Petersen, S. E. (2006). Intermanual transfer effects in sequential tactuomotor learning: Evidence for effector independent coding. *Neuropsychologia, 44*(6), 939–949.

Verwey, W. B. (1994). Evidence for the development of concurrent processing in a sequential keypressing task. *Acta Psychologica, 85*(3), 245–262.

Verwey, W. B. (1995). A forthcoming key press can be selected while earlier ones are executed. *Journal of Motor Behavior, 27*(3), 275–284.

Verwey, W. B. (1996). Buffer loading and chunking in sequential key pressing. *Journal of Experimental Psychology: Human Perception, and Performance, 22,* 544–562.

Verwey, W. B. (1999). Evidence for a multistage model of practice in a sequential movement task. *Journal of Experimental Psychology: Human Perception and Performance, 25*(6), 1693–1708.

Verwey, W. B. (2001). Concatenating familiar movement sequences: The versatile cognitive processor. *Acta Psychologica, 106*(1–2), 69–95.

Verwey, W. B. (2003). Effect of sequence length on the execution of familiar keying sequences: Lasting segmentation and preparation? *Journal of Motor Behavior, 35*(4), 343–354.

Verwey, W. B., and Wright, D. L. (2004). Effector-independent and effector-dependent learning in a discrete sequence production task. *Psychological Research, 68,* 64–70.

Walter, C. B., and Swinnen, S. P. (1994). The formation and dissolution of "bad habits" during the acquisition of coordination skills. In S. P. Swinnen, H. Heuer, J. Massion, and P. Casaer (Eds.), *Interlimb coordination: Neural, dynamical, and cognitive constraints* (pp. 491–513). San Diego, CA: Academic Press.

Watters, R. G. (1992). Retention of human sequenced behavior following forward chaining, backward chaining, and whole task training procedures. *Journal of Human Movement Studies, 22,* 117–129.

Whitacre, C. A., and Shea, C. H. (2000). Performance and learning of generalized motor programs: Relative (GMP) and absolute (parameter) errors. *Journal of Motor Behavior, 32,* 163–175.

Wightman, D. C., and Lintern, G. (1985). Part-task training strategies in simulated carrier landing final-approach training. *Human Factors, 29,* 245–254.

Wilde, H., and Shea, C. H. (2006). Proportional and nonproportional transfer of movement sequences. *Quarterly Journal of Experimental Psychology, 59*(9), 1626–1647.

Wilde, H., Magnuson, C. E., and Shea, C. H. (2005). Random and blocked practice of movement sequences: Differential effects on response structure and movement speed. *Research Quarterly for Exercise and Sport, 76,* 416–425.

Willingham, D. B., Wells, L. A., Farrell, J. M., and Stemwedel, M. E. (2000). Implicit motor sequence learning is represented in response locations. *Memory & Cognition, 28*(3), 366–375.

Wright, C. E. (1990). Generalized motor programs: Reexamining claims of effector independence in writing. In M. Jeannerod (Ed.), *Attention and performance XIII* (pp. 294–320). Hillsdale, NJ: Lawrence Erlbaum Associates.

9

Use of, Reaction to, and Efficacy of Observation Rehearsal Training

Enhancing Skill Retention on a Complex Command-and-Control Simulation Task

Anton J. Villado, Eric Anthony Day,
Winfred Arthur, Jr., Paul R. Boatman,
Vanessa Kowollik, Alok Bhupatkar,
and Winston Bennett, Jr.

INTRODUCTION

As noted in other chapters in this volume (e.g., Chapters 1, 3, 11, and 13), the extant empirical research on skill decay is limited. It is therefore not surprising to find a near absence of literature devoted to *enhancing* skill retention on cognitively complex tasks during periods of nonuse. One possible method of enhancing the retention of trained skills during a period of nonuse is repeating the initial training some time during the nonuse period (tantamount to shortening the nonuse interval). Although hands-on retraining may certainly enhance retention (Schendel and Hagman, 1982), employing such a program could be cost prohibitive. Research on alternative refresher training interventions that do not involve hands-on practice is limited and researchers and training professionals alike have little empirical guidance upon which to base the design of such refresher training programs.

Technological advances may provide the delivery of alternative types of refresher training. Internet-based training may be a more feasible and viable alternative to hands-on refresher training. Thus, there is a pressing need for research that introduces and tests training interventions designed to enhance skill retention during periods of nonuse, especially interventions that do not require full-scale hands-on retraining during the nonuse interval. Consequently, the purpose of the present study was to assess the use of post-acquisition observational rehearsal in maximizing retention and facilitating skill transfer and reacquisition after an *extended* period of nonuse using a complex command-and-control microworld simulation.

Given the lack of guidance in enhancing skill retention during periods of nonuse, the present study sought to accomplish four goals concerning a posttraining internet-based observational rehearsal training intervention. The first goal was to assess whether trainees will voluntarily engage in rehearsal if such an opportunity were available. Simply making a training program available does not mean that trainees will avail themselves of that training. A second goal was to determine whether trainees who engage in voluntary observational refresher training could be differentiated from those who do not. The ability to distinguish between trainees who will and will not has implications for both selection and the assignment of trainees to this type of training. The third goal was to document trainees' reactions to the internet-based observational refresher training. Finally, and most importantly, the fourth goal was to test the effects of the observational refresher training on various training outcomes. Specifically, we were interested in determining the efficacy of observational refresher training on skill retention, transfer, and reacquisition. In summary, our objective was to provide both researchers and training professionals with some guidance on alternatives to hands-on practice for the purpose of facilitating performance on a complex task after prolonged nonuse. So, using 192 paid participants who trained for approximately 10 hours on a command-and-control microworld simulation, we examined the level of participation, individual differences that were related to participation, and the reaction to a voluntary observational rehearsal nonuse training intervention. We also examined the efficacy of the voluntary observational based training intervention in enhancing skill retention in comparison to mandatory and no observational training. We found that only a small percentage (29 percent) of trainees utilized the voluntary training. Non-ability rather than ability-based individual differences were better able to differentiate those who availed themselves of the observational based training intervention from those who did not. In general, reactions to the internet-based refresher training were positive. Finally, the efficacy of the training was dependent on the training outcome. The observational based training intervention improved training transfer, but not retention nor reacquisition. The implications of our findings are discussed.

Posttraining Rehearsal

The progressive deterioration of knowledge and skills when they are not used over extended periods of time is a robust phenomenon (Arthur, Bennett, Stanush, and McNelly, 1998; Arthur et al., 1997). In addition, longer periods of nonuse are associated with lower levels of retention. One obvious strategy to enhance skill retention is to provide opportunities to perform the task during the nonuse interval, thereby shortening the interval between training and the time when the skill is used. However, performing a trained skill may not be possible or feasible for a variety of organizational, logistical, structural, and administrative reasons (Ford, Quiñones, Sego, and Speer Sorra, 1992; Noe, 1986; Peters and O'Connor, 1980). By their very nature, complex tasks introduce logistical constraints that may preclude hands-on-training during a nonuse period. For example, first responders may experience rather long nonuse intervals following training. Hands-on training may not only be costly (e.g., cost of support staff, and equipment), but also dangerous, given the environments in which hands-on training is likely to occur (e.g., mountain rescue operations, fire fighting). Therefore, some research has focused on the use of alternative strategies, such as mental rehearsal or imaginary practice (Driskell, Copper, and Moran, 1994).

Technology may provide a more feasible and viable alternative to hands-on refresher training. Logistical constraints could be eliminated or at least reduced by providing trainees with a train-anywhere-anytime option via internet-based training. Using internet-based training, trainees would be able to engage in training according to their own schedules and at their own pace. However, despite the apparent logistical advantages of internet-based training, it is not hands-on training. So, unless the task being trained requires human–computer interaction, internet-based training will not be capable of providing trainees with hands-on training. Therefore, other alternatives to hands-on training must be used when the trained skill does not require a computer. One such alternative is behavior modeling training or observational rehearsal.

Based on work in social learning, observational learning, and modeling (Bandura, 1986; Caroll and Bandura, 1990), learning by watching others (i.e., behavioral models) perform a task has shown positive effects for knowledge, skill, and attitude change within the context of training (Baldwin, 1992; Burke and Day, 1986; Custers et al., 1999; Shebilske, Jordan, Goettl, and Paulus, 1998; Taylor, Russ-Eft, and Chan, 2005). Ellis, Ganzach, Castle, and Sekely (2010) have obtained similar effects for watching filmed after-action reviews. The efficacy of observational learning combined with the technologies of the internet makes it a viable and possibly cost-effective alternative to other nonuse interval training interventions (e.g., practice or retraining during the nonuse interval). Rather than be required to repeat a costly and time-consuming training program or even a booster program, an observational learning training intervention would only require trainees to view models perform a task on a personal computer (e.g., see Ellis et al., 2010). Therefore, the purpose of the present study was to investigate the efficacy of two observational rehearsal training interventions (i.e., mandatory rehearsal and voluntary rehearsal compared to no rehearsal). Specifically, we sought (a) to investigate whether trainees would voluntarily train if an observational rehearsal training intervention were made available, and (b) to assess their reaction to the observational rehearsal training intervention.

Although making training available to trainees anywhere and at anytime is feasible with current technology, simply making training available may not yield desired outcomes (e.g., modified performance, knowledge, or attitudes). Research focused on learner control has found that trainees often fail to effectively use the control they are afforded (Schmidt and Ford, 2003; Steinberg, 1989; Tennyson, Christenson, and Park, 1984). When given the choice of whether or not to spend time training, there is great variability in those who do and do not train (Brown, 2001). In a study where trainees were brought to a central training facility, and provided with the time and resources (i.e., a computer with access to the training materials), Brown (2001) found that some employees skipped over practice opportunities or terminated their practice early and opted to leave the training facility. In fact, individual differences accounted for a significant portion of the variability in the amount of time trainees' trained. Specifically, achievement motivation and self-efficacy were related to various metrics of time spent training (Brown, 2001). Thus, simply providing training does not mean that trainees will take the opportunity to learn. The trainees' choice to engage in voluntary training is influenced by individual differences.

Recognizing poor use of time by trainees when given control over their learning, Schmidt and Ford (2003) identified three possible options to account for individual differences in training. First, one could ignore individual differences altogether and design training so that it provides guidance to the learner. A second approach would be to provide customized training tailored to each trainee based on their unique individual differences. And finally, Schmidt and Ford suggested that trainers could focus on changing the trainee (e.g., modifying trainee individual differences so that they foster voluntary practice). While these solutions may be tenable to training professionals at varying degrees, they all rest on the assumption that individual differences will demonstrate predictable relationships with trainees' decisions to engage in or ignore opportunities to voluntarily train. Therefore, a third purpose of this study was to assess whether specified individual differences could distinguish those who would and would not avail themselves of the training. We accomplished this by examining the role of achievement motivation, and self-efficacy (Brown, 2001), in addition to conscientiousness, openness to experience, cognitive ability, declarative knowledge, and level of skill before a period of nonuse. The theoretical basis for examining these non-ability individual differences in terms of training motivation stems from choice. That is, in contrast to ability, non-ability-based individual differences play a critical role in the decisions made by trainees, namely decisions of direction, level, and persistence of one's effort. Our general hypothesis was that non-ability individual differences will differentiate trainees who availed themselves of training from those would not. On the other hand, these two groups would not differ in terms of their mean standing on ability variables.

Effectiveness of Observational Rehearsal

A limitation of the skill decay literature in particular, and the training and educational literature in general, is the tendency to treat learning (i.e., skill acquisition), retention, transfer, and reacquisition as separate phenomena that are subsequently studied independently (Arthur et al., 1998; Schmidt and Bjork, 1992). In highlighting the limitations of this approach, Schmidt and Bjork (1992), for example, showed that training interventions that maximize performance during training may not necessarily be the most effective with regard to long-term outcomes. That is, training interventions that maximize skill acquisition may not necessarily lead to the best retention and transfer compared to other protocols that may yield slower speeds of acquisition. Thus, these authors argued that acquisition, retention, and transfer are inseparable and need to be considered together when conducting research on skill acquisition. In a similar vein, although skill transfer to novel performance demands can be distinguished conceptually from skill retention, transfer and retention are logically interconnected given that the need for skill transfer may arise after a period of nonuse. For instance, it is not difficult to envision scenarios where the sudden need to make use of a skill under novel circumstances arises when the skill has gone unutilized for an extensive period. Such is frequently the case in military, emergency rescue, and disaster relief operations.

A critical decision in behavior modeling training is whether the model should be of positive, negative, or both positive and negative behaviors. Although some research has suggested that including examples of negative models (i.e., ineffective performance) may be detrimental to learning (Bandura and Walters, 1963; Berliner, 1969), other research has shown that the inclusion of negative models in combination with positive models can enhance learning, particularly transfer (Baldwin, 1992; Taylor et al., 2005; Trimble, Nathan, and Decker, 1991). There are several reasons why including negative models may be beneficial to learning. For instance, including negative models promotes the "unlearning" of pre-existing negative habits and helps trainees avoid using ineffective strategies (Russell, Wexley, and Hunter, 1984). In addition, including negative models generates task-related interference, which forces the learner to more actively concentrate and refine information to comprehend underlying principles of the task (Battig, 1972, 1979). In a similar vein, including negative models enhances the distinctiveness of key learning points and the recognition of important behaviors (Baldwin, 1992; Jentsch, Bowers, and Salas, 2001). Based on the previous empirical support for observational learning and the use of both negative and positive models in facilitating transfer, we tested the general hypothesis that trainees would benefit from posttraining observational rehearsal. Specifically, in the voluntary and mandatory rehearsal conditions, trainees rehearsed by watching video clips of both effective and ineffective performance of the trained task.

METHOD

Participants

The sample for the present study was the 192 participants described in Villado et al. (Chapter 3 of this volume) and Day et al. (Chapter 11 of this volume). This sample (77 percent young adult males) was obtained from the campuses and surrounding communities of Texas A&M University and the University of Oklahoma.

Paper–Pencil Measures

Individual differences. Measures of conscientiousness, openness to experience, achievement motivation, self-efficacy, cognitive ability, and declarative knowledge were the same measures reported in Chapter 11, and so the reader is referred to Chapter 11 for a comprehensive and detailed description of these measures. Goldberg's 100 Unipolar Markers (Goldberg, 1992) was used to assess personality. Again, for purposes of this study, only the 20 items for conscientiousness and 20 items for openness to experience were examined. A 17-item scale adapted from Elliot and Church (1997) was used to assess the three achievement motivation dimensions—mastery, performance approach, and performance avoidance. Self-efficacy was measured using a 12-item measure based on items from scales used in several previous studies (e.g., Bell and Kozlowski, 2002; Martocchio and Judge, 1997; Nease, Mudgett, and Quiñones, 1999) as well as items developed specifically for this study. Cognitive ability was measured using the Raven's Advanced Progressive Matrices (APM; Raven, Raven, and Court, 1998). Finally, declarative knowledge was assessed using a 21-item 3-alternative test developed for this study.

Reaction Measure

Trainees' reactions to the internet-based observational rehearsal, which consisted primarily of watching online training videos, were assessed using a 16-item measure. The reaction measure included items that assessed both the trainees' affective and utility reactions, as well as the trainees' reactions to the design of the training videos. The items were responded to on a 1–5-point scale. The measure also included 4 open-ended questions that asked trainees' to report what they liked most and least about the videos, and why they did or did not view the training videos.

Performance Task—Jane's Fleet Command

As described in Chapter 3, the performance task was Jane's Fleet Command (Sonalysts, Inc., 2004, Air Force Research Laboratory ver. 1.55) which is a PC-based real-time micro-simulation of modern naval warfare featuring ships, aircraft, submarines, and airbases on land. It provides the user with the ability to wargame carrier battle group strategy, tactics, and resource allocations and enables flexible, immersed, and interactive training. Fleet Command is considered an ecologically valid laboratory analogue of the types of cognitive, information processing, and decision-making tasks present in operational command-and-control environments in military, civilian first-responder, and other similar settings. See Villado et al. (Chapter 3 of this volume) for a detailed description of Jane's Fleet Command.

Five missions (Missions A–E) were presented to trainees during the acquisition phase. These missions were progressively more difficult and complex. Trainees also completed the same missions in the same order during reacquisition. The same mission was used for the last test mission of acquisition, the test of retention, and the final test mission of reacquisition. After the test of retention and the last mission of the reacquisition phase, trainees completed a test of transfer (a sixth mission, Mission F). The test of transfer consisted of a very different mission involving both novel and over-whelming performance demands. Villado et al. (Chapter 3 of this volume) provides a detailed description of the training and test missions.

Procedure

Prior to training (acquisition phase), trainees completed the measures of personality and cognitive ability. During acquisition, participants completed approximately 10 hours of training on Fleet Command. Upon completion of the acquisition phase, trainees completed measures of achievement motivation, self-efficacy, and declarative knowledge, and continued their participation in their assigned observational rehearsal conditions. Trainees were assigned to one of two posttraining, observational rehearsal conditions—mandatory rehearsal ($n = 60$), voluntary rehearsal ($n = 76$)—and a control or no-rehearsal ($n = 56$) condition.

Trainees in the mandatory condition returned to the lab once a week during the 8-week nonuse interval to view a different after-action-review refresher video. These videos were developed to refresh trainees on specific aspects of Fleet Command (e.g., weapons employment, issuing orders, RADAR and Airborne Early Warning aircraft, RADAR jamming, and weapons use near friendly and neutral forces). The duration of these videos was 10 minutes on average. Each video began with an example of maladaptive or ineffective performance, followed by an explanation of why it was maladaptive or ineffective, and an example of adaptive or effective performance. The videos showed trainees the Fleet Command game screen, and trainees could see specific actions being executed while hearing (through headsets) a narrator describe and explain the actions. Trainees not only viewed the actions, they also viewed the consequences associated with the actions.

Trainees in the voluntary condition were given a logon identification number, which gave them internet access to the same after-action-review refresher videos. Although voluntary trainees had unlimited access to the videos, they were constrained to accessing the videos in sequential order. For example, once the first video was accessed and viewed, both the first and second videos were then available. Once the second video was accessed and viewed, the first three videos were then available, and so on. Trainees in the voluntary condition were not paid for their time spent viewing the videos. However, voluntary trainees were offered bonuses of $75 and $50 for the two highest scores achieved on the first mission performed upon immediately returning from the 8-week nonpractice period.

Trainees in the no-rehearsal condition were not given access to the videos nor were they made aware that the videos existed. Trainees in the no-rehearsal condition completed the acquisition phase and did not have an opportunity to rehearse during the 8-week nonuse interval.

Following the nonuse interval, trainees repeated the last mission of the acquisition phase (i.e., skill retention), followed by a novel mission (i.e., skill transfer). Trainees then repeated a single tutorial (i.e., tutorial review) and then completed approximately 4 hours of training (i.e., skill reacquisition). At the end of reacquisition, trainees repeated a variant of the novel mission (i.e., second test of skill transfer).

RESULTS

Engagement in Voluntary Observational Rehearsal

As previously stated, trainees were assigned to one of two posttraining, observational rehearsal conditions—mandatory rehearsal ($n = 60$) and voluntary rehearsal ($n = 76$)—as well as a control no-rehearsal ($n = 56$) condition. The first research question sought the answer to whether trainees would voluntarily train if training were made available. An evaluation of the amount of time trainees assigned to the voluntary condition spent watching the videos revealed a wide range of values (min = 0 minutes, max = 115 minutes). Only 22 of the 76 trainees (29 percent) in the voluntary condition actually viewed the videos.

Individual Differences Associated with Participation in Voluntary Observational Rehearsal

The second objective of this study was to determine whether specified individual differences would differentiate those who did and did not avail themselves of the voluntary training. Table 9.1 presents the descriptive statistics and standardized mean differences between trainees in the voluntary observational rehearsal condition who did and did not view the refresher videos. The general hypothesis that trainees would differ on non-ability variables (i.e., conscientiousness, openness to experience, achievement motivation, and self-efficacy) but not on ability measures (i.e., cognitive ability, declarative knowledge, skill prior to the nonuse interval) was partially supported. The overall standardized mean difference for non-ability measures was $d = 0.33$ whereas the standardized mean difference for ability measures was $d = 0.09$. However, not all non-ability measures demonstrated statistically different means across the two groups. Specifically, participants who volunteered to view the refresher videos described themselves as having a statistically significantly higher self-efficacy ($t[74] = 2.29, p < .05, d = 0.59$) than those who did not view the refresher videos. None of the other non-ability individual differences yielded statistically significant mean differences between those who did and did not view the videos. It is worth noting that although moderately large, the fairly small sample sizes precluded their achieving statistical significance.

TABLE 9.1

Descriptive Statistics, Standardized Mean Differences and Correlations for Non-Ability and Ability Measures and Selected Fleet Command Sessions

Measure	Did View Videos		Did Not View Videos		
	M	**SD**	**M**	**SD**	**d^a**
Non-Ability					
Personality					
Conscientiousness	128.41	18.38	120.89	21.98	0.37
Openess to Experience	134.00	13.78	131.24	18.32	0.17
Goal Orientation[b]					
Approach	3.69	0.87	3.48	0.87	0.24
Avoidance	2.39	0.85	2.31	0.83	0.10
Mastery	3.93	0.70	3.60	0.63	0.50*
Self–Efficacy[c]	3.98	0.58	3.61	0.67	0.59*
Average Non-Ability Effect					**0.33**
Ability					
Cognitive Ability	26.18	4.58	26.81	4.56	-0.14
Declarative Knowledge[c]	17.49	1.43	17.22	2.06	0.15
Skill Acquisition[d]	24.66	19.34	19.28	21.38	0.26
Average Ability Effect					**0.09**

Did view videos n = 22; did not view videos n = 54. [a]In computing the *d*s, the *did view videos* condition was treated as the experimental and the *did not view videos* condition as the control. [b]Mean of three administrations (Sessions 1, 4, and 9). [c]Third administration (Session 9). [d]Mission effectiveness score in the last acquisition session (session 9). * *p* < .05, two-tailed.

Reactions of Those Who Engaged in Voluntary Observational Rehearsal

The third research question sought to assess trainees' reactions to the voluntary observational rehearsal training intervention. Of the 22 trainees who voluntarily viewed the observational rehearsal videos, 18 provided their reactions to the videos. Affective reactions to the refresher videos were neutral (mean = 3.00, *SD* = 1.14). However, trainees found the refresher videos useful (mean = 3.56, *SD* = 0.59) and well designed (mean = 4.13, *SD* = 0.41). Trainees also responded to several open-ended questions. Responses to the open-ended questions were content coded by several of this chapter's authors. Trainees who watched the refresher videos reported that "being too busy" (44 percent) or "forgot to access the videos" (33 percent) were the primary reasons they did not watch the refresher videos. Trainees who did watch the refresher videos reported that the reasons they chose to watch them were to "refresh their memory" (56 percent) or "to learn" (33 percent). In response to the question, "What did you like most about the videos," 56 percent said the videos refreshed their memory, and 33 percent said they were easy to understand. Finally, in response to the question, "What did you like least about the videos," 61 percent of the participants who watched the videos said they were boring, and 17 percent said they contained no new information.

Effectiveness of Observational Rehearsal

The fourth and final objective of the study was to assess the effectiveness of the posttraining observational rehearsal videos. As previously stated, only 22 of the 76 trainees (29 percent) assigned to the voluntary condition actually viewed the videos. Although the 54 trainees who chose not to watch the videos were initially assigned to the voluntary condition, not having watched the videos meant that they were best described as being trainees like those in the no-rehearsal condition. Therefore, in evaluating the effectiveness of observational rehearsal, we combined the 54 trainees from the voluntary condition who did not view the videos with the trainees assigned to the no-rehearsal condition, resulting in the following sample sizes—mandatory rehearsal $n = 60$, voluntary rehearsal $n = 22$, and no-rehearsal $n = 110$. Subsequent analyses are based on these condition assignments. Table 9.2 presents the descriptive statistics and effect sizes for the observational rehearsal conditions for Sessions 9 through 16. There were no significant differences among the conditions at the end of acquisition (Session 9) before the rehearsal manipulation occurred, $F (2, 189) = 1.58$, $p > .10$, $\eta^2 = .02$.

We tested for differences in skill retention (Session 10), transfer (Session 11), and immediate reacquisition (Session 12) using ANCOVAs with the last acquisition session (Session 9) as the covariate. In contrast to our general hypothesis that trainees would benefit from observational rehearsal, the results showed no statistically significant differences regarding skill retention, $F (2, 188) = 0.36$, $p > .10$, $\eta^2 = .01$, or immediate reacquisition, $F (2, 188) = 0.36$, $p > .10$, $\eta^2 = .01$. However, the results indicated a significant effect for transfer performance, $F [2, 188] = 3.23$, $p < .05$, $\eta^2 = .04$. Results of a planned comparison supported our hypothesized advantage of observational rehearsal over no rehearsal in terms of skill transfer, showing that trainees who viewed the rehearsal videos (mandatory and voluntary conditions combined) obtained

TABLE 9.2

Descriptive Statistics and Effect Sizes for the Nonuse Rehearsal Conditions on Fleet Command Retention, Transfer, and Reacquisition Sessions

	Mandatory		Voluntary		No		
Session	Mean	SD	Mean	SD	Mean	SD	η^2
Acquisition							
9_E	17.61	18.71	24.66	19.34	16.73	18.78	.02
Retention							
10_E	13.34	18.90	18.12	17.15	15.60	17.34	.01
Transfer							
11_F	−10.26	14.26	−11.42	16.38	−16.70	16.86	.04*
Reacquisition							
12_B	21.26	25.34	19.05	18.54	19.98	19.01	.00
13_C	25.82	34.58	26.35	37.39	16.45	29.27	.02
14_D	7.52	33.26	4.64	31.50	3.16	44.49	.00
15_E	21.23	18.20	21.27	17.31	21.80	17.22	.00
Transfer							
16_F	−6.14	10.90	−9.73	12.07	−13.10	15.13	.05*

$N = 192$. The rehearsal manipulation began after Session 9. Mandatory Rehearsal ($n = 60$), Voluntary Rehearsal ($n = 22$), and No-Rehearsal ($n = 110$). Subscript uppercase letters indicate the mission performed in each session. *$p < .05$.

higher transfer performance scores than trainees who did not participate in observational rehearsal, $t(190) = 2.63$, $p < .01$, $d = 0.38$.

To examine the effects of observational rehearsal on reacquisition, we conducted a 3 (rehearsal condition) × 4 (training session) mixed ANOVA for Sessions 12 through 15. The main effect for training session was statistically significant, $F(3, 567) = 10.33$, $p < .01$, $\eta^2 = .05$. Neither the main effect for rehearsal condition, $F(2, 189) = 1.08$, $p > .10$, $\eta^2 = .01$, nor the interaction between rehearsal and session were statistically significant, $F(3, 567) = 1.58$, $p > .10$, $\eta^2 = .00$.

Finally, to examine the stability of the transfer performance effects observed on the first test of skill transfer (i.e., Session 11), we conducted two ANCOVAs on the second transfer mission (i.e., Session 16). The first ANCOVA used mission effectiveness scores from Session 9 as the covariate (the same covariate used previously). The results revealed a statistically significant difference among the rehearsal conditions, $F(2, 188) = 5.06$, $p < .01$, $\eta^2 = .05$. The second ANCOVA used mission effectiveness scores from Session 11 as the covariate and it also revealed a statistically significant effect, F (2, 188) = 3.33, $p < .05$, $\eta^2 = .03$. Similar to the effects from the first transfer mission, the results of a planned comparison showed that trainees who viewed the rehearsal videos (mandatory and voluntary conditions combined) obtained higher transfer performance scores than trainees who did not participate in observational rehearsal, t (190) = 3.02, $p < .01$, $d = .44$.

DISCUSSION

The purpose of the present study was to assess the effectiveness (and efficacy) of an internet-based observational rehearsal training protocol intended to enhance skill retention, transfer, reacquisition, and adaptability on a cognitively complex task. The first conclusion that we draw from our results pertains to the expectation that individuals would voluntarily participate in post-training rehearsal via the internet. The fact that only 29 percent of the trainees in our voluntary condition actually made use of the online videos was contrary to this expectation. With the advent of computer-based training, and the ease with which it can be delivered online (Sitzman, Kraiger, Stewart, and Wisher, 2006), providing opportunities for refresher training via the internet, at first glance, appears to be a viable option. However, the extent to which individuals will want to make use of such opportunities on a voluntary basis is a separate matter to consider. These findings parallel the conclusions drawn from previous research in the learner control literature (Schmidt and Ford, 2003; Steinberg, 1989; Tennyson et al., 1984). These results support the conclusion made by Schmidt and Ford (2003) that trainees often fail to effectively use the control they are afforded. Despite this rather dismal view of trainee participation in volitional training programs, we must point out that motivational theories of behavior may prove helpful in designing effective training programs with high degrees of learner control. Issues pertaining to motivation are particularly salient, and applying reinforcement (Skinner, 1969) and value-expectancy (Vroom, 1964) theories of motivation to address trainee participation in voluntary refresher training is a worthwhile avenue of future research. We acknowledge that although trainees in the voluntary condition were informed of and awarded $75 and $50 for the top two scorers on the retention test mission (i.e., Session 10), one could argue that our study did not provide the same sense of importance as an actual organizational training situation. Consequently, our study may have underestimated voluntary participation in online refresher training. Hence, this is an issue that warrants future research.

Second, non-ability individual differences differentiated those who did versus those who did not volunteer to engage in the observational rehearsal refresher videos. Ability-based individual differences were similar in both groups (i.e., those who did not volunteer to engage in the observational rehearsal refresher videos). This is consistent with our general hypothesis that non-ability individual differences (versus ability individual differences) would predict trainees' volunteering behavior. These findings provide several possibilities for the design and implementation of training, as noted by Schmidt and Ford (2003). Based upon the non-ability individual differences trainees, training may be matched to the trainee in order to maximize the utility of training. Whether this is in the form of assigning trainees to different delivery methods (mandatory versus voluntary rehearsal) or selecting trainees based on their propensity to engage in voluntary training, individual differences may be used to mitigate the low levels of engagement in volitional training.

The third conclusion that we draw from our results concerns trainees' reactions to an observational rehearsal intervention. Trainees had generally positive reactions to the rehearsal videos. Although this is encouraging, these results must be interpreted in the context of the rather low participation rates. That is, despite the positive evaluation of the refresher videos, relatively few trainees opted to view the videos. Therefore, if rehearsal interventions such as that presented here are used in operational settings, one may expect positive reactions by those who volunteer to use them; however, very few individuals may opt to use them.

The final conclusion that we draw from our data is that the observational rehearsal refresher videos had different effects on different training outcomes. These different effects on different training outcomes supports the statement that retention, transfer, and reacquisition are not surrogates of each other and cannot be used interchangeably (Arthur, Bennett, Edens, and Bell, 2003). Specifically, although our results did not support the general hypothesis that trainees would benefit from observational rehearsal during the extended nonpractice interval, they did demonstrate consistent benefits for observational rehearsal in terms of transfer performance. In the context of this manipulation, our objective was to examine the effectiveness of posttraining observational rehearsal as a means of enhancing skill retention and promoting transfer and reacquisition. We were particularly interested in how our observational rehearsal strategy, which combined both positive and negative models, facilitated transfer to a scenario involving novel performance demands. Posttraining observational rehearsal did not yield consistently significant benefits across tests of retention, transfer, and reacquisition. Specifically, posttraining observational rehearsal only had a positive effect on transfer performance, that is, adaptability. This beneficial effect on adaptability is consistent with Baldwin's (1992) research on mixed models in interpersonal-skills training, as well as Taylor et al.'s (2005) meta-analysis of the behavior modeling literature. Because previous research on the use of mixed models has been limited to interpersonal-skills training (Taylor et al., 2005), our use of a complex command-and-control task is a meaningful contribution to the extant literature.

In addition, although observational rehearsal did not have a beneficial effect on skill retention and reacquisition, the fact that it did not have a detrimental effect is noteworthy, because scholars of instructional design occasionally argue that incorporating both negative and positive models will detract from simple reproduction of learned skills (Baldwin, 1992). Thus, recognizing that we did not manipulate the presence and absence of negative models in our observational rehearsal videos because we did not have a positive model-only condition, the use of mixed-model observational rehearsal could be a viable means of facilitating adaptive performance (i.e., transfer) without degrading skill retention and reacquisition (i.e., reproduction). In summary, to echo Arthur et al.'s (2003) conclusions that different training evaluation criteria cannot be used interchangeably, the results of the rehearsal manipulations lead us to emphasize the importance of matching or ensuring that training interventions are targeted at specific outcomes.

Implications for Practice, and Conclusions

Given the lack of empirical research on skill decay and the near absence of literature devoted to enhancing skill retention on cognitively complex tasks during periods of nonuse, the study presented in this chapter provides guidance on alternatives to hands-on practice for the purpose of facilitating complex task performance after prolonged periods of nonuse. By utilizing the internet, internet-based observational rehearsal training may ostensibly be a viable intervention to enhance skill retention for complex tasks during extended periods of nonuse. However, as documented in this study, control over when and how often to participate in voluntary training may not and probably will not result in trainees utilizing the training resources available to them during a period of nonuse. Low levels of participation may therefore call into question the utility of implementing such a training intervention intended to enhance complex skill retention during a period of nonuse. Fortunately, as theory would suggest, non-ability individual differences (in contrast to ability-based individual differences) differentiated those who did versus those who did not participate in voluntary training. Training professionals may improve the utility of voluntary refresher training by considering those non-ability individual differences related to engaging in voluntary training. Whether non-ability individual differences are used to hire or place individuals into jobs, intentionally modified by the organization, or used to place individuals in voluntary (versus mandatory) training, these individual differences offer critical points of leverage for organizations.

The final objective of the present study was to assess the comparative effectiveness of post-acquisition observational rehearsal in maximizing retention and facilitating skill transfer and reacquisition after an *extended* period of nonuse using a complex command-and-control microworld simulation. When considering how to conduct training with the dual purpose of minimizing skill decay and promoting adaptability after extensive periods of nonuse, our findings suggest that training professionals should consider incorporating multiple techniques that separately target retention and adaptability. One intervention may not serve both purposes well, and finding potent combinations of interventions to address the dual purpose of facilitating retention and adaptability would appear to be a worthwhile challenge for future research.

REFERENCES

Arthur, W. Jr., Bennett, W. Jr., Edens, P. S., and Bell, S. T. (2003). Effectiveness of training in organizations: A meta-analysis of design and evaluation features. *Journal of Applied Psychology, 88*, 234–245.

Arthur, W. Jr., Bennett, W. Jr., Stanush, P. L., and McNelly, T. L. (1998). Factors that influence skill decay and retention: A quantitative review and analysis. *Human Performance, 11*, 57–101.

Arthur, W. Jr., Day, E. A., Bennett, W. Jr., McNelly, T. L., and Jordan, J. A. (1997). Dyadic versus individual training protocols: Loss and reacquisition of a complex skill. *Journal of Applied Psychology, 82*, 783–791.

Baldwin, T. P. (1992). Effects of alternative modeling strategies on outcomes of interpersonal skills training. *Personnel Psychology, 77*, 147–154.

Bandura, A. (1986). *Social foundations of thought and action: A social cognitive theory.* Englewood Cliffs, NJ: Prentice-Hall.

Bandura, A., and Walters, R. (1963). *Social learning and personality development.* New York: Holt, Rinehart, and Winston.

Battig, W. F. (1972). Intratask interference as a source of facilitation in transfer and retention. In R. F. Thompson and J. F. Voss (Eds.), *Topics in learning and performance* (pp. 131–159). New York: Academic Press.

Battig, W. F. (1979). The flexibility of human memory. In L. S. Cermak and F. I. Craik (Eds.), *Levels of processing in human memory* (pp. 23–44). Hillsdale, NJ: Lawrence Lawrence Erlbaum Associates.

Bell, B. S., and Kozlowski, S. W. J. (2002). Goal orientation and ability: Interactive effects on self-efficacy, performance, and knowledge. *Journal of Applied Psychology, 87*, 497–505.

Berliner, D. (1969). *Microteaching and the technical skills approach to teacher training.* (Technical Report No. 3). Stanford, CA: Stanford Center for Research and Development in Teaching. (ERIC Document Reproduction Service No. ED 034 707.)

Brown, K. G. (2001). Using computers to deliver training: Which employees learn and why? *Personnel Psychology, 54*, 271–296.

Burke, M. J., and Day, R. R. (1986). A cumulative study of the effectiveness of managerial training. *Journal of Applied Psychology, 71*, 232–245.

Carroll, W. R., and Bandura, A. (1990). Representational guidance of action production in observational learning: A causal analysis. *Journal of Motor Behavior, 22*, 85–97.

Custers, E. J. F. M., Regehr, G., McCulloch, W., Peniston, C., and Reznick, R. (1999). The effects of modeling on learning a simple surgical procedure: See one, do one or see many, do one? *Advances in Health Sciences Education, 4*, 123–143.

Day, E. A., Arthur, W. Jr., Villado, A. J., Boatman, P. R., Kowollik, V., Bhupatkar, A., and Bennett, W. Jr. (2013). Relating individual differences in ability, personality, and motivation to the retention and transfer of skill on a complex command-and-control simulation task. In W. Arthur, Jr., E. A. Day, W. Bennett, Jr., and A. Portrey (Eds.), *Individual and team skill decay: The science and implications for practice* (pp. 282–301). New York: Taylor & Francis.

Driskell, J. E., Copper, C., and Moran, A. (1994). Does mental practice enhance performance? *Journal of Applied Psychology, 79*, 481–492.

Elliot, A. J., and Church, M. A. (1997). A hierarchical model of approach and avoidance achievement motivation. *Journal of Personality and Social Psychology, 72*, 218–232.

Ellis, S., Ganzach, Y., Castle, E., and Sekely, G. (2010). The effect of filmed versus personal after-event reviews on task performance: The mediating and moderating role of self-efficacy. *Journal of Applied Psychology, 95*, 122–131.

Ford, J. K., Quiñones, M., Sego, D., and Speer Sorra, J. S. (1992). Factors affecting the opportunity to perform trained tasks on the job. *Personnel Psychology, 45*, 511–527.

Goldberg, L. R. (1992). The development of markers for the Big-Five factor structure. *Psychological Assessment, 4*, 26–42.

Jentsch, F., Bowers, C., and Salas, E. (2001). What determines whether observers recognize targeted behaviors in modeling displays? *Human Factors, 43*, 496–507.

Martocchio, J. J., and Judge, T. A. (1997). Relationship between conscientiousness and learning in employee training: Mediating influences of self-deception and self-efficacy. *Journal of Applied Psychology, 82*, 764–773.

Nease, A. A., Mudgett, B. A., and Quiñones, M. A. (1999). Relationships among feedback sign, self-efficacy, and acceptance of performance feedback. *Journal of Applied Psychology, 84*, 806–814.

Noe, R. A. (1986). Trainees' attributes and attitudes: Neglected influences on training effectiveness. *Academy of Management Review, 11*, 736–749.

Peters, L. H., and O'Connor, E. J. (1980). Situational constraints and work outcomes: The influence of a frequently overlooked construct. *Academy of Management Review, 5*, 391–397.

Raven, J. C., Raven, J., and Court, J. H. (1998). *A manual for Raven's Progressive Matrices and Vocabulary Scales*. London: H. K. Lewis.

Russell, J. S., Wexley, K. N., and Hunter, J. E. (1984). Questioning the effectiveness of behavior modeling training in an industrial setting. *Personnel Psychology, 37*, 465–481.

Schendel, J. D., and Hagman, J. D. (1982). On sustaining procedural skills over a prolonged retention interval. *Journal of Applied Psychology, 67*, 605–610.

Schmidt, A. M., and Ford, K. (2003). Learning within a learner control training environment: The interactive effects of goal orientation and metacognitive instruction on learning outcomes. *Personnel Psychology, 56*, 405–429.

Schmidt, R. A., and Bjork, R. A. (1992). New conceptualizations of practice: Common principles in three paradigms suggest new concepts in training. *Psychological Science, 3*, 207–217.

Shebilske, W. L., Jordan, J. A., Goettl, B. P., and Paulus, L. E. (1998). Observational versus hands-on practice of complex skills in dyadic, triadic, and tetradic training-teams. *Human Factors, 40*, 526–540.

Sitzmann, T., Kraiger, K., Stewart, D., and Wisher, R. (2006). The comparative effectiveness of Web-based and classroom instruction: A meta-analysis. *Personnel Psychology, 59*, 623–664.

Skinner, B. F. (1969). *Contingencies of reinforcement.* New York: Appleton-Century-Crofts.

Sonalysts, Inc. (2004). *Jane's Fleet Command Air Force Research Laboratory ver. 1.55* [Computer software]. Redwood City, CA: Electronic Arts.

Steinberg, E. R. (1989). Cognition and learner control: A literature review, 1977–1988. *Journal of Computer Based Instruction, 16*, 117–121.

Taylor, P., Russ-Eft, D., and Chan, D. (2005). A meta-analytic review of behavior modeling training. *Journal of Applied Psychology, 90*, 692–709.

Tennyson, R. D., Christensen, D. L., and Park, S. I. (1984). The Minnesota Adaptive Instructional System: An intelligent CBI system. *Journal of Computer Based Instruction, 11*, 2–13.

Trimble, S. K., Nathan, B. R., and Decker, P. J. (1991). The effect of positive and negative models on learning in behavior modeling training: Testing for proactive and retroactive interference. *Journal of Human Behavior and Learning, 7*, 1–12.

Villado, A. J., Day, E. A., Arthur, W. Jr., Boatman, P. R., Kowollik, V., Bhupatkar, A., and Bennett, W. Jr. (2013). Complex command-and-control simulation task performance following periods of nonuse. In W. Arthur, Jr., E. A. Day, W. Bennett, Jr., and A. Portrey (Eds.), *Individual and team skill decay: The science and implications for practice* (pp. 53–67). New York: Taylor & Francis.

Vroom, V. H. (1964). *Work and motivation.* New York: John Wiley & Sons.

AUTHORS' NOTES

This research was sponsored by contracts and grants from the U.S. Air Force Research Laboratory, Human Effectiveness Directorate, Warfighter Training Research Division, Mesa, AZ, the Defense Advance Research Project Agency, and the National Science Foundation awarded to Winfred Arthur, Jr. The views expressed herein are those of the authors and do not necessarily reflect the official position or opinion of the sponsors or their respective organizations.

10

Skill Decay, Reacquisition Training, and Transfer Studies in the Swedish Air Force

A Retrospective Review

Erland Svensson, Maud Angelborg-Thanderz, Jonathan Borgvall, and Martin Castor

OUTLINE

The chapter covers almost two decades of research—the 1970s and 1980s—performed by the Swedish Defence Research Establishment, FOA (nowadays the Swedish Defence Research Agency, FOI), and in close co-operation with the Swedish Air Force[1,2] (SwAF). This work was motivated by an interest in two questions. What are the relationships between experience on an aircraft system, absence from a task/system, speed of skill decay, reacquisition training, and operational performance? What are the transfer effects from simulated to real flight? To answer these questions, a series of studies, simulated and live, were conducted in the Swedish Air Force during the 1970s and 1980s, and the chapter presents a review of these activities. Early retired fighter pilots were compared with active pilots. Performance was the crucial measure. By means of structural equation modeling, valid and reliable performance measures of aircraft, radar, and weapon systems operations were generated and applied, and models of their causal relationships were developed. The pilots' mental workload, their effort, mood, and motivation were also measured. The more experience with and the less absence from the aircraft the pilots had, the better their operational performance. The non-linear relations found between time on system, absence from system, respectively, and performance, were used for optimal screening of pilots for operational reacquisition training. Once skillful, the pilots can be away from their systems for quite a while and make a successful comeback, provided that they get individualized and guided training, where the concrete results and performance measures are consistently used in briefings and as information feedback supervised by experienced instructors. The training procedures developed proved effective for keeping the pilots' motivation at constantly high levels. By means of structural modeling, significant predictions, from simulator to live flight, of the pilot's capacity and operational performance could be made. Lessons learned from these studies, and connections to training challenges of today conclude the chapter.

SKILL DECAY, REACQUISITION TRAINING, AND TRANSFER STUDIES IN THE SWEDISH AIR FORCE: A RETROSPECTIVE REVIEW

Almost all of our research was performed in accordance with successive requests from the Swedish Air Force. Early questions of interest to the Air Force concerned training criteria and training feedback in simulated training, and the need for research on cost-effective training was early foreseen. In the late 1960s, system aircraft simulators started to form an important part of the training program of the Swedish Air Force. This was a consequence of the introduction of the first system aircraft[3] (J35 Draken) in the SwAF. The Air Force was, for the time, notably well informed about the potential of simulation as a cost-effective means for systems training.

Before answering questions on skill decay and the effects of reacquisition training, we had to establish training objectives and performance criteria of an average Swedish "standard pilot" during missions in a single-seat fighter. In these studies, both simulator and aircraft were used. Some objective measures and recording devices were used, but most measures were based on questionnaires. The questionnaires comprised primarily aspects of manifest behavior or concrete actions and decisions made. What did the pilots do? What decisions did they make? How well did they perform with respect to prescribed standards?

It was early learned that it was desirable to point out the options and actions in a chronological order or sequence. We found that neither the instructors nor their students were used to verbalizing their knowledge (or lack of knowledge). We realized that we must focus on those actions and events that are of decisive importance for the outcome. It was found that assessing the pilots training standards is a prerequisite for performance feedback, and that immediate feedback is an indispensable requirement for effective training. We also learned that performance is a multifacetted and complex concept hard to capture and measure. These measurement problems, in terms of theoretical as well as practical aspects, are still central areas of research. Without reliable and valid performance measures, effects of time on or absence from tasks/systems, training, or transfer cannot be estimated.

We were dealing with tasks with all those dynamic characteristics which later have been described as naturalistic decision settings. The problems were ill-structured, the environment was uncertain and super-dynamic, the goals were shifting, the results were not coupled to actions in a simple way, and feedback was delayed. The questionnaires developed can be considered descriptions of optimal behavior or optimal systems handling against which the pilots' actual behavior should be compared. One general finding was that the use of the questionnaires altered the pilots' decisions, made them use more and other system functions, and, most important, made them more analytical.

In the objective towards making the training more efficient, the interviews and discussions with the experts of the systems (i.e., subject matter experts, SMEs) were of critical importance, and the method hinges on the participation of SMEs. Over time, we got a more complete understanding by means of analysis of the fighter pilot's job in two steps: analysis of the situations and of the actions within the situations, respectively. This analysis formed a basis for our development of performance measures (Angelborg-Thanderz, 1990).

A main advantage of our method was that it increased the pilot's skill to analyze the mission and his or her role in it (Angelborg-Thanderz, 1989; Thanderz, 1973). Nowadays—in the light of the research on situational awareness—this gave the pilots means to be aware of the whole situation: its demands and its course, where in the situation they currently were and where they had been earlier, and how they should proceed to be able to succeed. Theoretically, it would have been possible to make a complete list of all the situations a pilot in a single-seat fighter is confronted with, but from a practical point of view this list would have been useless. Instead, pilot proficiency tests were designed and developed on selected checklists corresponding to what was expected from a trained pilot and chosen with regard to enemy threats and existing weapon systems. They could be characterized as the blueprint describing the skills that pilots must achieve to be mission ready. Several similarities between the process of performance assessment described and the procedure of Mission Essential Competencies (Colegrove and Alliger, 2003; Colegrove and Bennett, 2006) can be found.

SKILL DECAY AND REACQUISITION TRAINING—A SIMULATOR STUDY

Our experiences on performance assessment, optimizing flight systems training, and how to train and maintain trained multi-purpose pilots came in handy when we were asked by the Commander in Chief (C-in-C) of the SwAF to investigate whether intermittent flight training could be a cost-effective procedure. In close cooperation with the Air Staff, 19 specific aspects (intercepts to destroy enemy aircraft) of the system missions were chosen to constitute the objective of a fully trained J35 Draken pilot, corresponding simulator training intercepts were developed and analyzed down to their components, and checklists created of the decisive ones. We identified 16 pilots who had not flown the J35 Draken fighter for a time varying from 6 months to 12 years. Their experience on the specific system (J35F) ranged from 380 to 2400 hours. The pilots were tested in the simulator. On the basis of their results our highly motivated participants were provided an intensive and individualized training program in the simulator, and then re-tested. Before and after training, they were compared with a control group of active pilots. The control group was selected to represent a cross section of system 35 pilots with respect to flight time on system, and skill (Angelborg-Thanderz, 1989, 1990).

As noted, performance measures were crucial. But could the pilot's mental workload owing to lack of training be so high that he would not be able to learn and use his knowledge and experience efficiently? One cannot expect a sound and solid performance, or an absence of stress reactions, from a pilot working under an overly heavy workload and performing on the edge of maximum ability. Would a combination of measures allow us to make more precise diagnoses and prognoses of performance? That is why the pilots' mental workload was measured. In addition, the pilots rated their effort, motivation, mood, difficulty, and risk of the missions both before and after the sorties. Data on the pilots' psycho-physiological reactions in terms of heart rate and excretion of adrenaline and nor-adrenaline was also collected (cf. Svensson, Angelborg-Thanderz, and Sjöberg, 1993; Svensson, Angelborg-Thanderz, Sjöberg, and Gillberg, 1988; Svensson, Angelborg-Thanderz, Sjöberg, and Olsson, 1997).

We have looked upon mental workload as a cost. What does performance cost in terms of mental workload? In the studies we consider the relationship between performance and mental workload (performance/mental workload) as a measure of efficiency.

The data set was quite extensive: 741 intercepts and 180 variables. As noted, the intercepts were analyzed down to their components and, accordingly, the checklists or questionnaires were comprehensive. The large number of items was reduced by means of factor analysis. Factors are optimal with respect to reliability and construct validity, and, accordingly, well suited as performance measures. To estimate and test causal models we used LISREL (analysis of Linear Structural Relationships; Jöreskog and Sörbom, 1984), which offers a powerful method for development and testing of structural models based on empirical data.

Results from the Simulator Study

Figure 10.1 presents the initial structural model of the relationships between the three factors or dimensions: aircraft operation, radar operation, and weapon operation.

The most powerful checklist variables were used as markers in the analyses. The analyses were based on deviations from optimal behavior or performance. Accordingly, the model shows that the pilots' deviations from optimal aircraft operation results in deviations in radar operation, which in turn, results in deviations in weapon operation. Twenty-five percent of the variance in radar operation performance was explained by the variance in aircraft operation. In the same way, 15 percent of the variance in weapon operation was explained by the variance in radar operation. Compared to single measures, the factors represent interrelated performance aspects with high reliability and empirical validity. Accordingly, we used these factors as measures of the pilots' deviation from optimal behavior or performance in the reacquisition training.

Directly after each intercept, the instructors rated the pilots' performance during the intercept in general terms. The pilots rated their performance in the same way, as well as their mental workload during the intercepts. Factor analyses showed that the instructor and pilot ratings form a performance factor.

How does time on system and absence from system affect the deviation scores from optimal performance? It was found that the two markers form a factor called trim on system (i.e., the longer the system experience and the shorter time of absence from the system, the better the trim).

Figure 10.2 presents the final model combining aircraft, radar, and weapon operations with trim on system, and general performance. It starts with trim

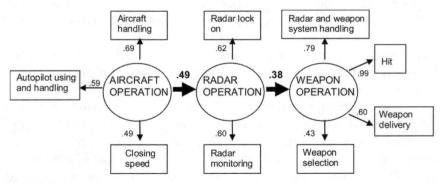

FIGURE 10.1

The initial structural model of the relationships between the factors: Aircraft Operation, Radar Operation, and Weapon Operation. $\chi^2 = 40.89$, $df = 26$, $p = .04$. Goodness of Fit Index (GFI) = .957. Adjusted GFI = .925. Root Mean Square (RMS) = .050. Squares denote manifest or measured variables, and ellipses latent variables or factors.

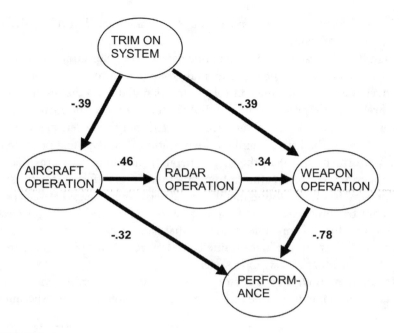

FIGURE 10.2

A combined structural model (markers excluded) of the relationships between the factors: Trim on System, Aircraft Operation, Radar Operation, Weapon Operation, and General Performance. χ^2 = 88.11, df = 59, p = .01. Goodness of Fit Index (GFI) = .93. Adjusted GFI = .90. Root Mean Square (RMS) = .048.

on system and ends with performance. The deviation scores of aircraft, radar, and weapon operations are mediating factors between trim on system and general performance. As can be seen, trim on system affects aircraft operation and weapon operation directly, and to the same extent. Trim on system also has an indirect effect on weapon operation via radar operation. In the same way, the variance in performance is explained directly by aircraft and weapon operation, and indirectly by aircraft operation via radar and weapon operations. The main effect on general performance is mediated by weapon operation, indicating that weapon system handling is in focus. The correlation between trim on system and general performance is .47 (p < .01), meaning that 22 percent of the variance in performance is explained by the variance in trim on system.

The models presented are based on data from intercepts performed after the reacquisition training program in the simulator; that is, when they were supposed to be ready for regular operational training as ordinary squadron members. What were the effects of the reacquisition training program? To what extent did their performance improve? Was their performance in accordance with the performance of the control group? Did their mental workload decrease as a function of training?

Figure 10.3 presents the means of deviation scores for aircraft, radar, and weapon operations for the experimental group before and after training, and the deviation scores for the control group. As noted from the models above, the three scores represent different, but related, aspects of performance.

Results from analyses of variance indicated that the experimental group, before training, had significantly more deviations from optimal performance (i.e., performed worse) in the three operation handling measures than the control group. However, after training, there were no differences between the two groups. It was also found that the initial performance gaps between before and after training were highest for weapon operation and lowest for aircraft operation. This was concluded to reflect that handling the platform (i.e., to fly the aircraft) was a basic, "over-trained," and more lasting task as compared to handling the radar and weapon systems.

In the same way, the instructor and pilot ratings of performance and the pilots' rating of mental workload, before and after training, for the experimental

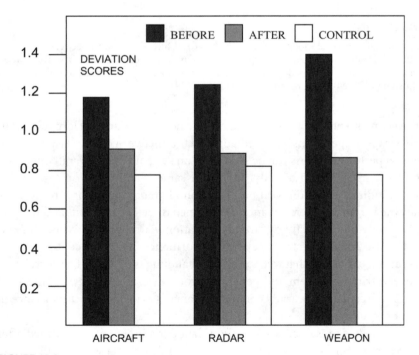

FIGURE 10.3

Means of deviations from optimal performance in aircraft, radar, and weapon operations handling for the experimental group before and after training, and for the control group. Notice that lower scores indicate better performance.

group were compared with the corresponding values for the control group. The results of these analyses indicated that the performance ratings were significantly lower for the experimental group before training compared to after training, but no differences were found between the experimental group after training and the control group. The results are presented in Figure 10.4.

The changes in mental workload of the experimental group did not show the same pattern as the performance changes. Certainly, their level of mental workload decreased significantly from before to after the training, but it was also significantly higher after training compared to the control group. Accordingly, the mental effort was higher for the experimental group for the same performance standard compared to the control group. When considering the pilots' efficiency as a function of the quotient performance/ mental workload, it was concluded that the efficiency and durability was lower for the experimental group (i.e., they had to work harder for the same performance).

What are the relationships between experience on an aircraft system, absence from the system, and the speed of skill decay? From the model analyses

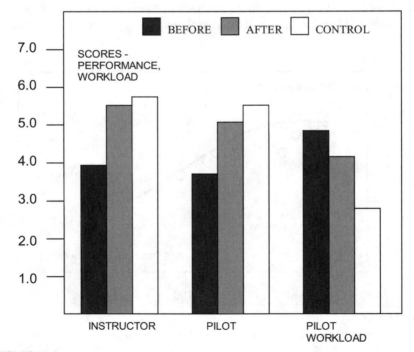

FIGURE 10.4

Means of instructor and pilot ratings of performance, and pilot workload ratings for the experimental group before and after training, and for the control group, respectively.

we found that absence from system (with a loading –.87) was a more important aspect than time on system (with a loading of .58) of the factor trim on system, and, accordingly, it was of specific importance for explaining the performance differences of the pilots.

Figure 10.5 presents the respective pilot's performance after training as a function of absence from the system. The circles represent the means of 18 instructor-rated intercepts per pilot. The performance scale format was from 1 to 7. As can be seen from the curve, the performance levels of the pilots can be described as a curve-linear function of absence from the system. Accordingly, the skill decay function of the pilots has a curve-linear form.

When comparing the mean performance of the control group (marked by the square), absence of shorter duration than about four years seemed not to affect the performance negatively. However, absence of longer durations had a negative effect on performance in terms of skill decay. Accordingly, the reacquisition training in the simulator was successful for those with absence no longer than about four years (in this case about 50 percent of the pilots in the experimental group).

Figure 10.6 presents the respective pilot's performance after training as a function of time on system (before reacquisition training). The circles represent the means of 18 instructor-rated intercepts per pilot. In this analysis we found

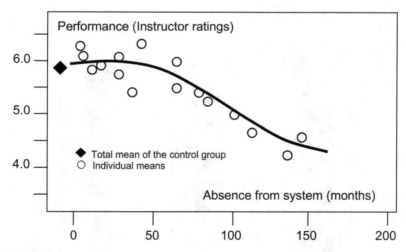

FIGURE 10.5

Instructor ratings (means of 18 intercepts per pilot, $n = 16$) of performance (scale format 1 to 7) after training as a function of absence from system in months. Open circles indicate individual means. The closed diamond indicates the total mean of the control group. The curve has been smoothed by means of distance weighted least squares regression analysis.

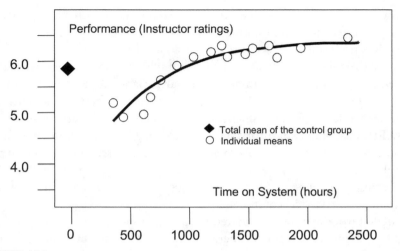

FIGURE 10.6

Instructor ratings (means of 18 intercepts per pilot, $n = 16$) of performance (scale format 1 to 7) after training as a function of time on system. Open circles indicate individual means. The closed diamond indicates the total mean of the control group. The curve has been smoothed by means of distance weighted least squares regression analysis.

that time on system also was a restricting condition, and that a certain least amount of operational flight time (about 1000 hours) was necessary for a performance level satisfying control group criteria.

From correlation analyses we found that the instructors' performance assessments, after the reacquisition training, correlated $-.64$ ($p < .01$) with absence from system and $.66$ ($p < .01$) with time on system. Accordingly, there is a covariation of about 40 percent between performance ratings and absence from system and time on system, respectively. It is interesting to note that the initial skill and training level in terms of hours on system has a substantial effect even after several years of absence from the system.

TRANSFER OF TRAINING—A LIVE FLIGHT STUDY

The results of the reacquisition training in the simulator were found to be of great interest and importance, and, accordingly, the C-in-C of the Swedish Air Force asked us to proceed to live flight studies. This gave an opportunity to follow the pilots from their initial reacquisition training in the simulator to their operational training in the air, and the transfer of training effects from simulation to live flight was here of particular interest.

Six of the 16 pilots from the simulation study were selected and provided operational reacquisition training in the air. In this second step of the study the pilots performed in all 154 flight missions (about 25 missions per pilot) and 78 variables were measured. Accordingly, the study was a repeated measures design, and the inter-individual variance as well as the intra-individual variance as a function of training formed the basis of the statistical analyses. Performance assessment was again a crucial measure in this study as well. It was found, not surprisingly perhaps, that it was easier to get information from a simulator than from an airborne single-seat aircraft. From the simulation study we knew that a simulator could very well be used for determining the pilot's skill and knowledge about the system and the direct handling of the tactical equipment.

Mental workload was considered of specific importance in a study of live flight. It has often been said that there is a genuine difference between simulated and live flight with respect to psychological stress and mental workload. Could the pilot's mental workload, owing to lack of training, be so high that he would not be able to use his knowledge, and utilize the training efficiently in the air? That is the main reason for measuring not only aspects of the pilots' performance but also their corresponding mental workload.

In most studies of man–machine systems, there has been a tendency to emphasize cognitive and perceptual functions and neglect emotional and motivational ones. However, there is evidence that these latter aspects are important as well, especially when participants must work under time pressure and high mental stress during live flights. Under some circumstances motivation can be the most important aspect. The negative effects of emotion coping on military flight performance have been modeled in Svensson et al. (1993).

Therefore, emotional and motivational factors were considered. The pilots rated their mental effort, motivation, and their moods, in terms of perceived activation, extraversion, and psychological stress.[4] Furthermore, the pilots also rated the difficulty and the risk of the missions. In other studies (Svensson et al., 1993; Svensson et al., 1997; Svensson et al., 1999; Svensson and Wilson, 2002) it has been found that these aspects are states changing as a function of the pilots' trim, temporary psychological status, and the demands of the situation. All the judgments and evaluations were made both before and after the flights. Data on the pilot's psycho-physiological reactions were also collected. As in the simulator study, the pilots were equipped with a portable Electro-Cardiograph (ECG) tape recorder. Excretion levels of adrenaline and nor-adrenaline were also determined before and after the flights. This means that we had access to a series of psycho-physiological correlates to our psychological—and performance—measures.

We used the same checklists as in the simulator again after the weapon system missions in the air. Objective measures from registration equipment in the aircraft concerning the pilots' operation of the weapon system were also collected. Performance assessments were collected from several sources: in addition to the pilot himself, from a wingman and from the operator of the target aircraft as well.

The reacquisition training program in the air consisted of three types of training missions: initial flight training missions, visual training missions, and systems training missions. The program comprised 25 flight missions per pilot in all, and was performed over a period of 3 weeks.

In addition to the pilots' performance in the air, and the transfer effects from simulation training to live flight, we were also interested in their development of skill as a function of the training program. How did their performance and mental workload change as a function of training? As noted, mental workload is critical with respect to the durability of the pilots' performance and skill.

Results from the Live Flight Study

The simulator results were confirmed in the air. Accordingly, after the training program, the performance of the six selected pilots was considered to be in accordance with the standards of the control group of operational pilots. Figure 10.7 presents instructor and pilot ratings of performance, and the pilots' ratings of mental workload before and after training, and in the air for the six selected pilots. It was found that the instructor performance ratings tended to be lower in the air as compared with the ratings after training, and that the pilot ratings were the same as after simulation training. There was no significant change in mental workload, but, somewhat surprisingly, the pilots tended to be less mentally loaded in the air as compared to the simulator after training.

These findings were obviously of central importance for the SwAF and as a consequence, a program for reacquisition training was started at Scania Air Force Base (Wing F10). Furthermore, another squadron for this training was raised at the wing. Accordingly, the initial topic had transformed from a research question to a practical implementation.

How did the performance in the simulator affect the performance in the air? By means of modeling ad modum LISREL, we estimated the optimal transfer effects. Figure 10.8 presents a model in which we used the performance ratings of the instructors, the performance ratings of the pilots as well as the pilots' ratings of their mental workload.

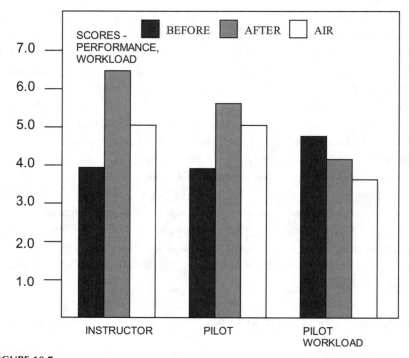

FIGURE 10.7

Means of instructor and pilot ratings of performance, and pilot workload ratings for the six pilots before and after training, and in the air, respectively.

As can be seen from the figure, the three markers form a factor called efficiency. The factor loadings for the performance measures are positive and the loadings for mental workload are negative. Accordingly, we have an efficiency measure ranging from high performance during low mental effort to bad performance during high mental effort. From the model we can see that there is a significant transfer effect (.40) from simulation to live flight. This means that 16 percent of the variance of operational performance in the air could be explained by the variance of performance in the simulator. No significant difference of the efficiency factors were found between simulation and air.

In a second model of transfer effects, emotional and motivational aspects were included, and a factor called "fighting spirit" with markers of the moods of activation and extraversion was formed. The factor reflects the pilots' motivation to act and cooperate.

From the model in Figure 10.9 we found that efficiency in the air was affected not only directly from the efficiency in the simulator, but also indirectly

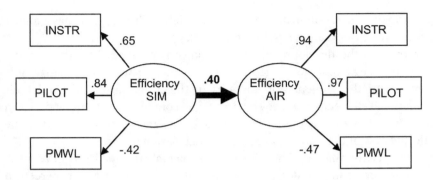

FIGURE 10.8

A model of the causal relationships between the factors' efficiency in simulation (Efficiency SIM) and efficiency in the air (Efficiency Air). $\chi^2 = 13.71$, $df = 8$, $p = 0.09$. Root Mean Square Residual (RMR) = 0.09. Goodness of Fit Index (GFI) = 0.94.

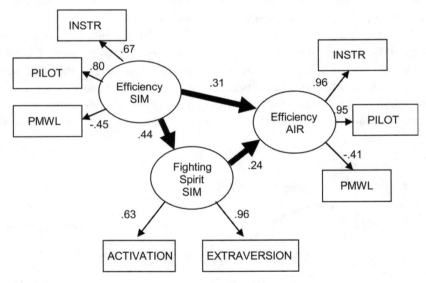

FIGURE 10.9

A model of the causal relationships between the factors' efficiency in simulation (Efficiency SIM), "fighting spirit" in simulation (Fighting Spirit SIM), and efficiency in the air (Efficiency Air). $\chi^2 = 34.27$, $df = 17$, $p = 0.01$. Root Mean Square Residual (RMR) = 0.09. Goodness of Fit Index (GFI) = 0.88.

by the "fighting spirit" factor. The combined effects of efficiency in the simulator and "fighting spirit" on efficiency in the air are .48. This means that 22 percent of the variance in efficiency in the air was explained by the variances in efficiency in the simulator and 'fighting spirit'. Accordingly, good performance in the simulator resulting in a high "fighting spirit" has a higher predictive power than the exclusive efficiency factor.

How was the development of their skills as a function of the training program? How did their performance and mental workload change as a function of the sequence of missions in the program, or how did their operational efficiency change? The design and content of the training program were adapted to the pilots' trim, and by means of trend analyses the effectiveness of the training program could be evaluated.

From factor analyses, an index of pilot mental workload was developed. The measure comprised aspects of mental and physical effort, perceived activation, psychological tension, and excretion of adrenaline. Accordingly, the algorithm of measures reflects psychological as well as psycho-physiological aspects of the workload. In the same way, performance variables (instructor and pilot ratings of performance and form) comprised the operational performance index. Figure 10.10 presents the changes of the workload and performance indices as a function of mission sequence.

In order to make a comparison possible between the two measures, they were standardized (Z-scores: $M = 0.0$, $SD = 1.0$). As can be seen, there is (a) a curve-linear relationship between mental workload and the sequence of missions, and (b) no relation between performance and sequence of training missions. The reason for the similar and "horizontal" performance level is that the training program followed a flight of stairs, in which the complexity

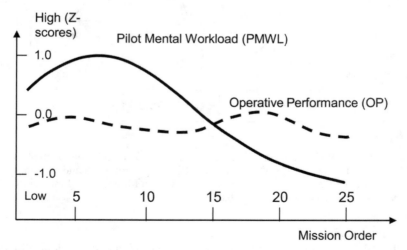

FIGURE 10.10

Changes in pilot mental workload, and operative performance as a function of mission order. The workload and performance measures are standardized (Z-scores: $M = 0.0$, $SD = 1.0$). The curves are smoothed by means of distance weighted least squares analyses.

of each stair (i.e., mission in the sequence) was adjusted to the pilot's current capability. Well-performed missions repeatedly gave similar and high performance ratings, and accordingly, no changes were to be expected over the sequence of missions. The similar performance ratings as a function of mission order, indicates that the flight of stairs of increasing complexity was well adapted to the pilots' ability to profit from the training.

When comparing the two curves of the figure, it is evident that the performance in the former part of the program demanded a significantly higher mental effort as compared with the corresponding performance level in the latter part. This change in the pilots' efficiency indicates that their performance increased in durability, and that their ability to handle complex information and critical situations increased.

CONCLUSIONS

The studies were conducted upon request of the user (i.e., the Swedish Air Force) and from the end user's perspective the results were of operational and practical importance. From our perspective as scientists, a series of lessons were learned. In retrospect, we believe that some methodological standpoints made during the 1970s and early 1980s are still of interest and importance.

From the task analyses of intercepts in flight missions, and the development of check-lists or questionnaires, the pilots' behavior (decisions and actions made) was considered as a process in which a behavior at a certain point or phase affects the behavior at the following ones. Accordingly, we became more interested in the processes behind the pilots' performance than in the manifest performance itself. The regulatory and compensatory processes of mental effort for optimal performance illustrate this view, and it has been used in later research on optimization of the training potential in simulations (Nählinder, 2009).

We considered the relationships between behavioral measures as important as the measures themselves, and working in terms of causal processes and covariations between variables, we believe, is a more powerful scientific procedure than that of classical experimental designs. For example, by means of classical techniques, we can confirm differences in dependent variables as a consequence of independent ones. By means of second generation statistical techniques, it can be estimated to what extent sets of variables affect each other.

The development of techniques, since these studies were conducted, for dynamic registration and measurement of behavioral aspects (measures of the operator) and technical aspects (measures of the system), makes the development of models with higher explanatory power than the ones presented here possible. Furthermore, the interactions between the dynamic changes of the system with the corresponding dynamic changes of the pilot can be modeled. A series of modern modeling studies of these interactions in military pilot performance are presented in Castor (2009).

The pilots demonstrated their knowledge and skill in the air, and their performance was close to their performance in the simulator after training. Even if pilots of a squadron are selected in several steps, and accordingly, a restricted variance in their performance is to be expected, we have quite often still found substantial variance. Even if we found less variance in the pilots' performance after reacquisition training, there were still substantial differences.

No differences in performance between the experimental group after simulator training and the control group were found. On the other hand, the mental workload was higher for the experimental group, and, accordingly, their efficiency was lower. However, mental workload of the pilots in the air was about the same as for the control group. It is reasonable to assume that mental workload and psychological stress should be higher in live flights as compared to corresponding simulated ones. However, we have, more than once, noticed that instructor evaluations of simulated missions are more stressing than operational missions in the air. Somewhat to our surprise, older pilots who had not been operational on their systems for several years were even better than the younger pilots in our control group. However, their performance had a higher "cost" in terms of higher workload.

It was found that handling the platform (i.e., to fly the aircraft) was a basic, "over-trained," and better retained task compared to handling the radar and weapon systems. Military aircraft of today are easier to fly but the burden of handling information and weapon systems are higher and, accordingly, we believe, the pilots' information and weapon systems handling are still mental bottlenecks.

A noticeable lesson learned in our training was the importance of correct and immediate feedback. We realized that assessing the pilots training standards was a prerequisite for performance feedback, which in its turn was an indispensable requirement for effective training.

Empirically based modeling has been in focus, and a series of models of pilot performance have been developed. From the models we were able to estimate the relative importance of the pilots' actions on the final outcome, and the models were of practical importance for the user. The finding that absence from the system was more important than time on system is an example. The extent to which system operation aspects as compared to aircraft operation aspects affect performance is another.

In the analyses of transfer effects, it was found that the pilots' efficiency in the simulator, to some extent, can explain the efficiency in the air and with our restricted arsenal of measures, about 20 percent of the variance could be explained. This seems not to be impressive, but an explanatory power of 100 percent is not to be expected. What is the maximum variance explainable? Well, the maximum explained variance is restricted by the reliability of measures used. If, for example, the reliability indices of the performance and workload measures are 0.80, then the maximum expected common variance between the measures in the simulator and the corresponding measures in the air is 0.64 (i.e., 0.80^2). Accordingly, a more appropriate estimate of the proportion transferred in the model of Figure 10.9, is $0.48^2/0.80^2$, (i.e., 0.36). Seen in this perspective 20 percent is considerable, and of practical importance.

Concerning skill decay and retention a conclusion of practical importance is that once skilled pilots can be away from their systems for quite a while and make a successful comeback, provided that they get individualized and guided training, where the concrete results and performance measures are consistently used in briefings and as information feedback supervised by experienced instructors. The remarkable skill perseverance or resistance to decay over time when appropriately trained was a memento to us. The linear functions of Figures 10.5 and 10.6 describing the operational performance as a function of absence from flight system and time on system, respectively, have been of particular value for the user. In fact, a new squadron manned by pilots selected and retrained according to our results was created by the SwAF.

A general conclusion concerns the importance of a close and interactive cooperation between the user and the researcher, in this case the SwAF and FOA (now FOI). The use of operational pilots and systems reduces validity problems with respect to generalization to populations and systems, and provides a possibility to address and investigate questions important for the Air Force. Unfortunately, the number of available operational pilots, even more so today than at the time of these studies, is too low to allow anything other than small-scale operational studies which inevitably reduces the generalization of results.

The studies described here were performed about 25 years ago at Scania Air Force Base. The aircraft used, J35 Draken, was the first system aircraft of the Swedish Air Force. Today, we study the operator function in the first fourth-generation high performance aircraft, JAS39 Gripen. The possibilities for logging systems as well as pilots have made considerable progress (cf. Castor, 2009). The development of measurement techniques in combination with the methodological development is believed to form a base for prosperous research on training in the future.

IMPLICATIONS FOR PRACTICE, AND CONCLUSIONS

The studies presented were all performed in accordance with successive requests from the SwAF. Accordingly, the links between research and practice are strong, and the implications for simulated and real operations straightforward. The results of these studies played an important role in the establishment of another fighter squadron at the Scania Air Force Base in Sweden, and the findings on skill decay and reacquisition training were implemented in the training programs at the simulation centers of the Air Force.

It has been said that nothing is as practical as a good theory. The structural models on operational performance and transfer of training substantiate this proverbial phrase. From the models it can not only be concluded that different skills and simulated training affect operational performance but also to what extent these aspects affect performance. This knowledge on the relative causal importance of different training aspects has been of great importance for the training programs of the Air Force.

It has been 25 years since the reported empirical studies were conducted and the characteristics of the missions have changed. Operating a modern fighter aircraft is more about making tactical decisions based on sensor information than handling the aircraft itself. Modern armed conflicts are characterized by ambiguous situations with continuously increasing complexity; for example, with regard to the identification and distinction of friend or foe, and possible actions as permitted by the Rules of Engagement (RoE) of an operation.

One contemporary example is the training at the SwAF Combat Simulation Centre (FLSC), where the team training of pilot decision making, situation awareness, and tactical execution skills over the past decade has shifted from home land defense scenarios only to include coalition peacekeeping and peace enforcement operations (peace support operations, PSO) at an international arena. As any training program must be based on a model of skill acquisition, FLSC has adopted a model influenced by Kolb's Experiential Learning Theory (Kolb, 1984), in the spirit that "learning is the process whereby knowledge and skills are developed through the transformation of experiences." In short, the practical implementation of this model is that the trainees train themselves using the tools provided in the facility with the support and guidance of instructors. The intention is to provide and maintain an environment that stimulates the motivation of deliberate practice and active learning among the trainees, improving their performance toward expertise levels (Ericsson and Charness, 1994; Ericsson, Krampe, and Tesch-Römer, 1993; Kozlowski, 1998).

The trainees are exposed to concrete experiences in the simulator, leading to observations and reflections during planning, execution, and debriefs. The trainees own influence over the training aims to stimulate them to assimilate their reflective observations into concepts that they can actively discuss, test, and explore.

In addition to delivering training according to a well-designed skill acquisition model, the content of the training must meet at least some part of the operational requirements to be meaningful and successful across environments, moving the trainees closer to operational expert performance (e.g., Ward, Williams, and Hancock, 2006). The PSO training scenarios at FLSC were carefully designed and evaluated with the support of senior pilots possessing extensive experience from operational deployments, before being implemented in the training program. To further develop the training, we have recently mapped the Mission Essential Competencies (MEC) (Alliger, Beard, Bennett and Colegrove, 2012; Alliger, Beard, Colegrove and Garrity, 2007; Colegrove and Alliger, 2003; Colegrove and Bennett, 2006) required for Swedish PSO Air to Air missions (Bennett et al., 2006). With the support of Air Force Research Laboratory (AFRL, 711 HPW/RH, Mesa, AZ), knowledge and skills essential for SwAF PSO and their developmental experiences across environments were identified and evaluated with regard to current training (note that an approach with similarities to the MEC process was used in the studies reported earlier in this chapter).

It is obvious from the PSO MEC process that additional knowledge and skills are required from the modern fighter pilots compared to the pilots of earlier days. The pilots of today train for new situations, in a partly new context, and for a more complex level of decision making. For example, the evaluation of an action against the current Rules of Engagement and Commander's Intent has been added on top of aircraft, sensor, and weapon operations. Whether mastery and resistance against decay for the new skill sets required by today's pilots will exhibit the same properties as in our earlier studies will indeed be interesting research questions.

The development of training programs and studies of skill acquisition, retention, transfer, and decay will be increasingly important in order to prepare today's pilots for current and upcoming operational requirements through the development of a deep comprehension of the conceptual structure of the diverse problem domain. This is expected to be an essential requirement in order to successfully transfer training experiences to manage live combat situations.

In a recent study, Alliger et al.'s (1997) augmented framework of Kirkpatrick's training criteria taxonomy (1959a, 1959b, 1960a, 1960b) formed the base for an extensive field training evaluation effort covering a simulator exercise preparing fast-jet fighter pilots for a live large force exercise (Castor, Borgvall, and Bennett, 2009). This represented a holistic evaluation approach where data was collected before, during, and after the preparatory simulator training and the live exercises on four different levels of training criteria: reactions, learning, transfer, and results.

In a meta-review of 53 articles, Arthur, Bennett, Stanush, and McNelly (1998) find evidence that performance on physical, natural, and speed-based tasks are less susceptible to skill decay than performance on cognitive, artificial, and accuracy-based tasks. The presented studies support these findings in the way that aircraft handling and maneuvering was found to be a better retained task compared to radar and weapon systems handling. The review also indicates that open-loop tasks such as continuous control are better retained, even for extended time periods (months or even years), than closed-loop discrete tasks. The tasks for a contemporary fighter pilot have, as mentioned earlier, radically changed over the last 20–25 years. Today there is a heavy emphasis on cognitively oriented tasks such as for example sensor and weapon systems handling, and decision making. Taking into account that understanding of the processes behind the acquisition, retention, transfer (and reacquisition) of skills are inseparable in order to understand the whole learning process (e.g., Schmidt and Bjork, 1992), there is a strong need for contemporary studies within this domain, similar to those described here but where an holistic view of the learning process, modern theory, and existing research results are integrated.

NOTES

1   The content of this chapter originates from the doctoral thesis Military Flight Training at a Reasonable Price and Risk by Dr. Maud Angelborg-Thanderz (1990).
2   The introduction is principally based on Thanderz (1973) and Angelborg-Thanderz (1989, 1990). It has, in part, also been presented in Angelborg-Thanderz and Svensson (1994) and Angelborg-Thanderz (1997).
3   In a military system aircraft computerized information, sensor, flight, and weapon systems, together with the operator, form an integral and interactive network in order to accomplish a certain task or mission.
4   Perceived activation, extraversion and psychological stress are dimensions from a mood adjective checklist (MACL) developed by Svensson (1978). Extraversion is closely related to activation and it reflects your momentary motivation to cooperate and to social interaction.

REFERENCES

Alliger, G. M., Beard, R., Bennett, W., Jr., and Colegrove, C. M. (2012). Understanding mission essential competencies as a job analysis method. In M. A. Wilson, W. Bennett, Jr., S. G. Gibston, and G. M. Alliger (Eds.), *The handbook of work analysis: Methods, systems, applications, and science of work measurement in organizations* (pp. 603–624). New York: Routledge.

Alliger, G. M, Beard, R., Bennett, W., Jr., Colegrove, C. M., and Garrity, M. (2007). *Understanding Mission Essential Competencies as a Work Analysis Method* (AFRL-HE-AZ-TR-2007–0034). Mesa, AZ: Air Force Research Laboratory.

Alliger, G. M., Tannenbaum, S. I., Bennett, W., Jr., Traver, H., and Shotland, A. (1997). A meta-analysis of the relations among training criteria. *Personnel Psychology, 50,* 341–358.

Angelborg-Thanderz, M. (1989). Assessing pilot performance in training simulators: A structural analysis. In *Proceedings of The Royal Aeronautical Society Spring Convention: Flight simulation: Assessing the benefits and economics* (pp. 8.1–8.9). London, United Kingdom: The Royal Aeronautical Society.

Angelborg-Thanderz, M. (1990). *Military flight training at a reasonable price and risk* (Stockholm School of Economics Dissertation No. 311). Stockholm, Sweden: Stockholm School of Economics.

Angelborg-Thanderz, M. (1997). Military pilot performance: Dynamic decision making in its extreme. In R. Flin, E. Salas, M. Strub, and L. Martin (Eds.), *Decision making under stress: Emerging themes and applications* (pp. 225–232). Aldershot: Ashgate.

Angelborg-Thanderz, M., and Svensson, E. (1994). The modern military pilot. A managing director rather than a martial warrior. *Military Simulation & Training, 2,* 41–47.

Arthur, W. Jr., Bennett, W. Jr., Stanush, P. L., and McNelly, T. L. (1998). Factors that influence skill decay and retention: A quantitative review and analysis. *Human Performance, 11,* 57–101.

Bennett, W., Jr., Borgvall, J., Lavén, P., Castor, M., Gehr, S. E., Schreiber, B., et al. (2006, June 21). *International mission training research (IMTR): Competency-based methods for interoperable training, rehearsal and evaluation.* In *Proceedings of the Simulation and Interoperability Standards Organization (SISO) European Interoperability Workshop 2006* (EuroSIW 2006) (Paper No. 06E-SIW-052). Retrieved October 5, 2009, from www.sisostds.org/index.php?tg=filemanandidx=listandid=2andgr=Yandpath=Simulation+Interoperability+Workshops%2F2006+Euro+SIW%2F2006+Euro+SIW+Papers+and+ Presentations.

Castor, M. (2009). *The use of structural equation modeling to describe the effect of operator functional state on air-to-air engagements outcomes* (Doctoral dissertation). Retrieved from Linköping University Electronic Press (Accession No. urn:nbn:se:liu:diva-17224).

Castor, M., Borgvall, J., and Bennett, W., Jr. (2009). Knowledge and skill-based evaluation of simulated and live training: From evaluation framework to field application. In *Proceedings of the International Symposium for Aviation Psychology 2009.* Dayton, OH: Wright State University.

Colegrove, C. M., and Alliger, G. M. (2003). Mission essential competencies: Defining combat readiness in a novel way. In NATO Research and Technology Organization (RTO) System Analysis and Studies Panel's (SAS) Symposium, *Air Mission Training*

Through Distributed Simulation *(MTDS)—Achieving and Maintaining Readiness (SAS-038)*. Brussels, Belgium: NATO RTO.

Colegrove, C., and Bennett, W., Jr. (2006). *Competency-based training: Adapting to warfighter needs* (AFRL-HE-AZ-TR-2006–0014). Mesa, AZ: Air Force Research Laboratory.

Ericsson, K. A., and Charness, N. (1994). Expert performance: Its structure and acquisition. *American Psychologist, 49*, 725–747.

Ericsson, K. A., Krampe, R. Th., and Tesch-Römer, C. (1993). The role of deliberate practice in the acquisition of expert performance. *Psychological Review, 100*, 363–406.

Jöreskog K. G., and Sörbom, D. (1984). *LISREL VI: Analysis of linear structural relationships by maximum likelihood, instrumental variables, and least squares methods* (Department of Statistics at Uppsala University). Uppsala, Sweden: Uppsala University.

Kirkpatrick, D. L. (1959a). Techniques for evaluating training programs. *Journal of ASTD, 13*, 3–9.

Kirkpatrick, D. L. (1959b). Techniques for evaluating training programs: Part 2-Learning. *Journal of ASTD, 13*, 21–26.

Kirkpatrick, D. L. (1960a). Techniques for evaluating training programs: Part 3-Behaviour. *Journal of ASTD, 14*, 13–18.

Kirkpatrick, D. L. (1960b). Techniques for evaluating training programs: Part 4-Results. *Journal of ASTD, 14*, 28–32.

Kolb, D. A. (1984). *Experimental learning: Experience as the source of learning and development*. Upper Saddle River, NJ: Prentice Hall.

Kozlowski, S. W. J. (1998). Training and developing adaptive teams: Theory, principles, and research. In J. A. Cannon-Bowers and E. Salas (Eds.), *Making decisions under stress: Implications for individual and team training* (pp. 115–153). Washington, DC: American Psychological Association.

Nählinder, S. (2009). *Flight simulator training: Assessing the potential* (Linköping Studies in Science and Technology Dissertation No. 1250). Linköping, Sweden: Linköping University.

Schmidt, R. A., and Bjork, R. A. (1992). New conceptualizations of practice: Common principles in three paradigms suggest new concepts for training. *Psychological Science, 3*, 207–217.

Svensson, E. (1978). *Mood: Its structure and measurement* (Doctoral thesis). University of Gothenburg, Gothenburg, Sweden.

Svensson, E., and Wilson, G. F. (2002). Psychological and psychophysical models of pilot performance for systems development and mission evaluation. *The International Journal of Aviation Psychology, 12*(1), 95–110.

Svensson, E., Angelborg-Thanderz, M., and Sjöberg, L. (1993). Mission challenge, mental workload, and performance in military aviation. *Aviation, Space, and Environmental Medicine, 64*, 985–991.

Svensson, E., Angelborg-Thanderz, M., Sjöberg, L., and Gillberg, M. (1988). Military flight experience and sympatho-adrenal activity. *Aviation, Space, and Environmental Medicine, 59*, 411–416.

Svensson, E., Angelborg-Thanderz, M., Sjöberg, L., and Olsson, S. (1997). Information complexity: Mental workload and performance in combat aircraft. *Ergonomics, 40*, 362–380.

Svensson, E., Angelborg-Thanderz, M., and Wilson, G. (1999). *Models of pilot performance for systems and mission evaluation: Psychological and psycho-physiological aspects* (AFRL-HE-WP-TR-1999–0215*)*. Dayton, OH: Air Force Research Laboratory.

Thanderz, M. (1973). *A study of pilot training on a modern weapon system* (Institute for Aviation Medicine, Flight Test Centre, Air Material Department, Defence Materiel Administration Rep. No. FMI-73–10). Linköping, Sweden: Defence Material Administration.

Ward, P., Williams, A. M., and Hancock, P. A. (2006). Simulation for performance and training. In K. A. Ericsson, N. Charness, P. J. Feltovich, and R. R. Hoffman (Eds.), *The Cambridge handbook of expertise and expert performance* (pp. 243–262). New York: Cambridge University Press.

11

Relating Individual Differences in Ability, Personality, and Motivation to the Retention and Transfer of Skill on a Complex Command-and-Control Simulation Task

Eric Anthony Day, Winfred Arthur, Jr., Anton J. Villado, Paul R. Boatman, Vanessa Kowollik, Alok Bhupatkar, and Winston Bennett, Jr.

INTRODUCTION

As discussed in Villado et al. (Chapter 3 of this volume), the extant empirical skill retention (decay) research is characterized by relatively simple tasks coupled with relatively short nonuse intervals. As such, it is not too surprising to find a paucity of empirical research relating individual differences to the retention and transfer of skill after extended periods of nonuse on cognitively complex tasks. Although training interventions could certainly be used to mitigate skill decay and promote skill transfer after periods of nonuse (e.g., Schendel and Hagman, 1982), identifying individual difference variables that predict skilled performance after extensive periods of nonuse could also serve as another means by which performance problems associated with nonuse can be addressed. Specifically, the selection of personnel for positions in which extended periods of downtime are common could be based on individual differences found to be predictive of long-term skill retention and transfer. Similarly, at the end of a given training period, individuals who are more likely to need remedial or booster training before being called into action after an extended period of nonuse can be identified. Furthermore, given that performance at the end of a specified acquisition period frequently does not reflect future performance in terms of skill retention and transfer (Schmidt and Bjork, 1992), it is imperative that the search for individual differences extend beyond assessments of skill at the conclusion of training. Consequently, research identifying the individual differences that are predictive of long-term skill retention transfer is worthwhile, especially research that involves or emulates real-world performance contexts such as those commonly associated with military reserve personnel and first responders.

Therefore, the purpose of the present study was to examine how well individual differences in ability, personality, and motivation predict skill retention and transfer after an *extended* period (i.e., 8 weeks) of nonuse[1] on a complex command-and-control microworld simulation. We also included a brief assessment of skill *reacquisition* as a criterion of interest. Cognitive ability was the primary ability factor investigated. We also examined how well a test of declarative knowledge at the end of a designated skill acquisition period predicted skill retention and transfer. Personality variables included conscientiousness and openness to experience. Motivation variables included self-efficacy and achievement motivation (i.e., mastery, performance approach, and performance avoidance goals) assessed at the end of skill acquisition. Transfer was operationalized in terms of adapting ones' skill to novel and overwhelming performance demands. Additionally, we examined the extent to which individual differences in ability, personality, and motivation yield incremental validity in the prediction of skill retention, transfer, and reacquisition beyond immediate assessments of posttraining skill.

So, after completing 10 hours of training on a computer-based command-and-control simulation as well as assessments of ability, personality, and motivation, 192 young adults returned after an 8-week nonuse interval and completed tests of skill retention, transfer, and reacquisition. (These were data stemming from the data collection effort described in Villado et al., Chapter 3 of this volume.) Although none of the individual differences consistently predicted performance across each of the skill-based criteria, skill acquisition and self-efficacy scores taken immediately at the end of training as well as cognitive ability were generally the strongest predictors of performance after nonuse, especially in relation to skill retention. Declarative knowledge and openness were less consistent predictors. Conscientiousness and achievement motivation provided no predictive value. The results are discussed in terms of the need for more ecologically valid research examining how individual differences are related to skilled performance after extensive periods of nonuse.

Ability Factors

The role of individual differences has been recognized as an important but under-studied issue in the skill retention literature (Arthur and Bennett, 1996; Arthur, Bennett, Stanush, and McNelly, 1998). Nevertheless, it is generally argued that higher ability individuals, compared to lower ability individuals, retain more knowledge and skill over periods of nonuse because they acquire more knowledge and skill in the same amount of time (Carron, 1971; Carron and Marteniuk, 1970; Farr, 1987; Fox, Taylor, and Caylor, 1969; Grimsley, 1969a, 1969b; Purdy and Lockhart, 1962; Schendel, Shields, and Katz, 1978; Vineberg, 1975). However, there is dissenting research suggesting that there is also a qualitative difference between higher and lower ability individuals that may explain the enhanced skill retention exhibited by higher ability individuals. Farr (1987), for example, suggested that the differential rates of decay observed between higher and lower ability individuals may be owing to higher ability individuals using more effective strategies to acquire knowledge and skills. This is consistent with Hall, Ford, Whitten, and Plyant (1983) who required Navy sailors to complete two self-paced courses in basic electricity and electronics to a criterion of mastery. After a nonpractice interval ranging from 18 to 34 days, Hall et al. found that higher ability sailors had significantly higher retention scores than lower ability sailors.

In short, cognitive ability has demonstrated a robust relationship with training and job performance (Ree, Carretta, and Teachout, 1995; Ree and Earles, 1991, 1992; Ree, Earles, and Teachout, 1994; Schmidt and Hunter, 1998). Research also has shown that this relationship is largely mediated via knowledge acquisition (Hunter, 1983; Schmidt and Hunter, 1993) such that individuals with greater levels of cognitive ability acquire more job and task knowledge, and it is this higher level of knowledge acquisition that leads to greater performance. This relationship is supported by research indicating that knowledge structures mediate the relationship between cognitive ability and skill-based performance (Day, Arthur, and Gettman, 2001). Research has also shown that measures of cognitive ability are predictive of adaptive performance (LePine, Colquitt, and Erez, 2000; Pulakos et al., 2002). Despite the preponderance of empirical support for the predictive value of cognitive ability, there is a lack of research examining the relationship between cognitive ability and skill retention and adaptive performance after an extended period of nonuse. Nevertheless, despite this lack of research, we tested the hypothesis that cognitive ability would predict and be positively associated with skill retention, transfer, and reacquisition after an extended nonuse period. We similarly tested the hypothesis that declarative knowledge and skilled performance at the end of a given training period would predict and be positively associated with skill retention, transfer, and reacquisition.

Non-ability Factors

The premise that performance is determined by a combination of ability, personality, and motivation is frequently discussed in the training literature. Although there is a host of non-ability individual differences shown to be associated with training outcomes (for a review, see Colquitt, LePine, and Noe, 2000), four variables associated with training motivation have received particular research attention over the last 20 years. These variables are conscientiousness, openness to experience, achievement motivation (also referred to as goal orientation), and self-efficacy. The common theoretical basis for the relationships between these variables and specified training outcomes is the cognitive and information-processing conceptualization of motivation which describes motivation as the combined effects of three choices or decisions, namely decisions pertaining to the direction, level, and persistence of one's effort. These decisions create differences in self-set goals, assessments and interpretations of situations, and reactions to these interpretations.

Personality. Within the framework of the five-factor model of personality (Digman, 1990), conscientiousness and openness to experience have been shown to be related to training performance and learning outcomes (Barrick and Mount, 1991; cf. Gully, Payne, Koles, and Whiteman, 2002; LePine et al., 2000). Conscientiousness is associated with behavioral tendencies such as dependability, perseverance, deliberation, and striving for success. Conscientious individuals are organized and systematic, set more challenging goals, and are more committed to these goals (Barrick, Mount, and Strauss, 1993; Hollenbeck and Klein, 1987). In addition, conscientiousness is related to the motivation to learn (Colquitt and Simmering, 1998). Therefore, we tested the hypothesis that conscientiousness would predict and be positively associated with skill retention, transfer, and reacquisition after extensive periods of nonuse.

Openness to experience pertains to proactive seeking of experience for its own sake as well as a tolerance for and exploration of the unfamiliar (Costa and McCrae, 1992). Individuals high on openness prefer novel situations because they offer variety, while individuals low on openness prefer familiar and routine situations. Because persons high on openness enjoy intellectually stimulating tasks, their thoughts tend to be focused on understanding the nature of an intellectual challenge rather than the possibility of failure. Accordingly, we tested the hypothesis that openness would predict and be positively associated with skill retention, transfer, and reacquisition after extensive nonuse.

Achievement motivation. Achievement motivation is broadly conceptualized as an implicit goal-oriented framework used by individuals to behave in learning and achievement settings (Dweck, 1986). Three dimensions of achievement motivation are widely researched—mastery, performance approach, and performance avoidance (McGregor and Elliot, 2002; VandeWalle, 1997). A mastery orientation involves a focus on improving one's competence by developing new skills—in other words, learning for the sake of learning. A performance-approach orientation refers to a focus on demonstrating one's competence to oneself and others. A performance-avoidance orientation involves a focus on avoiding demonstrating one's lack of competence.

Past research indicates that these three dimensions are related to a variety of achievement-related outcomes. In addition to adaptive cognitive processes such as self-regulation and deep cognitive engagement, numerous investigations have shown that a mastery orientation is positively correlated with attitudinal outcomes such as enjoyment and sustained interest as well as with grades and other performance-based outcomes (e.g., Button, Mathieu, and Zajac, 1996; Day, Radosevich, and Chasteen, 2003; Elliot and Church, 1997; Payne, Youngcourt, and Beaubien, 2007; VandeWalle, Brown, Cron, and Slocum, 1999). Although a performance-approach orientation sometimes yields positive relationships with achievement-related outcomes, links between performance orientations and achievement-related outcomes reflect motivational processes that are distinct from those associated with a mastery orientation (Elliot, McGregor, Holly, and Gable, 1999). For example, performance orientations tend to undermine intrinsic motivation and enjoyment in achievement settings (Elliot and Church, 1997; Elliot and Sheldon, 1997). With a concern for attaining extrinsic outcomes rather than learning and understanding per se, performance orientations tend to be associated with superficial learning strategies and performance-oriented thoughts that are unrelated to developing competence (Elliot and Church, 1997; Elliot and McGregor, 1999). In the present study, we tested the hypothesis that mastery orientation at the end of acquisition training would predict and be positively associated with skill retention, transfer, and reacquisition. Because empirical results have generally been mixed for performance-approach orientation, we did not test a directional hypothesis for this orientation. Performance-avoidance orientation, on the other hand, has been shown to yield inverse relationships with achievement- and performance-based outcomes (Day, Yeo, and Radosevich, 2003; Payne et al., 2007). Therefore, we tested the hypothesis that performance-avoidance orientation at the end of acquisition training would predict and be negatively associated with skill retention, transfer, and reacquisition.

Self-efficacy. Self-efficacy refers to a person's belief that he or she has the capacity to successfully perform specific behaviors or tasks (Bandura, 1977, 1986; Wood and Bandura, 1989). On the one hand, meta-analytic investigations have shown that self-efficacy is positively related to performance in a variety of work-related settings (Sadri and Robertson, 1993; Stajkovic and Luthans, 1998). In particular, it has been shown that self-efficacy plays a prominent role in training motivation, yielding positive associations with learning and performance throughout the training process and in posttraining transfer contexts (Bell and Kozlowski, 2008; Colquitt et al., 2000). On the other hand, there is a body of research suggesting that the causal roles played by self-efficacy may not be as straightforward and direct as many might think. For example, there is currently a debate in the literature regarding causality between self-efficacy and performance (Heggestad and Kanfer, 2005), and recent meta-analytic research has demonstrated that self-efficacy offers little if any main effect on performance after controlling for prior performance and other individual differences related to motivation and performance (Arthur, Bell, and Edwards, 2007; Judge, Jackson, Shaw, Scott, and Rich, 2007). Moreover, recent research (e.g., Vancouver and Kendall, 2006) has even demonstrated that under certain conditions self-efficacy may be negatively related to performance. However, we are unaware of any previous research in the literature that has examined the relationship between self-efficacy and performance after an extended period of nonuse. Thus, the present study contributes to the extant literature by investigating the predictive and incremental validity of self-efficacy assessed at the end of acquisition with respect to retention, transfer, and reacquisition after an extended period of nonuse after training. Accordingly, we tested the hypothesis that self-efficacy at the end of skill acquisition would predict and be positively associated with tests of skill retention, transfer, and reacquisition.

METHOD

Participants

The sample for the present study was the 192 participants described in Villado et al. (Chapter 3 of this volume). This sample (77 percent young adult males) from the campuses and surrounding communities of Texas A&M University and the University of Oklahoma completed approximately 10 hours of training on a cognitively complex command-and-control simulation task and assessments of ability, personality, and motivation. They then returned for tests of skill retention, transfer, and reacquisition after an 8-week nonuse interval.

Measures and Procedures

Performance task—Jane's Fleet Command. As described in Chapter 3, the performance task was Jane's Fleet Command (JFC) (Sonalysts, Inc., 2004, Air Force Research Laboratory ver. 1.55) which is a PC-based real-time micro-simulation of modern naval warfare featuring ships, aircraft, submarines, and airbases on land. Skilled performance on Jane's Fleet Command was operationalized as the mission effectiveness of test missions at the end of approximately 10 hours of training (i.e., skill acquisition), after an 8-week nonuse period (i.e., skill retention), on a novel mission (i.e., skill transfer), and after approximately 30 minutes of reacquisition training (i.e., skill reacquisition). Similar missions were used for the tests of acquisition, retention, and reacquisition. The test of transfer involved a very different mission consisting of both novel and overwhelming performance demands. The transfer mission was the most complex and difficult mission faced by trainees. It required trainees to implement all of the strategies and techniques presented in all of the preceding training sessions and test missions. Whereas in other missions trainees may have used proficiency in one area (e.g., sensor and weapons use, strike coordination, and resource management) to compensate for a deficiency in another area, effective performance on the test of transfer required proficiency in all tasks simultaneously. Furthermore, this transfer mission also presented trainees with an environment that was novel, both in terms of the platforms under their command and the strategy necessary to achieve the mission objectives and goals. This mission required trainees to employ new platforms with unique capabilities, search for and engage an enemy fleet that was defended unlike any other previous fleet they had engaged, while for the first time defending their fleet from two separate attacks simultaneously. Villado et al. (Chapter 3 of this volume) provide a more complete description of Jane's Fleet Command and the composition of training and test missions.

Cognitive ability. The Raven's Advanced Progressive Matrices (APM; Raven, Raven, and Court, 1998) was used to operationalize cognitive ability. The APM consists of 36 matrix problems arranged in an ascending order of difficulty. Each problem involves a logical pattern with a piece missing. The respondent's task is to select the piece that best completes the pattern from eight alternatives. Because its stimuli are nonverbal and do not require a specific knowledge base to be understood, the APM should not be heavily influenced by a respondent's acquired knowledge or reading ability (Saccuzzo and Johnson, 1995). This has led many experts to argue that it is among the purest available measures of general cognitive ability and complex reasoning (e.g., Carpenter, Just, and Snell, 1990; Humphreys, 1984). We used an administration time of 40 minutes. The test manual reports a test–retest reliability of .91 and strong evidence of convergent validity for APM scores. The APM was scored by summing the number of problems answered correctly. We obtained a Spearman-Brown odd–even split-half reliability of .84 for the APM scores. Trainees completed the APM prior to the start of training.

Declarative knowledge. We developed a 21-item 3-alternative multiple-choice test to assess knowledge of JFC instructions, procedural rules, and information presented during training. The test was scored by summing the number of items answered correctly. Trainees completed this test after completing their final mission at the end of acquisition (Session 9).

Personality. Goldberg's 100 Unipolar Markers (Goldberg, 1992) was used to assess personality. Using a nine-point scale (1 = extremely inaccurate; 9 = extremely accurate), trainees described themselves by rating a list of 100 adjectives. For purposes of this study, only the 20 items for conscientious-ness and 20 items for openness to experience were examined. Item responses were summed to derive the personality dimension scores. Coefficient alphas of .90 and .85 were obtained for the conscientiousness and openness scores, respectively. Trainees completed the Unipolar Markers prior to the start of training.

Achievement motivation. A 17-item scale adapted from Elliot and Church (1997) was used to operationalize the three task-specific achievement motiva-tion dimensions. Example items included, "It is important to me to do better at Fleet Command than the other trainees in this study" (performance approach), "I want to learn as much as possible about Fleet Command during this study" (mastery), and "I would prefer to avoid playing Fleet Command in front of someone else because I might perform poorly" (performance avoidance). Trainees responded using a 5-point scale (1 = strongly disagree; 5 = strongly agree). Item responses were averaged to derive each dimension score. Coefficient alphas of .94, .91, and .87 were obtained for the performance approach, mastery, and performance avoidance scores, respectively. Trainees completed the achievement motivation scales after completing their final mission at the end of acquisition (Session 9).

Self-efficacy. The self-efficacy scale used in this study was based on items from scales used in several previous studies (e.g., Bell and Kozlowski, 2002; Martocchio and Judge, 1997; Nease, Mudgett, and Quiñones, 1999) as well as items developed specifically for this study. The scale consisted of 12 items, including "I can meet the challenges of Fleet Command" and "I am confident that I have what it takes to perform Fleet Command well." Trainees responded using a 5-point scale (1 = strongly disagree; 5 = strongly agree). Item responses were averaged to derive the self-efficacy scores. A coefficient alpha of .93 was obtained for the self-efficacy scores. Trainees completed the self-efficacy scale after completing their final mission at the end of acquisition (Session 9).

RESULTS

Table 11.1 shows the means, standard deviations, and correlations for all the study variables. With the exception of skill transfer, the means and standard deviations indicate that performance scores were relatively stable across criteria. The tests of skill acquisition and retention reflect only a small decrement in performance after the 8-week nonuse interval ($d = -0.15$). Consistent with what might be expected when facing a novel mission with overwhelming performance demands, there was a substantial decrement in performance on the test of transfer after the test of retention ($d = -1.72$). Performance after a brief period of reacquisition training was at par with, in fact slightly better than performance on the test of skill acquisition prior to the 8-week nonuse interval ($d = 0.12$). Criterion scores were only slightly correlated with each other (mean $r = .18$).

We used a combination of statistical approaches in our examination of how well individual differences in ability, personality, and motivation predict skill retention, transfer, and reacquisition after a prolonged period of nonuse. First, we examined simple correlations. Second, we examined the incremental validity of our predictor variables beyond immediate assessments of post-training skill by computing partial correlations controlling for the influence of skill acquisition scores. Finally, we examined the unique predictive validity (i.e., contribution) of each individual difference variable by regressing skill retention, transfer, and reacquisition scores on all of the individual difference variables simultaneously. Table 11.2 shows the partial correlations and a summary of the regression results.

In terms of ability factors, the results show mixed support for our hypotheses. With respect to skill retention and transfer scores, cognitive ability yielded statistically significant correlations, incremental validity beyond skill acquisition, and unique predictive validity in the presence of all the individual difference variables. However, cognitive ability was not related to reacquisition scores. Declarative knowledge yielded statistically significant correlations and incremental validity beyond skill acquisition with transfer and reacquisition scores, but in the presence of all the individual difference variables, declarative knowledge only made a unique contribution to transfer scores. Declarative

TABLE 11.1

Means, Standard Deviations, and Correlations of Study Variables

Variable	M	SD	1	2	3	4	5	6	7	8	9	10	11
1. Cognitive ability	26.91	4.32	—										
2. Conscientious	122.51	21.20	-.10	—									
3. Openness	132.39	17.81	.10	.24**	—								
4. Performance approach	3.49	0.91	.06	.11	.10	—							
5. Mastery	3.62	0.72	.01	.12	.08	.43**	—						
6. Performance avoidance	2.45	0.90	-.09	.01	-.10	.26**	.18*	—					
7. Self-efficacy	3.65	0.75	.06	.12	.17*	.45**	.60**	-.19**	—				
8. Declarative knowledge	17.37	2.14	.22**	-.02	.19**	.15*	.06	-.18*	.30**	—			
9. Skill acquisition	17.91	18.89	.09	.07	-.01	.18*	.07	-.18*	.33**	.20**	—		
10. Skill retention	15.18	17.79	.22**	-.04	-.05	.10	.08	-.10	.25**	.11	.27**	—	
11. Skill transfer	-14.08	16.24	.15*	.03	-.16*	.02	.04	-.09	.12	.17*	.14*	.02	—
12. Skill reacquisition	20.28	21.05	.12	-.12	-.05	.06	-.01	-.14*	.22**	.21**	.25**	.28**	.11

$N = 192$. $*p < .05$, $**p < .01$, two-tailed.

TABLE 11.2

Partial Correlations and Regression Results

Variable	Retention		Transfer		Reacquisition	
	pr	β	*pr*	β	*pr*	β
Cognitive ability[a]	.21**	.21**	.14*	.14*	.10	.07
Conscientiousness[a]	−.06	−.03	.02	.10	−.13	−.11
Openness	−.05	−.10	−.16*	−.23**	−.05	−.08
Performance approach	.05	−.02	.00	−.03	.01	−.01
Mastery[a]	.06	−.07	.03	.00	−.03	−.15
Performance avoidance	−.05	.01	−.06	−.04	−.10	−.02
Self-efficacy[a]	.18*	.26**	.07	.07	.15*	.25**
Declarative knowledge[a]	.06	−.02	.14*	.15*	.17*	.12
Skill acquisition[a]	—	.18*	—	.07	—	.15*
R^2		.15**		.11*		.15**
Adjusted R^2		.11		.06		.10

$N = 192$. pr = correlations partialling out the influence of skill acquisition. [a]Levels of statistical significance reflect one-tailed tests based on hypothesized positive relationships. *$p < .05$. **$p < .01$.

knowledge was not related to retention scores. Skill acquisition yielded statistically significant correlations with retention, transfer, and reacquisition scores, but skill acquisition only made a unique contribution to retention and reacquisition scores.

The results generally show mixed support for our hypotheses pertaining to personality and motivational variables. On the one hand, the results show no support for our hypotheses concerning conscientiousness, openness, and achievement motivation. Conscientiousness yielded no statistically significant associations with any of the criterion scores. Openness was not related to retention or reacquisition scores. In sharp contrast to what was hypothesized, openness was inversely related to transfer scores. With the exception of the correlation between performance avoidance and reacquisition scores, achievement motivation variables did not yield statistically significant associations with any of the criterion scores.

On the other hand, the results are more supportive of our hypothesis for self-efficacy. With respect to skill retention and reacquisition scores, self-efficacy yielded statistically significant correlations, incremental validity beyond skill acquisition, and unique predictive validity in the presence of all the individual difference variables. However, self-efficacy was not related to transfer scores.

DISCUSSION

The extant literature on training and skilled performance contains little empirical research involving the performance of complex tasks after extensive periods of nonuse. For instance, the empirical literature on skill decay is replete with studies involving simple tasks and relatively short (less than 1 week, and much of the time less than 1 day or even 1 hour) nonuse intervals. As such, one could argue that the extant literature on training and skilled performance suffers from relatively poor ecological validity in relation to many real-world contexts in which periods of nonuse can be prolonged. Thus, this study makes an important contribution to the training and skilled performance literature by relating individual differences in ability, personality, and motivation to the performance of a cognitively complex command-and-control simulation after an extended, 8-week period of nonuse.

In looking at our findings overall, one general conclusion that could be made is that skill retention, transfer, and reacquisition on cognitively complex tasks are related yet meaningfully distinct phenomena. We base this conclusion on the relatively small intercorrelations among the criterion scores as well as the fact that none of the individual difference variables, even skill acquisition, was a robust predictor for all three criteria. The regression results showed that each criterion was associated with a different set of predictors. Skill retention was predicted by a combination of cognitive ability, self-efficacy, and skill acquisition. Skill transfer was predicted by a combination of cognitive ability, openness, and declarative knowledge. Skill reacquisition was predicted by a combination of self-efficacy and skill acquisition. Moreover, the combination of individual differences at most accounted for 15 percent of the variance in criterion scores. It would appear that accounting for the variance in the performance of dynamic and cognitively complex tasks after extensive periods of nonuse is a challenging undertaking.

Similar to what was reported in Villado et al. (2013) pertaining to skill decay across varying lengths of nonuse, we obtained relatively small and less consistent findings compared to those of more micro-scaled studies. In considering these differences in effects and the vital importance of minimizing skill decay and facilitating transfer and reacquisition in such applied contexts as military and rescue operations, we believe that substantially more ecologically valid research on skill decay is needed before strong practical recommendations can be made. In the sections below, we discuss our findings in reference to the extant literature, tentative practical recommendations, and directions for future research.

Relating Individual Differences to Skilled Performance after Prolonged Nonuse

Although cognitive ability is characterized in the scholarly literature as a strong and robust predictor of job and training performance (Ree et al., 1995; Ree and Earles, 1991), in this study cognitive ability was only a modest predictor of skilled performance after extensive nonuse. Nevertheless, cognitive ability did yield incremental validity beyond skill acquisition and declarative knowledge in the prediction of skill retention and transfer, thus supporting claims that the link between cognitive ability and skilled performance after nonuse is not fully mediated by knowledge (or skill acquisition) and there may be *qualitative* differences in learning strategies between high- and low-ability individuals (e.g., Farr, 1987). This incremental validity is also consistent with recent causal models of training performance that link cognitive ability both distally and directly to training outcomes (Bell and Kozlowski, 2008; Colquitt et al., 2000).

In contrast to recent research questioning the positive incremental value of self-efficacy in predicting future performance beyond prior levels of performance (e.g., Heggestad and Kanfer, 2005; Judge et al., 2007), our results showed significant incremental prediction for self-efficacy with respect to skill retention and reacquisition. One plausible explanation for this difference in reported findings may be the extensive nonuse period separating the assessment of self-efficacy and the tests of retention and reacquisition. Perhaps self-efficacy contains motivational properties not reflected in prior perform-ance that have more influence on performance after extensive nonuse rather than more immediate performance. Such a conclusion is consistent with research showing a direct link between self-efficacy and posttraining adaptive performance (e.g., Bell and Kozlowski, 2008; Kozlowski et al., 2001). Regardless, our observed incremental validity for self-efficacy warrants replication in future research, and the examination of specific mediating processes would also be informative.

The effects for mastery orientation were nonsignificant in terms of predicting performance after the extended nonuse period. These findings may not be too surprising given the relatively weak correlations found between mastery orientation and performance-based outcomes (Day et al., 2003; Payne et al., 2007). It may be more fruitful to consider more volition-based conse-quences of mastery orientation than actual performance-based outcomes (cf. Brown, 2001). The effects for conscientiousness and performance orienta-tions were consistently nonsignificant in our analyses. Although this might be expected for performance-approach orientation given the mixed results found across the body of previous research, the lack of significant negative relationships for performance-avoidance orientation is at odds with previous research (Payne et al., 2007). On one hand, the lack of effects for conscientiousness is inconsistent with previous studies linking conscientiousness to training outcomes (Barrick and Mount, 1991). On the other hand, the lack of effects might be expected in the light of more recent research (LePine et al., 2000) showing that some dimensions of conscientiousness (e.g., order, dutifulness, and deliberation) are differentially and negatively related to adaptability compared to other dimensions of conscientiousness (e.g., competence, achievement striving, and self-discipline).

Perhaps the most surprising result from this study was the inverse relationship between openness and skill transfer. Consistent with previous research showing positive relationships between openness and training outcomes (e.g., Barrick and Mount, 1991; Gully et al., 2002), we hypothesized a positive association between openness and skill transfer. The theoretical basis for this hypothesis stems from the motivational properties associated with openness, such as tolerance for and exploration of the unfamiliar, preference for variety, a preference for intellectually stimulating tasks, and a focus on understanding a challenge rather than on the possibility of failure (Costa and McCrae, 1992). With these motivational properties in mind, it is important to note that the transfer mission used in this study involved novel as well as *overwhelming* performance demands. Although the motivational properties associated with openness may be adaptive in the face of novel performance demands, we speculate that these motivational properties may be maladaptive in terms of immediately addressing overwhelming demands. In an overwhelming situation, individuals high in openness may search for optimal solutions or strategies whereas individuals low in openness may focus on simply performing actions that reasonably address the demands placed on them ("putting out fires"). Those high in openness are more likely to attempt a wide range of novel actions and even purposely make errors simply to better understand the situation. In an immediate sense, just taking action is likely more adaptive than searching for the optimal solution. This relationship between openness and performance under overwhelming demands may be exacerbated in the presence of novel demands, which was the case in the transfer missions used in this study. Furthermore, it may be that openness yields negative relationships with immediate performance under novel and overwhelming situations, but conversely it yields positive relationships with performance after greater exposure to the transfer situation. However, we acknowledge that this is largely speculative and hence call for future research to investigate the relationship between openness and the performance of complex tasks under novel and overwhelming demands.

An important boundary condition that qualifies our findings and any inferences that may be drawn from them is that there is a paucity of published empirical research examining the relationships between individual differences and performance on complex tasks after extended periods of nonuse (Arthur et al., 1998). Hence, additional studies that replicate and also constructively replicate our findings are required before any strong inferences and implications can be arrived at on the basis of the findings reported here.

The Nature of Acquisition in Research on Skill Retention and Performance after Extensive Nonuse

As discussed in Villado et al. (2013), we defined the skill acquisition phase as a fixed amount of training time (i.e., 10 hours of training) as opposed to a specified level of performance (e.g., 90 percent mission effectiveness, one errorless mission, or three errorless missions). Training to a specified level of performance and training for a fixed amount of time represent two distinct ways of defining the training acquisition phase. Related to this, it is plausible that individual differences in ability, personality, and motivation will differentially relate to skill retention, transfer, and reacquisition as a function of how the end of the acquisition phase of training is operationalized. For instance, training to a specified performance level or mastery may differentially influence individual differences on some variables—an example of which might be trainees' efficacy levels at the end of training. Thus, one could envisage a situation in which the range of individual differences in self-efficacy might be restricted with the resultant restriction in range subsequently attenuating the predictive validity of self-efficacy. Consequently, it would seem worthwhile for future research to examine how the predictive validities of individual difference variables are affected by different operationalizations of the training acquisition phase.

IMPLICATIONS FOR PRACTICE, AND CONCLUSIONS

A practical implication of our findings is that measures of cognitive ability could be considered as predictors of performance in positions that involve prolonged periods of downtime on critical tasks. In addition, these findings would also suggest that it is important to know not only trainees' skill levels at the end of acquisition prior to the nonuse interval, but also their efficacy levels. Thus, a recommendation is for training practitioners to use adequate measures of skill and self-efficacy during or after the completion of training to identify those individuals likely to require remedial or booster training.

Nevertheless, the modest predictive validity observed in the study for post-training skill and self-efficacy is a reminder of how criterion assessments taken upon the completion of training are not surrogates for more distal criteria (Alliger, Tannenbaum, Bennett, Traver, and Shotland, 1997; Schmidt and Bjork, 1992).

Indeed, after considering the modest predictive validity obtained in the present study, it would seem that substantially more research is needed to better understand the roles that individual differences play in performance after extended periods of nonuse. We recommend expanding the number and variety of individual differences (e.g., locus of control) as well as examining causal networks that include both distal and proximal predictors. Proximal predictors could include the same state attributes as in the present study but assessed longitudinally with some assessments occurring temporally closer (i.e., toward the end of the nonuse period) to tests of skill retention, transfer, and reacquisition. Proximal predictors could also include self-regulatory (e.g., goal-setting) and cognitive processes (e.g., metacognition and elaborative rehearsal) that might mediate the effects of more distal individual differences (e.g., conscientiousness, mastery orientation, and self-efficacy) and training interventions.

In sum, there is a near absence of empirical investigations concerning the relationships between individual differences and the performance of trained complex skills after extensive periods of nonuse. For instance, empirical investigations of retention and transfer typically involve simple tasks and short periods of nonuse. By using a cognitively complex criterion task and an 8-week nonuse interval, we attempted to conduct a more ecologically valid investigation than typically found in the extant skill decay literature. However, the laboratory nature and the predominantly student sample of this study limit the extent to which generalizations can be made to real-world contexts. Certainly, there is a need for field studies. Thus, we consider this study to be an initial step toward better understanding how individual differences relate to complex task performance after extensive nonuse intervals. We hope this study inspires researchers to use more ecologically valid designs in the future when studying the relationships between individual differences and performance after extensive nonuse.

NOTE

1   As reviewed in Villado et al. (Chapter 3 of this volume), this study is part of a larger project in which one of the objectives was to examine the relative levels of skill retention (decay) as a function of the length of the nonuse interval. To accomplish this objective, participants were randomly assigned to return once during one of the 8 weeks following training only to complete a test of skill retention. Therefore, the 8-week nonuse interval

discussed in the present study was not a pure nonuse interval. However, we believe this 8-week period can be reasonably considered a nonuse interval, because the amount of time to complete the test of retention during the 8-week interval was rather short relative to both the total 8-week time period (25 minutes compared to approximately 80,640 minutes) and the prior training period (25 minutes compared to approximately 600 minutes).

REFERENCES

Alliger, G. M., Tannenbaum, S. I., Bennett, W., Jr., Traver, H., and Shotland, A. (1997). A meta-analysis of relations among training criteria. *Personnel Psychology, 50,* 341–358.

Arthur, W. Jr., and Bennett, W. Jr. (1996). *Skill retention and decay: A meta-analysis [Final report].* (AL/HR-TR-1996-XXXX). AL/HRTD contract F41622–93-M-2342, Technical Training Division, Brooks AFB, TX.

Arthur, W. Jr., Bell, S. T., and Edwards, B. D. (2007). A longitudinal examination of the comparative criterion-related validity of additive and referent-shift consensus operationalizations of team efficacy. *Organizational Research Methods, 10,* 35–58.

Arthur, W. Jr., Bennett, W. Jr., Stanush, P. L., and McNelly, T. L. (1998). Factors that influence skill decay and retention: A quantitative review and analysis. *Human Performance, 11,* 57–101.

Bandura, A. (1977). *Social learning theory.* Englewood Cliffs, NJ: Prentice-Hall.

Bandura, A. (1986). *Social foundations of thought and action: A social cognitive theory.* Englewood Cliffs, NJ: Prentice-Hall.

Barrick, M. R., and Mount, M. K. (1991). The Big Five personality dimensions and job performance: A meta-analysis. *Personnel Psychology, 44,* 1–26.

Barrick, M. R., Mount, M. K., and Strauss, J. P. (1993). Conscientiousness and performance of sales representatives: Tests of the mediating effects of goal setting. *Journal of Applied Psychology, 78,* 715–722.

Bell, B. S., and Kozlowski, S. W. J. (2002). Goal orientation and ability: Interactive effects on self-efficacy, performance, and knowledge. *Journal of Applied Psychology, 87,* 497–505.

Bell, B. S., and Kozlowski, S. W. J. (2008). Active learning: Effects of core training design elements on self-regulatory processes, learning, and adaptability. *Journal of Applied Psychology, 93,* 296–316.

Brown, K. G. (2001). Using computers to deliver training: Which employees learn and why? *Personnel Psychology, 54,* 271–296.

Button, S. B., Mathieu, J. E., and Zajac, D. M. (1996). Goal orientation in organizational research: A conceptual and empirical foundation. *Organizational Behavior and Human Decision Processes, 67,* 26–48.

Carpenter, P. A., Just, M. A., and Snell, P. (1990). What one intelligence test measures: A theoretical account of the processing in the Raven Progressive Matrices test. *Psychological Review, 97,* 404–431.

Carron, A. V. (1971). Effect of ability upon retention of a balance skill as a function of initial ability level. *Perceptual and Motor Skills, 33,* 527–529.

Carron, A. V., and Marteniuk, R. C. (1970). Retention as a balance skill as a function of initial ability level. *Research Quarterly, 41,* 478–483.

Colquitt, J. A., and Simmering, M. J. (1998). Conscientiousness, goal orientation, and motivation to learn during the learning process: A longitudinal study. *Journal of Applied Psychology, 81*, 110–116.

Colquitt, J. A., LePine, J. A., and Noe, R. (2000). Toward an integrative theory of training motivation: A meta-analytic path analysis of 20 years of research. *Journal of Applied Psychology, 85*, 678–707.

Costa, P. T., Jr., and McCrae, R. R. (1992). *NEO-PI-R: Professional Manual. Revised NEO Personality Inventory (NEO-PI-R) and NEO Five-Factor Inventory (NEO-FFI).* Odessa, FL: Psychological Assessment Resources.

Day, E. A., Arthur, W. Jr., and Gettman, D. (2001). Knowledge structures and the acquisition of a complex skill. *Journal of Applied Psychology, 86*, 1022–1033.

Day, E. A., Radosevich, D. J., and Chasteen, C. S. (2003). Construct- and criterion-related validity of four commonly used goal orientation instruments. *Contemporary Educational Psychology, 28*, 434–464.

Day, E. A., Yeo, S., and Radosevich, D. J. (2003). *Comparing two- and three-factor models of goal orientation: A meta-analysis.* Poster presented at the 18th Annual Conference of the Society for Industrial and Organizational Psychology, Orlando, FL.

Digman, J. M. (1990). Personality structure: Emergence of the five-factor model. *Annual Review of Psychology, 41*, 417–440.

Dweck, C. S. (1986). Motivational processes affecting learning. *American Psychologist, 41*, 1040–1048.

Elliot, A. J., and Church, M. A. (1997). A hierarchical model of approach and avoidance achievement motivation. *Journal of Personality and Social Psychology, 72*, 218–232.

Elliot, A. J., and McGregor, H. A. (1999). Test anxiety and the hierarchical model of approach and avoidance achievement motivation. *Journal of Personality and Social Psychology, 76*, 628–644.

Elliot, A. J., and Sheldon, K. M. (1997). Avoidance achievement motivation: A personal goals analysis. *Journal of Personality and Social Psychology, 73*, 171–185.

Elliot, A. J., McGregor, H. A., Holly, A., and Gable, S. (1999). Achievement goals, study strategies, and exam performance: A mediational analysis. *Journal of Educational Psychology, 91*, 549–563.

Farr, M. J. (1987). *The long-term retention of knowledge and skills: A cognitive and instructional perspective.* New York: Springer-Verlag.

Fox, W. L., Taylor, J. E., and Caylor, J. S. (1969). *Aptitude level and the acquisition of skills and knowledges in a variety of military training tasks.* (HumRRO Technical Report 69–6). Alexandria, VA: Human Resources Research Organization.

Goldberg, L. R. (1992). The development of markers for the Big-Five factor structure. *Psychological Assessment, 4*, 26–42.

Grimsley, D. L. (1969b). *Acquisition, retention, and retraining: Effects of high and low fidelity in training devices.* (HumRRO Technical Report 69–1). Alexandria, VA: Human Resources Research Organization.

Grimsley, D. L. (1969a). *Acquisition, retention, and retraining: Training category IV personnel with low fidelity devices.* (HumRRO Technical Report 69–12). Alexandria, VA: Human Resources Research Organization.

Gully, S., M., Payne, S. C., Koles, K. L. K., and Whiteman, J. K. (2002). The impact of error training and individual differences on training outcomes: An attribute-treatment interaction perspective. *Journal of Applied Psychology, 87*, 143–155.

Hall, E. R., Ford, L. H., Whitten, T. C., and Plyant, L. R. (1983). *Knowledge retention among graduates of basic electricity and electronic schools.* (HumRRO Technical Report 149). Orlando, FL: Training Analysis and Evaluation Group, Department of the Navy.

Heggestad, E. D., and Kanfer, R. (2005). The predictive validity of self-efficacy in training performance: Little more than past performance. *Journal of Experimental Psychology: Applied, 11*, 84–97.

Hollenbeck, J. R., and Klein, H. J. (1987). Goal commitment and the goal-setting process: Problems, prospects, and proposals for future research. *Journal of Applied Psychology, 72*, 212–220.

Humphreys, L. G. (1984). General intelligence. In C. R. Reynolds and R. T. Brown (Eds.), *Perspectives on bias in mental testing* (pp. 221–247). New York: Plenum.

Hunter, J. E. (1983). A causal analysis of cognitive ability, job knowledge, job performance, and supervisor ratings. In F. Landy, S. Zedeck, and J. Cleveland (Eds.), *Performance measurement and theory* (pp. 257–266). Hillsdale, NJ: Lawrence Erlbaum Associates.

Judge, T. A., Jackson, C. L., Shaw, J. C., Scott, B. A., and Rich, B. L. (2007). Self-efficacy and work-related performance: The integral role of individual differences. *Journal of Applied Psychology, 92*, 107–127.

Kozlowski, S. W., Gully, S. M., Brown, K. G., Salas, E., Smith, E. M., and Nason, E. R. (2001). Effects of training goals and goal orientation traits on multidimensional training outcomes and performance adaptability. *Organizational Behavior and Human Decision Processes, 85*, 1–31.

LePine, J. A., Colquitt, J. A., and Erez, A. (2000). Adaptability to changing task contexts: Effects of general cognitive ability, conscientiousness, and openness to experience. *Personnel Psychology, 53*, 563–593.

Martocchio, J. J., and Judge, T. A. (1997). Relationship between conscientiousness and learning in employee training: Mediating influences of self-deception and self-efficacy. *Journal of Applied Psychology, 82*, 764–773.

McGregor, H. A., and Elliot, A. J. (2002) Achievement goals as predictors of achievement-relevant processes prior to task engagement. *Journal of Educational Psychology, 94*, 381–395.

Nease, A. A., Mudgett, B. A., and Quiñones, M. A. (1999). Relationships among feedback sign, self-efficacy, and acceptance of performance feedback. *Journal of Applied Psychology, 84*, 806–814.

Payne, S. C., Youngcourt, S. S., and Beaubien, J. M. (2007). A meta-analytic examination of the goal orientation nomological net. *Journal of Applied Psychology, 92*, 128–150.

Pulakos, E. D., Schmitt, N., Dorsey, Arad, S., Hedge, J. W., and Borman, W. C. (2002). Predicting adaptive performance: Further tests of a model of adaptability. *Human Performance, 15*, 299–323.

Purdy, B. J., and Lockhart, A. (1962). Retention and relearning of gross motor skills after long periods of no practice. *Research Quarterly, 33*, 265–272.

Raven, J. C., Raven, J., and Court, J. H. (1998). *A manual for Raven's Progressive Matrices and Vocabulary Scales*. London: H. K. Lewis.

Ree, M. J., and Earles, J. A. (1991). Predicting training success: Not much more than *g*. *Personnel Psychology, 44*, 321–332.

Ree, M. J., and Earles, J. A. (1992). Intelligence is the best predictor of job performance. *Current Directions in Psychological Science, 1*, 86–89.

Ree, M. J., Carretta, T. R., and Teachout, M. S. (1995). Role of ability and prior job knowledge in complex training performance. *Journal of Applied Psychology, 80*, 721–730.

Ree, M. J., Earles, J. A., and Teachout, M. S. (1994). Predicting job performance: Not much more than *g*. *Journal of Applied Psychology, 79*, 518–524.

Saccuzzo, D. P., and Johnson, N. E. (1995). Traditional psychometric tests and proportionate representation: An intervention and program evaluation study. *Psychological Assessment, 7*, 183–194.

Sadri, G., and Robertson, I. T. (1993). Self-efficacy and work-related behavior: A review and meta-analysis. *Applied Psychology: An International Review, 42,* 139–152.

Schendel, J. D., and Hagman, J. D. (1982). On sustaining procedural skills over a prolonged retention interval. *Journal of Applied Psychology, 67,* 605–610.

Schendel, J. D., Shields, J. L., and Katz, M. S. (1978). *Retention of motor skills: Review.* (Technical Paper 313). Alexandria, VA: U.S. Army Research Institute for the Behavioral and Social Sciences.

Schmidt, F. L., and Hunter, J. E. (1993). Tacit knowledge, practical intelligence, general mental ability, and job knowledge. *Current Directions in Psychological Science, 2,* 8–9.

Schmidt, F. L., and Hunter, J. E. (1998). The validity and utility of selection methods in personnel psychology: Practical and theoretical implications of 85 years of research findings. *Psychological Bulletin, 124,* 262–274.

Schmidt, R. A., and Bjork, R. A. (1992). New conceptualizations of practice: Common principles in three paradigms suggest new concepts in training. *Psychological Science, 3,* 207–217.

Sonalysts, Inc. (2004). *Jane's Fleet Command Air Force Research Laboratory ver. 1.55* [Computer software]. Redwood City, CA: Electronic Arts.

Stajkovic, A. D, and Luthans, F. (1998). Self-efficacy and work-related performance: A meta-analysis. *Psychological Bulletin, 124,* 240–261.

Vancouver, J., and Kendall, L. (2006). When self-efficacy negatively relates to motivation and performance in a learning context. *Journal of Applied Psychology, 91,* 1146–1153.

VandeWalle, D. (1997). Development and validation of a work domain goal orientation instrument. *Educational and Psychological Measurement, 57,* 995–1015.

VandeWalle, D., Brown, S. P., Cron, W. L., and Slocum, Jr., J. W. (1999). The influence of goal orientation and self-regulation tactics on sales performance: A longitudinal field test. *Journal of Applied Psychology, 84,* 249–259.

Villado, A. J., Day, E. A., Arthur, W. Jr., Boatman, P. R., Kowollik, V., Bhupatkar, A., and Bennett, W. Jr. (2013). Complex command-and-control simulation task performance following periods of nonuse. In W. Arthur, Jr., E. A. Day, W. Bennett, Jr., and A. Portrey (Eds.), *Individual and team skill decay: The science and implications for practice* (pp. 53–67). New York: Taylor & Francis.

Vineberg, R. (1975). *A study of the retention skills and knowledge acquired in basic training.* (HumRRO Technical Report 75–10). Alexandria, VA: Human Resources Research Organization.

Wood, R. E., and Bandura, A. (1989). Social cognitive theory of organizational management. *Academy of Management Review, 14,* 361–384.

AUTHORS' NOTES

This research was sponsored by contracts and grants from the U.S. Air Force Research Laboratory, Human Effectiveness Directorate, Warfighter Training Research Division, Mesa, AZ, the Defense Advance Research Project Agency, and the National Science Foundation awarded to Winfred Arthur, Jr. The views expressed herein are those of the authors and do not necessarily reflect the official position or opinion of the sponsors or their respective organizations.

12

Individual Difference Variables as Predictors of Error During Multitasking Training

Elizabeth M. Boyd and Frederick L. Oswald

INTRODUCTION

The retention of skills over extended periods of nonuse is important for individuals in many occupations, particularly those such as the military reserves and emergency response (Villado et al., this volume). It has generally been argued that individuals of higher ability will suffer less decay of learned skills over time (Farr, 1987). For the most part, however, individual differences characteristics other than general ability have not been considered with respect to skill decay and relationships more complex than the one between ability and eventual decay, although it has been acknowledged that more research on these issues is needed (Arthur, Bennett, Stanush, and McNelly, 1998). In addition, the literature on skill decay has been characterized by a focus on simple rather than complex tasks, which stands in stark contrast to the fact that occupations in which skill decay is often cited as being most important require skills that are highly complex and adaptive in nature. The purpose of the present chapter is to contribute to the literature on skill decay by making progress in both of these areas. This will be accomplished by exploring relationships between select cognitive and non-cognitive individual differ-ence characteristics and error during training of a complex skill. Specifically, results are presented from a study involving 102 university students who com-pleted training on a computerized multitasking simulation. The multitasking simulation recorded error data for two types of errors: errors of omission and errors of commission. Data were also collected on working memory, perceptual speed, conscientiousness, and anxiety during the multitasking simulation. Results of the study indicated that working memory was related to errors of commission, perceptual speed was related to errors of omission, and anxiety was related to both types of error.

Skill Decay and Individual Differences

Skill decay refers to the degradation of skills or knowledge over an interval of nonuse and may be contrasted with skill retention, which refers to the preservation of skills or knowledge over such an interval (Arthur et al., 1998). There is agreement in the skill decay literature that higher cognitive ability is associated with lower skill decay over time, either owing to the fact that individuals higher in ability acquire more knowledge during initial acquisition of skills or knowledge or owing to differences in retention strategies (Farr, 1987). There is reason to believe, however, that there may be value in exploring more complex relationships than the direct one between overall ability and eventual skill decay.

Considerations of individual differences and training performance have shown that individuals higher in ability or possessing certain personality characteristics have been shown to perform better during training (Ree and Earles, 1991). Although higher performance during training might seem as though it would be beneficial for the retention of skills, recent research has indicated that committing errors during training can actually increase transfer of training (Keith and Frese, 2005). Transfer of training is the application of trained skills to the work environment; it can be thought of in terms of skill decay because skill retention is essentially transfer over an extended period of nonuse (Kirkpatrick, 1987).

Why would error during training be beneficial? A consistent finding in the literature on risk taking is that potential losses are more salient than potential gains (e.g., De Dreu and McCusker, 1997). Similarly, mistakes or failures are likely to be more salient, and thus more memorable, than successes owing to their infrequency and their association with negative affect (e.g., Roese, 1997). As a result, committing an error helps promote the long-term retention of material encountered during training. Examples of errors leading to long-term retention are not difficult to come by. The first author of this chapter can recall a spelling bee from the fifth grade in which she was asked to spell the word "martyr" and failed to do so correctly; the rest of the words from that year's competition have long since been forgotten, but the missed word is emblazoned on her memory owing to its salience as an error.

Because committing errors while one is still in the stage of learning or being trained on a new skill has the potential to promote long-term retention, *not* committing such errors may actually have a negative impact on long-term transfer. If individuals possessing certain characteristics tend to commit fewer errors during training, then it may be the case that these individuals could be negatively impacted in terms of skill retention over time.

In past research exploring the relationship between error making during training and transfer of training, researchers have focused on the nature of training in inducing errors (e.g., Keith and Frese, 2005). Research has shown that error-encouragement training, where errors are prompted and encouraged rather than discouraged during training, shows a positive relationship with learning and transfer outcomes, as opposed to training where errors are discouraged or typical training methods. Although researchers have explored the role of individual differences and self-efficacy during error-encouragement training, the direct relationship between individual differences and error-making during training independently of interventions aimed at encouraging errors has not been studied empirically, and as such this will be the focus of the present study.

Complex Skills and Skill Decay

Although researchers have contributed a great deal to the issue of skill retention with respect to simple skills, research involving more complex or adaptive skills of the kind more likely to be needed in today's modern occupations is needed (Villado et al., this volume). Simple skills and complex skills are significantly different in nature, and in ways that have implications for skill retention and decay. For instance, Nembhard and Osothsilp (2002) found that variability among individuals on learning and forgetting increased as task complexity increased.

Multitasking is one complex skill that is becoming increasingly important in many occupations, and is particularly important in many of the occupations such as those mentioned above requiring the recall of trained skills. Multitasking can be generally described as the performance of multiple tasks in a relatively short time period, with shifts in attention among the tasks (Oswald, Hambrick, and Jones, 2007). Multitasking can be challenging not only as a result of the task demands themselves, but also owing to the additional process of organizing and prioritizing the tasks within a time span that may be either limited or unknown to the individual or team that is performing. A person's capability to adapt to changing task priorities may be critical to his or her performance during multitasking, and the failure to shift one's attention accordingly may result in serious performance errors.

For many individuals, multitasking has become an essential requirement of modern home and work life owing to general increases in the pace of life, broadening of work roles, and expectations for individual performance and productivity (Bühner, König, Pick, and Krumm, 2006). This is particularly true in occupations such as those discussed in this chapter, where emergency situations call not only for the usage of skills trained long ago, but also for multitasking and adaptive performance. For example, flight attendants involved in an emergency situation such as the US Airways Hudson River landing in January 2009 not only had to recall emergency management skills learned long ago during training, but also had to manage multiple task priorities such as keeping passengers calm, opening emergency exits, ensuring the evacuation of passengers, and attempting to prevent the flooding of the aircraft. Little research has addressed the issue of complex skill decay, and as such the present chapter will attempt to explore the training of a complex skill: performance at a computerized multitasking scenario.

The Nature of Multitasking and Error in this Context

Multitasking is a broad construct and it is not possible for any given multitasking simulation or scenario to represent all potential forms of multitasking. We will, however, highlight some of the major attributes of the type of multitasking on which we will focus in this chapter. The type of multitasking on which we focus is the type that would potentially be required by individuals in the military or in an emergency situation, in that it consists mainly of tasks that impose switches upon the multitasker rather than allowing him or her to choose when to switch.

In an emergency situation such as a fire, elements of the situation such as the condition of the burning structure or of fire victims change as a result of conditions external to the individual attempting to manage the situation (the emergency responder), necessitating that s/he switch from one task to another in response to these changing task priorities. This is in contrast to other forms of multitasking where the multitasker is essentially "in charge" of the switches, such as when an individual chooses to switch over to another task such as email while working on a writing assignment.

Error may be broadly defined as performing an action that deviates from an individual's intended performance. It is useful within the present context to differentiate between two forms of error: errors of commission and errors of omission. Errors of commission are defined as errors where an individual takes action, but the action taken is incorrect. Errors of omission are defined as errors where an individual fails to perform what would have been a correct action (Reason, 1990). Even the most cursory literature search shows that these two general forms of errors have been examined across numerous research disciplines such as decision making (e.g., Gilovich, Medvec, and Chen, 1995), medicine (e.g., Overhage, Tierney, Zhou, and McDonald, 1997), clinical psychology (e.g., Losier, McGrath, and Klein, 1996), human factors (Fields, Wright, and Harrison, 1995), and occupational safety (e.g., Wallace and Chen, 2006).

Both errors of commission and errors of omission have the potential to occur during the type of multitasking just described, and such errors are likely to be related to one's ability (or inability) to shift attention as task priorities change (see Figure 12.1). Within the multitasking framework discussed herein, errors of commission are defined as actions taken within individual tasks that deviate from the correct action. Errors of omission are defined as failing to recognize that a switch from one task to another should be made and allowing a task priority to lapse. A task priority is defined as an action that should have been taken within an individual task. The purpose of the present paper is to explore whether individual difference characteristics (both ability and non-ability factors) predict these errors during the training of multitasking. We will now present a theoretical rationale for the individual difference characteristics of interest in the present study, as well as our hypotheses.

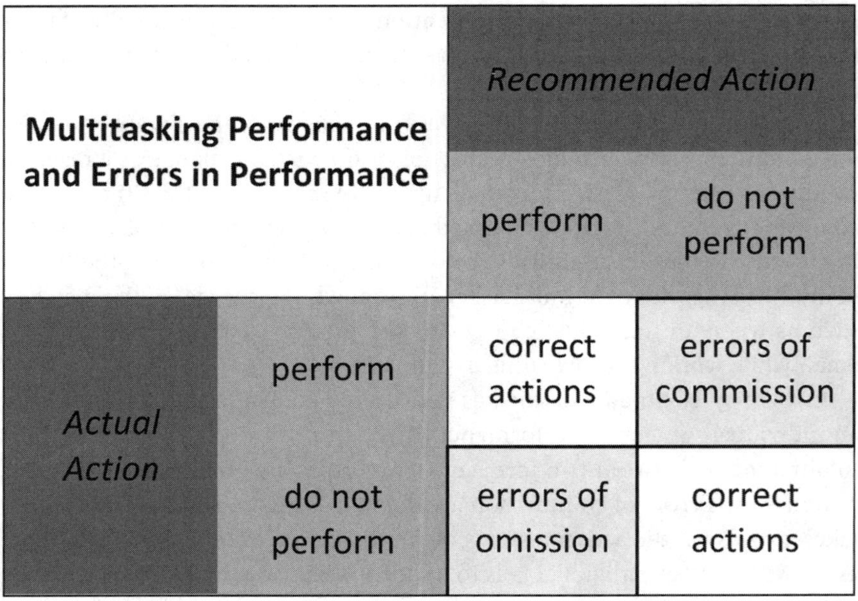

Multitasking Performance and Errors in Performance		Recommended Action	
		perform	do not perform
Actual Action	perform	correct actions	errors of commission
	do not perform	errors of omission	correct actions

FIGURE 12.1

Errors in multitasking performance.

Proposed Relationships

Cognitive characteristics. Past research on multitasking has established that two cognitive ability characteristics are of primary importance in predicting performance. Working memory is defined as the ability to actively maintain information in mind, and has been consistently shown to be associated with multitasking performance (Salthouse, Hambrick, Lukas, and Dell, 1996). Perceptual speed is both a cognitive and psychomotor factor defined as the ability to quickly and accurately identify (and often match or compare) objects, and has been shown to be positively related to performance at complex tasks involving multitasking (Ackerman, 1992; Ackerman and Cianciolo, 2002).

Because it reflects an individual's capacity to keep information in mind, *working memory* should be associated with the degree to which information about various task priorities and status is encoded, stored and retrieved while the tasks themselves are being performed. Therefore, individuals low in working memory, as a result of the fact that they have fewer resources for keeping information about tasks in mind, should have more difficulty switching between tasks. Because task switches within the multitasking context of this chapter are imposed rather than self-paced, working memory should not be related to errors of omission because when a shift in task priority occurs, the failure to notice the need to switch tasks should not depend on one's ability to keep task information in mind, but rather one's capacity for recognizing the shift and attending to the newly important task. Therefore, no prediction regarding working memory and errors of omission is made.

H1: Working memory will be negatively correlated with errors of commission. Because it reflects an individual's ability to quickly identify features of the external environment, people high in perceptual speed should be better able to quickly identify when a task priority has changed and when a switch is therefore needed. Failing to do so, by contrast, should result in failing to act when doing so is necessary. Recognizing that a task priority has changed and a switch must be made, however, does not guarantee that the correct action will be taken. Thus, it is possible that either an incorrect or a correct action could follow a switch to the correct task. Therefore, we make no prediction regarding the relationship between perceptual speed and errors of commission.

H2: Perceptual speed will be negatively correlated with errors of omission.
Non-cognitive characteristics. Conscientiousness is a personality trait reflecting an individual's tendency to behave in ways that are self-disciplined, careful, and diligent and has been shown to be a valid predictor of work performance across settings (e.g., Barrick and Mount, 1991). Although previous researchers

have not explored the relationship between conscientiousness and multitasking performance, there is reason to believe that conscientiousness may be related to errors in multitasking. Conscientious individuals are more likely to be paying attention to the task, rather than becoming distracted by other features of the environment or their own thoughts about unrelated issues. They are more likely to watch diligently for changes in task priority than are individuals low in conscientiousness, owing to their achievement-striving and disciplined nature and thus will be less likely to commit errors of omission. Similarly to the rationale provided for perceptual speed, noticing changes in task priority will not necessarily lead to the performance of the correct action, however, and thus we do not predict a relationship between conscientiousness and errors of commission.

H3: Conscientiousness will be negatively correlated with errors of omission. Finally, because multitasking places high demands on an individual in terms of managing task switches and interruptions, it has the potential to be highly anxiety-provoking (Delbridge, 2000; Oswald et al., 2007). Anxiety is a form of arousal that is unpleasant in nature, and is experienced in reaction to stressors that may be real or imagined (Lundqvist, 2006). State anxiety is determined by an interaction between an individual's level of trait anxiety and the amount of stress s/he is currently experiencing. Research has shown that experiencing high levels of state anxiety results in lowered performance on cognitive tasks owing to lowered working memory capacity (Eysenck and Calvo, 1992). Anxiety is predicted to be related to errors of commission, owing to the fact that individuals experiencing high levels of anxiety will have temporarily reduced capacity to remember information about tasks. Similar to working memory, anxiety is not expected to be related to errors of omission because it will not affect individuals' ability to attend to changes in task priority.

H4: Anxiety will be positively related to errors of commission.
Figure 12.2 provides a model that integrates the four hypotheses just described.

METHOD

Participants

Participants were 125 undergraduate students recruited from introductory psychology courses at Michigan State University, who participated voluntarily in exchange for course credit. Sixty-eight percent were female, 68 percent were

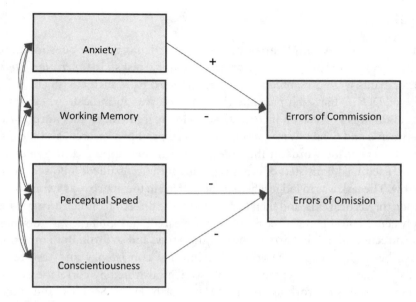

FIGURE 12.2

Model of hypothesized relationships.

18–19 years old, and 32 percent were 20–25 years old. The majority of the sample (75 percent) were non-Hispanic Caucasian, with the remaining portion being 10 percent Asian, 7 percent African American, and 4 percent Hispanic, with 4 percent classified as other/unidentified. Some participants were identified as outliers owing to their extreme (greater than 4 SDs from the mean) scores on multitasking performance, and some failed to complete a vast majority of the measures. Thus, these cases were excluded from the analyses and 102 participants made up the final sample used for analyses. The final sample was 73 percent female, 67 percent aged 18–19, 33 percent aged 20–25, 78 percent non-Hispanic Caucasian, 9 percent Asian, 4 percent African American, 4 percent Hispanic, and 5 percent other/unidentified.

Procedure

Participants were tested in a laboratory setting in small proctored groups of 4–10 individuals tested across two sessions approximately one week apart, each session taking approximately 1.5 hours. Predictor measures were assessed in Session one, while the criterion measure training session and measurement occurred during Session two. Measures relevant to the present paper are as follows:

Materials

Measures. In Session 1, after completing a demographic questionnaire, participants completed two working memory tasks. In *operation span*, participants were presented with equation–word pairs such as: "IS (12 / 3) + 3 = 6? DOG." For each pair like this, the task was to indicate whether the equation was correct or incorrect, and also to remember the word. After between 2 and 6 pairs were presented, a recall prompt appeared, and the task was to report the words in the order in which they appeared. In *symmetry span*, each trial consisted of a matrix, with some cells filled, followed by an arrow. The task was to judge whether the pattern in the matrix was symmetrical along the vertical axis, and then to remember the direction of each arrow. After between 2 and 6 pairs, a recall prompt appeared, and the task was to report the direction of the first arrow, the second arrow, and so forth. Both measures have been shown to have acceptable internal consistency and test–retest reliability as well as acceptable validity as demonstrated by correlations with other measures of working memory (Unsworth, Heitz, Schrock, and Engle, 2005).

After the working memory tasks, participants then completed two perceptual speed tasks. In *letter comparison*, stimuli were pairs of letters separated by a line such as "XJK ___ XRK." Participants were to write S on the line if the pairs were the same or D if they were different. In *pattern comparison*, the task was the same, except that the stimuli were geometric patterns. In both tasks, the goal was to make as many comparisons as possible in 30 seconds. Both measures have been previously established as having acceptable levels of both reliability and validity (Babcock and Salthouse, 1990). Following this set of cognitive tasks, participants completed a 10-item measure of conscientiousness. The measure consisted of statements such as "I am the life of the party" or "I feel comfortable around people." The participants' task was to rate each item on how well it described them, using a 5-point scale (strongly disagree–strongly agree; Goldberg, 1999).

Criterion task. In Session 2, participants first received an introduction to a computerized multitasking simulation called SynWin and were then given the chance to perform nine 5-minute blocks of SynWin (Elsmore, 1994). Block 1 was a "practice" block, Blocks 2–5 were "performance" blocks, and blocks 6–9 were "emergency" blocks. For the present study, data from the performance blocks (2–5) were used (in the emergency blocks, the pace was doubled and the payoff parameters changed). Although blocks 2–5 were labeled "performance" blocks, with the focus of long-term skill retention in mind, the fact that these blocks were administered immediately after the task was introduced to participants makes them more appropriately viewed in the training, rather than performance, context and that is how they will be considered in this chapter. Figure 12.3 provides a screenshot of the SynWin task.

SynWin is a "synthetic" work task that contains four computerized tasks that are presented simultaneously but that are performed through the shifting of attention among tasks. The tasks are *memory search, arithmetic, visual monitoring,* and *auditory monitoring.* The memory search task involves a set of letters that is presented for a short period of time. Following this presentation, a letter is shown and participants' task is to identify whether the letter was one of the letters shown as a part of the original list. If needed, participants are allowed to click the area where the list originally appeared and it will appear again, but this will deduct points from their score. The arithmetic task requires that participants add 2- or 3-digit numbers and is performed at the participant's own pace. The visual monitoring task involves a needle that moves across a fuel gauge, and participants' task is to click on the gauge before the needle reaches zero, which resets the gauge. The closer the needle gets to zero before being reset, the more points are given. The auditory monitoring task requires participants to respond to a higher-pitch tone by clicking on a button and to ignore a lower-pitch tone.

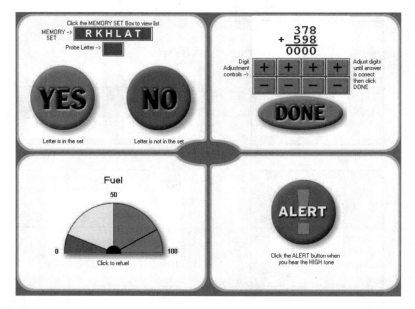

FIGURE 12.3

SynWin multitasking simulation.

Although one of the tasks used in our scenario is self-paced, three of the tasks impose a switch upon the multitasker by requiring action of him or her at a given time, with a time limit. As was described above, this type of multitasking is thought to resemble the type of multitasking engaged in by individuals in occupations where skill decay and retention have been discussed as important concerns. Further, the SynWin task has proven effective in past research investigating multitasking. Importantly, while participants engaged in the multitasking simulation, the SynWin software recorded mouse-click data on correct performance and on errors in performance over time that allowed us to track the data needed to test our hypotheses. Immediately following Block 5, participants completed a measure of state anxiety. The measure consisted of 20 words describing emotions (e.g., frustrated, calm). Participants indicated on a five-point scale the degree to which each of the emotions described how they felt during the SynWin task.

RESULTS

Results are displayed in the path model in Figure 12.4. Note that the correlations between the four exogenous variables (Table 12.1) were also modeled but were not depicted in the figure for greater simplicity. The four

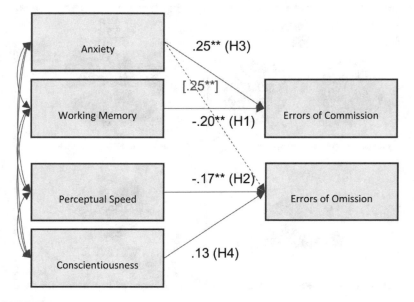

FIGURE 12.4

Results of structural equation modeling.

solid paths from exogenous to endogenous variables reflect our four hypotheses proposed between individual differences and errors of commission and omission. Three of the four paths were statistically significant and in the direction of the proposed hypotheses (all tests are t tests on the path coefficients, b, with $df = 16$): Working memory was negatively related to errors of commission ($b = -.20, p < .05$); perceptual speed was negatively related to errors of omission ($b = -.17, p < .05$); anxiety was positively related to errors of commission ($b = .25, p < .05$).

Our post hoc modification to the model indicated that anxiety was also significantly related to errors of omission ($b = .25, p < .05$; this path was constrained to be equal to the anxiety → errors of commission path). Conscientiousness was not found to be significantly related to errors of omission, though the trend was in the hypothesized direction ($b = .13, p > .05$). Fit indices indicated that the model fit very well overall, $\chi^2 (15, N = 102) = 2.03, p > .05$, CFI = 1, AGFI = .99, RMSEA < .005. This compares favorably with the proposed model, which fit the data slightly less well, $\chi^2 (15, N = 102) = 10.31, p > .05$, CFI = 1, AGFI = .95, RMSEA < .005, CFI = 1.00. The amount of variance accounted for in errors of commission and errors of omission were similar ($R^2 = .11$ and .12, respectively). Note that the variance accounted for in the error criteria is conservative in the sense that path analysis does not incorporate unsystematic errors of measurement that could attenuate modeled relationships. That said, the reliability estimates for our non-cognitive measures were high (.85 and .91), and reliability coefficients for these cognitive measures are typically high as well (often around .90).

TABLE 12.1

Descriptive Statistics, Reliabilities and Correlations

Scale	Mean	SD	1	2	3	4	5	6
Cognitive Variables								
1. Working Memory	.02	.85						
2. Perceptual Speed	.02	.76	.32*					
Non-cognitive Variables								
3. Anxiety	51.94	13.98	−.13	−.21*	.91			
4. Conscientiousness	34.36	6.81	−.15	−.04	−.18	.85		
MT Errors								
5. Errors of Commission	29.48	20.60	−.22*	−.07	.22*	.06		
6. Errors of Omission	16.38	21.39	−.10	−.24*	.31*	.09	.16	

*$p < .05$, two-tailed. Variables 1 and 2 are in z-score units, but the mean is not exactly 0 owing to removal of outliers. Alpha reliabilities are listed along the diagonal.

DISCUSSION

The present chapter contributes to the literature on skill decay and retention by exploring the role of individual differences on errors during the acquisition of a complex skill. To this end, the chapter presented a study that tested hypotheses regarding the role of various cognitive and non-cognitive individual-differences characteristics in predicting errors during multitasking training. As was hypothesized, working memory was found to be related to errors of commission, while perceptual speed was found to be related to errors of omission. Additionally, state anxiety during the multitasking scenario was found to be related to both types of error. Although the path from anxiety to errors of omission was not originally hypothesized, this path is reasonable, given recent models of the relationship between anxiety and performance. Eysenck, Derakshan, Santos, and Calvo (2007) proposed attentional control theory which claims that anxiety affects complex task performance primarily through the ability to control attention. Our empirical findings are consistent with this theory. Finally, conscientiousness was not related to either type of error, though we thought it may be related to errors of omission during multitasking (i.e., forgetting a task because of diligence paid to another task). We speculate that conscientiousness may instead interact with cognitive ability in predicting errors of omission, a subject of future research. In addition, because errors during training are known to relate to the transfer of training to the work environment, this study contributes to the skill retention literature in that it provides evidence that individual differences have the potential to impact skill decay in more complex ways than simply with the straightforward relationship between cognitive ability and eventual decay of skills or knowledge.

Limitations and Future Directions

Like all studies, this study is limited in a few important ways that should be discussed in relation to the findings. First, participants in this study were college students, and although this sample probably generalizes more strongly to populations such as incoming members of the military or new entrants into the workforce, further research must be done to examine the relationships found here in older and more diverse samples. This is particularly true given the negative association between perceptual speed and age (Salthouse et al., 1996). Second, the model tested in this paper was fairly simple as a result of sample size limitations. Future research should examine more complete models, including a variety of interactions and other situational and dispositional variables. Third, the study did not actually measure the outcome of retention over the long term. Future studies should assess this outcome, using errors during training as a mediator.

Implications for Practice, and Conclusions

Implications of this paper are that, for some individuals, training or initial job experiences may be less beneficial owing to the fact that errors, as they reflect a chance to learn and process new skills more thoroughly, may not occur as often. As a result, individuals higher in working memory or perceptual speed may be less likely to commit errors and thus, less likely to learn from them. For these individuals, training that encourages the making of errors early on before skills have been mastered may be especially beneficial for long-term retention. Future research is needed to explore this possibility.

In addition to individuals higher in these cognitive characteristics, we found that people who tend to experience higher levels of anxiety are more likely to commit errors. Although committing more errors may generally lead to more opportunities for long-term retention, these people may also require some type of intervention to be able to mitigate the anxiety that may interfere with performance as well as learning from their errors. All trainees may benefit from positive error framing and the notion that making errors is acceptable and an opportunity for learning. Again, the relationship between anxiety and errors is evident, and this relationship should be investigated further in future research.

It should be discussed that considerable debate has occurred in the literature over whether error management training benefits individuals as a result of the fact that they actually make more errors or owing to the more exploratory nature of the training. Similarly to the theoretical argument presented in the present chapter, many have proposed that errors themselves are helpful for learning owing to the fact that they provide developmental knowledge and feedback (Frese, 1995; Ivancic and Hesketh, 1995/1996). However, others have argued that most error encouragement training also includes an element of exploration that is not included in typical training, which confounds any differences detected between traditional and error management training (Keith and Frese, 2008). The exploratory element is proposed to increase learning by inducing a learning, rather than performance, orientation. Recent meta-analytic evidence, however, supports the notion that both the exploratory element of error encouragement training and the actual making of errors contribute unique and significant variance to training outcomes (Keith and

Frese, 2008). Therefore, it is clear that error making in and of itself is beneficial for training outcomes, supporting our earlier assertions.

In conclusion, in this chapter we have attempted to provide preliminary investigation of the relationship between error during multitasking training and both cognitive and non-cognitive individual differences. We framed our research within the context of skill decay and retention, proposing that the making of errors during training has the potential to impact retention positively over time. Although our study is limited in a few key ways, it is hoped that the current chapter provides a starting point for future research to further examine these issues and their relationships with the broader issues of skill decay and retention over time.

REFERENCES

Ackerman, P. L. (1992). Predicting individual differences in complex skill acquisition: Dynamics of ability determinants. *Journal of Applied Psychology, 77,* 598–614.

Ackerman, P. L., and Cianciolo, A. T. (2002). Ability and task constraint determinants of complex task performance. *Journal of Experimental Psychology: Applied, 8,* 194–208.

Arthur, W. Jr., Bennett, W. Jr., Stanush, P. L., and McNelly, T. L. (1998). Factors that influence skill decay and retention: A quantitative review and analysis. *Human Performance, 11,* 57.

Babcock, R. L., and Salthouse, T. A. (1990). Effects of increased processing demands on age differences in working memory. *Psychology and Aging, 5,* 421–428.

Barrick, M. R., and Mount, M. K. (1991). The Big Five personality dimensions and job performance: A meta-analysis. *Personnel Psychology, 44,* 1–26.

Buhner, M., Konig, C. J., Pick, M., and Krumm, S. (2006). Working memory dimensions as differential predictors of the speed and error aspect of multitasking performance. *Human Performance, 19,* 253–275.

De Dreu, C. K., and McCusker, C. (1997). Gain-loss frames and cooperation in two-person social dilemmas: A transformational analysis. *Journal of Personality and Social Psychology, 72,* 1093–1106.

Delbridge, K. A. (2000). Individual differences in multi-tasking ability: Exploring a nomological network. Unpublished doctoral dissertation, Michigan State University.

Elsmore, T. F. (1994). SYNWORK1: A PC-based tool for assessment of performance in a simulated work environment. *Behavior, Research Methods, Instruments, & Computers, 26,* 421–426.

Eysenck, M. W., and Calvo, M. G. (1992). Anxiety and performance: The processing efficiency theory. *Cognition & Emotion, 17,* 409–434.

Eysenck, M. W., Derakshan, N., Santos, R., and Calvo, M. G. (2007). Anxiety and cognitive performance: attentional control theory. *Emotion, 7,* 336–53.

Farr, M. J. (1987). *The long-term retention of knowledge and skills: A cognitive and instructional perspective.* New York: Springer-Verlag.

Fields, R. E., Wright, P. C., and Harrison, M. D. (1995). A task centered approach in analyzing human error tolerance requirements. *Second IEEE International Symposium on Requirements Engineering, RE95,* 18–26.

Frese, M. (1995). Error management in training: Conceptual and empirical results. In C. Zucchermaglio, S. Bagnara, and S. U. Stucky (Eds.), *Organizational learning and technological change, Series F: Computer and systems sciences* (Vol. 141, pp. 112–124). Berlin: Springer.

Gilovich, T., Medvec, V. H., and Chen, S. (1995). Commission, omission, and dissonance reduction: Coping with regret in the "Monty Hall" problem. *Personality and Social Psychology Bulletin, 21*, 182–190.

Goldberg, L. R. (1999). A broad-bandwidth, public domain, personality inventory measuring the lower-level facets of several five-factor models. In I. Mervielde, I. Deary, F. De Fruyt, and F. Ostendorf (Eds.), *Personality Psychology in Europe, Vol. 7* (pp. 7–28). Tilburg, The Netherlands: Tilburg University Press.

Ivancic, K., and Heskth, B. (1995/1996). Making the best of errors during training. *Training Research Journal, 1*, 103–125.

Keith, N., and Frese, M. (2005). Self-regulation in error management training: Emotion control and metacognition as mediators of performance effects. *Journal of Applied Psychology, 90*, 677–691.

Keith, N., and Frese, M. (2008). Effectiveness of error management training: A meta-analysis. *Journal of Applied Psychology, 93*, 59–69.

Kirkpatrick, D. L. (1987). Evaluation of training. In R. L. Craig (Ed.), *Training and development handbook: A guide to human resource development, 3rd ed.* (pp. 301–319). New York: McGraw-Hill.

Losier, B. J., McGrath, P. J., and Klein, R. M. (1996). Error patterns on the continuous performance test in medicated and non-medicated samples of children with and without ADHD: A meta-analytic review. *Journal of Child Psychology and Psychiatry, 37*, 971–987.

Lundqvist, C. (2006). Competing under pressure: State anxiety, sports performance, and assessment. Unpublished doctoral dissertation, Stockholm University.

Nembhard, D., and Osothsilp, N. (2002). Task complexity effects on between-individual learning/forgetting variability. *International Journal of Industrial Ergonomics, 29*, 297–306.

Oswald, F. L., Hambrick, D. Z., and Jones, L. A. (2007). Keeping all the plates spinning: Understanding and predicting multitasking performance. In D. H. Jonassen (Ed.), *Learning to solve complex scientific problems* (pp. 77–97). Mahwah, NJ: Lawrence Erlbaum Associates.

Overhage, J. M., Tierney, W. M., Zhou, X., and McDonald, C. J. (1997). A randomized trial of "corollary orders" to prevent errors of omission. *Journal of the American Medical Informatics Association, 4*, 364–375.

Reason, J. (1990). *Human error.* New York: Cambridge University Press.

Ree, M. J., and Earles, J. A. (1991). Predicting training success: Not much more than g. *Personnel Psychology, 44*, 321–332.

Roese, N. J. (1997). Counterfactual thinking. *Psychological Bulletin, 121*, 133–148.

Salthouse, T. A., Hambrick, D. Z., Lukas, K. E., and Dell, T. C. (1996). Determinants of adult age differences on synthetic work performance. *Journal of Experimental Psychology: Applied, 2*, 305–329.

Unsworth, N., Heitz, R. P., Schrock, J.C., and Engle, R.W. (2005). An automated version of the operation span task. *Behavior Research Methods, 37*, 498–505.

Villado, A. J., Day, E. A., Arthur, W. Jr., Boatman, P. R., Kowollik, V., Bhupatkar, A., and Bennett, W. Jr. (2013). Complex command-and-control simulation task performance following periods of nonuse. In W. Arthur, E. Day, W. Bennett, Jr., and A. Portrey (Eds.), *Individual and team skill decay: The science, and implications for practice* (pp. 53–67). New York: Taylor & Francis.

Wallace, J. C., and Chen, G. 2006. A multilevel integration of personality, climate, regulatory focus, and performance. *Personnel Psychology, 59,* 529–557.

AUTHORS' NOTES

We would like to thank Zach Hambrick and the members of the Skilled Performance Laboratory at Michigan State University for their help with data collection. This work was partially supported by a grant from the Navy Personnel, Studies, and Technology (NPRST; Contract #DAAD19–02-D-0001). All views contained herein are those of the authors and should not be interpreted as representing the official policies or endorsements, either expressed or implied, of NPRST or of the U.S. Government.

Part 3

Skill Decay and Retention at the Team Level

13

A Comparative Investigation of Individual and Team Skill Retention and Transfer on a Complex Command-and-Control Simulation Task

Winfred Arthur, Jr., Eric Anthony Day, Anton J. Villado, Ryan M. Glaze, Matthew J. Schuelke, Paul R. Boatman, Vanessa Kowollik, Xiaoqian Wang, and Winston Bennett, Jr.

INTRODUCTION

It has been noted that the extant skill retention literature has predominantly involved relatively simple tasks with rather short nonuse intervals (Arthur, Bennett, Stanush, and McNelly, 1998). In addition, this research has also focused almost exclusively on the performance of individuals. Thus, if the research on skill retention and transfer on complex tasks is limited, then the state of the extant literature is even more deficient in reference to *team* complex task skill retention and transfer since there appears to be a complete lack of attention to these issues in the context of team training. Indeed, excluding the works presented in the present volume (e.g., Cooke et al. 2013), we were unable to locate any published empirical or conceptual reports on this issue.

This notwithstanding, the study and understanding of skill and performance retention and transfer at the level of teams is particularly important. With the rapid pace of technology advancements and complexity, many work tasks now consist of cognitive and information-processing demands that are too diverse and complicated for most individuals to successfully accomplish alone.

Consequently, reliance on teams is now a pervasive reality in many military and civilian settings, and teams have become an integral part of organizational tasks and missions. With the continued increase in the use of teams in organizations, there has been commensurate interest in how to effectively train teams (Salas, Bowers, and Cannon-Bowers, 1995; Salas and Cannon-Bowers, 2001) with some studies (e.g., Bohlander and McCarthy, 1996; Day et al., 2005; Salas, Dickinson, Converse, and Tannenbaum, 1992) assessing differences between effective and ineffective teams, and others (e.g., Arthur et al., 2005; Arthur, Villado, and Bennett, 2012; Day et al., 2005; Swezey and Salas, 1992) developing guidelines for team training. Thus, an investigation of the retention and transfer of complex skills in the context of teams is an important logical extension of the investigation of these phenomena that have typically been studied at the individual level. Hence, the fundamental differences between individual and team performance necessitates the need for research comparing individual versus team retention and transfer after extended periods of nonuse. Using 231 paid participants who trained in three-person teams ($N = 77$ teams) on a command-and-control task, we examined the comparative effectiveness of two practice schedules in terms of end-of-acquisition performance, retention after an 8-week nonuse interval, and transfer performance. Furthermore, we compared two protocols, individual- and team-level protocols, which used the same task and practice schedules to assess the extent to which the spacing of practice effect generalized from individuals to teams. The results indicated that teams and individuals displayed differing levels of skill acquisition and transfer, but similar levels of retention. Furthermore, the spacing of practice had a larger effect on individuals than teams. Finally, both teams and individuals displayed smaller levels of skill decay after an extended period of nonuse than researchers may be inclined to anticipate. The primary conclusion based on our findings is that teams engender features and characteristics not found in individuals and these features and characteristics influence processes associated with skill acquisition, retention, and transfer.

ASPECTS OF TEAMS THAT MAY ENGENDER DIFFERENT RETENTION AND TRANSFER PROCESSES

Because teams consist of two or more individuals who work interdependently, have specific role assignments, perform specific tasks, and interact and coordinate to achieve a common goal, an additional task and job characteristic not present with individuals is the nature and degree of interdependence that is required for the successful performance of the task or job (Arthur, Villado, and Bennett, 2012; Arthur et al., 2012; Kozlowski and Ilgen, 2006; Wageman,

2001). Indeed, *some* degree of interdependence is that which distinguishes teams from groups and the presence of interdependence, in turn, introduces two additional concepts to the functioning of teams, namely the distinction between taskwork and teamwork. Taskwork refers to the team's efforts to understand and perform the requirements of the job, tasks, and equipment to be used. Teamwork, on the other hand, refers to the team's efforts to facilitate interaction among team members in the accomplishment of the team's tasks. Thus, teamwork consists of behaviors required for cooperative functioning and focuses on team interaction processes such as coordination, monitoring, backing up, and conflict management (Marks, Mathieu, and Zaccaro, 2001). Furthermore, unlike taskwork, the knowledge, skills, and abilities underlying effective team processes are generally considered more generic instead of being task or domain specific (Stevens and Campion, 1994, 1999).

The presence of interdependence and the role of teamwork processes suggest that there are aspects or characteristics of teams that may engender retention and transfer processes and outcomes that are quite different from those observed for individuals. For instance, meta-analytic studies have demonstrated the importance of affective and motivational states such as team cohesion (e.g., Beal, Cohen, Burke, and McLendon, 2003; Mullen and Cooper, 1994) and collective efficacy (e.g., Gully, Incalcaterra, Joshi, and Beaubian, 2002) to team performance and outcomes. Likewise, meta-analytic studies (i.e., DeChurch and Mesmer-Magnus, 2010a, 2010b; Mohammed, Ferzandi, and Hamilton, 2010) have reaffirmed and highlighted the role that team cognition plays in team effectiveness. Team cognition is "an emergent state that refers to the manner in which knowledge important to team functioning is mentally organized, represented, and distributed within a team and allows team members to anticipate and execute actions" (DeChurch and Mesmer-Magnus, 2010a, p. 33). The two team cognition constructs that have been generally investigated are shared mental models and transactive memory systems.

Shared or team mental models generally refers to that which is *held in common* by team members. Thus, team mental models are "organized mental representations of the key elements within a team's relevant environment that are shared across team members" (Mohammed et al., 2010, p. 877) that allow teams to operate in complex, dynamic, and uncertain performance environments with the extant literature generally indicating that teams that have more similar and accurate mental models are likely to be more effective than teams that do not (DeChurch and Mesmer-Magnus, 2010a, 2010b; Mohammed et al., 2010).

As distinguished from team mental models, team transactive memory systems pertain to knowledge that is *distributed* among team members (Kozlowski and Ilgen, 2006). Thus, transactive memory pertains to an awareness within a team of who knows what—that is, where specific knowledge resides within the team. Like team mental models, meta-analytic studies (i.e., DeChurch and Mesmer-Magnus, 2010a, 2010b) have reaffirmed the importance of team transactive memory to team effectiveness.

In summary, there are several team-related variables, such as interdependency, teamwork, cohesion, collective efficacy, shared mental models, and transactive memory, that are not present in the context of individuals. In addition, these variables and phenomena have been shown to be important to team performance. Consequently, given these conceptual differences, it is not unreasonable to question the extent to which our knowledge and understanding of individual skill and performance retention and transfer generalizes to teams. For instance, it is conceivable that mechanisms associated with the sharedness of mental models and transactive memory may result in compensatory factors across team members to mitigate against the manifestation of skill loss after extended periods of nonuse. Thus, team mental models, along with phenomena such as interpositional knowledge (i.e., knowledge regarding other team members' roles), may result in situations where knowledge gaps at the level of the individual are rapidly filled in by other team members such that the team as a whole displays limited performance decrements after extended nonuse intervals.

Conversely, in the absence of empirical data to the contrary, one could also envisage a situation where the complexities associated with performing as a team, such as managing and maintaining the taskwork and teamwork interdependencies, are so tasking that extended periods of nonuse result in synergistic downward effects that exacerbate the loss of teamwork and taskwork skills and performance more so than is generally observed for individuals. So, whereas in the present study we do not directly investigate specific team cognition variables and the roles they play, clearly their presence in team contexts and absence in individual contexts introduces a set of dynamics that make the comparative investigation of individual versus team skill retention and transfer over extended nonuse periods a worthwhile initial first step in furthering the understanding of these effects at the team-level, particularly in the context of complex skills.

Accordingly, the objectives of the present study were to (1) investigate and document the comparative levels of retention and transfer for individuals and teams on the same complex command-and-control simulation task; and (2) investigate the comparative effectiveness of the spacing of practice in terms of individual versus team skill acquisition, retention, and transfer. Concerning the second objective, Arthur et al. (2010) have shown that for individuals learning a complex command-and-control simulation task, longer interstudy intervals led to higher levels of skill at the end of training and after nonuse than shorter interstudy intervals; the goal here was to test for these effects in the context of teams.

SPACING OF PRACTICE

The spacing of practice is an important consideration in the design of training programs because it is a robust design feature that has been shown to play an important role in learning (Cepeda et al., 2008; Donovan and Radosevich, 1999; Kornell and Bjork, 2008; Rohrer and Taylor, 2007; Schmidt and Bjork, 1992). The spacing of practice is typically discussed in the context of massed versus distributed practice conditions. As clarified by Cepeda et al. (2006), "when the study time devoted to any given item is not subject to any interruptions of intervening items or intervening time, [then] learning is said to be *massed* . . . . In contrast, learning is spaced or *distributed* when a measurable time lag (1 s or longer) separates study episodes for a given item" (p. 354). Specifically, within the context of Cepeda et al.'s (2006) definition, it is nearly impossible to envisage a complex or real-world organizational task where learning sessions or training episodes are not separated by measurable time lags (1 second or longer; p. 354)—which is consonant with the observation that investigations of the massed versus distributed distinction have historically used simple tasks that are amenable to interstudy episodes that are "not subject to any inter-ruptions of intervening items or intervening time" (Cepeda et al., 2006, p. 354). Consequently, in terms of complex skill acquisition (i.e., amount of skill acquired) and the associated use of distributed practice protocols, the more germane issue is the relative length of the time lag (i.e., the interstudy interval— less versus more space) between training sessions or episodes and whether said varying lengths are associated with different levels of acquisition and retention.

We were unable to locate any studies that investigated the comparative effectiveness of varied interstudy intervals in distributed practice schedules in terms of acquisition and retention performance on a *cognitively complex* task over an *extended* nonuse interval for individuals *and* teams. However, Arthur et al. (2010) reported such a comparison for individuals (only) and their results indicated that longer interstudy intervals led to higher levels of skill at the end of training and after nonuse than shorter interstudy intervals. Consequently, the objective of the present study was to extend this work to teams and present a comparative evaluation of teams and individuals in the context of the effectiveness of two distributed practice protocols in terms of performance immediately following training, after an 8-week nonuse interval, and transfer. We also acknowledge that although our primary focus is on retention and transfer after extended periods of nonuse, acquisition is by definition a part of any such investigation since it serves as a reference point for tests of retention. Thus, we present tests of acquisition as well.

METHOD

Participants

To accomplish the research objectives, the data collected as part of an individual-level training protocol were compared to data collected as part of a team-level protocol.[1] The individual-level sample consisted of 192 participants (22 percent female) with a mean age of 20.94 years ($SD = 3.67$). A detailed description of the sample is presented in Villado et al. (Chapter 3 of this volume).

The initial team-level sample consisted of 231 participants (20.35 percent female; 3.42 percent did not report their sex) from the university and campus communities of Texas A&M University and the University of Oklahoma. Participants were assigned to three-person teams in either a shorter or longer interstudy interval condition. Participants were paid $12.00 per hour of participation and competed for performance bonuses of $80, $40, and $20, which were awarded to each member of the teams with the three highest average task performance scores, respectively. Seventeen teams did not complete the study owing to at least one member of the team withdrawing from the study (22.08 percent attrition). Six teams withdrew from the shorter interstudy interval condition (15.38 percent attrition), and 11 teams withdrew from the longer interstudy interval condition (28.95 percent attrition). The attrition rates did not significantly differ across conditions (χ^2 [1, $N = 77$] $= 2.06$, $p > .05$). The final sample consisted of 183 individual participants in 61 three-person teams (shorter interstudy interval $n = 33$ teams; longer interstudy interval $n = 28$ teams). Thirty-four of the participants were female (18.58 percent; 1.09 percent did not report their sex) and the mean age of the participants was 20.53 years ($SD = 1.82$; 3.28 percent did not report their age).

Performance Task

The performance task was Jane's Fleet Command (Sonalysts, Inc., 2004, Air Force Research Laboratory ver. 1.55). Jane's Fleet Command may be configured as a single- or multi-user simulator. So, whereas for the individual-level protocol, Fleet Command was configured as a single-user simulator with a single trainee charged with managing the entire fleet, trainees in the team-level protocol operated Fleet Command in a multi-user (i.e., networked) configuration with three trainees, each managing a specific function of the fleet. A detailed description of Fleet Command for the individual-level protocol is presented in Villado et al. (Chapter 3 of this volume). Consequently, the following description focuses on the modifications to the performance task for the team-level protocol.

Trainees in the team-level protocol used three networked computers to manage one fleet. Each trainee was assigned a specific role within a team—either the Surface, Air, or Electronic Warfare Commander role. Each role had a combination of common and specialized functions within the team and was provided with role-specific resources (e.g., platforms, weapons). Trainees assigned the role of Surface Warfare Commander were responsible for (a) surface and sub-surface platforms in the fleet (e.g., cruisers, destroyers, mine sweepers, and submarines), (b) all ship-based combat operations, and (c) defending the team's surface ships. Surface Warfare Commanders were also equipped with the only aircraft in the fleet outfitted with long-range RADAR. Thus, the Surface Warfare Commander was responsible for communicating enemy positions to the other team members whose radars were unable to detect enemies at a long range. Surface Warfare Commanders were typically assigned a combination of 10 surface and sub-surface platforms, two airborne early warning aircraft (i.e., aircraft with long-range RADAR), and two ship-based helicopters.

Trainees who served as Air Warfare Commanders controlled and coordinated the fastest aircraft available to the team, and the only aircraft capable of air-to-air combat. These aircraft were also capable of conducting air-to-ground combat operations. Trainees in these roles were assigned approximately 16 aircraft and a platform from which to launch the aircraft (i.e., either a land base or an aircraft carrier). Air Warfare Commanders were responsible for intercepting enemy aircraft, and destroying enemy air and ground targets.

Trainees assigned the role of Electronic Warfare Commander were responsible for jamming enemy ground, ship, air, and weapon RADAR systems. Additionally, aircraft assigned to Electronic Warfare Commanders were capable of executing air-to-ground and air-to-ship combat operations. Trainees serving in the role of Electronic Warfare Commanders were assigned the responsibility of conducting the electronic warfare component of a mission and assisting with air-to-ground and air-to-ship combat operations. Electronic Warfare Commanders were typically assigned 12 aircraft and a platform from which to launch the aircraft (i.e., either a land base or an aircraft carrier or both).

Because Fleet Command was configured as a multi-user simulator for the team-level protocol, participants completed a team task analysis questionnaire

(Arthur et al., 2005) to confirm that the Surface, Air, and Electronic Warfare Commander roles were indeed interdependent. The results indicated that on a 1–5 point scale, participants' perceived this task as being characterized by a high degree of overall team-relatedness ($M = 4.06$, $SD = 0.63$) and workflow ($M = 3.83$, $SD = 0.87$) with a composite mean (i.e., sum of the team-relatedness and team workflow ratings) of 3.97 ($SD = 0.96$). Thus, the degree of interdependence was perceived to be fairly high and the type or form of interdependence was characterized as reciprocal interdependence.

Procedure

Table 13.1 provides an overview and summary of the training protocol and procedures. These were basically the same as those used for the individual-level data collection with team-specific elements or differences as warranted. (A detailed description of the individual-level procedures is presented in Villado et al.—Chapter 3 of this volume; however, because the description that follows applies to both the individual- and team-level procedures, there may be some redundancies in the descriptions.)

The difference between "longer" and "shorter" interstudy intervals is, of course, relative and this difference can vary in terms of both the number of trials in a session and the amount of time between sessions (Cepeda et al., 2006). We used two interstudy intervals and so our conditions differed in terms of the amount of time between sessions. Table 13.1 provides an overview of the procedural differences between them as well as a summary of the study's training procedures. Both conditions involved a mix of interstudy intervals. In the longer interstudy condition, all of the interstudy intervals between training sessions lasted 23 hours with the exception of a 71-hour interval (i.e., a weekend) halfway through training between Sessions 4 and 5. In the shorter interstudy condition, intervals alternated between 2 minutes and 22 hours with 2-minute intervals between Sessions 1 and 2, 3 and 4, 5 and 6, and 7 and 8; and 22-hour intervals between Sessions 2 and 3, 4 and 5, 6 and 7, and 8 and 9.

Upon being recruited, trainees were informed during a screening and scheduling session that they would be training to perform a complex decision-making computer-based performance task. The screening session also entailed the completion of a demographic and contact form, and a video-game experience measure. The intention of the video-game experience measure was to exclude trainees who reported extensive experience and familiarity with Fleet Command. No participant reported having any exposure to Fleet Command, and therefore, no one was eliminated on this basis. Trainees were selected into the study based on their availability and then randomly assigned to a condition. Although we attempted to assign all the trainees randomly to their respective

TABLE 13.1

Overview of Training Procedures

Longer Interstudy Interval (2 Weeks of Acquisition Training [10 Sessions])		Shorter Interstudy Interval (1 Week of Acquisition Training [10 Sessions])	
Schedule	**Activity**	**Schedule**	**Activity**
Week 1 Monday	Session 0 (JFC Baseline Test, instructions, and tutorial; Mission A)	Week 1 Monday	Session 0 (JFC Baseline Test, instructions, and tutorial; Mission A)
	Session 1 (JFC tutorial and practice)		Session 1 (JFC tutorial and practice; Mission A)
			Session 2 (JFC tutorial and practice; Mission A)
Tuesday	Session 2 (JFC tutorial and practice; Mission A)	Tuesday	Session 3 (JFC tutorial and practice; Mission B)
			Session 4 (JFC tutorial and practice; Mission B)
Wednesday	Session 3 (JFC tutorial and practice; Mission B)	Wednesday	Session 5 (JFC tutorial review and practice; Mission C)
			Session 6 (JFC practice; Mission C)
Thursday	Session 4 (JFC tutorial and practice; Mission B)	Thursday	Session 7 (JFC practice; Mission D)
			Session 8 (JFC practice; Mission D)
Friday	Session 5 (JFC tutorial review and practice; Mission C)	Friday	Session 9 (JFC practice and End-of-Acquisition Test; Mission E)
Week 2 Monday	Session 6 (JFC practice; Mission C)	8-Week Nonpractice Interval	
Tuesday	Session 7 (JFC practice; Mission D)	Monday	Session 10 (JFC Long-Term Retention Test; Mission E)
Wednesday	Session 8 (JFC practice; Mission D)		Session 11 (JFC Transfer Test; Mission F)
Thursday	Session 8 (JFC practice; Mission D)		
Friday	Session 9 (JFC practice and End-of-Acquisition Test; Mission E)		
Week 2 Monday	Session 10 (JFC tutorial review and practice; Mission C)		
Tuesday	Session 6 (JFC practice; Mission C)		
Wednesday	Session 7 (JFC practice; Mission D)		
Thursday	Session 8 (JFC practice; Mission D)		
Friday	Session 9 (JFC practice and End-of-Acquisition Test; Mission E)		
8-Week Nonpractice Interval			
Monday	Session 10 (JFC Long-Term Retention Test; Mission E)		
	Session 11 (JFC Transfer Test; Mission F)		

JFC = Jane's Fleet Command.

training conditions, random assignment was not always possible owing to difficulties encountered with accommodating participants' weekly schedules and 4-month calendars. Examination of the baseline mission effectiveness scores (Session 0) indicated that the training conditions were roughly equivalent at the start of training for both individuals, t (interstudy interval [190]) = 0.20, $p > .05$, $d = 0.03$, and teams, t (interstudy interval [69]) = 0.02, $p > .05$, $d = 0.01$.

Prior to training on the first day of the study, trainees completed the baseline mission (Session 0) of Fleet Command. For this baseline mission (Mission A), trainees were simply given time to read the standard mission briefing which specified the goals and objectives of the mission. No other instructions were provided. After completing the baseline mission, trainees then received instruction and tutorials on how to "play" Fleet Command. Training was delivered by an instructor who guided trainees through the training sessions as trainees followed along on their individual workstations using a fully functional Fleet Command mission. It is important to note that all trainees completed all of the tutorials, and thus were fully cross-trained. Following the training portion of a session, trainees then completed practice missions. Sessions followed the training sequence presented in Table 13.1. Sessions were scheduled to be an hour long. For sessions that had practice and test missions, the hour-long session consisted of 20 minutes of practice and 25 minutes of testing. Acquisition training took place over a 2-week period in the longer interstudy interval condition compared to 1 week in the shorter interstudy interval condition. After an 8-week nonuse interval, participants returned to the lab for the retention and transfer tests.

As indicated in Table 13.1, three different JFC missions were used to assess baseline performance (Mission A), end-of-acquisition performance and long-term retention (Mission E), and transfer (Mission F). Because it was their first exposure to the game and to give them some opportunity to play the game without being immediately "killed," Mission A was designed to be less difficult than Mission E which required trainees to implement and deploy all the systems and strategies that had been learned and practiced in the preceding training sessions (i.e., Sessions 1–8). The mission played during Session 11 (Mission F; also considered to be the transfer mission) was the most complex and difficult and required trainees to implement all of the strategies and techniques presented in all of the preceding training sessions. Thus, whereas in other missions trainees may have used proficiency in one area (e.g., sensor and weapons use, strike coordination, and resource management) to compensate for a deficiency in another area, effective performance on Mission F required proficiency in all tasks simultaneously. Furthermore, Mission F also presented trainees with an environment that was novel, both in terms of the platforms under their command and the strategy necessary to achieve the mission objectives and goals. This mission required trainees to employ new platforms with unique capabilities, search for and engage an enemy fleet that was defended unlike any other fleet to which they had been previously exposed, while for the first time defending their fleet from two separate attacks at once. A progressive-part training approach was used during the practice sessions such that three different missions were used to train participants on the various systems and strategies.

JFC scores and data analytic procedures

For each mission, Fleet Command generates a mission effectiveness score that represents the total points earned during the mission. Points are earned for completing mission objectives and destroying enemy platforms; and lost when own-platforms and neutral platforms (i.e., non-military platforms) are destroyed. The total points earned is then divided by the total number of points possible for the specified mission. The ratio of points earned to the points possible is multiplied by 100 to rescale the value to approximate a percentage of points earned during the mission. However, because one could lose more points than earn during a mission (e.g., an unharmed enemy destroying all friendly platforms), one could earn a score less than –100 but not greater than 100. Furthermore, because Fleet Command was configured as a multi-user simulator for the team-level protocol (i.e., Surface, Air, and Electronic Warfare Commander roles), Fleet Command assigned points to each role such that the team score had to be obtained by summing the scores across the three roles. Subsequently, this made the individual and team Fleet Command scores *directly* non-comparable. So, instead of the expected 2 (individual vs team) × 2 (shorter vs longer interstudy interval) repeated measures (baseline, end-of-acquisition, retention, transfer) analysis of variance (ANOVA) approach, we primarily analyzed the data in terms of within-subjects comparative improvements (and decrements) in performance in a session over the immediately preceding session as well as in terms of separate between-subjects comparisons of interstudy interval for individuals and teams.

Finally, owing to technical computer problems experienced during the team data collection, performance data were lost for some participants within a team, and sometimes, the whole team. So, to obtain a viable data set, the decision was made to impute missing data if only one member of the team's data were lost. An outcome of this is that the sample sizes vary across sessions for the team-level data since teams that were missing data for two or more members for a specified session were not included in the analyses for that session. Data imputation was accomplished by predicting the missing value for the team member based on the condition and role assignment for the specified session. In summary, 93 out of 732 data points (12.43 percent) were imputed.

RESULTS

End-of-Acquisition

Table 13.2 and Table 13.3 present the descriptive statistics and standardized mean differences (d) for the interstudy interval conditions for the baseline, end-of-acquisition, retention, and transfer tests, for the individual and team protocols, respectively. These effects are also illustrated in Figure 13.1. To address the research questions of interest, we first examined the change in baseline and end-of-acquisition scores for each interstudy interval condition in the individual and team protocols. In the individual protocol, both the longer interstudy interval, $t(99) = 24.44, p < .001, d = 3.30$ (one-tailed), and the shorter interstudy interval, $t(91) = 23.45, p < .001, d = 3.32$ (one-tailed), achieved higher end-of-acquisition scores over the baseline. A similar pattern of results was obtained for the team protocol although the magnitude of improvement for both the longer interstudy interval $t(34) = 5.17, p < .001, d = 1.33$ (one-tailed), and the shorter interstudy interval, $t(35) = 3.44, p < .01, d = 0.91$ (one-tailed), was less than half of that obtained for the individual protocol.

In addition, in contrast to the individual protocol where the magnitude of improvement was fairly similar for the two interstudy intervals ($d = 3.30$ vs. 3.32), for the team protocol, the magnitude of improvement for the longer interval ($d = 1.33$) was larger than that for the shorter interval ($d = 0.91$).

With respect to end-of-acquisition test-game performance, individuals in the longer interstudy interval achieved higher scores compared to individuals in the shorter interstudy interval, $t(190) = 1.65, p < .05, d = 0.24$ (one-tailed). However, there was not a statistically significant difference in performance between teams in the longer versus shorter interstudy interval conditions, $t(69) = 0.34, p > .05, d = 0.08$ (one-tailed).

Long-term Retention

Long-term retention comparisons were first examined in terms of the difference between end-of-acquisition and long-term retention performance. As would be expected, the results presented in Table 13.2 (and Figure 13.1) for the individual protocol indicate that long-term retention performance for both the longer, $t(99) = -0.50, p > .05, d = -0.06$ (one-tailed), and shorter

TABLE 13.2

Descriptive Statistics and Standardized Mean Differences Between Acquisition Schedules on Fleet Command Sessions—Individual Protocol

Session	Longer Interstudy Interval				Shorter Interstudy Interval				Total			
	N	Mean	SD	d	N	Mean	SD	d	N	Mean	SD	d
Baseline	100	-89.74	42.83	—	92	-90.97	41.60	—	192	-90.33	42.14	—
End-of-Acquisition	100	20.06	19.45	3.30*	92	15.58	18.07	3.32*	192	17.91	18.89	3.31*
Long-Term Retention	100	19.02	16.81	-0.06	92	11.01	17.98	-0.25	192	15.81	17.79	-0.11
Transfer	100	-13.63	16.08	-1.98*	92	-14.56	16.49	-1.48*	192	-14.08	16.24	-1.75*

N = number of individual participants. *d*s were computed such that the previous session to each focal session served as the control (e.g., for long-term acquisition, end-of-acquisition served as the control). Thus, positive *d*s indicates a performance improvement in the subsequent session over the previous session. * *p* < .05, one-tailed.

TABLE 13.3

Descriptive Statistics and Standardized Mean Differences Between Acquisition Schedules on Fleet Command Sessions—Team Protocol

Session	Longer Interstudy Interval				Shorter Interstudy Interval				Total			
	N	Mean	SD	d	N	Mean	SD	d	N	Mean	SD	d
Baseline	39	-17.52	28.11	—	38	-18.01	44.84	—	77	-17.76	37.07	—
End-of-Acquisition	35	11.91	12.69	1.33*	36	13.11	16.86	0.91*	71	12.52	14.86	1.06*
Long-Term Retention	17	11.54	12.39	-0.03	15	10.03	15.77	-0.19	32	10.83	13.86	-0.12
Transfer	31	-2.98	15.24	-1.01	33	-0.67	19.32	-0.58	64	-1.79	17.37	-0.77*

N = number of three-person teams. *d*s were computed such that the previous session to each focal session served as the control (e.g., for long-term acquisition, end-of-acquisition served as the control). Thus, positive *d*s indicate a performance improvement in the subsequent session over the previous session. * *p* < .05, one-tailed.

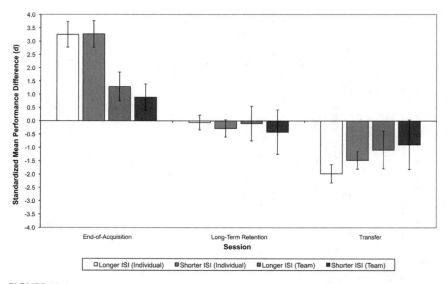

FIGURE 13.1

Fleet Command standardized mean improvement scores over previous sessions. Error bars represent one standard error of the mean.

interstudy intervals, t (91) = −1.86, $p < .05$, $d = -0.25$ (one-tailed) was lower than the end-of-acquisition performance. However, the long-term retention decrement for the longer interstudy interval was not statistically significant whereas the performance decrement for the shorter interstudy interval was statistically significant. Furthermore, it is worth noting that the amount of skill decay for the shorter interstudy interval ($d = -0.25$) was four times that for the longer interval ($d = -0.06$).

Like the end-of-acquisition results, a similar pattern of results was obtained for the team protocol. Thus, the results presented in Table 13.3 (and Figure 13.1) indicate that although the effects were not statistically significant, long-term retention performance for both the longer, t (16) = −0.25, $p > .05$, $d = -0.03$ (one-tailed), and shorter interstudy intervals, t (14) = 1.44, $p > .05$, $d = -0.19$ (one-tailed) was lower than the end-of-acquisition performance. And again, the amount of skill decay for the shorter interstudy interval ($d = -0.19$) was about six times that for the longer interval ($d = -0.03$). It is also worth noting that for both interstudy intervals, the amount of skill loss in the team protocol appeared to be slightly lower than that for the individual protocol.

With respect to retention test-game performance, the longer interstudy interval led to higher levels of performance after the long-term retention interval for individuals, t (190) = 3.19, $p < .001$, $d = 0.47$ (one-tailed). However, for teams, there was no statistically significant difference in performance between longer and shorter interstudy intervals, $t(30) = 0.30$, $p > .05$, $d = 0.11$ (one-tailed).

Transfer

Transfer performance comparisons were first examined in terms of the difference between long-term retention and transfer performance. The results indicated that individuals in both the longer, $t(99) = -14.58$, $p < .001$, $d = -1.98$ (one-tailed), and shorter, $t(91) = -9.79$, $p < .001$, $d = -1.48$ (one-tailed), interstudy intervals displayed statistically significant decrements in performance. Teams in the longer, $t(13) = 0.25$, $p > .05$, $d = -1.01$ (one-tailed) and shorter, $t(14) = 1.44$, $p > .05$, $d = -0.58$ (one-tailed) interstudy interval conditions did not display statistically significant performance decrements.

The general pattern of results that emerges from an examination of Tables 13.2 and 13.3 and Figure 13.1 is that for both interstudy intervals, although both individuals and teams displayed performance decrements on the transfer mission, the effect appeared be more profound for individuals (longer and shorter interstudy interval ds = -1.98 and -1.48, respectively) than for teams (longer and shorter interstudy interval ds = -1.01 and -0.58, respectively).

The results of between-groups analyses suggest that there was not a statistically significant difference in transfer performance scores between individuals in the longer and shorter interstudy intervals, $t(190) = 0.40$, $p > .05$, $d = 0.06$ (one-tailed). Similarly, the transfer scores for teams in the longer and shorter interstudy intervals were not statistically significantly different, $t(62) = 0.53$, $p > .05$, $d = 0.13$, (one-tailed).

DISCUSSION

The extant skill retention literature has primarily focused on individuals performing simple tasks and uses relatively short nonuse intervals (Arthur et al., 1998). In a meta-analysis examining the effects of practice schedules, Cepeda et al. (2008) reported that only seven out of 254 studies examined retention intervals longer than one week. Thus, much of the skill retention and the spacing of practice literatures do not reflect the types of tasks and training environments found in organizations. Indeed, organizations are increasingly using teams to achieve their objectives. Furthermore, teams often perform cognitively complex tasks and are expected to perform at high levels of proficiency after extended periods of nonuse. The stark differences between the types of tasks and training environments examined in the extant literature and those in organizational settings has led researchers to question the extent to which results from studies using simple tasks generalize to complex tasks (Arthur et al., 2010) and the extent to which training interventions that are effective for individuals are effective for teams. As such, an objective of the present study was to investigate and document the comparative levels of retention, and transfer for individuals and teams on the same complex command-and-control simulation task. A second objective was to investigate the comparative effectiveness of the spacing of practice in terms of individual versus team skill acquisition, retention, and transfer. On the basis of the results of the current study, three broad summary statements can be made—(a) teams and individuals differed in terms of rates of skill acquisition and extent of transfer, (b) spacing of practice seemed to have a smaller effect for teams than for individuals, and (c) both teams and individuals displayed less skill loss on a complex task after an extended nonuse interval than typically expected.

Team Skill Acquisition, Retention, and Transfer

The general pattern of results suggests that training interventions may differentially influence individual and team performance. Specifically, teams displayed smaller performance gains from baseline to end-of-acquisition ($d = 1.33$ and 0.91 for the longer and shorter interstudy intervals, respectively) compared to individuals ($d = 3.30$ and 3.31 for the longer and shorter interstudy intervals, respectively). One potential explanation for these results is that teams must engage in both task- and team-oriented activities such as developing shared mental models and transactive memory during skill acquisition. However, these team-oriented activities and processes may allow teams to perform better in terms of retention and transfer performance. Although teams experienced only slightly less skill loss than individuals both in the longer ($d = -0.03$ versus -0.06) and shorter ($d = -0.19$ versus -0.25) interstudy interval conditions, teams displayed a much greater extent of transfer (i.e., smaller performance decrements) compared to individuals (-1.01 versus -1.98 for the longer interstudy interval and -0.58 and -1.48 for the shorter interstudy interval). Thus, these results suggest that the features and characteristics of teams (e.g., interdependencies, team process variables) may mitigate skill loss and, in particular, lessen the negative impact of novel performance demands.

Differential Effects of the Spacing of Practice for Teams and Individuals

The spacing of practice is one of several methodological factors that have been identified to influence skill acquisition, retention, and transfer (Arthur et al.,

2003; Cepeda et al., 2006; DeCecco, 1968). The superiority of longer over shorter interstudy intervals is somewhat of a received doctrine. However, the preponderance of research demonstrating the superiority of longer interstudy intervals is based primarily on simple motor tasks (Donovan and Radosevich, 1999; Lee and Genovese, 1988), or simple cognitive tasks (Cepeda et al., 2006; Janiszewski, Noel, and Sawyer, 2003; cf. Cepeda et al, 2008) in the context of individual training. Longer interstudy intervals may foster skill acquisition, retention, and transfer through increased mental rehearsal, decreased fatigue and increased effort (Digman, 1959), and increased information processing and retrieval practice (Schmidt and Bjork, 1992). Given these mechanisms by which the spacing of practice effects occur, it is not unreasonable to posit that the characteristics and features of teams may influence the relationship between practice spacing and skill acquisition, retention, and transfer.

The results of the current study suggest that longer interstudy intervals had a larger effect on individuals than for teams. Specifically, the longer interstudy interval resulted in higher performance at the end of acquisition ($d = 0.24$) and after an extended period of nonuse ($d = 0.47$) compared to the shorter interstudy interval condition. However, there was not a statistically significant difference between the longer and shorter interstudy intervals for transfer ($d = 0.06$). For the team protocol, there were no differences between the longer and shorter interstudy interval conditions for acquisition ($d = 0.08$), retention ($d = 0.11$), or transfer ($d = 0.13$).

A potential explanation for these results is that the teams engaged in more tasks (i.e., taskwork and teamwork tasks) than trainees in the individual condition (i.e., taskwork only), and that the additional tasks performed by teams increased the overall complexity of the task as a whole. In a meta-analysis investigating the effects of the spacing of practice on individual performance, Donovan and Radosevich (1999) concluded that task complexity moderated the relationship between practice spacing and performance, such that simple tasks displayed larger effect sizes ($d = 0.97$) compared to complex tasks ($d = 0.07$). Thus, the current results would support the supposition that some characteristics or features of teams may mitigate the effect of the spacing of practice.

Skill Decay after an Extended Nonuse Interval

The final broad summary statement that can be made on the basis of the present study's results is that the amount of skill decay on a complex command-and-control task was not as large as one might expect based on the research on simple tasks. For example, Arthur et al.'s (1998) meta-analysis reported a performance decrement d of -0.65 after 28 to 90 days of nonuse. However, the results of the present study suggest individuals experienced comparatively less skill decay ($d = -0.11$). Similar results were found for teams ($d = -0.12$). One plausible explanation for why complex tasks may be more resistant to skill decay is that complex tasks are inherently open-looped in nature and engender dynamic stimulus-response patterns (cf. Wang et al. (2013), Chapter 4, this volume). This in turn requires deeper and more controlled processing that may lead to less skill decay compared to superficial, automatic processing (Arthur et al., 1998; Schmidt and Bjork, 1992).

Directions for Future Research

The current study investigated the comparative effectiveness of longer versus shorter interstudy intervals in the context of both individual and team training. We recognize that organizations often use practice schedules that are much shorter (e.g., 8 hours of training in 1 day) than the schedules used in the current study. Future research could investigate a broader range of schedules to determine the optimal interstudy interval. We suspect that the optimal interstudy interval would vary as a function of several task features (e.g., complex versus simple tasks, individual versus team tasks), training design features (e.g., part versus whole training, degree of overlearning), and the outcomes of interest (e.g., skill acquisition, retention, transfer). We also believe that the interstudy interval length and performance probably display a nonlinear relationship such that, at some point, a longer interstudy interval will lead to decreases in skill acquisition, retention, and transfer.

Although we invoked several team processes in explaining the current results, team process variables were not measured. Thus, an investigation of the extent to which team process variables (e.g., transactive memory, shared mental models) mitigate skill loss and contribute to skill transfer may hold promise as an avenue for future research. Specifically, although transactive memory (e.g., Moreland, 1999; Zhang, Hempel, Han, and Tjosvold 2007), shared mental models (e.g., Edwards, Day, Arthur, and Bell, 2006), and other team cognition variables continue to garner research attention, these concepts and phenomena have not been applied to the issue of team performance after extended periods of nonuse.

Implications for Practice, and Conclusions

In summary, team training engenders a myriad of variables and processes (e.g., team interdependence, team mental models, team-efficacy) that are not present in individual training. As such, researchers and practitioners question the extent to which training principles generalize from individual to team training contexts. In the context of team skill retention and transfer, it is easy to envision a situation where team-related variables mitigate skill loss and facilitate transfer. Conversely, it is as easy to envisage situations where, given the increased complexity of operating in a team and managing teamwork and taskwork interdependencies, teams would experience greater skill loss over an extended period of nonuse. The results of the current study suggest that although teams displayed similarly small performance decrements after an extended period of nonuse compared to individuals, teams displayed substantially smaller decrements on a test of transfer compared to individuals. It is also important to note that teams displayed less performance gains during skill acquisition compared to individuals.

The lack of spacing effects for teams suggests that the benefits associated with longer interstudy intervals at the individual level may not generalize to team training contexts. Specifically, the results of the present study suggest that longer interstudy intervals may mitigate skill loss after an extend period of nonuse for individuals. However, for teams, the differences between the longer and shorter intervals at retention was not statistically significant. Thus, the administrative difficulty and costs associated with longer interstudy intervals may not be warranted when team performance is the primary outcome of interest. However, it is important to note that this conclusion is based on a single study, and future research needs to replicate these findings.

Our comparison of individual and team transfer performance suggests that teams may perform better than individuals in novel and changing task environments. Indeed, the ability of teams to adapt in complex, changing environments is a principal benefit of using teams (Burke et al., 2006; LePine, 2003) and some researchers consider adaptability to be a defining feature of teams (e.g., Salas et al., 1992). Because teams consist of multiple individuals, teams may possess higher levels of knowledge, skills, and performance capabilities compared to individuals and be better equipped to perform in novel environments. Kozlowski, Gully, Nason, and Smith (1999) argued that teams undergo team compilation which involves the process of building or aggregating these knowledge, skills, and performance capabilities during training and performance. Team compilation entails both individual processes (e.g., acquisition of role-specific knowledge and skills) and team processes (e.g., negotiation, identification, and affective and motivational states), and these team processes may facilitate better adaptive performance. For example, research suggests that role adaptation during novel performance is positively related to performance (LePine, 2003).

Team cognition is another characteristic of teams that may facilitate adaptive performance. When faced with novel situations, teams may have to perform the task without prior planning. Shared mental models allow teams to coordinate and anticipate team members' actions without explicit planning or communication (Cannon-Bowers, Salas, and Converse, 1993). For example, Marks, Zaccaro, and Mathieu (2000) found that team mental model similarity predicted task performance in two novel performance environments ($r = .38$ and .30).

The present study contributes to the extant team adaptation literature by directly assessing the extent to which individuals and teams adapted to a novel performance environment using the same command-and-control simulation task after an 8-week nonuse interval. Specifically, teams displayed smaller performance decrements ($d = -0.77$) compared to individuals ($d = -1.75$) in terms of transfer. Thus, teams may appear to have an advantage over individuals in situations where novel and dynamic performance demands are the norm.

NOTE

1   The individual-level data and analyses are presented in Arthur et al. (2010), The effect of distributed practice on immediate posttraining, and long-term performance on a complex command-and-control task, *Human Performance, 23*, 428–445.

REFERENCES

Arthur, W. Jr., Bennett, W. Jr., Stanush, P. L., and McNelly, T. L. (1998). Factors that influence skill decay and retention: A quantitative review and analysis. *Human Performance, 11*, 57–101.

Arthur, W. Jr., Day, E. A., Villado, A. J., Boatman, P. R., Kowollik, V., Bennett, W. Jr., and Bhupatkar, A. (2010). The effect of distributed practice on immediate posttraining, and long-term performance on a complex command-and-control task. *Human Performance, 23*, 428–445.

Arthur, W. Jr., Edwards, B., Bell, S., Villado, A., and Bennett, W. Jr. (2005). Team task analysis: Identifying tasks and jobs that are team based. *Human Factors, 47*, 654–669.

Arthur, W. Jr., Glaze, R. M., Bhupatkar, A., Villado, A. J., Bennett, W. Jr., and Rowe, L. (2012). Team task analysis: Differentiating between tasks using team-relatedness and team workflow as metrics of team task interdependence. *Human Factors, 54*, 277–295.

Arthur, W. Jr., Villado, A. J., and Bennett, W. Jr. (2012). Innovations in team task analysis: Identifying team-based task elements, tasks, and jobs. In M. A. Wilson, W. Bennett, Jr., S. G. Gibson, and G. M. Alliger (Eds.), *The handbook of work analysis in organizations: The methods, systems, applications, and science of work measurement in organizations* (pp. 641–661). New York: Routledge/Psychology Press.

Beal, D. J., Cohen, R. R., Burke, M. J., and McLendon, C. L. (2003). Cohesion and performance in groups. A meta-analytic clarification of construct relations. *Journal of Applied Psychology, 88*, 989–1004.

Bohlander, G. W., and McCarthy, K. (1996). How to get the most from team training. *National Productivity Review, 15*, 2535.

Burke, C. S., Stagle, K. C., Salas, E., Pierce, L., and Kendall, D. (2006). Understanding team adaptation: A conceptual analysis and model. *Journal of Applied Psychology, 91*, 1189–1207.

Cannon-Bowers, J. A., Salas, E., and Converse, S. (1993). Shared mental models in expert team decision making. In N. J. Castellan Jr. (Ed.), *Individual and Group Decision Making: Current Issues* (pp. 221–246). Hillsdale, NJ: Lawrence Erlbaum Associates.

Cepeda, N. J., Pashler, H., Vul, E., Wixted, J. T., and Rohrer, D. (2006). Distributed practice in verbal recall tasks: A review and quantitative synthesis. *Psychological Bulletin, 132*, 354–380.

Cepeda, N. J., Vul, E., Rohrer, D., Wixted, J. T., and Pashler, H. (2008). Spacing effects in learning: A temporal ridgeline of optimal retention. *Psychological Science, 19*, 1095–1102.

Cooke, N. J., Gorman, J. C., Duran, J. Myers, C. W., and Andrews, D. H. (2013). Retention of team coordination skill. In W. Arthur, Jr., E. A. Day, W. Bennett, Jr., and A. Portrey (Eds.), *Individual and team skill decay: The science and implications for practice* (pp. 344–363). New York: Taylor & Francis.

Day, E. A., Arthur, W. Jr., Bell, S. T., Edwards, B. D., Bennett, W. Jr., Mendoza, J. L., and Tubre, T. C. (2005). Ability-based pairing strategies in the team-based training of a complex skill: Does the intelligence of your training partner matter? *Intelligence, 33*, 39–65.

DeCecco, J. P. (1968). *The psychology of learning and instruction: Educational psychology*. Englewood Cliffs, NJ: Prentice Hall.

DeChurch, L. A., and Mesmer-Magnus, J. R. (2010a). The cognitive underpinnings of effective teamwork: A meta-analysis. *Journal of Applied Psychology, 95*, 32–53.

DeChurch, L. A., and Mesmer-Magnus, J. R. (2010b). Measured shared team mental models: A meta-analysis. *Group Dynamics: Theory, Research, and Practice, 14*, 1–14.

Digman, J. M. (1959). Growth of a motor skill as a function of distribution of practice. *Journal of Experimental Psychology, 57*, 310–316.

Donovan, J. J., and Radosevich, D. J. (1999). A meta-analytic review of the distribution of practice effect: Now you see it, now you don't. *Journal of Applied Psychology, 84*, 795–805.

Edwards, B. D., Day, E. A., Arthur, W. Jr., and Bell, S. T. (2006). Relationships among team ability composition, team mental models, and team performance. *Journal of Applied Psychology, 91*, 727–736.

Gully, S. M., Incalcaterra, K. A., Joshi, A., and Beaubien, J. M. (2002). A meta-analysis of team efficacy, potency, and performance. Interdependence and level of analysis as moderators of observed relationships. *Journal of Applied Psychology, 87*, 819–832.

Janiszewski, C., Noel, H., and Sawyer, A. G. (2003). A meta-analysis of the spacing effect in verbal learning: Implications for research on advertising repetition and consumer memory. *Journal of Consumer Research, 30*, 138–149.

Kornell, N., and Bjork, R. A. (2008). Learning concepts and categories: Is spacing the "enemy of induction"? *Psychological Science, 19*, 585–592.

Kozlowski, S., and Ilgen, D. (2006). Enhancing the effectiveness of work groups and teams. *Psychological Science in the Public Interest, 7*, 77–124.

Kozlowski, S. W. J., Gully, S. M., Nason, E. R., and Smith, E. M. (1999). Developing adaptive teams: A theory of compilation and performance across levels and time.

In D. R. Ilgen and E. D. Pulakos (Eds.), *The changing nature of work performance: Implications for staffing, personnel actions, and development* (pp. 240–292). San Francisco: Jossey-Bass.

LePine, J. A. (2003). Team adaptation and postchange performance: Effects of team composition in terms of members' cognitive ability and personality. *Journal of Applied Psychology, 88,* 27–39.

Marks, M. A., Mathieu, J. E., and Zaccaro, S. J. (2001). A temporally based framework and taxonomy of team processes. *Academy of Management Review, 26,* 356–376.

Mohammed, S., Ferzandi, L., and Hamilton, K. (2010). Metaphor no more: A 15-year review of the team mental model construct. *Journal of Management, 36,* 876–910.

Moreland, R. L. (1999). Transactive memory: Learning who knows what in work groups and organizations. In L. Thompson, D. Messick, and J. Levine (Eds.), *Shared cognition in organizations: The management of knowledge* (pp. 3–31). Hillsdale, NJ: Erlbaum.

Mullen, B., and Cooper, C. (1994). The relationship between group cohesion and performance: An integration. *Journal of Applied Psychology, 115,* 210–227.

Rohrer, D., and Taylor, K. (2007). The effects of overlearning and distributed practise on the retention of mathematics knowledge. *Applied Cognitive Psychology, 20,* 1209–1224.

Salas, E., and Cannon-Bowers, J. A. (2001). The science of training: A decade of progress. *Annual Review of Psychology, 52,* 471–499.

Salas, E., Bowers, C., and Cannon-Bowers, J. A. (1995). Military team research: 10 years of progress. *Military Psychology, 7,* 55–75.

Salas, E., Dickinson, T. L., Converse, S. A., and Tannenbaum, S. I. (1992). Toward an understanding of team performance and training. In R. W. Swezey and E. Salas (Eds.), *Teams: Their training and performance* (pp. 3–29). Norwood, NJ: Ablex.

Schmidt, R. A., and Bjork, R. A. (1992). New conceptualizations of practice: Common principles in three paradigms suggest new concepts in training. *Psychological Science, 3,* 207–217.

Sonalysts, Inc. (2004). *Jane's Fleet Command* [Computer software]. Redwood City, CA: Electronic Arts.

Stevens, M. J., and Campion, M. A. (1994). The knowledge, skills, and ability requirements for teamwork: Implications for human resource management. *Journal of Management, 20,* 503–530.

Stevens, M. J., and Campion, M. A. (1999). Staffing teams: Development and validation of a selection test for teamwork settings. *Journal of Management, 25,* 207–228.

Swezey, R. W., and Salas, E. (1992). Guidelines for use in team training development. In R. W. Swezey and E. Salas (Eds.), *Teams: Their training and performance* (pp. 219–245). Norwood, NJ: Ablex.

Villado, A. J., Day, E. A., Arthur, W. Jr., Boatman, P. R., Kowollik, V., Bhupatkar, A., and Bennett, W. Jr. (2013). Complex command-and control simulation task performance following periods of nonuse. In W. Arthur, Jr., E. A. Day, W. Bennett, Jr., and A. Portrey (Eds.), *Individual and team skill decay: The science, and implications for practice* (pp. 53–67). New York: Taylor & Francis.

Wageman, R. (2001). The meaning of interdependence. In M. E. Turner (Ed.), *Groups at work: Advances in theory and research* (pp. 197–217). Hillsdale, NJ: Lawrence Erlbaum Associates.

Wang, X., Day, E. A., Kowollik, V., Schuelke, M. J., and Hughes, M. (2013). Factors influencing knowledge and skill decay after training: A meta-analysis. In W. Arthur,

Jr., E. A. Day, W. Bennett, Jr., and A. Portrey (Eds.), *Individual and team skill decay: The science, and implications for practice* (pp. 68–116). New York: Taylor & Francis.

Zhang, Z., Hempel, P. S., Han, Y., and Tjosvold, D. (2007). Transactive memory system links work team characteristics and performance. *Journal of Applied Psychology, 92,* 1722–1730.

AUTHORS' NOTES

This research was sponsored by contracts and grants from the U.S. Air Force Research Laboratory, Human Effectiveness Directorate, Warfighter Training Research Division, Mesa, AZ, the Defense Advance Research Project Agency, and the National Science Foundation awarded to Winfred Arthur, Jr. The views expressed herein are those of the authors and do not necessarily reflect the official position or opinion of the sponsors or their respective organizations.

14

Retention of Team Coordination Skill

Nancy J. Cooke, Jamie C. Gorman, Jasmine Duran, Christopher W. Myers, and Dee Andrews

INTRODUCTION

Teams and Cognitive Tasks

Teams and teamwork are beginning to dominate industrial, academic, and military settings. Seldom are tasks accomplished by individuals acting alone. Furthermore, tasks are becoming increasingly complex with considerable cognitive demands that have rendered individual skill inadequate and have necessitated a variety of skills that are brought to the task by a heterogeneous group of specialists. Moreover, team composition changes regularly and even intact teams may experience lengthy periods without practice (e.g., incident command teams). Teams may be expected to retain teamwork skills over long periods of nonuse. The question of team skill and its decay is critical.

But is skill decay in teams something more than, or different from, the aggregated skill decay of all individuals on the team? In this chapter we make the case that it is—that there is skill decay at the team level of analysis. Specifically, in previously collected data, we examine the relative contributions of individual performance decay and loss of team interaction skills to predict team performance decay. Results indicate that team performance decay and/or retention is accounted for by differences in team member interaction, rather than individual competency. These results support the view that team performance is more than the sum of individual team member performance, and that differences in team retention can be attributed to team interaction processes. These findings have implications for team training for long-term retention.

Studies of Skill Decay

Research on acquisition and retention of individual skills dates back to 1885 and the work of Hermann Ebbinghaus on nonsense syllable forgetting (1885/1913). Numerous studies since that time have documented the decay or loss of individual skill using verbal, motor, and procedural tasks and have examined interventions to stave off the loss of skill after a break in performance (Bahrick, 1984; Driskell, Copper, and Willis, 1992; Fendrich et al., 1988; Hammerton, 1963; Neumann and Ammons, 1957; Semb, Ellis, and Araujo, 1993).

Retention of skill is important to the military for maintenance of combat readiness while keeping training time and costs to a minimum (Farr, 1987; Prophet, 1976; Sabol and Wisher, 2001; Wisher, Sabol, and Ellis, 1999). For instance, U.S. Army personnel will undergo hours of marksmanship training, yet may go for weeks or months before firing a weapon again (Thompson, Smith, Morey, and Osborne, 1980). Other studies have examined the retention of skills learned in basic training (McDonald, 1967), weapon assembly/disassembly (Hagman and Rose, 1983), tank gunnery skills (Goldberg, Drillings, and Dressel, 1981; Marmie and Healy, 1995), and flight (Mengelkoch, Adams, and Gainer, 1960) and have generally found that skill retention is dependent on variables such as training time, mastery criteria, and interval length.

Virtually all of this work has focused on skill acquisition and retention at the individual level. Indeed the study of cognitive processing has focused on the individual as the unit of analysis; but there are specific challenges associated with empirical studies of skill decay in teams. It is difficult to keep experimental teams together long enough to measure losses in skill over extended periods of time. For teams that stay together in a natural, operational setting (e.g., Air Operation Center teams) it is difficult to control the amount of exposure teams get to the operational tasks between experimental sessions. Consequently, the team literature has little to say about team skill decay and how to best mitigate its effects.

Team Cognition

Although there has been little empirical work on team-level skill decay, there has been considerable research on team-level cognition or "team cognition" (Cooke, Gorman, and Winner, 2007a; Salas and Fiore, 2004). Team cognition refers to cognitive processing or cognitive activity that is carried out by teams—typically three or more individuals working interdependently toward a common goal (Salas, Dickinson, Converse, and Tannenbaum, 1992).

Consider the Air Operation Center, a central hub of military command-and-control that requires hundreds of personnel acting in a coordinated fashion to execute military plans. Teams in this setting make decisions, plan, assess the situation, and solve problems as coordinated units. These are cognitive activities performed by teams. Similarly consider the surgical team consisting of surgeon, anesthesiologist, and nurse. The individuals need to interact to accomplish the surgical task as an effective team. The team as a whole is capable of performing well or failing, apart from individual performance. Indeed team training focuses on improving performance of the team. The acquisition and decay of cognitive skill at a team level are functions of team cognition.

There are two ways that researchers have characterized team cognition. The predominant way is to describe and measure team cognition in terms of an aggregate of the cognition of the individual team members (Blickensderfer, Cannon-Bowers, and Salas, 1997; Converse, Cannon-Bowers, and Salas, 1991; Langan-Fox, Code, and Langfield-Smith, 2000; Mathieu et al., 2000; Stout, Cannon-Bowers, Salas, and Milanovich, 1999). This "aggregate" approach for instance, assumes that team knowledge or a "shared mental model" is the aggregate of what each team member knows. According to this view, team skill decay would be best predicted by the aggregate of the skill decay of every individual on the team.

Alternatively, team cognition can be characterized as an emergent property of teammate interactions or process (Cooke, Gorman, and Rowe, 2009). According to this "Interactive Team Cognition" view, team cognition may result in team members "connecting the dots" and coming up with new knowledge that never existed for any one individual. Namely, interaction is at the heart of team-level performance, where interactivity defines individuals as team-members rather than a collection of individuals. Team skill decay per this view would depend more on the preservation of effective team interactions via communication or coordination, rather than individual skill sets.

Team Skill Decay

In this chapter we explore team skill decay in the context of the Aggregate and Interactive perspectives of team cognition. Given that there is a team performance decrement after a retention interval, the Aggregate viewpoint would predict that this is primarily owing to individual skill loss. According to the Interactive Team Cognition perspective, the decrement would be primarily attributed to loss of team-level skill such as communication or coordination.

In accord with Interactive Team Cognition theory we hypothesize that decrements in team performance can largely be accounted for by differences in interactions across team members measured using process metrics. A process metric differentiates teams by focusing on team-member interactions. That is, we assume that most of the variance in team performance outcome is accounted for by team member interaction, rather than individual competency (i.e., reminiscent of the 2004 Olympic basketball team, a team of experts does not obtain high performance on individual merits alone; they must interact with each other). Process metrics can be contrasted with measures of knowledge. We assume that knowledge plays a relatively minor role in predicting team performance decrements, relative to process. In order to address the question of whether or not change in teamwork and taskwork knowledge accounts for team performance decrements, knowledge metrics based on accuracy of team members reaching consensus are also examined.

SOME EMPIRICAL EVIDENCE

We had an early glimpse of possible team-level skill decay in a team study conducted for other purposes and have more recently examined skill decay more directly. Data from both studies were collected in the context of a three-person simulation of Unmanned Aerial Vehicle (UAV) ground control (Cooke and Shope, 2004). In this simulation, three team members work collaboratively to take photos of reconnaissance targets. There are three roles assumed by three team members who are initially naive to the simulation and task. The Air Vehicle Operator (AVO) controls the aerial vehicle from the ground and monitors aircraft systems. The Payload Operator (PLO) controls the camera equipment and monitors camera systems. The Data Exploitation, Mission Planning, and Communications (DEMPC) operator navigates and plans the mission. The synthetic task that involves interaction among these three interdependent roles (e.g., the camera focus set by the PLO is dependent on the aircraft altitude set by the AVO which is dependent on threats and mission constraints sent by the DEMPC) was developed as a testbed for studying team cognition.

In a typical experiment three participants are randomly assigned to one of the three roles and then presented with training on that role in the form of PowerPoint slides and tests. After successful completion of this training, a hands-on check of some of the basic skills is conducted. The team then participates in a series of 40-minute missions.

There are a number of measures taken during and apart from the missions. Team performance is reflected in a composite score of weighted outcomes collected automatically during the mission (e.g., time each individual spent in an alarm state, time each individual spent in a warning state, number of critical waypoints acquired, and the number of targets successfully photographed). Penalty points for each of these components are weighted a priori in accord with importance to the task and subtracted from a maximum score of 1000. Team performance data were collected for each of the ten missions.

Each individual role within a team (AVO, PLO, and DEMPC) also had a composite score based on various mission variables including time spent in alarm or warning state as well as variables that were unique to that role. Penalty points for each of the components were weighted a priori in accord with importance to the task and subtracted from a maximum score of 1000. The most important components for the AVO were time spent in alarm state and course deviations, for the DEMPC they were critical waypoints missed and route planning errors, and for the PLO, duplicate good photos, time spent in an alarm state, and number of bad photos were the most important components. *Individual performance* data were collected for each role in each mission.

The scores for each individual role and for the team were based on different weightings of different outcome variable composites and though they may share some score components, they are not directly comparable to each other or to the team score. The team is provided with the performance score feedback at the end of every mission and an indication of how the three individual role scores and team score compare to the average role and team scores collected thus far in the lab.

Serendipitous Findings on Team Skill Decay

In an early experiment conducted at New Mexico State University with 11 three-person ROTC teams, team performance suggested the possibility of team skill decay (Cooke, Kiekel, and Helm, 2001; Cooke, Shope, and Kiekel, 2001). (Data for two teams are not included in these analyses owing to missing data and another team was excluded on the basis of an outlying score at Mission 8.) Figure 14.1 displays the average team performance of the eight teams who participated in a series of ten 40-minute or less missions over the course of three experimental sessions. Missions 3 and 4 were separated by a 24–48 hour interval. But Missions 7 and 8 were separated by Spring Break and consequently longer intervals ranging from 4–11 weeks. We noticed in these data that some of the teams with longer intervals seemed to experience skill decay.

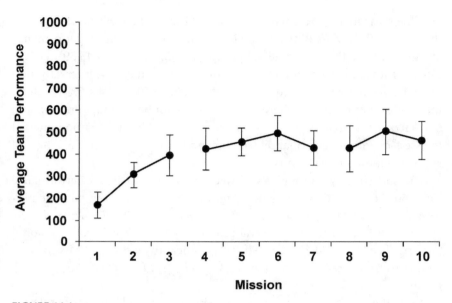

FIGURE 14.1

Average three-person team performance and standard error ($N = 8$) across 10 simulated UAV missions with breaks after Mission 3 and Mission 7.

We examined the retention data more closely from these teams. In order to observe the effects of retention interval on team performance during Session 3 (i.e., Missions 8–10), the teams were split into two groups based on the median number of weeks between Sessions 2 and 3. These groups can be seen in Table 14.1.

A baseline level of performance was established from missions completed in the first two experimental sessions. All teams taken together ($n = 8$), asymptotic levels of performance were achieved at Mission 3 and did not significantly change until after Mission 6. Therefore, Mission 6 was used as a

TABLE 14.1

Descriptive Statistics of Teams in Short and Long Retention Interval Groups.

Retention Interval Group	Mean (number of weeks)	Standard Deviation	Min	Max	N
Short (4–7 weeks)	5.86	.82	4.71	6.57	4
Long (8–11 weeks)	9.32	.71	8.71	10.86	4

baseline measure of performance (Mission 7 involved a scenario change and therefore slightly more difficult than initial missions). The mean performance at Mission 6 for the short interval group (M = 534.02, SD = 45.39) did not differ significantly from the mean performance for the long interval group (M = 442.99, SD = 90.98), $t(6)$ = 1.79, p > .10, SE = 50.84 d = 1.5. Therefore, the baseline performance criterion was the same for both groups and Mission 6 was next compared to Mission 8 which occurred after the retention interval to assess retention performance decrement differences between the long and short retention interval teams.

The short interval group's (4–7 week interval) Mission 8 performance (M = 506.76, SD = 61.45) was not significantly different from baseline performance (M =534.72, SD = 45.39), $t(3)$ = −.58, p = > .10, SE = 47.03, d = .58 (See Figure 14.2). The long interval group's (8–11 week interval) Mission 8 performance (M = 380.62., SD = 90.19.) significantly declined at Mission 8 in comparison to baseline performance (M = 442.99, SD = 90.98) $t(3)$ = −5.27, p < .05, d = −.79

Next, the baseline performance (Mission 6) for both the short interval and long interval groups was compared to Mission 9 performance. The short interval group's Mission 9 performance (M = 567.29, SD = 73.67) was not significantly different from baseline performance (M = 534.72, SD = 45.39), $t(3)$ = .729 p > .10, SE = 45.63, d =.63. For the long interval group, baseline performance (M = 442.99, SD = 90.98) was not significantly different compared to Mission 9 performance (M = 458.25, SD = 132.32), $t(3)$ = .453, p > .10, SE = 33.67, d = −.16.

Baseline performance for the short interval group (M = 534.72, SD = 45.39) was not significantly different from Mission 10 performance (M = 536.45, SD = 53.48) $t(3)$ = -.062, p >.10, SE 39.88, d = -.06. Baseline performance for the long interval group (M = 442.99, SD = 90.98) was not significantly different from Mission 10 performance (M = 399.78, SD = 68.89) $t(3)$ = 2.06, p > .10, SE = 20.97, d = .62.

Overall, these preliminary results indicate that the long interval group experienced a significant decrement in performance immediately after the retention interval, while the short interval group did not. It is also interesting to note that this decrement in performance was short lived, as the long interval groups were able to achieve baseline levels of performance in subsequent missions (Mission 9).

This result however, needs to be interpreted with caution because there was no random assignment of teams to the two conditions, given that this was not a factor intentionally manipulated. Therefore, there may be other factors associated with long-retention-interval teams that account for the drop in

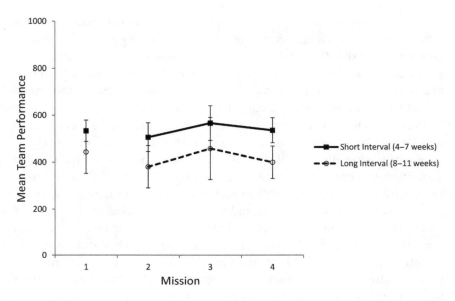

FIGURE 14.2

Mean team performance and standard deviation for teams that returned for Session 3 after a short or long interval.

performance. For instance, the teams who took more time to return after the break and thus were part of the long-retention interval, may also have been less motivated than the teams who returned more quickly. Therefore the individual and team contributions to team skill decay after a long-retention interval were more formally examined in a different experiment that held retention interval constant at 8–10 weeks for all teams and manipulated team training regime. In this report we focus on the contribution of individual and team factors to skill decay after the interval. A full report on the training manipulation and its effects can be found in (Cooke et al., 2007b).

Contributions to Team Skill Decay

An experiment was conducted at Arizona State University in which 32 three-person teams collaborated for two sessions on nine UAV missions (five and four missions for each respective session) separated by an 8–10 week retention interval (Cooke et al., 2007b). The 26 teams who completed the two sessions were randomly assigned to one of three types of team coordination training (Procedural ($n = 8$), Cross-training ($n = 10$), and Perturbed ($n = 8$)). Procedural training teams were presented with written instructions to communicate using a set of rules regarding who talks to whom about what and when. Cross-training involved having team members learn about the information needs of fellow teammates. Perturbed training involved deliberate changes to the simulation to block routine coordination. The results of this manipulation are reported elsewhere (Cooke et al., 2007b; Gorman, Cooke, and Amazeen, 2010; Gorman et al., 2007) and are not the focus of this paper. For all teams, Session 2 was scheduled 8–10 weeks after Session 1.

In addition to team and individual performance measures, a set of process and knowledge measures was taken and analyzed in terms of process or knowledge decrements after the retention interval. Process measures included coordination scores, team process ratings assigned at specific times during the course of the missions, and some team situation awareness measures. Knowledge measures of taskwork and teamwork were taken after Missions 1 and 6. The process measures were included to test whether metrics based on measures of team-member interactions accounted for significant team performance variance. The knowledge variables were included to examine the possibility that team performance decrements were related to changes in team knowledge. The experimental protocol is summarized in Table 14.2.

Measures

Team and individual performance scores were derived for each of the nine missions as in the prior experiment using composites of weighted mission outcome variables. Absolute values of performance scores are not directly comparable across the two experiments reported here owing to a modification in the scoring routine in the second experiment in order to account for changes in workload. Specifically, number of targets visited and photographed was

TABLE 14.2

Experimental Protocol. (Session 2 occurred 8–10 weeks following Session 1.)

Session 1	Session 2
Consent Forms	Skills Refresher
Task Training	Mission 6
Mission 1	Knowledge Measures
Knowledge Measures	Mission 7
Mission 2	Mission 8
Mission 3	Mission 9
Mission 4	Demographics
Mission 5	Debriefing

All measures but knowledge measures were taken in the context of the task.

modified to number of targets visited and photographed per minute (Cooke et al., 2007b).

During the experiment, a trained observer used custom software to log predetermined *coordination* events for each target. Specifically, the observer logged whether the DEMPC informed the AVO and PLO of upcoming targets (e.g., restrictions, effective radius), whether the PLO and AVO negotiated airspeed and altitude at the target, and whether the AVO was told by the PLO that the photograph taken at the target was acceptable (thus indicating to the AVO that the team is clear to move to the next waypoint). The observer was also able to indicate if a particular communication event did not occur, if information was repeated, if there was uncertainty about whether a particular event occurred (in order to review the videotape and make confirmations that the event in question did or did not occur), and make comments at each particular target. Each time an observation was logged it was associated with a time stamp. In addition, team coordination ratings described in the next section were entered using this software.

A procedural model of coordination is presented in Figure 14.3 and basically involves a sequence of three events that typically occur at each target. The DEMPC tells the AVO information (I) concerning upcoming target restrictions, the AVO and PLO then negotiate (N) the appropriate altitude and airspeed for taking the photograph through back-and-forth negotiation, and the PLO gives the DEMPC and AVO feedback (F) that the target has been photographed. Implementation of the procedural model by teams was computed as a coordination score based on the timing of these three events. Specifically, the coordination score is calculated by: $t(F_i) - t(I_i)/t(F_i) - t(N_i)$ which basically examines the relationship among the procedural model constituents at each target waypoint.

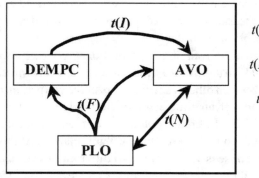

$t(I)$ – Information Initiated

$t(N)$ – Negotiation Initiated

$t(F)$ – Feedback Initiated

Optimal sequence is:
I, N, F

FIGURE 14.3

Procedural model (standard operating procedure) for photographing UAV ground targets.

A transition point ($\beta = 1$) separates these two qualitatively different states of poor coordination ($\beta < 1$) or good coordination ($\beta > 1$). Specifically, in the "bad" region either 'N' precedes 'I,' or 'F' precedes either 'I' or 'N' or both. When 'N' precedes 'I' this is indicative of a "backlog" of information. In the "good" region, all components are in the proper sequence for the procedural model, with larger values indicating more "front-loading" of information in terms of establishing the 'I' component well before the target is approached.

Ten percent of the missions were randomly selected to be independently coded by a second observer. For the missions selected, a second observer played back the video recording to log the coordination and assign process ratings for each target that the team photographed. After excluding all cases in which one observer provided a rating and the other had not, there were 199 coordination ratings provided by both sets of observers. Ratings were paired by team, mission, and target and the intraclass correlation coefficient was estimated. Based on the results, we rejected the null hypothesis that the coordination ratings assigned by the different observers were independent ($ICC = .474$, $F(198, 199) = 2.80$, $p < .001$).

The observer who logged coordination events and an additional experimenter also rated *team process* on a scale ranging from 0 to 4 with 4 indicating "excellent" process and 0 indicating "poor" process. The rating was based on the timing of communications, number of repeated communications, situation awareness behaviors, and whether the team followed and included all elements of the procedural model for that particular target.

Team Situation Awareness was measured using the Coordinated Awareness of Situation by Teams (CAST) measure (Gorman, Cooke, and Winner, 2006). This measure is taken on three levels, wherein the team responds to some unusual circumstance, or a CAST roadblock. A roadblock is defined experimentally as any manipulation introduced during the course of performance that can result in performance decrement if not successfully coordinated and acted upon by the team. CAST measures the coordinated perception and action of a team responding to a roadblock.

The first part of the CAST measure is firsthand perception—who responds independently to the unusual circumstance; the second is coordinated perception—which team members tell other team members of their experience; the third is coordinated action—given the roadblock, how does the team address it? Each of these levels can be coded (by an experimenter) according to an optimal response with respect to a roadblock manipulation. A non-response is zero, whereas a response is 1. According to different channels of communication (e.g., AVO→PLO), a response can be coded as 1—if the channel is employed with respect to the roadblock, or 0—if the channel is NOT employed with respect to the roadblock. In our case we have a three-member team, so an optimal response would either be a three-element vector for unique perspectives (i.e., action or not with respect to each team member), or it could be a six-element vector (the number of possible communication channels) for shared perspectives (i.e., AVO→PLO, AVO→DEM, PLO→ AVO, PLO→DEM, DEM→AVO, and DEM→PLO). Each element of the observed vector can then be compared to an "optimal" vector determined by expert judgment. The 1s and 0s are coded as hits and false alarms according to signal detection theory in addition to whether or not the roadblock was overcome by the team.

Approximately 10 percent of missions (12 Missions) were randomly selected and rated by a second experimenter. Inter-rater reliability was assessed in two ways. First, component agreement (agreement between ratings of perception, coordinated perception, and action) was calculated between ratings provided by the two experimenters using Cohen's Kappa; there were 165 paired observations ($\kappa = .68$, $z = 8.72$, $p < .001$). Next, outcome agreement (agreement between ratings of whether or not the team overcame the SA roadblock) was calculated between the two experimenters; there were a total of 12 paired observations ($\kappa = .83$, $z = 2.93$, $p < .01$).

Taskwork knowledge was assessed through individual relatedness ratings on pairs of eleven task-related terms (e.g., altitude, focus, zoom, shutter speed, fuel). These task-related terms formed 55 concept pairs, which were presented in one direction only, one pair at a time. Pair order was randomized and order within pairs was counterbalanced across participants.

Team members made relatedness ratings of the 55 concept pairs on a six-point scale that ranged from unrelated to highly related. By submitting these ratings to Knowledge Network Organization Tool (KNOT), using parameters $r = $ infinity and $q = $ n-1, an individual Pathfinder network (Schvaneveldt, 1990) was derived for each of the team members. These networks reduce and represent the rating data in a graph structure with concept nodes standing for terms and links standing for associations between terms. The individual taskwork networks were scored against a key representing overall knowledge, and against role-specific keys, but in this analysis we use only overall taskwork knowledge accuracy. The referent network for overall accuracy was based on data from the highest scoring teams in our previous studies. The accuracy of an individual's overall knowledge was determined by comparing each individual network to this empirical referent using a network similarity metric based on the proportion of shared links. These individual overall knowledge scores were aggregated to form a team score for overall accuracy.

Teamwork knowledge was assessed using a teamwork questionnaire. The teamwork questionnaire consisted of a scenario in which each individual participant was required to indicate which of 16 specific communications were absolutely necessary in order to achieve the scenario goal. To calculate each individual's overall accuracy, the responses were compared to an answer key, which classified each of the 16 communications into one of the three following categories: (1) the communication is NEVER absolutely necessary to complete the scenario goal; (2) the communication could POSSIBLY be necessary to complete the scenario goal (e.g., as considered by novices); or (3) the communication is ALWAYS absolutely necessary to complete the scenario goal. Each communication was worth 2 points, which yielded a maximum of 32 points possible per team member. Participants either checked each communication, indicating that it was absolutely necessary to complete the scenario goal, or left it blank, indicating that it was not absolutely necessary. A perfect score was achieved by only checking those communications that were ALWAYS absolutely necessary and leaving all other communications blank. Team overall knowledge was the mean of the three team members' overall accuracy scores.

Results Pertinent to Team-level Skill Decay

Team performance scores averaged across the teams in each condition are presented in Figure 14.4. Complete results from this experiment are reported in Cooke et al., 2007b). Here we focus on retention of team skill. We hypothesized that the retention interval would result in a significant decline in team performance. At Mission 5, all teams were presented with a situation awareness roadblock that may have affected team performance; therefore, Mission 4 was selected for use as the baseline score. A decrement score was generated for each team by subtracting a pre-manipulation baseline score (Mission 4) from the post-manipulation score (Mission 6). These decrement scores were indicative of degree of team performance decrement (negative score) and served as the dependent variable in the following tests. There was a decrement in team performance from Mission 4 ($M = 459.72$, $SD = 63.42$) to Mission 6 ($M = 412.53$, $SD = 91.10$). A paired sample t-test revealed that team performance diminished significantly between Missions 4 and 6 (t (25) $= -2.96$, $p < .01$, $SE = 15.96$, $d = .58$). The performance decrement was not significantly different for the treatment groups (F (2, 23) $= 0.93$, $p > .10$, $MSe = 6657.57$, $d = .08$).

Two of the team member roles also exhibited performance decrements. The AVO role exhibited a significant decrement (t (25) $= -4.39$, $p < .001$, $SE = 9.69$, $d = .86$) from Mission 4 ($M = 902.33$, $SD = 70.10$) to Mission 6 ($M = 859.81$, $SD = 89.02$). The DEMPC role also exhibited a significant decrement (t (25) $= -2.35$, $p < .05$, $SE = 35.07$, $d = .86$) from Mission 4 ($M = 799.38$, $SD = 248.20$) to Mission 6 ($M = 717.16$, $SD = 319.75$). The PLO

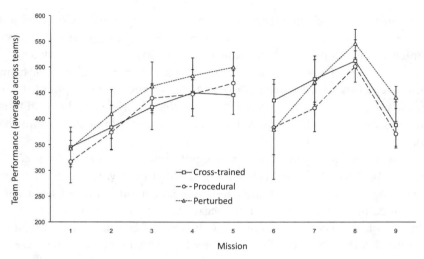

FIGURE 14.4

Mean team and standard error performance across all missions. Missions 5 and 6 were separated by an 8 to 10 week retention interval.

role did not exhibit a significant decrement (t (25) = 1.93, $p > .10$, SE = 5.55, $d = .38$) from Mission 4 (M = 875.15, SD = 37.60) to Mission 6 (M = 885.87, SD = 24.21).

The team performance decrement was regressed on the comparable individual performance decrements for the three UAV-STE team members in order to test the hypothesis that variance in individual performance decrements accounts for the variance in team performance decrements. Recall that the team performance score is not based on the individual scores, but that components of the individual scores are shared with the team score. Retention interval, which ranged from 8 to 10 weeks in duration was statistically controlled by including the number of days between Mission 4 performance and Mission 6 performance. This was tested using the regression model (all variables are decrement scores except interval):

Team performance = constant + AVO performance + PLO performance

+ DEM performance + Interval + error

This baseline model made up of individual decrements failed to reach significance (F (4, 20) = 2.018, MSe = 5880.23, $p > .10$, R^2 = .29). None of the individual predictors in this model were significant.

After this model was fit, we introduced process and knowledge variables to the same baseline model by entering decrement variables for: Team Situation

Awareness (hits and false alarms over all CAST components), Coordination Score (averaged over targets in a mission), Process Ratings (averaged over targets in a mission), Teamwork Knowledge Accuracy, and Taskwork Knowledge Accuracy. These process and knowledge variables were also in the form of decrement scores between Mission 4 and 6, with the exception of the knowledge scores which were taken twice (after Missions 1 and 6) and thus the knowledge decrements were based on these two administrations of the measure.

This second regression model was significant ($F(10, 14) = 2.71$, $p < .05$, $MSe = 4011.88$, $R^2 = .66$; Table 14.3). Two process variable decrements (coordination and team SA hits) were significant predictors of team performance decrement. The curious negative relation between performance decrements and coordination decrements needs to be interpreted in light of the fact that the mean coordination scores for all teams and missions were all greater than 1, the qualitative transition point, indicating that coordination sequence was appropriate for all teams. Differences on the positive end of the scale are only indicative differences in the relative timing of information components. In the case of skill decay it appears that bigger changes in coordination timing (e.g., scores greater than 1 before the break and closer to 1 after the break) are associated with smaller performance decrements.

None of the knowledge decrements significantly predicted team performance decrement. Compared to the baseline model, when accounting for decrements in the process variables, the AVO decrement and the length of retention interval significantly predicted team performance decrement. This suggests that accounting for process decrements may free up variance in team decrement that can then be accounted for in individual decrements and team-level differences (i.e., length of retention interval).

IMPLICATIONS FOR PRACTICE, AND CONCLUSIONS

Teams are a ubiquitous feature of nearly every type of military operation, and team effectiveness is often tied to an operation's success or failure. Work from our lab indicates that team skill in a three-person UAV control task decays after a period of 10–13 weeks or sooner. It could be that team skill decay results from the decay of individual skills—the amount of individual skill decay across participants predicts the skill decay of the team. Alternatively, our data indicate that team skill decay results from the decay of skills associated with team interaction (e.g., team coordination and team situation awareness) in concert with the decay of individual skills.

TABLE 14.3

Multiple Linear Regression for Individual Performance and Process Decrements Predicting Team Performance Decrement

Predictors ($df = 14$)	M	SD	Decrement Size (d)	Slope (B)	SE	Beta	t	Semipartial r^2
AVO perf	42.52	49.4	0.86	0.87	0.32	0.53	2.70*	0.18
PLO perf	-10.71	28.31	-0.38	1.14	0.57	0.4	2.02	0.10
DEMPC perf	82.23	178.81	0.46	0.02	0.09	0.05	0.27	0.00
Interval (days)	NA	NA	NA	6.93	2.67	0.53	2.59*	0.16
Team SA (hits)	0.01	0.31	0.03	127.91	48.11	0.48	2.66*	0.17
Team SA (false alarms)	0.09	0.13	0.69	112.27	114.19	0.18	0.98	0.02
Process	0.23	0.86	0.27	12.87	20.13	0.13	0.64	0.01
Coordination	-0.35	1.29	-0.27	-42.72	17.82	-0.67	-2.40*	0.14
Knowledge (task)	-0.01	0.05	-0.20	67.68	353.23	0.04	0.19	0.00
Knowledge (team)	-0.97	3.22	-0.30	3.86	4.89	0.15	0.79	0.02

Model $R^2 = .66$; * $p < .05$.

Individual performance decreases after an individual stops performing a task for some amount of time, and the longer the period without practice the greater the decrement in performance. Performance decrements are typically attributed to decaying cognitive processes resulting in the skill, such as memory retrievals and task proceduralization. Interestingly, team performance also decreases after time off from a task, and decrements follow the same general pattern as decrements from individuals.

Naturally, it is a small step to assuming that team performance decrements result from the decay of individual teammates' skills. It is a simple explanation as there is already evidence that individuals' performance decreases with time away from the task, so it is not hard to imagine that a decrease in individual performance will result in a decrease in team performance. The results from the analyses presented in this chapter support an alternative account of team performance decrements.

We examined how well individual skill decay and team skill decay predicted team performance. Our first regression model only included decrements to individual skill, and did not predict drops in team performance. Our second regression model produced statistically reliable predictions of team performance with the addition of variables that captured changes of team coordination and situation awareness after taking time off from the task. Interestingly, decrements in individual teammates' performance became a significant contributor to the predictions only after adding team coordination and situation awareness variables. These results indicate that the dynamics of teammate interactions are an important factor affecting team performance. Furthermore, the decay of individual teammates' task-specific skills also contributes to decrements in team performance. Together, these results support the view that a team is not necessarily equal to the sum of its parts and that skill decay in teams is not simply the loss of its parts.

What are the implications of this work for team effectiveness? The results presented here indicate that at least in this three-person military simulation, team skill decays over time without practice and that this decay cannot solely be attributed to decay experienced by each individual team member. Team interactions are associated with this loss in team skill. Additional experimentation is needed to determine whether the linkage between team interaction and team skill decay is causal in nature; however, the results suggest that initial or refresher training should not neglect team training that exercises coordination, communication and team situation awareness.

REFERENCES

Bahrick, H. P. (1984). Semantic memory content in permastore: Fifty years of memory for Spanish learned in school. *Journal of Experimental Psychology: General, 113,* 1–29.

Blickensderfer, E., Cannon-Bowers, J. A., and Salas, E. (1997). *Training teams to self-correct: An empirical evaluation.* Paper presented at the Meeting of the Society for Industrial and Organizational Psychology, St. Louis, MO (April 10–13).

Converse, S., Cannon-Bowers, J. A., and Salas, E. (1991). Team member shared mental models. *Proceedings of the 35th Human Factors Society Annual Meeting* (pp. 1417–1421). Santa Monica, CA: Human Factors and Ergonomics Society.

Cooke, N. J., and Shope, S. M. (2004). Designing a synthetic task environment. In S. G. Schiflett, L. R. Elliott, E. Salas, and M. D. Coovert (Eds.), *Scaled worlds: Development, validation, and application,* (pp. 263–278). Aldershot: Ashgate.

Cooke, N. J., Shope, S. M., and Kiekel, P.A. (2001). *Shared-knowledge and team performance: A cognitive engineering approach to measurement.* Technical Report for AFOSR Grant No. F49620–98–1-0287.

Cooke, N. J., Gorman, J. C., and Rowe, L. J. (2009). An Ecological Perspective on Team Cognition. In E. Salas, J. Goodwin, and C. S. Burke (Eds.), *Team effectiveness in complex organizations: Cross-disciplinary perspectives and approaches,* pp. 157–182. SIOP Organizational Frontiers Series. New York: Taylor & Francis.

Cooke, N. J., Gorman, J. C., and Winner, J. L. (2007a). Team cognition. In F. Durso, R. Nickerson, S. Dumais, S. Lewandowsky, and T. Perfect (Eds.), *Handbook of applied cognition* (2nd ed.) (pp. 239–268), Chichester: John Wiley & Sons.

Cooke, N. J., Kiekel, P. A., and Helm E. (2001). Measuring team knowledge during skill acquisition of a complex task. *International Journal of Cognitive Ergonomics: Special Section on Knowledge Acquisition, 5,* 297–315.

Cooke, N. J., Gorman, J. C., Pedersen, H. K., Winner, J. L., Duran, J., Taylor, A., Amazeen, P. G., and Andrews, D. (2007b). *Acquisition and retention of team coordination in command-and-control.* Technical Report for AFOSR Grant FA9550–04–1-0234 and AFRL Award No. FA8650–04–6442.

Driskell, J. E., Copper, C., and Willis, R. P. (1992). Effect of overlearning on retention. *Journal of Applied Psychology, 77,* 615–622.

Ebbinghaus, H. (1913). *Memory; A contribution to experimental psychology.* H. A. Rueger and C. E. Bussenius, Trans. New York: Teachers College, Columbia University.

Farr, M. J. (1987). *The long-term retention of knowledge and skills: A cognitive and instructional perspective.* New York: Springer-Verlag

Fendrich, D. W., Healy, A. F., Meiskey, L., Crutcher, R. J., Little, W., and Bourne, L. E. (1988). *Skill maintenance: Literature review and theoretical analysis.* Technical report AFHRL-TP-87-73. Brooks Air Force Base, Texas: Air Force Human Resources Laboratory.

Goldberg, S. L., Drillings, M., and Dressel, J. D. (1981). *Mastery training: Effect on skill retention.* Technical report 513. Alexandria, VA: Army Research Institute for the Behavioral and Social Sciences.

Gorman, J. C., Cooke, N. J., and Amazeen, P. G. (2010). Training adaptive teams. *Human Factors, 52,* 295–307.

Gorman, J. C., Cooke, N. J., and Winner, J. L. (2006). Measuring team situation awareness in decentralized command and control systems. *Ergonomics, 49,* 1312–1325.

Gorman, J. C., Cooke, N. J., Winner, J. L., Duran, J. L., Pedersen, H. K., and Taylor, A. R. (2007). Knowledge training versus process training: The effects of training protocol on team coordination and performance, *Proceedings of the Human Factors and Ergonomics Society 51st Annual Meeting*, Baltimore, MD, 382–386.

Hagman, J. D., and Rose, A. M. (1983). Retention of military tasks: A review. *Human Factors*, 25, 199–213.

Hammerton, M. (1963). Retention of learning in a difficult tracking task. *Journal of Experimental Psychology*, 66, 108–110.

Langan-Fox, J., Code, S., and Langfield-Smith, K. (2000). Team mental models: Techniques, methods, and analytic approaches. *Human Factors*, 42, 242–271.

McDonald, R. D. (1967). *Retention of military skills acquired in basic combat training.* Technical Report 67-13. Alexandria, VA: Human Resources Research Office.

Marmie,W. R., and Healy, A. F. (1995). The long-term retention of a complex skill. In A.F. Healy and J. L. E. Bourne (Eds.). *Learning and memory of knowledge and skills: Durability and specificity* (pp. 30–65). Thousand Oaks, CA: Sage.

Mathieu, J. E., Goodwin, G. F., Heffner, T. S., Salas, E., and Cannon-Bowers, J. A. (2000). The influence of shared mental models on team process and performance. *Journal of Applied Psychology*, 85, 273–283.

Mengelkoch, R. F., Adams, J. A., and Gainer, C. A. (1960). *The forgetting of instrument flying skills as a function of the level of initial proficiency.* NAVTRADEVCEN TR-71-16-18, Port Washington, NY: U.S. Naval Training Device Center.

Neumann, E., and Ammons, R. B. (1957). Acquisition and long-term retention of a simple serial perceptual-motor skill. *Journal of Experimental Psychology*, 53, 159–161.

Prophet, W. W. (1976). *Long-term retention of flying skills: A review of the literature.* HumRRO Final Technical Report FR-ED(P) 76–35. Alexandria, VA: Human Resources Research Organization.

Sabol, M. A., and Wisher, R. A. (2001). Retention and reacquisition of military skills. *Military Operations Research*, 6, 59–80.

Salas, E. and Fiore, S. M. (Eds., 2004). *Team cognition: Understanding the factors that drive process and performance.* Washington, D.C.: American Psychological Association.

Salas, E., Dickinson, T. L., Converse, S. A., and Tannenbaum, S. I. (1992). Toward an understanding of team performance and training. In R. W. Swezey and E. Salas (Eds.), *Teams: Their training and performance* (pp. 3–29). Norwood, NJ: Ablex.

Schvaneveldt, R. W. (1990). *Pathfinder associative networks: Studies in knowledge organization.* Norwood, NJ: Ablex.

Semb, G., Ellis, J., and Araujo, J. (1993). Long-term memory of knowledge learned in school. *Journal of Educational Psychology*, 85, 305–316.

Stout, R. J., Cannon-Bowers, J. A., Salas, E., and Milanovich, D. M. (1999). Planning, shared mental models, and coordinated performance: An empirical link is established. *Human Factors*, 41, 61–71.

Thompson, T. J., Smith, S., Morey, J. C., and Osborne, A. D. (1980). *Effects of improved basic rifle marksmanship training programs.* ARI Research Report 1255, Alexandria, VA: U.S. Army Research Institute for the Behavioral and Social Sciences.

Wisher, R. A., Sabol, M. A., and Ellis, J. A. (1999). *Staying sharp: Retention of military knowledge and skills.* ARI Special Report #39. Alexandria, VA: U.S. Army Research Institute for the Behavioral and Social Sciences.

AUTHORS' NOTES

This work was sponsored partly by grants FA9550–07–1–0081 and FA9550–04–1–0234 from the Air Force Office of Scientific Research and partly by the Air Force Research Laboratory's Warfighter Readiness Research Division (AFRL Award Number FA8650–04–6442). The authors would like to thank Nia Amazeen, Harry Pedersen, Amanda Taylor, and Jennifer Winner for their contributions to the larger project.

15

Team Performance Decay

Why Does It Happen and How to Avoid It?

Deborah DiazGranados, Elizabeth H. Lazzara, Rebecca Lyons, Samuel R. Wooten, II, and Eduardo Salas

INTRODUCTION

Throughout history, teams have played a central role in society. From early hunters, to sports settings, to common organizational tasks, the use of teams has allowed humans to perform feats that individuals working alone could not accomplish. Furthermore, recent technological advances and the globalization of organizations have contributed to a transformation in the nature of work, exemplified by the modern organization's extensive dependence on teams. Also, teams can contribute to an organization by increasing organizational productivity. One suggested reason for this increased productivity is based on the view that a team's ability is the compilation of knowledge, skills, attitudes, and experiences of each of the team's members, thus, providing a greater tool kit from which the team may draw.

Given the prevalence of team use, understanding how these units operate and the factors associated with their success has become colloquial. Over the last 25 years, teams have been examined from several perspectives including the optimal composition of teams (e.g., Halfhill, Nielsen, Sundstrom, Weilbaecher, 2005), team size (e.g., Pearce and Herbik, 2004), team training methods (e.g., Ellis, Bell, Ployhart, Hollenbeck, and Ilgen, 2005), and team member selection (e.g., Morgeson, Reider, and Campion, 2005), along with a host of other factors. Yet ultimately, each of these questions is examined with an underlying interest in the optimization of team performance.

Although numerous articles advise on the training and performance enhancement of teams, the literature has neglected to account for the fact that even the most capable teams fail to perform at optimal levels. Such decreases in level of performance are what we refer to as team performance decay. Although the common practice has been to respond to decreases in performance after they have occurred, we argue this approach to be insufficient, especially given the number of teams that currently operate in critical, high risk environments, where performance slips may be fatal for either the team members or others (e.g., medical teams, fire crews, military units). It would be advantageous to battle team performance decay proactively, thus, circumventing the consequences of performance decay; however, to do this, we must first understand the sources of performance decrement. Therefore, the present chapter addresses the concept of team performance decay and the factors at the environmental, task, and team level associated with its occurrence. However, before discussing performance decay and its sources, we must first consider team performance itself.

The Basics of Team Performance

Team performance has been defined as the behavioral, attitudinal, or cognitive actions of a team (Salas, Stagl, Burke, and Goodwin, 2007), as represented through the display of individual competencies, teamwork competencies, and integrated team-level actions (Kozlowski and Klein, 2000). Although organizational leaders often focus on performance outcomes (e.g., profits), it is the variation of a teams' performance process (i.e., how teams reach a given outcome) which is of interest for the present discussion.

In order for a collective, such as a team, to successfully perform, the individuals on the team must first have the ability to perform the action. Thus, team members must have both sufficiently learned the relevant knowledge and skills and have the capability of retrieving this content from memory when needed. Research examining the learning and retention of individual skills suggests there are several issues that influence the degree to which content is absorbed and made available for recall. Specifically, such relevant factors include method of presentation, depth of encoding, and the cues that allow the retrieval of such information.

Ability is an essential component of team performance, but team members must also be able to integrate with other team members as required by their task. Unique to team performance, it is suggested that beyond the typical individual motivation factors, motivation for team performance is influenced through a social identification with the team (van Knippenberg, 2000). Therefore, team members must have the ability to accomplish their work, team members must be motivated, and they must be able to interact effectively and interdependently while working towards the team's goal. Our discussion will now turn to the presentation of understanding and defining team performance decay.

Team Performance Decay

Understanding incidents of team performance decay is critical. Not only do these events result in the immediate consequence of performance loss, but research has also indicated that incidents of team failure affect subsequent team performance as well. For example, Reisel and Kopelman (1995) examined National Football League statistics over three seasons in an effort to better understand the ways in which individuals respond to failure. To bolster their predictions on how teams would respond to failure, Reisel and Kopleman considered the theories of reactance and learned helplessness. The theory of reactance (Trice, Elliott, Pope, and Tryall, 1991) predicts that after a failed performance there is an attempt to regain control of the situation by trying harder to improve performance. Based on the theory of reactance, the authors hypothesized that after a large loss, subsequent team performance would improve because team members would exert more effort; therefore, the authors believed that it would be unlikely that performance would decline. Alternatively, the theory of learned helplessness (Abramson, Seligman, and Teasdale, 1978) suggests that individuals experience a sense of helplessness when outcomes are perceived to be beyond their control. Drawing upon this theory, a competing hypothesis was proposed that the greater a team's loss, the greater the decay in performance in subsequent performance events. Results indicated that not only were negative performance events related to the likelihood for future negative performance events, but also performance decrements were greater when the opponent of the game following the loss was perceived as a challenging team. Hence, poor performance contributed to both immediate and future consequences for the team and organization.

Before we proceed with our discussion about team performance decay, it is important that we first present our definition of team performance decay. Formally, we define team performance decay as a negative change in performance from a previously demonstrated effective team-based performance level. Team performance decay may result from changes in any individual, task, team, organizational, or environmental factor that influences team performance. This decay may be attributable to a loss of trained or acquired knowledge, skills, or attitudes (KSAs) after a long or short period of nonuse as well as a team's failure to execute previously trained or exhibited teamwork processes (e.g., communication, coordination, cooperation). Thus, at the most basic level, team performance decay represents any performance period over which a team is achieving at a lower level than that at which they were previously performing.

Related to the concept of team performance decay, two papers (i.e., Milanovich, Salas, Cannon-Bowers, and Muñiz, 2000; Sims and Salas, 2007) have addressed "team derailment," a specialized, extreme component of the broader team performance decay process. Specifically, team derailment is limited to the severe performance decay of a highly effective team (e.g., the 1972 crash of Eastern Air Lines Flight 401 by a highly experienced crew, costing the 99 aboard their lives). These distinctions of decay magnitude and team proficiency are not required within the present discussion. We extend beyond previous discussions of complete team performance breakdowns but recognize them as a base for our discussion. The remainder of this chapter will discuss environmental and task characteristics as well as the team (e.g., communication, coordination, cooperation) factors associated with the decay of team performance and how each of these factors could contribute to the occurrence of negative shifts in performance. Additionally, recommendations for preventing incidents of team performance decay are provided.

Having defined team performance decay, we will elaborate on elements that may contribute to its occurrence. Because team performance decay is such a complex phenomenon, it stands to reason that multiple factors influence the rate at which skills decay. A team is not solely at fault when its skills degrade. In fact, we propose that the team is merely one facet of why performance decays. In addition to the team, we posit that environmental and task factors impact and may contribute to team performance decay. To acquire a better understanding for what contributes to this decay, we will expand upon the environmental, task, and team level components below in greater detail. We refer the reader to Table 15.1 for a summary of the propositions we present in the following sections.

Environmental Level

Teams do not perform in isolation, but rather they are one element within a multifaceted system. Thus, it is critical to understand the contextual factors that can impact team performance. We begin our discussion by elaborating on the environmental cues that can affect teams as well as the influence of organizational support.

Environmental Cues

The environment and the context in which skills are both acquired and retrieved significantly impact the rate of decay (Tulving, 1983). Specifically,

TABLE 15.1

Identified factors and propositions related to team performance decay

Proposition	Level	Factors
1. The rate of decay is slower when environmental cues during training are similar in the transfer environment.	Environmental	Environmental Cues
2. If resources are limited and the two environments cannot be highly similar, reduce the rate of decay by augmenting the training with appropriately designed, context specific training simulations.		
3. Organizational support such as offering reinforcements, modeling behavior, and mentoring subordinates can reduce team performance decay.		Organizational Support
4. A shorter retention interval will reduce team performance decay because it reduces the time in which the team is absent of skill practice and feedback.	Task	Retention Interval
5. Overlearning increases automaticity which in turn decreases the likelihood of team performance decay.		Overlearning
6. Overlearning decreases team performance decay by increasing trainees' confidence via greater levels of self-efficacy and lower levels of anxiety to perform.		
7. Opportunities to practice which will enhance retention will reduce team performance decay.		Practice
8. Teams that practice and have established transactive memory systems will reduce their likelihood of team performance decay.		
9. Constructive, timely, and meaningful (i.e., relevant and specific to the trainee) feedback will reduce team performance decay.		Feedback
10. Designing open-looped tasks reduce team performance decay owing to inherent characteristics such as repeated practice, integrated tasks, and resource intensity.		Closed- vs. open-looped
11. Team performance decay can be reduced for procedural type tasks by enhancing procedures with cues that allow team members to recognize subsequent steps.		Procedural
12. Physical practice tasks results in higher degrees of skill retention for physical tasks.		Cognitive vs. Physical
13. Mental rehearsal (i.e., recurrent training) promotes overlearning thereby reducing the detrimental effects of team performance decay.		
14. Designing work systems for teams that involve either low levels of workload or extremely high workloads will influence attention, motivation, and fatigue, and thus result in team performance decay.		Workload and Fatigue

TABLE 15.1 *continued*

Proposition	Level	Factors
15. During times of nonuse or extreme workload levels, improving the team's level of motivation to continue learning can reduce team performance decay.	Team	Task Motivation
16. Improving motivation to maintain knowledge and skills will decrease the susceptibility to team performance decay.		
17. Teams that develop their expertise by engaging in deliberate practice will reduce the potential for the occurrence of team performance decay.		Expertise
18. A team must exhibit a shared mental model in order to effectively coordinate and maintain performance.		Shared Mental Model
19. Cross-training help to improve and build shared mental models that will reduce team performance decay.		
20. Communication of all types (i.e., verbal or non-verbal) is necessary for individuals in a team to coordinate and prevent team performance decay.		Communica-tion
21. Team members' trust in one another improves the capabilities of the team by improving their coordination, thus reducing the potential for team performance decay to occur.		Trust
22. Team performance decay can be reduced if the team members feel psychologically safe to make suggestions or recommendations to the team.		Psychological Safety
23. A leader who effectively coordinates and synchro-nizes team members during performance can reduce the probability of team performance decay.		Team Leadership
24. By engaging in mutual performance monitoring, a team is aware of their progress, which in turn can minimize team performance decay.		Mutual Performance Monitoring
25. Backup behavior has a direct impact on team performance decay in that if a team member is in need of assistance and no backup behavior is provided, the team's performance is likely to decay.		Backup Behavior
26. Team performance decay can be minimized via team adaptation. Team adaptation allows a team to recognize deviations from an expected action and to readjust behaviors accordingly.		Adaptability
27. Promoting team learning through knowledge sharing and team self-correction can foster team adaptation and result in minimizing team performance decay.		
28. The preference for working with others and the perception of team interdependency is necessary for any team (intact or ad hoc) to prevent team performance decay.		Team Orientation

skills are retained better when the transfer environment is highly similar to the environment where the skills were initially learned (Arthur, Bennett, Stanush, and McNelly, 1998). In an applied setting, this translates to performance decay being minimized if the equipment used during training resembles the equipment used on the actual job site. Klein (1998) states that training in context-specific environments is likely to develop such team competencies as problem solving, communication, coordination, or management of unanticipated events. Performance is more resistant to decay because the similarities in the environment trigger cues making information readily available and easier to retrieve from memory (Cann and Ross, 1989; Schab, 1990). Although it is ideal that the elements within the training environment be identical to the components within the performance environment, it is not always plausible for the two environments (i.e., the training and performance environment) to possess identical cues.

Frequently, organizations do not have the available resources and time to manage the implementation of high-fidelity simulations (i.e., simulations that utilize very realistic materials and equipment to represent the task in the transfer environment). Thus, Dahlstrom, Dekker, van Winsen, and Nyce (2009) argue that this problem can be solved with low-fidelity simulations. When appropriately designed, low-fidelity simulators can maximize limited training resources. Although materials and equipment used in low-fidelity simulations do not precisely replicate those used on the job, they can be an effective training tool when task and context relevance is maintained. Therefore, we propose that if the two environments (i.e., training and performance environment) are highly similar, then the rate of decay will be lower than if the two environments are distinct from one another. Furthermore, if resources are limited and the two environments cannot be highly similar, bolster the training with appropriately designed, context-specific training simulations.

Proposition 1: The rate of decay is slower when environmental cues during training are similar in the transfer environment.

Proposition 2: If resources are limited and the two environments cannot be highly similar, reduce the rate of decay by augmenting the training with appropriately designed, context specific training simulations.

Organizational Support

In addition to environmental cues, organizational support will impact performance decay. If the organization encourages utilizing trained skills on the job, performance levels will be maintained. Organizations can encourage the utilization of trained skills on the job by providing opportunities for practice. However, we will elaborate on this point later in this chapter. Furthermore, organizations can show support by not just implementing the appropriate policies and procedures but by providing rewards for skill use and optimal performance. Verbal praise or monetary compensation for specific desired behaviors, versus an outcome-based criteria, can act as an incentive to sustain performance (Rouiller and Goldstein, 1993). Additionally, supervisors can support the sustainment of skills by mentoring subordinates and modeling desired behaviors (McConnell, 2005). Such supervisor involvement indicates the value placed on the performance of these skills by the organization and encourages individuals to place similar emphasis on their performance. Skills used frequently are less susceptible to decay.

Proposition 3: Organizational support such as offering reinforcements, modeling behavior, and mentoring subordinates can reduce team performance decay.

Task Level

In addition to the environment, characteristics of the task also impact the potential for a team to experience performance decay. We specifically address factors that influence performance within the areas of retention interval, training, and task type.

Retention Interval

The retention interval refers to the time interval between training and when a skill is performed on the job (Stothard and Nicholson, 2001). As skills must be used to be maintained, such periods of nonuse are strongly correlated with performance decay. Typically, the longer the interval between training and performance without any opportunities to practice, the more likely a team will experience performance decays (Naylor, Briggs, and Reed, 1968). This is because without practice, we tend to be more forgetful and develop poor habits as time passes. However, the greatest decline in performance occurs primarily in the beginning (i.e., between learning and the first opportunity for performance); after which point, the rate of decay slows and eventually plateaus (Kassin, Ellsworth, and Smith, 1989; Wixted and Ebbesen, 1991). The reason why the retention interval is so powerful and performance is not sustained over time is owing to the inability to practice and the lack of feedback (Driskell, Willis, and Copper, 1992; Ford, Quiñones, Sego, and

Speer Sorra, 1992). Teams who are able to perform shortly after competencies are initially acquired, thus, having a small retention interval, are less likely to display performance decrements. However, it is not the duration alone that affects performance; the retention interval is moderated by other factors (e.g., task type and individual characteristics). We will discuss the moderating components in greater detail in a later section.

Proposition 4: A shorter retention interval will reduce team performance decay because it reduces the time in which the team is absent of skill practice and feedback.

Training

It is evident that the retention interval is a significant factor in the decay of performance. One facet influencing the sustainability of skills over a given retention interval is how the skills were initially trained. Although the specific training strategy is not necessarily relevant, whether or not the training program was developed around the science of training is important (see Salas and Cannon-Bowers, 2001). Training that is scientifically sound will optimize learning, and skills will be more proficient; therefore, they will be more resistant to decay. It is important to remember that the amount of training will not determine performance. More is not always better. Rather, training needs to be grounded in science (e.g., based on a thorough organizational and task needs analysis) in order to sustain team performance. Specific aspects that pertain to training (e.g., overlearning, practice, feedback) are discussed in more detail below.

Overlearning. Although training is an important element to performance decay, overtraining is even more influential. We agree with Driskell and colleagues (1992) that a form of overlearning can be referred to as deliberate overtraining to an established criterion. Moreover, the effectiveness of over-learning will depend on the validity of this criterion, which is an overlooked issue in the cognitive/experimental literature. Ebbinghaus (1913), an expert in this field, conducted some of the early studies regarding overlearning. His research provided evidence for the importance and effectiveness of overlearning on retention. Subsequently, the notion of overtraining to minimize decay has been supported by additional researchers (Arthur et al., 1998; Driskell et al., 1992; Farr, 1987; Krueger, 1929, 1930; Schendel and Hagman, 1982). The theory underlying overlearning, as it pertains to retention, is that the extended training increases automaticity. When trained skills become automatic their performance is less cognitively demanding, and teams are thereby less susceptible to degradation (Anderson, 1983). Wisher, Sabol, and Ellis (1999) have similarly argued that overlearning is designed to enhance long-term retention and reduce the need for sustainment training (see also Fletcher, 2004).

In addition, overlearning fosters retention simply because it necessitates more practice and opportunities to receive feedback. Trainees are capable of maintaining performance levels because they are more confident; therefore, trainees possess greater self-efficacy and experience less anxiety to perform (Mulvey and Klein, 1998). Thus, a team's aggregate level of confidence in their ability to accomplish a task is directly related to an individual team member's self-confidence levels.

Proposition 5: Overlearning increases automaticity which in turn decreases the likelihood of team performance decay.

Proposition 6: Overlearning decreases team performance decay by increasing trainees' confidence via greater levels of self-efficacy and lesser levels of anxiety to perform.

Practice. As mentioned above, merely practicing a skill can enhance retention and simultaneously reduce decay. Practice provides opportunities to perform. The more opportunities that are provided and the more competencies are repeated and rehearsed, the slower the rate of decay (Stothard and Nicholson, 2001). The underlying theory is that performance is maintained through reinforcement and conditioning. The correct response to a certain stimuli is learned through repetition (Egenfeldt-Nielsen, 2007). Practice opportunities should not only be offered during training but also on the job. As eluded to earlier in this chapter, this is an opportunity for organizations to encourage and support the demonstration of skills learned in training on the job.

Performing tasks in the work environment that were learned during training increases the transfer of training, which ultimately impacts the ability to sustain performance. A team that not only practices during training but also performs together in the work environment will be able to retain learned KSAs. These performance benefits are attributable to transactive memory systems, a shared system for encoding, storing, and retrieving information (Wegner, Erber, and Raymond, 1991). Research has suggested that groups with more developed transactive memory systems perform better than their counterparts (Lewis, 2004; Moreland and Myaskovsky, 2000). Furthermore, according to Ren (2004), groups with transactive memory systems have established more efficient means of implicit coordination because team members are more aware of each member's knowledge and skills.

Proposition 7: Opportunities to practice that will enhance retention will reduce team performance decay.

Proposition 8: Teams that practice and have established transactive memory systems will reduce their likelihood of team performance decay.

    Feedback. Feedback is an essential part of learning; thus, it is also an integral part of retention. Feedback is designed to identify areas of performance that are both completed correctly and the areas that still need improvements. Hence, effective feedback allows trainees to identify existing strengths and weaknesses in their performance, and to adjust their strategies in subsequent performance periods (Sims and Salas, 2007). To optimize learning, feedback should be constructive and meaningful to the trainees. In other words, feedback should be task specific and directed at specific behaviors exhibited by the trainee, instead of being personal and targeting the trainee. Furthermore, feedback should be relevant to the trainee and his or her specific performance, and not general statements about performance, so that it possesses more meaning. Feedback that is more personally relevant to the trainee is more likely to be remembered and incorporated in future performance episodes. In addition, the timing and frequency of feedback during skill acquisition should be carefully considered. Feedback that immediately follows performance has both advantages and disadvantages (Schmidt and Bjork, 1992). Frequent feedback has the benefit of improving performance by providing guidance towards correct behavior. On the other hand, frequent feedback can be disadvantageous because team members can become dependent upon it to perform the task. In addition, it can disrupt information processing during skill acquisition. We argue that providing feedback to a team is critical. However, determining the appropriate timing and frequency of feedback based on the context and the task is just as critical.

Proposition 9: Constructive, timely, and meaningful (i.e., relevant and specific to the trainee) feedback will reduce team performance decay.

Task Type

Closed-looped vs. open-looped. Closed-looped tasks involve fixed-sequenced tasks with a distinct beginning and end. On the other hand, open-looped tasks involve continuous responses that are repeated. In a review of the skill retention literature, Arthur et al. (1998) surmised that open-looped tasks produce better results even in the face of lengthy temporal phases, an established source of performance decay (Hufford and Adams, 1961; Mengelkoch, Adams, and Gainer, 1960; Smith and Matheny, 1976). Furthermore, Arthur et al. (1998)

proposed that the heightened levels of integration inherent in open-looped tasks provide an edge over closed-looped tasks with regard to retention. However, the results indicated that higher levels of retention were present in closed-looped tasks. Even though the results of this study appear to show that closed-loop tasks are better at preventing retention, open-loop tasks have the advantage of integrating tasks and repeating practice.

Proposition 10: Designing open-looped tasks reduces team performance decay owing to inherent characteristics such as repeated practice, integrated tasks, and resource intensity.

Procedural. Tasks comprised of coherent steps involving cognitive and/or motor skills are said to be procedural in nature. Previous studies suggest that retention is better for continuous tasks (Hurlock and Montague, 1982). Hurlock and Montague add that cues may constitute an important characteristic of organized tasks by facilitating recollection of the next step in the procedure, and thus, allowing a seemingly complex and fragile procedural task to be strengthened. However, the effects of procedural skills on retention have resulted in mixed reviews (Healy et al., 1992). For example, high retention has been demonstrated for tasks such as target detection (Healy, Fendrich, and Proctor, 1990), mental multiplication (Fendrich, Healy, and Bourne, 1993), and data entry (Fendrich, Healy, and Bourne, 1991); whereas, low retention has been reported for tasks such as memory for numerical calculation (Crutcher and Healy, 1989), vocabulary learning (Crutcher and Ericsson, 1988), and components of memory for course schedules (Wittman, 1989).

Proposition 11: Team performance decay can be reduced for procedural type tasks by enhancing the procedures with cues that allow team members to recognize subsequent steps.

Cognitive vs. physical. The difference between a physical task (e.g., muscular strength and coordination) and cognitive task (e.g., problem solving and mental operations) is evident by characterization. What is less obvious is which type of task better withstands performance decay. Conflicting evidence exists as to which task is more resistant. For example, Ryan and Simons (1981) investigated practice type (i.e., physical practice, mental practice, or no practice) with two motor tasks that varied in demand (i.e., cognitive or motor). Results suggest that participants in the physical practice condition performed significantly better than those in other conditions on the motor task, while the mental practice condition performed as well as the physical condition with regard to the cognitive task. Furthermore, while a meta-analysis by Arthur et al. (1998) of the skill retention and skill decay literature found that cognitive skills were less prone to performance decay, a preceding meta-analysis by Driskell et al. (1992) concluded that motor skills were more resistant. There is support for Driskell and colleagues finding wherein tasks that rely primarily on cognitive processes are more susceptible to decay (Childs and Spears, 1986). Therefore, in order to sustain performance it is imperative to not only consider the type of task but also the type of practice as well.

Childs and Spears (1986) offer recurrent training as a method to forestall the loss of proficiency. Consequently, another technique that we recommend to reduce performance decay is the use of mental rehearsal (Farr, 1987; Glisky, Williams, and Kihlstrom, 1996; Kim, Singer, and Radlo, 1996). Conversely, if mental rehearsal is not initiated, then the possibility exists where physical skills will be better retained than cognitive skills (Arthur et al., 1998). Case in point is the saying "it is like riding a bicycle" which can be interpreted as the physical skill is not truly lost but simply dormant. Thus, it is plausible to assert that an individual who has not recently ridden a bicycle will not use mental imagery to practice riding during the time of nonuse. For non-routine or complex tasks that elicit both physical and cognitive resources, a team's performance can be facilitated by members both using mental imagery to practice and also by practicing as a team.

Proposition 12: Physical practice results in higher degrees of skill retention for physical tasks.

Proposition 13: Mental rehearsal (i.e., recurrent training) promotes over-learning thereby reducing the detrimental effects of team performance decay.

Workload and fatigue. Workload is the degree to which cognitive, physical, and/or emotional systems are stressed perhaps owing to environmental changes. Optimally, all extremes should be avoided whenever possible, but the reality is that many jobs entail high levels of workload that place great demands on the worker and contribute to physical or mental fatigue (e.g., physicians, nurses). Thus, while we discuss workload as a task feature that influences performance, we acknowledge its interconnection with the individual and the construct fatigue.

In examining the effects of workload in spaceflights on skill maintenance, Sauer, Wastell, and Hockey (1997) presented insightful observations. Problems associated with low level workloads, in the context of long-term temporal phases, are lapses of attention and a decline of motivation. Within this same context, problems with regards to high workload emerge and include narrowed attention and increased tension and fatigue. Overall, manifestations of performance decay appear both in extremely high workload levels (i.e., impaired performance and well-being) and in low levels of workload (i.e., loss of task involvement and risk of distraction). High levels of workload affect an individual's performance (Beith, 1987; Hart and Hauser, 1987), and thus, affect the team's ability to coordinate effectively (Bowers, Braun, and Morgan, 1992; Kidd, 1961; Williges, Johnston, and Briggs, 1966).

Proposition 14: Designing work systems for teams that involve either low levels of workload or extremely high workloads will influence attention, motivation and fatigue, and thus results in performance decay.

Team Level

Factors that impact team performance decay have been discussed on the environmental and task level. It is now time to discuss team level factors that can contribute to the occurrence of team performance decay. Several team researchers have stated that for teams to succeed they must display the mastering of two types of skills: taskwork and teamwork (Gersick, 1988; Morgan et al., 1986; Kozlowski et al., 1996). Morgan et al. explained that taskwork skills are skills that are related to the operations-related activities performed by the team and teamwork skills are the "behavioral and attitudinal" responses that team members need so that they can function effectively. Salas et al. (2006) in their discussion of creating a "dream team," implied that it is not sufficient that team members be only technical experts (i.e., taskwork) but they must also be experts at teamwork. The previous discussions on contributing factors that are related to team performance decay focused primarily on the topic of taskwork; however, in this section, we present two team member attributes relevant to taskwork performance, and the teamwork components that contribute to effective team functioning will be discussed. We outline the primary coordinating mechanisms of teamwork and draw upon Salas, Sims, and Burke's (2005) presentation of the Big 5 of teamwork to guide our discussion of the team level aspects that impact team performance decay.

Team Member Attributes

At both individual and team levels, task performance can be influenced by attributes of those performing the task. At the team level, it is often some form of compilation of attributes across individuals that matters. We address two attributes with potential implications for team skill decay.

Task motivation. When tasks become more familiar and thus monotonous or perhaps during overlearning, individuals can experience ebbs and flows in their motivation levels to complete their task, continue learning, and maintain their skill level. A lack of motivation has been demonstrated to influence skill retention and achieving an expert level of performance (Boyle and Ackerman,

2004). Furthermore, a person's motivation to acquire knowledge or skill is linked to the degree of subsequent learning especially in the event of task difficulty or task failure (Dweck and Leggett, 1988; Elliot and Dweck, 1988). The literature on goal orientation suggests that an individual can hold either a learning orientation or a performance orientation. Learning orientation is characterized when an individual is motivated to master the information, and performance orientation is characterized by individuals who are motivated to achieve a prescribed score in order to avoid negative feedback (Dweck, 1986; Dweck and Leggett, 1988). This is relevant to performance decay in that it can affect an individual's motivation to complete a task during times of task inactivity and also with regard to degree of workload level. Team performance is then hampered when members experience a lack of motivation especially in times of inactivity and extreme degrees of workload.

Proposition 15: During times of nonuse or extreme workload levels, improving the team's level of motivation to continue learning can reduce team performance decay.

Proposition 16: Improving motivation to maintain knowledge and skills will decrease the susceptibility to team performance decay.

Expertise. Expertise is comprised of an individual's ability to perform repeatedly and reliably at high levels on a specific set of tasks (Salas, Rosen, and DiazGranados, 2010). The mechanisms by which this expertise is developed are the cognitive, behavioral, and attitudinal adaptations to the demands of the performance domain. Expertise is domain specific and highly sensitive to task constraints and contextual cues (Chi, 2006). Experts know more about the specific domain and have developed a keen sense of identifying patterns of cues that correlate within the domain. But how do individuals develop their knowledge and their sensitivity to cues and patterns? The simplest of answers to this question is deliberate practice.

Bloom and Sosniak (1985) attributed the expertise found in surgeons, concert pianists, and tennis players to thousands of hours of experience and reflection (for an illustration of the idea of practice leading to success see the 10,000 hour rule in Ericsson, Charnes, Feltovich, and Hoffman, 2006 or Gladwell, 2008). Another line of research has dedicated itself to understanding how people make decisions in field settings. Such research has been applied to help quickly develop expertise and apply it to a task. One of the most cited models of decision making is the Recognition-Primed Decision (RPD) making model which suggests that people can use their experiences to evaluate their situation, recognize goals, cues and expectancies, and determine the correct course of action (Klein, 1998). By utilizing previous experiences and understanding the decision-making process, teams can achieve better performance, which can minimize the potential for team performance decay.

Proposition 17: Teams that develop their expertise by engaging in deliberate practice will reduce the potential for the occurrence of team performance decay.

Coordinating Mechanisms

In the teams' literature there has been mention of factors that are known to be coordinating mechanisms (Salas, Sims, and Burke, 2005) or transformers (Shiflett, 1979) of teamwork. These factors in general have been discussed as variables that incorporate the resources of the team or, as Salas and colleagues (2005) explain, they are variables that ensure that the Big 5 of teamwork is functioning. In the following section, the factors that we outline as coordinating mechanisms are shared mental models, communication, trust, and psychological safety.

Shared mental models. Shared knowledge is a construct involving all team members, which can contribute to the effective coordination of team members. Shared knowledge can contribute to task accomplishment by facilitating the effective coordination of information into useful and salient means to accomplish a task. Ideally, a team should possess a shared mental model (SMM) of a task. SMMs are defined as knowledge structures consisting of clustered, shared, and accurate information held by team members (Cooke et al., 2004). Shared mental models can be held for a variety of constructs including: equipment, task, team, team interaction, and problem/situation models. Research shows that both shared team-based mental models and shared task-based mental models are positively related to team processes and outcomes (Mathieu et al., 2000). Shared mental models are beneficial because they help team members coordinate and adapt their behavior and actions (Cannon-Bowers, Salas, Converse, 1993). Furthermore, SMMs allow team members to interpret the environment and the task in a similar manner which fosters effective decision making (Cannon-Bowers and Salas, 2001). For teams to be able to accomplish their task, the individuals need to share their task mental model as well as their team mental model. What this means is that the team members not only know their specific task, but also share a broader understanding of the team's task as a whole, member roles, and who is responsible for specific tasks.

One technique that will specifically improve SMM development among team members is cross-training. Cross-training occurs when each team member is trained on the tasks and responsibilities of the other team members. We suggest utilizing cross-training to reduce ambiguity and improve role clarity and expectations. Without shared knowledge between team members, the coordination between members could be disastrous. Ultimately, when team members possess a SMM they are more likely to develop transactive memory systems; therefore, they are able to operate from a common conceptual framework that lets them perceive, interpret, and respond to environments that may be dynamic or ambiguous and do so in a coordinated, synchronous fashion (Schlechter, Zaccaro, and Burke, 1998).

Proposition 18: A team must exhibit a shared mental model in order to effectively coordinate and maintain performance.

Proposition 19: Cross-training will help to improve and build shared mental models which will reduce team performance decay.

Communication. Communication refers to the information exchange between team members irrespective of the medium (McIntyre and Salas, 1995; Salas and Cannon-Bowers, 2000). It is not uncommon for a message to be relayed by an individual only to result in a misunderstanding of the intended message. Misunderstandings can result from the specific verbiage used (e.g., incorrect use of proper phraseology) or contextual reasons (e.g., faulty communication equipment, high stress situation causing confusion). Imagine an air-traffic controller who does not understand the message from a pilot that the airplane's fuel tank is approaching dangerously low levels. This breakdown in communication within a team could potentially result in team performance decay and detrimental effects.

There are two forms of communication. Both implicit and explicit forms of communication can be used by team members. Implicit communication occurs when team members voluntarily offer information; on the other hand, explicit communication occurs as a result of an explicit request for information (Serfaty, Entin, and Volpe, 1993; Serfaty, Entin, and Johnston, 1998). Research has demonstrated that in times of high stress (e.g., in novel situations or situations constrained by time) teams are more likely to utilize implicit communication, because explicit communication takes up too much time (Entin and Serfaty, 1999; Stout, Cannon-Bowers, Salas, and Milanovich, 1999). Implicit communication is greatly supported by transactive memory systems.

Researchers have determined that much like individuals, teams process information to perform their tasks (Hastie, 1986; Hinsz, Tindale, and Vollrath, 1997; Hinsz, Vollrath, Nagao, and Davis, 1988). The information processing that occurs within a team involves the communication of ideas, information, or cognitive processes among the team members, and this sharing of information affects group-level outcomes (Hinsz et al., 1997). Thus, communication is the method by which teams translate individual-level understanding into team-level dynamic representations that guide the coordination of a team (Cooke, Salas, Kiekel, and Bell, 2004).

Proposition 20: Communication of all types (i.e., verbal or non-verbal) is necessary for individuals in a team to coordinate and prevent team performance decay.

Trust. Trust has been defined as the expectation that the way others' act will be positive to one's own interest (Dirks, 1999; Mayer, Davis, and Schoorman, 1995; Robinson, 1996). Trust in a team setting pertains to the perception that individuals on a team will perform certain actions that are important and protect the interests of their team and its members (Webber, 2002). Owing to the interdependent nature of teams, trust is essential to maintaining team performance. Trust is important to teamwork such that team members' trust in one another will impact their actions in accomplishing a task. For example, hypothetically imagine an American football team. The quarterback must trust his offensive linemen to protect him so that he can effectively and precisely throw the football to his intended receiver. If the quarterback does not trust his linemen, the quarterback may, owing to fear of being tackled, throw the ball prematurely, which could result in an incomplete play or, worse, an interception.

Research has repeatedly shown that one of the most important determinants of effective performance in teams is trust (Axelrod, 1984; Cummings and Bromiley, 1996; Kramer, 1999; Salas et al., 2005). Trust can enable a team member to focus on their own performance-related issues (e.g., pre-preparation, maintaining skill, continued improvement) rather than being concerned about what the other team members are doing to prepare for their task or to maintain or improve their skills. In addition, trust facilitates the desire to share information among team members (Jones and George, 1998). Individuals on a team will be more inclined to disseminate vital information if they trust their teammates will value their input (Bandow, 2001). Furthermore, individuals will be more cooperative and participative if they are capable of trusting and relying on their team members to meet the shared goals.

Conversely, a lack of trust can be detrimental to achieving the team goal. When individuals do not trust their team members, their cognitive resources will be allocated to vigilantly monitoring their team members rather than utilizing their cognitive abilities to perform the tasks to accomplish the team goal. Furthermore, they may experience stress and fatigue if their attention is focused on other team members as opposed to the task at hand. Additionally, a lack of trust can lead to misinterpreting the actions and doubting the intentions of fellow team members, which can lead to decays in team performance. If team members not only trust one another to perform their designated roles and complete the assigned tasks, but also assist in the accomplishment of the team goal, regardless of the elements impacting the team, team performance decay can be averted.

Proposition 21: Team members' trust in one another improves the capabilities of the team by improving their coordination, thus reducing the potential for team performance decay to occur.

Psychological safety. Team psychological safety as defined by Edmonson (1999) is the shared belief that the team is safe from risk taking, such that any member of the team can speak up or provide suggestions without any negative repercussions (e.g., rejection or punishment). The confidence team members have that they are "safe" is closely related to team trust and respect. Consider another example, this time an advertising team tasked with the development of a new commercial. It is easy to imagine the scenario that this team meets in a conference room suggesting ideas during a phase of collaboration and brain storming in order to develop their final idea to be presented to their client. If the members on this team do not feel safe to share their thoughts and suggest their ideas, the potential of the team will be limited. In order for the potential of the team to be maximized every team member must feel safe that they will not be punished or ridiculed for any idea that is given. Moreover, an action team's psychological safety should lead to the freedom to propose to teammates how to prepare for the future and try novel approaches to the task.

Research by Kahn (1990) demonstrated that psychological safety is one of three psychological conditions that affect how people fulfill their role in an organization. Moreover, research has also shown that psychological safety promotes work engagement (May, Gilson, and Harter, 2004). Effective coordination among team members is required to minimize team performance decay. For effective coordination to occur, team members must be able to feel comfortable asking questions or seeking help from team members.

Proposition 22: Team performance decay can be reduced if the team members feel psychologically safe to make suggestions or recommendations to the team.

Teamwork Components: The Big 5

Salas et al. (2005) were the first to present what is known as the "Big 5" of teamwork. They present a focal set of teamwork components that a team should have in order to complete their task. We present those five components in relation to how they can prevent team performance decay. In our discussion it is important to keep in mind that our intent is to portray these components as critical for a team to be effective. That is, we assume that each individual has the KSAs to accomplish the task; thus, they have acquired the necessary skills to perform. We focus on post acquisition and propose that it is because a team lacks these teamwork components that a team can suffer from performance decay.

Team leadership. The team leader has a great impact on team performance (Stewart and Manz, 1995). A team leader who does not guide a team towards the accomplishment of the team's goal has not only failed his/her job, but also may be the reason for the ineffective team performance. A team leader has the capability of facilitating the coordinating behaviors that a team needs. Moreover, an effective leader provides the direction for collective action which aids teams to maintain a state of minimal process loss (Gardner and Schermerhorn, 1992; Jacobs and Jaques, 1990; Zaccaro, Heinen, and Shuffler, 2009).

For example, imagine a surgical team where the assigned leader is the lead surgeon. The success of the team is not limited to each individual knowing and doing their job, but rather the leader has to synchronize and combine each individual's contributions to the surgery so that they, as a team, can successfully accomplish their task. If the leader fails to communicate to the other team members the status of the patient or the immediate needs during the surgery, the result, in this case, can be quite drastic.

Proposition 23: A leader who effectively coordinates and synchronizes team members during performance can reduce the probability of team performance decay.

Mutual performance monitoring. Since teams work interdependently, it is common to have a scenario where several team members are engaging in different actions simultaneously in order to work toward the same goal. Mutual performance monitoring refers to the fact that team members are aware of each other's work without it interrupting their own work (McIntyre and Salas, 1995). If a team successfully engages in mutual performance monitoring, they are all aware of how they, as a team, are progressing to meet their goal. It is not a method of correcting any one member's performance, but rather it is a proactive measure team members can take to ensure that the team is on track to successfully accomplishing their goal.

Proposition 24: By engaging in mutual performance monitoring, a team is aware of their progress, which in turn can minimize team performance decay.

Backup behavior. In addition to the direct benefits of mutual performance monitoring in reducing team performance decay, team members engaging in monitoring will also be more alert to the needs of their teammates, and thus, able to reallocate resources and provide assistance to an individual member.

This assistance or administering of additional resources to a team member in need has been defined as backup behavior (Marks, Mathieu, and Zaccaro, 2001; Porter et al., 2003). It is reasonable to hypothesize that a team that engages in backup behaviors will experience less team performance decay, and teams that do not will be more susceptible to team performance decay. For example, if a member of a project team has become overloaded with a specific feature of the project, other members who have the available resources can provide them with assistance in order to maintain progress towards the overall goal.

Proposition 25: Backup behavior has a direct impact on team performance decay in that if a team member is in need of assistance and no backup behavior is provided, the team's performance is likely to decay.

Adaptability. As discussed under backup behavior, the team should have the ability to determine when there is a need to reallocate their resources, specifically when one particular member needs the assistance. However, adaptability is a complete change on the entire team level. For instance, the clearest example we can offer is a medical team. Doctors often follow specific protocol when diagnosing the ailments of their patients. The protocol they follow is largely determined by the patient's symptoms. If the symptoms of the patient lead the medical team to implement a specific treatment but in reality the symptoms are a mask for a completely different medical issue, then the team must change their type of treatment and not be functionally fixated on one course of action. Adaptability is not only the ability to recognize that there are deviations from an expected action but also the ability to readjust behaviors accordingly (Priest, Burke, Munim, and Salas, 2002). Burke et al. (2006) state that team adaptation "manifests itself as a modification of existing structures . . . or behavioral goal-directed actions" (p. 1190).

Burke et al. (2006) note that team adaptation resembles the construct of team learning (Edmonson, 1999) such that team learning is the process by which permanent changes occur in the behavioral potential of the team as a result of members acquiring, sharing, and combining knowledge. However, they also highlight a critical distinction between the two constructs. Team learning is the cognitive event that develops knowledge and can impact the behavioral potential of a team. Although team learning is essential for team adaptation, it is insufficient for a team to develop their adaptability. Certain methods such as team self-correction or knowledge sharing can help to foster a team-learning environment. We direct the interested reader to Burke, Salas, and DiazGranados (2008) for a more detailed discussion on methods (e.g., storytelling, action learning, and communities of practice) that can promote team learning.

Proposition 26: Team performance decay can be minimized via team adaptation. Team adaptation allows a team to recognize deviations from an expected action and to readjust behaviors accordingly.

Proposition 27: Promoting team learning through knowledge sharing and team self-correction can foster team adaptation and result in minimizing team performance decay.

   Team orientation. The final component of what is known as the "Big 5" of teamwork is team orientation. The difference between this factor and the other four is that this component is attitudinally based. However, this does not lessen its importance. For individuals to be team oriented, there are two requirements: (1) the individuals should prefer to work in team settings and (2) the individuals on the team should clearly understand that it is the inputs from all members that move them towards the execution of a goal (i.e., perceptions of team interdependency; Driskell and Salas, 1992). A lack of team orientation can occur in any team, whether it is a team that has worked together before (i.e., an intact team) or a newly developed team (i.e., an ad hoc team). In either case, once a team member believes they do not need their teammates to accomplish their goal, the potential of the team decreases, and the team is susceptible to team performance decay.

Proposition 28: The preference for working with others and the perception of team interdependency is necessary for any team (intact or ad hoc) to prevent team performance decay.

WHAT CAN PREVENT TEAM PERFORMANCE DECAY?

We have defined team performance decay as a negative change in team-based performance from a previously demonstrated level. In addition, we have proposed environmental, task, and team level factors that may contribute to decay in team performance. Having highlighted several factors likely to influence team performance decay, we now turn the discussion toward the prevention of team performance decay. In the following sections, applicable strategies for preventing team performance decay are presented. The proposed strategies focus on three broad categories related to maintaining team performance: (a) the development and implementation of training, (b) team functioning, and (c) ways in which the organization can be proactive in preventing team performance decay. For an overview of these recommendations, we refer the reader to Table 15.2.

TABLE 15.2

Strategies for the Prevention of Team Performance Decay

Strategy Focus	Strategy	Example	Source
Training	Basic learning is not enough. . . design training to support the overlearning of critical skills	• Offer many opportunities to practice and provide effective feedback	Driskell, Willis, and Copper (1992); Salas and Cannon-Bowers (2001)
	Establish a schedule for refresher training, considering the degree of overlearning, the type of task, and the retention interval	• Minimize the amount of time between training and performance periods • On average, refreshers should be implemented every 3 weeks	Driskell, Willis, and Copper (1992); Stothard and Nicholson, 2001
	Align contextual cues in team training with those existent in the performance environment	• Feedback in the midst of a training exercise should be avoided if it is not part of the performance environment	Arthur, Bennett, Stanush, and McNelly (1998)
Team Functioning	Team members should learn and practice as a team, and collectively evaluate each performance in an effort towards improvement	• Conduct an after-action reviews following team performance, involving all team members • Review both positives and negatives of performance	Driskell, Hughes, and Oser (1998)
	Teach team members to monitor their teammates' task related behaviors	• Make team members aware of task related behaviors critical for performance so that potential problems can be identified and averted or resolved in a timely manner	Marks and Panzer (2004); Salas, Sims, and Burke (2005)

TABLE 15.2 *continued*

	Recommendation		Reference
	Establish clear roles and expectations for performance	• Clearly define each team member's roles and expectations to the entire team so that team members can identify when assistance and back-up behaviors are needed	Cannon-Bowers, Tannenbaum, Salas, and Volpe (1995)
	To motivate team members set difficult, specific, yet attainable goals for team performance	• Goal setting is most effective for learning-oriented team members • Set difficult goals to facilitate more effective performance strategies	Locke and Latham (2002); LePine (2005)
The Organization	Organizational leaders can reduce team performance decay by ensuring that teams are provided with the required resources for successful performance	• Supplies should be available and accessible to the team	Gladstein (1984)
	Encourage the use of team behaviors most related to team performance by formally evaluating the behaviors that matter most	• Incorporate behaviors related to effective team performance in the team's performance appraisal	Rouiller and Goldstein (1993)
	Reinforce the behaviors related to effective performance by tying compensation and rewards to evaluated behaviors	• Compensate the team based on the performance of behaviors related to success rather than the outcomes themselves • Monetary compensation is not always necessary, verbal recognition can go a long way	Kerr (1975); Lawler (2003)

Training Related Strategies

As noted earlier in this chapter, some incidents of team performance decay may be attributable to the loss of trained or acquired KSAs, most commonly after a period of nonuse. Based on the science of training, it is known that the manner in which a training program is designed and implemented can contribute greatly to training effectiveness, the transferability of trained skills from the training environment to the job, and also the degree to which trained content is retained over time. Thus, we first address several strategies relevant to team training that we propose can help prevent the decay of team performance.

As training is the initial acquisition of knowledge, it is during this time that it is critical for individuals to learn the skills necessary to accomplish a task. Although basic training may provide team members with the ability to perform at a required level, we recommend that for purposes of preventing team performance decay, individual and team training should go beyond the basic "can do" level of learning (i.e., developing just enough to be able to perform the task). Rather, consistent with theories of overlearning, we propose that when training newly acquired skills, a training program should be structured to require repetitive practice well beyond that needed for basic skill mastery (e.g., Schendel and Hagman, 1982). In a meta-analytic review of the over-learning literature, Driskell, Willis, and Copper (1992) reported overlearning to have a moderate overall effect on retention; thus, as discussed previously, overlearning has been demonstrated as a means of prevention against per-formance decay. Specifically, this strategy is proposed to help prevent team performance decay attributed to the loss of trained or acquired KSAs.

Yet, despite the observations that overlearning can enhance retention intervals, Driskell and colleagues (1992) further identified several moderating factors of the relationship between overlearning and retention that may impact the benefits of overlearning on retention, and thereby influence the likelihood of team performance decay. Meta-analytic evaluations suggested that the degree of overlearning, the type of task performed, and the length of the retention period between the practice and performance periods moderate the relationship between overlearning and retention. More specifically, the average effect of overlearning on retention nearly tripled from 50 percent overlearning to 200 percent overlearning. However, in relation to the type of task performed, although positive effects of overlearning were observed for both cognitive and physical tasks, on average, overlearning was less effec-tive for the retention of physical tasks. Additionally, the duration of retention benefits from overlearning was demonstrated to be limited, with benefits reduced by approximately 50 percent after 19 days if no refresher training was conducted. Based on these results, Driskell and colleagues suggested that if overlearning is to be used as a means of avoiding decay, refresher training should be conducted approximately every 3 weeks.

Finally, in considering the appropriateness of overlearning as a means for helping to prevent team performance decay within a given organization, one should consider the costs required by the additional "over-training" in comparison to the benefits to retention. If the benefits of overlearning for a specific task are rather limited and the additional training/practice opportunities are costly (as they generally are), it is likely in the best interest of the organization to select a more cost-effective prevention strategy.

Strategy 1: Basic learning is not enough ... design training to support the overlearning of critical skills.

Strategy 2: Establish a schedule for refresher training, considering the degree of overlearning, the type of task, and the retention interval.

The extent to which a team can apply skills developed in training on the job, or transfer these skills from one performance environment to another, is also influential in the prevention of performance decay. One critical source of problems with performance transferability across different environments is when the contextual cues a team relies on to perform a task are not consistent across all performance environments. In terms of performance decay, such decrements are likely to be observed when cues relied upon by a team for performance are not provided. This implies that to avoid team performance decay as a result of poor training transfer, or a lack of skills transferability across various performance settings, organizations should ensure that the environmental cues that contribute to effective team performance are also incorporated in team training exercises (Arthur et al., 1998). Furthermore, training should avoid the inclusion of cues in training that are inconsistent with the performance environment. For example, if the performance environment does not offer feedback to teams during task performance, organizations should limit the amount of feedback or the guidance an instructor provides a team during training practice sessions (i.e., mid-task). Individuals may become dependent on specific cues or prompts for task performance during training, such that when they are removed, performance declines.

Strategy 3: Align contextual cues in team training with those existent in the performance environment.

Strategies Related to Team Functioning

Improving the effectiveness of team training design and implementation is just one area an organization can target for the prevention of team performance decay. Even if training was perfectly designed, not all performance decay is attributable to the loss of trained or acquired KSAs. Rather, as inferred from many of the environmental, task, and team-level factors already addressed, decay is also observed if individuals are simply unwilling or unmotivated to perform the task. As the manner in which a team operates can have a strong influence on team performance, we now address several decay prevention strategies related to features of the way in which a team functions.

One factor related to a team's function that is important to keep in mind as we are discussing team performance is that it is not sufficient to only be concerned with the degree to which team members maintain their individual skill levels. However, the team has to also maintain an adequate level of team skill. For this reason, one of our suggestions for reducing the occurrence of team performance decay is to ensure that teams practice and train together. In addition, feedback that is appropriately provided should be directed to the team. A suggested practice is to provide the team with an opportunity to perform together and also to discuss their performance after the completion of the task (i.e., conduct a debrief or after action review). The military and the healthcare industries are two examples of industries that commonly use what is called the after action review (see Driskell, Hughes, and Oser, 1998). During this session, teams review their performance and discuss room for improvement, lessons learned, and task and team strategies that were effective and ineffective. The conduction of an after action review or debrief serves as yet another form of training in that the team learns to evaluate their own performance and continually develop their collective knowledge bank of effective and ineffective performance strategies. By discussing the actions that may have led to failure, the team can determine their weaknesses, whether those come in the form of individual skill levels or teamwork skills.

Strategy 4: Team members should learn and practice as a team, and collectively evaluate each performance in an effort towards improvement.

Also important for the prevention of performance decay is to teach team members to monitor their teammates' task-related behaviors. Monitoring as a team function, has been defined as "observing the activities and performance of other team members" (Dickinson and McIntyre, 1997, p. 27) and is often recognized for its positive influence on critical team processes such as situational awareness, team coordination, and feedback (see Salas et al., 2005 for additional information related to these processes). Related to team performance, Marks and Panzer (2004) empirically demonstrate a relationship between team monitoring and performance. In other words, the authors suggest that team monitoring can positively influence team coordination and feedback. Furthermore, the authors theoretically explain this relationship in that when team members are closely monitoring one another, they are able to identify potential problems and remedy them either before they occur, or at a minimum, to address them immediately. Thus, any problems that can be averted will mitigate team performance decay that otherwise would likely occur.

In addition, setting clear roles and expectations for performance also contribute to more effective team monitoring and an ability to prevent team performance decay in that clearly defined roles assist team members in effective coordination (Cannon-Bowers, Tannenbaum, Salas, and Volpe, 1995), thus reducing the likelihood of team coordination problems that could lead to performance decay. Also, related to early detection of problems, an individual must first understand the role a teammate is performing in order to be able to identify when a teammate needs assistance and provide appropriate backup.

Strategy 5: Teach team members to monitor their teammates' task related behaviors.

Strategy 6: Establish clear roles and expectations for performance.

As addressed in a previous section of this chapter, the motivation level of individual team members, as well as a team's overall motivation level influences team performance. Over time it is common for a team's motivation to vary. Subsequently, in periods in which motivation is waning, performance decay is also likely to be observed. This relationship suggests that performance can be sustained (and its decay avoided) through methods that enhance motivation. Related to team functioning, several decades of evidence support goal setting as a powerful motivational influence (e.g., Locke and Latham, 2002). Moreover, goal setting has been suggested as the primary mechanism through which other motivational methods, such as rewards, influence performance (Latham and Locke, 1979). It is generally suggested that goals are most effective when they are challenging, specific, and attainable. Furthermore, though beneficial to all individuals, goal setting is suggested to be most effective for teams composed of learning-oriented individuals.

Though primarily studied at the individual level, in the last decade there has been increasing discussion of goal setting at the team level. For example, LePine (2005) conducted a study to examine the influence of goal difficulty on team performance and adaptation. Results suggested that team members with a high learning orientation, when assigned a difficult goal, developed more efficient strategies for their role than did members in groups assigned an easy goal. Thus, these team members were generally able to adapt when faced with an unexpected problem. In contrast, team members with a high performance orientation were relatively unlikely to adapt their role strategies when a problem arose. To the degree that setting difficult team goals helps to improve the performance strategies used by team members, the decay of performance should be minimized.

Strategy 7: To motivate team members, set difficult, specific, yet attainable goals for team performance.

Strategies for the Organization

As a final set of prevention strategies, we address the organizational factors that may contribute to the prevention of team performance decay. Organizations can play an important role against team performance decay by taking a few proactive measures. Organizational leaders often hold the role of policy makers and those who control the distribution of rewards; thus, we argue that such individuals are in a position to help prevent performance decay based on the policies they set, the sources of motivation they utilize, and the overall organizational culture. For example, one of the most direct ways in which an organization can help prevent team performance decay is by ensuring a team has access to all the necessary resources. Therefore, a high performing team may suddenly demonstrate performance decay without any apparent changes in the team's abilities or behaviors, but rather owing to a lack of the resources required to effectively perform the task. A lack of available or accessible resources or supplies can prevent the team's capability of performing successfully (Gladstein, 1984). Thus, an organization can most effectively avoid such performance decay by monitoring a team's needs and ensuring these needs are met.

Strategy 8: Organizational leaders can reduce team performance decay by ensuring that teams are provided with the required resources for successful performance.

Performance appraisals, along with compensatory incentives or other rewards, can also send a message regarding the organization's expectations for a team and can serve to motivate a team to work actively to avoid performance decay. Organizations can demonstrate the importance of teamwork behaviors by including performance relevant behaviors in team evaluations. For example, organizations can send a clear, positive message by making compensation partially dependent on the performance of such behaviors

(Kerr, 1975; Lawler, 2003). Furthermore, if team members know their compensation will be influenced by their performance on specific skills, it will help to motivate individuals to maintain these skills. Additionally, in designing a reward system, the system must be perceived as fair, and team members must be able to trust that if they perform at the required levels the organization will actually provide the specified rewards.

Rewards are represented by many forms. They can refer to monetary compensation or acknowledgements via verbal praise. In addition to the use of rewards, organizations can implement policies or procedures that facilitate team performance. For example, create policies and procedures that are in line with training systems in order to support the implementation of skills learned during training. Moreover, organizations should support the work that is conducted within teams. An organization can recognize the importance for individuals to work on a team and can relay this message to all individuals of that organization. By rewarding both individual members and the team as a whole, teams are more likely to exhibit KSAs, which will ultimately sustain performance.

Strategy 9: Encourage the use of team behaviors most related to team performance by formally evaluating the behaviors that matter most.

Strategy 10: Reinforce the behaviors related to effective performance by tying compensation and rewards to evaluated behaviors.

IMPLICATIONS FOR PRACTICE, AND CONCLUSIONS

Performance decay is a real and important issue for teams, and no team is immune. All teams are susceptible to decay over time. Thus, there are several implications for practice that can be extracted from the literature addressed within this chapter. First, organizations, managers, and human resource professionals should be aware of team performance decay. Organizations and those performing within teams must be made aware that performance decay is possible, and its prevention requires conscious, sustained attention. It is easy for organizations to narrow their attention and development efforts to low performing teams. Top performing teams are then left to continue without any intervention. Although this approach helps to fix immediate problems, it does little to ensure sustained performance. Top performing teams are not immune to the requirements of maintaining high levels of performance. Top performing teams must maintain the knowledge, skill, and ability levels that make it possible for them to perform at high levels. We argue that team performance can more effectively be maintained through proactive efforts that act against performance decay. Putting measures in place to prevent decay has the potential to help organizations sustain high performing work teams and avoid the costs resulting from performance decay episodes.

A second implication for practice is that organizations will benefit from expanding the toolkits used to promote effective performance. As mentioned, for many organizations, team performance decay is primarily addressed reactively. When performance falls below organizational expectations, the common response is to implement training to bring skills back up to an acceptable performance level. While training is often a sufficient means of teaching and refreshing skills, it is far from a sufficient solution to the broader problem of team performance decay. This review has suggested a variety of organizational-, task-, and team-level factors with implications for performance decay. Thus, additional emphasis can be placed on promoting skill maintenance following training through practice and feedback, ensuring teams have the resources required for performance, and supporting teams in the use of teamwork skills. Recognition that performance decay results from a combination of factors, and providing support at the organization, task, and team levels will help to circumvent performance decay.

Finally, as collaboration technologies continue to advance, teams are increasingly composed of individuals from multiple locations. Because these distributed teams conduct most, if not all, of their tasks virtually, the risk for decay is significantly multiplied. One issue arises in that distributed team members are limited in their capacity to directly monitor one another, which adds challenges to leadership and often leads to delay in the identification of problems when they occur. Furthermore, training for distributed teams, particularly on teamwork skills, is still a relatively underdeveloped practice. Efforts are needed to continue in the development of effective teamwork training methods for distributed teams. Also, organizations must ensure that such teams are provided with collaboration systems that effectively support teams in their use of teamwork skills. By treating the prevention of performance decay as an integral component in organizational practice, the consequences of such incidents can be greatly reduced.

On an individual level, it has been a well circulated myth that once a sports figure who is on top of his/her game appears on a magazine cover, his/her performance begins to decline. Does the general idea of this myth apply to a team as well? Once a team has proven that they can perform well or even exceptionally well, does their performance decline for no particular reason? While performance levels of effective teams may remain largely stable, this chapter addresses factors contributing to performance decay from the team's general level of performance. A team's performance does not decay for one specific reason alone, but rather it can be the result of a host of reasons. We have discussed several factors contributing to such incidents of performance decay, along with recommendations for the prevention of such incidents. Factors were identified at the environmental, task (e.g., retention interval, training), and team (e.g., trust, communication) levels, all of which are important to an interdependently working team.

Although substantial effort and resources are invested annually in the development of such teams, less concern is directed towards maintaining the performance of already effective teams. The challenge for today's organizations is to create teams that can sustain high levels of performance. Organizations must consider the impact that all factors have on a team's ability to maintain effective performance. It is not only critical to create teams that have expert task knowledge and experience but it is also crucial for teams to be experts at teamwork as well. The purpose of this chapter was to not only provide some food for thought when examining the reasons for a team's performance decline, but also to provide organizations with some applicable strategies to prevent the occurrence of team performance decay. The factors highlighted in this chapter indicate that organizations and managers alike should pay attention to the individuals who comprise the team, the training the team receives, as well as the context in which the team performs, since all elements may contribute to team performance decay.

REFERENCES

Abramson, L. Y., Seligman, M. E. P., and Teasdale, J. D. (1978). Learned helplessness in humans: Critique and reformulation. *Journal of Abnormal Psychology, 87*, 49–74.

Anderson, J. R. (1983). Retrieval of information from long-term memory. *Science, 220*, 25–30.

Arthur Jr., W., Bennett Jr., W., Stanush, P. L., and McNelly, T. L. (1998). Factors that influence skill decay and retention: A quantitative review and analysis. *Human Performance, 11*, 57–101.

Axelrod, R. (1984). *The evolution of cooperation.* New York: Basic Books.

Bandow, D. (2001). Time to create sound teamwork. *The Journal for Quality and Participation, 24*, 41–47.

Beith, B. H. (1987). Subjective workload under individual and team performance conditions. *Proceedings of the Human Factors Society 31st Annual Meeting*, 66–71.

Bloom, B., and Sosniak, L. (1985). *Developing talent in young people.* New York: Ballantine Books.

Bowers, C. A., Braun, C., and Morgan, B. B., Jr. (1992). *Workload and team performance.* Paper presented at the University of South Florida Workshop on Team Performance Measurement, Tampa, FL.

Boyle, M. O., and Ackerman, P. L. (2004). Individual differences in skill acquisition. In A. Williams and N. Hodges (Eds.), *Skill acquisition in sport: Research, theory, and practice* (pp. 84–102). London: Routledge.

Burke, C. S., Salas, E., and DiazGranados, D. (2008). The role of team learning in facilitating team learning adaptation within complex environments: Tools and strategies. In V. I. Sessa and M. London (Eds.), *Work group learning: Understanding, improving and assessing how groups learn in organizations*. New York: Lawrence Erlbaum Associates.

Burke, C. S., Stagl, K. C., Salas, E., Pierce, L., and Kendall, D. (2006). Understanding team adaptation: A conceptual analysis and model. *Journal of Applied Psychology, 91,* 1189–1207.

Cann, A., and Ross, D. A. (1989). Olfactory stimuli as context cues in human memory. *American Journal of Psychology, 102,* 91–102.

Cannon-Bowers, J. A., and Salas, E. (2001). Reflections of shared cognition. *Journal of Organizational Behavior, 22,* 195–202.

Cannon-Bowers, J. A., Salas, E., and Converse, S. (1993). Shared mental models in expert team decision making. In N. J. Castellan, Jr. (Ed.), *Individual and group decision making: Current issues* (pp. 221–246). Hillsdale, NJ: Lawrence Erlbaum Associates.

Cannon-Bowers, J. A., Tannenbaum, S. I., Salas, E., and Volpe, C. E. (1995). Defining team competencies and establishing team training requirements. In R. Guzzo, E. Salas, and Associates (Eds.), *Team effectiveness and decision making in organizations* (pp. 333–380). San Francisco, CA: Jossey-Bass.

Chi, M. T. H. (2006). Two approaches to the study of experts' characteristics. In K. A. Ericsson, N. Charness, R. Hoffman, and P. J. Feltovich (Eds.), *The Cambridge handbook of expertise and expert performance* (pp. 21–30). New York: Cambridge University Press.

Childs, J. M., and Spears, W. D. (1986). Flight-skill decay and recurrent training. *Perceptual and Motor Skills, 62,* 235–242.

Cooke, N. J., Salas, E., Kiekel, P. A., and Bell, B. (2004). Advances in measuring team cognition. In E. Salas and S. Fiore (Eds.), *Team cognition: Understanding the factors that drive process and performance.* Washington, D.C.: APA Books.

Crutcher, R. J., and Ericsson, K. A. (1988). A componential analysis of the keyword method. *American Educational Research Association Convention.*

Crutcher, R. J., and Healy, A. F. (1989). Cognitive operations and the generation effect. *Journal of Experimental Psychology, 15,* 669–675.

Cummings, L. L., and Bromiley, P. (1996). The organizational trust inventory (OTI). *Trust in organizations: Frontiers of theory and research, 302,* 330.

Dahlstrom, N. Dekker, S., van Winsen, R., and Nyce, J. (2009). Fidelity and validity of simulator training. *Theoretical Issues in Ergonomics Science, 10,* 305–314.

Dickinson, T. L. and McIntyre, R. M. (1997). A conceptual framework for teamwork measurement. In M. T. Brannick, E. Salas, and C. Prince (Eds.), *Team performance assessment and measurement: Theory, Methods, and Applications* (pp. 19–44). Mahwah, NJ: Lawrence Erlbaum Associates.

Dirks, K. T. (1999). The effects of interpersonal trust on work group performance. *Journal of Applied Psychology, 84,* 445–455.

Driskell, J. E., and Salas, E. (1992). Collective behavior and team performance. *Human Factors, 34,* 277–288.

Driskell, J. E., Hughes, S., and Oser, R. (1998). Optimizing the after action review. *Florida Maxima Corporation.*

Driskell, J. E., Willis, R. P., and Copper, C. (1992). Effect of overlearning on retention. *Journal of Applied Psychology, 77,* 615–622.

Dweck, C. S. (1986). Motivational processes affecting learning. *American Psychologist, 41,* 1040–1048.

Dweck, C. S., and Leggett, E. L. (1988). A social-cognitive approach to motivation and personality. *Psychological Review, 95,* 256–273.

Ebbinghaus, H. (1913). *Memory: A contribution to experimental psychology.* New York, New York: Teacher's College.

Edmondson, A. (1999). Psychological safety and learning behavior in work teams. *Administrative Science Quarterly, 44,* 350–383.

Egenfeldt-Nielsen, S. (2007). Third generation educational use of computer games. *Journal of Educational Multimedia and Hypermedia, 16,* 263–281.

Elliot, E. S., and Dweck, C. S. (1988). Goals: An approach to motivation and achievement. *Journal of Personality and Social Psychology, 54,* 5–12.

Ellis, A. P., Bell, B. S., Ployhart, R. E., Hollenbeck, J. R., and Ilgen, D. R. (2005). An evaluation of generic teamwork skills training with action teams: Effects on cognitive and skill-based outcomes. *Personnel Psychology, 58,* 641–672.

Entin, E. E., and Serfaty, D. (1999). Adaptive team coordination. *Human Factors, 41*(2), 312.

Ericsson, K. A., Charness, N., Feltovich, P. J., and Hoffman, R. R. (Eds.). (2006). *Cambridge handbook on expertise and expert performance.* Cambridge, UK: Cambridge University Press.

Farr, M. J. (1987). *The long-term retention of knowledge and skills: A cognitive and instructional perspective.* New York: Springer-Verlag.

Fendrich, D. W., Healy, A. F., and Bourne, L. E. (1991). Long-term repetition effects for motoric and perceptual procedures. *Journal of Experimental Psychology: Learning, Memory, and Cognition, 17,* 137–151.

Fendrich, D. W., Healy, A. F., and Bourne, L. E. (1993). Mental arithmetic: Training and retention of multiplication skill. In C. Izawa (Ed.), *Cognitive psychology applied* (pp. 111–133). Hillsdale, NJ: Lawrence Erlbaum Associates.

Fletcher, J. D. (2004). *Cognitive readiness: Preparing for the unexpected.* Alexandria, VA: Institute for Defense Analyses.

Ford, J. K., Quiñones, M. A., Sego, D. J., and Speer Sorra, J. S. (1992). Factors affecting the opportunity to perform trained tasks on the job. *Personnel Psychology, 45,* 511–527.

Gardner, W. L. I., and Schermerhorn, J. R. (1992). *Strategic operational leadership and the management of supportive work environments.* Westport, CT: Quorum.

Gentile, J. R., Monaco, N., Iheozor-Ejiofor, I. E., Ndu, A. N., and Ogbonaya, P. (1982). Retention by "fast" and "slow" learners. *Intelligence, 6,* 125–138.

Gersick, C. J. (1988). Time and transition in work teams: Toward a new model of group development. *Academy of Management Journal, 31,* 9–41.

Gladstein, D. L. (1984). Groups in context: A model of task group effectiveness. *Administrative Science Quarterly, 29,* 499–517.

Gladwell, M. (2008). *Outliers: The story of success.* New York: Little, Brown and Co.

Glisky, M. L., Williams, J. M., and Kihlstrom, J. F. (1996). Internal and external mental imagery perspectives and performances on two tasks. *Journal of Sports Behavior, 19,* 3–18.

Halfhill, T., Nielsen, T. M., Sundstrom, E., and Weilbaecher, A. (2005). Group personality composition and performance in military service teams. *Military Psychology, 17,* 41–54.

Hart, S. G., and Hauser, I. R. (1987). Inflight application of three pilot workload measurement techniques. *Aerospace and Environmental Medicine, 58,* 402–410.

Hastie, R. (1986). Experimental evidence on group accuracy. In B. Grofman and G. Owen (Eds.), *Decision research* (Vol. 2, pp. 129–157). Greenwich, CT: JAI Press.

Healy, A. F., Fendrich, D. W., and Proctor, J. D. (1990). Acquisition and retention of a letterdectection skill. *Journal of Experimental Psychology, 16,* 270–281.

Healy, A. F., Fendrich, D. W., Crutcher, R. J., Wittman, W. T., Gesi, A. T., Ericsson, K. A., et al. (1992). The long term retention of skills. *Essays in honour of William Estes: From learning processes to cognitive processes, 2,* 87–118.

Hinsz, V. B., Tindale, R. S., and Vollrath, D. A. (1997). The emerging conceptualization of groups as information processes. *Psychological Bulletin, 121,* 43–64.

Hinsz, V. B., Vollrath, D. A., Nagao, D. H., and Davis, J. H. (1988). Comparing the structure of individual and small group perceptions. *International Journal of Small Group Research, 4,* 159–168.

Hufford, L. E., and Adams, A. (1961). The contribution of part-task training to the relearning of a flight maneuver. *Report No. NAVTRADEVCENTR297–2.*

Hurlock, R. E., and Montague, W. E. (1982). Skill retention and its implications for nay tasks: An analytic review. *NPRDC Special Rep. No.82–21.*

Jacobs, T. O., and Jaques, E. (1990). *Measures of leadership.* West Orange, NJ: Leadership Library of America.

Jones, G. R., and George, J. M. (1998). The experience and evolution of trust: Implications for cooperation and teamwork. *Academy of Management Review,* 531–546.

Kahn, W. A. (1990). Psychological conditions of personal engagement and disengagement at work. *Academy of Management Journal, 33,* 692–724.

Kassin, S. M., Ellsworth, P. C., and Smith, V. L. (1989). The "general acceptance" of psychological research on eyewitness testimony: A survey of experts. *American Psychologist, 44,* 1089–1099.

Kerr, S. (1975). On the folly of rewarding A, while hoping for B. *The Academy of Management Journal, 18,* 769–783.

Kidd, I. S. (1961). A comparison of one-, two-, and three man work units under various conditions of workload. *Journal of Applied Psychology, 45,* 195–200.

Kim, J., Singer, R. N., and Radlo, S. J. (1996). Degree of cognitive demands in psychomotor tasks and the effects of the five-step strategy on achievement. *Human Performance, 9,* 155–169.

Klein, G. (1997). The recognition-primed decision (RPD) model: Looking back, looking forward. In C. E. Zsambok and G. Klein (Eds.), *Naturalistic decision making*: Lawrence Erlbaum Associates.

Klein, G.A. (1998). *Sources of power: How people make decisions.* Cambridge, MA: MIT Press.

Kozlowski, S. W., and Klein, K. J. (2000). A multilevel approach to theory and research in organizations: Contextual, temporal, and emergent processes. In *Multilevel theory, research, and methods in organizations: Foundations, extensions, and new directions* (pp. 3–90). San Francisco, CA: Jossey-Bass.

Kozlowski, S. W., Gully, S. M., McHugh, P. P., Salas, E., and Cannon-Bowers, J. A. (1996). A dynamic theory of leadership and team effectiveness: Developmental and task contingent leader roles. *Research in Personnel and Human Resources Management, 14,* 253–305.

Kramer, R. M. (1999). Trust and distrust in organizations: Emerging perspectives, enduring questions. *Annual Review of Psychology, 50*, 569–598.

Krueger, W. C. F. (1929). The effect of overlearning on retention. *Journal of Experimental Psychology, 12*, 71–78.

Krueger, W. C. F. (1930). Further studies in overlearning. *Journal of Experimental Psychology, 13*, 152–163.

Lance, C. E., Parisi, A. G., Bennett, W. R., Teachout, M. S., Harville, D. L., and Welles, M. L. (1998). Moderators of skill retention interval/performance in eight U.S. air forced enlisted specialties. *Human Performance, 11*, 103–123.

Latham, G. P., and Locke, E. A. (1979). Goal setting: A motivational technique that works. *Organziational Dynamics, 8*, 68–80.

Lawler, E. (2003). Reward practices and performance management system effectiveness. *Organizational Dynamics, 32*, 396–404.

LePine, J. A. (2005). Adaptation of teams in response to unforeseen change: Effects of goal difficulty and team composition in terms of cognitive ability and goal orientation. *Journal of Applied Psychology, 90*, 1153–1167.

Lewis, K. (2004). Knowledge and performance in knowledge-worker teams: A longitudinal study of transactive memory systems. *Management Science, 50*, 1519–1533.

Locke, E. A., and Latham, G. P. (2002). Building a practically useful theory of goal setting and task motivation: A 35-year odyssey. *American Psychologist, 57*, 705–717.

McConnell, C. R. (2005). Motivating your employees and yourself. *The Health Care Manager, 24*, 284–292.

McIntyre, R. M., and Salas, E. (1995). Measuring and managing for team performance: Emerging principles from complex environments. In R. A. Guzzo and E. Salas (Eds.), *Team Effectiveness and Decision Making in Organizations* (pp. 9–45). San Francisco, CA: Jossey-Bass Publishers.

Marks, M. A., and Panzer, F. J. (2004). The influence of team monitoring on team processes and performance. *Human Performance, 17*, 25–41.

Marks, M. A., Mathieu, J. E., and Zaccaro, S. J. (2001). A temporally based framework and taxonomy of team processes. *Academy of Management Journal, 26*, 356–376.

Mathieu, J. E., Heffner, T. S., Goodwin, G. F., Salas, E., and Cannon-Bowers, J. A. (2000). The influence of shared mental models on team process and performance. *Journal of Applied Psychology, 85*(2), 273–283.

May, D. R., Gilson, R. L., and Harter, L. M. (2004). The psychological conditions of meaningfulness, safety and availability and the engagement of the human spirit at work. *Journal of Occupational and Organizational Psychology, 77*, 11–37.

Mayer, R. C., Davis, J. H., and Schoorman. (1995). An integrative model of organizational trust. *Academy of Management Review, 20*, 709–734.

Mengelkoch, R. F., Adams, J. A., and Gainer, C. A. (1960). The forgetting of instrument flying skills as a function of the initial level of proficiency (Report No. NAVTRADEVCEN 71-16-18). Port Washington, NY: US Naval Training Device Center.

Milanovich, D. M., Salas, E., Cannon-Bowers, J. A., and Muniz, E. J. (2000). Understanding the team derailment process: A look at team skill and attitude deficiencies. In M. M. Beyerlein, D. A. Johnson, and S. T. Beyerlein (Eds.), *Advances in interdisciplinary studies of work teams: Team development* (Vol. 7, pp. 187–206). Greenwich, CT: JAI Press.

Moreland, R. L., and Myaskovsky, L. (2000). Exploring the performance benefits of group training: Transactive memory or improved communication? *Organizational Behavior and Human Decision Processes, 82,* 117–133.

Morgan, B. B., Jr., Glickman, A. S., Woodward, E. A., Blaiwes, A., and Salas, E. (1986). *Measurment of team behaviors in a navy environment* (NTSC Tech. Rep. No. 86–014). Orlando, FL: Naval Training Systems Center.

Morgeson, F. P., Reider, M. H., and Campion, M. A. (2005). Selecting individuals in team settings: The importance of social skills, personality characteristics, and teamwork knowledge. *Personnel Psychology, 58,* 583–611.

Mulvey, P. W., and Klein, H. J. (1998). The impact of perceived loafing and collective efficacy on group goal processes and group performance. *Organizational Behavior and Human Decision Processes, 74,* 62–87.

Naylor, J. C., Briggs, G. E., and Reed, W. G. (1968). Task coherence, training time, and retention interval effects on skill retention. *Journal of Applied Psychology, 52,* 386.

Pearce, C. L., and Herbik, P. A. (2004). Citizenship behavior at the team level of analysis: the effects of team leadership, team commitment, perceived team support, and team size. *The Journal of Social Psychology, 144,* 293–310.

Porter, C. O. L. H., Hollenbeck, J. R., Ilgen, D. R., Ellis, A. P. J., West, B. J., and Henry, M. (2003). Backup behaviors in teams: The role of personality and legitimacy of need. *Journal of Applied Psychology, 88,* 391–403.

Priest, H. A., Burke, C. S., Munim, D., and Salas, E. (2002). Understanding team adaptability: Initial theoretical and practical considerations. Paper presented in the *Proceedings of the Human Factors and Ergonomics Society, 46,* 561–545.

Reisel, W. D., and Kopelman, R. E. (1995). The effects of failure on subsequent group performance in a professional sports setting. *The Journal of Psychology, 129,* 103–113.

Ren, Y. (2004). *Why and when does transactive memory matter.* Paper presented at the 10th Annual Organization Science Winter Conference (OSWC), Steamboat Springs, CO.

Robinson, S. L. (1996). Trust and breach of the psychological contract. *Administrative Science Quarterly, 41,* 574–599.

Rouiller, J. Z., and Goldstein, I. L. (1993). The relationship between organizational transfer climate and positive transfer of training. *Human Resource Development Quarterly, 4,* 377–390.

Ryan, E. D., and Simons, J. (1981). Cognitive demand, imagery, and frequency of mental rehearsal as factors influencing acquisition of motor skills. *Journal of Sport Psychology, 3,* 35–45.

Salas, E., and Cannon-Bowers, J. A. (2000). The anatomy of team training. In S. Tobias and J. D. Fletcher (Eds.), *Training and retraining: A handbook for business, industry, government, and the military* (pp. 312–335). New York: MacMillan Reference.

Salas, E., and Cannon-Bowers, J. A. (2001). The science of team training. *Annual Review of Psychology, 52,* 471–499.

Salas, E., Rosen, M. A., and DiazGranados, D. (2010). Expertise-based intuition and decision making in organizations. *Journal of Management, 36,* 941–973.

Salas, E., Sims, D. E., and Burke, C. S. (2005). Is there a 'big five' in teamwork? *Small Group Research, 36,* 555–599.

Salas, E., Rosen, M. A., Burke, C. S., Goodwin, G. F., and Fiore, S. (2006). The making of a dream team: When expert teams do best. In *The Cambridge handbook of expertise and expert performance* (pp. 439–453). New York: Cambridge University Press.

Salas, E., Stagl, K. C., Burke, C. S., and Goodwin, G. F. (2007). Fostering team effectiveness in organizations: Toward an integrative theoretical framework. In *Modeling complex systems* (pp. 185–243). Lincoln, NE: University of Nebraska Press.

Sauer, J., Wastell, D. G., and Hockey, R. J. (1997). Skill maintenance in extended spaceflight: Human factors analysis of space and analogue work environments. *Acta Astronautica*, *39*, 579–587.

Schab, F. R. (1990). Odors and the remembrance of things past. *Journal of Experimental Psychology: Learning, Memory, and Cognition*, *16*, 648–655.

Schendel, J. D., and Hagman, J. D. (1982). On sustaining procedural skills over a prolonged retention interval. *Journal of Applied Psychology*, *67*, 605–610.

Schlechter, T. R., Zaccaro, S. L., and Burke, C. S. (1998). Toward and understanding of the shared mental models associated with proficient team performance. *Meeting of the American Psychological Society*, Washington, D.C.

Schmidt, R. A., and Bjork, R. A. (1992). New conceptualizations of practice: Common principles in three paradigms suggest new concepts for training. *Psychological Science*, *3*, 207–217.

Serfaty, D., Entin, E. E., and Johnston, J. H. (1998). Team coordination training. In J. A. Cannon-Bowers and E. Salas (Eds.), *Making decisions under stress: Implications for individual and team training* (pp. 221–246). Washington, DC: American Psychological Association.

Serfaty, D., Entin, E. E., and Volpe, C. (1993). *Adaptation to stress in team decision-making and coordination*. Paper presented at the Human Factors and Ergonomics Society 37th Annual Meeting, Santa Monica, CA.

Shiflett, S. (1979). Toward a general model of small group productivity. *Psychological Bulletin*, *86*, 67–79.

Sims, D. E., and Salas, E. (2007). When teams fail in organizations: What creates teamwork breakdowns? In J. Langan-Fox, C. L. Cooper, and R. J. Klimoski (Eds.), *Research companion to the dysfunctional workplace: Management challenges and symptoms* (pp. 302–318). New York: Edward Elgar Publishing.

Smith, J. F., and Matheny, W. G. (1976). *Continuation versus recurrent pilot training* (No. Final Report, Nov. 1974- Oct. 1975). Brooks AFB, TX: Air Force Human Resources Lab.

Stewart, G. L., and Manz, C. C. (1995). Leadership for self-managing work teams: A typology and integrative model. *Human Relations*, *48*, 747–770.

Stothard, C., and Nicholson, R. (2001). *Skill acquisition and retention in training: DSTO support to the Army ammunition study* (No. DSTO-CR-0218). Edinburgh, South Australia: DSTO Electronics and Surveillance Research Laboratory.

Stout, R. J., Cannon-Bowers, J. A., Salas, E., and Milanovich, D. M. (1999). Planning, shared mental models, and coordinated performance: An empirical link is established. *Human Factors*, *41*, 61–71.

Trice, A. D., Elliott, K. A., Pope, N. J., and Tryall, T. (1991). Self-efficacy as a moderator of the effects of failure at a mathematics task. *Journal of Social Behavior and Personality*, *6*, 597–604.

Tulving, E. (1983). *Elements of episodic memory*. New York: Oxford University Press.

van Knippenberg, D. (2000). Work motivation and performance: A social identity perspective. *Applied Psychology: An International Review*, *49*, 357–371.

Webber, S. S. (2002). Leadership and trust facilitating cross-functional team success. *Journal of Management Development*, *21*, 201–214.

Wegner, D. M., Erber, R., and Raymond, P. (1991). Transactive memory in close relationships. *Journal of Personality and Social Psychology, 61*, 923–929.

Williges, R. C., Johnston, W. A., and Briggs, G. E. (1966). Role of verbal communication in teamwork. *Journal of Applied Psychology, 6*, 473–478.

Wisher, R., Sabol, M. A., and Ellis, J. A. (1999). *Staying sharp: Retention of military knowledge and skills* (No. ARI Special Report 39). Alexandria, VA: US Army Research Institute for Social and Behavioral Sciences.

Wittman, W. T. (1989). A long-term retention advantage for spatial information learned naturally and in the laboratory. Unpublished doctoral dissertation, University of Colorado, Boulder, CO.

Wixted, J. T., and Ebbesen, E. B. (1991). On the form of forgetting. *Psychological Science, 2*, 409–415.

Zaccaro, S. J., Heinen, B. A., and Shuffler, M. L. (2009). Team leadership and team effectiveness. In E. Salas, J. Goodwin and C. S. Burke (Eds.), *Team effectiveness in complex organizations: Cross-disciplinary perspectives and approaches* (pp. 83–111). San Francisco, CA: Jossey-Bass.

Part 4

Summary

16

A Look From "aFarr" (1987)

The Past, Present, and Future of Applied Skill Decay Research

Winfred Arthur, Jr. and Eric Anthony Day

INTRODUCTION

In the 25 years since Farr's (1987) seminal review of research on the long-term retention of knowledge and skills and almost 15 years since Arthur, Bennett, Stanush, and McNelly's (1998) meta-analysis, it appears to us that not a lot of empirical research has been devoted to the study of knowledge and skill retention outside the more basic, cognitive-experimental work on memory and motor learning. We see two major reasons for this lack of research attention. First, from a purely practical perspective, there are substantial logistical challenges associated with recruiting and training participants, and of course retaining and retesting them after extensive periods of nonuse. This is particularly the case with applied research, given that the chosen task domain typically involves a complex performance environment that reflects some real-world context. Such task domains require many hours of training, often distributed across several days if not a few weeks, and the tasks themselves must be selected with a consideration that participants will not have opportunities to practice the task during a designated nonuse period. Second, from a theoretical perspective, many researchers may not perceive the need for more empirical work given that the preponderance of basic research points to "decay" as a matter of interference with retrieval processes rather than sheer nonuse. From this viewpoint it could be argued that decay is not much of a problem with many contemporary real-world tasks. Moreover, for simple tasks, the practical implications appear fairly straightforward. If a task simply entails retrieving declarative knowledge (i.e., basic facts or information), then why not just instruct individuals to "Google it" on a hand-held electronic device rather than being concerned with training individuals to develop richly encoded memory stores? If a task involves the accurate and efficient execution of a mundane set of procedures, then such tasks could be identified before training as candidates for frequent refresher training. With these practical and theoretical issues in mind, researchers may not see much of a payoff in conducting applied research on skill retention with protocols involving complex tasks and extensive periods of nonuse.

Nevertheless, it is our position that future research on skill retention is warranted and that the payoffs could be substantial from both applied and scholarly perspectives. We see the biggest payoffs accruing from addressing two issues in particular: (1) how to build durable and efficient yet adaptable skills (a potential retention–transfer tradeoff?), and (2) filling notable gaps in the extant literature. In this final chapter, we expound on these two issues by first reviewing the major conclusions that can be drawn from an integrative look across all the chapters in this volume in relation to the state of the science reflected in Farr's (1987) review. On the basis of this exposition, we then identify and discuss a set of specific issues that we believe would be most propitious to address in future applied research on skill retention.

FROM THE PAST TO THE PRESENT

Reification

Much of the applied research on knowledge and skill retention over the last 25 years as well as the content of the works in the present volume reflects a reification of many of Farr's (1987) major conclusions (see also Arthur et al., 1998). For example, (1) decay is more a matter of competition between relevant and irrelevant information and processes stored in memory rather than simply the forgetting of information and processes through the passage of time (Chapters 2, 7, 8); (2) retention rates are largely task dependent with retention being stronger for tasks that are more organized, meaningful, and open-looped (i.e., complex) compared to tasks that predominantly involve a discrete set of procedures or declarative knowledge (Chapters 2, 3, 4, 7, 9, 10, 13, 14, and 15); and (3) retention is generally greater with more practice, elaborative rehearsal, and greater mastery of the task (Chapters 2, 4, 8, 10, and 15).

The first conclusion is particularly important in that it reflects how knowledge and skill decay represent a *process* contrary to its common usage in the applied training and industrial/organizational (I/O) psychology literatures (as is represented in many of the chapters in this volume as well) as an *outcome*. The process and outcome distinction is an important one because, as noted by Gronlund and Kimball (2013), although the construct of decay is expedient as a colloquial description of what happens to memory over time, as a process variable, decay is inadequate as "an explanation of forgetting because the mechanism by which a memory [or skill] weakens is never specified" (p. 14). And as further highlighted in their quotation of McGeoch (1932), "'Rust does not occur because of time itself, but rather from oxidation processes that occur with time.' To be viable, decay explanations of forgetting must specify the oxidation process" (pp. 32–33). From a process perspective, Levy, Kuhl, and Wagner (2010) proposed five mechanisms of forgetting: (1) failure to encode, (2) disrupted consolidation, (3) retrieval competition, (4) resolving retrieval competition, and (5) ineffective retrieval cues. And as noted by Gronlund and Kimball, most researchers reject the first two mechanisms because forgetting is considered to be "the inability to recall something now that could be recalled on an earlier occasion" (Tulving, 1974, p. 74). With this process perspective, it becomes clear as to why researchers often fail to find a simple relationship between retention and length of nonuse (Chapters 2, 3, and 4). The second two conclusions indirectly speak to this, given that retention depends on task characteristics and the degree and quality of original skill acquisition.

We believe the overriding implication in considering the Gestalt of the three previously noted conclusions is that the science of knowledge and skill retention should focus on retrieval processes and interference, particularly with respect to the distinction between retention and transfer. Phrased another way, we believe that the state of the science on knowledge and skill decay reflects a move toward building adaptive expertise rather than simply preventing decay (e.g., Bell and Kozlowski, 2009). Not only does theory and empirical research reflect this state of affairs, but a move toward building adaptive expertise also reflects the more dynamic nature of today's (and even more so the future's) global, technologically sophisticated, and service-oriented work environment.

Although retention and transfer are related, empirical evidence also shows they are meaningfully distinct (Chapters 2, 7, 8, 9, 11, 13, and 15) and in some respects, there may even be a trade-off (interference) between the two, as extensive practice (if not overlearning) leads to a restructuring and consolidation of knowledge and skill components, consequently creating automated retrieval processes that can at times interfere with the learning of new information and processes or the retrieval of other memory stores that may be better used to address novel performance demands (Chapters 2 and 8). As reflected in the title of Healy et al.'s Chapter 7 in this volume, we need better theories that address the distinction between retention and transfer while keeping in mind the practical issue of "training for efficient, durable, and flexible performance." This issue is elaborated on later in our discussion of future research needs.

Progress

In his review, Farr (1987) explicitly listed 11 future research needs. However, for the most part, very little research has been undertaken in the last 25 years to address them. What research that *has* been undertaken in relation to Farr's listed needs has been mostly in the cognitive-experimental literature on memory and motor learning. Specifically, progress has been made with respect to the need for (a) better algorithms for predicting retention by way of computational modeling (Chapters 2 and 6); (b) a clearer understanding for how "motor memory" is represented through theory and research on embodied cognition (Chapter 2) and the dynamic roles of visual–spatial and motor systems (Chapter 8); (c) clearer definitions of "distinctiveness" and "discriminability" of memory traces through research on interference and the diagnosticity of retrieval cues, the distinctiveness of stored memory in terms of recollection versus familiarity processes, and the joint influence of prior knowledge and distinctive processing in expert memory (Chapter 2); and (d) better understanding of the "quality" versus "quantity" of learning in terms of practice conditions that involve "desirable difficulties" (Chapter 2), the need to assess learning with a variety of measures including measures of both retention and transfer (Chapters 7, 8, 9, 10, 11, and 13), both knowledge and skill-based criteria (Chapters 4, 5, 7, 11, and 14), tests of recognition and recall (Chapter 2), different types of errors (Chapter 12), and perhaps even indices of variability coupled with mean or maximal performance scores (Chapter 5). In contrast, less progress has been made in terms of (a) developing more fine-grained definitions of the dimensions of task complexity to inform the "memorability" of a task (Chapter 4), (b) deciding when to provide refresher training and how to sequence and streamline it (i.e., having a well-established protocol that is fairly efficient and generalizable; Chapters 4, 6, 9, and 15), and (c) relating individual differences in ability, motivation, knowledge, and skill to long-term retention and transfer (Chapter 11).

There are obviously a number of critical research issues that were *not* listed by Farr (1987). One of these—which has received almost no research attention —is knowledge and skill retention and decay in teams, a topic of particular import given the ever-growing importance of teams in today's civilian and military work environments. With this in mind, the empirical works reflected in Chapters 13 and 14 of the present volume as well as the guiding set of propositions provided in Chapter 15 lay the foundation for building an agenda for future research on team performance decay and adaptability. In Chapter 13, Arthur et al. showed that team performance decay on a complex command-and-control simulation after an 8-week period of nonuse was similarly low compared to individual performance, but that team performance did not suffer nearly as much under novel and over-whelming performance demands (i.e., test of transfer) compared to individual performance. In other words, while rates of retention may not differ between team and individual levels, teams seem better suited for dealing with novel situations. In Chapter 14, Cooke, Gorman, Duran, Myers, and Andrews showed how the variance in overall team performance decay on a complex decision-making simulation was linked to losses in teamwork performance (i.e., coordination) rather than losses in individual taskwork performance. We speculate that this result stems from teamwork having a greater susceptibility to interference because, on one hand, the dimensions of teamwork are fairly broad and generic (i.e., helping, coordinating, backing-up, communication, performance and systems monitoring) across team environments, but on the other hand, the specific manner in which these actions should be manifested most likely varies across specific team environments. And although Cook et al. did not investigate this issue, teamwork may also have greater susceptibility to interference, given that team membership is oftentimes very transient and the distribution of generic teamwork roles may change as membership changes and the specific manner in which teamwork roles are performed likely varies across individuals. In Chapter 15, DiazGranados, Lazzara, Lyons, Wooten, and Salas provide specific propositions regarding the nature of team performance decay as well as strategies for proactively mitigating team performance decay, many of which directly speak to the importance of teamwork processes. Several specific issues pertaining to team performance decay are reviewed later in this chapter in the discussion of future research needs.

Lessons Learned Toward Building Durable and Efficient Yet Adaptable Performance

To recapitulate, the body of empirical literature makes it clear that skill decay is (1) a process largely involving interference with the retrieval of needed information and performance processes, (2) dependent on task characteristics, (3) dependent on how practice and instruction leads to the development of a coherent knowledge and skill structure, and (4) is related to but meaningfully distinct from skill transfer (i.e., adaptability). Specifically, while extensive and repetitive hands-on practice and overlearning (drilling practice) leads to the development of well-retained skill, such skill is not as adaptable as that acquired through more elaborative, thought-provoking instruction and practice conditions. Sheer quantity of practice and overlearning facilitates the transition from executive control (slow and deliberate) processes to more automated (quick and efficient) processes as learners acquire declarative knowledge and compile the knowledge into a set of performance procedures. In this respect and in simplistic terms (perhaps overly simplistic), the acquisition of complex skills appears to reflect a processing of components or skill parts toward the development of a more singular structure or whole pattern of responses. In the context of motor learning, learning goes from an abstract understanding to something that is more literal (Shea and Kovacs, 2013). It appears that, to a large degree, the components or parts of a complex skill must be integrated in order for effective, durable, and efficient performance to develop. Such a singular, integrated structure can be generalized across a variety of performance demands and facilitate transfer when the structure is grounded in a set of key themes and underlying principles, and the novel performance demands do not necessitate a major restructuring of the skill components. Otherwise, transfer will not benefit from the singular, integrated structure.

When novel performance demands require deviation from the acquired knowledge and skill structure, transfer is likely better facilitated from a discrete understanding of components and parts as opposed to just having a consolidated structure. In this vein, we believe the key to building durable and efficient yet adaptable performance lies in the development of coherent knowledge and skill structures while at the same time maintaining a fair amount of integrity in the components and parts. In Healy et al. (2013) and Day et al. (2013), declarative knowledge was shown to be facilitative of transfer but not retention. In Shea and Kovacs (2013), random practice led to the development of a singular response pattern that was more generalizable than blocked practice, but not if the test of transfer required a new response structure. Although there is a fairly well-established empirical literature supporting the superiority of random and variable practice over blocked and constant practice (Schmidt and Bjork, 1992), this latter finding by Shea and Kovacs uniquely shows the limits to random practice's transfer effectiveness. Shea and Kovacs' research with part versus whole practice (part–whole versus whole–part) is pivotal to our proposition that the integrity of the components and parts is an important factor. This research by Shea and Kovacs showed how part–whole practice appears to be a viable way to promote retention and adaptability by facilitating the development of a needed complex behavioral response pattern, while at the same time maintaining relatively independent codes for different parts of the skill that could be used as the building blocks for learning new skills or adapting previously learned skills.

Obviously, emphasizing more part–whole training (and part-training in the context of performing the whole task (Gopher, Weil, and Siegel, 1989)) in the acquisition and practice of complex skills is one of the major practical implications of our proposition that maintaining the integrity of skill components and parts is critical to the transfer of knowledge and skill. Cross-training and imparting interpositional knowledge (Marks, Sabella, Burke, and Zaccaro, 2002) are parallels to part–whole training at the team level. We also believe that elaborative rehearsal should include an explicit consideration of specific components and parts (including specific pieces of declarative knowledge) in relation to one another and in relation to how they fit in the overall structure. Furthermore, once a reasonable level of skilled performance has been acquired, elaborative rehearsal could also include relating components of the skill (and pieces of declarative knowledge) and the overall structure to components of other skills and areas of knowledge previously learned outside of training. Here, prior knowledge would be used to more deeply encode skill components in a manner that would facilitate transfer and not interfere with skill acquisition or retention (see Gronlund and Kimball, 2013). Indeed, elaborative rehearsal has a rich history in memory research and knowledge retention (Craik and Lockhart, 1972), but we also believe that it can be used via an emphasis on components to facilitate transfer as well.

Another implication is that training and instruction should not be guided by the idea of transitioning learners from a declarative stage to a more automated stage, such that task knowledge and information are regarded simply as tools for facilitating skill acquisition. Rather, task knowledge and information should also be emphasized as tools needed to adapt to novel performance demands vis-à-vis developing a learning or mastery orientation as opposed to a performance orientation (Dweck, 1986). Hence, tests of knowledge and skilled performance should be equally emphasized in training evaluation.

Task analysis could also be used to guide the development of durable and efficient yet adaptable performance. Traditionally, in the applied skill decay literature, the purpose of task analysis is to identify which knowledge and skills are most susceptible to decay and, consequently, are the best candidates for overlearning and refresher training. In considering decay as a process involving interference with a goal of facilitating adaptable performance, the focus of task analysis must change and be expanded to involve not only the knowledge and skills to be trained but also the conditions (including specific tasks) characterizing the nonuse period as well as the conditions when the trained knowledge and skills are most likely to be needed. First, conditions and tasks likely to be performed during known periods of nonuse should be analyzed to identify possible sources of interference. In turn, the sources of interference might be removed or identified as possible candidates for purposeful forgetting (see Gronlund and Kimball, 2013) when individuals are later called upon to perform the critical tasks learned prior to the nonuse period. Second, task analysis could be used to distinguish areas of knowledge or aspects of a skill that are likely more in need of future restructuring versus those that should be held intact as core to the domain. If pure retention is deemed more important for certain areas, then overlearning and refresher training may be more appropriate, whereas training that induces elaborative rehearsal and self-regulation may be more appropriate for areas where flexibility and adaptability are needed. In this respect, specific areas of declarative knowledge could be targeted as most likely to facilitate adaptable performance.

We also believe that coupling mental imagery and rehearsal with hands-on practice is another viable means toward building durable and efficient yet adaptable performance. Although meta-analytic evidence has long supported the effectiveness of mental rehearsal toward the acquisition and retention of knowledge and skill (Driskell, Copper, and Moran, 1994; see also Farr, 1987), complementing hands-on practice with the imagining and mental rehearsal of performance under different circumstances could promote the develop-ment of a well-integrated response structure that is also easily adaptive. Specifically, after hands-on practice is conducted under conditions that facilitate the acquisition of a needed skill structure, trainees could be instructed to imagine how performance circumstances might be different in the future and accordingly mentally rehearse how they would modify what they have learned. In the vein of part–whole training, they could even be instructed to imagine how different skill components would need to be altered discretely or in relation to other components in order to most effectively adapt to new and changing circumstances. Given the importance of declarative knowledge to successful transfer, trainees could even be instructed to explicitly consider which specific facts about the task are most important to consider in the imagined circumstances. Such mental simulations could be shared in a facilitated group discussion, whether the goal is individual learning or team performance.

Ultimately, we believe the above recommendations could facilitate transfer through multiple mechanisms. They likely facilitate (a) the development of more deeply encoded memory traces and more coherent and flexible mental models, (b) the use of self-regulation processes (i.e., metamemory), and (c) the use of mental rehearsal of future performance during periods of nonuse. In these ways, mental rehearsal furthers knowledge and skill development and promotes planning for future performance episodes and contingencies (Driskell et al., 1994; Gronlund and Kimball, 2013; Vealey and Greanleaf, 2010).

NOTEABLE GAPS IN THE LITERATURE AND AVENUES FOR FUTURE RESEARCH

Integrative Theory Development

As the applied research on training and development has increasingly emphasized the need for a better understanding of the processes associated with knowledge and skill transfer and the development of adaptable performance, not only do we see a need to bridge skill decay research with research on transfer and adaptable performance, but we also see a need to build bridges with other areas of research not commonly associated with training and development. First, it would be worthwhile to consider theories of intuitive expertise that integrate the seemingly opposing theoretical traditions of naturalistic decision making and heuristics and biases (Kahneman and Klein, 2009). Such an integration would be helpful toward improving our understanding of the potential tradeoff between retention and adaptability as a result of extensive practice and overlearning. Although research on naturalistic decision making has shown how experts in the field quickly and effectively approach novel circumstances through a sequence of first applying existing mental models, then monitoring progress, and subsequently improvising as needed, there is considerable empirical evidence showing how judgments and decisions made by experts are often undermined by heuristics and biases. Second, we also believe the time has come for applied research on training and development to incorporate theory and methodology from the creativity literature, which has a rich history of both basic and applied empirical research (Zhou and Shalley, 2011). As with the preceding, the creativity literature offers much promise for addressing the ostensible tradeoff between retention and adaptability given (a) creative ideas are defined as ones that are both novel (i.e., original) and useful, and (b) both domain knowledge and skill (i.e, expertise) and more generic creative skills are key components to creative performance.

We propose that the most worthwhile path for building better theory on skill retention and adaptability would be one in which the adaptive learning perspective emphasized in contemporary applied training research is integrated with theory on intuitive expertise and creativity while being grounded in the fundamentals of memory theory and cognitive psychology. To illustrate the potential of this integration, we consider the role of mental models in skilled performance and adaptability (Chi, Feltovich, and Glaser, 1981; Collins and Gentner, 1987; Day, Arthur, and Gettman, 2001; Johnson-Laird, 1983; Schuelke et al., 2009). A coherent mental model of a domain that reflects guiding rules and principles (i.e., representing expertise) facilitates the recognition of relevant situational cues and subsequently the retrieval of appropriate processes in the face of unexpected and seemingly novel circumstances. This automated sequence of recognition and retrieval when faced with unexpected and seemingly novel circumstances is an aspect of adaptability, but it also frees up cognitive resources (i.e., working memory) for another aspect of adaptability— when the situation in fact demands novel action, performance in a manner that has never previously been exhibited. Metamemory, involving cognitive (e.g., metacognition) and motivational (e.g., self-evaluation) aspects of self-regulation (Bell and Kozlowski, 2009), is required to check for the possibility of needed changes in light of how overconfidence and biases might have led to an initial failure to fully process the nature of the original demands posed by the novel situation. If performance is deemed not effective by the individual, then creativity is needed. The individual now must identify what "parts" of the existing mental model are still relevant and then retrieve information, whether they be principles, strategies, procedures, or more discrete facts, from other existing domain mental models to possibly combine with the originally retrieved mental model (i.e., conceptual combination or expansion (Finke, Ward, and Smith, 1992; Leung, Maddux, Galinsky, and Chui, 2008; Mobley, Doares, and Mumford, 1992)). In turn, the individual must experiment with and ultimately develop new processes that would be applied, thus creating a new mental model that would enable further application and adaptability. In this vein, creativity is not so much "going outside the box" as is often and colloquially stated, but is instead, more often along the lines of "combining boxes" or "combining the content of boxes." As part of this process, the individual must also retrieve information from a metamemory mental model of how to cope with new challenges, change, and perhaps even "start from scratch." Accordingly, we also believe that any empirical search for individual difference variables that might be important and differentially related to retention and adaptive performance would be well served by causal theories couched in terms of intuitive expertise and creativity by emphasizing a combination of domain-specific and generically useful skills and bases of knowledge.

The Meaning and Role of "Desirable Difficulties"

A few years after Farr's (1987) review of the retention literature, reviews from the cognitive-experimental and motor learning literature (e.g., Schmidt and Bjork, 1992) showed how the conditions that maximized acquisition often did not translate into better retention or transfer. Put another way, there was reasonable consensus from the basic research literature that those practice conditions that better facilitated performance on tests of retention and transfer did not always exhibit the best performance during practice or immediately at the end of practice. Such practice conditions that better facilitated retention and transfer yet slowed skill acquisition or downgraded performance during practice became known as "desirable difficulties." Indeed, the discovery of desirable difficulties was a watershed moment in the science of learning (Schmidt and Bjork, 1992).

However, there is also a fair amount of tautology to the notion of desirable difficulties. Desirable difficulties are those instructional conditions that promote the use (i.e., practice) of "transfer-appropriate" processing. Although transfer-appropriate processes can refer to just about any specific cognitive process or set of processes needed for effective performance in some transfer condition, more generic transfer-appropriate processes have been suggested by researchers (e.g., Schmidt and Bjork, 1992) and include (a) deeper, more elaborative rehearsal of task information, (b) metacognitive or metamemory activities, and (c) reconstruction of what was previously learned, also referred to as retrieval-based learning (Karpicke, 2012). Nonetheless, the specific processes relevant in some future instance when transfer is needed are not always well known. In other words, training for adaptable performance largely translates into training for the unexpected or unknown. But how can we be certain of what the transfer-appropriate processes are if what we are training for is the unexpected or unknown?

Like the science of personnel assessment and selection for so many years, this question reflects how the science of training and development appears to us to suffer from a "criterion problem" (Austin and Villanova, 1992). We see several interrelated ways to address this question. First, we need a theory of transfer or adaptable performance and, as previously mentioned in the preceding section, the most viable theoretical approach would reflect an integration of several research literatures. We believe that the construct of skill transfer or adaptable performance is most likely multidimensional in nature and thus needs to be clearly conceptualized and operationalized as such (cf. Barnett and Ceci, 2002). Second, and following this multidimensional perspective, it is logical that empirical studies addressing skill learning should include a clear description and explanation of what the tests of transfer or adaptable performance used represent in relation to some clear conceptualization or taxonomy of transfer, detailing the specific processes needed to effectively transfer or adapt what was originally learned to the transfer test conditions. Accordingly, to better understand the limits of what has been learned, we also recommend that multiple tests of transfer be used in applied research, going beyond the commonly used design that simply involves two posttraining performance tests reflecting a "near" versus "far" or "analogical" versus "adaptive" transfer distinction. Such distinctions are not only simplistic in their representation of real-world novel performance demands, they are also conceptually vague in terms of what adaptive performance entails.

Third, empirical investigations should include measurement of the specific actions and cognitive processes used during tests of transfer. Scientifically it is not enough to simply show which instructional or practice conditions were associated with higher scores on tests of transfer or what antecedent variables were correlated with transfer scores. Researchers should strive to determine the extent to which specific cognitions and behaviors are associated with higher transfer scores. For example, without the measurement of specific cognitive and behavioral actions used during transfer performance, it is difficult if not impossible to know if the more successful performers simply did a better job of maintaining the same exact actions and cognitive processes used or if they actually made changes to—in fact adapted—the actions and cognitive processes previously learned in some novel manner. Did they simply do a better job of "getting by," or did they improvise in some way, restructuring (not just reconstructing) components previously learned or abandoning specific components in favor of others? If some sort of improvisation occurred, did it involve the incorporation of knowledge or skill acquired outside the original learning context?

Fourth, applied empirical studies should include tests of retention coupled with manipulations of interference (following the logic of basic memory research paradigms, including a control condition of "no" interference) alongside tests of transfer to better elucidate the processes that distinguish retention performance from adaptive performance. Once we have a sound conceptualization of adaptive performance and better designed empirical investigations that include a variety of tests of transfer with tests of retention, and measures of specific cognitions and actions used on tests of retention and transfer, we can empirically better link desirable difficulties to retention and adaptive performance by way of distal "transfer-appropriate" processes occurring in training, and proximal cognitive and behavioral actions used in transfer. In other words, we believe it is important to capture the extent to which the processes enacted during cases of successful retention and adaptive performance simply match the processes occurring during acquisition as a function of incorporated desirable difficulties (similar to the logic of an identical elements framework), or perhaps that the desirable difficulties facilitated the development of a wide-ranging knowledge base and a coherent mental model. For example, do random or variable practice conditions facilitate retention and transfer (in general and differentially) because they give trainees practice at reconstruction (retrieval) and adjusting to different circumstances (metamemory) or because they lead to the development of a rich, varied, and deeply encoded knowledge base that is organized in terms of a coherent set of guiding rules and principles? In this manner, not only will we have a more concrete understanding of which difficulties are more "desirable" than others, but we can then also build causal theories of retention and adaptive performance that are more firmly grounded on the criterion side of the equation.

THE KNOWLEDGE AND SKILL DECAY CURVE: PREDICTING AND INFORMING THE TIMING AND SEQUENCING OF REFRESHER TRAINING?

Skill or knowledge decay or loss can be graphically illustrated as the amount of retention plotted against the time elapsed since original learning. This classic retention curve is usually negatively accelerated; the curve falls most quickly during the time immediately following acquisition and declines more and more gradually over time. Consequently, a power function seems most adept at summarizing knowledge and skill loss—one "loses" a lot of information at first but the rate of loss slows over time. This is in contrast to an exponential function that reflects a constant rate of loss (e.g., Meeter, Murre, and Janssen, 2005; Wixted and Carpenter, 2007; but see Bahrick, 1992). However, it is important to note that, although the length of the retention interval (i.e., the nonuse interval) has been cited as a powerful factor in retention (e.g., Annett, 1979; Farr, 1987; Gardlin and Sitterley, 1972; Hurlock, and Montague, 1982; Naylor and Briggs, 1961; Prophet, 1976), as previously discussed, it is, albeit, a factor that may operate through mechanisms other than time per se (Naylor and Briggs, 1961). Furthermore, it has been argued by some (e.g., Naylor and Briggs, 1961) that there is not one single decrement function curve, but rather that decrement is specific to the task and situation.

It is intuitively obvious that there is immense inherent value to developing techniques for predicting the amount of knowledge and skill decay for various periods of nonuse. Among others, such models, algorithms, or equations can then be used to inform the timing and sequencing of refresher training. However, as illustrated by Arthur and Bennett (1996), who generated decay curves on the basis of meta-analytic data, there is not one single decay function curve but rather the rate and magnitude of decay is specific to the task and situation. Nevertheless, said decay curves, generated through the use of computational modeling (Gronlund and Kimball, 2013), could be used to predict the course of decay as a function of task-type, the cognitive demands, the conditions of learning the task, and the frequency and/or types of interference. Such a model would permit the plotting of the shape and end point of an individual's learning curve and provide some guidance as to recommendations for the timing and sequencing of refresher training and of what sort.

Task Complexity

A core set of factors that influence the decay of knowledge and skills over extended nonuse periods have been identified in the extant literature. Building off Farr (1987), Arthur et al. (1998) categorized them as methodological and task-related factors. Methodological factors can be modified in the design of the training or learning environment to enhance retention. Examples of these factors include the degree of overlearning, instructional design and training methods (e.g., spacing of practice), conditions of retrieval, the training evaluation criteria, and the method of testing. In contrast, task-related factors are inherent characteristics of the task and are typically not amenable to modification by the trainer or researcher. Examples include characteristics such as the distinction between closed- versus open-looped tasks, physical versus cognitive tasks, task complexity, and whether said tasks are individual- versus team-based.

Although the amount or degree of initial learning and the length of the nonuse interval appear to be two important determinants of knowledge and skill loss (Farr, 1987; Hurlock and Montague, 1982; Schendel, Shields, and Katz, 1978; Wright, 1973), their effects are not independent of task-related factors (Arthur et al., 1998; Wang et al., 2013). Complexity and interdependence are important task characteristics that have received limited, if any, attention in the extant literature. Because task interdependence is peculiar to team training contexts, it is discussed in the "Individual vs. Team Training" section of this chapter.

As noted in a number of chapters in the present volume (see also Arthur et al., 1998, and Farr, 1987), the extant skill decay literature has been characterized by the use of relatively simple tasks. Concomitantly, it is also noteworthy that several reports in the present volume (e.g., Arthur and colleagues, Cooke et al., and Svensson et al., Wang et al.) observed relatively limited loss for their complex tasks. Collectively, these results suggest that the amount of decrement on cognitive, complex tasks may not be as large as researchers are inclined to accept or has been typically observed for simple tasks.

There are a number of reasons why more cognitively complex tasks would be associated with less skill loss compared to simple tasks. For instance, it is possible that the dynamic stimulus–response patterns associated with complex tasks along with their open-looped nature inherently induces deeper, more elaborative processing, which in turn leads to greater skill retention compared to superficial, rote processing (Arthur et al., 1998; Craik and Lockhart, 1972; Schmidt and Bjork, 1992). Likewise, cognitively complex tasks may be inherently more meaningful (i.e., natural), and meaningfulness may lead to higher levels of motivation as well as deeper, more elaborative processing (Wexley and Latham, 2002). Furthermore, individuals may be more naturally inclined to mentally rehearse tasks that are more meaningful during periods of nonuse (cf. Driskell et al., 1994; Ryan and Simons, 1981).

There may be methodological explanations as well. For example, complex tasks involve more task parameters compared to simple tasks (Bonner, 1994; Wood, 1986), and complexity may be directly proportional to longer performance episodes. So, to fully capture performance with complex tasks, longer tests of performance are required to allow all task parameters to run their course. Longer tests of retention naturally provide individuals with the opportunity to reacquaint themselves with the task. For instance, the performance tests used by Arthur and colleagues in the respective chapters of this volume lasted 25 minutes, which is in sharp contrast to the typical skill retention study which entails a simple task with a performance test lasting no more than a few minutes. Cooke et al.'s performance task was 40 minutes long, and Svensson et al.'s task was even longer. So, the amount of time involved in performance tests is likely to be positively correlated with task complexity. Hence, we suspect that complex tasks may actually display less decay owing to the amount of time required to perform the task. Specifically, the length of time required to perform the task provides the opportunity for individuals (and teams) to reacquaint themselves with the task while performing the task. Therefore, complex tasks may appear more resistant to skill loss because they provide inherent opportunities to reacquire skill on the retention test.

Farr (1987) also discusses the notion that the different components (i.e., subtasks) of complex tasks may have different decay rates. This then raises the issue of whether the performance of subtasks that may have suffered less decay facilitates the recall and performance of other subtasks during the performance of the task on the retention trial. Such a phenomenon, if empirically demonstrated, may serve as another reason why complex tasks appear to display lower levels of decay than simple tasks.

So, on one hand, one could speculate that skill loss may be less of a concern with respect to cognitively complex tasks. On the other hand, given the potentially dire consequences associated with poor performance in many real-world contexts, additional research is needed before strong conclusions can be made regarding the extent to which skill on cognitively complex tasks is not as susceptible to loss over extended periods of nonuse. This need for additional research is especially pressing considering the dearth of research on skill loss involving complex tasks coupled with extended periods of nonuse.

The Nature and Operationalization of Acquisition and Retention

As Farr (1987) notes, "[t]he separation between the learning phase and the retention phase is arbitrary, in the sense that we can only determine whether a person has successfully learned something by having him demonstrate its retention" (p. S-4). The import of this observation is reflected in the pivotal role that the amount or degree of initial learning, and correspondingly, the effect of overlearning play in the amount of subsequent knowledge and skill decay over extended nonuse intervals. Hence, the question of when does acquisition end and retention and transfer begin is central to discussions of decay and loss. In their meta-analysis of the skill decay literature, Arthur et al. (1998) commented on this issue as well. They noted the lack of consensus concerning the criteria used to determine the point at which acquisition ceases and retention and reacquisition begin. Arthur et al. described several metrics of performance that have been used in the literature to identify the end of skill acquisition; some studies have used an accuracy criterion (e.g., one errorless trial), whereas other studies have required trainees to complete a specified amount of material or train for a certain amount of time. Training to mastery (i.e., training to a specified level of accuracy) and training for a fixed amount of time represent two distinct dimensions of performance. Furthermore, in terms of permitting comparisons across studies, the former appears to be an absolute criterion while the latter is a relative criterion. So, while we recognize the methodological challenges and costs associated with taking a mastery approach to acquisition, especially in lab-based research, it is fair to say that it is methodologically more robust and consequently, permits more rigorous loss- and retention-related conclusions if trainees are trained to mastery (experimental control) instead of trying to control for trainee variability or differences in acquisition statistically by using procedures such as the analysis of covariance.

Individual vs. Team Training

As noted by Arthur et al. (2013), because teams consist of two or more individuals who work interdependently, have specific role assignments, perform specific tasks, and interact and coordinate to achieve a common goal, there are aspects to teams that engender retention and transfer processes and outcomes that are quite different from those observed for individuals. Some of these characteristics are manifested in the form of concepts and phenomena such as taskwork versus teamwork, task interdependence, transactive memory (and team member substitution), team composition, and interpositional knowledge.

The extant team training literature draws a distinction between taskwork and teamwork, whereby teamwork refers to the team's efforts to facilitate interaction among team members (with a focus on process factors) in the accomplishment of team tasks (e.g., see Cooke, Gorman, Duran, Myers, and Andrews, 2013). In contrast, taskwork refers to the team's efforts to understand and perform the requirements of the job, tasks, and equipment to be used. Consonant with this distinction and with a focus on taskwork in the context of team training, team task analysis, and team performance, Arthur and colleagues have conceptualized taskwork interdependence (i.e., "teamness") in terms of (a) the extent to which and (b) the manner in which team members must exchange information and resources (i.e., work together) to successfully complete their tasks and jobs (Arthur et al., 2005; Arthur et al., 2012a; Arthur, Villado, and Bennett, 2012; Van Der Vegt, Emans, and Van de Vliert, 2000). Arthur and colleagues operationalize the former as team-relatedness and the latter as team workflow. Hence, team-relatedness speaks to the extent to which working with members of the team is required for optimal task or job performance ("not at all required for optimal performance" to "very much required for optimal performance"). In contrast, team workflow is operationalized in terms of which of five workflow patterns (i.e., not a team task or activity, pooled or additive, sequential, reciprocal, or intensive interdependence) best characterizes the way that work and/or information between team members flows for the optimal performance of each task or activity. And although they have been found to be moderately correlated, Arthur and colleagues have nevertheless also shown team-relatedness and team workflow to be distinct facets of taskwork interdependence. Arthur and associates have also noted that similar to other task characteristics, an analysis of task and job interdependence can be used to inform the design of personnel-related and human resource development interventions such as training. Thus, team-relatedness and team workflow ratings have been demonstrated to be predictive of team performance (Arthur et al., 2005; Arthur et al., 2012; Munoz, Jarrett, Arthur, and Schurig, 2012), and are also efficacious as outcome variables in the assessment of the effectiveness of team training interventions (Kyte, 2009; Munoz et al., 2012).

The relevance of task interdependence to knowledge and skill retention resides in the fact that it is logically associated with the conceptual underpinnings of transactive memory, the embeddedness of knowledge and skills within individual team members, their degree of teamness, and the differential forgetting rates by individuals, all of which are posited to play a role in the performance of teams at retention sessions. Transactive memory, as a team cognition construct, is conceptually closely rated to task interdependence. Transactive memory refers to a "cognitively interdependent system for encoding, storing, and retrieving information that combines the knowledge possessed by each individual with the shared awareness of who knows what" (Mohammed, Ferzandi, and Hamilton, 2010, p. 882). Thus, one can envisage a situation where one is likely to see less manifest team skill loss in a situation where the team has an intensive interdependence workflow pattern that will have associated with it more distributed transactive memory (Moreland, 1999). Likewise, the converse would be true for a team with a pooled or additive workflow pattern, and restricted transactive memory. Whereas the preceding propositions are theoretically grounded, empirical tests of their veracity or lack thereof, coupled with subsequent assessments of their applied and practical implications are called for.

As previously noted, teamwork (in contrast to taskwork) is recognized as a second dimension of team performance that consists of behaviors that are required for cooperative functioning and focuses on team process variables such as cooperation, coordination, and cohesion (Barry and Stewart, 1997; Dickinson and McIntyre, 1997; Glickman et al., 1987; Morgan et al., 1986). Furthermore, unlike taskwork skills, teamwork and team process skills are considered to be generic instead of being task- or job-specific (Stevens and Campion, 1994, 1999). However, in spite of the fact that they can be argued to be as important as taskwork factors, especially in situations of high levels of interdependence where they would be pivotal to the effective functioning of teams, with the exception of Cooke et al. (2013), we are unaware of any studies that have investigated the decay of teamwork skills and competencies. This is clearly a gap in the literature that warrants attention.

Furthermore, to the extent that individual differences, both cognitive and noncognitive have been demonstrated to be predictive of skill acquisition and retention, one would likewise expect the composition of teams on these variables to also play an important role in the skill acquisition (Bowler, Woehr, Rentsch, and Bowler, 2010; Day et al., 2005) and subsequently, retention and transfer over extended nonuse intervals as well. However, to the best of our knowledge, the latter has yet to be empirically investigated and is a rich avenue for future research.

In summary, there are several team-related variables, such as teamwork, task interdependence, transactive memory, shared mental models, and inter-positional knowledge that are not present or germane in the context of individual performance. Given these differences, it is not unreasonable to question the extent to which our knowledge and understanding of individual skill retention and transfer generalizes to teams. For instance, it is conceivable that mechanisms associated with the sharedness of mental models and transactive memory may result in compensatory factors across team members to mitigate against the manifestation of skill loss after extended periods of nonuse. Thus, team mental models, along with phenomena such as interpositional knowledge (i.e., knowledge regarding other team members' roles), may result in situations where knowledge gaps at the level of the individual are rapidly filled by other team members such that the team as a whole displays limited performance decrements after extended nonuse intervals. Conversely, in the absence of empirical data to the contrary, one could also envisage a situation where the complexities associated with performing as a team, such as managing and maintaining the taskwork and teamwork interdependencies, are so tasking that extended periods of nonuse result in synergistic downward effects that exacerbate the loss of teamwork and taskwork skills and performance more so than is generally observed for individuals. In spite of the above speculative propositions, as has been previously noted in this chapter and others in this volume, at odds with the burgeoning volume of research on team performance and team training, there has been very limited research, if any, that has investigated the role of these team factors in the retention and transfer of knowledge and skills in teams.

CONCLUSION

In conclusion, there are several avenues for future research resulting from gaps in the extant literature. Attention to these gaps will go a long way to advancing our knowledge and understanding of skill and knowledge loss. Overarching the specific issues previously discussed is the general need to engage in research that has higher levels of ecological validity with a focus on more complex tasks, coupled with using longer, more realistic nonuse intervals. In addition, there should be efforts to use more "absolute" operationalizations of end-of-acquisition, such as training to mastery instead of training for a fixed amount of time. Given the noticeable differences in the role of additional conceptual factors—such as taskwork versus teamwork, task interdependence, transactive memory (and team member substitution), team composition, and interpositional knowledge—that are germane in the context of team training and performance, the need for a dedicated program of research on skill and knowledge loss and retention in teams cannot be overstated. Finally, it is important to recognize and maintain the distinction between processes of retention and processes of adaptive transfer through future research that better links desirable difficulties to retention and adaptive performance by way of distal "transfer-appropriate" processes occurring in training with proximal cognitive and behavioral actions used during tests of retention and transfer.

REFERENCES

Annett, J. (1979). Memory for skill. In M. M. Gruneberg and P. E. Morris (Eds.), *Applied problems in memory* (pp. 215–247). London: Academic Press.

Arthur, W. Jr., and Bennett, W. Jr. (1996). *Skill retention and decay: A meta-analysis* [Final report] (AL/HR-TR-1996). AL/HRTD contract F41622–93-M-2342, Technical Training Division, Brooks AFB, TX.

Arthur, W. Jr., Bennett, W. Jr., Stanush, P. L., and McNelly, T. L. (1998). Factors that influence skill decay and retention: A quantitative review and analysis. *Human Performance, 11,* 57–101.

Arthur, W. Jr., Day, E. A., Villado, A. J., Glaze, R. M., Schuelke, M. J., Boatman, P. R., Kowollik, V., Wang, X., and Bennett, W. Jr. (2013). A comparative investigation of individual and team skill retention and transfer on a complex command-and-control simulation task. In W. Arthur, Jr., E. A. Day, W. Bennett, Jr., and A. Portrey (Eds.), *Individual and team skill decay: The science, and implications for practice* (pp. 321–343). New York: Taylor & Francis.

Arthur, W. Jr., Edwards, B., Bell, S., Villado, A., and Bennett, W. Jr. (2005). Team task analysis: Identifying tasks and jobs that are team based. *Human Factors, 47,* 654–669.

Arthur, W. Jr., Glaze, R. M., Bhupatkar, A., Villado, A. J., Bennett, W. Jr., and Rowe, L. (2012a). Team task analysis: Differentiating between tasks using team-relatedness and team workflow as metrics of team task interdependence. *Human Factors, 54,* 277–295.

Arthur, W. Jr., Villado, A. J., and Bennett, W. Jr. (2012b). Innovations in team task analysis: Identifying team-based task elements, tasks, and jobs. In M. A. Wilson, W. Bennett, Jr., S. G. Gibson, and G. M. Alliger (Eds.), *The handbook of work analysis in organizations: Methods, systems, applications, and science of work measurement in organizations* (pp. 641–661). New York: Routledge/Psychology Press.

Austin, J. T., and Villanova, P. (1992). The criterion problem 1917–1992. *Journal of Applied Psychology, 77,* 836–874.

Bahrick, H. P. (1992). Stabilized memory of unrehearsed knowledge. *Journal of Experimental Psychology: General, 121,* 112–113.

Barnett, S. M., and Ceci, S. J. (2002). When and where do we apply what we learn? A taxonomy for far transfer. *Psychological Bulletin, 128,* 612–637.

Barry, B., and Stewart, G. L. (1997). Composition, process, and performance in self-managed groups: The role of personality. *Journal of Applied Psychology, 82,* 62–78.

Bell, B. S., and Kozlowski, S. W. J. (2009). Toward a theory of learner-centered training design: An integrative framework of active learning. In S. Kozlowski, and E. Salas (Eds.), *Learning, training, and development in organizations* (pp. 263–300). New York: Routledge.

Bonner, S. E. (1994). A model of the effects of audit task complexity. *Accounting, Organizations and Society, 19,* 213–234.

Bowler, M. C., Woehr, D. J., Rentsch, J. R., and Bowler, J. L. (2010). The impact of aggressive individuals on team training. *Personality and Individual Differences, 49,* 88–94.

Chi, M., Feltovich, P., and Glaser, R. (1981). Categorization and representation of physics problems by experts and novices. *Cognitive Science, 5,* 121–152.

Collins, A. M., and Gentner, D. (1987). How people construct mental models. In D. Holland and N. Quinn (Eds.), *Cultural models in thought and language* (pp. 243–265). Cambridge, UK: Cambridge University Press.

Cooke, N. J., Gorman, J. C., Duran, J., Myers, C., and Andrews, D. (2013). Retention of team coordination skill. In W. Arthur, Jr., E. A. Day, W. Bennett, Jr., and A. Portrey (Eds.), *Individual and team skill decay: The science, and implications for practice* (pp. 344–363). New York: Taylor & Francis.

Craik, F. I., and Lockhart, R. S. (1972). Levels of processing: A framework for memory research. *Journal of Verbal Learning and Verbal Behavior, 11*, 671–684.

Day, E. A., Arthur, W. Jr., and Gettman, D. (2001). Knowledge structures and the acquisition of a complex skill. *Journal of Applied Psychology, 86*, 1022–1033.

Day, E. A., Arthur, W. Jr., Bell, S. T., Edwards, B. D., Bennett, W. Jr., Mendoza, J. L., and Tubre, T. C. (2005). Ability-based pairing strategies in the team-based training of a complex skill: Does the intelligence of your training partner matter? *Intelligence, 33*, 39–65.

Day, E. A., Arthur, W. Jr., Villado, A. J., Boatman, P. R., Kowollik, V., Bhupatkar, A., and Bennett, W. Jr. (2013). Relating individual differences in ability, personality, and motivation to the retention and transfer of skill on a complex command-and-control simulation task. In W. Arthur, Jr., E. A. Day, W. Bennett, Jr., and A. Portrey (Eds.), *Individual and team skill decay: The science, and implications for practice* (pp. 282–301). New York: Taylor & Francis.

Dickinson, T. L., and McIntyre, R. M. (1997). A conceptual framework for teamwork measurement. In M. T. Brannick, C. Prince, and E. Salas (Eds.), *Team performance assessment and measurement* (pp. 15–43). Mahweh, NJ: Lawrence Erlbaum Associates.

Driskell, J. E., Copper, C., and Moran, A. (1994). Does mental practice enhance performance? *Journal of Applied Psychology, 79*, 481–492.

Dweck, C. S. (1986). Motivational processes affecting learning. *American Psychologist, 41*, 1040–1048.

Farr, M. J. (1987). *The long-term retention of knowledge and skill: A cognitive and instructional perspective.* New York: Springer-Verlag.

Finke, R. A., Ward, T. B., and Smith, S. M. (1992). *Creative cognition: Theory, research, and applications.* Cambridge, MA: MIT Press.

Gardlin, G. R., and Sitterley, T. E. (1972). *Degradation of learned skills: A review and annotated bibliography* (D180–15081–1, NASA-CR-128611). Seattle, WA: Boeing.

Glickman, A. S., Zimmer, S., Montero, R. C., Guerette, P. J., Campbell, W. J., Morgan, B. B., and Salas, E. (1987). *The evolution of team skills: An empirical assessment with implications for training* (NTSC Tech. Report No. 87–016). Arlington, VA: Office of Naval Research.

Gopher, D., Weil, M., and Siegel, D. (1989). Practice under changing priorities: An approach to the training of complex skills. *Acta Psychologica, 71*, 147–177.

Gronlund, S. D., and Kimball, D. R. (2013). Remembering and forgetting: From the laboratory looking out. In W. Arthur, Jr., E. A. Day, W. Bennett, Jr., and A. Portrey (Eds.), *Individual and team skill decay: The science, and implications for practice* (pp. 14–52). New York: Taylor & Francis.

Healy, A. F., Wohldmann, E. L., Kole, J. A., Schneider, V. I., Shea, K. M., and Bourne, L. E. Jr. (2013). Training for efficient, durable, and flexible performance in the military. In W. Arthur, Jr., E. A. Day, W. Bennett, Jr., and A. Portrey (Eds.), *Individual and team skill decay: The science, and implications for practice* (pp. 176–204). New York: Taylor & Francis.

Hurlock, R. E., and Montague, W. E. (1982). *Skill retention and its implications for navy tasks: An analytical review* (NPRDC Special Report 82–21). San Diego, CA: Navy Personnel Research and Development Center.

Johnson-Laird, P. N. (1983). *Mental models: Towards a cognitive science of language, inference, and consciousness.* Cambridge, MA: Harvard University Press.

Kahneman, D., and Klein, G. (2009). Conditions for intuitive expertise. *American Psychologist, 64*, 515–526.

Karpicke, J. D. (2012). Retrieval-based learning: Active retrieval promotes meaningful learning. *Current Directions in Psychological Science, 21*, 157–163.

Kyte, T. B. (2009). Crew resource management training's effect on railroad crews' perceptions of task interdependence and teamwork (Doctoral dissertation, Texas A&M University. 2008). *Dissertation Abstracts International, 69*, 0419–4217.

Leung, A. K., Maddux, W. Galinsky, A. D., and Chui, C. Y. (2008). Multicultural experience enhances creativity: The when and how. *American Psychologist, 63*, 169–181.

Levy, B. J., Kuhl, B. A., and Wagner, A. D. (2010). The functional neuroimaging of forgetting. In S. Della Sala (Ed.), *Forgetting* (pp. 135–163). Hove, UK: Psychology Press.

McGeoch, J. (1932). Forgetting and the law of disuse. *Psychological Review, 39*, 352–370.

Marks, M. A., Sabella, M. J., Burke, C. S., and Zaccaro, S. J. (2002). The impact of cross-training on team effectiveness. *Journal of Applied Psychology, 87*, 3–13.

Meeter, M., Murre, J., and Janssen, S. (2005). Remembering the news: Modeling retention data from a study with 14,000 participants. *Memory & Cognition, 33*, 793–810.

Mobley, M. I., Doares, L. M., and Mumford, M. D. (1992). Process analytic models of creative capacities: Evidence for the combination and reorganization process. *Creativity Research Journal, 5*, 125–155.

Mohammed, S., Ferzandi, L., and Hamilton, K. (2010). Metaphor no more: A 15-year review of the team mental model construct. *Journal of Management, 36*, 876–910.

Moreland, R. L. (1999). Transactive memory: Learning who knows what in work groups and organizations. In L. Thompson, D. Messick, and J. Levine (Eds.), *Shared cognition in organizations: The management of knowledge* (pp. 3–31). Hillsdale, NJ: Lawrence Erlbaum Associates.

Morgan, B. B., Glickman, A. S., Woodward, E. A. Blaiwes, A. S., and Salas, E. (1986). *Measurement of team behaviors in a Navy environment* (NTSC Tech. Report No. 86–014). Orlando, FL: Naval Training Systems Center.

Munoz, G. J., Jarrett, S., Arthur, W. Jr., and Schurig, I. (2012). *Revisiting a questionnaire-based approach to team task analysis.* Poster presented at the 27th Annual Conference of the Society for Industrial and Organizational Psychology, San Diego, CA.

Naylor, J. C., and Briggs, G. E. (1961). *Long-term retention of learned skills: A review of the literature* (ASD TR 61-390). Columbus: Ohio State University, Laboratory of Aviation Psychology.

Prophet, W. W. (1976). *Long-term retention of flying skills: A review of the literature* (HumRRO Final Report 76–35). Alexandria, VA: Human Resources Research Organization (ADA036077).

Ryan, E. D., and Simons, J. (1981). Cognitive demand, imagery, and frequency of mental rehearsal as factors influencing acquisition of motor skills. *Journal of Sport Psychology, 3*, 35–45.

Schendel, J. D., Shields, J. L., and Katz, M. S. (1978). *Retention of motor skills: Review* (Technical Paper 313). Alexandria, VA: U.S. Army Research Institute for the Behavioral and Social Sciences.

Schmidt, R. A., and Bjork, R. A. (1992). New conceptualizations of practice: Common principles in three paradigms suggest new concepts in training. *Psychological Science, 3,* 207–217.

Schuelke, M. J., Day, E. A., McEntire, L. E., Espejo, J., Boatman, P. R., Kowollik, V., and Wang, X. (2009). Relating indices of knowledge structure coherence and accuracy to skill-based performance: Is there utility in using a combination of indices? *Journal of Applied Psychology, 94,* 1076–1085.

Shea, C. H., and Kovacs, A. J. (2013). Complex movement sequences: How the sequence structure affects learning and transfer. In W. Arthur, Jr., E. A. Day, W. Bennett, Jr., and A. Portrey (Eds.), *Individual and team skill decay: The science, and implications for practice* (pp. 205–239). New York: Taylor & Francis.

Stevens, M. J., and Campion, M. A. (1994). The knowledge, skills, and ability requirements for teamwork: Implications for human resource management. *Journal of Management, 20,* 503–530.

Stevens, M. J., and Campion, M. A. (1999). Staffing teams: Development and validation of a selection test for teamwork settings. *Journal of Management, 25,* 207–228.

Tulving, E. (1974). Cue-dependent forgetting. *American Scientist, 62,* 74–82.

Van der Vegt, G., Emans, B., and Van de Vliert, E. (2000). Team member's affective responses to patterns of intragroup interdependence and job complexity. *Journal of Management, 26,* 633–655.

Vealey, R. S., and Greanleaf, C. A. (2010). Seeing is believing: Understanding and using imagery in sport. In J. M. Williams (Ed.), *Applied sport psychology* (6th ed.) (pp. 267–299). New York: McGraw-Hill.

Wang, X., Day, E. A., Kowollik, V., Schuelke, M. J., and Hughes, M. G. (2013). Factors influencing knowledge and skill decay in organizational training: A meta-analysis. In W. Arthur, Jr., E. A. Day, W. Bennett, Jr., and A. Portrey (Eds.), *Individual and team skill decay: The science, and implications for practice* (pp. 68–116). New York: Taylor & Francis.

Wexley, K. N., and Latham, G. P. (2002). *Developing and training human resources in organizations* (3rd ed.). Upper Saddle River, NJ: Prentice Hall.

Wixted, J. T., and Carpenter, S. K. (2007). The Wickelgren power law and the Ebbinghaus savings function. *Psychological Science, 18,* 133–134.

Wood, R. E. (1986). Task complexity: Definition of the construct. *Organizational Behvior and Human Decision Processes, 37,* 60–82.

Wright, R. H. (1973). *Retention of flying skills and refresher training requirements: Effects of non-flying and proficiency flying* (HumRRO Technical Report 73–32). Alexandria, VA: Human Resources Research Organization: Alexandria, VA.

Zhou, J., and Shalley, C. E. (2011). Deepening our understanding of creativity in the workplace: A review of different approaches to creativity research. In S. Zedeck (Ed.), *Handbook of industrial and organizational psychology: Volume I, Building and developing the organization* (pp. 275–302). Washington, D.C.: American Psychological Association.

Author Index

Subject Index